GEOGRAPHICAL INFORMATION SYSTEMS

VOLUME 2 : APPLICATIONS

GEOGRAPHICAL INFORMATION SYSTEMS

PRINCIPLES AND APPLICATIONS

EDITED BY
DAVID J MAGUIRE,
MICHAEL F GOODCHILD
AND
DAVID W RHIND

Copublished in the United States and Canada with
John Wiley & Sons, Inc., New York

Longman Scientific and Technical,
Longman Group UK Ltd
Longman House, Burnt Mill, Harlow,
Essex CM20 2JE, England
and Associated Companies throughout the world.

*copublished in the United States and Canada with
John Wiley & Sons, Inc., 605 Third Avenue, New York,
NY 10158*

© Longman Group UK Limited 1991

All rights reserved; no part of this publication may be reproduced, stored in a retrieval system, or transmitted in any form or by any means, electronic, mechanical, photocopying, recording, or otherwise without either the prior written permission of the Publishers or a licence permitting restricted copying in the United Kingdom issued by the Copyright Licensing Agency Ltd, 90 Tottenham Court Road, London W1P 9HE.

Trademarks
Throughout this book trademarked names are used. Rather than put a trademark symbol in every occurrence of a trademarked name, we state that we are using the names only in an editorial fashion and to the benefit of the trademark owner with no intention of infringement of the trademark.

First published 1991
Reprinted 1992
Reprinted 1993

British Library Cataloguing in Publication Data
Maguire, David J.
  Geographical information systems: Principles and applications
  I. Title II. Goodchild, Michael F.
  III. Rhind, David W.
  910.901

  ISBN 0-582-05661-6

Library of Congress Cataloging-in-Publication Data
Maguire, D. J. (David J.)
  Geographical information systems / by D. J. Maguire,
  Michael F. Goodchild, and David W. Rhind.
    p.   cm.
  Includes bibliographical references and index.
  Contents: v. 1. Principles – v. 2. Applications.
  ISBN 0-470-21789-8 (USA only)
  1. Geographical information systems.
  I. Goodchild, Michael F. II. Rhind,
  David. III. Title.
  G70.2.M354 1991
  910'.285–dc20   91-3724
                                         CIP

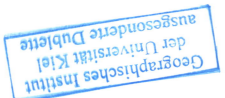

Set in Great Britain by Fakenham Photosetting Limited.

Printed and Bound in Great Britain at the Bath Press, Avon

Dedicated to the memory of

DAVID S SIMONETT

1926–90

David Simonett was born in Australia in 1926. After earning a Doctorate at the University of Sydney, he became a leading pioneer in the field of Remote Sensing, holding faculty positions at the University of Kansas, the University of Sydney and the University of California, Santa Barbara. He was director of land use applications at Earth Satellite Corp from 1972 to 1975.

As Chair at Santa Barbara from 1975, he was able to build one of the foremost Geography programs in the US, culminating in 1988 with the establishment of the National Center for Geographic Information and Analysis. The Santa Barbara site of the Center was renamed the David Simonett Center for Spatial Analysis in 1990 in recognition of his role in its creation. He received the Honours Award from the Association of American Geographers and the Victoria Medal from the Royal Geographical Society.

David Simonett lost a courageous fight against cancer on December 22, 1990 in the course of the preparation of his contribution to this book. The editors dedicate this book to his memory and to the outstanding role he has played in the development of the field of Geographical Information Systems.

VOLUME 1 : PRINCIPLES

Preface	*xiii*
List of contributors	*xvii*
Acknowledgements	*xxvii*

Section I Overview

Introduction *D J Maguire, M F Goodchild and D W Rhind*	3–7
1. An overview and definition of GIS *D J Maguire*	9–20
2. The history of GIS *J T Coppock and D W Rhind*	21–43
3. The technological setting of GIS *M F Goodchild*	45–54
4. The commercial setting of GIS *J Dangermond*	55–65
5. The government setting of GIS in the United Kingdom *R Chorley and R Buxton*	67–79
6. The academic setting of GIS *D J Unwin*	81–90
7. The organizational home for GIS in the scientific professional community *J L Morrison*	91–100
8. A critique of GIS *R T Aangeenbrug*	101–7

Section II Principles

Introduction *M F Goodchild, D W Rhind and D J Maguire*	111–17

VOLUME 1 : PRINCIPLES

(a) Nature of spatial data

9. Concepts of space and geographical data **119–34**
   A C Gatrell

10. Coordinate systems and map projections for GIS **135–46**
    D H Maling

11. Language issues for GIS **147–63**
    A U Frank and D M Mark

12. The error component in spatial data **165–74**
    N R Chrisman

13. Spatial data sources and data problems **175–89**
    P F Fisher

14. GIS and remote sensing **191–213**
    F W Davis and D S Simonett

(b) Digital representation

15. Computer systems and low-level data structures for GIS **215–25**
    Wm R Franklin

16. High-level spatial data structures for GIS **227–37**
    M J Egenhofer and J R Herring

17. GIS data capture hardware and software **239–49**
    M J Jackson and P A Woodsford

VOLUME 1 : PRINCIPLES

18.	Database management systems *R G Healey*	**251–67**
19.	Digital terrain modelling *R Weibel and M Heller*	**269–97**
20.	Three-dimensional GIS *J F Raper and B Kelk*	**299–317**

(c) Functional issues

21.	The functionality of GIS *D J Maguire and J Dangermond*	**319–35**
22.	Information integration and GIS *I D H Shepherd*	**337–60**
23.	Cartographic modelling *C D Tomlin*	**361–74**
24.	Spatial data integration *R Flowerdew*	**375–87**
25.	Developing appropriate spatial analysis methods for GIS *S Openshaw*	**389–402**
26.	Spatial decision support systems *P J Densham*	**403–12**
27.	Knowledge-based approaches in GIS *T R Smith and Ye Jiang*	**413–25**

VOLUME 1 : PRINCIPLES

(d) Display issues

28. Visualization   **427–43**
    B P Buttenfield and W A Mackaness

29. Computer name placement   **445–56**
    H Freeman

30. Generalization of spatial databases   **457–75**
    J-C Muller

(e) Operational issues

31. GIS specification, evaluation and implementation   **477–88**
    A L Clarke

32. Legal aspects of GIS   **489–502**
    E F Epstein

33. Managing an operational GIS: the UK National On-Line Manpower Information System (NOMIS)   **503–13**
    M J Blakemore

34. Spatial data exchange and standardization   **515–30**
    S C Guptill

Consolidated bibliography   *531–591*
List of acronyms   *593–598*
Author index   *599–613*
Subject index   *615–649*

VOLUME 2 : APPLICATIONS

Preface   *xiii*
List of contributors   *xvii*
Acknowledgements   *xxvii*

Section III Applications

Introduction   **3–10**
D W Rhind, D J Maguire and M F Goodchild

(a) National and international GIS programmes

35. A USGS perspective on GIS   **11–22**
    L E Starr and K E Anderson

36. Development of GIS-related activities at the Ordnance Survey   **23–38**
    M Sowton

37. National GIS programmes in Sweden   **39–46**
    L Ottoson and B Rystedt

38. The development of GIS in Japan   **47–56**
    S Kubo

39. Land and Geographical Information Systems in Australia   **57–70**
    J F O'Callaghan and B J Garner

40. GIS and developing nations   **71–84**
    D R F Taylor

(b) Socio-economic applications

41. Land information systems   **85–99**
    P F Dale

42. GIS and utilities   **101–14**
    R P Mahoney

43. Car navigation systems   **115–25**
    M White

44. Counting the people: the role of GIS   **127–37**
    D W Rhind

45. GIS and market analysis   **139–51**
    J R Beaumont

VOLUME 2 : APPLICATIONS

(c) Environmental applications

46. Soil information systems
    P A Burrough — **153–69**

47. Integration of geoscientific data using GIS
    G F Bonham-Carter — **171–84**

48. Multisource, multinational environmental GIS: lessons learnt from CORINE
    H M Mounsey. — **185–200**

49. Environmental databases and GIS
    J R G Townshend — **201–16**

50. Global databases and their implications for GIS
    D M Clark, D A Hastings and J J Kineman — **217–31**

(d) Management applications

51. GIS and public policy
    H W Calkins — **233–45**

52. Urban GIS applications
    R Parrott and F P Stutz — **247–60**

53. Land resource information systems
    K C Siderelis — **261–73**

54. Land management applications of GIS in the state of Minnesota
    A Robinette — **275–83**

55. GIS in island resource planning: a case study in map analysis
    J K Berry — **285–95**

56. Integrated planning information systems
    D J Cowen and W L Shirley — **297–310**

Section IV Epilogue

Epilogue — **313–27**
D W Rhind, M F Goodchild and D J Maguire

Consolidated bibliography — *329–389*
List of acronyms — *391–396*
Author index — *397–411*
Subject index — *413–447*

PREFACE

The idea for a book on Geographical Information Systems (GIS) came shortly after the Portland Association of American Geographers conference in 1987. It was clear from the papers presented in Portland and at similar meetings in 1986 and 1987 that GIS, although still a rapidly developing field, had reached a level of maturity sufficient to make production of a large reference compendium a feasible task. In 1988, the editors were appointed and in late 1988 they began to recruit authors. Manuscripts were delivered, edited and revised in early 1990. Final editing took place in late spring and summer 1990 and *Geographical Information Systems: principles and applications* was finished at the end of 1990.

At the outset, the aim of the book was to assemble a team of international experts to write a major reference work on GIS. The book was designed to be a benchmark volume, that could be used as a reference against which trends in the field might be assessed. Indeed, it was suggested that the book should carry a 'health warning' to the effect that, after the early 1990s, it should only be read in conjunction with the proceedings of the latest AUTOCARTO, GIS/LIS or International Spatial Data Handling Symposium conferences; one would thus provide the general context and long term view, the other to contribute specific details of current developments. The authors were selected primarily because of their expertise, but the editors were also keen to choose a set of authors who reflected the geographical distribution of work effort and the sometimes disparate views of GIS. The North America/UK bias is an inevitable manifestation of these processes. This is not however in any way intended to decry the important work in Australasia, continental Europe and many other places.

Bearing in mind that the book was to be a reference volume, authors were asked to write around 5000 words (excluding references) on the fundamental enduring principles of their topic, rather than current trends which may lack substance and longevity. The variations in the length of the resulting chapters in part represent authors' views of their subject's perceived size and importance. Authors were asked to pitch their chapters at a level suitable for advanced undergraduates, postgraduates, professionals and research workers. Thus, each of the contributions is a mixture of overview, review and purview, with both a pedagogic and a research element.

The choice of topics was a difficult one. It proved impossible, even in 56 chapters, to cover the field of GIS comprehensively. The initial list of topics was refined several times by the editors and additional chapters were commissioned following initial editing, in an attempt to cover the main areas adequately. Inevitably however, the final list still has its limitations, reflecting the restrictions imposed by space, time and the differential development of GIS. Ideally, the geographical coverage might have been extended to include more on Africa, South America and planets other than Earth. The book only briefly touches on temporal GIS, the atmosphere and oceans. In Section III, **Applications**, it would also have been interesting to have more on economic and organizational issues, particularly some examples of where GIS has failed or been uneconomic. Nevertheless, the editors believe that the selection captures the main thrust of the spirit and purpose of GIS in the early 1990s.

The organization of the book has purposely been kept simple. Even so, in one or two cases the chapters contain material relevant to more than one section or subsection. Subjects such as data capture, error, the raster-vector dichotomy, generalization and visualization which pervade many aspects of GIS are discussed in a large number of chapters from a variety of perspectives and the authors present interesting comparisons of their role and importance.

The book has four main sections offering an **Overview** of GIS and covering the fundamental **Principles** and key **Applications**. In a final brief section the editors provide an **Epilogue** to the main work. Each of the four sections begins with an introduction by the editors which discusses the context of the work and shows how the chapters link together. In these introductions, the editors have also attempted to offer some critical remarks about the material and GIS in general. The material is split into two volumes. The first includes the preliminary material and the **Overview** and **Principles** sections; the second includes the **Applications** and **Epilogue** sections. Both volumes contain an author and subject index, a list of acronyms used and a consolidated bibliography.

Section I, **Overview**, contains eight chapters which provide the context of GIS. The section begins with discussion of the definition of GIS: other chapters discuss the main intellectual, technical and organizational forces which have had, and which continue to have, a profound impact on the development of GIS.

Section II, **Principles**, has five subsections: Nature of spatial data; Digital representation; Functional issues; Display issues; and Operational issues. The six chapters dealing with the nature of spatial data examine the characteristics, sources and problems of using and interacting with data. The six digital representation chapters deal with the way geographical data are captured, stored and structured. The seven chapters on functional issues show how data can be integrated, manipulated and analysed using GIS. The penultimate subsection contains three chapters that examine issues involved in the display of data. The final subsection, on operational issues, has four chapters that look at the economic, legal and managerial implications of using GIS. This is a crucially important yet often undervalued aspect of GIS. Together the chapters in this section constitute a major synthesis of important past and recent work on the principles of GIS.

Section III, **Applications**, has four subsections: National and international GIS programmes; Socio-economic applications; Environmental applications; and Management applications. The six chapters covering national and international programmes overview the current state of GIS development at national, continental and world scales. In the remaining three subsections of Section III, selected GIS applications are organized thematically. This list is clearly not comprehensive and never could be given the diversity of interests of GIS users. The application areas were chosen to represent the main broad application areas of GIS in the early 1990s. These applications are a mixture of general overviews of application areas and specific examples which highlight the everyday aspects of using GIS. Hopefully, readers will be able to generalize about the main advantages and disadvantages of the GIS approach from this material.

Section IV, **Epilogue** which concludes the volume has been written by the editors. It is an essay which examines the internal state of GIS and its wider context. Some predictions for the future are also presented in this final chapter.

This book has been written with a wide variety of users in mind. The list of people interested in GIS includes professionals in the commercial sector, government workers, specific application-oriented end-users, academics and students. Each of these groups has different interests and will find different parts of the book more relevant than others. It is tempting to try and summarize which areas of the book are relevant for each group. All the editors' experience shows, however, that in fact the differences between these groups is not as great as might at first be imagined. Successful professional organizations often prefer to hire people with a general education rather than specific training, academics are forced to try and make money by acting as system developers and consultants, and many users and students are not as narrow minded, naive and misguided as many imagine. Awareness, in its many forms, is relevant to us all.

A compendium such as this is to some extent the result of a democratic process, each author contributing an individual viewpoint and piece of a much larger puzzle. At the same time, the editors have been conscious of the need to provide a focus and direction, and to ensure that the whole is greater than the sum of the individual parts. The editors' invisible and visible hand has been used throughout to maintain consistency, avoid overlap and develop a coherent view. *Geographical Information Systems: principles and applications* is a statement about GIS in the early 1990s. The editors are responsible for the overall message, but we thank all the individual authors for providing the substance of what we wanted to say.

Many people have contributed a great deal of time, effort and forbearance to the production of this book. The editors would especially like to record their gratitude to the following key individuals. The diagrams were expertly and imaginatively drawn by Mrs Kate Moore of the Department of Geography at the University of Leicester. The author and subject indexes and list of acronyms were compiled by Mr Craig Wood of the Computers in Teaching Initiative Centre for Geography at the University of Leicester. Ms Vanessa Lawrence of Longman Scientific and Technical was responsible for commissioning the book and has been with the project over the 4 years from conception to delivery. She deserves great credit for her vision, persistence and considerable ability in coping with the editors. Finally, we thank our wives Heather, Fiona and Christine who sacrificed a lot, though they did discover the Green Parrot.

David J Maguire
Michael F Goodchild
David W Rhind

January 1991

LIST OF CONTRIBUTORS

THE EDITORS

David J Maguire
Formerly Lecturer in GIS, University of Leicester. Currently Technical Director, ESRI UK. Research interests include data integration, areal interpolation, database design and GIS education.

ESRI (UK)
Doric House
23 Woodford Road
Watford
WD1 1PB
UK

Michael F Goodchild
Professor of Geography at the University of California Santa Barbara and Co-Director of the National Center for Geographic Information and Analysis. Current research interests include the generic issues of GIS such as accuracy, spatial decision support systems and data structures for global GIS.

Department of Geography
University of California
Santa Barbara
California
93106
USA

David W Rhind
Formerly Professor of Geography, Birkbeck College, London. Currently Director General and Chief Executive of the Ordnance Survey of Great Britain. Author of over 100 papers on GIS and related topics. Current research interests include the generalization of spatial databases, environmental information systems, multimedia GIS and data charging and access issues.

Ordnance Survey
Romsey Road
Maybush
Southampton
SO9 4DH
UK

THE AUTHORS

Robert T Aangeenbrug
Professor of Geography and Chair at the University of South Florida, Tampa. Director of the Center for Spatial and Environmental Analysis. Research interests include urban and natural resource systems modelling and GIS education.

Department of Geography
University of South Florida
Tampa
Florida
33620–8100
USA

K Eric Anderson
Head of Eastern Mapping Division of the US National Mapping Agency, the US Geological Survey National Mapping Division, and Chairman of the International Cartographic Association's Commission on Advanced Technology.

Head of Eastern Mapping Division.
United States Geological Survey
Reston
Virginia
22092
USA

John R Beaumont
Professor in Management and Head of the School of Management at the University of Bath. Member

of the Council of the Economic and Social Research Council and Chairman of their Research and Resources Advisory Group and Regional Research Laboratories Steering Committee.

School of Management
University of Bath
Claverton Down
Bath
BA2 7AY
UK

Joseph K Berry

Associate Professor in the Department of Forest and Wood Sciences, Colorado State University, and Principal in Berry and Associates, Consultants in GIS Technology. Board member, Spatial Information Systems Corporation. Interested in applications fully incorporating map analysis techniques into the decision-making process.

Department of Forestry & Wood Sciences
Colorado State University
Fort Collins
Colorado
80524
USA

Michael J Blakemore

Executive Director of NOMIS at the University of Durham. Research interests in data quality and the development of integrated access to national and international geographical information.

NOMIS
Unit 3P
Mountjoy Research Centre
University of Durham
DH1 3SW
UK

Graeme F Bonham-Carter

Research Scientist, Geological Survey of Canada and Adjunct Professor of Geology, University of Ottawa. Current research interests in the applications of GIS for modelling in geology.

Mineral Resources Division
Geological Survey of Canada
601 Booth Street
Ottawa
Ontario
K1A OE8
Canada

Peter A Burrough

Professor of Physical Geography and Geographical Information Systems at the University of Utrecht, the Netherlands. Chairman of the Netherlands Centre for Geographical Information Processing and the Steering Committee of EGIS (European GIS Congress Organization). Research interests include the development and application of GIS technology for environmental modelling with special attention to the use of non-exact techniques such as geostatistics and error propagation, fuzzy reasoning and fractals in groundwater and surface water models, soil, water and air pollution and land evaluation.

Department of Physical Geography
Faculty of Geographical Sciences
University of Utrecht
Heidelberglaan 2
PO Box 80115
Utrecht
The Netherlands

Barbara P Buttenfield

Assistant Professor in the Department of Geography, State University of New York at Buffalo. Researcher and member of the Scientific Policy Committee of the National Center for Geographic Information and Analysis. Research interests include map generalization and scale dependent geometry, and the use and design of GIS graphics for analysis and illustration.

NCGIA-Buffalo
301 Wilkeson Quad
State University of New York at Buffalo
Buffalo
New York
14261
USA

Richard Buxton

Principal Associate in the Government Services Division of Coopers & Lybrand Deloitte and manager of the government sector GIS consultancy practice. Special interests include GIS strategy in central and local government and the cost/benefit analysis of GIS investment in the public sector.

Coopers and Lybrand Deloitte
Plumtree Court
London
EC4A 4HT
UK

List of Contributors

Hugh W Calkins
Associate Professor of Geography, State University of New York at Buffalo. Research Scientist at the National Center for Geographic Information and Analysis. Active in development and use of GIS for town planning and local government since the mid 1960s.

NCGIA-Buffalo
301 Wilkeson Quad
State University of New York at Buffalo
Buffalo
New York
14261
USA

Roger Chorley
Chairman of the Committee of Enquiry into the Handling of Geographic Information and member of the House of Lords Select Committee on Science and Technology. Past President of the Royal Geographical Society and President of the Association for Geographic Information and the National Trust. Former Senior Partner and currently advisor, Coopers & Lybrand Deloitte.

The National Trust
36 Queen Anne's Gate
London
SW1H 9AS
UK

Nicholas R Chrisman
Associate Professor of Geography at the University of Washington, Seattle. Previously spent ten years at the Harvard Laboratory for Computer Graphics and Spatial Analysis and five years at the University of Wisconsin, Madison.

Department of Geography
University of Washington
406 Smith Hall
Seattle
Washington
98195
USA

David M Clark
Scientific Assistant to the Director of the National Geophysical Data Center, part of the National Oceanographic and Atmospheric Administration. Research interests include GIS applications for the study of the Earth system and global change, and integrated vector/raster GIS.

NGDC/NOAA
325 Broadway
Boulder
Colorado
80303
USA

Andrew L Clarke
Marketing Manager, Australian Surveying and Land Information Group, Canberra. Experience in surveys for the Australian and Antarctic mapping programmes, development of national digital spatial databases, and acquisition and management of GIS.

Australian Surveying and Land Information Group
PO Box 2
Belconnen
ACT 2616
Australia

J Terry Coppock
Emeritus Professor of Geography at the University of Edinburgh. Currently Editor of the *International Journal of Geographical Information Systems*.

Department of Geography
University of Edinburgh
Drummond Street
Edinburgh
EH8 9XP
UK

David J Cowen
Professor of Geography and Director of the Humanities and Social Sciences Computing Laboratory at the University of South Carolina. US delegate to the IGU Commission on GIS and member of the National Research Council Mapping Sciences Committee.

Department of Geography
University of South Carolina
Columbia
South Carolina
29208
USA

Peter F Dale
Professor of Land Surveying at East London Polytechnic. Member of the AGI council. Past President of the Royal Institution of Chartered Surveyors Land Surveyors' Division. Research interests in Land Information Systems especially in developing countries.

List of Contributors

Department of Land Surveying
Polytechnic of East London
Longbridge Road
Dagenham
Essex
RM8 2AS
UK

Jack Dangermond
President of ESRI Inc., Redlands California, the developers of ARC/INFO. Author of many papers on GIS and influential in its development.

ESRI Inc
380 New York Street
Redlands
California
92373
USA

Frank W Davis
Associate Professor in the Department of Geography, University of California Santa Barbara. Research interests include biogeography, plant ecology, ecological modelling using remote sensing and GIS.

Department of Geography
University of California
Santa Barbara
California
93106
USA

Paul J Densham
Assistant Professor of Geography, State University of New York at Buffalo, and Research Scientist in the NCGIA. Research interests include spatial decision support systems, locational analysis and parallel algorithms.

Department of Geography
114 Wilkeson Quad
State University of New York at Buffalo
Buffalo
New York
14261
USA

Max J Egenhofer
Research Assistant Professor at the National Center for Geographic Information and Analysis. Research interests include the design of database management systems for GIS, spatial query languages and spatial reasoning.

NCGIA
Department of Surveying Engineering
University of Maine
Orono
Maine
04473
USA

Earl F Epstein
Professor of Natural Resources, Ohio State University. Trained as a scientist (PhD Physical Chemistry) and in Law (JD). Interests include legal, economic and institutional development of GIS and LIS.

School of Natural Resources
Ohio State University
2021 Coffey Road
Columbus
Ohio
43210–1085
USA

Peter F Fisher
Lecturer in GIS at the Department of Geography, Leicester University. Research interests include many aspects of error in geographical data, especially soils and remotely sensed data, and geographical applications of artificial intelligence.

Department of Geography
University of Leicester
University Road
Leicester
LE1 7RH
UK

Robin Flowerdew
Lecturer in Geography at the University of Lancaster and North West Regional Research Laboratory. Interested in statistical applications in geography, especially population and urban geography.

Department of Geography
University of Lancaster
Bailrigg
Lancaster
LA1 4YB
UK

Andrew U Frank
New England ACSM Professor in Land Information Studies and Associate Director of the National Center for Geographic Information and Analysis at

the University of Maine. Research interests include database management systems, methods to represent geometrical properties in a database, software engineering and user interfaces for GIS.

NCGIA
119 Boardman Hall
University of Maine
Orono
Maine
04473
USA

Wm. Randolph Franklin

Associate Professor in the Electrical, Computer, and Systems Engineering Department, Rensselaer Polytechnic Institute, Troy. Research interests include algorithms and data structures for efficient processing of large geometric databases on parallel machines.

Electrical, Computer & Systems Engineering Department
Rensselaer Polytechnic Institute
Troy
New York
12180
USA

Herbert Freeman

State of New Jersey Professor of Computer Engineering, Rutgers University, and Director, CAIP Machine Vision Laboratory. Research interests include computer image processing, machine vision, pattern recognition, computer graphics and computerized cartography.

CAIP Center
Rutgers University
PO Box 1390
Piscataway
New Jersey
08855–1390
USA

Barry J Garner

Professor and Head of the School of Geography at the University of New South Wales. Chairman of the National Committee for Geography, Australian Academy of Science and member of the Australian Survey and Mapping Industries Council. Research interests include the application of GIS techniques in urban and regional analysis and GIS education.

School of Geography
University of New South Wales
PO Box 1
Kensington
NSW
2033
Australia

Anthony C Gatrell

Senior Lecturer in the Department of Geography, Lancaster University and Co-Director of the ESRC-funded North West Regional Research Laboratory. Interested in the applications of GIS techniques in environmental and geographical epidemiology.

North West Regional Research Laboratory
Department of Geography
Lancaster University
Lancaster
LA1 4YB
UK

Stephen C Guptill

Scientific Advisor for Geography and Spatial Data Systems, National Mapping Division, US Geological Survey. Research studies concentrate on conceptual modelling of geographical and cartographical features, scale-independent databases, spatial accuracy, and the design of advanced GIS.

USGS National Mapping Division
Office of Research
519 National Center
Reston
Virginia
22092
USA

David A Hastings

Chief, Data Integration and Remote Sensing, National Geophysical Data Center, NOAA, USA. Current research uses GIS for combining disparate data layers into optimally integrated regional and global databases.

NGDC/NOAA
325 Boulder
Colorado
80303
USA

Richard G Healey

Lecturer in Geography at the University of Edinburgh. Research interests in parallel processing and database applications of GIS.

Department of Geography
University of Edinburgh
Drummond Street
Edinburgh
EH8 9XP
UK

Martin Heller
Researcher at the Department of Geography, University of Zurich. Lectures in GIS architecture, computational geometry and computer graphics. Current research focuses on object design for adaptive terrain modelling.

Department of Geography
University of Zurich
Winterthurerstrasse 190
CH 8057
Zurich
Switzerland

John R Herring
Senior Systems Consultant in the GIS, Mapping and Energy Division of Intergraph Corporation. Responsible for supporting product development in GIS, mapping and related fields. Played a major role in Intergraphs's TIGRIS research project.

Intergraph Corporation
Mail Stop IW17A2
One Madison Industrial Park
Huntsville
Alabama
35807–2174
USA

Michael J Jackson
Managing Director of Laser-Scan Limited and formerly Head of the Natural Environment Research Council Thematic Information Services.

Laser-Scan Limited
Science Park
Milton Road
Cambridge
CB4 4FY
UK

Brian Kelk
Formerly Assistant Director responsible for Information and Marketing, now Head of Geosciences Information Technology, British Geological Survey.

British Geological Survey
Keyworth
Nottingham
NG12 5GG
UK

John J Kineman
Environmental scientist and ecologist, working for the National Geophysical Data Center, National Oceanic and Atmospheric Administration on global environment data projects for national and international global change programmes. Research interests include global ecological monitoring and analysis and developments in global applications.

NGDC/NOAA
325 Broadway
Boulder
Colorado
80303
USA

Sachio Kubo
Professor of Geography, Keio University. Research interests include 'intelligent GIS' and multimedia GIS.

Keio University
Faculty of Environmental Information
5322 Endo
Fujisawa
Kanagawa
Japan

William A Mackaness
Research Associate for the National Center for Geographic Information and Analysis, University of Maine. Research interests include human-computer interaction and automated map design.

NCGIA
University of Maine
348 Boardman Hall
Orono
Maine
04469–0110
USA

Robert P Mahoney
Director of Business Information Management, a company providing independent GIS consultancy services. Extensive experience in utility mapping as Project Manager for the British Gas South Eastern Digital Records Trial and British Gas corporate evaluation project. A major contributor to the Ordnance Survey Digitizing and Quality Assurance procedures.

Business Information Management
14 Kings Avenue
Denton
Newhaven
East Sussex
BN9 0NA
UK

Derek H Maling
Author of many papers and several influential books on map projections and cartography. Now retired and living in Wales.

Tredustan Hall
Defynnog
Brecon
Powys
LD3 8YH
UK

David M Mark
Professor of Geography at SUNY Buffalo and Chair of the Scientific Policy Committee of NCGIA. Current research interests include spatial cognition, human-computer interaction and geographical data structures.

NCGIA-Buffalo
Department of Geography
State University of New York at Buffalo
Buffalo
New York
14261
USA

Joel L Morrison
Assistant Division Chief for Research in the National Mapping Division of the USGS at Reston Virginia. Past President of the International Cartographic Association and the American Congress on Surveying and Mapping. Currently Secretary of AM/FM International (North American Division).

USGS
MS 519
National Center
Reston
Virginia
22092
USA

Helen M Mounsey
Senior Associate in GIS and related matters at one of the largest multi-national management consultants. Formerly a lecturer in GIS at Birkbeck College, University of London.

Coopers and Lybrand Deloitte
Plumtree Court
London
EC4A 4HT
UK

Jean-Claude Muller
Professor and Chairman of the Department of Cartography, International Institute for Aerospace Survey and Earth Science (ITC). Research interests include generalization of spatial databases, expert system guidance and decision support systems for geoinformation production, map design and modelling in GIS.

Department of Cartography
International Institute for Aerospace Surveys and Earth Sciences (ITC)
PO Box 6 7500 AA
Enschede
The Netherlands

John F O'Callaghan
Chief of the CSIRO Division of Information Technology, which contains the Centre for Spatial Information Systems, Canberra. Research interests include image processing, visualization, GIS and decision support systems.

Division of IT
CSIRO
PO Box 1599
Macquarie Centre
North Ryde
New South Wales
2113
Australia

Stan Openshaw
Professor of Geography, Technical Director of the North East Regional Research Laboratory and member of the Centre for Urban and Regional Studies. Author of several books and many papers on quantitative geography, particularly with respect to medical and urban geography and nuclear power.

Department of Geography
University of Newcastle
Daysh Building
Newcastle upon Tyne
NE1 7RU
UK

List of Contributors

Lars Ottoson
Head of research and development department at the National Land Survey and member of its board of executive directors. Main GIS interest is the introduction of new techniques in production of maps and geographical databases. Swedish and Scandinavian representative on CERCO working groups and for many years secretary of the Swedish Cartographic Society.

National Land Survey
Lantmaterigatan 2
S-801 82
Gavle
Sweden

Robert Parrott
Director of Research and Information Systems, San Diego Association of Governments (SANDAG). Twenty years experience in conducting surveys and acquisitions for San Diego County and California Mapping Applications, the development of Regional Digital Spatial Databases and Management of Geographical Information Systems for growth management and land use and facility planning.

San Diego Association of Governments
401 B. St. Suite 800
San Diego
California 92101
USA

Jonathan F Raper
Lecturer in Geography at Birkbeck College and Director of the Apple Mapping Centre. Research interest in 3-D GIS spatial languages and interfaces.

Department of Geography
Birkbeck College
University of London
7–15 Gresse Street
London
W1P 1PA
UK

Alan Robinette
Assistant Commissioner for the Minnesota State Planning Agency with lead responsibility for the Land Management Information Center, a data clearing house and service centre for GIS in the State.

Minnesota State Planning Agency
300 Centennial Office Building
658 Cedar Street
St Paul
Minnesota
55155
USA

Bengt Rystedt
Head of the information systems division within the R&D department of the National Land Survey of Sweden. Main interests are design, specification and applications of national geographical databases. Chairman of the ICA Commission on National Atlases and the GIS section of the Swedish Cartographic Society.

National Land Survey
Lantmaterigatan 2
S-801 82
Gavle
Sweden

Ifan D H Shepherd
Principal lecturer in GIS and GIS Laboratory Director at Middlesex Polytechnic. Teaches computer cartography, remote sensing, GIS, computer applications and human-computer interfacing, and manages an authorized training centre for Autocad. Current research interests include the adaptation and integration of desktop software for GIS use, cartographic generalization, hypermedia, and alternative realities.

School of Geography and Planning
Middlesex Polytechnic
Queensway
Enfield
Middlesex
EN3 4SF
UK

W Lynn Shirley
Project Manager at the Humanities and Social Sciences Computer Laboratory at the University of South Carolina. More than 12 years experience in GIS.

Department of Geography
University of South Carolina
Columbia
South Carolina
29208
USA

Karen Siderelis

Head of Center for Geographic Information and Analysis which has provided GIS support and expertise to state agencies for more than a decade.

Center for Geographic Information and Analysis
NC Department of Environment, Health, and Natural Resources
512 North Salisbury Street
PO Box 27687
Raleigh
North Carolina
27611–7687
USA

David S Simonett*

Formerly Professor of Geography at the University of California Santa Barbara and Co-Director of the National Center for Geographic Information and Analysis.

Department of Geography
University of California
Santa Barbara
California
93106
USA
* Deceased

Terence R Smith

Professor of Computer Science and Professor of Geography, University of California Santa Barbara. His various research interests include the development of theoretical bases for logic-based and object-based spatial database systems, as well as implementation aspects of such systems and their application to the modelling of complex geographic phenomena.

Department of Computer Science
University of California
Santa Barbara
California
93106
USA

Michael (Sam) Sowton

Head of Research and Development in the Ordnance Survey since 1983. Chairman of the UK National Transfer Format (NTF) Steering Committee. Experience in surveying and mapping in Great Britain and overseas with Military Survey, the Ordnance Survey and the Directorate of Overseas Survey. Currently responsible for projects concerned with the development of digital mapping and topographic databases.

Ordnance Survey
Romsey Road
Maybush
Southampton
SO9 4DH
UK

Lowell E Starr

Chief of the National Mapping Division of the US National Mapping Division of the US Geological Survey until his retirement in February 1991. Since then he has been working in the private sector.

USGS National Mapping Division
521 National Center
Reston
Virginia
22092
USA

Frederick P Stutz

Professor of Geography, San Diego State University in San Diego, California. Experience in building information systems and conducting mapping for land use management and transportation problem solutions for the California Department of Recreation, California Department of Transportation and the City and County of San Diego. Federal research contracts were awarded by the US Department of State, Aid for International Development, US Department of Health and Human Services, US Department of Commerce, the National Oceanographic and Atmospheric Administration and the Environmental Protection Agency.

Department of Geography
San Diego State University
San Diego
California
92182
USA

D R Fraser Taylor

Professor of Geography and International Affairs, Carleton University, Ottawa, Canada, and Associate Dean (International) and Director of Carleton International. Research interests include the preparation and design of maps for computer screens, computer cartography in spatial planning processes in developing nations and the development of the theory and practice of the 'New Cartography'.

Department of Geography
Carleton University
Ottawa
K1S 5B6
Canada

C Dana Tomlin
Formerly Associate Professor of Natural Resources, Director of the Natural Resources Information Laboratory and Assistant Director of the Center for Mapping at The Ohio State University and Associate of the Harvard Forest at Harvard University. Currently Associate Professor Department of Landscape Architecture, University of Pennsylvania. Interested in the development and application of digital cartographic modelling capabilities.

Department of Landscape Architecture
University of Pennsylvania
210 South 34th Street
Rm 119 Meyerson Hall
Philadelphia
19104–6311
USA

John R G Townshend
Professor and Chair, Department of Geography, University of Maryland College Park. Previously Director of the NERC Unit for Thematic Information Systems, Department of Geography, University of Reading UK. Research interests include applications of remote sensing and integration of remote sensing with other data sets.

Department of Geography
Room 1113 Lefrak Hall
University of Maryland
College Park
Maryland
20742
USA

David J Unwin
Senior Lecturer in Geography at the University of Leicester, Co-Director of the Midlands Regional Research Laboratory and Director of the Computers in Teaching Initiative Centre for Geography. Research interests in spatial analysis and GIS education.

Department of Geography
University of Leicester
University Road
Leicester
LE1 7RH
UK

Robert Weibel
Senior Software Engineer, Prime Wild GIS, Zurich. Also Lecturer in GIS at the Department of Geography, University of Zurich. Research interests include digital terrain modelling, automated map generalization, and computer graphics and cartographic visualization.

Prime Wild GIS AG
Hohlstrasse 192
CH-8040
Zurich
Switzerland

Marvin S White Jr
Vice-President, Research and Development at ETAK Inc, a company concerned with navigation and digital geography.

ETAK Inc
1430 O'Brien Drive
Menlo Park
California
94025
USA

Peter A Woodsford
Chairman of Laser-Scan Limited and Chairman for 1991 of the UK Association for Geographic Information.

Laser-Scan Limited
Science Park
Milton Road
Cambridge
CB4 4FY
UK

Ye Jiang
Doctorate candidate in Department of Computer Science, University of California Santa Barbara.

Department of Computer Science
University of California
Santa Barbara
California
93106
USA

ACKNOWLEDGEMENTS

Graeme Bonham-Carter acknowledges that much of the GIS computer work reviewed in his chapter was carried out by Danny Wright. Frits Agterberg played a major role in the study and reviewed the manuscript. Gordon Watson, Andy Rencz, Ramesh Reddy and Alan Goodacre are also thanked for their contributions. Graeme Bonham-Carter's chapter is Geological Survey of Canada Contribution Number 44789.

Peter Burrough acknowledges that sincere thanks are due to all colleagues who over the years have contributed to the successful introduction of quantitative methods and GIS in soil and land resource survey. Thanks are especially due to A. Mateos for permission to use the data in Figs 46.5 and 46.6, to Alfred Stein of the Department of Soil Science and Geology of the Agricultural University, Wageningen, The Netherlands for Figs 46.7, to R. A. MacMillan, Alberta Research Council, Canada for Plate 46.1, S. de Jong, V. Jetten and E. J. Henkens of the Department of Physical Geography, University of Utrecht for Plate 46.2 and Arnold Bregt of the Winand Staring Centre for Integrated Land, Soil and Water Research, Wageningen, The Netherlands for Plate 46.3.

Nicholas Chrisman acknowledges US National Science Foundation Grant SES 87–22084 which provided partial support for this contribution.

Terry Coppock and David Rhind owe a considerable debt to many people in writing about the history of GIS; the list is too long to enumerate. They have both gained immensely from discussions since the 1960s with fellow enthusiasts, often in the most unlikely of places. They trust that they have contributed to a useful result.

Frank Davis and David Simonett acknowledge that Mark Friedl and John Estes provided useful comments on the draft manuscript.

Max Egenhofer acknowledges the support from NSF for the NCGIA under grant number SES 88–10917, Digital Equipment Corporation under TP–765536 and Intergraph Corporation.

Andrew Frank and David Mark acknowledge that their chapter represents part of Research Initiative #2, 'Languages of Spatial Relations', of the National Center for Geographic Information and Analysis, supported by a grant from the National Science Foundation (SES 88–10917); support by NSF is also gratefully acknowledged. Valuable comments on an earlier draft were provided by Max Egenhofer, Michael Gould and Werner Kuhn.

Randolph Franklin acknowledges that his work was supported by NSF Presidential Young Investigator grant CCR–8351942. Partial support for this work was also provided by the Directorate for Computer and Information Science and Engineering, NSF grant CDA–8805910. Equipment at the Computer Science Department and Rensselaer Design Research Center at RPI was used for the work. Part of the work was conducted using the computational resources of the Northeast Parallel Architectures Center (NPAC) at Syracuse University, which is funded by and operates under contract to DARPA and the Air Force Systems Command, Rome Air Development Center (RADC), Griffiss Air Force Base, NY, under contract F306002–88-C-0031. Part of the research reported here was made possible through the support of the New Jersey Commission on Science and Technology and the Rutgers University CAIP Center's Industrial Members.

Acknowledgements

Herbert Freeman acknowledges that most of his chapter is based on the research activities of the author and two of his graduate students, John Ahn and Jeffrey Doerschler. Other graduate students who contributed to the research effort were Andy Heard, Vinciane Lacroix, John Nastelin and Bradford Nickerson. The work was supported by the National Science Foundation under grants ECS84-07900 and DMC-8518621; this support is gratefully acknowledged.

Anthony Gatrell is associated with the North West Regional Research Laboratory at Lancaster University, funded by the Economic and Social Research Council. The University and ESRC are thanked for their financial support of the RRL initiative. Colleagues at Lancaster have provided a stimulating intellectual environment, for which the author is most grateful. Michael Goodchild (Santa Barbara) and David Unwin (Leicester) helped improve an earlier version, though any remaining fuzzy thinking is his and not theirs!

Richard Healey acknowledges the support of the Economic and Social Research Council in funding the Regional Research Laboratory for Scotland and thanks are due to Anona Lyons for drawing the original versions of the diagrams.

Brian Kelk acknowledges that he publishes with the permission of the Director, British Geological Survey.

David Maguire and Jack Dangermond acknowledge the contribution of Jonathan Raper and Nicholas Green in formulating the GIS functionality classification.

David Rhind thanks David Pearce and Chris Denham at the Office of Population Censuses and Surveys in Britain and Bob Marx at the Bureau of Census who helped provide material and insight for the chapter. The UK Economic and Social Research Council funded part of the work of the South East Regional Research Laboratory and this review emanates from that work.

Karen Siderelis acknowledges first, and foremost, the superb CGIA staff; in particular her chapter could not have been written without the assistance of Scott Carr, Timothy R. Johnson, Zsolt Nagy and Thomas N. Tribble. Thanks are also due to the client organizations whose work is summarized including the Albemarle-Pamlico Estuarine Study, the UNC Sea Grant College Program, the NC Hazardous Waste Management Commission and the NC Board of Science and Technology. Finally, Dr. Walter Clark, Dr. Earl Mac Cormac, Dr. Bill Dunn, Darrell Hinnant, Dr. Robert Holman, Prof David Rhind and Tom Scheitlin have all been most helpful in ways which they should know!

John Townshend acknowledges that much of the material used in his chapter on the distinctive problems of environmental data sets arose through the activities of the NERC Working Group on Geographic Information, which the author chaired. The contributions of the members of the working group (G. Darwell, A. Laughton, B. Kelk, C. Milner, J. Plevin and D. Pugh) are gratefully acknowledged.

Several US authors are associated with the National Center for Geographic Information and Analysis sites at the University of California Santa Barbara; the State University of New York at Buffalo; and the University of Maine. Michael Goodchild acknowledges the role that the US National Science Foundation has played in establishing and funding the NCGIA through grant SES 88-10917, and in supporting the activities of himself, Andrew Frank, David Mark, Terence Smith, Frank Davis, David Simonett, Max Egenhofer, Paul Densham, Je Yiang, Barbara Buttenfield, William Mackaness, Hugh Calkins and many others.

We are grateful to the following for permission to reproduce copyright figures and tables:

American Congress on Surveying & Mapping for fig. 13.6 from fig. 1 (Beard & Chrisman, 1988); American Society for Photogrammetry & Remote Sensing for table 13.4 from table 1M (Merchant, 1987) copyright 1987 by the American Society for Photogrammetry & Remote Sensing; Butterworth & Co. (Publishers) Ltd. for fig. 13.3 from fig. 2.1, p. 8 (Parry & Perkins, 1987); the editor, *Cartographica* (University of Toronto Press) for fig. 13.1a from fig. 1 (Gardiner, 1982); Environmental Systems Research Institute, Inc. for figs 22.4 & 22.6 from figs 4 & 1 (ESRI, 1989 © 1991 Environmental Systems Research Institute, Inc.); the author, J

Acknowledgements

Hogg for fig. 9.5 from figs 2–5 (Gahegan & Hogg, 1986); London Regional Transport (L. T. Museum) for fig. 9.4; Longman Group UK Ltd. for figs 13.1b & 13.2 from figs 32, 126, 129, 165, pp. 46, 160, 161, 192 (Keates, 1989); the author, Dr. D H Maling for fig. 9.6 from fig. 14.4 (Maling, 1989); McGraw–Hill Inc. for fig. 45.5 from fig. 6, p. 24 (Rapp & Collins, 1987 copyright 1987 McGraw–Hill Inc.); National Joint Utility Group for fig. 42.3; Swiss Federal Office of Topography for figs 19.3, 19.9, 19.10, 19.12, 19.13, 19.15–17; Taylor & Francis Ltd. and the respective authors for figs 13.5 from fig. 7, p. 93 (Rhind & Clark, 1988), 13.8 from fig. 2, p. 245 (Flowerdew & Green, 1989) and table 13.1 from table on p. 132 (Tobler, 1988); the author, Prof. I P Williamson for figs 39.1 & 39.2 from figs 1 & 2 (Williamson & Blackburn, 1987).

While every effort has been made to trace the owners of copyright material, in a few cases this has proved impossible and we take this opportunity to offer our apologies to any copyright holders whose rights we may have unwittingly infringed.

We are grateful to the following for permission to reproduce copyright photographs:

Altek Corporation for plate 17.1; DATANET Plus Mapping and Land Management Information Center (LMIC) for plate 54.8; René L'Eplattenier for plates 19.4, 19.5; Intergraph (UK) Limited for plate 17.6; Laser–Scan Limited for plates 17.5, 17.7, 17.8, 17.9, 17.10; Land Management Information Center (LMIC) for plates 54.6, 54.10; E Meier, University of Zurich and ESA/Earthnet for plate 19.2; Minnesota Board of Water and Soil Resources and Land Management Information Center (LMIC) for plate 54.2; Minnesota Department of Natural Resources for plates 54.7, 54.11, 54.13; Minnesota Geological Survey for plate 54.14; Minnesota Pollution Control Agency and Land Management Information Center (LMIC) for plates 54.1, 54.5, 54.9; N Quarmby and the NERC Unit for Thematic Information Systems for plate 49.4; David A Reece, Knoxville Utilities Board for plate 42.1; Rochester–Olmstead County Planning and Land Management Information Center (LMIC) for plates 54.3, 54.4; Scan Graphics for plates 17.2, 17.3; SPOT Image Corporation © 1989 CNES for plates 56.8, 56.9; Tangent Engineering, Inc. for plate 17.4; G Wadge and the NERC Unit for plates 49.5, 49.6.

While every effort has been made to trace the owners of copyright material in a few cases this has proved impossible and we take this opportunity to offer our apologies to any copyright holders whose rights we may have unwittingly infringed.

SECTION III

APPLICATIONS

Introduction	3–10	(c) **Environmental applications**		
D W Rhind, D J Maguire and M F Goodchild		46. Soil information systems *P A Burrough*	153–69	

(a) National and international GIS programmes

35. A USGS perspective on GIS 11–22
    L E Starr and K E Anderson

36. Development of GIS-related activities at the Ordnance Survey 23–38
    M Sowton

37. National GIS programmes in Sweden 39–46
    L Ottoson and B Rystedt

38. The development of GIS in Japan 47–56
    S Kubo

39. Land and Geographical Information Systems in Australia 57–70
    J F O'Callaghan and B J Garner

40. GIS and developing nations 71–84
    D R F Taylor

(b) Socio-economic applications

41. Land information Systems 85–99
    P F Dale

42. GIS and utilities 101–14
    R P Mahoney

43. Car navigation systems 115–25
    M White

44. Counting the people: the role of GIS 127–37
    D W Rhind

45. GIS and market analysis 139–51
    J R Beaumont

(c) Environmental applications

46. Soil information systems 153–69
    P A Burrough

47. Integration of geoscientific data using GIS 171–84
    G F Bonham-Carter

48. Multisource, multinational environmental GIS: lessons learnt from CORINE 185–200
    H M Mounsey

49. Environmental databases and GIS 201–16
    J R G Townshend

50. Global databases and their implications for GIS 217–31
    D M Clark, D A Hastings and J J Kineman

(d) Management applications

51. GIS and public policy 233–45
    H W Calkins

52. Urban GIS applications 247–60
    R Parrott and F P Stutz

53. Land resource information systems 261–73
    K C Siderelis

54. Land management applications of GIS in the state of Minnesota 275–83
    A Robinette

55. GIS in island resource planning: a case study in map analysis 285–95
    J K Berry

56. Integrated planning information systems 297–310
    D J Cowen and W L Shirley

SECTION III

INTRODUCTION

D W RHIND, D J MAGUIRE AND M F GOODCHILD

Sections I and II have demonstrated the capabilities of GIS methodologies and techniques. Even though a number of significant research problems remain, much use of these systems is now routine. Indeed, the applications of GIS are limited only by awareness of the possibilities, the imagination of those in charge of the facilities and the costs involved. Fortunately, most of the costs are falling and awareness is growing. Given all this, it is scarcely surprising that numerous possible applications could have been chosen to illustrate the breadth of applications.

Despite the inevitable difficulties involved in making a selection of topics and authors, the material that follows represents the most comprehensive planned overview of GIS applications to date. The structure is an obvious one: the first subsection is a short survey of selected national and international developments including the developing countries as a single group. The other three subsections provide overviews of socio-economic, environmental and management application areas. Each deals with specific systems currently in operation in selected organizations. Two considerations dictated the choice of most examples in Section III. The first is that the individual systems selected had, of necessity, to have been in operation for a substantial period in order to obtain proof of their benefits. The second was the need to obtain multiple views on similar topics. Thus three chapters have been included on land and resource management (by Siderelis, Robinette, and Cowen and Shirley) and another three on environmental databases (by Mounsey, Townshend, and Clark, Hastings and Kineman). Yet, in each case, the authors both confirm and contradict each other's viewpoint providing different views (e.g. at different scales of viewing and from differing perspectives) of the same general area.

The nature of GIS and the responsibilities of organizations running them are such that many themes occur even within one chapter: thus Mounsey's chapter could readily be considered as a description of multinational GIS collaboration, of environmental databases in general or of a particular system. Such multiple linkages are not only inevitable – they are desirable because GIS applications are typically multidisciplinary and multipurpose. Moreover, such an 'enabling technology' as GIS frequently has important implications for the internal organization of the agency concerned (as Starr and Anderson point out in Chapter 35). For both reasons – the ubiquitous nature of the applications and the effect on the structure of the host organization of the use of GIS – GIS is already demonstrably a revolutionizing concept and technology.

NATIONAL DEVELOPMENTS IN OFFICIAL MAPPING AND GIS

The first subsection contains chapters on the nature and pace of developments in a selection of countries, together with the formal national objectives where they can be ascertained. In this work, considerable emphasis is placed upon the role of national mapping agencies since, in most countries, national mapping agencies provide the spatial framework over which GIS applications are 'draped'; geodetic control and subsequent topographic mapping are normally essential preliminaries to successful exploitation of GIS. The first two chapters demonstrate the international convergence which is occurring between national mapping agencies. Thus Lowell Starr and Eric Anderson (US Geological Survey or USGS) in Chapter 35 and Michael Sowton (Ordnance Survey of Great Britain or OS) in Chapter 36 both make clear the evolution of their agencies. Both USGS and OS started by producing paper maps using traditional manual means, moved through a stage where computers were seen simply as a means of producing the same products faster and/or cheaper, to the present day where the database is regarded as the central concept and maps are spun off to meet either standard or special user requirements.

These first two contributions also exemplify the enormous diversity of character which may exist in national mapping agencies; indeed, in many respects, the USGS and the OS represent opposites within those agencies which are active in base mapping. The USGS only produces digital data as large as 1 : 24 000 in scale and complete coverage of the country is currently only available in up-to-date form at 1 : 100 000 scale; in Britain, complete coverage of the country is available at 1 : 10 000 scale and 70 per cent of the land area is covered by mapping at 1 : 1250 or 1 : 2500 scale. Keeping the topographical data up to date is becoming a topic of major importance for USGS; it is the only one that matters for OS and the mapping of few – if any – populated areas under their jurisdiction is more than a year out of date. Perhaps the best explanatory factors for these differences are history and the 30 : 1 ratio in the sizes of the countries. But the society in which the surveys are embedded also controls what is done. Within the federal system, it is not the role of a national government to make detailed local maps (a situation replicated in what was the Federal Republic of Germany where IfAG, the national mapping agency, was only able to make topographic maps at 1 : 200 000 and smaller scales). By contrast, and despite the changes in the 1980s, OS resides in a highly centralized state and, in practice, enjoys a virtual state monopoly to work at the large scales – its surveyors have a statutory right of access to land. Yet, astonishingly, it is in the United Kingdom that commercialization of the products has gone much the furthest; the OS is on a path to complete recovery of all operating costs from revenue while this seems never to have been contemplated seriously in the United States, where data collected at the taxpayer's expense are distributed at little more than the cost of copying. Compare, for instance, the cost of purchasing 1 : 625 000 scale data from OS (quoted at about US$80,000 in 1988) with the $28 cost of the 1 : 2 million scale data for the (much larger) United States. It is not the role of the authors to make judgements about which is the better system; it is merely noted here that an increasing emphasis on cost recovery from sales of data seems to be occurring in many countries across the world and that few national mapping agencies are exempt from it. The consequences for use of GIS are obvious.

If topographic mapping is the framework within which GIS normally function, the nature of the data collecting agency and its concerns with non-topographical data vary considerably throughout the world. In Sweden, as Lars Ottoson and Bengt Rystedt point out in Chapter 37, the Landmateriet or National Land Survey has been in existence since 1615 and has much broader roles than USGS or OS. In particular, it has extremely close relationships with the cadastral system for recording land ownership. To those from other countries, the Swedish (and other Scandinavian) data holdings are astonishing. Publicly accessible registers of individuals and their addresses are cross-referenced to others of property ownership; to these are now being added detailed property boundaries in computer form. The situation may be contrasted with that in which details on individuals are held by banks and private sector firms in the United States, the United Kingdom and elsewhere, for credit rating and other purposes (see Chapter 45 by John Beaumont). In the Swedish case, however, the system is run openly by the state. Finally, it is appropriate to point out the great early contributions of the Swedes to GIS through such work as that of Hägerstrand in the 1950s – even if GIS did not then exist as a name!

Land Information Systems (or LIS) are now part of the fabric of the administration in many countries, as Peter Dale points out in Chapter 41. Nowhere is this more true than in Australia where, as John O'Callaghan and Barry Garner illustrate in Chapter 39, the land registration process has driven much of the GIS work. In passing, it is worth noting here the controversy which has grown up in the use of terminology. For Dale and McLaughlin (1988), the functions and uses of a LIS are enormously varied but centre on the handling of detailed data pertaining to the land (and sea!); by interpolation, they seem to regard GIS rather differently, suggesting it deals with less detailed environmental data, usually derived from small-scale maps. Such a view may accurately reflect the ideas of many land surveyors. On the other hand, Maguire, in Chapter 1, and others have argued that LIS and AM/FM are now normally regarded as special-purpose GIS (which may well be operated independently of a more complex GIS, depending on the needs of the task). Australia illustrates one type of system evolution perfectly: LIS become adopted first since they are part of the everyday, low level (but essential) functions of the state and more analytical uses of (typically) aggregated versions of the data follow. O'Callaghan and Garner in Chapter 39 also discuss the official tendency to review and reorganize national mapping organizations: in Australia, the former NATMAP and other federal government mapping agencies were reorganized into AUSLIG, the Australian Survey and Land Information Group in the late 1980s.

For many observers of the GIS scene, the role of Japan has been an enigma. All know of the country's role in diversifying the uses of high technology, especially to Japan's economic benefit. Sachio Kubo in Chapter 38 indicates the long history of the Japanese geographers' involvement in the conceptualization of GIS-type analyses and the extensive data collection by official agencies. Yet, to date, little software or even hardware used in GIS has emanated from Japan. He attributes this uncharacteristic situation primarily to the early concentration on gridded databases and to disagreements between official agencies. None the less, the highly sophisticated systems created by some of the major utilities and the setting up of major research projects such as the National Museum of Cartography and the Global Environmental Change project suggest that Japanese developments will repay close attention in the future.

There is a common perception that GIS is largely a First World activity and that developing countries in particular have played little role in GIS, or even that they have no need for sophisticated GIS. Such a view is belied by such papers as that by Chen Shupeng (1987). He pointed out the fragile equilibrium in which China's environment exists and how readily this may be disturbed, with catastrophic effects for the populace. GIS have been used in Chen's Laboratory for Resource and Environmental Information Systems in Beijing for a number of years, as well as elsewhere in the country, to model, predict and report the behaviour of natural systems. Chapter 40 in this volume, by Fraser Taylor, takes the process further: he describes the declining state of natural environments and wealth in some parts of the world, and indicates how GIS can – at least in theory – help in minimizing avoidable problems. He argues against the notion of 'quick technological fixes': in his view, 'technological imperialism' occurs through the supply of systems by (often well-meaning) agencies in North America and Europe to those who live and work in different social, political and environmental circumstances. The need for 'indigenization of GIS and high technology' – and as soon as possible – is the moral of his chapter.

SOME PARTICULAR APPLICATIONS OF GIS

From the galaxy of applications which might have been selected, three particular categories have been isolated. These cover the assembly and use of basic spatial data about the land, its people and the infrastructure on and under it (broadly socio-economic applications); the environmental dimension; and management issues relating to the first two categories. Each is now introduced in turn.

GIS and land, people and infrastructure

The importance of LIS in particular countries has already been indicated. In Chapter 41, Peter Dale describes the origins and growth of LIS in general terms and concentrates on several common key factors in their success, such as the need for professionally authenticated standards in managing data guaranteed by statute and the assessment of costs and benefits. For him, the organizational and management issues are crucial to the role of such GIS. Interestingly – and fruitfully – some examples in his chapter also appear in the chapters by Ottoson and Rystedt (Chapter 37) and O'Callaghan and Garner (Chapter 39). However, the material is often used to illustrate different points, reflecting again the web of inter-connections that typify GIS activities.

If the description of the ownership of parcels of land is fundamental to the functioning of most societies, the use of that land is also vital information for many purposes. Arguably, the most influential users of land and GIS thus far have been the utilities. As Kubo points out in Chapter 38, Tokyo Gas alone has 6.7 million subscribers. The second chapter in subsection (b), Chapter 42, is by Rob Mahoney. He describes the explosive growth in the use by utility industries of GIS, starting often with simple mapping tools under the Automated Mapping/Facilities Management banner and evolving into full information systems as the mapping functions are grafted on to other business concerns. What stands out from Mahoney's overview is that the tasks within different utilities vary considerably and hence demand inputs such as topographical mapping in different forms. In addition, the utilities' technical, operational and legal problems are greater than is often understood by those outside the industry.

The inventory of land ownership and of utilities' plant is among the most basic and critical needs in developed and developing countries alike. Navigation, however, is just as basic. In this book, there is insufficient space to consider how the rapid technological developments have aided marine navigation. But, in Chapter 43, Marvin White describes how competing groups in the motor industry have come to believe that car guidance systems may be a major selling point. A plethora of Japanese, US and European groups have designed and built prototype systems, and a few of them have been marketed. The essence of the earliest systems is the combined use of digital maps of the street network and some form of dead reckoning derived from the distance and orientation of travel of the vehicle, updated periodically as available. Subsequent systems may be aided by beacons on lamp-posts, which can indicate roads which are temporarily closed, etc.; use of the Global Positioning System may, in the future, provide instantaneous absolute position fixing to avoid many of the hazards of dead reckoning, especially in urban areas with much electromagnetic flux. With over 500 million cars on the roads, the potential market is large and the rewards for commercial success considerable. The opportunity is by no means restricted to the provision of hardware and software. Publishing concerns run by individuals such as Murdoch and Maxwell have become involved in the field of data provision through the purchase of firms like Etak and Bartholomews.

A knowledge of where the people live and work and how the numbers and characteristics of the populace as a whole differ from place to place is addressed by David Rhind in Chapter 44. On the basis of census and other figures, many nations monitor the effects of policy, plan school building and other infrastructure provision and create areas which Members of Parliament represent in democratic fora; such a knowledge of population also often forms the basis of resource distribution from the nation state to local government and serves as the basis for thriving private sector businesses (e.g. Chapter 45 by John Beaumont). Such data collection is often expensive and may have unexpected 'knock-on' effects: the preparations for the 1990 Census in the United States, for instance, involved spending over $170 million on hardware and software. The resulting TIGER program provides nation-wide topographic detail hitherto unavailable in that country. More important still, the accuracy and outcome of the data collection process may be critical: Detroit, for instance, sued the US Bureau of Census in 1990 when preliminary figures suggested the city's population was 980 000, that is 20 000 people short of a threshold for claiming certain federal grants. Rhind describes the different methods of assembling population and related socio-economic data and the role of GIS in the data collection and analysis.

While White is concerned with navigating from one known position to another, specified by a user, and Rhind is concerned with ways to enumerate the population accurately, in Chapter 45 John Beaumont is concerned to hunt through space and find all of those populated areas that meet certain criteria. His concern is with market analysis and he shows how GIS has a role in all four of the 'Ps' in the marketing mix: product, price, place and promotion. Like Dale, he stresses the need for further work on how to graft the technology on to individual organizations, many of which have multi-million or even multi-billion dollar turnovers and which operate in a highly competitive environment; securing competitive edge through use of GIS is the way they must proceed – but the GIS must be tailored to fit with the business and be usable routinely by those in the industry.

The environmental dimension

Perhaps the ubiquitous concern of scientists, politicians and other human beings at large in the late 1980s and early 1990s is that for the fate of the environment. Concern for the environment ranges from that for areas immediately surrounding people's homes up to the global scale. GIS have already made useful contributions to the collection, analysis and understanding of information on the environment and promise much more success. For this reason, a group of five chapters, comprising subsection (c), describes different aspects of this use of these systems.

In Chapter 46, Peter Burrough begins the group by introducing ideas on the nature of soils, that most apparently simple yet undefinable of all basic substances. From this, he describes the evolution in the way soil scientists have tried to collect information on soils, and to record and model the nature and variation of soils within GIS. Seeing the problem as essentially a geostatistical one, he describes efforts to treat the soil not as a set of polygons, within which all soils are supposed to be identical, but rather as a property varying continuously across space and, interestingly, with scale. Inevitably and logically, this involves discussion of optimal spatial interpolation. He concludes with examples of the application of GIS in mapping and modelling soil properties.

Graeme Bonham-Carter takes up this theme of the inherent variability of natural phenomena in Chapter 47. He asks how it is possible to know which factors give rise to measured values of a certain phenomenon (such as the concentration of gold in a rock) at different places in space. From observations made at sets of sample points, plus background information in geological map and other form, he integrates the data sources and deduces promising areas for further prospecting. Such modelling is facilitated by particular spatial data structures and the use of 'state of the art' statistical modelling tools.

However complex is the real world, there is a need to attempt to understand it if it is to be managed sensibly. Nowhere is this more complicated than at the multinational level. Chapter 48, by Helen Mounsey, describes the GIS-based CO-oRdinated INformation on the European environment (CORINE) project of the European Commission (the civil or public service of the 12 nation Community) as an exemplar. CORINE produced a spatially coherent environmental database for use as input to policy making. Its creation demanded cooperation between multiple groups in each of the member countries and, unlike many other projects, it was policy driven. But, like many other projects, it was under-financed and hardware, software, policy and data needs evolved continuously as it proceeded. From this experience, Mounsey extracts more general issues and conclusions on building and using a GIS in such (typical) conditions of adversity!

Mounsey's chapter deals with detailed data held for an area of about 2.3 million km^2 and largely assembled from existing map-based and ground-collected data. Yet a striking change in the 1980s was the realization that changes to weather, climate, the fauna and flora and other resources of the earth could only be understood by starting with the viewpoint of the whole planet (ESSC 1988). Publications such as the Bruntland Report (WCED 1988) inculcated the idea of inter-dependency among communities across the world and the desirability of 'sustainable development' (though that proved hard to define in practice and even harder to achieve). Such interest led to great interest in monitoring global change. John Townshend in Chapter 49 describes the range of environmental data sets now extant and stresses the shortcomings of traditional GIS in dealing with the three-dimensional and four-dimensional data commonly in use in this field. After summarizing the characteristics of the different types of environmental data, he assesses the problems encountered in carrying out meaningful linkage of data sets. The role of GIS methods is described through five, highly contrasting examples. He concludes (like authors of some other chapters) that GIS has much potential – some of which is now being realized – for contributing to understanding the environment but that a lack of awareness, substantial costs and existing discipline-specific, rather than widely available, computer tools are delaying factors.

The final contribution to subsection (c) is Chapter 50 by David Clark, David Hastings and John Kineman of the US National Oceanic and Atmospheric Administration (NOAA). Like Townshend, they concentrate on the global picture but, unlike him, they are based in an organization whose remit is the collection and dissemination of environmental data. Organizations active in this field include the US National Aeronautics and Space Administration (NASA), NOAA, the European Space Agency (ESA) and corresponding agencies elsewhere in the world; Clark et al. describe the need for GIS for global monitoring, a selection of the most important programmes for data collection and analysis, the shortcomings of existing systems and the avenues which researchers are now pursuing to match scientific needs and aspirations to financial and technical realities.

Management using GIS

While the management of GIS is itself a topic of some importance (and is partly covered by Michael Blakemore in Chapter 33), much more important is its use in planning and resource management generally. The final subsection (subsection (d)) thus deals with a set of examples of how this has or can be achieved. It begins with Chapter 51 by Hugh Calkins. He sets out a model of how decision making is achieved in the creation of public policy. Calkins sees three major categories of GIS use in policy analysis: to determine where and when public policies are needed; to aid in the formulation of public policies; and to analyse the extent to which public policies are successful and have achieved the goals and objectives intended. His systems model is illustrated by use in the evaluation of alternative land use allocations in a town that is experiencing explosive growth in population. Calkins shows how general policy statements may be converted into the quantified and specific thresholds which the existing types of GIS can handle. While it cannot be shown in a book, the dynamic aspects of such models are also important and can be brilliantly encapsulated by combining GIS and gaming simulations; a first version of this sort of tool is provided by the SimCity simulation (Joffe and Wright 1989) and Maguire (1989) presents some other examples.

A particularly important application area of GIS is the management of urban areas. In Chapter 52, Robert Parrott and Fred Stutz exemplify this through the example of GIS use in the San Diego Association of Governments (SANDAG). Though the detailed uses of such systems for urban areas will vary between (and even within) countries because of legal, fiscal and administrative differences in the roles of local government, the SANDAG example is one in which information-based planning strategies covering both the long and the short term have long been used. The principles underlying it are thus relevant to many other urban environments. A primary use of GIS has been for modelling purposes; the four sample applications described illustrate the use of GIS for finding land for development, emergency planning, determining the ideal location for fire stations, and assistance in crime control and documentation.

Four further chapters then demonstrate the way in which GIS have been used in land and natural resource management in three US states and on a small island. The three US examples demonstrate how effective use can be made of GIS over extended periods by local government. The choice of governments may appear quixotic but has a rationale: all three demonstrate successful uses; all three have faced a variety of tasks over the years, and all three come from one particular type of government – a US state – so that comparisons of the different approaches can be made. That the two superficially similar chapters by Karen Siderelis (North Carolina) and Alan Robinette (Minnesota) cite no identical applications demonstrates the range of applications to which GIS can be put in such governments, rather than inspired editing by Maguire, Goodchild and Rhind! Finally, by way of introduction to this group, it is entirely coincidental that two of the states concerned happen to be adjacent (though belief in the importance of geography and the likelihood of innovations spreading by local contagion suggest it should not be a matter of coincidence).

Karen Siderelis, in Chapter 53, first defines Land Resource Information Systems (LRIS) and the features that distinguish them from other application areas of GIS. She also defines the various user groups of such systems and describes the types and characteristics of data that the systems handle. The bulk of her chapter, however, comprises a description of three major case studies illustrating the value of LRIS in a variety of practical ways: these are the Albemarle–Pamlico estuarine study, state-wide screening for a hazardous waste management facility and the location of an optimal proposed site for the Superconducting Super Collider. A key component of her account is the way in which databases within the North Carolina Center for Geographic Information and Analysis had to be assembled initially on a project-by-project basis, necessitating much long-range planning and ingenuity to establish the credibility of an ongoing geographical database.

In Chapter 54, Alan Robinette describes how

Minnesota is a large state with over 20 years' experience in the application of GIS to environmental management. As elsewhere, it has been necessary to grapple with the conflict between breadth and depth in the inventory and analysis of cultural and natural resources. Decisions are needed on issues ranging from state-wide land suitability to clean-up of pollution at an individual site. The chapter describes a conceptual hierarchy of planning decisions and the appropriate scale and resolution of data required to support these decisions. Case studies in five topical areas are described which exemplify the concept of 'telescoping' to the appropriate levels of decision and geography.

Many of the developments described thus far have been based upon significantly sized computers (mainframes to workstations) and have been carried out where skills should be in (relative) abundance. In complete contrast, in Chapter 55 Joe Berry describes a self-contained and more local project on resource planning using an IBM PC machine, which was actually carried out in the US Virgin Islands. He demonstrates how a model was built by combining information gained from map and other sources and, from it, 'best' allocations of land use were generated after making a number of subjective decisions; the sensitivity of the results to these decisions is evaluated by re-running the model with different parameters.

The last part of subsection (d), Chapter 56 by Dave Cowen and Lynn Shirley, attempts to summarize and extend the lessons derived from its predecessors. It examines those tasks typically performed by planners, which involve spatial data handling and the consequences in terms of data sets and GIS functionality. It assesses, in a critical way, the GIS resources currently available and the needs for a Spatial Decision Support System – thereby linking back to Chapter 26 by Paul Densham and other earlier chapters in this book. The final part of Chapter 56 utilizes a wide-ranging case study of a major GIS project in South Carolina to demonstrate how USGS Digital Line Graphs, Bureau of Census TIGER files and remotely sensed data from SPOT and Landsat can be integrated into a single system that successfully addresses many of the obstacles normally associated with the use of GIS in planning.

It was said at the outset that Section III was about the use of GIS in managing areas, environments and societies. Inevitably, however, the system-specific management issues which have emerged within the chapters include the pragmatic decision making necessary at all stages, leading to the need to build wide area (e.g. state-wide) information services 'bottom-up' from the data files created for specific projects. Throughout all the papers, the hard decisions which need to be made by politicians and government officers are stressed. Ultimately, these involve a yes or no decision but the choice is based upon geographical intelligence provided by the GIS and other factors, all qualitatively combined. Moreover, information provided late (especially in competitive situations such as bidding for the site for the Super Collider) is as useless as wrong information.

Two missing items

That the papers in this section are disparate is undeniable – that was in part a design aim. To our disappointment, however, we were unable to find adequate representation of two types of material which we sought to include and this, in itself, says something about the present state of the GIS market. The first shortcoming is that, of the existing literature, only two papers which describe GIS that failed, are known to the editors. The first, by Giles (1987), was published in China and the second, by Openshaw *et al.* (1990), was presented at the 1990 Association for Geographic Information annual conference in the United Kingdom. Understandably, few people want to confess to failure; yet such papers are instructive for others. In the absence of careful documentation, all that the editors can do is to record our strong impression – based upon discussions with many individuals – that the most common reasons for failure are now organizational weaknesses or political naivety, rather than technical factors.

The second type of 'missing' material is actually covered in part by Drew Clarke in Chapter 31 and is touched upon by Jack Dangermond in Chapter 4. This describes the need for careful cost/benefit analyses – or investment appraisals – of GIS. In an ideal world, each applications paper would have included such a section but many systems have grown by evolution and, typically, have come to be applied to tasks that were not originally anticipated. Moreover, many of the benefits seen by system implementors are claimed to be unquantifiable. In these circumstances, it would be surprising if the system design was optimal. Much information on system evaluation does of course exist, notably inside management consultants, but is usually commercial in confidence. Many studies are now beginning in this area, such as that by the economist, Didier (1990); it is to be hoped that future editions of this book will contain more material of this type. Since such appraisals are now demanded even by governments before undertaking environmental actions (see Pearce, Markandya and Barbier 1989), they will need to become a standard part of all work in GIS.

REFERENCES

Chen Shupeng (1987) Geographical data handling and GIS in China. *International Journal of GIS* **1** (3): 219–28.

Dale P F, McLaughlin J D (1988) *Land Information Management*. Oxford University Press, Oxford

Didier M (1990) *Utilité et valeur de l'Information Géographique*. CNIG Economica, Paris

ESSC (1988) *Earth System Science : a program for global change*. Report prepared by the Earth System Sciences Committee for the National Aeronautics and Space Administration, Washington DC.

Giles R H (1987) The creation, uses and demise of a Virginia USA Geographical Information System. *Proceedings of the International Geographical Union GIS Workshop Beijing, China*. IGU, pp. 507–24

Joffe B A and Wright W (1989) SimCity : Thematic mapping + City management Simulation = an entertaining, interactive gaming tool. *Proceedings of GIS/LIS '89*. ACSM\ASPRS\AAG\URISA\AM/FM, Bethesda Maryland, pp. 591–600

Maguire D J (1989) *Computers in Geography*. Longman, London

Openshaw S, Cross A, Charlton M, Brunsdon C, Lillie J (1990) Lessons learnt from a post-mortem of a failed GIS. *Proceedings of AGI '90*, AGI, London, pp. 2.3.1–2.3.5

Pearce D, Markandya A, Barbier E B (1989) *Blueprint for a Green Economy*. Earthscan Publications, London

WCED (1987) *Our Common Future*. World Commission on Environment and Development. Oxford University Press, Oxford

A USGS PERSPECTIVE ON GIS

L E STARR AND K E ANDERSON

The United States Geological Survey (USGS) is a national earth science agency with responsibility for gathering, analysing and presenting information on the US geology, water resources and topography. USGS operates with a budget of over $500 million and over 8000 people involved in scientific programmes throughout the nation and around the world. The Survey comprises five divisions which conduct and support its programmes: Geologic, Water Resources, National Mapping, Information Systems, and Administrative.

Researchers in the USGS have long been involved in the application of computers to earth science problems including digital cartography, spatial database design and GIS. The USGS is responsible for the US National Digital Cartographic Data Base (NDCDB) and, as one of the earliest users of topological data structures, has led the effort to establish spatial data standards in the United States. These efforts are based on a recognition of the emerging need for large volumes of spatial data and the growing interdependence among users, data producers and system developers. The rapid evolution of the technological base has led to a fundamental change in philosophy: digital cartographic data were seen initially simply as by-products of the mapping process, but the long-term objective now is the establishment of an all-digital production capability. Ultimately, the combined capability of Geographical and Land Information Systems and integrated spatial databases will provide great scope for the transformation of land and resources management, planning and science.

As the lead United States federal agency in mapping and earth science, the Survey must stay in the forefront of the development of automated cartographic systems and GIS. As a consequence, advanced software and hardware systems must always be available to the agency's scientists if new technologies are to be successfully employed for USGS earth science data collection and dissemination and for research based upon the data. Based, then, upon the USGS experience and vision of the future needs, this chapter provides a perspective on the future of GIS within – and externally as influenced by – national mapping agencies.

THE USGS MISSION

The USGS, through its National Mapping Program (NMP), provides a diversity of cartographic, geographical and remotely sensed data, products and information services for the United States and US territories and possessions. The products of the Program include several series of standard topographic maps in both graphic and digital form, photoimage maps, land use and land cover maps and associated data, geographical names information, geodetic control data and remotely sensed data (USGS 1986).

The Survey is charged with meeting the topographic mapping needs of the nation for federal and state agencies, commercial companies and individual citizens. While many users build their own maps to meet their specific needs, the most common starting point is the base topographic information compiled by the Survey. It is the task of the USGS to conduct the control surveys, undertake field completion, cartographically finish and print the maps. These tasks are primarily focused on the 1 : 24 000-scale series. Other map series include those at the 1 : 100 000, 1 : 250 000 and 1 : 500 000 scales; these have hitherto been derived by manual cartographic means from the primary series. However, just as the USGS achieved the milestone of national cartographic coverage at the 1 : 24 000 scale, it was experiencing a dramatic increase in the need for map revision and a demand for digital cartographic data. Most of these increased needs are rooted in the equally dramatic spread in the use of GIS by federal, state and local government users of USGS maps and the National Digital Cartographic Data Base or NDCDB.

For over 10 years, the USGS has used – and continues to use – GIS software produced both internally within the US Government and by commercial vendors. GIS software is used for test and evaluation, for data collection and validation, and for the conduct of earth science studies of many types. However, because of the recent explosion in use of GIS among its map information users, the Survey now frequently conducts cooperative GIS evaluations, studies and demonstration projects of mutual interest with other government agencies. In addition to the advancement of scientific knowledge, these projects assist the cooperating organizations to incorporate the relevant parts of the NDCDB and other relevant earth science information into the local databases used for their own GIS applications.

The USGS also needs to foster development of improved technology. It does this in various ways; for instance, it recently began to develop specifications for the applications-oriented GIS technology that will be needed early in the next century. Some of this technology will be needed to support the large earth science research projects (e.g. on global change; see Clark, Hastings and Kineman 1991 in this volume; Townshend 1991 in this volume) that are expected to be in progress at that time. So far as internal needs are concerned, the technology under development by the National Mapping Division (NMD) is needed to accelerate the completion of the NDCDB, shorten the time span of standard map revision cycles, and produce the special-purpose thematic map products required to support narrowly focused earth science research projects of the Survey.

ORIGINS OF THE SURVEY'S INVOLVEMENT IN GIS

Though one inevitably influenced the other, it is convenient to separate out the evolution within the Survey of data products and the software tools exploited or developed.

Evolution of the Survey's data products

The USGS has a long tradition of research in techniques of gathering, analysing and displaying cartographic and earth science information, including photogrammetry, advanced surveying techniques and the applications of computers to the mapping sciences (Thompson 1988). Early experiments in digitizing topographic maps established the feasibility of digital cartography (McEwen 1979; Southard and Anderson 1983; Starr and Guptill 1985). In the mid-1970s, the transition to digital data production began with the collection of digital map data from the graphic source materials produced by the NMP. Initial efforts used manual digitizing techniques, although the Survey moved to interactive systems and scanning technology in the late-1970s. At that time, the production of standard topographic maps from digital data was not cost effective, but the emerging use of GIS – especially those set up by other agencies with land management responsibilities within the Department of the Interior – created an immediate user community for digital cartographic data which the USGS needed to satisfy.

In response to these needs, the Survey created two products for distribution to GIS users. One was the digital elevation model or DEM (USGS 1987). So far as USGS is concerned, a DEM (see Weibel and Heller 1991 in this volume) is a rectangular array of points, each of which is assigned an elevation value, that covers a standard quadrangle area (see Plates 35.1–35.3). Originally produced to support the production of orthophotomaps, DEMs became of great value to many users through the use of software to generate perspective views and to carry out volumetric computations. DEMs have been primarily produced via profiling on stereoplotters or automatic correlation instruments like the Gestalt PhotoMapper. Only with the recent advancements in production techniques has the digitizing of contours to support DEM production become a viable option (Anderson and Callahan 1990).

The second product created in this period was the digital line graph or DLG (USGS 1990). The term DLG arises from the adoption of a graph-theoretic view of the elements of a planimetric map and the use of such concepts to develop effective data validation techniques. As a result of such efforts in the early 1970s, USGS implemented topological validation techniques when it began DLG production in 1977 (McEwen and Jacknow 1980; McEwen 1980; McEwen and Calkins 1982). Because of the strong need for specific categories of data by users, production efforts focused only on the categories needed rather than digitizing all the information on a map. Throughout the 1980s, the goal of meeting users' needs for digital data rather than satisfying internal needs was the dominant philosophy. In this respect, the USGS experience and aims have differed significantly from those of the Ordnance Survey, which had only modest external demand for its data up to the mid-1980s but significant internal requirements (see Sowton 1991 in this volume).

As the various products were developed, it became necessary to establish an efficient mechanism for distributing these data. The Survey established the National Digital Cartographic Data Base as an archival and distribution mechanism for digital cartographic data (McEwen and Jacknow 1980; McEwen 1981). The NDCDB also provides indexing and meta-data for its contents and is in a state of continual evolution to meet the growing needs of the user community.

Since then, the Survey has been developing systems and procedures continuously in order to expand and enhance digital data production. In 1980, a comprehensive review was conducted of the then production systems and their capabilities for digital cartographic and geographical data production, and production improvements were made. Major system modifications were not made at that time: the system was considered to be stable and maintainable over the short term, although it was judged to be inadequate to meet the projected long-term requirements for digital data. The opportunity to gain several years of experience, while allowing technology to advance and become more cost effective, was judged to be the appropriate next step towards the ultimate goal of modernization necessary to build and maintain the NDCDB (Starr and Anderson 1980; McEwen 1982).

Software used by the Survey

The USGS experience with GIS software began in the early 1970s with an internally developed system, the Geographical Information Processing System (GIPS). This system was designed for the validation and analysis of vector land use and land cover data. GIPS was composed of large computer applications programs that functioned primarily in a batch processing environment with an information base on magnetic tapes. An enhanced version of this system, the Geographical Information Retrieval and Analysis System or GIRAS (Mitchell *et al.* 1977), is still used by the NMD for validation and error analysis of machine-digitized polygonal data collected in support of the Division's land use and land cover mapping program (Plate 35.4).

The earlier GIPS and GIRAS technology was supplemented in 1980 by the Map Overlay and Statistics System (MOSS), a more sophisticated GIS that was developed during the late 1970s by two companion agencies in the Department of the Interior. This new system included both vector and raster polygon processing support, polygon overlay, and geographical coordinate conversion capability – features absent from the earlier systems. It also operated in an interactive processing environment which permitted visual examination of digital graphic data through a graphic display. An enhanced version of MOSS is still in widespread use for natural resource inventory and public lands management programs in several agencies of the Department of the Interior.

During this time period, software systems for handling remotely sensed digital imagery were also being developed. These included the Geological Survey's Mini Image Processing System (Chavez 1984) and ELAS, a raster-based GIS and image processing system developed under the auspices of NASA and NSTL. In the late 1980s, NASA

Goddard and the USGS were involved in the joint development of the Land Analysis System (LAS). This is used by agency scientists working on small-scale mapping applications which involve the use of multi-spectral remotely sensed satellite imagery for geological applications, land use and land cover mapping and for other multidisciplinary scientific studies.

In 1981, the USGS acquired the first of several commercially marketed GIS that were tested and evaluated during the 1980s. Through a competitive procurement in 1984, the ARC/INFO system was selected for support of the national water resource analysis, monitoring and management programs of the USGS. By the end of 1989, this GIS was installed and in use in more than 25 Survey facilities throughout the United States.

CURRENT USGS PRODUCTS

The USGS produces a variety of earth science products, reports, maps and digital data of value to GIS users. Perhaps the most widely used products are the topographic maps produced at 1 : 24 000 (Plate 35.5), 1 : 100 000, and 1 : 250 000 scales. These frequently serve as the base on which other, problem-specific data are compiled. The information on these maps is clearly of enhanced value to GIS users when available in digital form. In response to this need for digital versions of the information held in the paper maps, the Survey established the National Digital Cartographic Data Base (NDCDB). The status of this database and of the paper map coverages from which it is partially derived is shown in Table 35.1. In addition, however, digital orthophotographs (Plate 35.6) are of increasing importance, especially in urban areas.

A particular characteristic of the United States is that information generated by public funds is not subject to copyright regulations. In some other countries, the creation and provision of national data sets is more tightly controlled because the base map series and digital data derived from that series are copyrighted by the government (see, for instance, Sowton 1991 in this volume). This copyright facilitates the establishment of cooperative ventures between the government and the private sector. In Japan, for example, digital information representing the highway system is being prepared by the Japan Digital Road Map Association, a consortium led by the Geographical Survey Institute (a government agency) and supported by 21 other members from the private sector (Kubo 1991 in this volume; White 1991 in this volume). Information collected by the Association (under a copyright agreement with the Geographical Survey Institute), including the initial data digitized from the maps as well as updates, is shared by all members (such as Toyota, Honda and Nissan).

Contrast this with the situation in the United States where multiple sets of digital highway data exist. Some of these data sets have been created by government agencies and some by the private sector. Many have been derived from USGS source material. Because significant resources are needed to satisfy the requirements for basic data coverage and the maintenance of current data, it would seem to be in the best interest of all parties to eliminate duplication of basic data sets and to find innovative ways for data to be shared across the commercial and government sectors.

Table 35.1 Status of the USGS map coverage and of the NDCDB in September 1990

USGS Quadrangles in paper map form

Scale	Format	Number of maps
1 : 24 000	7.5′ × 7.5′	53 721
1 : 100 000	1° × 30′	1 805
1 : 250 000	2° × 1°	635

Status of the 1 : 24 000 scale NDCDB

Categories	Available
Public Land Survey System	12 064
Boundaries	14 464
Transportation	4 265
Hydrography	4 220
Hypsography	931
Man-made structures	145
Surface cover	53
Non-vegetative surface	51
Survey control and markers	81
Digital elevation models	21 248

APPLICATIONS OF GIS WITH USGS

Four of the five USGS divisions are involved in GIS activities ranging from theoretical studies of more effective data structures to the everyday application of existing tools to specific mission-oriented problems. This diversity of interests, systems and applications results in an innovative environment for attacking problems of significant size.

The Information Systems Division (ISD) works with, and evaluates the capabilities of, new technological developments in advanced computer hardware such as optical disks, concurrent processors and supercomputers. It is involved in the development of GIS applications using existing microcomputer technology. Less prosaically, it is also involved in the development of an Earth Science Information Network to link a series of information databases with a number of public contact points plus the development of an Earth Science Data Directory to provide on-line access to USGS central repositories of detailed information about earth science data. Finally, it is studying the feasibility of artificial intelligence for GIS technology.

The Geologic Division (GD) uses GIS for geologic and related geographical information management, manipulation and display. The GIS capabilities used by GD include gridded contouring of continuous data (Weibel and Heller 1991 in this volume), feature extraction, overlay, linking of spatial location to non-spatial attribute data and combined display of raster and vector data presentations. These GIS capabilities are used to process geologic data, including the management of multiple large data sets containing diverse attribute data, and for updating data sets as new scientific data are collected.

The Water Resources Division (WRD) is by far the largest user of commercially marketed GIS software in the USGS. The WRD has installed GIS hardware and software in many locations throughout the United States and has linked all of these GIS facilities through a telecommunications system known as GEONET. The primary WRD applications of GIS technology include analysis and production of a National Water Summary, boundary mapping for assignment of irrigation water rights, support of groundwater modelling studies and analysis of aquifer and water use databases.

The National Mapping Division (NMD) conducts basic and applied research in techniques for spatial data analysis, manipulation and display. Moreover, it is charged to devise methods of applying technological advances in GIS technology to the solution of earth science and resource management problems. At the time of writing, research in GIS technology is conducted in spatial database design, modelling of cartographic entities and objects, the implementation of prototype spatial operators, development of standard exchange formats for dissemination of digital cartographic and geographical data, test and evaluation of new GIS technology and development of advanced vector and raster data manipulation interfaces (see, for example, Guptill *et al.* 1990).

The USGS has consolidated selected components of its GIS equipment and software in interdisciplinary regional research and applications development laboratories located at five locations across the United States. These facilities provide a unique interdisciplinary environment where day-to-day contact – at both the informal and technical levels – between specialists in geology, geophysics, hydrology, geography, cartography and computer science enhances their skills and improves the communication required for interdisciplinary applications. This consolidation also makes a full range of GIS hardware and software available at key locations where they are available for organizationally or geographically dispersed projects. Moreover, these tools can be used for assisting new projects of the USGS and other government agencies where there may be little experience using GIS, and in design, initiation and implementation of pilot projects utilizing GIS technology or methodologies. The tools available range from PCs with CD-ROM readers, through powerful workstations to large minicomputers. Software packages such as ARC/INFO, SPANS, GRASS, ERDAS, 3-D modelling and other visualization and analysis tools are available. In addition, the laboratories provide access to specialized equipment such as scanning systems, graphics workstations or CD-ROM mastering systems.

The USGS works with other Department of the Interior bureaux and federal and state agencies in cooperative GIS development or demonstration projects of mutual interest. Among the more interesting examples of such joint projects is an undertaking with the National Center for Health Statistics (NCHS) which will explore the application of GIS and DLG data in creating a national health statistics database. NCHS will contribute expertise in statistical modelling to explore the relationship between human health and the geochemical environment. This type of project is providing valuable practical experience for USGS research personnel, enabling a better response to digital data user needs of the future, and practical experience in the use of DLG cartographic data (Guptill *et al.* 1990) for GIS applications. This experience is of particular importance because data in the DLG structure has been provided to many map information users for a wide variety of applications. As the USGS and its data users gain experience with this data structure in practical applications, issues related to current coding schemes, vertical and horizontal data integration, accuracy of data and data dissemination formats can be addressed on the basis of demonstrable user needs and practical experience.

EVOLVING TECHNOLOGY

Early in the 1980s, the Census Bureau approached the Survey for assistance in building the geographical base to support the 1990 population census. After initial pilot studies were completed, an agreement was reached to build jointly a database from the transportation and hydrography layers of the USGS 1 : 100 000-scale series of maps (USGS 1989). At the time of agreement, over 30 per cent of the maps remained to be completed in graphic form. As a consequence, USGS had both to complete the graphics and digitize all the maps in a three-year time-frame in order to meet the required schedule. Fortunately, the 1 : 100 000-scale series had been designed in the 1970s specifically to be more easily digitized than traditional cartographic products – roads and streams were depicted by single-line symbology and continuous and extensive feature separations were made rather than merely colour separates.

The basic production process involved raster scanning and editing of the separates, followed by interactive editing, tagging and topological validation. The inevitable focus of attention produced by a project of this magnitude and such a tight schedule resulted in process improvements which, over the course of the whole project, reduced the production time for individual data elements by 70 per cent overall. Many small ideas, such as pre-scan inspections by experienced cartographers to colour code recognizable trouble spots, led to significant advances in throughput. While the USGS coded attributes on to the hydrography layer, the Census Bureau was responsible for the attribute coding of the transportation layer, all to standard USGS specifications. The successful completion of this project was the beginning of the creation of the TIGER database used effectively in the 1990 Census (see Rhind 1991 in this volume).

In the mid-1980s, the Survey undertook a major new system development effort, termed MARK II. This is employing advanced technologies and production procedures in order to satisfy National Mapping Program requirements through to the year 2000 (Anderson and Callahan 1990). Specific tasks of this development effort are to:

- expand and improve mass digitization capabilities;
- modify data structures to support increased content and improved access requirements;
- develop a digital revision capability;
- further develop product generation capability for standard, derivative and specialist digital products;
- improve quality control; and
- support advanced analysis and applications.

The Survey's aim is that, by the year 2000, the NDCDB should contain digital data representing the content and accuracy of the primary map series and other smaller scale series. This database will serve as a central archive of digital data for dissemination to the user community and also as a working database for the production of standard USGS maps.

A comprehensive management strategy is critical to the success of the MARK II project. With the completion of initial primary map coverage of the nation, many state agencies are seeking cooperative agreements with NMD to acquire digital data for use in GIS activities. The 'knock-on' impact of a large number of such cooperative projects on other programme goals and objectives must be assessed. Major reimbursable programmes of national importance will also play an increasing role in the execution of the National Mapping Program. The challenge is to strike a balance among existing programmes and new cooperators and reimbursable programmes, making it possible to conduct major projects requiring large amounts of data quickly. Examples of the latter are the production of Digital Terrain Elevation Data (DTED) for the US Defense Mapping Agency and the production of 1 : 100 000-scale DLG data for the Department of Energy. The MARK II technology is also being designed to accommodate the growing user requirements; but at the same time, new contract proposals, work-share and data-share arrangements will also need to be explored as a means of achieving this balance.

Management of the MARK II effort is being accomplished through changes in the organizational structure of the Division. The research staff has been realigned to effect the overall coordination and management of the development effort. The MARK II effort is divided into developmental components and modules. Component management has been assigned to headquarters staff offices while module management responsibilities are assigned to production-oriented centres throughout the Division.

The transition of the National Mapping Program into one centred on a digital database requires extensive development of both graphic and digital standards. Issues being addressed during this development include database design, digitizing procedures, data accuracy and content, symbology and product generation rules, graphic and digital revision and data applications and transfer. One of the elements recognized early in the Mark II development was the need for a more sophisticated data model that enabled more elaborate applications than do the simple topological data models. The need to support cartographic symbolization and generalization, as well as GIS applications and modelling, led to the examination of feature-oriented data models. After careful review and analysis, such a data model was adopted and named the Digital Line Graph-Enhanced or DLG-E (Guptill 1990).

In addition, the Division is leading the development of a Digital Cartographic Data Standard, including a Spatial Data Transfer Specification, which is being proposed as a national standard (USGS 1991). The development of new technologies in the USGS mapping systems represents a major commitment of both human and financial resources over at least the next six years. This planned commitment of over US $100 million is expected to accelerate significantly the transition of the Survey's cartographic production operations from a largely graphic production line to an all-digital one.

The technological and programmatic changes that the National Mapping Program has encountered during the 1980s have tested and challenged the organizational structure. In response to the pressures encountered, it has been necessary to implement a more flexible structure that provided clear-cut areas of responsibility and yet enabled the increased levels of communication necessary to balance the variety of programmes under way. This led to the separation of the budgeting and fiscal accounting from the actual production management activities. It elevated the status of coordination and requirements-gathering activities because of the long-term dependency on the success of such efforts. Finally, it resulted in a dispersion of research and development activities away from headquarters and into other organizational units to increase the level of staff involvement and to draw upon the resources of those with production experience.

INTER-DEPENDENCY BETWEEN THE SURVEY AND OTHER ORGANIZATIONS

Federal and State agencies annually report their cartographic requirements, for maps in graphic form as well as for map-related data in digital form, to the Geological Survey through the Office of Management and Budget Circular A-16 process. This formal solicitation process allows the agencies to identify their requirements by type of product, geographical area of interest and year of need.

The primary purpose of the A-16 process is to minimize duplication of effort and costly single-purpose mapping activities among federal agencies. However, not every requirement of every agency can be met through this process. The A-16 solicitation in 1988 yielded requests from 11 federal agencies and 34 states for primary map revision, intermediate-scale mapping, thematic maps and digital data production. Of these requests, primary map revision and digital data production accounted for about 7000 and 5000 standard quadrangle maps respectively. With the overlap of these graphic and digital requirements, about 9000 quadrangles will need to be put into the Division's near-term production schedules. The highest priority requirements exceed current production capacities by a factor of four.

Despite this shortfall in capacity, the Division has largely been successful in these coordination efforts. A number of agencies have entered into reimbursable or cooperative agreements with the Division and the shared costs and work have expedited mutually beneficial cartographic production. During 1988, the Division entered into 78 reimbursable agreements with 37 federal agencies and into joint funding agreements with 43 state agencies in 33 states.

Many states are becoming sophisticated GIS users and are requesting more digital cartographic data. Concurrently, the huge growth in the use of GIS in federal agencies has also dramatically increased the federal need for the Survey's digital data. This interest in digital map products and the variety of National Mapping Program spatial data activities have resulted in increased user enquiries regarding NMD data, assistance services and cooperative activities. These increasing interests heighten the need to communicate information to users on the use of existing products, the evaluation of new products, the identification of future needs and the development of plans for technical assistance. In the past, the great bulk of NMD coordination efforts has been focused on agencies at the federal and state levels, but USGS products and services are being used increasingly by local agencies; it is now important to broaden coordination efforts and to improve communication with county agencies.

Several major trends for Division products and services emerged from the analysis of the most recent A-16 solicitation. The need for digital data appears to be the most urgent specific requirement, particularly for hypsography DLGs, more accurate DEMs and land use and land cover data for support of GIS applications. Other stated requirements include an acceleration of the primary map revision programme, production of high-resolution orthophotoquads in conventional and digital form, image maps, digital state bases and county maps; revised versions of the existing 1:250 000-scale land use and land cover map series based on the 1:100 000-scale map series are also required.

As the MARK II programme began to evolve, it became important to substantiate the benefits attributed to the programme and also to determine the appropriate revision cycle for primary maps. To meet these needs, the Primary Mapping Economic Analysis study was undertaken (Amos et al. 1987, 1988). This study used an interview technique with a large sample of users to learn more about the uses and needs for maps and data. The results of the analyses show that net benefits are maximized with a production level of between 10 000 and 17 000 quadrangles revised per year. From a policy point of view, the fact that positive net benefits are maximized at a specific level of production does not automatically justify the associated expenditure. This analysis, however, showed conclusively that economic benefits of map revision are positive and are large over a wide range of production levels. Clearly, the current USGS target of revising 5600 maps per year is conservative and net benefits would be significantly larger with an even higher production level.

The construction of the NDCDB requires a high degree of data inter-changeability between the proliferation of numbers and types of GIS that populate, maintain and use the information in the database. The wide variety of applications for which the data are used also requires a high degree of standardization in the content and quality of the information in the base. Under the impact of these two requirements, together with other strategic planning considerations, the traditional USGS National Mapping Program is evolving rapidly.

The Survey's coordination role

In 1983, the Office of Management and Budget (OMB) established the Federal Interagency Coordinating Committee on Digital Cartography (FICCDC). The Geological Survey was designated to chair this committee. FICCDC was charged with facilitating the coordination of the collection and exchange of digital map data, with an emphasis on base map information (Federal Interagency Coordinating Committee on Digital Cartography

1989). Throughout the 1980s, the increasingly important role of digital spatial data in the federal government became ever more clear. In 1989, the Director of OMB requested that FICCDC provide him with an analysis of the FICCDC mission in relation to an expanded role of coordinating federal use of digital spatial data. In addition, he requested a review of OMB Circular A-16 on Coordination of Surveying and Mapping Activities, plus recommendations for potential revisions to it; the latter were to incorporate federal activities relating to digital spatial data. The end result of these activities was the issue on 19 October 1990 of a revision of Circular A-16 by the Director of OMB.

The revised Circular expands the breadth of spatial data coordination, assigns leadership roles to federal departments for coordination activities related to certain categories of data, and establishes an interagency coordinating committee to provide policy guidance and oversight to these activities. The objective of this interagency committee, named the Federal Geographic Data Committee (FGDC), is to promote the coordinated development, use, sharing and dissemination of surveying, mapping and related spatial data. The Circular assigns the responsibility for chairing the committee to the Department of Interior. It is intended that FGDC will support domestic surveying and mapping activities, aid the use of GIS and assist users in meeting their programme objectives through:

- promoting the development, maintenance and management of distributed database systems that are national in scope for surveying, mapping and related spatial data;

- encouraging the development and implementation of standards, exchange formats, specifications, procedures and guidelines;

- promoting technology development, transfer and exchange;

- promoting interaction with other existing federal coordinating mechanisms that have an interest in the generation, collection, use and transfer of spatial data;

- publishing periodic technical and management articles and reports;

- performing special studies and providing special reports and briefings to OMB on major initiatives involving spatial data technologies and agency programmes;

- ensuring that Circular A-16 related activities support national security, national defence and emergency preparedness programmes;

- reporting annually to OMB.

In consultation with federal agencies and other appropriate organizations, the new committee will establish such standards, procedures, interagency agreements and other mechanisms as are necessary to carry out its government-wide coordinating responsibilities and will recommend to OMB any revisions to Circular A-16 and exhibits.

FUTURE DIRECTIONS

'The United States must make better use of its scientific and technical information (STI) resources, if it wishes to be competitive in world markets and maintain its leadership.' Thus concluded a recent report of the US Congress, Office of Technology Assessment (1990:1). The report stated that the success of the federal STI programme will depend on progress in several areas: the availability and use of technical standards for databases and documents, so that information can be electronically moved among agencies and users with ease and efficiency; the indexing of databases and documents; the funding of basic STI activities in agency research and development budgets; and user involvement in agency STI programmes, so that federal STI is disseminated in user-friendly formats that meet user needs. The report noted the importance of STI when it argued (1990:5) 'The list of designated presidential science technology priorities, such as science education, technology transfer, high-performance computing and networking, international competitiveness, and global change, justifies additional emphasis on STI.'

A similar theme is sounded in *Spatial Data Needs: the future of the National Mapping Program* (Mapping Science Committee, National Academy of Science 1990). The report was prepared by the Mapping Science Committee of the National Academy of Science, at the request of the Director of the Geological Survey. The Committee was asked to examine the needs for the geographical and cartographic data provided by the National Mapping Division, to provide advice on the Division's programmes of mapping research and development, to examine the scope of the Division's activities in GIS and to recommend the appropriate role for the Division in assembling and maintaining digital databases from other sources. In response, the Committee offered six recommendations to the Geological Survey concerning the National Mapping Division:

- expand the Division's role in developing the NDCDB to include management and coordination, standard setting and enforcement, data production, cataloguing, and data dissemination and related services;
- increase the Division's activities to provide a larger number of classes of spatial data;
- speed the expansion of the NDCDB by encouraging work- and cost-sharing programmes and instituting a digital data donor programme throughout the public and private sectors;
- expand the Division's efforts to establish and promulgate digital spatial data quality standards;
- begin the development of a national spatial database that would be an enhancement of the NDCDB, would be feature-oriented and accessible on-line by the year 2010;
- expand the Division's research activities in digital cartography, GIS, and remote sensing and image processing.

The National Mapping Division intends to remain a key contributor to an increasingly information-based society; its response to these recommendations is enshrined in goals set out below, to be accomplished within the next 10 years (Starr 1990).

Enhancement of the National Digital Cartographic Data Base

During the 1990s, the Division will continue the development of the NDCDB and the MARK II modernization effort. It will augment the loading of the NDCDB through increased cooperative activities with other federal, state and local governments and with the private sector. The objective is to create an up-to-date NDCDB from which both digital data and automatically generated graphic output can be provided to the user community.

Promulgation of standards

In order for cooperative data collection and revision programmes to be successful, the Division must continue its efforts to establish and promulgate standards for data format and quality and set minimum content levels. The new Federal Geographical Data Committee will facilitate the development and implementation of standards which are applicable to a broad range of spatial data.

Management of spatial databases

In the period up to the year 2000, the Division will be challenged in many areas related to database management. One of the biggest challenges will be the development of a conceptual framework for a national spatial data infrastructure, of which the NDCDB will be an important part. The Federal Geographical Data Committee envisages the development of a National GEO-DATA System which would be a collection of independently held and maintained federal digital spatial databases. The scope of this system would include those federal agencies willing to meet certain criteria, such as standards for data transfer and conformity with minimum quality and content requirements, plus establishment of agency mechanisms for quality control, collection specifications, classification specifications and records disposition.

The conduct of research

The Division's research activities throughout the planning period will most likely continue to be a mix ranging from basic scientific research to improve our understanding of cartography and spatial data representation to studies on the adaptation of technological innovations into the mapping and spatial database management missions of the Survey.

CONCLUSIONS

The USGS National Mapping Program is undergoing a major technological and programmatic transition that is both exciting and challenging. Central to this transition is the development of the National Digital Cartographic Data Base. This will become the focus of the agency's future mapping activities, including maintenance and revision of the primary map series. Another important factor in this transition will be the development and maintenance of the GIS-related scientific knowledge and expertise required to conduct the Survey's large and complex earth science research and analytical studies. The provision of advice to the agency's data users on GIS, which incorporate and exploit NDCDB data in resource management and analysis activities to meet their own local interests, is also certain to be a priority. This transition involves dealing with organizational issues that will tax the USGS mapping resources to the maximum, yet will provide rewarding professional and scientific experiences. Progress thus far has necessitated comprehensive changes to existing practice, including structural change in the way and location in which research and development is carried out and a recasting of the way in which user needs are determined and assessed. Though the changes involved may be difficult, successful resolution of these issues will enable the US Geological Survey to accomplish both of its missions at least as far ahead as the new millennium: to carry out earth science research and to support federal, state and local government, and private user requirements for cartographic, geological and hydrological data products in both graphic and digital form.

REFERENCES

Amos L L et al. (1987) *Primary Mapping Economic Analysis, Phase One*, Internal report. US Geological Survey, Reston Virginia
Amos L L et al. (1988) *Primary Mapping Economic Analysis, Phase Two*, Internal report. US Geological Survey, Reston Virginia
Anderson K E, Callahan G M (1990) The modernization program of the US Geological Survey's National Mapping Division. *Cartography and Geographic Informations Systems* **17** (3): 243–8

Chavez P S (1984) *US Geological Survey Mini Image Processing System*. USGS Open File Report 84–880
Clark D M, Hastings D A, Kineman J J (1991) Global databases and their implications for GIS.In: Maguire D J, Goodchild M F, Rhind D W (eds.) *Geographical Information Systems: principles and applications*. Longman, London, pp. 217–31, Vol 2

Federal Interagency Coordinating Committee on Digital Cartography (1989) *Co-ordination of Digital Cartographic Activities in the Federal Government*. FICCDC

Guptill S C (ed.) (1990) *An Enhanced Digital Line Graph Design*. US Geological Survey Circular 1048
Guptill S C, Boyko K J, Domaratz M A, Fegeas R G, Rossmeissl H J, Usery E L (1990) *An enhanced Digital Line Graph Design*. US Geological Survey Professional Paper 1048, Washington DC

Kubo S (1991) The development of GIS in Japan. In: Maguire D J, Goodchild M F, Rhind D W (eds.) *Geographical Information Systems: principles and applications*. Longman, London, pp. 47–56, Vol 2

Mapping Science Committee, National Academy of Science (1990) *Spatial Data Needs: the future of the National Mapping Program*. National Academy Press, Washington DC
McEwen RB (1979) US Geological Survey digital cartographic data aquisition. In: *Mapping Software and Cartographic Data Bases*. Havard Library of Computer Graphics, pp. 136–42
McEwen R B (1980) USGS Digital Cartographic Applications Program. *Journal of Surveying and Mapping Division*. ASCE, **106** (1): 13–22
McEwen R B (1981) *A National Digital Cartographic Data Base*. Computer Graphics in Transportation, The Princeton University Conference
McEwen R B (1982) Observations and Trends in Digital Cartography. *Proceedings ISPRS Commission IV Symposium*. ASP, Falls Church Virginia, pp. 419–31
McEwen R B, Calkins H W (1982) Digital Cartography in the USGS National Mapping Division: a comparison of current and future mapping processes. *Cartographica* **19**: 11–26
McEwen R B, Jacknow H R (1980) USGS Digital Cartographic Data Base. *Proceedings of AUTOCARTO4*. SPRS, Falls Church Virginia, pp. 225–35
Mitchell W B, Guptill S C, Anderson E A, Fegeas R G, Hallam C A (1977) *GIRAS – a geographic information retrieval and analysis system for handling land use and land cover data*. US Geological Survey Professional Paper 1059

Rhind D W (1991) Counting the people: the role of GIS.

In: Maguire D J, Goodchild M F, Rhind D W (eds.) *Geographical Information Systems: principles and applications*. Longman, London, pp. 127–37, Vol 2

Southard R B, Anderson K E (1983) A National Program for Digital Cartography. *AUTOCARTO5 Proceedings*. ACSM, Falls Church Virginia, pp. 41–9

Sowton M (1991) Development of GIS-related activities at the Ordnance Survey. In: Maguire D J, Goodchild M F, Rhind D W (eds.) *Geographical Information Systems: principles and applications*. Longman, London, pp. 23–38, Vol 2

Starr L E, Anderson K E (1982) Some Thoughts on Cartographic and Geographic Information Systems for the 1980s. *Pecara VII Symposium Proceedings*. ASP, Falls Church Virginia, pp. 41–55

Starr L E, Guptill S C (1984) The US Geological Survey and the National Digital Cartographic Data Base. *Proceedings from the FIG International Symposium*. Edmonton Alberta, pp. 166–75

Starr L E (1990) USGS National Mapping Division: preparing for the Twenty-First Century. *Proceedings of GIS/LIS '90*. AAG/ACSM/AM/FM/ASPRS/URISA, Bethesda Maryland, pp. 872–81

Thompson M M (1988) *Maps for America*, 3rd edn. US Government Printing Office, Washington DC

Townshend J R G (1991) Environmental databases and GIS. In: Maguire D J, Goodchild M F, Rhind D W (eds.) *Geographical Information Systems: principles and applications*. Longman, London, pp. 201–16, Vol 2

United States Congress, Office of Technology Assessment (1990) *Helping America Compete: the role of federal scientific and technical information*. US Government Printing Office, Washington DC

USGS (1986) *Goals of the US Geological Survey*. US Geological Survey Circular 1010

USGS (1987) *Digital Elevation Models*. US Geological Survey Data Users Guide 5

USGS (1989) *Digital Line Graphs from 1 : 100 000-Scale Maps*. US Geological Survey Data Users Guide 2

USGS (1990) *Digital Line Graphs from 1 : 24 000-Scale Maps*. US Geological Survey Data Users Guide 1

USGS (1991) *The Spatial Data Transfer Format*. US Geological Survey National Mapping Division, Washington DC

Weibel R, Heller M (1991) Digital terrain modelling. In: Maguire D J, Goodchild M F, Rhind D W (eds.) *Geographical Information Systems: principles and applications*. Longman, London, pp. 269–97, Vol 1

White M (1991) Car navigation systems. In: Maguire D J, Goodchild M F, Rhind D W (eds.) *Geographical Information Systems: principles and applications*. Longman, London, pp. 115–25, Vol 2

DEVELOPMENT OF GIS-RELATED ACTIVITIES AT THE ORDNANCE SURVEY

M SOWTON

This chapter complements Chapter 35 by Starr and Anderson in describing the evolution of concepts, techniques and user needs in regard to the work of the Ordnance Survey (OS) in Britain. The main characteristic of OS map coverage is that almost all of the country is available at the very large scales of 1 : 1250 or 1 : 2500 and these maps are continuously updated. The author describes the evolution of digital mapping in OS from its origins in the late 1960s to the present day, setting this in the context of government policy and OS's mission. The difficulties of assessing market needs and balancing these against apparently simpler requirements within OS are set out and the role of advice from external bodies is examined. A final, major section on recent developments covers plans and actions for the national topographic database, based upon topologically structured vector data; the feasibility of generating a 'scale free' database is examined and rejected – at least in the short term – and additional use of digital products derived from smaller scale maps is predicted.

INTRODUCTION

The Ordnance Survey of Great Britain (OS) is the national mapping agency for England, Scotland and Wales and is based in Southampton. It is a completely separate organization from the Ordnance Survey of Northern Ireland, based in Belfast, and the Ordnance Survey of the Republic of Ireland which is based in Dublin. All three mapping agencies have a common origin in the British Military Board of Ordnance, but only in OS Dublin are direct links with the military still preserved. OS is a government department with its own accounting officer reporting directly to environment ministers. Despite this reporting arrangement, it is separate from the Department of the Environment and negotiates directly with Treasury officials on financial matters.

The original surveys of OS in 1791 concentrated on mapping at one inch to one mile (1 : 63 360) and later at six inches to one mile (1 : 10 560), but modern mapping has been concerned with much larger scales (Seymour 1980). In 1990, the OS map coverage of Great Britain was as shown in Table 36.1.

In addition to the topographic mapping of Great Britain, OS publishes a large number of atlases and guidebooks in collaboration with various map and book publishers.

Controversy has long been the hallmark of the OS digital mapping work (Rhind 1990). For instance, concern has frequently been expressed about the way in which OS developed its digital mapping techniques and at an apparent lack of progress when applications elsewhere seemed to be moving ahead faster than in the Survey. However, the role of a national mapping agency which is also a government department is to provide a surveying

Table 36.1 Ordnance Survey map products (mid-1990).

Scale	No. of sheets	Size/area covered
1 : 1250	57 395	0.5 km × 0.5 km sheets – urban areas
1 : 2500	163 357	1 km × 1 km sheets – developed rural areas
1 : 10 000	10 160	5 km × 5 km sheets – full cover of GB mainly derived from larger scales, but by basic survey in mountain and moorland areas
1 : 25 000	1 374	10 km × 20 km sheets
1 : 50 000	204	40 km × 40 km sheets (nominal size)
1 : 250 000	9	approximately 250 km × 200 km sheets
1 : 625 000	2	approximately 500 km × 500 km sheets

Table 36.2 Ordnance Survey digital map products (mid-1990). (see Plates 36.1–36.7)

Scale	No. of sheets	No. digitized	% digitized
1 : 1250	57 395	49 736	86.7
1 : 2500	163 357	31 326	19.2
1 : 10 000	10 160	43	0.4
1 : 25 000	1 374	0	0.0
1 : 50 000	204	1	0.5
1 : 250 000	9	9	100.0
1 : 625 000	2	2	100.0
Total	232 501	81 117	34.8

and mapping service to the nation as a whole; it must avoid serving the interests of any particular group to the detriment of others. Given finite resources, this demands compromise and the avoidance of high risk strategies. Thus, in the late 1960s, decisions relating to the application of the newly emerging CAD/CAM technology to digital mapping – to which it was not wholly suited – had to be taken against a background of competing work programmes, unproven technology and a need to produce cost-effective solutions. That a programme of digital mapping development was started when the major preoccupation of the Department at that time was a commitment to complete the revision and overhaul of the maps of Great Britain by 1980, was entirely due to the far-sighted decisions of the then Director General, Major General B St G Irwin. Supported by champions for the emerging technology, he sought to assess whether computerization would be a cost-effective way of supporting the existing mapping programme. The references cited in this chapter include the names of the significant contributors to this assessment and no serious study of the development of digital mapping in OS could be carried out without recourse to their original papers.

Such progress as was made in the late 1960s and early 1970s was based on two acts of faith: that a viable map production tool would emerge (which would include the cost-effective derivation of smaller scale maps) and that there would be a demand for the data for other purposes from outside of OS. During this period – which lasted until 1972 – the Survey collaborated with the Experimental Cartographic Unit of the Royal College of Art but later developed its own systems for the production of digital maps, largely due to the primary need for the production of high quality maps but also due to considerations of cost.

This need to use the digital processes to produce a high quality map has again generated criticism about the speed at which OS has progressed. Yet few would fail to acknowledge that, without the excellence of these maps and the processes by which they were kept up to date, there would have been no basis for the advantageous position in which Great Britain finds itself today: no less than 70 per cent of the country is covered by maps at 1 : 1250 or 1 : 2500 scale, these are mostly under continuous revision and the whole country is covered by recently completed 1 : 10 000-scale maps. Nor would there have been a basis of financial support through which the system could be developed. To this day, the revenue of OS depends on the quality and availability of its graphic products and it is now true to say that the quality of the digital data being produced owes a great deal to this pursuit of cartographic excellence.

What follows will give some insight into how OS has progressed up to the time of writing, when digital data are available for 89 per cent of the urban 1 : 1250 maps and 19 per cent of the rural 1 : 2500 maps (Table 36.2; Plates 36.4–36.7). While concentrating on the development of digital mapping, the issues of GIS and the supporting role which digital maps play will also be considered. For the most part, the story is one of large-scale mapping (in the English sense of the phrase – in other countries 1 : 25 000 and 1 : 50 000 scale maps are often described by this term). Although the Utopian dream of 'scale-free' data for mapping purposes may not exist, some remarks will be made about the way in which scale is treated at present and how OS will provide for the user who has a wider interest in spatial relationships.

THE ORDNANCE SURVEY MISSION

Until recently, the overall mission of the OS had remained unchanged for many years. It had developed in response to changing requirements, first military and then almost entirely civil. There had been a changing emphasis from small scales (1 : 625 000–1 : 25 000) to large scales (1 : 10 000–1 : 1250) and from manual to digital methods with requirements to produce derived mapping and conventional graphics from the digital data.

In 1987, the role of OS was reviewed in the light of government policy and customers' perceptions of what OS should be providing and a mission statement and corporate objectives were published (Ordnance Survey 1988a). These spelt out a clear need to recover a sizeable proportion of the operating costs while providing an adequate service to the nation and at the same time giving customers value for money.

The overall role of OS is to provide a survey and mapping service with responsibility for keeping the topographic mapping of England, Scotland and Wales up to date. There is also a requirement to provide topographic information in forms that customers require. It is acknowledged that this can only be done economically through complete digital coverage at large scales as a first priority, followed at a later date by that derived from smaller scales mapping. Sufficient safeguards have been introduced so that those customers who still require graphic products (and who currently still provide the predominant share of OS revenue) are not adversely affected by the digital programme. In addition, there is a government-imposed requirement to recover an ever-increasing proportion of the total OS operating costs. Since 1971, following the report of the Janes Committee (Department of the Environment 1971), OS has followed a policy of maximizing revenue on all products to recover an increasing proportion of its costs in accordance with guidelines agreed with HM Treasury. From a level of about 30 per cent in the early 1970s, the total recovery has risen to 59 per cent of all expenditure (Ordnance Survey 1989), an increasing proportion of which is now being achieved through the most recent developments in digital mapping.

THE EVOLUTION OF OS DIGITAL MAPPING AND GIS SUPPORT

All organizations are constrained and guided by their past, especially those involved in serving the nation as a whole and in building large databases of long-term utility. National mapping organizations exemplify these categories. For this reason, a brief summary will be given of the way in which concepts, skills, techniques and data have evolved in OS in the last two decades.

The first steps

In the late 1960s, an internal study of the possibilities of using digital techniques was carried out, spurred on by the emerging computer processes for automating the traditional engineering and architectural drawing processes. From this review, it was considered that similar techniques could be adapted to the process of large-scale map production in general and, more specifically, to the derivation of 1 : 10 000 and 1 : 25 000-scale maps from the digitized data. In order to prove this approach, a collaborative experiment was carried out with the Experimental Cartographic Unit of the Royal College of Art. The object of the Bideford experiment (as it was known), was to establish the feasibility, but not the cost effectiveness, of converting OS large-scale plans into computer-compatible form on magnetic tape and of drawing smaller scale maps from the data (Bickmore 1971). At about the same time, OS also investigated the possibilities of producing digital data directly from shaft encoders attached to the lead-screws of a Wild A8 Autograph with a view to producing digital contours for incorporation into the proposed digitally derived 1 : 10 000 and 1 : 25 000-scale maps (Sowton 1971).

An OS evaluation of the economics of the Bideford experiment proved unfavourable and showed that costs outweighed the technical desirability of producing derived maps in this way. Consequently, a decision was made that the future emphasis of digital experimentation would be on the production of large-scale map graphics from digital data and that the problem of derivation of smaller map scales from these data would have to await a cost-effective solution (Gardiner-Hill 1971). At this time, it was also concluded that digital photogrammetry was uneconomic due partly to the excessive quantities of data generated in stream mode digitizing and the reduction in output caused by the additional tasks imposed upon the operators of the plotting machines. Development of derived scale mapping and photogrammetric digitizing were not to be resurrected until a decade later.

It is interesting to note that OS started digitizing maps at the other end of the scale range at the same time as the large-scale experiments were in progress. In 1970, for instance, an outline map of the country was experimentally digitized from 1 : 1 250 000-scale maps for the British Oxygen Company as a base on which to present its management statistics. Details of this early example of a GIS base map were published in the widely distributed Calcomp Newsletter (Gardiner-Hill 1971). Following this experiment, a digital data set was created from the 1 : 625 000 Route Planning Map with the idea of supporting users in the field of operations research in their attempts to solve problems such as optimization of delivery routes and depot siting (Gardiner-Hill 1972). While consideration was given to updating these data, the limited capability of plotters then in existence ruled out the possibility of creating the reproduction material for the printed map by digital means. The current 1 : 625 000 data set, which is described later, is not a child of this original data set whose fate is unknown.

The digital dream

Once the decision not to proceed with automated generalization had been taken, a major part of the potential benefits to be derived from digital mapping vanished. Subsequent experiments were, therefore, designed to establish viable production methods whereby the digital data could be used to support the production of paper maps – and yet be of value for traditional users of OS maps who were developing new digital systems of their own for recording map-related data (Gardiner-Hill 1974). In these circumstances, there could be little justification for the creation of digital data to support an embryonic demand external to OS if a cost-effective solution to the Survey's own graphic production process could not be found.

Perseverance with the early processes for the capture of digital data using cumbersome 'blind digitizing', off-line editing and subsequent re-digitizing eventually resulted in a pilot flow-line which could capture digital data and reproduce the exacting linework and text specification. However, the requirements for symbolization and house fills (although possible on the system) required so much additional digitizing work and time on the plotters that a decision was taken to return the digital plots to a cartographic flow-line for the addition of symbols and other ornamentation by conventional cartographic means. Notwithstanding this, the result was a satisfactory blend of new technology and conventional methods which, although not entirely cost effective for the graphic output, did produce adequate digital data for use by experimental digital systems for recording inventories of distribution plant. The main problem for OS in the early 1970s lay in obtaining a suitable plotter with the ability to reproduce the digital data accurately and give satisfactory quality for the making of reproduction material as well as revision documents. This problem was finally solved using the Master Plotters designed by Ferranti and the digital map production flow-line was launched in 1973 (Atkey and Gibson 1975).

Having met the internal needs of the Survey, the next stage was the consideration of a marketing strategy for the digital data. In the early 1970s, there were few potential customers who had the equipment to exploit the data; those who did have it were only willing to embark on small exercises in testing the potential of digital mapping, thus requiring only a few sheets of data. The result was that OS was faced with a large number of expressions of interest, but with few concrete and substantial proposals. In the face of this uncertainty, the production of digital mapping became a sprinkling of small pockets of digital data throughout the country designed to generate interest; these were insignificant in the creation of consolidated blocks of digital data. It was some time before significant demand for large areas of data emerged. Indeed, it was not until the early 1980s that sales reached 1000 digital maps per year. It is only since 1985 that sales have risen significantly: in 1988/89 they reached 22 000 maps from a data bank of about 59 000 (Ordnance Survey 1989).

It was recognized of course that sales have been constrained by the availability of data and OS has tried to tailor its digitizing programme to include areas where there is a firm commitment from users. It seems an invariable rule that one user's area of interest does not coincide with another's (water authority areas are not coterminous with county boundaries for instance) and this, together with the size of the digitizing task, has led to digitizing agreements with specific utilities in which they digitize their area of interest to an agreed OS specification. This has speeded up the digitizing process, so that it is now possible to expand specific digitized areas to create large blocks. Even so, only seven counties were approaching full digital cover at the end of 1989 (Table 36.2). However, it is expected that digitizing of the 1 : 1250 maps will be completed in 1991. Thus far, the major factor in the take-up of digital data has been availability of data, not necessarily the price.

The final event in this period of evolution was the suggestion in 1974 that there might be a need for data with more structure than that included in the rudimentary cartographic feature-coded ('spaghetti') vector strings which were being created in the pilot production flow-line. As a result, a trial area was selected and a contract let to produce a topologically structured data set for an information system (see below).

It is from these beginnings that subsequent events make a logical progression up to the present day, a period during which the processes described earlier evolved and became refined with the introduction of more efficient data specifications, interactive editing and improvements in techniques. However, the basic philosophy in OS remains that expressed by Brigadier E P J Williams, namely, to produce digital data which will also produce good graphic maps (Williams 1971). The issue of derived mapping still remains unresolved, but the advent of structured data may produce the answer to this enigma of large-scale digital data (as will be described later).

The Dudley Project

In 1974, a feasibility study was commissioned by the Department of the Environment (DoE) for Great Britain (Northern Ireland is administered separately) to 'investigate the different needs of potential users of OS large-scale digital map data in local authorities, public undertakings, central government and elsewhere'. The feasibility study identified the need to create land and property gazetteers and databases of properties, roads and highways. It identified the possibility of recording public utility networks as the major uses for large-scale OS digital data. The provision of data to meet these requirements could probably have been provided by different and more complex digitizing procedures, but it was decided that a more practical solution was to retain the simplest possible digitizing method and restructure the data subsequently by software to meet the requirements for data outside the normal, internal OS uses. Consequently, a development project (also funded by DoE) was commissioned to produce software to restructure the OS digital map data so that it could be used in computer-based analysis as well as in mapping.

The first phase of the project involved the actual reorganization of the map data. The process required all line intersections to be identified and, from them, nodes and the links between nodes were created. The next phase of the project was to create software which, in effect, provided a number of user languages to allow the formation of objects required by different classes of user from the links in the data. However, for reasons of cost, it was decided to proceed only with the user language which defined the property (land) category: although this was the most difficult to create, it was also considered to have the widest range of application. The facilities provided by this user language included: the extraction of land parcels by type within a given area of search, together with the perimeter coordinates; a unique reference number; the area of the parcel; and a serial number. While the process was supposed to be fully automatic and used the feature codes in the coordinate strings data to assist in the formation and classification of the land parcels, it frequently failed when operating on standard digital data in which the polygons had not been closed and, consequently, a number of interactive editing processes were incorporated into what had been intended to be an automated software solution (Thompson 1978).

The methodology was ultimately applied to an area in the metropolitan borough of Dudley, close to Birmingham (hence the name Dudley Project) and the restructured data and land parcels were successfully used in what was basically a GIS trial using ICL's LAMIS system (later developed into PLANES). In addition, also in the Dudley area, a block of this topologically structured data was provided for a trial of information exchange between organizations providing utility services (these are distinct from local government in Britain); this trial, referred to as the NJUG Dudley Project, successfully demonstrated the use of digital map data in an information exchange system based on a single central processor to which the various utilities were linked (Mahoney 1991 in this volume).

Both these trials were highly significant in the development of applications for OS digital map data. To some extent, the utility project has had the greater impact because it focused attention on the importance of using a common digital map base for recording utility plant records and the consequent need for OS to produce such data as quickly as possible. The structured data project, however, was more significant in terms of the actual use of the digital maps and the benefit which could accrue from their various uses, even though it was overshadowed by the utility project where the maps were only used as a background to the utility plant records. The land parcel element of the Dudley Project was undoubtedly the precursor of GIS in Great Britain, but was probably too advanced for the 'state of the art' in computer software and hardware at that time (Sowton and Green 1984).

Reviews of Ordnance Survey's digital mapping

The OS Review (or Serpell) Committee

In January 1978, a Review Committee under the chairmanship of Sir David Serpell was commissioned to review the long-term policies and activities of OS and the ways in which they were to be funded. Among many aspects of OS production, the Committee studied the requirements and financing of digital mapping. In its recommendations (HMSO 1979), the Committee supported the need for OS to continue with its digital mapping programme in spite of the higher cost of digital production when compared with conventional methods. The Committee also supported the need to develop the technology and accepted the OS proposals that a two-stage approach should be adopted, with the first stage concentrating on the development of the current digital flow-lines. Prior to proceeding to the second stage (which was to be an acceleration of the existing programme), it was recommended that an external assessment should be made of the outcome of the investigatory first stage. For an alternative review of this and other digital mapping reports, see also Chorley and Buxton (1991 in this volume).

The House of Lords' study

In 1983, a House of Lords' Select Committee on Science and Technology under the chairmanship of Lord Shackleton studied the subjects of remote sensing and digital mapping. Their recommendations, although critical of some aspects of OS progress, included significant support for digital mapping and the acceleration of the OS digitizing programme (HMSO 1983; Rhind 1986)

The government response to the Serpell Committee's report, which had been delayed for five years, coincided with the publication of the Select Committee's report and increased the impact of the special emphasis which both reports placed upon the need to speed up the digitizing of the large-scale mapping. At about this same time, OS concluded the experimental development of the digital flow-lines on which the Serpell Committee had recommended the need for external assessment. Consequently, Professor D W Rhind and Dr R A S Whitfield were commissioned in the latter part of 1983 to carry out a review of the OS digital mapping system and make recommendations prior to an approach to the Treasury for additional funds to accelerate the digital mapping programme. Their report concluded that there was justification in the proposals to press ahead with digitizing and that the OS proposals were a reasonable compromise in terms of rapidity of cover and geographical priorities. They made a number of detailed recommendations, most of which were implemented before an approach was made to the Treasury for additional funds which were granted in mid-1984 and used to fund a programme of external contracts for digital data (Rhind and Whitfield 1983).

Included in the House of Lords' report were specific recommendations relating to the production of small-scale digital data which some evidence to the Committee indicated to be urgently required. Before embarking on this work, OS decided to determine through a market survey the digital user requirement, the scales to be used and the potential revenue. The results of this exercise were inconclusive, but showed that the most promising prospect would be at 1 : 50 000-scale and, as a result, a single sheet of data for experimental purposes was produced.

The Committee of Enquiry into the Handling of Geographic Information

As a direct outcome of the recommendations of the House of Lords' Select Committee, the Government established in 1985 a Committee of Enquiry, under the chairmanship of Lord Chorley, into the Handling of Geographic Information (Rhind and Mounsey 1989; Chorley and Buxton 1991). The recommendations from this Committee added considerably to the already growing pressure on OS to increase the output of digital map data and within the recommendations were important proposals for OS to collaborate with its major customers to produce digital data (DoE 1987).

Late in 1987, high level negotiations took place between the senior management of OS and senior executives representing the utilities (gas, water, telephone and electricity). These negotiations established a basis for agreement whereby OS customers for digital data in those areas not yet digitized could obtain the data they needed by letting their own digitizing contracts. Resale of such data by OS (as part of the National Topographic Database) would then benefit both parties to the agreement. In order to establish standards for data produced in this way and ultimately to create more general standards which could be applied to the production of all digital data, a new feature code (or attribute) specification was created and a jointly agreed Quality Control Procedure was devised (National Joint Utilities Group 1988; see also Mahoney 1991 in this volume). The latter was based upon statistical sampling of various aspects of the data and hence eliminated subjective interpretations.

The evolution of OS data

Data formats and storage

Research and development work was done in the late 1970s on structured data and, more recently, it has been used in pilot production. But the basic structure of the digital map data continues to reflect the early concept that the digital mapping process was primarily a means of map production. While the very earliest specification has evolved to some extent, there have been few changes and the original data remain unchanged in organization. The data are divided into sheet units, each stored in separate files. Each file contains header information which specifies, among other things, the digitizing scale, survey and digitizing dates and information about updates. The map data follow the header information. Each line, point, text string or symbol is held as a separate feature. The nature of the feature is described by a feature code (e.g. fence, Bench Mark, road edge). The position and geometry of the feature are described by a series of coordinates which define locations on the National Grid (x and y coordinates only) for Britain. A line is defined by sufficient coordinates to give its location precisely at source scale (1 : 1250, 1 : 2500 or 1 : 10 000) and curves are held as a large number of short vectors. Points along a curve are digitized according to the skill and judgement of the digitizing operator and a mathematical spline (McConalogue 1970) is used during subsequent computer processing to generate sufficient additional points to achieve an apparently smooth curve. These additional points are permanently stored, together with the originally digitized points. This procedure is considered more efficient than generating the additional points as part of the plotting routines because it ensures that data sets are complete and do not depend on customers having access to the appropriate spline generation software.

Until 1987, the data in the OS data bank were stored in the archive sheet by sheet in files held on magnetic tape, using binary rather than character representation. Data sets were transferred to customers using a transfer format termed DMC, along with an associated Fortran plot program called D09 supplied free to purchasers of digital data. The D09 program allowed customers to plot a facsimile map from the data. DMC evolved into OSTF (Ordnance Survey Transfer Format) and a sophisticated version of this (OSTF+) is used to transfer data between systems within OS. Eventually it was accepted that the ICL 1906–based mapping system had to be re-written for use on the replacement 2966 computer and a new version of the system – though still based on feature-coded strings – was produced. This version, called DMV, was further modified for use on an ICL 3960 computer. In DMV, the data are stored on magnetic disk in emulated magnetic tape format. Data from this data bank have been used as input to the structuring software used to create data for the pilot topographic database (see below).

While DMC, OSTF and OSTF+ are still available to transfer data, the OS is now committed to sole use of a new National Transfer Format (NTF). NTF was originally designed in 1985 and, after widespread comment on draft proposals, the initial version (1.0) became available in 1987. Like DMC and OSTF before, NTF is based on the transfer of feature-coded vector data using four levels of increasing complexity (see Guptill 1991 for further discussion of transfer standards). Unlike the other transfer systems used by OS, NTF also has limited provision for raster data. For internal transfers, a version of NTF level 4 is being developed. Although originally designed by an OS-led working party (Sowton and Haywood 1986), responsibility for administration and future development of NTF was transferred to the newly formed Association for Geographic Information in 1989 (see Chorley and Buxton 1991 in this volume; Morrison 1991 in this volume).

Feature coding

In the earliest stages (i.e. around 1970), the OS adopted an extremely simple feature coding system which was applied to features by the digitizing operators through a menu on a digitizing table. For direct production of graphics from the digital data, the initial coding system was very effective. However, because the process of derived mapping needed to hold information about the treatment of data at smaller scales, it was considered that this could be most efficiently done by adding more feature codes; eventually these codes were combined into dual and sometimes multiple feature codes for a single entity. The consequence of this was a more effective derived mapping process, but at the expense of slower initial data capture caused by the increased interpretation and selection required on the part of the digitizing operators. With few external customers and little guidance from potential users of data for purposes other than map production, the coding system was developed to support and improve this application. It continued to develop along these lines until early 1987, when over 160 feature codes were available, although only a small proportion (typically 20 to 30) occurred on any one map.

At that time, the main application for digital data appeared to be as background maps for inventories of plant for the gas, electricity, telephone and water industries. This view was supported and emphasized by the report of the Chorley Committee (DoE 1987) which recommended that OS should adopt a less elaborate feature coding specification based on the now-superseded National Joint Utilities Group (NJUG 12) specification (National Joint Utilities Group 1986).

Since the number and range of feature codes held had just been increased to produce derived mapping, it was considered by OS that a reduction could only be adopted if an alternative way to achieve derived mapping could be found. An OS database study was, among other things, undertaken to look at the possibilities of using topologically structured data (hereafter denoted simply as 'structured data') to reduce the burden of feature coding. The report concluded that many of the feature codes were totally unnecessary and that their functions could be carried out through cartographic attributes attached to the links in the data. The first proposal, known as OS 1987, contained a little over 40 feature codes; this was significantly more than the NJUG 12 proposal which had 15 feature codes – and even that number was said to be more than required by most of their users. However, a compromise feature code specification (Ordnance Survey 1988b; National Joint Utilities Group 1988) was agreed by OS and NJUG 12 was withdrawn. OS 1988 contains 35 feature codes and has been adopted as an acceptable content for OS large scale digital map data. For cartographic purposes, the OS has added additional feature codes which are used to fill polygons with symbols and stipples by software, thereby eliminating all manual cartographic processes from the production of large scale digital maps to existing specifications.

Data quality

In addition to the negotiations with the utility organizations over feature coding, data quality was also considered. For some time prior to this, OS had been criticized – mainly by the utilities – about the lengths to which the Department went to preserve the graphic specification. This criticism was not supported by the local authorities who, although wishing to see production rates increase, also wished to have the content, accuracy and graphic quality of OS maps preserved in the digital data. Some of the critics felt that the checking processes used by OS caused digital production rates to be lower than they might be if less subjective checking procedures were to be adopted.

A statistical sampling procedure was suggested which, after modification and testing, was agreed as a quality control procedure to be used for digital contracts by the utilities. In the light of experience, it was accepted that OS would have to make a visual check of the data to establish its suitability for map production; this check is now combined with minor corrections, thereby further improving the success rate for the acceptance of data. The quality control procedure is published in the National Joint Utilities Group's pamphlet number 13 (National Joint Utilities Group 1988) and has now been adopted by OS for its own contract and internal digitizing.

Digitizing methods

The first digitizing equipment used by OS for digital mapping comprised 'blind tables' (i.e. without any visual display of the progress of digitizing). On these, an operator digitized each point sequentially or followed a line with a cursor. Both methods produced vector data after processing, but line following was found to be less accurate and often produced excessive amounts of data which had subsequently to be compressed or excised. Using the cursor and a menu, the operator assigned classification codes to the various map features. Since there was no screen display, checks for errors and completeness could not be carried out until a hard copy plot had been made. Corrections were made using the same blind process and off-line batch editing methods (Gardiner-Hill 1972). With the advent of editing workstations, the editing and capture processes were improved but the work, whether blind or interactive, still depended on digitizing point by point or line following.

From 1970 onwards, in an endeavour to improve the output of digital data, automatic line following and scanning methods were periodically tested but none proved effective, due in part to the failure of the equipment to cope with the graphical survey methods used for revision and the nature of the large-scale map detail. Extensive tests were made with two alternative systems, but no cost savings could be demonstrated to justify changing from the manual point digitizing methods.

The possibility of producing raster data from the surveyor's field document (known as a Master Survey Drawing or MSD) to fulfil a potential market requirement is again being investigated in 1990. The solution depends on the scanner being able to record the detail from the MSD which is part printed and part revised in pen and ink. So far, the pen-drawn lines have defeated the scanning systems available or the operations have been so demanding in operator intervention that the result has not been cost effective. In 1989, a system using automatic image enhancement was investigated; thus technology may yet create an acceptable raster product from a MSD.

Revision

Although various survey techniques have been used over the years to create the large scale maps, they are still kept up to date by predominantly graphical survey methods, supported by instrumental survey and some photogrammetry. The up to date survey of an area is held in a local field office as an inked plot on a plastic MSD. This method has proved to be extremely cost effective and digital revision methods have been designed to maintain this process as well as to incorporate output from field instruments and photogrammetry.

It was realized at an early stage in the development of digital mapping that the digital data would become valueless unless they were kept up to date to the same level as the MSDs. With the increase in the number of digital maps available, digital revision processes have been introduced which complement the existing graphic field methods. A Digital Field Update System (DFUS) has been developed which allows surveyors to digitize their graphic survey, input the data directly into the relevant data file and plot the survey on to the MSD. In recent modifications, the MSD is no longer required and the surveyor works on a graphic plot taken from the data bank, subsequently digitizing the surveyed change into the database with no hard-copy record or MSD being retained. Since 1989 in those areas where digital field update is being introduced, the maps will be updated without MSDs and this revision will rely entirely on digital processes (Coote 1988). Regardless of the source of revision data (i.e. from DFUS, instrumental survey or photogrammetry), the data and their source will be recorded directly into the database. As soon as the database has been updated, the data or a plot from them are available to the next customer.

In order to take this update process further and to introduce digital methods into graphic field work, a Portable Interactive Editing System (PIES) has been developed. This allows a surveyor to enter surveyed detail directly into the digital data on the ground and have a visual display of the result immediately. Thus all the work and corrections can be done on site. The PIES equipment will interface directly with the DFUS equipment for the transfer of data into and out of the data bank. This development will allow each surveyor to have a personal recording system and should reduce the number of more expensive DFUS workstations needed.

For structured vector data, it will be essential to revise links and polygons without upsetting the structure of the existing data or introducing inconsistencies. The editing process must not only maintain an accurate survey and keep the data 'clean', but must also preserve the topology. Thus, for a land parcel to be subdivided, the system must be able to incorporate the dividing link or links, split the existing links where appropriate, create new nodes and, finally, record the new polygons and flag the previous polygon as no longer current data. It is essential to develop a mechanism to do this, either working directly on the structured data or through a process of restructuring after editing. The flagged data could be used to obtain historic data from the database. OS is investigating the introduction of such structured data editors at the time of writing.

The final requirement in the editing process will be the ability to transfer only the changes – and not the complete edited map file – to those customers purchasing updates. This is not a particularly difficult technical problem, but the solution will involve consideration of the mechanics of the recipient systems and how their data are linked to the OS map data. Of far more significance are the administrative processes which have to record which customers receive updates, the frequency or the content of change they receive, when last updated and so on. Undoubtedly 'change only' update will happen, but there are many non-technical considerations which may make its introduction later rather than sooner.

Derived mapping

The Bideford experiment (see above) was a technical success, but only addressed the problem in a largely rural environment. However, it did show that it was possible to produce 1 : 25 000-scale maps to the existing specification from 1 : 2500 digital data (Cobb, 1970, contains illustrations that demonstrate this point). Later work also showed that an acceptable 1 : 10 000-scale map could be created from urban 1 : 1250 data. Not only was the map of an acceptable quality, but the process was demonstrated to be cost effective. Difficulties arose, however, because the conventional 1 : 10 000-scale map specification was designed to produce 1 : 25 000 maps by photographic reduction. The digitally produced 1 : 10 000-scale map could not meet the specification for this photographic process. Further work revealed that digitally produced 1 : 25 000-scale maps covering urban areas were too detailed to be acceptable and the feature coding system was not sufficiently versatile to accomplish all the generalization required. The additional interactive editing made the combined costs of the two map series greater than production by conventional methods. The separation of the two series was not possible because the revision of the 1 : 25 000 maps depended upon the revision of the 1 : 10 000 maps and it was not economic to break the dependence of the 1 : 25 000 on the 1 : 10 000 mapping until a cost-effective method for revising the 1 : 25 000 maps could be found (Gibson 1974).

With the advent of topologically structured vector data on a production basis during 1989, the production process of the derived 1 : 10 000 series has increased in efficiency and recent results show that 1 : 1250 and 1 : 2500 data can be used to produce acceptable 1 : 10 000 graphics (Plate 36.3). At the same time, investigations into the production and revision of 1 : 25 000 maps as an independent series using conventional processes are showing promising results. Thus it appears as if up to date 1 : 10 000 graphics will be an economic possibility in the near future where structured data exist, with the 1 : 25 000 mapping being maintained through conventional processes until a more robust production method for 1 : 25 000 maps from structured digital data can be developed.

To go beyond 1 : 25 000 scales from the large-scale map base with the derived mapping process is not thought feasible at present. However, it may yet be possible to use expert systems to create the generalization necessary (see Muller 1991 in this volume) but, for the immediate future, if a commercially viable demand for 1 : 50 000 and smaller scale data emerges, it will be met by the creation of data sets for each application rather than creating a 'scale-free' comprehensive database with full map-making capabilities.

RECENT OS DEVELOPMENTS

The late 1980s saw considerable developments in the technology available, a growth in user demand and the financial requirement to maximize use of the topographic archive for as many purposes as possible. For these and other reasons, OS has made significant changes in recent years.

The Database Project

Considerations about a database – as opposed to the existing OS collection of files of large-scale data or a data bank – started before 1979 (Thompson 1979) but it was not until 1985 that the requirements, the content and use of a large-scale database were systematically studied. Between 1985 and 1987, the principles behind the establishment of a database were investigated. The database study team recommended the need for a relational database and, during the final stages of their investigations, a prototype relational database was set up using RDB on a Digital Equipment Corporation VAX 11/780 which was subsequently transferred on to a small Britton Lee (now Sharebase) database machine to test the validity of their recommendations. The study concluded that significant benefits would arise to both OS and its customers from having:

- a completely digital large-scale map archive;
- topologically structured data;
- the addition to the topographic data of management and process data.

Furthermore, as a result of these changes in data specification, it was predicted that there would be additional benefits if database management procedures replaced file management and also if more on-line communications were introduced. The implementation plan for such a database contained three main elements. These were to:

- develop a fully automated production system for large scale maps which would eliminate all manual intervention;
- create a pilot area to test the conclusions of the database study;
- carry out marketing and research and development projects to examine the implications that might arise from the full implementation of a database management system based on the conclusions of the study (Haywood 1987).

In January 1988, the implementation plan of the Database Project was accepted and approval was given to proceed with the creation of a pilot topographic database for the purpose of obtaining production experience in:

- relational database management of the topographic data to identify improvements in data handling and the benefits to be derived from the storage of information related to the data, such as survey methods, date of survey, etc.;
- topologically structured data with object building capabilities and attribute attachment;
- automated map production using the structured data to eliminate all conventional cartographic processes.

Although it would have been simpler to implement a pilot database in a single block, it was realized that no single area could provide sufficient variety of users to test all the various advantages on which the final adoption of such a system would depend. As a consequence, three test areas were established. The project was a compromise between testing database applications, the implementation of new map production processes and the creation and use of structured data for use within GIS projects. In addition, it was anticipated that new graphic products from the digital data and new data products could also be introduced.

The final report of the project has been considered by the OS Management Board and approval given for the continued support of such structured data users in the pilot areas, pending the collection of more information about the potential market for structured data. In the meantime, a study of the requirements for a replacement of the existing DMV digital mapping system has been approved; it will take account of the requirements for handling structured topographic data and the cost implications. It has also been agreed that structured data will be provided to customers on a full-cost basis. The final report of the project team emphasized the need for structured data for the economic production of graphics, the increased ability to market a variety of new graphic products and the commercial potential of new digital products, particularly those supporting in-car navigation. In 1990, the benefits to be derived from these recommendations and the market for structured data are being assessed.

Use of structured data inside OS

At an early stage in the database study, it was realized that topologically structured data would be a valuable asset for internal purposes and not only as an improved data product for GIS purposes. Unlike the earlier, labour-intensive way in which structured data were produced for the Dudley Project, the process now relies on software which creates unique junctions and eliminates all gaps and overshoots in the data within set tolerances. Anything outside these tolerances is flagged and is examined on a workstation. The structured data are produced from this by digitizing some additional information, mainly polygon points, and creating a link and node structure by software with some interactive editing. Polygon objects are built by software using the polygon points which, because they can readily be re-generated automatically, can then be discarded. The attributes of these polygons can then be used to control the filling of areas with symbols, other ornamentation or colour. The topological relationships thus identified are explicitly stored in the database along with attributes deduced from the original data. Positioned text, previously used for cartographic purposes, is attached as an attribute to the points, links, nodes and other objects to which it actually pertains. This linking or object building creates the significant polygons on which cartographic and information processes depend (Haywood 1988).

Use of structured data outside OS

At the time of writing (mid-1990), only a small number of trials of structured data are in progress, the most important being in Tameside (Greater Manchester) where a GIS trial is starting to demonstrate the advantages of having a central database using a structured data set with all the borough's functions being linked. It is thus too early to say what level of general demand will arise from the results of these trials. But it is now clear that a great deal of interest is being generated and one successful GIS, which can be demonstrated by a local authority, may cause a surge of demand. Clearly, the extra costs of producing structured data ahead of demand is a risk but the demonstrated uses of structured data within OS may show sufficient benefits to outweigh the additional production costs even without support from an external market being required in the short term.

Graphic products from the data

It has been recognized for some time that digital data will only be a valuable asset for OS if they can be harnessed to produce not only a range of digital products, but also a range of graphic products, some of which emulate to a great degree or improve upon current products. Graphic products are currently sold in three main forms. The first is a printed copy which, as time passes, becomes more and more out of date until a new edition is produced. The second is an enlargement from 35 mm microfilm output and is known as SIM (Survey Information on Microfilm); it may contain some revised detail. And the third is a direct copy from the MSD produced in the survey office, being known as SUSI (Sale of

Unpublished Survey Information). SUSI allows the customer to have access to the most up-to-date mapping but has a lower quality than lithographically printed standard products. Comparable services have to be available from the digital data as part of a fully viable digital process. With certain changes to the map specification and through the use of structured data, it is now possible to produce an acceptable map without manual cartographic processes and this can be plotted either on a paper or transparent base from which a printing plate could be made. The modified specification has been accepted by OS's consultative committees; all new editions at 1 : 1250 are being produced in this way and 1 : 2500 production will start during 1990. Thus, 20 years after the original OS experiments, all of the basic scale maps for the non-mountainous areas of Britain are being produced entirely by automated means.

As an extension of this process, a new service called Superplan has been introduced which, by manipulating the data, can permit the user to obtain a product for non-standard areas or scales, which suppresses unwanted details and adds new symbols and colours. Some, but not all, of these variations rely upon the availability of topologically structured data; hence customers wishing to have non-standard products to their own layout, scale and specification can – within limits – have such a plot on demand. However, where structured data are not available, symbols and colour cannot be added. A variation of the full Superplan service using feature-coded vector data is available in London. For these services to be viable, it is essential that the digital data are maintained up to date and, as described earlier, revision processes to do this for 'normal' vector data are available and processes to deal with structured data are being developed.

Additional Digital Products

From the structured digital data, three experimental products have been created which have gained modest acceptance by customers. These have been given provisional names:

- OSBASE: the standard structured digital map, usable as a base for GIS and graphic plot production.

- OSLAND: a product based on OSBASE with all the land parcels and highway polygons closed and referenced. It is anticipated that this data set would also include additional feature codes, reference numbers and postal addresses.

- OSCAR: a data set related to the road network for use in navigation systems and to solve road-related management and maintenance problems. This data set includes road names, and classifications linked to each network segment; it may eventually include post-codes.

Geographical information for vehicle navigation

The use of digital map data to support various vehicle-related applications for geographical information has increased in importance since 1987. OS has been actively producing data for in-car navigation by combining the OSCAR data with smaller scale data. Production of data in link and node form for this application is now a matter of routine, but storage and update techniques are still being developed.

Navigation in this context is also taken to include:

- pre-journey route planning;

- delivery scheduling;

- fleet command and control; and

- traffic management.

OS has supplied data from a variety of scales ranging from 1 : 625 000 to large scales to support these applications (Smith 1989). As a consequence, commercial products such as Autoroute have appeared; this runs on a PC, provides tabular and map output on routes selected on multiple criteria and retails for about £200 (US$400).

Small-scale digital data

The Chorley Committee recommended that the longer term objective for OS should be to achieve a 'scale-free' digital database rather than a family of databases derived from maps compiled at a variety of scales. At the present time, it appears that this will not be achieved for many years until a breakthrough in the generalization process is made. While interactive generalization is now possible, it is extremely time consuming and the result is no less costly than re-digitizing the data from existing cartographic products. It seems, therefore, that for some years at least, scale will be considered in steps and the OS Topographic Database will only be 'scale free' between the 1 : 1250 and the 1 : 10 000 scales. Thus a series of single scale databases will exist although it may be possible or even essential to create a bridge between 1 : 25 000 and 1 : 50 000 scales at an early stage.

OS started its investigations into database technology through the creation of a database compiled from the 1 : 625 000-scale maps. This project culminated in the successful production of the 1986 Routeplanner maps from digital data (Plate 36.1). From then onwards, data sets from this scale were produced first for experiment and, finally, for sale as commercial products. In addition, 1 : 250 000-scale data have been produced as a co-venture with a commercial partner and these data were launched on the market in 1990 (Plate 36.2).

As a result of market research projects, data for a single 1 : 50 000 map have been digitized to determine reactions to the data content and specification (Ordnance Survey 1984, 1985). However, this experiment has proved that digital data at this scale need a special specification and users are not interested in a complicated data set which can merely reproduce the 1 : 50 000-scale mapping exactly. A project is now in hand to create a new specification for data at this scale which it is hoped will create interest, particularly with GIS users. The data may contain additional features, for example field boundaries and network data, such as rivers, not needed to produce mapping; they may also leave out some less important items.

Data sets are unlikely to be produced at 1 : 25 000 scale unless a way of automatically generalizing the large-scale data can be developed. Data for this scale would be quite considerably generalized and therefore might not serve any real purpose for GIS users who would already have available 1 : 50 000 data to the new specification as well as 1 : 10 000-scale data.

The Ministry of Defence and OS have come to an agreement in which contours from the 1 : 50 000 scale map are digitized and marketed. Sales have been low but this reflects, among other things, the lack of coverage to date. In addition, Digital Elevation Models derived from these contours and hydrological information are now available.

GEOGRAPHICAL INFORMATION SYSTEMS

The OS is not directly involved in GIS, but provides essential digital map data sets on which such systems depend. The essential nature of a GIS is that it should be capable of linking a variety of data through spatial links. A GIS is a system which allows the capture, updating and display of a number of previously unconnected data sets, bringing them into a common reference system for spatial analysis from which relationships can be identified and decisions made. In order to do this, a common spatial reference framework is required and it is this which the OS digital maps provide for GIS. Through the topologically structured data, it is possible to link non-cartographic data to polygon seeds and individual links in the map data, and to manipulate the various data sets as one.

While it is sometimes forgotten that the output of a GIS need not be a map, none the less when a map *is* required a GIS should be capable of producing a good quality map either on a screen or on a plotter in order to give credibility to the results displayed. Moreover, high cartographic quality is taken for granted by British customers. The OS digital data provide the quality required; it has the area 'seeds' and 'hooks' needed to link other spatially related data to the map data through the reference system (the National Grid) and it ensures the correct relationship between systems based on OS mapping. Perhaps the most important factor, however, in linking data sets is that the digital mapping is kept up to date and users of OS data may obtain updates based on the amount of change which has occurred or on a specified elapsed time or some combination of both (Haywood 1989). Demand for this option is difficult to quantify because user comments thus far are more concerned with initial digitizing (as well as digitizing their own records) and, as a result, demand for update has been limited as yet. This scenario is expected to continue for some time while users gain sufficient experience to put a value on having up to date data for the manipulation of various data sets.

CONCLUSIONS

The Ordnance Survey is faced with a number of decisions about the way forward with digital mapping and the early 1990s should provide the answers to many of the unresolved questions which arise out of recent investigations. Clearly, the OS will go forward as a digital data producer with a requirement to service the newly emerging GIS: it will also continue to meet less sophisticated requirements for data and also to produce graphic products for a wide range of non-digital map users.

The only certainty is that the current digital mapping system has to be replaced by a new system with a database capable of storing and producing data for a wide range of applications. What is not clear, however, is whether there is a requirement for structured data and object building within the database or whether this should be a special product created 'on-demand' from the digital data. The requirements for structured data within OS and among its major customers are just emerging and some answers to this uncertainty are expected during 1990. Fortunately, OS is now able to create structured data and the production and handling of such data are routine.

Whether a demand for raster data products will emerge is uncertain but, in areas where vector data already exist, a demand for this type of data could be rapidly met. What has still to be solved is a way to create up-to-date raster data where vector data have not yet been created and where the demand for vector data may not arise for some time. Current investigations suggest raster data can be scanned from the MSDs and that the resulting data sets can be converted by software to vector data if necessary and without difficulty. What cannot be foreseen is whether raster technology will move towards an intelligent raster (where each pixel has a relationship to its neighbour and to which attributes can be attached) and the conversion of graphics to vector data via raster data will become almost completely automatic, with rule-based systems for assigning feature codes.

Finally, in Great Britain at least, it seems likely that the demand for small-scale digital data will increase to become a major data requirement of GIS users carrying out macro-spatial data analyses. The problem here will be the relationship between the large-scale micro-analysis and the overall macro-consolidation. Will it be necessary to convert between the various map databases or will the treatment of scale in separate databases be adequate for the wider issues of GIS and hence solve the 'scale-free' issue? OS has come a long way since the late-1960s but there are still exciting times ahead in the 1990s.

REFERENCES

Atkey R G, Gibson R J (1975) Progress in automated cartography. *Proceedings of the Conference of Commonwealth Survey Officers*. Cambridge, August 1975. Ministry of Overseas Development. Paper J3

Bickmore D P (1971) Experimental maps of the Bideford area. *Proceedings of the Conference of Commonwealth Survey Officers*. Cambridge, August 1971. Foreign and Commonwealth Office. Paper E1, pp. 217–23

Chorley R, Buxton R (1991) The government setting for GIS in the United Kingdom. In: Maguire D J, Goodchild M F, Rhind D W (eds.) *Geographical Information Systems: principles and applications*. Longman, London, pp. 67–79, Vol 1

Cobb M C (1970) Changing map scales by automation. *Geographical Magazine* **4** (3): 786–8

Coote A M (1988) Current developments in field-based digital mapping systems at Ordnance Survey. *Proceedings of Mapping Awareness Conference*. Miles Arnold, Oxford

DoE (Department of the Environment) (1971) Inter-departmental Committee, chaired by J. D. W. Janes. *Report of the Committee on the Ordnance Survey 1970–71*. Unpublished

DoE (Department of the Environment) (1987) *Handling Geographic Information – Report of the Committee of Inquiry chaired by Lord Chorley*. HMSO, London

Gardiner-Hill R C (1971) Automated cartography in the Ordnance Survey. *Proceedings of the Conference of Commonwealth Survey Officers*. Cambridge, August 1971. Foreign and Commonwealth Office. Paper E3, pp. 235–41

Gardiner-Hill R C (1972) *Professional Paper New Series No. 23*. Ordnance Survey, Southampton

Gardiner-Hill R C (1974) The cosmetics of computer cartography. *Proceedings of the 7th International Conference on Cartography*. International Cartographic Association, Madrid

Gibson R J (1974) The production of 1 : 10,000 scale mapping from large scale database. In: Wilford-Brickwood, Bertrand and van Zuylen (eds.) *Working Group Oceanic Cartography Commission III*. International Cartographic Association, Enschede, pp. 121–32

Guptill S C (1991) Spatial data exchange and standardization. In: Maguire D J, Goodchild M F, Rhind

D W (eds.) *Geographical Information Systems: principles and applications*. Longman, London, pp. 515–30, Vol 1

Haywood P E (1987) The OS Topographic Database Study – the first stage report. In: Haywood P E (ed.) *Proceedings of Spatially-Oriented Referencing Systems Association (SORSA) Symposium, Durham*. Ordnance Survey

Haywood P E (1988) Structured digital data at OS. *Land and Minerals Surveying* **6** (3): 151–6

Haywood P E (1989) Structured topographic data – the key to GIS. *Proceedings of Association of Geographic Information Conference*, Birmingham, October 1989. AGI, London, pp. B1.1–1.4

HMSO (Her Majesty's Stationery Office) (1979) *Report of the Ordnance Survey Review Committee*. Chaired by Sir David Serpell. HMSO, London

HMSO (Her Majesty's Stationery Office) (1983) *Report of the Select Committee on Science and Technology – Remote Sensing and Digital Mapping*. Chaired by Lord Shackleton. HMSO, London

Mahoney R P (1991) GIS and utilities. In: Maguire D J, Goodchild M F, Rhind D W (eds.) *Geographical Information Systems: principles and applications*. Longman, London, pp. 101–14, Vol 2

McConalogue D J (1970) A quasi-intrinsic scheme for passing a smooth curve through a discrete set of points. *Computer Journal* **13** (4): 392–96

Morrison J L (1991) The organizational home for GIS in the scientific professional community. In: Maguire D J, Goodchild M F, Rhind D W (eds.) *Geographical Information Systems: principles and applications*. Longman, London, pp. 91–100, Vol 1

Muller J-C (1991) Generalization of spatial databases. In: Maguire D J, Goodchild M F, Rhind D W (eds.) *Geographical Information Systems: principles and applications*. Longman, London, pp. 457–75, Vol 1

National Joint Utilities Group (1986) *NJUG Specification for the Digitisation of Large Scale OS Maps. No. 12*. NJUG, London

National Joint Utilities Group (1988) *Quality Control Procedure for Large Scale Ordnance Survey Maps Digitised to OS 1988. No. 13*. NJUG, London

Ordnance Survey (1984) *Report of the Small Scales Digital Map User Needs Study*. OS, Southampton

Ordnance Survey (1985) *Report of the Investigation into Demand for Digital Data from 1 : 50 000 Mapping*. OS, Southampton

Ordnance Survey (1988a) *Annual Report 1987/88*. OS, Southampton

Ordnance Survey (1988b) *Ordnance Survey's Contractors' Specification for Digital Mapping*. OS, Southampton

Ordnance Survey (1989) *Annual Report 1988/89*. OS, Southampton

Rhind D W (1986) Remote sensing, digital mapping and Geographical Information Systems: the creation of government policy in the UK. *Environment and Planning C: Government and Policy* **4**: 91–102

Rhind D W (1990) Topographic databases derived from small scale maps and the future of Ordnance Survey. In: Foster M, Shand P J (eds.) *The AGI Yearbook 1990*. Taylor & Francis, London, pp. 187–96

Rhind D W, Mounsey H M (1989) The Chorley Committee and 'Handling Geographic Information'. *Environment and Planning A* **21**: 571–85

Rhind D W, Whitfield R A S (1983) *A Review of the OS Proposals for Digitising the Large Scale Maps of Great Britain*. Consultancy report – unpublished.

Seymour W A (ed.) (1980) *A History of the Ordnance Survey*. Dawson, Folkestone

Smith A B (1989) Geographical Information for European Vehicle Navigation Systems. In: Perry (ed.) *Proceedings of Government Computing 1989 (GC 89)*. HMSO, London. pp. 15–17.

Sowton M (1971) Automation in cartography at the Ordnance Survey using digital output from a plotting machine. *Bildmessung und Luftbildwesen* **39** (1): 41–4

Sowton M, Green P (1984) Digital map data for computerised land and utility information systems. *Proceedings 10th European Symposium for Urban Data Information Systems – Urban Data Management and the End Users*. Padua, pp. 34–49

Sowton M, Haywood P E (1986) National standards for the transfer of digital map data. In: Blakemore M J (ed.) *Proceedings of AUTOCARTO London I*. Royal Institution of Chartered Surveyors, London, pp. 198–311

Thompson C N (1978) Digital mapping in the Ordnance Survey 1968–1978. In: Allam (ed.) *Proceedings of the International Society for Photogrammetry Commission IV International Symposium – New Technology for Mapping*. Ottawa, pp. 195–219

Thompson C N (1979) The need for a large scale topographic database. *Proceedings of the Conference of Commonwealth Survey Officers, July 1979*, Foreign and Commonwealth Office. Paper F4

Williams E P J (1971) Digitisation of Large Scale Maps. *Proceedings of ICA Commission III meeting, Paris*. ICA, Paris, Paper II/a

NATIONAL GIS PROGRAMMES IN SWEDEN

L OTTOSON AND B RYSTEDT

Scandinavian societies differ in several important aspects from many others and this has affected the national developments in GIS. Most notably, there is a long tradition of holding personal and land-related information in registers open to public inspection with explicit links between items in certain of the registers. This chapter describes the Swedish Land Data Bank register in particular and how it has been converted to computer form. It also describes a programme for creating and disseminating national geographical databases, the progress in creating the new National Atlas of Sweden in electronic form, the setting up of regional GIS centres and the Swedish research and development council for land information development.

EARLY DEVELOPMENTS

Sweden has a very long tradition of keeping registers: the first land registers date from the beginning of the fifteenth century. A complete register for rural areas is preserved from the sixteenth century. The main reason for establishing this register was for tax purposes and, since economic activities rather than properties were taxed in towns, the land register for urban areas was not established until the beginning of this century. Mapping and population registration also have a long tradition in Sweden. The National Land Survey (NLS) was born in 1628 and Statistics Sweden in 1749. For centuries, all of the registers had to be kept by pen and ink methods and periodically totally re-drawn. Nevertheless, computers and information technology were recognized at an early stage as efficient tools for management of these registers and for a wider use of their contents (see Rhind 1991 in this volume for further discussion about population registers).

Although the term GIS was not known at that time, it can be claimed that the first work in the GIS area was done in 1955 by Professor Torsten Hägerstrand at the University of Lund (Hägerstrand 1955, 1967). He suggested that coordinates should be registered for the centroid of each residential building. He found, however, that there are no unique identifiers for buildings and that the division of land into parcels or 'real properties' provides the foundation for spatial referencing. In fact, the 'real property' designation is a common identifier for the most important registers of property, population and firms. By linking these registers to each other, a considerable amount of data could be spatially referenced by the coordinates of the real property to which they are connected. Hägerstrand illustrated this by examples of population maps (Fig. 37.1). He also estimated the lack of accuracy when the centroids of real properties were chosen in place of the coordinates of residential buildings as the spatial reference in the population register.

Hägerstrand's work was followed by other studies. Nordbeck's study from 1962 on point referencing of areal data, for instance, is still valid. He found that the lower left corner of the real property number (Fig. 37.2) is a good estimation of the centroid's position. Nordbeck's method was chosen when digitizing point references for the real properties in the Swedish Land Data Bank System

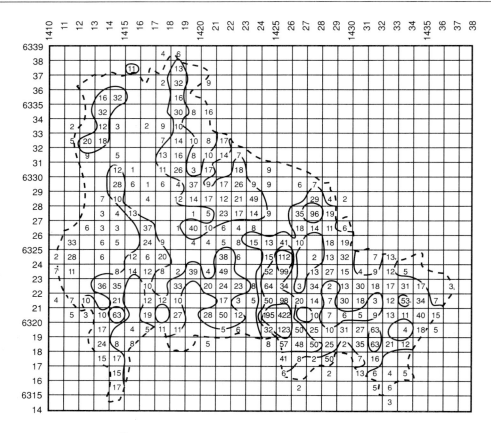

Fig. 37.1 Inhabitants per km^2 in the municipality of Moheda according to the 1940 population census. Isarithms as to 10, 50 and 100 inhabitants per km^2. Break downs by age and occupation are possible (Hägerstrand 1955: p. 241).

was started in 1969. In total, the 1960s was a very fruitful decade for research and development on GIS in Sweden. Based upon the results, several proposals were brought to Parliament at the end of the decade and the main decisions were:

- computerization of the central population register;
- initiation of the Land Data Bank System;
- establishment of a spatially referenced data bank for public roads.

In addition, the National Land Survey took the first steps in computer-assisted cartography during the late 1960s (Ottoson 1977).

CURRENT STRATEGIES

Although GIS was recognized early in Sweden, it has not been taken into widespread use. There has been a lack of hardware, software, geographical data and technical competence among staff. Today, however, there is no reason to worry about hardware and software. Both are now available at reasonable prices to those with knowledge about the suitability of various combinations. But building up the database and developing competence in using the system – as well keeping databases up to date – remain major problems. Based on these observations, NLS has taken a series of initiatives and set up the following:

- Geographical Data of Sweden (GSD) – a

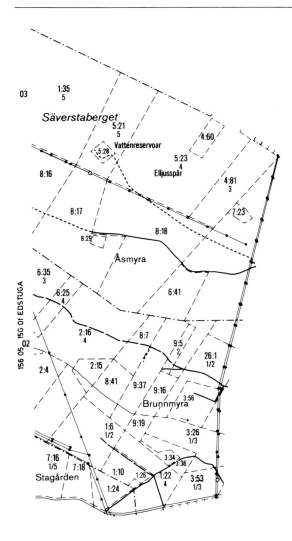

Fig. 37.2 The figure shows part of the property map at the scale of 1 : 10 000. For point referencing of land parcels in the Swedish Land Data Bank the left foot point of the property designation number is chosen as the point to digitize.

programme for creating 'national geographical databases';

- National Atlas of Sweden as a comprehensive national GIS;

- GIS regional centres for cooperative growth and use of GIS resources;

- ULI – a research and development council for land information technology.

Geographical Data of Sweden (GSD)

Historically, Swedish official mapping activities were focused on the production of printed maps and when information handling was introduced, it was designed expressly for that purpose. Some years ago, however, a broader approach was adopted to include responsibility for providing basic geographical digital data in a form suitable for the activities of other users and producers of land information. In Sweden, NLS is responsible for directing and coordinating the establishment of geographical databases by central and local authorities (Ottoson 1987). This task is performed through discussions and cooperation with other organizations and by initiatives in standardization, research and development. The most important geographical databases today are discussed below.

NLS has established two gridded national elevation databases at differing resolutions. These data are obtained primarily through photogrammetric methods and are used for such tasks as orthophoto mapping and visibility studies. The first grid was established during the 1970s and covers the entire country at a 500 m grid interval. Elevations are stored in 25 × 25 km blocks corresponding to standard NLS topographic map sheets. The second elevation database, with a 50 m grid spacing, is tied to 5 × 5 km Economic Map sheets and is now complete and comprises 19 000 grids. Basic topographic information for the country is also provided in digital form by NLS. One of these databases covers the entirety of Sweden and is used mainly for the production of small (1 : 1 000 000 and smaller)-scale thematic maps. It contains administrative boundaries of the counties, municipalities and parishes; hydrographic details such as shorelines, lakes, islands and rivers; urban area outlines; and public roads and railways. Another data set used for map presentation at scales of 1 : 200 000 to 1 : 500 000 contains the same features but in greater detail, plus place names and some other planimetric information. Although the entire data set is not yet complete, most features are available for all of Sweden. NLS has also produced a database of all place names found in the 1 : 50 000 scale Topographic Map Series. The costs of data acquisition were shared equally by NLS, the Defence Forces and the Swedish Alarm Company (which handles emergency calls and alerts the rescue units). The database is now complete and contains about 500 000 place names with coordinates, category codes and administrative affiliations.

A hydrographic database has been established through cooperation between NLS and the Swedish Meteorological and Hydrological Institute (SMHI). It contains boundary data on all water bodies, basins and islands (larger than 1 km^2) and rivers, streams and brooks. This database was completed during 1987 and constitutes the geographical reference material in the SMHI information system known as the Swedish Water Archive.

The National Road Administration's national highway database contains technical and administrative information on the Swedish highways and the coordinates of road intersections. An extension of this database, to include accurate X, Y and Z coordinates of highway centre lines, is now under construction through cooperation between NLS and the Road Administration. Data are acquired from small scale (1 : 150 000) aerial photographs using analytical photogrammetric instruments. The database will be completed in two steps: initially the primary highways will be digitized and then all other roads. All road crossings in the country have been given unique identifiers which makes it possible to link geometric road data to attribute data available in the highway database. In addition, NLS has started to build up a road database by digitizing the 1 : 50 000 Topographic Map Series. This base will contain all public and private roads by the end of 1991.

A national flight information data bank covering the whole country is maintained cooperatively by NLS, the Air Staff and the Board of Civil Aviation. It includes the information needed to produce air navigation charts and background for flight supervision equipment. Furthermore, NLS has established raster-formatted land use/cover databases by scanning the 1 : 250 000 scale topographic map feature separates. Thus, land data in seven classes are available as 50×50 m pixels.

The Land Data Bank System described in a later section of this chapter includes coordinates for a centroid of each individual real property unit, but not for the property border lines. Property lines, however, have for some years been registered sheet by sheet in the production of the 1 : 10 000 scale Economic Map Series (Szegö 1987). A standard concept for a National Property Line Base was proposed by NLS in March 1990. The proposed database will include geometry and topology, not only for property lines but also for the boundaries of land use zones, regulated areas and easements. Attribute data will be achieved by linkage to the registers of the Land Data Bank. It is proposed that the database will be built in coordination with the production of the Economic Map Series and, when appropriate, with the large-scale mapping conducted by the local authorities. The production time is estimated as nine years and the cost is predicted as 800 million Swedish Kronor (US$130 million). Before the proposal is finally sent to the government, a more thorough investigation of costs, benefits and organization will be made in conjunction with the Association of Local Authorities.

Generally, NLS employs computer-assisted methods in the production of feature separates for the official Economic and Topographic Map Series at scales ranging from 1 : 10 000 to 1 : 100 000, as well as for general maps at smaller scales. The digital information collected for these maps is stored in databases which are available to any user. Large-scale mapping (greater than 1 : 10 000 scale) is a responsibility of the municipalities but is normally carried out using digital methods by NLS or private companies. These maps typically include features such as geodetic points, buildings and property boundaries.

The National Atlas of Sweden

The first Atlas of Sweden was produced between 1953 and 1971. It is now out of date and the creation of a new one has been discussed for many years. In September 1986, NLS proposed that government funds should be made available for the production of a new, modern national atlas of Sweden. The atlas would consist of 20 volumes and be produced during the period 1987–96. The proposal passed Parliament and the first two volumes were published in 1990.

A national atlas is a geographical description of a country in the form of thematic maps with attached text, statistical data in the form of tables, diagrams and other illustrations of different kinds. Its purpose is to make an objective and scientific presentation of the nation in its natural and man-made aspects. But a modern atlas is not only an atlas in its bound book form: it must also be a set of geographical databases and an information system with versatile mapping and analysis functions. That will be achieved in the Swedish case by production of PC-atlases, which basically are to be used as small scale GIS in schools and public libraries (Rystedt 1987).

Regional GIS centres

Geographical data processing is very demanding in terms of both hardware and software; skilled personnel are also needed to operate a geographical information system. The regionalization of the technical systems of the National Land Survey has at least minimized these problems. Furthermore, the digital mapping programme described above has resulted in several databases containing basic digital geographical data. That means that the time is now opportune to set up regional GIS centres founded on regional cooperation, with resources of different government agencies and local authorities being pooled into a cooperative organization. Three such centres had been set up by 1990. The first was located in the county of Norrbotten, the northernmost province of Sweden. This centre is jointly owned by the local authorities in the county, the County Administration Board, the Regional Board of Forestry, Satimage (the state satellite data-receiving organization) and the Regional Land Survey. The centre uses the equipment and software of the Regional Land Survey at a fixed price of 600 000 Kronor (US$100 000) annually. The owners contribute together an additional 300 000 Kronor (US$50 000) annually to cover the costs of project management and purchase of satellite data.

In general, the first three years of each GIS centre will be a test period for the personnel to become familiar with the new technology and to carry out several pilot projects. After that period, the long-term conditions of operation will be finalized. Plans exist for the creation of four or five more centres.

ULI – Council for Research and Development in Land Information Technology

After an initiative taken by the Director General of NLS, a working group was set up to study the need for research and development (R&D) in land information. The report of the group (Aglinfou 1986) described the most important need as pertaining to collection, analysis and presentation of geographical information. The ultimate goal was to provide a basis for planning R&D collaboration between government agencies, universities and private companies in the area of LIS/GIS. Although certain parts of the field had previously been covered in relation to research in remote sensing and information technology programmes, this is the first time a unified programme for LIS/GIS R&D has been proposed in Sweden. Based on the report, the Council for R&D in Land Information Technology (ULI) was established. At present, ULI has some 80 members paying an annual fee to fund the management of the council.

Targeted areas where ULI will promote further research and development are database construction, digitizing, standardization problems, presentation systems, data communication and cost/benefit analysis. Of these, standardization and data transfer have been given first priority. It is recognized, however, that R&D is necessary within all these fields if future GIS is to fulfil the expectations of the user community.

THE LAND DATA BANK SYSTEM

The registration of real property and land is currently being automated in Sweden (Piscator 1987). An electronic data processing (EDP) system called the Land Data Bank System (LDBS) is being implemented to facilitate the registration of real property and land, and to make the information more readily available for other purposes (such as urban and regional planning and taxation). A governmental agency, the Central Board of Real Estate Data (CFD), was established to develop, implement and operate the new system. NLS and the National Court Administration, on the other hand, are responsible for the content and maintenance of LDBS.

By January 1991, almost 3 million out of the 4

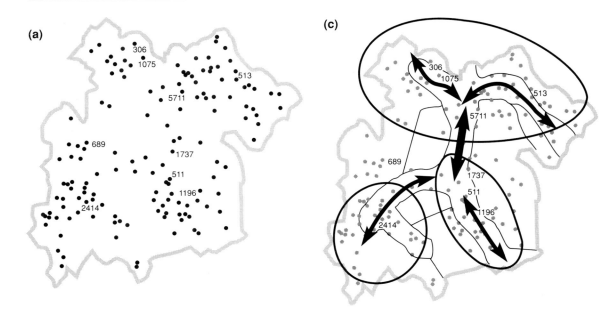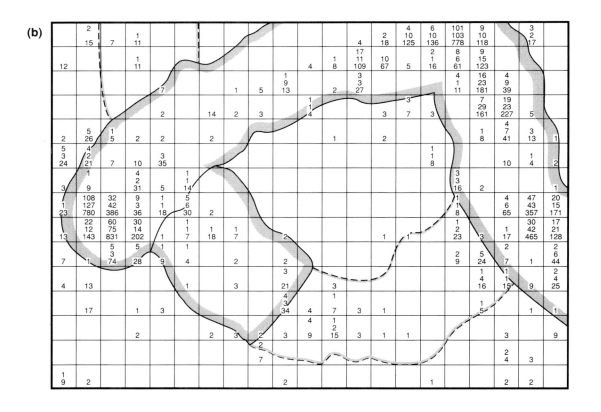

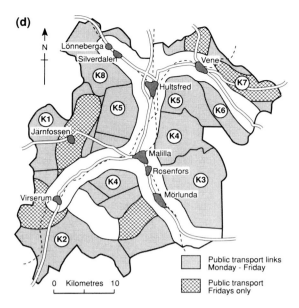

Fig. 37.3a–d The figures show in brief how population maps can be used in public transport planning. Spatially referenced population data are obtained by linking the coordinate register of the Swedish Land Data Bank with the population register of Statistics Sweden (Szegö 1987, pp. 92–93).
a The figure shows a dot map. The number represents the population of built-up areas, while each dot represents 10 persons in a rural area.
b A square grid net map with grid size one by one km showing the population distribution for different age groups.
c The population maps are used in an analysis of communication needs. This figure shows the result of the analysis.
d The figure shows the public communication plan of the municipality of Hultsfred. The corridors have regular bus services. In other areas complementary transport is provided, mostly via local taxis.

million real property units in Sweden were registered in the LDBS. The remaining real property units are currently being transferred to the system at a rate of 330 000 units per year. Thus, all units will be entered by the mid-1990s at a total cost of 240 million Kronor (US$40 million) and another 150 million Kronor (US$25 million) to improve the registers.

The LDBS runs on a central computer and its database is divided into two main registers: the Real Property Register (RPR) and the Land Register (LR). The RPR contains facts on area, centroid coordinates, land use and plans. The LR stores information on legal and economic matters, including the real property units, ownership, mortgages and assessed property values. Registration is made on-line, checks are performed and stamp duty and fees calculated automatically. In addition, the information contained in the Real Property and Land Registers is available to the public. Thus, local authorities, brokers, insurance companies, planning groups and other organizations that deal with real property information can get direct access to the LDBS by renting equipment from CFD or by connecting their own EDP-systems. As of January 1991, some 15 000 terminals and printers were connected to the system.

Modern techniques facilitate the handling and integration of large volumes of data from different sources. Consequently, the introduction of an official designation for real property units has made it possible to integrate different official registers for general use. With respect to the LDBS, integration with registers – including the Land Taxation Register and statistical registers from the National Tax Board and Statistics Sweden (census and housing data) – is achieved at the production stage. The results are either stored in the LDBS, and become an integral part of that register, or displayed as thematic maps and used for planning and reports.

Sweden has 284 local authorities responsible for the management of units as large as 19 000 km^2 in the far north and as small as 20 km^2 in densely populated areas. These authorities administer social services and public utilities and play a key role in the provision of housing. Information on real properties stored in the LDBS can be valuable in decision making and planning on the local level. For this reason, local authorities are capable of obtaining LDBS data by direct access through remote terminals, by ordering extracts or maps for specific purposes or by subscribing to the LDBS update service.

To make use of the unique fact that official statistics on population, housing and agriculture can readily be geocoded through the various interlinked registers, CFD has developed a system for computer-assisted cartography (Szegö 1987). These statistics may be presented as dot, grid or isarithmic maps accompanied by geographically structured tables and lists (Figs. 37.3a–d). When linking registers there is a risk that personal or economic confidentially might be violated. The Swedish data law and the secrecy law are the instruments to protect against that danger. Each organization which handles a register with personal or personally related data, has to register that information at the Data Inspection – a governmental agency with power to restrict and regulate the contents and use of personal registers. Population mapping, where only age and sex are used, is relatively harmless. The debate is more concerned with use of the 'deep' registers for long-term studies and especially the medical ones. So far, no severe abuse has been discovered.

CONCLUSIONS

The development of GIS in Sweden began early but partially mirrors development elsewhere. The long tradition of openness of public registers of land and people has facilitated data linkage to provide a variety of products. Even in Sweden, however, the confidentiality of high resolution (and hence often personal) data has given rise to public concern. As a result, strong legislation has been enacted to protect the citizen. Without doubt the government, especially the National Land Survey, has played a key role in the development of GIS. Today GIS is widely used for managing the enormous natural and significant socio-economic resources of Sweden.

REFERENCES

Aglinfou (1986) *Program för forskning och utveckling inom landskapsinformationsområdet.* LMV-rapport 1986:13 ISSN 0280–5731. Gävle, Sweden

Hägerstrand T (1955) *Statistiska primäruppgifter, flygkartering och 'dataprocessing'-maskiner. Ett kombineringsprojekt. Svensk Geografisk Årsbok 1955.* Lund, Sweden

Hägerstrand T (1967) The computer and the geographer. *Transactions of the Institute of British Geographers* **42**: 1–20

Nordbeck S (1962) Location of areal data for computer processing. *Lund Studies in Geography Series C* (2). Lund, Sweden

Ottoson L (1977) Information systems at the National Land Survey of Sweden. *Cartographica Monograph* 20: 104–14

Ottoson L (1987) *A programme for National Geographic Data Bases in Sweden.* LMV-rapport 1987:8, ISSN 0280–5731. Gävle, Sweden

Piscator I (1987) The Swedish Land Data Bank and its use by local authorities. *Proceedings of Land Use Information in Sweden.* Swedish Council for Building Research, Stockholm Sweden. ISBN 91–540–4665–3, pp. 56–68

Rhind D W (1991) Counting the people: the role of GIS. In Maguire D J, Goodchild M F, Rhind D W (eds.) *Geographical Information Systems: principles and applications.* Longman, London, pp. 127–37, Vol 2

Rystedt B (1987) *The New National Atlas of Sweden.* LMV-rapport 1987:17, ISSN 0280–5731. Gävle, Sweden

Szegö J (1987) Geocoded real property data in urban and regional planning. *Proceedings of Land Use Information in Sweden.* Swedish Council for Building Research, Stockholm Sweden. ISBN 91–540–4665–3, pp. 87–94.

THE DEVELOPMENT OF GIS IN JAPAN

S KUBO

The development of GIS in Japan dates from long before the term was used formally. This chapter takes a chronological view of Japanese developments, starting with analytical work carried out in the 1930s, through a period in which the central and local governments assembled large grid-based geographical data sets to the present-day situation. The interactions between different Japanese agencies are described, as are the major developments in the utility industries. Plans for large research projects such as the 'National Museum of Cartography' and the 'Global Environmental Change' project are outlined. It is concluded that, while Japan has pioneered certain aspects of GIS, it has been untypically slow to capitalize upon these early successes and its strengths in high technology.

PREHISTORY

In the 1930s, Japanese geographers were pioneers in spatial analysis, especially in the use of Digital Terrain Models (DTM), grid analysis and spatial pattern analysis. Torahiko Terada, a professor of geophysics in the University of Tokyo and also well known as a science essayist, was an inventor of a series of statistical analyses in geoscience. Terada (1930) used DTM to analyse slope erosion mechanisms on high mountains. His work influenced young geographers in the University of Tokyo. Yoshimura (1930), a graduate student of that university at the time, developed stochastic analyses in human geography and Matsui (1930) used grid-based data to analyse cultural landscapes. Murata discussed the statistical analysis of randomness using point pattern techniques in 1930 while Matsui also applied point pattern analysis to scattered villages in Tonami region (Matsui 1931) and a hilly area near to Tokyo (Matsui 1933).

In the late 1930s, discussions occurred on quantification in human geography. Vigorous debates were continued in journals and in association meetings, especially between Matsui and Ishida, a social geographer of Hitosubashi University. Later, however, this pre-war quantitative geography was much reduced by the wartime classicism and by newly evolved geopolitics. Strong post-war Marxist influence finally eradicated spatial analysis from Japanese geography. Only a few researchers used quantitative methods in the 1950s and these were no more than adaptations of the pre-war methodology. A re-evaluation of spatial analysis took place in the late 1960s influenced by the quantitative revolution in the United States. Geographers again started to use grid analysis and quantitative methods, especially for land use analyses (e.g. Birugawa *et al.* 1964)

HISTORY

A number of important developments occurred in different sectors in the 1970s. These are now considered in turn.

National and local government actions in the 1970s

Throughout the 1960s, Japan experienced a remarkable economic growth but paid a high price in severe urban and environmental problems. Japan at that time was often called 'the polluted islands' by its inhabitants. Requirements for a modern and 'scientific' planning methodology became strong in the eyes of planners in different levels of government and scientists. A more geographical view was requested in drawing up the third comprehensive national development plan.

Grid analysis was then revived. Ohtomo, a geographer in the Statistics Bureau, was responsible for the production of 1 km grid-based data from the 1965 population census which was an instant success. This attracted the interest of geographers, planners and people in government. Fortunately, however, some other geographers, planners and government officials also became interested in computer analysis and display of spatial data at this time through the influence of developments in computer mapping in North America (especially SYMAP from Harvard University and other early GIS developments).

In the early 1970s, hundreds of scientific papers and government reports using grid analysis were published and many agencies and local governments followed the Statistics Bureau in creating grid data. In the early stages, there were several discussions on the ideal grid shapes and sizes. National agencies used a rectangular grid of 45 seconds by 30 seconds (which equates to a 1131 by 924 metre dimension in Tokyo but the size obviously differs by latitude). However, some prefectures and many municipalities including Tokyo, Osaka and Nagoya preferred a 500 by 500 metre or 250 by 250 metre square grid. The majority of arguments were related to the location of grids on existing maps. A 1:25 000 scale map by the Geographical Survey Institute (GSI) covers seven and a half minutes of longitude (approximately 9.8 to 12.7 km) and five minutes of latitude (approximately 9.25 km). A one-tenth part of this in both directions makes a rectangular grid with approximately 1 square kilometre area. Large cities started to use 1:2500 planning maps, in which each sheet covers 3 km in the longtitudinal direction and 2 km in the latitudinal direction. Finally, a rectangular-shaped grid was authorized as the Japan Standard Grid System by the Administrative Management Agency and defined as a part of the Japan Industrial Standard (JIS). Figure 38.1 shows the definition of it. Despite this, the adoption of a square grid by users was not prohibited. Some local governments, including Tokyo Metropolitan Government, still use a square grid. Even in the JIS, X,Y coordinates for the origin of the grid, the grid shape and the grid size were defined but there is no standardized definition of the data format. Later, this became one of the problems in utilization of the National Grid Data.

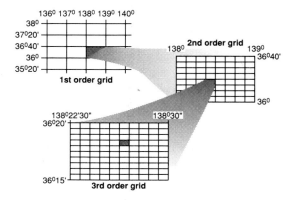

Fig. 38.1 Definition of the Japan Standard Grid System used in establishing grid databases.

In 1974, the National Land Agency – a newly established agency to coordinate national and regional development – took over the responsibility of producing a grid database. NLA received a budget for database creation from the Ministry of the Treasury and redistributed the resources to several agencies, including the GSI, the Ministry of Agriculture, Forestry and Fishery (MAFF), and the Ministry of International Trade and Industry (MITI). The resulting database consists of census information, geographical data sampled from existing 1:25 000-scale maps and large-scale (1:7500 or 1:15 000) colour aerial photography and meteorological observation data. The census information is very extensive, including data from the population and agriculture censuses (carried out every five years), the enterprise census and the retail and wholesale census (carried out every three years), and several other censuses such as those of industry and housing. The geographical data include DTMs and details of landforms, land use, soil, geology and other items. Some data are held in point, line, polygon or network form; for instance, administration boundaries are in polygon form, river systems in line form and public facility location in point form. There is, however, no standard description or standard format for point, line and polygon data: some data are simply held as strings of X, Y coordinates while others have a topological structure.

Nearly a hundred local governments, from large prefectures like Tokyo to small country towns, adopted the grid system in the 1970s. Consequent upon this boom in grid-based analysis, the Ministry of Construction wished to develop a standard system for urban planning and management. The Urban Information System (UIS) Project was started in 1975 as a seven-year scheme. Two cities, Kita-Kyushu and Nishinomiya, were selected as test sites. In Kita-Kyushu, the city and Hitachi together developed a grid analysis system named ADAMS for a Hitachi mainframe computer. The system was used for macro-level planning and training city officials. In Nishinomiya, a point-based system was developed for tax assessment. The major fault of the system was that it did not hold any vector data – even for roads.

Universities

The 'grid boom' also occurred in the universities. In the mid-1970s, some geographical information systems were developed in universities to use the (by then) available national and local grid data. Wadatsumi, a geologist in Osaka Metropolitan University, developed GEODAS. The most advanced feature of this software was the spatial thesaurus for geocoding. In 1976, a group of geographers, planners and architects received a grant from the Ministry of Education for a fundamental study of GIS. Watanabe, an architect in the Waseda University, developed a spatial language called MAL. Morozumi and also Kijima (1983) evaluated spatial errors according to the size of the grid employed and discussed the optimum grid size. They also developed a grid base GIS named KUMAP. Kubo (1980) developed a vector/raster-based GIS ALIS using a mainframe-micro workload-sharing architecture which was designed to solve cost and man–machine interface problems. Okudaira, a professor of Urban Engineering in the University of Tokyo, made theoretical contributions on grid analysis.

Non-government sectors

Some non-government organizations became interested in grid analysis. For instance, the Housing Corporation (a semi-government organization) used grid analysis for site selection for large scale housing development, but it did not use GIS. One of the successful GIS applications in private companies at the time was a simulation of the upgrading of gas calorific value in Tokyo area. Major Japanese gas companies started to change from coal gas to natural gas in the late 1970s. One of the objectives of raising the calorific value was to send more energy using the same underground pipes in order to satisfy increasing demand for gas. In 1977, Tokyo Gas, the world's second largest gas company – which serves 7 million customers in Tokyo and its suburbs – simulated the future gas demands using the standard grids to devise a plan for calorific change. In the same year, Tokyo Gas started to develop AM/FM.

GENERAL TRENDS IN THE EARLY AND MID-1980s

The first half of the 1980s was an era of recession due to high oil prices and a strong yen, which strongly affected the Japanese export-oriented industries. Consequently, the national and local governments suffered serious financial problems, along with many countries in the Western world; in this period, no new policy was introduced.

The end of the 'grid boom'

The grid boom gradually disappeared among increasing levels of disappointment. People found that, in spite of great efforts and the high costs spent in reproducing grid data from the original census information or coloured land use maps, the results from grid analysis were no more or less than those from conventional analysis. Planners complained of the quality of grid data, especially in regard to the coarse spatial resolution and the mechanical nature of the division of 'real' areas. The cost of computation was also a problem. The 1970s was the era of mainframes. Microcomputers only appeared in the late 1970s and, for several years, had 8 bit CPUs and 64 kb memories which are too small for GIS. Many of the earliest even had audio tapes instead of hard disks as backing store! Until the early 1980s at least, then, expensive and unfriendly large mainframes (using punched cards, lineprinters, XY plotters and no CRTs) were the only computers then available in most universities, governments and private companies. Software was an even larger problem. In the 1970s, there were no commercial GIS. National agencies and local governments ordered software for geoprocessing from mainframe computer makers such as Fujitsu, IBM, NEC and Hitachi, but the software provided was only an assortment of fragmentary programs and far from a 'system'.

Thus, over a 15-year period, the national government pioneered many developments and spent over 20 000 million yen (about US$150 million) creating the grid data and GIS. It is clear that the software produced was not a commercial success. Moreover, the data – while voluminous and detailed – also had inherent problems. The major problem with the national database is not its quality, its spatial resolution or its difficult-to-use format, but rather the government policy to close it off from public utilization. Permission to use the data was given only to national and local government officials (or its contractors) and full-time researchers in universities. Requests from private organizations for access to the data have been ignored for years. Furthermore, redistribution of data was strictly prohibited so that every user had to ask for permission (and had to pay) to transfer data to others. This policy resulted in several unfortunate situations so far as later GIS development in Japan is concerned. Tomatsuri (1985) pointed out that this policy prevented GIS diffusion in universities. In the case of GEODAS and ALIS, although systems themselves were public domain and distributed through university computer centres, most users could not access data supplied by governmental organizations. The policy also prevented commercial GIS development. With the small numbers of users in the government and university domains, private firms could not generate business opportunities in commercial GIS development through use of the data collected at taxpayer's expense.

National government activities

Through the 1980s, the NLA continued to create the nation-wide grid database. Although the agency spent a large budget on database creation, until the mid-1980s NLA did not have a GIS in its office. Thus valuable data gathered and held by NLA could not be used by the planning sections even in the same agency. In the mid-1980s, NLA ordered a 'custom tailored' GIS from Fujitsu. But the concepts underlying the resulting GIS (named ISLAND) were those of the 1960s, with poor graphics (an X,Y plotter was the only graphic device for ISLAND) and almost no man–machine interface. The period required to create a single map was often overnight and the quality was often not high! Almost no attention was paid by the Japanese government to contemporary GIS developments in the United States. Although many agencies were interested in geoprocessing, they persisted in using mainframes and *ad hoc* software.

Activities in municipalities

The business upturn in the mid-1980s was accompanied by a revived concentration of urban functions in the Tokyo area and skyrocketing land prices; serious social and political problems again began to appear. Once more, effective control policies and planning methodologies were sought. The first municipal government to introduce vector-based GIS was that of Abiko City (population 111 659), which is located 40 km north east of Tokyo and which had tripled its population in 20 years. In 1982, Abiko decided to introduce a GIS; after three years of surveying the market, a GIS from Nippon Electric Corporation (NEC), one of the giants in computers, was selected and started operation. The vendor saw GIS as an 'added value' feature for mainframes in local governments. NEC's product, WING, was the first Japanese-made comprehensive GIS on the market. It has topological structure, a relational database and other modern GIS characteristics. However, it became obvious that the introduction of this GIS was not a total success: WING runs on a mainframe computer and consumes quite large amounts of resources. As a consequence, the GIS runs only at night. Another problem with WING was that it did not have any interfaces with the non-geographic data held by the city government. Real-time population statistics can be generated from a residential register database and land use data can be extracted from the property tax database but unfortunately WING did not have any real-time interface program to those databases.

NEC's competitor, Fujitsu, did much the same in Matsudo City (population 427 473) which is also located in the north-eastern suburbs of Tokyo. As a result of the poor reputations of its earlier GIS (ISLAND and PLANET), Fujitsu created a new mainframe-based GIS entitled ARISTOWN. This system was also sold to Numazu City, where Fujitsu has its largest R&D division. Kawasaki, an industrial city neighbouring Tokyo, introduced a GIS from IBM which has its software division in that city.

By the mid-1980s, therefore, most municipalities had selected mainframe-based GIS; no municipality selected the then norm in the rest of the world, a super minicomputer-based system. The reasons for this choice are not only budgetary, shortage of disk space and a lack of the necessary personnel skills. They also arise from the prevalent belief that software is a 'giveaway' or a free good. Many municipalities introduced GIS not because they really needed one, but because GIS was becoming a fashion and they could get the software almost free when they bought new mainframes. As a consequence, very small budgets were established for buying software even if an organization really needed a GIS. This unfortunate tradition is still prevalent in the late-1980s. For example, Fujitsu offered to supply software at a price of one yen in a competitive tender for a basic AM/FM design for Hiroshima City. This tradition has been another obstacle for GIS business in Japan.

In 1985, the Ministry of Construction started the 'UIS II' project, four years after the first UIS project ended. The goal of this new project is to develop a comprehensive GIS for both planning and for AM/FM purposes. There are four phases in the project: a survey of requirements for a municipal GIS; the establishment of a standard database format; the development of data acquisition systems; and the implementation of pilot GIS operations in selected cities. Okayama, Koshigaya, Ohgaki and several other cities were chosen as test sites.

Private industries

The major users of spatial information systems among private users are the utilities. Gas, electric power and telephone corporations have begun to introduce facility management systems. One of the motivations for introducing such systems was a gas explosion in 1970. A bulldozer used for constructing a subway in downtown Osaka destroyed a gas pipeline 300 mm in diameter and a spark from the engine of the gas company's emergency vehicle created a tragic explosion. Seventy-nine people were killed, more than 380 were injured and 101 houses were burnt out. In court, lawyers insisted that the main reason for this accident was the chaotic arrangement of pipelines underground and a lack of proper plans of them – both being consequences of rapid urban developments. Similar accidents but causing less damage occurred in Tokyo in 1969 and in Shizuoka. After these accidents, MITI compelled the utilities to make underground plans for their network at 1 : 500 scale. In 1977, Tokyo Gas, which keeps 27 000 sheets of blueprints, started to develop a VAX-based AM/FM system in-house and completed it in 1988. In 1989, Tokyo Gas linked the AM/FM system and an IBM mainframe-based customer database to complete the corporate strategic information system. Osaka Gas followed the example of Tokyo Gas but selected IBM mainframes. Seibu Gas in Kyushu Island, Hokkaido Gas, Keiyo Gas, Shibata Gas and several other gas companies have purchased systems either from Tokyo Gas or Osaka Gas.

Japan's seven regional electric power companies also keep very large numbers of large-scale wiring diagrams. In Japan, almost all power supply cables are carried on pylons, not installed underground. Recently, the strength of public opinion concerning the landscape has created a large demand for moving these aerial cables underground. MITI and local governments support this movement of opinion because power companies, at least until late 1990, were receiving the benefits of low oil prices and high exchange rates for the yen: as a consequence, many more maps showing the layouts of such power cables will have to be made. The third motive for power companies introducing AM/FM is that these companies plan to enter the information and communication market, with telephone systems, cable television and value-added networks.

Nippon Telephone and Telegram (NTT) was converted into a private corporation in 1986 and this became one of the reasons for introducing AM/FM.

For many years, NTT did not pay charges for running telephone lines along streets but, since becoming a private company, it has had to pay such charges to local and national governments. NTT has asked them to refund these charges so that it can build digital cartographic databases which both the government and NTT can use.

Universities

A three-year GIS project funded by the Ministry of Education and named 'Intensive Utilization of Geographic Information' started in 1985. This project aimed to develop and spread GIS in geographical research. One of the outcomes from this project was TRINITY, a future-oriented multimedia GIS. Computer scientists also became interested in GIS and spatial analysis. Sakauchi and Ohsawa, computer scientists in the University of Tokyo, made a series of studies on AI-based automated raster scanning of paper maps. Iri *et al.* (1986) wrote a book on computer geometry and geoprocessing. Agui and Nakajima, who had been working mostly on computer animation, initiated studies on automated cartographic production and database design for vehicle navigation.

THE LATE 1980s

The same structure will be followed as hitherto, that is GIS developments and (in this case) prospects will be described for the different sectors.

National Agencies

The Ministry of Agriculture, Forestry and Fishery (MAFF) has been interested in distributing GIS to branch offices and to farming cooperatives. Low productivity and high labour costs have been the major reasons for a higher price of agriculture products than in other countries; this has been one of the focal points in Japan–United States trade conflicts. The Ministry wishes to improve the structure of Japanese agriculture to meet today's conditions of a global economy, an inadequate labour force and the need for environmental preservation. Several different systems were made for MAFF. PASCO, a surveying firm, made a workstation-based GIS and Kokusai, another surveying firm, developed a PC-based GIS for local farming consultants. One of the most interesting GIS applications in MAFF is the agricultural meteorological information system installed in Iwate and Hiroshima Prefectures. The systems, linked with AMEDAS (Automated MEteorological Data Acquisition System, operated by the Meteorological Agency through a large network of robot sensors), analyse and forecast local weather based on the 1 km standard grid. The systems are effective in preventing damage from late spring frost (*osojimo*) damage and a low temperature wind in summer (*yamase*). MAFF is the largest land owner in Japan since more than 70 per cent of Japan's land is mountains. Private forestry companies, such as Sumitomo Forestry, have already introduced GIS for forestry management. In MAFF, however, though the importance of forestry management systems have been repeatedly discussed, such a system has not been introduced at the time of writing.

Several more agencies are considering the introduction of GIS. The Ministry of Transportation has been discussing the use of GIS for water front development control. The National Police Agency is planning to introduce a criminal information system. The Statistics Bureau introduced GIS for mapping for the 1990 Census.

Prefectures

Because of the rapid expansion of metropolitan areas and redevelopment projects in the late 1980s, major prefectures introduced GIS for comprehensive planning. In the greater Tokyo region, planning departments of Tokyo, Kanagawa, Saitama and Chiba prefectures introduced ARC/INFO at that time. Prefectures are more responsible for social and economic planning than for physical planning and a major function for them is coordination of municipalities. In Kansai (western Japan) region, Osaka and Hyogo prefectures also installed a GIS.

Environmental problems again became an issue in the 1980s. The Environment Protection Department in Tokyo acquired a Fujitsu raster GIS called PLANET for data analysis and Kanagawa and Chiba introduced workstation-based raster GIS for environmental mapping. Okinawa, the southernmost sub-tropic islands in Japan, introduced ARC/INFO for environmental planning. Hokkaido, the undeveloped northern island, uses GIS for forest management and planning.

Emergency management is another emerging application of GIS in municipalities. The Ministry of Home Affairs encourages them to introduce emergency management systems (EMS) to fire departments within major cities. An EMS displays maps with detailed information (building types, flammable objects, immobile people) of the disaster areas. It automatically produces a dispatch plan for firefighters and fire vehicles. Maps and floor plans of buildings are sent to the vehicles of fire commanders through radio facsimile while the cars are on the way to the scene of the accident. Some EMSs also simulate fire diffusion to analyse the most effective arrangement of fire hoses. The EMSs are considered effective in cases of large-scale disasters, especially earthquakes. The fire department of Nagoya City introduced an EMS made by Fujitsu in 1987 and Osaka will introduce a system from IBM. Hitachi and Toshiba also sell EMSs to major cities.

Municipalities

According to a survey by *PIXEL* magazine in 1988 (Kawauchi 1988), three Japanese mainframe companies (Fujitsu, Hitachi and NEC) had sold more than 100 GIS systems to local governments. It is quite interesting that this figure does not match the number of cities using GIS. As mentioned earlier, a GIS tends to be treated as 'giveaway' software so that the sales figure does not show real demand or diffusion of GIS. It is certain, however, that more municipalities are interested in GIS – particularly for property taxation, school and social education and environment protection. The main problems of introducing GIS to local governments are costs of digital cartographic data and insufficient skilled GIS operators.

Private industries

PC-based GIS and desktop mapping evolved in the late 1980s following the rapid development of PCs themselves. Zenrin, a map publisher in Kyushu, has been producing large-scale (1 : 1500) *jutaku chizu* (house maps) for more than 30 years for most cities. *Jutaku chizu* is a great aid to delivery businesses, policemen, local governments and other services in a country with disordered address systems. Zenrin updates *jutaku chizu* every year and, to minimize workloads for updating, the company introduced an automated mapping system. This enabled Zenrin to distribute large-scale digital cartographic data. Z-map, a PC-based GIS kit, includes a CD-ROM containing a large-scale digital data file of every individual household in 1987, a package of basic handling software, a GIS construction kit and a sample program. The package does not, however, include database software. This kind of PC GIS is used for area marketing, especially by banks, insurance agents, car dealers and retail services as well as for election campaigns. Equivalent products are now on the market produced by several vendors, including NTT.

Stellar, a small software house in Tokyo, developed a PC- and workstation-based GIS construction kit for strategic information system applications. One of the interesting applications of this kit is a strategic information system in Lion, one of the largest soap and detergent manufacturing companies in Japan. Lion formed a nation-wide network of point-of-sale registers through its dealers. One of the aims of the network is to collect sales data and process them by GIS to relate to marketing campaigns.

Data sharing and ROADIC

Because of the increasing utilization of AM/FM in utilities, exchange and sharing of data became essential. In 1985, the Department of Roads in the Ministry of Construction set up a new organization entitled the Road Administration Information Centre (or ROADIC). This semi-government organization aims to maintain databases of roads and utilities in 11 cities each with a population of over 1 million (Fig. 38.2). The Centre converts and updates a road database under contracts with road departments of national and local governments. Utility enterprises provide piping and wiring data to the centre and, in return, they have access to both the road database and the total utility database. Moreover, they can exchange data with governments and other utility enterprises. Governments can access databases in order to manage roads as well as to charge utilities for using those roads. Construction of a pilot system was started in July 1987 at the Kanagawa branch (which maintains databases for Yokohama and Kawasaki) using NTT's INS SPACER and became operational in 1989. In other cities, operation was started in fiscal year 1990. In the Tokyo branch, TUMSY by Tokyo Gas is used as the basic software and, in Osaka, IIS-MAP is used. There is a plan to use this database for city planning, property assessment and other purposes in the future but, at the present moment, this plan appears difficult to implement because of institutional problems between and within ministries.

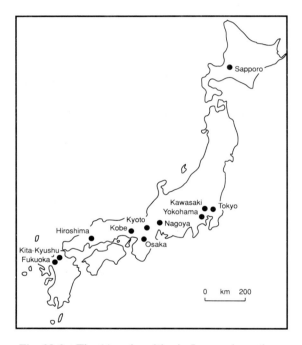

Fig. 38.2 The 11 major cities in Japan where the Road Administration Information Centre (ROADIC) has set up a database of roads and utilities.

Automobile navigation systems

The Toyota Crown, a flagship in the small car line of Toyota, was transmuted through a full model change into the Corona in 1987; the top model in the new range was equipped with a navigator (see White 1991 in this volume). Although there are still many arguments about whether an automobile navigation system can be helpful, Japanese industry and government agencies are moving rapidly to make its use routine. There are two major competitive groups: AMTECS, led by the National Police Agency, and a group organized by the civil engineering sections in the Ministry of Construction. The existence of two groups is not surprising since the National Police Agency and the Ministry of Construction have been in dispute on traffic control and guidance on highways since the first expressway was built in the early 1960s.

Despite this, the basic concepts in the two groups are similar. The location of an automobile is identified by X,Y coordinate information from global positioning satellites (GPS) and on signposts and from sensors within the automobile. Signposts send real-time information on traffic condition and parking facilities. A digitized map is stored in a CD-ROM together with auxiliary information (e.g. location of restaurants with the contents of their menus). A CRT displays the trace of the vehicle on a map and a voice synthesizer gives turning information and warnings. GPS will be used only as an auxiliary, because the radio wave from GPS may not be received in urban areas and dual transmission between ground and running vehicles is required. It is not yet certain whether automobile navigation systems will be accepted by Japanese or other drivers, but it is obvious that automobile companies like them because they can legitimate higher price tags on new cars.

The Digital Road Map Association, a non-profit organization dedicated to making available digital cartographic data for vehicle navigation, has been established. It has completed digitizing of major roads from 1 : 25 000 scale maps. This database will be sold on CD-ROMs and magnetic tapes. Although this database is the first nation-wide digital cartographic data, the database structure is not ideal for GIS uses.

Legal issues

Problems of data security and copyright have become critical issues in the public opinion (see Epstein 1991 in this volume). Over 400 local communities have security Acts and more than 700 have rules relevant to the operation of GIS. In some local communities, it is stipulated in law that data collected for a specific purpose must not be used for other purposes – without exception. Interpreting the statement strictly, a planning map cannot be used for tax assessment and a register of residents cannot be used for making population statistics. Such constraints would be a major obstacle to future use of integrated GIS in local governments. The focal point of the copyright problem is whether the Geographical Survey Institute (GSI) can claim copyright on digital maps or not. GSI only publishes small- and mid-scale maps; large-scale maps are mostly published by local governments. With paper maps, when publishers reproduce or use GSI maps as a base map, they must ask GSI for permission. However, in digitizing a GSI map, there is still a question as to whether permission is needed? So far as large-scale maps are concerned, copyright problems are even more complex. GSI claims partial copyright for use of its public survey data and, in many cases, it is not clear whether copyright belongs to local governments or to the survey companies involved.

GIS research centres

On 21 April 1988, the Science Council of Japan issued a recommendation to the then Prime Minister of Japan, Mr Noboru Takeshita, for the establishment of the National Museum of Cartography. The recommendation insists that, in the era of globalization, it is an urgent international and national requirement to have a centre to collect, store, process, retrieve and provide domestic and international geographical information including maps, charts, atlases, aerial photographs, ground landscape photographs, satellite images and various statistics. Although the recommendation carries the name of a 'museum', it implies something totally different from show cases of old maps. It is a research and education centre for geographical information. The museum is intended to have five major functions: it will be a map library; a research centre on geographical information and spatial analysis; a map exhibition and centre for social education; a database service; and, finally, a centre for training and graduate-level education. The recommendation is being processed by the National Council of Science and Technology. By 1990, nine ministries and national agencies had expressed their interest in the establishment of the museum. Several prefectures and cities have already offered to host the facility. The main hurdle to its implementation is a strict policy for reducing the numbers of government employees enforced by the Japanese Government.

In general, it is clear that research into future GIS and data collection is required to cope with post-modern society and the dramatic technological changes now occurring. A plan to establish a semi-governmental GIS research institute has been discussed by the national government, several leading companies in Japan and universities. As a result, a new research centre will start in 1992.

The GIS for Environmental Change Research project

A new GIS project funded by the Ministry of Education started in 1990. The project, entitled 'GIS for Environmental Change Research', aims to understand 100 years of environmental change in Japan since modernization in the late nineteenth century. An environmental database will be constructed through joint efforts by geographers and researchers from other disciplines. ARC/INFO is being used as a standard platform. This project relates to the International Geosphere–Biosphere Programme (IGBP) of the International Council of Scientific Unions and to the Human Dimensions of Global Change Programme (HDGCP). The total budget for three years is estimated to be 500 million yen (US$4 million). In 1990, the GIS software was installed at nine universities from Hokkaido to Kyushu.

CONCLUSIONS

It will be obvious from all of the above that Japan has long been involved in many facets of GIS and pioneered many aspects, notably in assembling large databases from many different sources. Unhappily, some of the developments were not notably successful and, for a time, decision makers in the country ignored the major advances being made in the United States and elsewhere. This phase is now over and a number of important industrial, research and governmental initiatives in GIS and related areas are now under way.

REFERENCES AND FURTHER READING

The references given below are those cited in the text and others to provide a wide range of information on the totality of developments in Japan.

Association for Promotion of Electronic Industries (1989) *Cartographic database standard*, Tokyo

Birugawa S, Yamamoto S, Okuno T, Kinto Y, Asano Y (1964) Distribution patterns of agricultural land use intensity and crop types. *Tokyo Geography Papers* **8**: 153–86

Epstein E F (1991) Legal aspects of GIS. In: Maguire D J, Goodchild M F, Rhind D W (eds.) *Geographical Information Systems: principles and applications*. Longman, London, pp. 489–502, Vol 1

Geographical Survey Institute (ed.) (1989) *Digital Mapping*. Kashima Shuppankai, Tokyo

Iri M, Okabe A, Koshizuka T, Yomono H (1986) *Computer Geometry and Geoprocessing*, Special publication of *BIT* magazine. Kyoritu Shuppan, Tokyo

Kamata et al. (1989) *Introduction to Cartographic Analysis*. Nikkan Kogyo Shinbun, Tokyo

Kawauchi (ed.) (1988) Recent computer mapping systems. *PIXEL*, Gazou Joho Shori Centre, Tokyo

Kijima Y (1983) *Urban Image*. Seichosha, Kumamoto

Kubo S (1980) Recent trends in geographic data processing. *Jinbun Chiri* **32** (4): 40–62

Kubo S (1987) The development of geographical information systems in Japan. *International Journal of Geographical Information Systems* **1**: 243–52

Kubo S (ed.) (1987–89) *Proceedings AUTOCARTO JAPAN 3–5*. Autocarto Japan Organizing Committee, Tokyo

Kubo S (1990) *GIS and the Population Census*. Bureau of Census, Tokyo

Land Agency (ed.) (1986) *Geographic Information System*. The Printing Bureau, The Ministry of Finance, Tokyo

Matsui I (1930) Relations between grade and cultural landscape around Kamimizo. *Geographical Review of Japan* **6**: 1599–627

Matsui I (1931) Statistical observation of scattered village in Tonami Plain. *Geographical Review of Japan* **7**: 459–75

Matsui I (1933) Some problems in spatial distribution, especially in Tama Hill. *Geographical Review of Japan* **8**: 359–1627

Ministry of Construction (1987) *The Urban Information Database*. Keibun Shuppan, Tokyo

Murai S (ed.) (1986) *Proceedings of AUTOCARTO JAPAN 2*. Autocarto Japan Organizing Committee, Tokyo

Murata T (1930) A method for analysing distribution of scattered village. *Geographical Review of Japan* **6**: 1744–53

Murayama Y (1990) *Regional Analysis*. Kokon Shoin, Tokyo

NICOGRAPH (ed.) (1988) *Computer Mapping*. Nihon Keizai Shinbunsha, Tokyo

Nishikawa O, Kubo S (1986) Intensive Utilisation of Geographic Information, In: Hirayama H (ed.) *Perspectives and Tasks Towards an Information Society*. The Science Council of Japan, Tokyo, pp. 131–40

Terada T (1930) Statistical methods on distribution of slopes using maps. *Geographical Review of Japan* **6**: 653–61

Tomatsuri Y (1985) Geographic research and data base. *Jinbun Chiri* **37** (3): 270–86

White M (1991) Car navigation systems. In: Maguire D J, Goodchild M F, Rhind D W (eds.) *Geographical Information Systems: principles and applications*. Longman, London, pp. 115–25, Vol 2

Yoshimura S (1930) A method for area measurement and its example. *Geographical Review of Japan* **6**: 1569–84; and 1708–43

LAND AND GEOGRAPHICAL INFORMATION SYSTEMS IN AUSTRALIA

J F O'CALLAGHAN AND B J GARNER

The most striking feature about the development of GIS in Australia is the emphasis given to Land Information Systems. This chapter describes the development of these systems in the Australian states, the major role taken by the federal government as a coordinating agency and the national strategy for land information management. The GIS developments in environmental and natural resource applications have been relatively modest although these are predicted to increase in importance. Substantial further developments are expected in the socio-economic aspects of GIS, driven largely by the private sector. A thriving research and education programme is now in existence. The chapter ends with a summary of the national prospects and concludes that user needs, existing organizational infrastructures, training programmes and local skills could well ensure that Australia becomes a major player in GIS.

INTRODUCTION

Australia has been particularly responsive to the opportunities and challenges presented by the developments in spatial information technology during the past decade. In large part this is undoubtedly a product of its geography: a large land mass sparsely settled, its population overwhelmingly concentrated in the state capital cities, a fragile physical environment and a well-developed economic infrastructure. Added to this, Australia has increasingly been characterized by a social and political climate open to the adoption and innovation of new technology. With respect to information technology, Australia is assuming an important role internationally in such areas as telecommunications services, financial information systems and remote sensing. This international profile is now being extended to the development and application of land and geographical information systems, in both the public and private sectors.

To date, the most active players in GIS have been in the public sector, particularly government agencies at the state level. Under the federal structure of government in Australia, the six state and two territory governments have jurisdiction over all the major areas in which land and geographical information systems (LIS/GIS) are typically applied: biophysical resources, social services, planning and economic development, transportation, provision of utilities and, especially, land titles and registration. The role of the federal government in Canberra is by and large one of coordination, regulation and setting national policies and priorities. The division of responsibilities that results means that it is difficult to identify a truly national picture of recent developments. There are few nation-wide programmes at the present time in any case and most initiatives at the state level are at an early stage of implementation.

Against this background, the aim of this chapter is to provide a generalized overview of the main areas of development and application of LIS/GIS in Australia. Most of the details of this overview may be found in the references, especially the annual *Urban and Regional Planning Information Systems (URPIS)* volumes (AURISA 1976ff.). Relevant research papers can also be found in the *International Journal of Geographical Information Systems* and in the *Proceedings of the International Spatial Data Handling Symposia*. The major topics covered here are land information systems, environment and natural resource applications, digital topographic mapping, social and economic applications, and research and education. Likely trends in future developments and application areas are discussed in the conclusion.

LAND INFORMATION SYSTEMS

From a national perspective, the most visible and well-coordinated area of LIS/GIS application has undoubtedly been that of land information management which has been developed by the state and territory governments during the past decade. Land information, particularly that embodied in the cadastre, has been increasingly recognized by state governments as a valuable resource, the administration and management of which is fundamental to effective decision making (see Dale 1991 in this volume for a wider discussion of this topic).

Australia has a sophisticated and tightly controlled system of recording land ownership, based in large part on the Torrens system of land registration. The title to land is supported by government guarantees, hence property (land parcel) records are complete and comprehensive in all states and territories. Well-established procedures exist for clarifying uncertainties in land ownership. With this detailed and historically complete database, it is not surprising that state governments have been primarily engaged in building computerized LIS with a cadastral emphasis. In all cases, these have grown out of manual parcel-based land administration systems established primarily for title registration and land valuation.

Building on concepts and initiatives dating from the late 1970s, each of the states and territories has operational cadastre-based LIS although there are still wide variations in coverage, structure and implementation, reflecting geographical differences in political and institutional environments. The most advanced systems are found in Western Australia, South Australia and the Northern Territory. Historical trends and current developments in state-wide LIS are discussed in AURISA (1985), Williamson (1986), Williamson and Blackburn (1987), the annual Proceedings of the URPIS Conferences (AURISA 1976ff.), and Annual Reports of the Australian Land Information Council (ALIC 1988ff.). In all cases, the primary responsibility for LIS development and implementation rests with the Lands Departments, or their equivalent, in each state and territory although other departments and agencies (e.g. Valuer Generals' Departments) are usually involved as well. All states have established the infrastructure and are formulating policies for the effective administration and management of their LIS, the common components of which are summarized in Fig. 39.1.

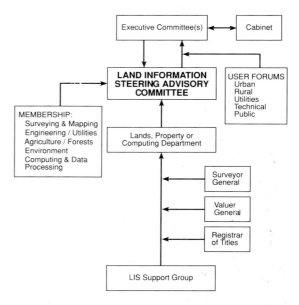

Fig. 39.1 Components of a Land Information System in Australian States (Source: Williamson and Blackburn 1987).

The primary objective of all the systems has been the development of computerized LIS embracing textual and graphic information for legal and fiscal administration (e.g. land taxation) and this is the major area of current application. The systems have typically been based on two data sets describing attribute and spatial data, related by two-way linkages via textual details, pointers (like parcel identifiers) and some form of spatial reference, as shown schematically in Fig. 39.2. In some jurisdictions, these systems are being augmented by the activities of the large utility organizations, for example the Melbourne and Metropolitan Board of Works in Victoria has a LIS which exchanges and combines data with various state and local government agencies to create a single large integrated data set (Matheson 1986).

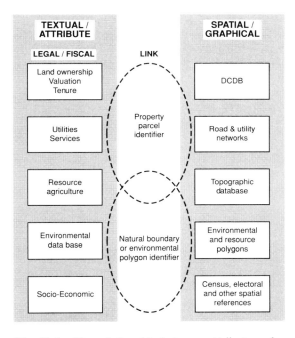

Fig. 39.2 The relationship between attribute and spatial data in Land Information Systems (Source: Williamson and Blackburn 1987).

The emphasis on data sharing between government agencies as a way of accessing large amounts of data is now a widely accepted concept in LIS developments at the state level in Australia, given the administrative and technical nightmare of establishing large-scale centralized single land databases. The key physical component in the conceptual and technological strategies for developing shared systems is the LIS Hub which is designed to manage the transfer of data, maintain data accuracy and provide a management mechanism to ensure that only authorized and correct data are made available to the system's different users (see Black, Sambura and Salijevic 1986; Eather 1986).

A leading example of the application of the Hub concept at the state level is the New South Wales LIS which has been progressively put in place since 1985 by the State Land Information Council – the government body responsible for the development and control of the system. The Hub serves two principal functions – system interlinking and data administration. Currently data from the Land Titles Office, Valuer General's Department, Lands Department, Water Board and the Land Tax Office are linked through the Hub (see Fig. 39.3). For a particular data item, the most appropriate source agency has been identified and designated as the 'Data Trustee'. Only the Trustee can change data items in the system, thus ensuring accuracy and the maintenance of data management standards in the system (Hart 1988).

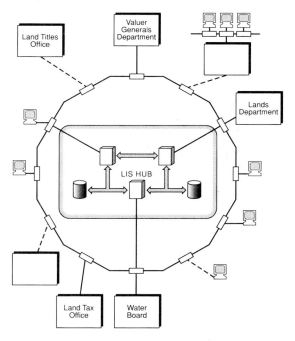

Fig. 39.3 The concept of the LIS Hub.

The New South Wales Hub is compartmentalized operationally into three main sub-projects. Project RAPID deals with the textual and attribute data. The Spatial Reference System handles map-based data and provides the link to the attribute information to give the system its spatially related enquiry capability. The communication sub-project involves the hardware and software necessary to link the participating agencies with the Hub itself. By the early 1990s, it is anticipated that the state's 3 million land titles will have been converted to the Automated Land Titles system. In addition, all of the land parcel maps in the Sydney metropolitan area and Wollongong will be computerized by the Water Board and the Lands Department will have completed the computerization of the land parcel maps of the non-metropolitan area of the state. At the same time, data from other government agencies (such as Soil Conservation and Mineral Resources) will be added progressively to the system in order to form the basis of an integrated state-wide land information management system.

Similar initiatives in land information management have also been taken by the federal Government although its effort has been more that of coordination in the collection, storage, and dissemination of land information between government departments, rather than developing systems *per se*. The responsible body is the Commonwealth Land Information Support Group (CLISG), a unit of the Australian Surveying and Land Information Group (AUSLIG), Department of Administrative Services. AUSLIG, formed in August 1987 following a rearrangement of federal government departments, comprises the former Australian Survey Office and Division of National Mapping, and now includes the Australian Centre for Remote Sensing. It is the federal government's primary source of advice and information on geodesy, mapping (apart from defence needs), surveying and remote sensing in Australia. It also provides technical support and undertakes specialist application projects for federal departments, although to date its involvement in the applications of GIS have been limited to small-scale exploratory pilot projects (e.g. see Phillips and Blackburn 1989).

The roles of CLISG are to increase coordination of the federal government's land information; to support national coordination of land information (in this capacity it acts as secretariat for the Australian Land Information Council); to provide advice on land information matters including monitoring developments in land information both in Australia and overseas; and to undertake special projects on an *ad hoc* basis. One of these special projects is AUSNOMA, a pilot project started in 1988 to develop a computerized query-based place name gazetteer for the 2500 names on the 1:5 million scale General Reference Map of Australia for the Committee for Geographical Names in Australia.

One of the major initiatives taken by the federal government through CLISG has been the creation of a directory (LANDSEARCH) containing details about federal data sets. The directory approach seems to facilitate more effective use of existing data sets held by the various government departments; to foster higher levels of information exchange between them; and to provide a basis for improved cooperation in policy formulation and decision-making. *LANDSEARCH 1* (AUSLIG 1985) lists over 830 items of land-related data held by the federal government. A second volume with improved geographical referencing, published in 1989, is available in an on-line version on a national computer network.

THE NATIONAL STRATEGY FOR LAND INFORMATION MANAGEMENT

A recurrent problem under a federal system of government is the coordination of activities concerning national and regional land-related issues. To overcome these problems, governments have taken a number of formal initiatives since the mid-1980s to improve national and regional coordination of land information by promoting and implementing cooperative arrangements and policies. The Australian Land Information Council (ALIC), established in March 1986 as the coordinating body for land information in Australia, provides the formal mechanism to achieve national coordination in LIS development and land information management.

The key roles of ALIC are to:

- address land information issues and policies at the national level;
- support the development and implementation of national guidelines and standards for land information management;
- provide a national forum for the sharing of

experiences and exchange of information on land information management policies at the national level;
- produce annual reports on LIS developments in Australia.

Members of ALIC are the Chairs of the Land Information Steering Committees from each state and territory, the Commonwealth Surveyor General and the Chief of the Australian Defence Force. New Zealand has observer status.

As part of the effort to bring about higher levels of coordination between jurisdictions and agencies in land information management, ALIC endorsed in December 1987 a set of policies and procedures which now form the National Strategy for Land Information Management (ALIC 1987). The strategy is viewed as a major accomplishment in promoting inter-governmental cooperation in Australia where land-related issues have traditionally been a sensitive matter between federal and state governments. The aims of the National Strategy are:

- to encourage cost-efficient access to land information throughout Australia to provide a solid basis for effective decision making on the social and economic use of land at all levels of government and by the private sector;
- to develop and provide mechanisms for efficient data transfer.

In order to achieve these aims by the mid-1990s, the strategy identifies a number of key issues and a set of policies and procedures has been developed to address them. In summary, these are:

1. Policy issues relating to the administrative and political environment:
   (a) breaking down barriers to inter-government/inter-agency cooperation;
   (b) land information and people – access to information, confidentiality and security;
   (c) responsibilities for data integrity;
   (d) improving mechanisms for data access, pricing and availability;
   (e) clarifying relationships and roles between the public and private sectors in matters relating to land information;
   (f) identification of appropriate strategies for creating, marketing and promoting land information products;
   (g) improving education and training for the land information industry.
2. Procedural issues relating to the technical environment:
   (a) preparation of nationally compatible land-related data standards;
   (b) improving methods and techniques for data capture, organization and exchange;
   (c) maximization of the development and use of technologies for managing land information.

The responsibility for implementing and maintaining the National Strategy rests with ALIC and its participating jurisdictions. In this capacity, and especially as this relates to implementation and procedural issues, ALIC works closely with Standards Australia in the development of land information exchange, data standards and data handling procedures. It has referred data standards on land use classification and street address standards for endorsement and implementation (planned late-1990), and is an active participant in the Australian Standards Committee IT/4 – Geographical Information Systems, established in 1987. The sub-committee on geodata exchange formats is currently examining the proposed US standard for digital cartographic data transfer based on ISO 8211 for use in Australia (see Guptill 1991 in this volume).

In future, it is anticipated that the National Strategy will encompass a broader range of databases, applications and governmental agencies, and that the distinction between LIS and GIS and between national, regional and local scales will be less apparent. The National Strategy is thus envisaged to be an evolving one.

ENVIRONMENTAL AND NATURAL RESOURCE APPLICATIONS

Given the nature of Australia's physical geography, its natural resource wealth and major environmental problems such as land degradation, it is perhaps surprising that there have been relatively few major applications of GIS to date in the area of natural resources and the environment – at least as compared with other countries. The indications are, however, that applications in these areas will increase significantly in the next five years or so in both the public and private sectors.

The predominant concern of the state government coordinating bodies is to develop jurisdiction-wide parcel-based LIS. Because of this, systems based on environmental and natural resources data have generally been the responsibility of individual government departments and agencies. All states are now actively engaged in building GIS for a range of environmental applications, especially in forest management, water resources, agriculture, soil conservation (especially for farm plans and catchment management), mineral resources, nature conservation and the management of national parks. The extent of developments and applications in these areas nationally can be gauged from the increasing number of papers that have been presented at the annual URPIS conferences during the past five years. Key contributions are summarized in abbreviated form in Table 39.1.

The systems in place so far vary in sophistication and coverage. Most are at an early stage of implementation, reflecting the more recent concern with GIS applications in these areas; developments have generally been uncoordinated and not formally integrated with the state-wide LIS effort. As the concept of state-wide GIS is enlarged to include environmental, natural resource and socio-economic databases however, greater attention will need to be given to integrating the separate developments within the overall framework of the National Strategy for Land Information Management.

Recognizing this and the need to widen the scope of national coordination of land information, ALIC convened the first National Workshop on Natural Resources Data Management in June 1989. The objectives of the Workshop were to:

- document key inter-agency and inter-jurisdiction projects involving natural resources data, particularly in the assessment of land degradation, land capability and a range of environmental issues including the greenhouse effect;
- identify existing data management and coordination processes directed at natural resources data;
- identify key issues involved in the management and use of natural resources data.

Table 39.1 URPIS papers relating to environmental and natural resource applications of GIS in Australia, 1985–89.

Abbreviated Title of Paper and Location (State)	Reference
The application of GIS to environmental planning (SA)	Stubbs T J *URPIS* **13**, 1985
Information systems for national parks management: the New South Wales approach (NSW)	Kessel S R *et al.* *URPIS* **13**, 1985
The Crown Lands study (QLD)	Wesche J *URPIS* **14**, 1986
The Flinders Range management review (SA)	Simpson P *URPIS* **15**, 1987
Using a state-wide natural resources GIS to support management (VIC)	Alexander D *URPIS* **15**, 1987
Implementing an agricultural LIS (TAS)	Fenn G *URPIS* **15**, 1987
The NSW mineral resources LIS (NSW)	Lucas R R *URPIS* **15**, 1987
Development of the rainforest GIS (QLD)	Stanton G *et al.* *URPIS* **16**, 1988
The impact of GIS on forest management (TAS)	Fenn G *URPIS* **17**, 1989
GIS – the ALCOA experience (WA)	Barber G G *URPIS* **17**, 1989
The use of GIS in forest inventories (TAS)	Bowen P J *et al.* *URPIS* **17**, 1989

Source: AURISA 1976ff.

SA = South Australia, NSW = New South Wales, QLD = Queensland, VIC = Victoria, TAS = Tasmania, WA = Western Australia. *URPIS = Proceedings of the Urban and Regional Planning Information Systems Annual Conferences*, Published by AURISA, Sydney.

Recent initiatives taken by the federal government have highlighted the need for environmental and natural resource applications of GIS, as well as providing mechanisms for better national coordination of data. The latter is seen as serving both domestic needs and, importantly, those for Australia's participation in international programmes such as the International Geosphere Biosphere Programme and the Human Dimensions of Global Environmental Change Programme (Clark, Kinneman and Hastings 1991 in this volume). In one of these initiatives, the Bureau of Mineral Resources commenced in 1988 a major upgrading of its digital spatial databases to aid its research and resource assessment projects. These databases include mineral deposits, coal deposits, geophysical and petroleum exploration and development data – areas in which there has been a major effort already by the private sector (e.g. in such companies as BHP Minerals, CRA and Western Mining). The Bureau has also commenced a pilot project to explore the feasibility of establishing a national integrated geoscience spatial database for which cooperation with the private sector will be important.

The federal government announced in May 1988 the formation of the National Resources Information Centre (NRIC) within the Department of Primary Industries and Energy. The principal aim of the Centre is to provide the means to enable rapid identification, access to, and integration of the available data to support government decision making concerning natural resources management (especially land use conflicts of national significance) and public policy formulation for the national estate. The Centre is planned to be fully operational in 1991 and one of its major objectives is to develop a computerized register of sources of national information within a GIS framework (Johnson, Mott and Robey 1989). In achieving this, the Centre will draw upon existing facilities, especially those of the Bureau of Rural Resources and the Bureau of Mineral Resources – both of which are heavily involved in the collection and use of natural resources and environmental data.

A subsequent initiative in 1989 was the establishment of an Environmental Resources Information Network (ERIN) within the federal government portfolio embracing arts, sport, the environment, tourism and territories. ERIN's mission is to provide geographically related environmental information for planning and decision making within the portfolio which encompasses the Divisions of Natural Heritage and Environment Protection, Conservation, and Tourism and several statutory authorities including the Australian Heritage Commission, the Australian National Parks and Wildlife Service and the Great Barrier Reef Marine Park Authority. A recent consultant's report on the user requirements for ERIN has provided directions for the development of GIS facilities within the ERIN unit and the portfolio in general.

One of the roles for these organizations is in the development of national inventories. For example, NRIC is assisting with the National Forest Inventory which is a joint enterprise between the federal and state governments. When complete, the inventory will comprise a central geographically-referenced database of the nation's forest resources. In a similar project, the Australian Heritage Commission is supporting the preparation of a National Wilderness Inventory, a digital database designed to assist in the identification and management of remote natural areas (Lesslie, Mackey and Preece 1988).

The creation of truly integrated national environmental and natural resources databases is currently a contentious issue in Australia and will affect future GIS applications in national programmes. The 'state of the art' technology now available, particularly in remote sensing, provides the pre-conditions for the creation of a national resources information system (Plate 39.1), and arguments have been provided in support of such developments (e.g. see Cocks and Walker 1987). Given the size of Australia, however, it is questionable whether data could ever be captured in sufficient detail to be really useful in the applications context or whether the benefits of such an undertaking could warrant the enormous cost. Better coordination of databases being developed by the state governments might be more appropriate, particularly for applications which involve environmental issues transgressing jurisdiction boundaries. Such coordination is being pursued within the framework of the National Strategy and through the establishment of special bodies.

A pioneering example of the latter approach was the formation in 1988 of the Murray–Darling Basin Commission – a jointly sponsored initiative by the federal government and the state governments of South Australia, Victoria, and New South Wales. The Murray–Darling Basin covers one-seventh of the area of Australia and encompasses three state jurisdictions. The region has a rich natural resource base, accounting for about one-third of the national output from rural industries. It is also an area of critical problems, notably deteriorating water quality (especially from salinity), soil erosion and widespread land degradation – all in an area of national ecological significance. The costs of these problems for agriculture alone are estimated to be over A$260 million (US$200 million) a year. The Commission's primary roles are to support strategic planning and improved management of the region's natural resource base and to develop mechanisms for coordinating the activities of the 30 separate agencies with responsibilities in the region, within the framework of the Natural Resources Management Strategy. A key component of this Strategy is the creation of a GIS for the Basin. Feasibility studies are being undertaken at the time of writing to identify the key problems in developing such a system, most of which are similar in nature to those encountered in developing state-wide LIS. They are, however, accentuated by the need for inter-jurisdiction collaboration to define common referencing systems, develop standardized data sets, clarify custodianship and provide effective mechanisms for data linkage and exchange (Smith and Eden 1989).

DIGITAL TOPOGRAPHIC MAPPING

The federal government is responsible for small-scale topographic mapping (at scales of 1 : 100 000 and smaller) across the country as a whole; it is also responsible for mapping at all scales in the Northern Territory and in selected, more isolated parts of the continent especially where information is essential for defence needs. This responsibility is shared between AUSLIG, the Royal Australian Army Survey Corps and the Navy Hydrographic Service. The last of these is responsible for producing all hydrographic and bathometric charts for the Australian region, including Papua New Guinea and large parts of the Indian, Pacific and Southern Oceans.

Defence needs thus contribute substantially to the national archive of base topographic and hydrographic data. Significant production systems in all areas are now based on digital technology and an increasing proportion of new products is being produced in digital form. The main systems for capturing and handling digital topographic and related spatial data are the Hydrographer's Autochart and related systems, the Air Force's digital systems at the Aeronautical Information Services and Central Photographic Establishment, and the Army's Automap system. In this last system, the database includes vegetation, relief, drainage and some cultural information at the 1 : 25 000 scale. Its prime use is currently the production of 1 : 50 000 scale topographic maps of areas of defence significance. The future needs for a defence-wide GIS will rely heavily on inputs from the various military mapping activities in conjunction with civil authorities (Laing and Puniard 1989). The Australian Defence Forces are currently investigating GIS applications (Babbage 1989) for defence purposes and in 1989 started a 12-month pilot study based at Darwin which includes a wide area of defence significance in the Northern Territory, in order to assess how effectively GIS technology may meet future needs and to identify the quality of available data and the extent to which they are accessible. In contrast, the digital topographic mapping programmes within the States (at scales below 1 : 100 000) are generally not well advanced, but substantial progress has been made in South Australia.

SOCIAL AND ECONOMIC APPLICATIONS

Compared with the progress made in environmental and natural resource applications in Australia during the recent past, there has been relatively little systems development or major applications in planning, transportation, or the socio-economic area broadly defined. The exception is in utilities and facilities management, an area which has rapidly developed along with Land Information Systems since the early 1980s. All state and territory government agencies concerned with electricity, water and sewerage services have at least basic utilities management systems in place, with the emphasis now being on integrating these data with the respective LIS. The status and development of systems for electricity supply in Australia has been reviewed by Hurle (1989).

An indication of the range of social and economic applications of GIS in Australia during the past five years is given by the presentations at the annual URPIS conferences, representative examples from which are summarized in abbreviated form in Table 39.2.

Table 39.2 URPIS papers relating to social and economic applications of GIS in Australia, 1985–89.

Abbreviated Title of Paper and Location (State)	Reference
The Urban Two project (WA)	Devereux D *URPIS* **13**, 1985
Land use modelling based on GIS (AUST)	Walker P A *et al.* *URPIS* **14**, 1986
Road Traffic Authority of Victoria location-based systems (VIC)	Cascales G *URPIS* **14**, 1986
The Country Centres project: assessing regional comparative advantage (AUST)	Parvey C A *et al.* *URPIS* **15**, 1987
Application of LIS for land use planning in Western Australia (WA)	Rogers M B *URPIS* **16**, 1988
COMFIS – a community facilities information system for planning (ACT)	Williamson S M *URPIS* **16**, 1988
Using GIS to target markets for financial institutions (WA)	Roberts N *URPIS* **16**, 1988
The impact of LIS in land use planning (WA)	Rogers M B *URPIS* **17**, 1989

Source: AURISA 1976

SA = South Australia, NSW = New South Wales, QLD = Queensland, VIC = Victoria, TAS = Tasmania, WA = Western Australia. *URPIS = Proceedings of the Urban and Regional Planning Information Systems Annual Conferences*, Published by AURISA, Sydney.

The incorporation of socio-economic applications in a GIS framework, together with environmental concerns, is possibly best represented in Australia by the Regional Geographical Information Systems Project (REGIS) established in 1985 by the Queensland government. This project was initially designed to investigate the feasibility of wide-scale GIS applications in the state and comprises a number of separate pilot projects being implemented in the northern part of the state in the hinterland of Cairns. Specific tasks being addressed include the monitoring of land use change and suburban development in an area of declining irrigation agriculture; evaluation of the location of tourist facilities and the impact of tourism on local economies; and the investigation of the applicability of integrated spatial databases for local government planning and administration. A major emphasis in all the projects is to evaluate the problems in accessing data located in Brisbane from Cairns using a satellite-based communications network (Q-Net) for voice, picture, and data transmission which was established in 1987. This highly innovative approach to long-distance data exchange is unique in Australia at the present time and REGIS was awarded the Exemplary Systems in Government Award in 1987 by URISA, the US-based Urban and Regional Information Systems Association (Perrett, Lyons and Moss 1989).

A key factor inhibiting widespread social and economic applications has undoubtedly been the lag in availability of census products in digital form, coupled with the fact that in Australia there is no equivalent to the DIME and TIGER files used by the US Bureau of Census (Rhind 1991 in this volume). The Australian Bureau of Statistics (ABS), the agency responsible for national censuses, has however been engaged in a major programme of upgrading the collection, processing and publication of census data in digital formats. The major censuses have been progressively converted to the Australian Standard Geographical Classification (Brauer 1985). Since 1981, the five-yearly Census of Housing and Population has been available in digital form for mainframes and selected data are now available on floppy diskettes. The release in 1988 of CDATA 86, a package designed for desktop computers, is a significant development. This package comprises a range of items from the 1986 Census plus selected 1981 data on CD-ROM, together with a commercial PC-based colour mapping system which permits a wide range of statistical profiles and maps to be produced for a number of different spatial units including post-code areas. This ongoing initiative, to be expanded for the 1991 Census, together with the growth of digital mapping programmes being introduced by state governments and private sector companies, will undoubtedly lead to a substantial effort in the application of GIS for social and economic studies in the immediate future.

Evidence of this trend is already apparent in the private sector where major applications are being developed, particularly in the banking and finance industry, marketing, the retail sector, and by urban planning consultants. In contrast, public authorities have generally lagged behind, particularly in the application of GIS in the health and welfare sector, social service provision, and urban and regional planning at the state level. Several local governments, however, are now actively engaged in social and economic applications within the major urban areas. The Council of the City of Sydney, for example, has been a pioneer in the applications of computerized systems in planning and land use for over a decade (Nash 1986, 1988).

RESEARCH AND EDUCATION

Australia has been actively engaged in research in GIS, including both hardware and software development, during the past decade and is currently intensifying its research effort although this is not yet particularly well coordinated nationally. There is no equivalent in Australia, for example, of the US National Center for Geographic Information and Analysis established in 1988 by the National Science Foundation or the Regional Research Laboratories in the United Kingdom created in 1987 by the Economic and Social Research Council. Nor has there yet been any major national inquiry into spatial data handling equivalent to the Committee of Enquiry on the Handling of Geographic Information in the UK (DoE 1987). For the most part, research in LIS and GIS is carried out independently by government organizations and higher education institutions, although the national academies are now beginning to play a more active role in linking research organizations, the scientific community and government in the policy context.

The major aim of the federal government's research effort is the Commonwealth Scientific and Industrial Research Organization (CSIRO). Several of its divisions have been actively engaged for many years in research and development in GIS and broader aspects of spatial modelling and data handling. The Division of Building, Construction and Engineering based in Melbourne has had a long history of research in spatial modelling and data handling, particularly in urban land use, transport and infrastructure planning and mapping. Over the years, several packages have been developed, many of which have now also been made available for microcomputers (see Newton, Taylor and Sharpe 1988). Representative major research contributions include TOPAZ, an urban activity location model (Brotchie, Dickey and Sharpe 1980); LAIRD, a package for assessing impacts of retail development (Roy and Anderson 1988); MULATM, a traffic network planning package (Taylor 1988); and LAMM, a microcomputer mapping package (Newton and Crawford 1988). These packages have been used in a variety of application areas.

The Division of Wildlife and Ecology in Canberra has similarly been engaged during the past decade in a wide-ranging research effort in information systems for environmental applications. ARIS, the Australian Resources Information System (Walker and Cocks 1984; Cocks, Walker and Parvey 1988) is a continental scale, computerized GIS designed to answer questions about the location of specified combinations of biophysical and socio-economic data using polygon and grid-cell formats. The system currently includes ten separate databases including the Australian Resources Data Bank containing over 400 biophysical data items. ARIS has been used over the years in a variety of studies by the federal government including site selection for new cities, mapping the effects of the location and orientation of the AUSSAT communication satellite, rangeland management, and the analysis of the coastal zone and changing vegetation patterns resulting from the greenhouse effect. More recently, research has been directed towards integrating cartographic and spatial modelling techniques with inductive modelling capabilities in a prototype system called the Spatial and Inductive Modelling Package for Land Evaluation or SIMPLE (Walker and Moore 1988). This system has enabled rule-based induction techniques to be applied towards analysing wildlife distributions (e.g. kangaroos, koalas).

The Division of Water Resources in Canberra has also had a history of developing GIS, stemming from early work on a combined cadastral and environment system for land use planning in the 1970s. Major contributions include ADAPT, a rule-based system for deriving zoning schemes (Davis and Grant 1987); ONKA, a policy analysis decision support system that draws upon ARC/INFO coverages (Davis, Nanninga and Clark 1989); and ARX, a spatial expert system that can be coupled to ARC/INFO (Davis, Whigham and Grant 1988). The latter, now a working prototype, is being applied to assist the Australian Army manage the Puckapunyal Training Area in Victoria (Cuddy et al. 1989) and to assess trafficability conditions in northern Australia (Davis and Laut 1989).

The Division of Information Technology has established a Centre for Spatial Information Systems in Canberra to undertake research leading to the design, implementation and application of systems for processing spatially referenced data. Research projects include GIS involving distributed spatial databases, decision support systems emphasizing spatial optimization and inferencing and image processing systems concentrating on terrain analysis and visualization. The Division is collaborating with industry to market and support the products of its research. Several commercially available software packages have been developed to date including SIRO-DBMS, a spatial database toolkit (Abel 1989) and ITA, a system for location-allocation tasks (Horn, O'Callaghan and Garner 1988).

Telecom Research Laboratories in Melbourne are engaged in GIS research for their corporate body, Telecom Australia, which is responsible for basic telecommunications facilities in Australia. The research is aimed at using GIS technology for demand studies, network planning and particularly the key role telecommunications will play in networking spatial information systems in future (Cavill and Greener 1988; Edney and Cavill 1989). Finally, as far as federal bodies are concerned, the Defence Science and Technology Organization is also involved in developing military GIS, concentrating to date on the analysis and integration of image-based data in decision support systems (Nichol et al. 1987).

Research in GIS is now well established at Australian universities and colleges. A 1989 survey of education and research in LIS/GIS indicated that some 34 separate institutions were engaged in research and offer degree or diploma courses in many facets of LIS/GIS (AURISA 1989). Many centres have been established, the most significant being the Australian Key Centre in Land Information Studies in Queensland. Established in 1986 by the federal government as part of its Key Centre initiative to provide a focus for teaching and research in areas of national importance, the Centre is built around the facilities and expertise of the Department of Geographical Sciences, Queensland University; the Queensland Centre for Surveying and Mapping Studies; and the Research and Development Unit, Queensland Department of Geographic Information. The Key Centre is engaged in a range of research, education, and training programmes in remote sensing, digital mapping and spatial information systems. Other universities with a national profile in research and applications in GIS and remote sensing include the Department of Surveying and Land Information, the University of Melbourne; the Centre for Resource and Environmental Studies at the Australian National University, Canberra; and the School of Geography and Centre for Remote Sensing, University of New South Wales, Sydney (Garner 1986).

RETROSPECT AND PROSPECT

Apart from the significant advances that have been made in the development of LIS by state governments – developments which are now nationally coordinated through the Australian Land Information Council and which must be viewed as a major success in inter-government collaboration – development in and applications of GIS are effectively at an early stage and fragmentary in scope compared with those in many other countries. However, with an infrastructure progressively being developed and a significant research and development effort now established, Australia is embarking on a major expansion of GIS activities in the coming decade in all application areas – both public and private.

The role of government agencies at state and federal levels will continue to be significant although the results of a 1988 national survey indicate clearly that the technology and its application is already rapidly extending into the activities of local government (see Murphy et al. 1988). Mechanisms and structures have been put in place to assure more effective coordination within and between jurisdictions in establishing and accessing databases, the sharing of which is expected to become commonplace in the next five years. Important in this regard is the question of the custodianship of data in shared and networked systems; the indications are that Australia is well advanced by international standards in coming to grips with this problem.

Apart from an intensification of effort at all levels of government and in the private sector – especially in environmental and natural resource applications at varying geographical scales – the major development will undoubtedly be in the advancement of systems for social and economic applications. GIS will become commonplace in urban and regional planning, housing, social services, and the health sector. At present, none of these major areas of government activity is taking advantage of the potential that GIS offers for monitoring performance, decision making and policy formulation. In this regard, however, the Australian experience is possibly little different to that of most other advanced countries.

Perhaps the major area of change, however, is likely to occur in the private sector, for which favourable taxation arrangements concerning investments in technology in recent years are already beginning to bear fruit. The banking and finance sector in Australia, for example, is now among the world leaders in the rate of adoption of information technology and its application, the extension of which in the geographical domain is already apparent. Similar trends are emerging in retailing and wholesaling – particularly in the food sector – and in the mining companies which have traditionally played a dominant role in national economic development. The private sector is also actively engaged in developing new kinds of databases, for example address matching systems which (in conjunction with the wider availability of national census data in digital forms) will inevitably provide new opportunities for all applications areas, particularly in marketing and survey research. These developments will be strengthened and facilitated by the emergence in Australia of an indigenous computer software industry, albeit at a small scale by international standards.

All of these anticipated developments will rely heavily on the supply of a skilled labour force in GIS and information technology – the building blocks for which have already been put in place in the education sector and in manpower training programmes that are progressively being introduced nationally. The future for Australia looks bright indeed; the indications are that it will rank among the world leaders in experience, initiative and the widespread development and application of geographical information systems technology in all areas of application in the coming decade.

REFERENCES

Abel D J (1989) SIRO-DBMS: a database tool-kit for geographical information systems. *International Journal of Geographical Information Systems* **3**: 103–16
ALIC (1987) *National Strategy for Land Information Management.* ALIC Secretariat, Canberra
ALIC (1988ff.) *Annual Report.* Australian Land Information Council, Canberra
AURISA (1976ff.) *URPIS – Proceedings of the Urban and Regional Planning Information Systems Annual Conferences.* Australasian Urban and Regional Information Systems Association Inc., Sydney
AURISA (1985) *Report of the Working Group on Statewide Parcel-based Land Information Systems in Australasia.* Australasian Urban and Regional Information Systems Association Inc., Sydney
AURISA (1989) *Towards the Implementation of a National Strategy for Education and Research in Land and Geographic Information Systems.* Australasian Urban and Regional Information Systems Association Inc., Sydney
AUSLIG (1985) *LANDSEARCH 1: Directory of Commonwealth Land Related Data.* Commonwealth Department of Local Government and Administrative Services, Canberra

Babbage R (1989) Planning the future of defence geographic information systems. In: Ball D, Babbage R (eds.) *Geographical Information Systems: Defence Applications.* Pergamon Press, Sydney, pp. 232–42
Black J, Sambura A, Salijevic R (1986) The conceptual and technological framework for the New South Wales Land Information System. *URPIS – Proceedings of the Urban and Regional Planning Information Systems Annual Conferences*, Volume 14. Australasian Urban and Regional Information Systems Association Inc., Sydney, pp. 356–67
Brauer A (1985) Introduction to the Australian Standard Geographical Classification. *URPIS – Proceedings of the Urban and Regional Planning Information Systems Annual Conferences*, Volume 13. Australasian Urban and Regional Information Systems Association Inc., Sydney, pp. 365–97
Brotchie J F, Dickey J W, Sharpe R (1980) *TOPAZ – General Planning Model and its Applications at the Urban and Facility Planning Levels.* Springer-Verlag, Heidelburg

Cavill M V, Greener S (1988) Introducing Geographic Information Systems Technology: concepts, approval and implementation. *URPIS – Proceedings of the Urban and Regional Planning Information Systems Annual Conferences*, Volume 16. Australasian Urban and Regional Information Systems Association Inc., Sydney, pp. 323–30

Clark D M, Hastings D A, Kineman J J (1991) Global databases and their implications for GIS. In: Maguire D J, Goodchild M F, Rhind D W (eds.) *Geographical Information Systems: principles and applications.* Longman, London, pp. 217–31, Vol 2

Cocks K D, Walker P A (1987) Edging towards a nation-wide resources information system for Australia. *Proceedings of the 21st Conference of the Institute of Australian Geographers, Perth*, pp. 319–25

Cocks K D, Walker P A, Parvey C A (1988) Evolution of a continental-scale geographical information system. *International Journal of Geographical Information Systems* **2**: 263–80

Cuddy S M, Laut P, Davis J R, Whigham P A, Goodspeed J, Duell T (1989) Modelling the environmental effects of training on a major Australian army base. *Proceedings SSA IMACS Biennial Conference on Modelling and Simulation, Canberra*

Dale P F (1991) Land information systems. In: Maguire D J, Goodchild M F, Rhind D W (eds.) *Geographical Information Systems: principles and applications.* Longman, London, pp. 85–99, Vol 2

Davis J R, Grant I W (1987) ADAPT: A knowledge-based decision support system for producing zoning plans. *Environment and Planning B* **14**: 53–66

Davis J R, Laut P (1989) An expert system to estimate trafficability in a remote region of Australia. *AI Applications in Natural Resource Management* **3** (1): 17–26

Davis J R, Nanninga P M, Clark R D S (1989) A decision support system for evaluating catchment policies. *Proceedings of the Conference on Computing in the Water Industry, Melbourne*, pp. 205–9

Davis J R, Whigham P A, Grant I W (1988) Representing and applying knowledge about spatial processes in environmental management. *AI Applications in Natural Resource Management* **2** (4): 17–25

Department of the Environment (DoE) (1987) *Handling Geographic Information.* Report to the Secretary of State for the Environment of the Committee of Inquiry into the Handling of Geographic Information, Chairman Lord Chorley. HMSO, London

Eather P T (1986) The HUB – the Queensland approach to land information system development. *URPIS – Proceedings of the Urban and Regional Planning Information Systems Annual Conferences*, Volume 16. Australasian Urban and Regional Information Systems Association Inc., Sydney, pp. 198–208

Edney P, Cavill M (1989) The Melbourne Knowledge Precinct GIS pilot project. *URPIS – Proceedings of the Urban and Regional Planning Information Systems Annual Conferences*. Volume 17. Australasian Urban and Regional Information Systems Association Inc., Sydney, pp. 325–31

Garner B J (1986) Geographical information systems technology at the University of New South Wales. *AURISA News* March/June: 3–5

Guptill S C (1991) Spatial data exchange and standardization. In: Maguire D J, Goodchild M F, Rhind D W (eds.) *Geographical Information Systems: principles and applications.* Longman, London, pp. 515–30, Vol 1

Hart A (1988) The New South Wales Land Information System in action. *URPIS – Proceedings of the Urban and Regional Planning Information Systems Annual Conferences*, Volume 16. Australasian Urban and Regional Information Systems Association Inc., Sydney, pp. 25–39

Horn M, O'Callaghan J F, Garner B J (1988) Design of integrated systems for spatial planning tasks. *Proceedings of the 3rd International Symposium on Spatial Data Handling.* International Geographical Union, Columbus, Ohio, pp. 107–16

Hurle G (1989) The status of development of facility management systems within the Australian electricity supply industry. *URPIS – Proceedings of the Urban and Regional Planning Information Systems Annual Conferences*, Volume 17. Australasian Urban and Regional Information Systems Association Inc., Sydney, pp. 350–8

Johnson B D, Mott J J, Robey T (1989) Providing effective access to resources information – progress towards a national directory of Australian resources data. *URPIS – Proceedings of the Urban and Regional Planning Information Systems Annual Conferences*, Volume 17. Australasian Urban and Regional Information Systems Association Inc., Sydney, pp. 260–5

Laing A W, Puniard D J (1989) The Australian Defence Force requirements for land-related information. In: Ball D, Babbage R (eds.) *Geographical Information Systems: defence applications.* Pergamon Press, Sydney, pp. 61–79

Lesslie R G, Mackey B G, Preece K M (1988) A computer-based method of wilderness evaluation. *Environmental Conservation* **15** (3): 225–32

Matheson G (1986) The implementation of a facilities information system with a major utility organisation. *URPIS – Proceedings of the Urban and Regional Planning Information Systems Annual Conferences*, Volume 14. Australasian Urban and Regional Information Systems Association Inc., Sydney, pp. 203–25

Murphy P A, Zehner R B, Robertson P A, Hirst R (1988) *Computer Use by Local Government Planners: an Australian perspective.* School of Town Planning University of New South Wales, Sydney

Nash K (1986) The application of computers to planning tasks in the city of Sydney. *Australian Planner* **24**: 19–23

Nash K (1988) The Sydney City Council Land Information System – a decade on, the dream and the reality. *URPIS – Proceedings of the Urban and Regional Planning Information Systems Annual Conferences*, Volume 16.

Australasian Urban and Regional Information Systems Association Inc., Sydney, pp. 1–13

Newton P W, Crawford J R (1988) Microcomputer-based geographic information and mapping systems. In: Newton P.W, Taylor M A P, Sharpe R (eds.) *Desktop Planning: microcomputer applications for infrastructure and services planning and management.* Hargreen, Melbourne, pp. 31–43

Newton P W, Taylor M A P, Sharpe R (eds.) (1988) *Desktop Planning: microcomputer applications for infrastructure and services planning and management.* Hargreen, Melbourne

Nichol D G, Fiebig M J, Whatmough R J, Whitbread P J (1987) Some image processing aspects of a military geographic information system. *Australian Computer Journal* 19 (3): 154–60

Perrett P, Lyons K J, Moss O F (1989) Overview of GIS activities in Queensland. In: Ball D, Babbage R (eds.) *Geographical Information Systems: defence applications.* Pergamon Press, Sydney, pp. 152–79

Phillips M, Blackburn J (1989) The Chrysalis Project: a regional GIS over Jervis Bay. In: Ball D, Babbage R (eds.) *Geographical Information Systems: defence applications.* Pergamon Press, Sydney, pp. 204–31

Rhind D W (1991) Counting the people: the role of GIS. In: Maguire D J, Goodchild M F, Rhind D W (eds.) *Geographical Information Systems: principles and applications.* Longman, London, pp. 127–37, Vol 2

Roy J R, Anderson M (1988) Assessing impacts of retail development and redevelopment. In: Newton P W, Taylor M A P, Sharpe R (eds.) *Desktop Planning: microcomputer applications for infrastructure and services planning and management.* Hargreen, Melbourne, pp. 172–9

Smith L, Eden R (1989) GIS and natural resource management: the Murray–Darling Basin *URPIS – Proceedings of the Urban and Regional Planning Information Systems Annual Conferences*, Volume 17. Australasian Urban and Regional Information Systems Association Inc., Sydney, pp. 452–60

Taylor M A P (1988) Computer models for traffic systems applications. In: Newton P W, Taylor M A P, Sharpe R (eds.) *Desktop Planning: microcomputer applications for infrastructure and services planning and management.* Hargreen, Melbourne, pp. 264–98

Walker P A, Cocks K D (1984) Computerised choropleth mapping of Australian resources data. *Cartography* 13 (4): 243–52

Walker P A, Moore D M (1988) SIMPLE – an inductive modelling and mapping tool for spatially-oriented data. *International Journal of Geographical Information Systems* 2 (4): 347–63

Williamson I P (1986) Trends in land information system administration in Australia. In: Blakemore M J (ed.) *Proceedings of AUTOCARTO London 1.* Royal Institution of Chartered Surveyors, London, pp. 71–82

Williamson I P, Blackburn J W (1987) Current developments in Land Information Systems in Australia. *Proceedings of the 21st Conference of the Institute of Australian Geographers, Perth*, pp. 289–97

40

GIS AND DEVELOPING NATIONS

D R F TAYLOR

The purpose of this chapter is to discuss GIS in the developing world. The central argument is that, although GIS has potential to be of utility in the struggle for development, that potential has not yet been realized and there are many problems to be overcome. Some of the problems are technical in nature but the bulk of them are social, economic and political. It is argued that the current developments in GIS are primarily technology-driven and that such an approach has limited relevance to the problems of development in the countries of Africa, Asia and Latin America. GIS technology is not scientifically objective and value free. It is an artefact of industrial and post-industrial society. Its structures, technologies and applications are products of the needs of these societies. If it is to be used in the context of development then it must be introduced, developed, modified and controlled by indigenous people who understand the social, economic and political context of the situation as well as the technical capabilities of GIS. This may involve some quite different GIS configurations and solutions from those already successful in the developed nations. It poses special problems of technology transfer and education and training. The chapter begins by looking at the developing nations and the challenges facing them. A brief description is then given of the introduction of GIS to the developing world, including a description of current applications. Special attention is given to China and India to illustrate the central argument. The chapter concludes with some general comments on GIS and the future in developing nations.

THE CHALLENGE OF DEVELOPMENT

The term 'developing nations' is a euphemism used by the rich to describe the poor. The terminology itself expresses optimism suggesting that progress towards an improved quality of life is taking place. Although difficult to define, 'development' is generally agreed to comprise a series of components including increased economic growth, improved equity and distribution of the fruits of that growth, control by the population of their own destiny and the achievement of qualitative transcendental values. Development cannot be defined in purely quantitative terms and differs over both time and space. It is best defined in terms of the aspirations and values of people in their own social context and, in this sense, is probably only really meaningful at the sub-national scale.

For many parts of the world there is no compelling evidence that 'development', however defined, is taking place. Africa, for example, is generally held to be in crisis and, over the decade of the 1980s, the quality of life for the majority of the continent's inhabitants has been declining in both relative and absolute terms. Increasing degradation would be a better description than 'development' of the current trends. The Secretary General of the Economic Commission for Africa has outlined (Adedeji 1989) the major features of this debilitating crisis which he sees as having three major manifestations:

- a deterioration in the main macro-economic indicators;
- a disintegration of productive mechanisms and infrastructural facilities: and

- an accelerating decline in social welfare provisions such as education, health and housing.

To his list could be added an increasing deterioration of the physical environment. The figures he quotes are disturbing to say the least. Between 1980 and 1988, per capita income in Africa fell steadily by 2.6 per cent per annum and wage employment fell by 16 per cent. GDP per capita in 1978 was US $854; by 1988 it was US $565. In 1978, the per capita growth rate was 3.03 per cent; in 1988, it was −0.88 per cent. Growth rates in all sectors are dropping and Africa's inflation rates are rising. The debt burden has risen from US $48 300 million in 1978 to over US $230 000 million in 1988 and debt servicing obligations now exceed 100 per cent of export earnings in several African countries. The scale of the debt servicing problem has reached such a level that, despite ODA (Official Development Assistance) flows, there is a net flow of capital from developing to developed countries in many instances. The terms of trade have continued to deteriorate, resulting in an annual loss of approximately 10 per cent of export earnings. Adedeji's comment is that 'The cumulative toll of this unremitting decline for a whole decade on our society is clear and unmistakable. The number of countries classified as least developed among the developing world – the wretched of the earth as they have been categorized – increased from 17 in 1978 to 28 in 1988. And more, I regret to say, are knocking at the door to join. Whereas in 1960 Africa had 124 million illiterates, in 1985 the illiterate population had increased to 162 million; almost one-fifth of all the illiterate females in the world are in Africa' (Adedeji 1989:11).

Unfortunately the extreme situation in Africa is not unique in the developing world. In December 1988, UNICEF released its report *The State of the World's Children* with the comment that:

> 'For almost 900 million people, approximately one-sixth of mankind, the march of human progress has now become a retreat. In many nations, development is being thrown into reverse. And after decades of steady economic advance, large areas of the world are sliding back into poverty. Throughout most of Africa and much of Latin America average incomes have fallen by 10 to 25 per cent in the 1980s. . . . In the 37 poorest nations, spending per head on health has been reduced by 50 per cent and on education by 25 per cent over the last four years. In almost half of the 103 developing countries for which recent data are available, the proportion of six to 11-year-olds enrolled in primary school is falling. . . . The slowing down of progress and the reversal of hard won gains is spreading hardship and human misery on a scale and of a severity unprecedented in the postwar era. . . . For most of the countries of Africa, Latin America and the Caribbean, almost every economic signal points to the fact that development has been derailed. Per capita GNP has fallen, debt repayments have risen to a quarter or more of all export earnings, share in world trade has dropped and productivity of labour has declined . . .'
>
> (UNICEF 1988:1).

The picture, although depressing, is not one of unrelieved gloom. In Asia there have been success stories such as those of the four Asian tigers, the NICs (newly industrialized countries) Korea, Taiwan, Hong Kong and Singapore. The two most populous countries in the world, China and India, have made impressive progress, although in the latter case macro-economic growth statistics mask severe and growing inequities between rich and poor. In both nations, population growth continues to be a problem despite progress on birth control which, in the case of China, has involved measures which severely limit individual freedom. Where large absolute numbers are involved, population increases of even moderate proportions create enormous problems – especially where the factors of production, such as arable land, are limited. For many nations, rapid economic growth must take place simply to maintain the *status quo*. In this respect, the progress made in many Asian nations is tenuous and there are real limits to their growth.

It is not surprising that, in these circumstances, the environment has come under increasing pressure. The issues involved have been well described in the Brundtland Report (World Commission on Environment and Development 1987). Environmental degradation by the people of many developing nations is not an act bred simply out of ignorance and greed but often out of desperation and the need for survival. As the title of the Brundtland Report – *Our Common Future* –

suggests, the problems of the environment cannot be isolated in space because (as one example) when areas of tropical rain forest are felled, the impact is felt on a world scale. Although the environmental problems of surplus, such as those of pollution by industrialized societies, are quite different from the environmental problems of poverty, there is an inexorable link between the two.

The same, of course, applies to many of the other problems facing developing nations. In the same month as the UNICEF study was published, the OECD released its half yearly report (OECD 1988) and the contrast between the two documents is striking. The OECD report showed an annual growth rate in excess of 4 per cent for member nations. The leading non-communist industrial economies were reported to be at their 'most buoyant' since the early 1970s and 'the brisk expansion has been widespread. Investment in industry has been growing especially fast' (OECD 1988). The major problems which were identified were growing protectionism and the imbalance among the major industrial trading blocks. Little mention was made of the impact of the policies which have led to this resurgence of growth on the economies of developing nations – yet many observers, including UNICEF, have pointed out that the crisis in developing nations '... is happening not because of any one visible cause but because of an unfolding economic drama in which the industrialized nations play a leading role' (UNICEF 1988:1).

There are those who argue that the success of the 'First World' has been built on the exploitation of the 'Third World' and that this is continuing in new and more subtle ways long after the period of formal colonialism and imperialism is over (see Fanon 1963; Amin 1973; Rodney 1974; Hart 1988). Although these analytical perspectives are controversial, there is no doubt that relationships between the First and Third Worlds have been unequal for centuries and continue to be so today. An understanding of these relationships is critical to an understanding of the context of development. In this respect, 1989 and 1990 have seen changes that will make the development context even more complex. The 'Second World' of the Soviet Union and Eastern Europe has undergone dramatic changes. As a result, almost overnight a revolutionary change is taking place in the relationships between the First and Second Worlds.

It is not yet clear what impact this will have on Third World nations, but the initial signs are not promising. It is likely that at least a portion of ODA will be re-defined and re-directed and that commercial loans and private investment, which have virtually disappeared from Africa (and to a lesser extent from Latin America), will be encouraged to seek new outlets in the Second World. Technology transfer, ODA and private loans and investment are important elements in the First World–Third World relationship. The emergence of a new player – the Second World – and the demands that this new player is likely to make will inevitably affect developing nations although the nature and extent of that impact remains to be seen.

GIS are a First World technology and their utilization in the Third World will depend, to some extent at least, upon the ways in which technology transfer takes place. If the First World finds new and more politically compelling outlets for its interests, the present nature and scale of that technology transfer may change. Thus, to understand GIS in developing nations, it is necessary to understand the challenges and context of development which is itself a constantly changing panorama. This is not primarily a technical problem.

THE INTRODUCTION OF GIS IN DEVELOPING NATIONS

The first GIS was developed in Canada in the 1960s and was based on mainframe technology. Even in the context for which it was developed, this GIS was not an immediate success story. The history of this development is outlined elsewhere in this volume (see Coppock and Rhind 1991). One of the early pioneers of GIS, Roger Tomlinson, has argued that in North America the year 1988 marks the cross-over point when GIS proved to be a really viable and useful technology (Tomlinson 1989a).

In developing nations, apart from a few research applications and exploratory pilot projects, the technology was not seriously applied prior to 1980. The 1980s, however, have seen a steady expansion of the application of the technology in developing nations, especially after 1986. This has largely been a result of rapid technological change in a number of related fields. Developments in remote sensing have been particularly important in making vastly increased amounts of data available, especially on the environment. The increasing power of the microcomputer has also been a key factor, together with the fact that costs of hardware per unit of computing power continue to decrease. The year 1986 saw a quantum leap in this respect with the introduction of the Intel 386 chip which one author (Bryden 1989) claims had as dramatic and revolutionary an effect on GIS as the impact of the changes in Eastern Europe had on the world political scene. Added to this has been the development of more efficient software systems and new storage devices such as CD-ROM, WORM and other optical disk technologies (see Goodchild 1991 in this volume).

Applications of GIS technologies in developing nations, especially those based on microcomputer technology, have exploded during the latter part of the 1980s (see Edralin 1990) but, when applications are examined, they are often found to be initiatives funded or supported by international aid agencies and many are pilot or research projects as opposed to operational systems. They also tend to be controlled by outsiders, not by indigenous scientists. A few examples will be used to illustrate this characteristic.

The United Nations system has been particularly active in the introduction and use of GIS. The United Nations Environmental Programme based in Nairobi and Geneva has been developing the Global Resource Information Data Base (GRID) which is being used to support UN efforts to collect and manage environmental information for planning and decision-making purposes (Clarke, Hastings and Kinneman 1991 in this volume). GRID is part of the UN system-wide Global Environmental Monitoring System (GEMS) which was established in 1985 to help rationalize the considerable volumes of data on environmental issues being collected from different sources. GEMS works through other United Nations agencies and international organizations in five key areas: climate and the atmosphere; oceans and regional seas; renewable natural resources; pollutant effects on the health of both humans and ecosystems; and long-range transportation of air pollutants. The major software used is ARC/INFO and in November 1988 the program received a multi-million dollar donation of hardware from IBM UK Ltd and software from ESRI to support its work. The GRID analysis of the African environment has been useful in monitoring the extent of environmental degradation. It is a good example of the 'top-down' approach to GIS.

As a second example, the Asian Institute of Technology (AIT) in Bangkok, which is supported by UN funds, is another agency which has been involved in the development and application of GIS especially in the Asian region. Particular attention has been given to training. The AIT approach has been very much of a 'bottom-up' one, with the emphasis on the use of existing resources (Dias 1987, 1989). The Human Settlements Development group at AIT has been particularly active in developing appropriate GIS approaches. The work of Yapa (1988, 1989) is an interesting approach developed initially at AIT and subsequently at his home base in the Pennsylvania State University. The approach used is decentralized and PC-based; 'the idea was to provide capabilities in map drawing and database management by linking existing popular, off-the shelf, commercial software' (Yapa 1988:215; see also Shepherd 1991 in this volume). Yapa developed the CARP system (Computer Assisted Regional Planning) which is a set of linkage routines written in BASIC which integrate AUTOCAD with DBASE to provide a simple low cost system designed to run an IBM-compatible PC with a memory of 640 kb. A digitizing tablet, a graphics monitor and an adapter are also required with a hard disk of at least ten megabytes recommended (Yapa 1989). The first experimental use of CARP was in 1987 in the Hambantota District of Sri Lanka, where a project on Integrated Rural Development supported by NORAD is underway. Yapa argued that CARP was extremely useful and 'is now in constant use as the basis for monitoring planning projects and carrying out routine work in district planning offices' (Yapa 1989: 32–3). The visual output from the system was found to be especially valuable, as was the fact that local languages could be used as text.

The work of AIT is built on a particular view of how GIS should be introduced. This conviction received considerable support at a UNESCO Seminar on Information Systems for Sub-National Planning held at Visakhapatnam in India in December 1985. The seminar agreed a series of resolutions, one of which has become known as the 'Visakhapatnam Declaration' which states that

'... multi-level, decentralized planning, as a means of achieving goals of development and equity with self-reliance be encouraged, facilitated and coordinated through the establishment of a matched set of authority and information structures that are supported by effective, economical and compatible computerized information systems' (RRDN 1986).

Another agency active in the introduction of GIS to developing nations is ITC. Although ITC is primarily a training institution, it also carries out research and contract work in the GIS field in developing nations and has developed its own microcomputer-based GIS called ILWIS (Integrated Land and Watershed Management Information System). Stefanovic, Drummond and Muller (1989:451) from ITC suggest 'both conceptually and practically, a GIS may be the superstructure on a CAC (Computer-Assisted Cartography) system and the bottom-up approach finds some favour at ITC because of its practical usefulness'. There is, however, also support at ITC for a 'top-down' approach to GIS (Jerie, Kure and Larsen 1980). Much of ITC's work is supported by aid funds from both national and international agencies and, in addition to its own ILWIS system, ITC introduces Third World trainees to a wide variety of existing GIS systems.

Nijkamp and De Jong (1987) have provided a good overview of the applications of GIS in developing nations, especially those applications emanating from ITC. They comment that 'coherent and integrated spatial planning is rare, and systematic use of information in computerized systems is uncommon. In the few cases registered, the GIS has usually a limited domain and is implemented and maintained in the framework of a development project led by expatriate experts' (Nijkamp and De Jong 1987:103). They then examine five projects: the use of the vector-based Dutch SALADIN system in an energy assessment project in West Java; an application of the raster-based MAP (Map Analysis Package) system to land use evaluation in Kisii District in Kenya; the monitoring of land use change in Moneragala District in Sri Lanka using the raster-based GIS USEMAP developed at ITC; landscape ecological planning in Colombia using ITC's Image Processing Lab GIS; and, finally, the use of CRIES (Comprehensive Resource Inventory and Evaluation System) in the Central American and Caribbean countries. This last system is supported by USAID, the US Department of Agriculture and Michigan State University. Their overview found that most of the applications were experimental and that none was a fully integral part of the ongoing planning.

In October 1989 an international conference on GIS Applications for Urban and Regional Planning was held in Indonesia (Edralin 1990), organized by the UN Centre for Regional Development together with the government of Indonesia. One hundred participants from 12 nations, together with representatives from a number of UN agencies, reviewed the experience of developing countries (especially those in Asia) in the use of GIS. The country-based case studies presented described a number of innovative uses in Indonesia, Thailand, Malaysia, India, Sri-Lanka, China and Hong Kong, together with several examples of microcomputer-based GIS in planning. These included (Edralin 1990) details of the REDATAM software developed by the Latin American Demographic Centre of the UN Economic Commission for Latin America and the Caribbean (UN/ECLAC). Although more recent and comprehensive than the overview by Nijkamp and De Jong, the report of this meeting reveals that GIS are still in the pilot or experimental stage and that '... many issues remain unresolved in the design and use of GIS' (Edralin 1990:1). The innovative *potential* of the technology was accepted but the primacy of its role as a support mechanism in planning was repeatedly reiterated.

The private sector entered the GIS market in a serious way in 1981 when what is billed as the first commercial GIS, ESRI's ARC/INFO, was introduced by ESRI of Redlands, California. Since that time, growth in commercial GIS systems has been rapid. Both the number of vendors and the variety of systems offered has proliferated into the hundreds and shows no signs of abating. These systems are being aggressively marketed and promoted in developing nations and the private sector will play an increasing role in how GIS evolves in the Third World. Most of the systems being purchased at present are being obtained by government agencies and often the purchase is supported in part by ODA funds from a variety of donors. The bulk of the applications are of the 'top-down' type and some are both imaginative and interesting. Issues of *ARC News* (ESRI's widely circulated GIS 'newspaper') for 1989 and 1990, for example, include illustrations of a variety of new uses in the Third World such as a major LIS project for Hong Kong, cadastral mapping of land holdings in Thailand, mineral exploration in Colombia, an LIS Conceptual Design Study for Oman and a major nation-wide project for providing environmental support for nomadic peoples in Saudi Arabia.

Vendors typically deliver a 'turn-key' system which usually includes a training component. The vendor will maintain and update the system for a price if required, but the use of that system is then in the hands of the purchaser. This approach assumes that the purchaser has a clear idea of why the GIS will be useful and how it will be applied to the development task at hand. This demands a considerable base of indigenous knowledge and expertise which, in practice, is not always present. GIS are a new technology in developing nations. Their introduction, whether in 'top-down' or 'bottom-up' fashion, is coming mainly from the outside and so far it has been largely marginal to the solution of the development challenges outlined earlier in this chapter. A necessary, but perhaps not sufficient, first step is for indigenous scientists and decision makers to gain a greater degree of knowledge and control of this technology. Sundaram (1987), following Rada (1982), has argued that the crucial question is how to obtain this 'socio-economic command'. He comments that 'information technology is a reality, and a rapidly expanding one. The question, therefore, is how to master the changes and deal with these issues to the best advantage for development strategies. What is needed is a socio-economic command of the development of science and technology' (Sundaram 1987:55). If this is not achieved, there will continue to be a 'mismatch' between the tasks which can be performed by GIS and the reality of the current application situation. To examine some of the dilemmas involved, the situation in the two most populous developing nations, China and India, will be examined.

GIS IN CHINA AND INDIA

Both China and India have a long history of involvement in geographical information processing and the collection of spatial data prior to the computer era. Chinese and Indian written records both record the achievements of ancient scientists in their countries. In the Vedic literature in India, Chadha points out that 'just before the beginning of the Christian era, the Brahmand Purana and the Arth Shastra of Kautilya contained the basic concept of map making. A manual known as Sulva Sutra (an article on mensuration) contained techniques of surveying and mensuration of areas. Sher Shah Suri and Todar Mal had revenue maps prepared on the basis of land survey' (Chadha 1989:2–3). The situation in China is even more impressive. References to maps in China go back thousands of years but the earliest maps which have been found date from the second century BC. From these early beginnings, the Chinese use of geographical information, in both graphic and tabular form, developed in a fascinating way as the work of Needham (1959, 1981) illustrates.

Both countries came into early contact with the West and this had differing impacts. In India, the British established the Survey of India (SOI) in 1767, a full 18 years before the equivalent in Britain itself and SOI has continued as one of the premier mapping organizations in the world ever since. Although China did not become a colonial possession as did India, it was no less deeply affected by the exploitation of foreign powers, such as England, France, Germany and the United States, and much was lost as a result.

With a long tradition of collecting geodata and a shared desire to modernize, it is not surprising that both nations are examining GIS and the role it might play in their development process. Their approaches and experience are, however, quite different and neatly illustrate the central arguments of this chapter.

The situation in India

India has not yet fully come to terms with GIS and its role in the development process although ambitious plans are in place. The Survey of India, utilizing substantial funds provided by UNDP, has obtained two sophisticated GIS systems and intends to build a digital topographic database for the country at two basic scales – 1 : 250 000 and 1 : 50 000. The Digital Cartographic Data Base is to be the building block for a national GIS system on which other government agencies can build according to their needs. This is very much a 'top-down', long-term approach. It is part of the Government of India's overall plan for information management and its application to the development process. In 1984, the Planning Commission of the Government of India constituted task forces in agriculture, water resources, forestry, soils and land use, urban and rural studies, and geology and oceanography. A separate task force on a National Natural Resources Information System (NNRIS) studied the recommendations of the other task forces and proposed that a national information system be established. Another separate task force looked at the Cartographic Representation of Data. It was from this group, CARD, that the recommendation originated to establish a Digital Cartographic Data Base to which data from all other government organizations could be tied. CARD also suggested increased use of remote sensing to collect data (Misra 1989). The task force on NNRIS recommended that the proposed Natural Resources Information System be established under the Department of Science and Technology as the Natural Resources Data Management System. This is intended to be a computer-based Decision Support System (see Densham 1991 in this volume) to help in the planning and management of natural resources at the micro-level (district and below) and ten pilot district-based data centres have been established. In 1989, the System purchased ARC/INFO to carry out experimental work in three of the 10 centres. Sundaram (1987) reported that 13 of the Advanced Technical Institutes in the country are collaborating in the work and that five pilot projects have been chosen for district planning utilizing an integrated composite software package called GRIDS. He also reported on GIS applications in urban and regional planning on a Computerized Rural Information Systems Project (CRISP) at the district level through the National Informatics Centre. The Centre has developed a satellite-based communication system called NICNET which will be totally operational by 1990 (Kumar 1989) and will greatly facilitate the transmission of messages and data. Impressive strides have also been made in remote sensing and India launched its own satellite IRS IA in March 1988 and utilizes Landsat, SPOT and other imagery extensively (Saxena 1989).

India has also developed a strong indigenous computer manufacturing industry and has '... a very powerful processing tool in the form of PC-AT/386 computer with 387 math co-processor which is indigenously available at a modest price in the market, off the shelf' (Naithani 1989:240). Small indigenous GIS systems are emerging such as ISROVISON for urban planning in the Delhi Metropolitan Area (Rao et al. 1989) and micro-based pilot projects at the rural district level are also emerging (Chappuis and Golbéry 1984; Krishnayya 1986). Project Vasundharsa (Parthasaradhi and Krishnanunni 1989) is an excellent example of a well-designed regional scale GIS for mineral exploration and prognosis utilizing a raster-based approach.

All of the above demonstrates that at least some of the necessary scientific and technical infrastructure is in place, but as yet GIS has made no appreciable contribution to development in India and is unlikely to do so unless certain problems can be overcome. Some of these are technical. As yet, GIS systems cannot effectively handle very large databases. Dobson has commented 'it is clearly the case that the spatial data handling systems that are available today are simply not capable of dealing with large databases.... Since we have just begun to realize the promise of spatial data handling and have not yet created any really significant databases, how will we ever realize the promise that our endeavours contain for solving significant problems related to world famine, disease control and a host of other social tragedies? Certainly not with today's "robust systems"!' (Dobson 1988:8–9). This is a major problem for India which the current approaches do not appear to have fully considered, although it is clear that the problem has been identified (Nag 1987; Parthasaradhi and Krishnanunni 1989). The suggestion has been made that at least six different databases at various levels and scales will be required since '... no single level of database would meet all of the diverse requirements of planners for macro-, regional and micro-level planning for the management of resources' (Parthasaradhi and Krishnanunni 1989:321). These problems are not, of course, unique to developing nations, but in countries like India both population size and geographical extent compound the scale of the problem.

A second major problem is what Dobson calls '... the psoriasis of the data handling world: the cost of data collection' (Dobson 1988:6). In the case of India, there is a huge amount of data currently collected, but little of it is in machine-readable form and the costs of input are astronomical. It is also of extremely variable quality. This was identified as a major problem at the UNCRD seminar (see above and UNCRD 1990); Edralin (1990) and Harper and Manheim (1989) estimated that 80 per cent of the cost of implementing GIS in developing nations is attributable to database development. Remote sensing is an obvious answer for some types of data but is not without its problems, including that of error which is attracting increasing attention. Even in the First World the situation is unsatisfactory: 'spatial data handling systems process data with high precision, so it is perhaps surprising to find that the results of query or analysis frequently conflict with ground truth' (Goodchild and Wang 1988:97). Where the quality of the data is suspect, as in many cases in the developing world, the situation is much worse.

In many developing countries the problems of data collection are compounded by the rapid rates of change, especially in cities which may be growing at up to 7 per cent per annum. Ramachandran (1990) has drawn attention to cities such as Bankok which converts 32 square kilometres of land per year into urban uses and issues about 50 000 new titles for land parcels in the same period. Overall, the land area covered by Third World cities is predicted to expand by at least 50 per cent between 1990 and 2000.

Despite the importance of these technical problems, they are not the major barriers to the development of GIS in India. Bureaucratic and political factors loom large. For reasons of national security, existing maps are classified documents in India. In addition, all publishers of maps must receive certification for their products from the Survey of India. The maps of any part of India on a scale of 1:4 million or larger, including simple reprinting of such maps beyond six months of the certification, require clearance from the Ministry of Defence before final printing. Publication of maps indicating incorrect external boundaries is an offence under the Criminal Law (Amendment) Act of 1961. Gulati (1989) presented the dilemma such a policy poses: 'maps for about 40% of the geographical areas of the country fell under the restricted or secret category defined by the Survey of India. Quite a large number of even these restricted maps are not available to official agencies for defence reasons. As a result, mapping on an all-India level is not possible on scales larger than 1 : 250 000 by thematic mapping (user) organizations. For example 60% of India's forests lie in the restricted zone and 'if a similar restriction policy is adopted by Survey of India in respect of use and dissemination of 1 : 250 000-scale digital data, then the propagation of digital cartography and GIS technology to achieve an operational status in India is doubtful'.

A second institutional problem is the fact that so many organizations are involved in data collection and in policies on land and water in India; as Misra indicated, 'a "single window" solution which is rather urgently required is not in sight' (Misra 1989:224). He has proposed a new bureaucratic organization, a National Surveys Coordinating Committee, to resolve this problem but, in listing the membership required, he reveals the scale of the problem. The body would have to have as full members no less than 15 organizations, 16 ministries, five training and research institutes, three professional bodies and four regional remote sensing organizations. To be effective, observers from 17 other organizations would also be required. It has often been argued that GIS are an integrating technology and that, for a GIS to be effective, a considerable degree of organizational and institutional integration is required. This will be a real challenge in India and success will be difficult to achieve.

A third problem of this type is ensuring that a 'top-down' model of GIS reaches the level where the needs are greatest – the village. 'The Nation's planners have already accepted the village panchayats as the basic unit for development activity in the country. It should be our ultimate aim to ensure that the products of Digital Cartography reach this ultimate unit for aid in planning and development' (Arur, Narayan and Gopalan 1989:14). According to Pandey, Dave and Kumar (1989), there is very limited evidence that this is likely to take place and, even if the database derived from 1 : 50 000-scale maps is made available, the scale may be too small to deal with the planning needs at the village level.

C. B. Singh posed some disturbing but important questions at a 1989 seminar where he stated

> 'the modern techniques and the pace of their adoption should be devised so as to suit the specific conditions our country is facing. We cannot afford running in the mad race of

developed countries for modernisation, ignoring our specific constraints and the need-based requirements. It's high time that some introspection is done in this vital field. . . . Indian economy is passing through a very crucial stage of crisis. There are competitions, compulsions, priorities and commitments in a number of fields, which cannot be overlooked. Research and development is a very essential part of national planning and should get due priority, but wider implementation of any technique should be embarked upon only after proven adaptability. The amount of indigenisation achieved has to be made a deciding factor for this purpose.'

(Singh 1989:425).

From this proposition stems a number of direct questions. Is a comprehensive centralized national GIS the best solution to the development challenges facing the Indian nation or is a more decentralized, micro-based 'bottom-up' approach based on systems for planners at the village level such as that suggested by AIT more appropriate? What is the best mix between 'top-down' and 'bottom-up' approaches? Is the importation of 'black box' technological solutions from Europe and North America more effective than the development of indigenous expertise? What level of indigenous expertise is required to gain 'socio-economic command' of this technology?

The Chinese approach

One developing nation which appears to have addressed these questions is China and an examination of the development of GIS in that nation is relevant to the fundamental issues facing all developing countries. The most recent comprehensive description of the progress of GIS in China is given by Chen (1987) and in the *Proceedings of the International Workshop on Geographic Information Systems*, held in Beijing in May 1987 (LREIS 1987).

China established a Laboratory of Resource and Environment Information Systems in February 1985. The Laboratory is a cooperative effort by the Institute of Geography of the Chinese Academy of Sciences and the State Planning Commission; the Government of China provided substantial funds to establish the Laboratory which acts as a focal point for research in GIS for China. Despite this, GIS in China is applications-driven. 'The justification for geographic information systems lies in the socio-economic benefits which they bring. The needs of users are the basic consideration in the design of systems' (Chen 1987:225). A series of regional experiments was, therefore, organized at various scales and for various applications to test the technology and to demonstrate its utility to China.

The county, of which there are over 2300, is considered to be a key administrative unit in China and it is at this scale where microcomputer technology and GIS systems based on the micro are being introduced. The importance of comprehensive information for local level planning has been appreciated and the plan is to have a micro-based GIS in every county to aid in decision making. At present, there are only a few such systems in operation such as that in Daxing county (Li and Sun 1986) and Fushui county (Zhong and Zhong 1987) but their popularity is growing. They utilize hardware and software developed in China. At the urban level, several systems have been developed such as that for Dukou in Sichuan Province based on a 125-metre grid and for Tianjin utilizing a 500-metre grid; other systems are under development. River basin systems have been built for the upper reaches of the Chanjian river, for the Jinshajiang river and for the Hwang Ho where a multi-level information system was almost complete in 1989. The most superficial knowledge of Chinese history indicates that water management and flood monitoring are of critical importance. At the provincial level, a multi-variable GIS is being built for Jiangsu Province (Sun, Wang and Tang 1987) and there are also impressive national-level systems, such as the China Tourism Resource Information System (Yan, Zhou and Shi 1987) and the National Agricultural Information System (Zhang and Kou 1987).

The national strategy is for a balance between local, regional and national applications of GIS; careful thought is being given to techniques and procedures for data normalization and standardization. A unique coding methodology has been devised for county names and a database of the administrative units of the county has been built. This formed the base for the impressive *Population Atlas of China* (Chinese Academy of Sciences 1987) and is being used in the new *Economic Atlas of China* project. Using a grid system based on latitude and longitude, the first stage of a national database has been established. Chen commented that

> on the basis of an analysis of experience in other countries and the lessons that could be learned from them, it was realized that the needs for data sharing to permit national and macro-level decisions could hardly be met with dispersed and unconnected regional systems. On the other hand, a solely national system might be unable to function for many regional tasks because data were over-generalized. A dual system combining both national and regional components in a multi-level structure, with an emphasis on national control but without neglecting regional initiatives, seemed the most appropriate approach to developing a geographical information system for China.
> (Chen 1987:224).

It is also worth noting that GIS in China is being built on three technical foundations: series mapping (which provides the topographic and thematic map base for GIS); the processing of remote sensed imagery where China has an impressive record; and computer-assisted cartography. In all of these technologies China moved early to build its own indigenous capabilities including production of its own hardware including digitizers, plotters, multispectral scanners and synthetic aperture side-scan radar. It also launches its own satellites and has an impressive array of platforms of various types. Chinese specialists were sent overseas for training in the 1970s and indigenous research capabilities have been systematically developed and expanded. The country has the capability to assess and analyse imported hardware and software and to adapt that technology to its own situation. Impressive indigenous software systems such as PURSIS (Zheng, Ren and Cheng Ji-Cheng 1989) have also been developed.

GIS AND THE FUTURE IN DEVELOPING NATIONS: SOME CONCLUSIONS

GIS is still very marginal to the development process even in China where most progress has been made. As a technology, GIS has inherent limitations and cannot in itself solve problems. It has taken 20 years in Europe and North America for the promise of GIS to begin to be realized in applications of some substance and, even now, as Jack Dangermond (one of the pioneers of GIS) has commented 'we're having a hard time introducing even simple GIS technologies into cities; maybe we're just suppressing the capabilities of people and institutions to absorb this technology. But it's also possible that we're trying to introduce the technology into some situations where it doesn't – at least not yet – belong. Given that possibility, we need to be careful that we are not overwhelmed by approaches that have little to offer except the latest technology' (Dangermond 1988:18). The need for such care is nowhere more evident than in developing nations where resources are scarce and poverty, ignorance, disease and environmental degradation are reaching crisis proportions. Can GIS contribute in a meaningful way or are they a technology which is inappropriate to conquering these problems? In Europe and North America, GIS use is expanding at a time where there is a growing need to manage information and in some senses it is a 'post-industrial' technology. It cannot simply be transferred to the developing world and be expected to perform functions for which it was not principally designed.

In developing nations, special attention must be given to the relevance of the products of any GIS to the understanding, analysis and solution of these pressing problems of socio-economic development. If the immediate relevance and utility of GIS are not apparent, it is unlikely that the technology will be adopted. But a question of fundamental importance is who decides what is relevant and useful. If GIS are to be useful and effective, then they must be introduced by indigenous scientists who understand both the technological and the socio-economic context in which the systems are to operate. Ideally, the technology should be 'indigenized' and adapted to the needs and capabilities of the particular situation in which it is to be used. Approaches which depend upon foreign donors, expatriate experts or foreign firms are least likely to succeed. The bulk of existing applications, especially in Africa and Latin America, are of this type. Only in Asia, and especially in China, is there any evidence of an indigenization of GIS technology. The contrast between India and China is quite marked in this respect. The approach used by China contains elements of a model which could be adapted by other developing countries. It might also be reasonable for countries too small to develop their own indigenous expertise to look to countries such as China as a source of technological transfer in the GIS field, rather than to the United States, Europe or Canada. China's pragmatic raster-based systems, utilizing remotely sensed data with databases of a manageable size may be more useful than 'Cadillac vector-based systems' designed for North American or European realities (but see also Kubo 1991 in this volume).

Appropriate technology is perhaps best defined as that most appropriate to the task at hand. In some instances, this will be the highest and most modern technology available: in others, more simple solutions will be appropriate. As the applications described in this chapter illustrate, 'appropriateness' comprises a number of issues including: cost in relation to foreign exchange; dependence on technology and sources of data controlled from the outside; the replacement of labour by capital in situations of high unemployment; and variables such as prestige and face which vary from society to society. A judicious mix of new and existing techniques is required. GIS technologies are not necessarily labour-replacing. China's National Agricultural Information System, for example, employed over 400 000 people in data collection between 1979 and 1986 (Zhang and Kou 1987). China has also used labour-intensive techniques to field-check the accuracy of remote sensing imagery. If data collection costs are a major part of GIS, then developing nations might consider using their large supply of human resources for this task. It might have the additional advantage of involving people in the solution of their own problems and the collection of data of a quality and nature not available from other sources.

The choices made should not be technology-driven. The technology is not the issue: it is the use made of that technology which is of overwhelming importance in developing nations. India has adopted some of the most sophisticated GIS hardware and software available but institutional and organizational barriers exist to the effective utilization of that technology. Although it is true that the development of microcomputer technology at ever-decreasing costs has had a positive impact on the availability for GIS in developing nations, it is quite possible that micro-based systems can be just as inappropriate as their mainframe or mini-based predecessors.

GIS cannot be seen in isolation from the development policies and approaches of governments, especially as these relate to technology. As Stefanovic et al. (1989:451) have commented '..the political environment within which a GIS is to be established has considerable bearing on whether or not the "top-down" or "bottom-up" approach is adopted'. In some instances, a decentralized approach to GIS will be the most effective solution, especially for rural development planning where a micro-based system in the hands of the individuals directly involved makes a great deal of sense. In others, such as the need for environmental monitoring and protection or flood and irrigation control over vast areas, then a 'top-down' national approach is required. It is clear that in developing countries a mixture of both approaches is appropriate, depending upon the particular situation. It is also apparent that there is value in ensuring that coordination and data sharing can take place in a meaningful way in both directions. Again, the Chinese model is a good example and the Indian model an example of the problems which a lack of coordination can bring. Unfortunately, in the developing world, the latter case is more common than the former.

Finally, it must be recognized that not all governments have the welfare of the poorest segments of their society and the development of the nation as their only priority in introducing GIS. Information is power and management of that information can be of importance to national security and control. As Guevera has commented in the Latin American context

> it has been said that information is knowledge and knowledge is power; but knowledge is not beneficial if the power it generates does not enrich a nation as a whole... Let's look into geoinformation for development.... There are few successful GIS installations in Latin America. There are many new ones. It is my belief that GIS technology represents a viable way to help our Latin American nations regain their economic and social strength. A GIS technical conscience has to be created so ideas like the Agro-Land Reforms can become a reality.
>
> (Guevera 1989:16).

The optimistic view of GIS technology is that it has the potential to be of utility in the development process. But, as yet, that potential remains to be fully demonstrated. This demonstration must come from the scientists and decision makers of developing nations themselves it if is to be meaningful in the development process.

REFERENCES

Adedeji A (1989) *The African Alternate Framework to Structural Adjustment.* Public Lecture, University of Ottawa, Canada, 23 October 1989

Amin S (1973) *Neo-Colonialism in West Africa.* Penguin Books, London

Arur M G, Narayan L R A, Gopalan N (1989) Challenges of the 90's for Digital Cartography in India. *IX INCA International Seminar on Digital Cartography and Potential Users.* Pre-session Proceedings. Survey of India, Dehra Dun, pp. 7–14

Bryden R (1989) GIS: an industry perspective. *Workshop on Strategic Directions for Canada's Surveying, Mapping, Remote Sensing and GIS Activities.* November 1989. Ottawa

Chadha S M (1989) Presidential Address. *IX INCA International Seminar on Digital Cartography and Potential Users.* Pre-Session Proceedings. Survey of India, Dehra Dun, p. 7

Chappuis A, Golbéry L (1984) Un atlas regional, outil d'aide a la décision en Inde. *Paper read to the 12th International Cartographic Conference, Perth, Australia*

Chen S (1987) Geographical data handling and GIS in China. *International Journal of Geographical Information Systems* **1** (3): 219–28

Chinese Academy of Sciences, Institute of Geography (1987) *Population Atlas of China.* Oxford University Press, Oxford

Clark D M, Hastings D A, Kineman J J (1991) Global databases and their implications for GIS. In: Maguire D J, Goodchild M F, Rhind D W (eds.) *Geographical Information Systems: principles and applications.* Longman, London, pp. 217–31, Vol 2

Coppock J T, Rhind D W (1991) The history of GIS. In: Maguire D J, Goodchild M F, Rhind D W (eds.) *Geographical Information Systems: principles and applications.* Longman, London, pp. 21–43, Vol 1

Dangermond J (1988) A review of digital data commonly available and some of the practical problems of entering them into a GIS. *Paper read to the International Geographical Union Conference, Sydney, Australia*: 18

Densham P J (1991) Spatial decision support systems. In:

Maguire D J, Goodchild M F, Rhind D W (eds.) *Geographical Information Systems: principles and applications.* Longman, London, pp. 403–12, Vol 1

Dias H D (1987) Varying information needs for local and regional planning and their implications for planning. *Regional Development Dialogue* **8** (1): 24–8

Dias H D (1989) Initiatives in GIS applications at the Asian Institute of Technology. *Paper given to the International Conference on Geographical Information Systems: approaches for urban and regional planning.* Ciloto, Puncak, Indonesia

Dobson M (1988) Digital cartography in the world of commercial publishing. *Proceedings of the 3rd International Symposium on Spatial Data Handling.* International Geographical Union, Columbus, Ohio, pp. 1–8

Edralin J (1990) Conference Report. *International Conference on Geographical Information Systems: Application for Urban Regional Planning.* Nagoya, UNCRD

Fanon F (1963) *The Wretched of the Earth.* New York, Grove Press

Goodchild M F (1991) The technological setting of GIS. In: Maguire D J, Goodchild M F, Rhind D W (eds.) *Geographical Information Systems: principles and applications.* Longman, London, pp. 45–54, Vol 1

Goodchild M F, Wang, Min-Hua (1988) Modeling error in raster based spatial data. *Proceedings of the 3rd International Symposium on Spatial Data Handling.* International Geographical Union, Columbus, Ohio, pp. 97–106

Guevera J A (1989) Latin America: geo-information for development. *ARC News* **11** (3): 16

Gulati A K (1989) Digital cartography or GIS for resource management and mapping. IX *INCA International Seminar on Digital Cartography and Potential Users.* Pre-Session Proceedings. Survey of India, Dehra Dun, pp. 128–37

Harper E A, Manheim M L (1989) Geographic information systems in transportation planning. *Paper given to the International Conference on Geographical Information Systems: approaches for urban and regional planning.* Ciloto, Puncak, Indonesia

Hart J (1988) Keynote Address. *Proceedings of The International Symposium on the Challenge of Rural Poverty: How to Meet It.* Feldafing, FRG, FAO and DSE, pp. 21–4

Jerie H C, Kure J, Larsen H K (1980) A system approach to Geo-Information Systems. *ITC Journal* 4, International Institute for Aerospace Survey and Earth Science, Enschedé

Krishnayya J G (1986) *C MAPS (Core System) Specifications.* Research and Systems Institute, Pune, India

Kubo S (1991) The development of GIS in Japan. In:

Maguire D J, Goodchild M F, Rhind D W (eds.) *Geographical Information Systems: principles and applications*. Longman, London, pp. 47–56, Vol 2

Kumar R S (1989) A case for Survey-Net. *IX INCA International Seminar on Digital Cartography and Potential Users*. Pre-Session Proceedings. Survey of India, Dehra Dun, pp. 182

Li, X Z, Sun Y (1986) The research of agricultural information systems at a county level. *Resource and Environment System No 1*. LREIS, Beijing

LREIS (1987) *Proceedings of International Workshop on Geographic Information System, Beijing '87*. Laboratory of Resource and Environmental Information Systems, Academica Sinica, Beijing

Misra P (1989) Survey of India identification of user needs. *IX INCA International Seminar on Digital Cartography and Potential Users*. Pre-session Proceedings. Survey of India, Dehra Dun, pp. 223–35

Nag P (1987) A proposed base for a Geographical Information System for India. *International Journal of Geographical Information Systems* **1** (2): 181–7

Naithani K K (1989) The SOI PC/AUTOCAD Photogrammetric Monoplotter System: a tool for rural-urban mapping. *IX INCA International Seminar on Digital Cartography and Potential Users*. Pre-session Proceedings. Survey of India, Dehra Dun, pp. 239–46

Needham J (1959) *Science and Civilization in China*, Volume 3. Cambridge University Press, Cambridge

Needham J (1981) *The Shorter Science and Civilization in China* (Abridged C A Ronan), Volume 2. Cambridge University Press, Cambridge

Nijkamp P, De Jong W (1987) Training needs in information systems for local and regional development and planning. *Regional Development Dialogue* **8** (1): 72–119

OECD (1988) *Activities of the OECD, Report of the Secretary General*. OECD Publications, Paris

Pandey M K, Dave V S, Kumar S (1989) Relevance of application of digital cartography for development planning process in India. *IX INCA International Seminar on Digital Cartography and Potential Users*. Pre-session Proceedings. Survey of India, Dehra Dun, pp. 304–19

Parthasaradhi, E U R, Krishnanunni K (1989) Specifications of a digital topographic base for GIS applications: some experiences from project Vasundharsa. *IX INCA International Seminar on Digital Cartography and Potential Users*. Pre-session Proceedings. Survey of India, Dehra Dun, pp. 320–8

Rada J (1982) The microelectronics revolution: implications for the Third World. *Development Dialogue* **2**: 41–67

Ramachandran A (1990) The global strategy for shelter: a new challenge for surveys. *Keynote address to the XIX Congress of the International Federation of Surveyors*, Helsinki

Rao M K, Pathan S K, Matieda I Cm, Majumder K L, Yogarajan N, Padmavathy A S (1989) Development of a Geographic Information System around ISROVISION. *IX INCA International Seminar on Digital Cartography and Potential Users*. Pre-session Proceedings. Survey of India, Dehra Dun, pp. 502–3

Rodney W (1974) *How Europe Underdeveloped Africa*. Howard University Press, Washington

RRDN (1986) *Rural Regional Development Newsletter*. AIT, Bangkok

Saxena M (1989) Satellite remote sensing for thematic maps. *IX INCA International Seminar on Digital Cartography and Potential Users*. Pre-session Proceedings. Survey of India, Dehra Dun, pp. 400–5

Shepherd I D H (1991) Information integration and GIS. In: Maguire D J, Goodchild M F, Rhind D W (eds.) *Geographical Information Systems: principles and applications*. Longman, London, pp. 337–60, Vol 1

Singh C B (1989) Indian perspective for automatic cartography – a poser. *IX INCA International Seminar on Digital Cartography and Potential Users*. Pre-session Proceedings. Survey of India, Dehra Dun, pp. 424–6

Stefanovic P, Drummond J, Muller J C (1989) ITC's response to the need for training in CAC and GIS. *IX INCA International Seminar on Digital Cartography and Potential Users*. Pre-session Proceedings. Survey of India, Dehra Dun, pp. 450–60

Sun Y, Wang R, Tang Q (1987) Automated cartographic system for population maps. *Proceedings of International Workshop on Geographic Information System, Beijing '87*. LREIS, Beijing, pp. 402–13

Sundaram K V (1987) Integrated approach to training for the establishment and use of information systems for subnational development planning. *Regional Development Dialogue* **8** (1): 54–70

Tomlinson R (1989a) Recent trends in GIS technology. *Workshop on Strategic Directions for Canada's Surveying, Mapping, Remote Sensing and GIS Activities*, November 1989, Ottawa

Tomlinson R (1989b) Canadian GIS experience. *CISM Journal* **43** (3): 227–32

UNICEF (1988) *The State of the World's Children*. UNICEF Publications, New York

World Commission on Environment and Development (1987) *Our Common Future*. Oxford University Press, Oxford

Yan S, Zhou M, Shi Z (1987) Chinese Tourism Resource Information System. *Proceedings of International Workshop on Geographic Information System Beijing '87*. LREIS, Beijing, pp. 377–83

Yapa L S (1988) Computer-aided regional planning: a study in rural Sri Lanka. *Environment and Planning B* **15**: 285–304

Yapa L S (1989) Peasants, planners and microcomputers

in the Third World. *Earth and Mineral Sciences* **58** (2): 31–3

Zhang Q, Kou Y (1987) A study on the information system for agricultural resources and economy. *Proceedings of International Workshop on Geographic Information System Beijing '87*. LREIS, Beijing, pp. 90–4

Zheng W, Ren F, Cheng Ji-Cheng (1989) Building of micro-GIS tool and its application. *Proceedings of International Conference in Urban Planning and Urban Management*. University of Hong Kong, Hong Kong, pp. 299–314

Zhong S, Zhong E (1987) A preliminary research on Land Resources Information System (LRIS) at Fushui County. *Proceedings of International Workshop on Geographic Information System Beijing '87*. LREIS, Beijing, 433–7

41

LAND INFORMATION SYSTEMS

P F DALE

This chapter takes the view that land information is central to most human activities and that Land Information Systems – defined as GIS technology plus institutional arrangements – are essential to handle the numerous tasks involved. After a brief historical review of land record systems and their objectives, the cost/benefit aspects and data quality implications of use of LIS are examined. This is followed by a review of the different characteristics of land parcel-based systems and the roles that they fulfil. The chapter then discusses the institutional and organizational aspects of LIS and concludes with a review of the management aspects, including the stages involved in procurement and implementation of such a system.

THE ORIGINS OF LAND INFORMATION SYSTEMS

'Land is the source of all material wealth. From it we get everything that we use or value, whether it be food, clothing, fuel, shelter, metal, or precious stones. We live on the land and from the land, and to the land our bodies or ashes are committed when we die. The availability of land is the key to human existence, and its distribution and use are of vital importance. Land records, therefore, are of great concern to all governments. The forming of land policy, and its execution, may in large measure depend on the effectiveness of "land registration", as we conveniently call the making and keeping of these records.' The same author (Simpson 1976) went on to add: '. . . land registration is only a means to an end. It is not an end in itself. Much time, money, and effort can be wasted if that elementary truth be forgotten.' In general, then, land registration may be seen as one facet – but a vital one – of the general problem of managing land information.

The origins of land record management and hence of Land Information Systems go back to antiquity. Units of measurement of land date from earlier than 4000 BC in Egypt while one of the earliest dimensioned plans comes from Babylonia, dating from the third dynasty of Ur, in the reign of Ibi-Sin. This shows a group of land parcels, that is areas of land representing all or part of an individual's estate (Fig. 41.1). Records dating back to before 1000 BC show that the land measurers were recording the land, the owner's name, the area of each property, its location and the tax due. In Egypt, from very early times, duplicate registers were kept in the Treasury and the Royal Granary. The recognition of the need for back-up copies of files, therefore, dates back 3000 years (Lyons 1931).

The Romans were well known for their prowess in surveying. Indeed, some authorities claim that the origin of the word 'cadastre' and the associated activity of cadastral surveying goes back to the Latin *capitastrum*, describing a register of units of territorial taxation (Dowson and Sheppard 1952). A cadastre is an information system that uses the land parcel as the basic spatial unit. Although a nation-wide land data system was established in Denmark in 1660 (Trollegaard 1985), the modern use of the term 'cadastre' is generally thought to date from the eighteenth century in Austria. The term, however, became better known when Napoleon introduced a cadastral system throughout France and then to much of his empire to expedite revenue collection. While its origins lie in tax collection, the principles underlying the cadastre have been adopted around the world and the terms 'legal cadastre' or 'juridical cadastre' are sometimes

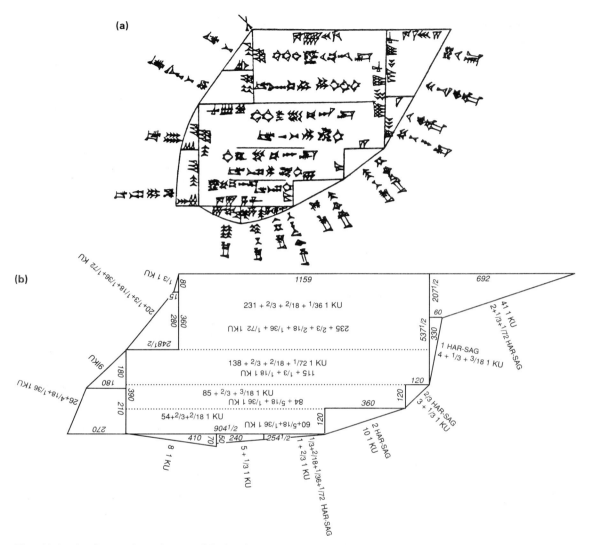

Fig. 41.1 Ancient cadastral maps: (a) plan in dimensionless units drawn on a clay tablet of size 12.7 × 10.8 cm; (b) the same plan as plotted to scale.

used to describe the compilation of land ownership records. Cadastral surveys, maps and plans now refer not only to the measurement and recording of land for fiscal purposes, but also to the registration of title to land where no tax collection may be involved.

In the 1950s, the term 'multipurpose cadastre' began to be applied to a broader range of land-related information, including the recording of underground services and utilities. By the 1970s, the terms 'Land Information System' and 'multipurpose cadastre' were being used synonymously by some commentators, for instance in the United States. Since then, the distinction has been made that a multipurpose cadastre relates specifically to records based on the proprietary land parcel and is a subset of the wider meaning of LIS (which may not necessarily be land parcel-based). Table 41.1 shows a list of data types that may appear in a multipurpose cadastral record. LIS, however, may also contain records of natural features such as soils, or of man-made constructions such as pipelines or overhead cables (Dale and McLaughlin 1988). LIS then is an approach to managing data not only at the local level (Leick 1982), but also at state and federal levels (NRC 1980, 1983).

THE EMERGENCE OF THE COMPUTERIZED LIS

The 1960s saw the first developments in digital mapping (see Coppock and Rhind 1991 in this volume). In 1971, during the XIII Congress of the Fédération Internationale de Géomètres (FIG), a study group was set up to engage in the problematic nature of Land Information Systems (Eichhorn 1981). In 1978, some 50 papers were presented at the FIG International Symposium on Land Information Systems at the Technical University of Darmstadt. These papers covered such topics as data acquisition and data processing, through the reorganization of rural areas and urban land development, to the management of environmental resources in both developed and developing countries. The term 'Geographical Information System' was not used at that meeting.

In 1981, a special Commission of the FIG was established to handle the whole question of LIS. It adopted the following definition:

> A Land Information System is a tool for legal, administrative and economic decision-making, and an aid for planning and development which consists, on the one hand, of a database containing spatially referenced land-related data for a defined area and, on the other hand, of procedures and techniques for the systematic collection, updating, processing, and distribution of the data. The base of a Land Information System is a uniform spatial referencing system for the data in the system which also facilitates the linking of data within the system with other land-related data.

In this definition, land is seen to include all land covered by water so that hydrographic data were included. The definition was inevitably a compromise between the terminology used in different countries and the semantics of different languages. It has been criticized on a number of counts – for example that the term 'tool' is restrictive and that a LIS should be seen more as a

Table 41.1 Examples of data in a multipurpose cadastre.

1. Parcel definition – description and identifying reference; associated maps
2. Land tenure data – type and term of tenure, rights and restrictions including encumbrances and charges; caveats and court orders; details of owners
3. Land value data – rental and assessment value; rents due or received; property rates or tax assessment due or received; stamp duty on transfer
4. Land use – rural or urban classification of use; soils, geological and geophysical data; hydrological data; vegetation, wildlife and conservation data; land use zoning, including pollution controls; site restrictions
5. Buildings and other construction data – floor space or leasable area; number of rooms; building height and number of stories; architectural style; type of construction materials; age of buildings
6. Infrastructure – water, sewerage, gas, electricity, telephone billings
7. Population and census data – number and age of inhabitants; socio-economic classification; employment data
8. Administration – health, safety and emergency services data; local authority management data.

'resource' (Hamilton and Williamson 1984). One of its strengths, however, lies in the final sentence where it anticipates networking and the linking of varied data sets.

In more recent times, LIS have been defined as combinations of human and technical resources, together with a set of organizing procedures, which result in the collection, storage, retrieval, dissemination and use of land information in a systematic manner. In such a concept, the form of any LIS is closely concerned with the uses to which the spatial data are put; thus the environment within which decision making takes place becomes an integral part of the system. Where there is a failure to address institutional and organizational arrangements, there tends to be a failure to solve the problems that LIS address.

Some of those who have adopted this broad-based view have tended to regard GIS as the technological component of Land Information Systems, comprising the hardware and software (DOI 1989). The Chorley Report (DoE 1987) defined a GIS as a series of technical operations and noted that a GIS is normally considered to involve computer technology. LIS extend beyond the technology and are not necessarily involved with computers although, because of the volumes of data that must be handled, computerization has tended to become an integral component. In this chapter, a distinction will, therefore, be made between LIS – which is seen as a system embracing institutional arrangements and the form and use of the appropriate technology – and GIS – which is seen as a set of hardware and software tools. This view is not shared by all. Maguire (1991 in this volume), for example, argues that a GIS is an integrated collection of computer hardware, software, data and liveware which operate in an institutional (i.e. organizational) context. Maguire (1991 in this volume) and others prefer to see LIS as a special, application-specific, case of the generic type GIS. The difference between the present author and Maguire is merely one of terminology.

Computerized LIS became linked to GIS through a 'bottom-up' approach. At that time, those concerned with land information management faced two different technical issues which were being independently addressed, namely the management of alphanumeric data and – quite separately – the handling of graphical data. The manipulation of alphanumeric data, such as lists of property owners and their rights in land, was essentially a one-dimensional problem in which the data could normally be handled sequentially. The handling of graphical data – such as the plans showing the extent and location of adjoining properties – involved work in two dimensions. The management of truly three-dimensional data (as distinct from data held in different layers) was, even by the end of the 1980s, still of low priority in LIS though it was becoming important in parts of GIS (Raper and Kelk 1991 in this volume).

In the early days of computerized LIS, the main problems related to the need to handle large volumes of alphanumeric data and to digitize large numbers of maps to which the textual data could be linked. The overall objective was, and in general remains, to improve land record management. Even by 1990, however, there were few LIS that held sufficient volumes of data for their effective use as an information (rather than as a data management) system. Only a few small local systems had reached that critical mass where it had become possible to use the data effectively to monitor changes or to model trends. This is not surprising since the volumes of paper-based data in common use in the 1970s and 1980s were large in the context of what it was possible to encode and handle by machine at that time. In the United Kingdom by 1989, for instance, Her Majesty's Land Registry held over 12 million registered titles, each accompanied by text and a map extract. There were over 6.4 million searches made of the register during that year (HMLR 1990). In the same year (Crawley and Nitze 1989; Mahoney 1991 in this volume), the UK Electricity Boards were dealing with 22 million homes and businesses, 100 million connections, 1.65 million kilometres of underground mains and 300 000 kilometres of overhead lines. Some 19 000 kilometres of new or replacement mains were being installed annually and 1.7 million new or replacement services were being provided. Over 2 million holes were being dug in the roads by utilities each year. Under PUSWA (the Public Utilities Street Works Act – see Mahoney 1991 in this volume), over 100 000 pieces of paper were generated daily for circulation to interested parties. Only computerization can be seen as offering hope for the proper management of such records.

LIS COSTS AND BENEFITS

Those responsible for the management of land information must inevitably acquire, store, analyse, retrieve and disseminate large volumes of data; they must also keep them up to date and as complete as possible. Failure to keep the records accurate and up to date has tangible economic and social consequences. There is an unrecoverable cost to digging a hole in the road at the bottom of which there is nothing of interest. Life itself may be at stake if the ownership of land is uncertain since disputes over land are a common cause of social tension – many wars, for example, are fought over the possession and control of territory. Dealing in land is a complex, expensive and emotive issue since the 'territorial imperative' (Ardrey 1966) affects most cultures and peoples.

Many land acquisition and development

programmes have been seriously delayed and additional costs have been incurred through the inadequacies of mapping and of the associated land records. Estimates suggest that up to 40 per cent of urban development programmes in Less Developed Countries (LDCs) and in excess of 50 per cent for low cost housing and shelter programmes have run into difficulties because of a lack of adequate reliable land records. The reasons for this stem from a combination of political, institutional and technical issues (Holstein 1988). Many of the records and maps that exist, especially in the LDCs, are out of date and hence can give rise to unnecessary additional expense when used as the basis for planning and implementing land development programmes. The digitization of already inaccurate and out-of-date records and maps, and the creation of incorrect data sets manifestly cannot help to solve the problems of urban management. Likewise, land information that is initially correct but is not kept up to date can give rise to long-term costs since development programmes can in consequence be delayed.

One function of LIS is to improve efficiency and thereby make financial savings through the prevention of waste. The cost of implementing LIS can often be offset by savings that come from reducing the level of land disputes or by increasing the rate of land tax collection. Additional benefits of LIS can come from the income generated by providing client communities with spatial information, for instance through the publication and marketing of maps. Unfortunately, most societies have yet to recognize the true cost of spatial data since maps and surveys have tended to be provided at subsidized rates – for instance by national mapping agencies or by petroleum companies who may even provide maps for free. The market for LIS goods and services has therefore been distorted, making cost recovery for LIS more difficult.

An example of the benefits of LIS comes from South Australia where the operation of the Land Ownership and Tenure System (LOTS) has generated revenue that is around 300 per cent of its running costs (Sedunary 1988). The basic component of LOTS is the Title System that consists of a title file, plan or allotment index and ownership files for all the 800 000 land parcels in the state. On a daily basis, the system automatically generates details of transactions which are then passed to the Valuation System (there are approximately 600 000 rateable properties) and on to the Sales History System, Land Tax and Engineering and Water Supply Revenue Systems. When established in 1979, LOTS handled 7000 enquiries in the first year; in 1988 it was handling up to 14 000 on-line enquiries per day. Although the number of access points is limited by the number of terminals that are connected into the system (some 700 in nearly 200 different sites), members of the public are entitled to gain access to enquire about any specific piece of land.

Within the United Kingdom – where, due in part to the lack of a cadastre, the distinction between a GIS and a LIS has been blurred – some of the major potential benefits of LIS and the application of GIS technology are in managing resources in local government. Detailed studies on the use of land information within a local authority (or government) were undertaken by the Local Authorities' Management Services and Computer Committee (LAMSAC 1989). Many uses of the data have been found and potential beneficiaries listed (Buxton 1989; Bromley and Coulson 1989). Estimates have suggested that approximately 80 per cent of the data held within a local authority can be related to some spatial component such as the postal address or property identifier. Some of the potential benefits to a local authority from use of a LIS are shown in Table 41.2.

DATA QUALITY

LIS must be capable of handling data with a high and demonstrable degree of reliability, hence the technical operations must be subject to quality control. Such systems frequently deal with discrete items of data, each with its own required level of accuracy. Error in any one item of the data may cause financial hardship or involve matters of the law. Unfortunately, the quality of data is not easy to define and hence to monitor (e.g. see Chrisman 1991 in this volume). Some attributes of spatial data, such as their accuracy and precision, their completeness and currency, their unit costs, their security from interference and the speed with which they can be handled can, to an extent at least, be quantified. Other qualities of the data, such as their clarity and their suitability to the purposes of the

Table 41.2 LIS applications giving rise to benefits for UK local authorities (= local governments) as reported by LAMSAC (1989).

Archaeological site recording and monitoring

Building asset management
Building permit control

Central government reporting
Communication through maps and graphics
Competitive tendering
Compulsory purchase orders
Customer billing

Demographic analysis
Development control

Emergency planning
Emergency services management
Environmental control and enforcement
Environmental impact assessment

Financial control
Fire services management
Footpath maintenance

Health and safety control
Highway maintenance

Land-based taxes
Land ownership records
Land searches for local land charges
Land use management
Linkage of multiple data sets

Minerals management
Monitoring contracts
Monitoring energy use
Monitoring of the land market

Physical planning
Police management and crime pattern analysis
Pollution control
Population forecasting
Pupil data for school resource planning

Resource optimization in general
Road traffic orders
Route planning (e.g. refuse (trash) collection)

Site finding
Social services optimization and management
Street light maintenance

Targeting mail shots
Traffic accident analysis
Traffic modelling to predict traffic flows
Transport planning in general
Tree preservation orders

Utilities (water, sewers, gas, electricity and telephones)

Valuation and property assessment

user, are less definable but are equally important. The land information manager must be concerned with all these qualities of data, especially where the information within the system is being treated as a corporate resource and shared within one or more organizations.

Data may be held in alphanumeric or graphical form, the graphical elements being associated with at least one attribute of the data. The quality of graphical data is directly related to the cost and effectiveness of their survey and transformation into digital form. Under pressure to digitize existing (particularly large-scale) mapping as quickly as possible, many organizations have been tempted to sacrifice quality for quantity. The speedy, accurate and comprehensive conversion of all types of data into digital form is the major unsolved problem in LIS (see Jackson and Woodsford 1991 in this volume). Much time and expense is involved in such data conversion, especially in digitizing maps, and often accounts for over 80 per cent of the up-front cost in setting up a system. Given the normal pressures to make a system operational and revenue-generating, so-called 'quick and dirty' solutions to the data conversion problem have considerable appeal but failure, for instance, to maintain geometrical standards in digitizing leads to difficulties later on when data sets are compared or overlaid.

The quality of the attributes of data is more difficult to define than is their position in space. Ambiguities in the definition of each item may create difficulties for a decision maker in the interpretation of the data. There may be significant differences, for instance, when using a term such as 'square metres of floor space', between the area that is available for use and could (by way of example) be covered by a carpet, and the total horizontal area, including walls and pillars. Similarly, the land parcel used for legal conveyance may differ in extent from that used for taxation purposes – legally, for example, a property may extend to the centre of a road while, for tax purposes, it may be bounded by the road edge. Depending on the context in which the user of the data operates, different interpretations may be required.

From a legal perspective, land includes 'all appurtenances attached thereto'. Thus it includes the buildings that stand upon the land and the soils and minerals beneath it (although the rights to minerals and hydrocarbons and even fishing may be excluded from the specific land owner's title and be retained by the original owner, typically the nation itself). The boundaries to each property may be more or less precisely defined while the accuracy of the coordinates of the boundary lines as held in database registers may or may not have legal significance. Thus, in England and Wales, there is a 'general boundaries' rule that treats the lines recorded on maps and plans as indicating only the approximate position of the legal boundary (Fig. 41.2(a)). In many countries, however, the survey record purports to show and guarantee the precise location of the boundary and hence the survey content of the parcel record is of much greater importance (Figure 41.2(b)).

From an economic perspective, the value of land is more difficult to define. The market price may change depending on such externalities as interest rates and social perceptions. The value of the property for insurance purposes may be significantly different from the market price since the former value is based on construction costs. The value of the land for tax assessment, on the other hand, may be derived from considerations such as land use and its potential for income generation. The land information manager, when communicating with the decision maker, must anticipate such variations in the meaning of land value and the purposes for which land value data are to be used. Clearly, then, the quality of the information that is derived from raw data is not just a technical matter.

LAND PARCEL-BASED SYSTEMS

The basic spatial unit in many LIS is the land parcel. Once each land parcel has been defined upon the ground – and this is no easy task where land disputes are rife – it must be surveyed and mapped (Dale 1976). The costs of survey are often high relative to local land values and, in extreme cases (typically in some developing countries), the cost of producing a cadastral plan for an individual land parcel may exceed the value of the ground that it represents. The overall cost is compounded by delays resulting from the surveying and mapping process. In many countries, the time required to complete the registration or transfer of title to land may extend to months or even years because of a lack of resources or inadequate management.

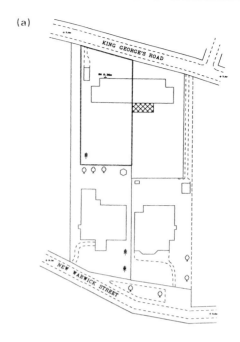

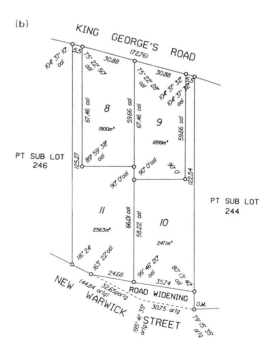

Fig. 41.2(a) and **(b)** Examples of a cadastral plan showing legal and surveyed boundaries.

Because of deficiencies in the administration of land, development often takes place outside the formal government sector. In some cities in less developed countries, as much as 75 per cent of development may take place in the informal sector – without planning control and with no adequate sanitation or the provision of suitable access to the land. The rate of urban expansion can be between 4 and 6 per cent per annum which means that many cities will double in size within the next 10 to 15 years (Harris 1989). Under such circumstances, the land information needed to guide urban infrastructure development must be updated rapidly and continuously if the development is to be controlled. How to do this with the minimal resources that are normally available in Less Developed Countries (LDCs) is a problem that has not yet been solved (see Taylor 1991 in this volume).

One of the most important applications for LIS is in land titling, the process of granting certificates of title to land owners. Some of the benefits of more secure land titles are listed in Table 41.3 (Dale and McLaughlin 1988). Thailand provides a good example of a major initiative to establish a national land titling programme (Angus Leppan 1989). The initial phase of such a project is to produce base maps, usually from aerial photography. These maps are used in adjudication, a legal process of determining land rights on the ground. The details of the property boundaries are recorded on the base maps and details of the tenure noted. This provides the basic spatial and alphanumeric framework for a LIS. More sophisticated systems, such as that operated by the Swedish Central Board for Real Estate (Andersson 1987; Ottoson and Rystedt 1991 in this volume), record more detail about the property, but may have less graphical information; others, such as the cadastral-based systems in Australia, contain precise spatial data and digitized cadastral maps (O'Callaghan and Garner 1991 in this volume).

In order to fund local development, many countries raise revenue through land taxation. Land, in particular the land parcel, is a basis of wealth and, therefore, a suitable resource for governments to tax. It has the added advantage that it is immovable so that tax evasion can be minimized. In principle, therefore, the cadastre provides a simple and effective way to manage tax collection and its use as such is being promoted in a number of countries.

Table 41.3 Benefits of a land registration system (from Dale and McLaughlin 1988).

- Certainty of ownership
- Security of tenure
- Reduction in land disputes
- Improved conveyancing
- Stimulation of the land market
- Security for credit
- Monitoring of the land market
- Facilitating land reform
- Management of State lands
- Greater efficiency in land taxation
- Improvements in physical planning
- Support for land resource management

Land tax assessment may be based on the productive capacity of the land or upon the value of the improvements, such as the buildings that have been erected upon it. Estimates of the yield from agricultural land, as was the custom in India, or the potential rental value of urban properties, as was previously the basis for domestic rating in the United Kingdom, may also be used. LIS facilitate the monitoring of prices by allowing easier comparison between different locations and different quality of land use. They structure the data and can be used to ensure that no property is omitted in the tax gathering – in a small pilot study in Indonesia, for example, 50 per cent more revenue was collected following the introduction of a LIS.

In many developed countries, the public utilities have been the driving force behind improved record management and the speedy digitization of large-scale maps and plans. The tangible benefits to the utilities of what has become known as Automated Mapping and Facilities Management (AM/FM) are high since the volumes of data that they handle are large. Benefits include better management of the physical infrastructure, better billing arrangements and closer liaison with the local government in designing new service networks conforming with planning data (Yarrow 1989; Mahoney 1991 in this volume).

A new application of LIS is the management of

complex buildings and areas such as shopping precincts. The traditional approach to LIS has been at the macro-level – either across the whole country or at least within a whole urban area, such as a city or large town. LIS applied to small areas, such as to individual complex buildings or to relatively self-contained shopping precincts, have however begun to emerge. Similarly, the management of property portfolios with a small number of spatially dispersed properties has provided opportunities for the land information manager. The data handling problems are much the same as in more extensive systems since an individual room has its own form of land use, and its own utilities such as water and electricity; each room may have its own rental value and will be subject to its own maintenance cycle. Thus, in comparison with national or urban systems, the problems may differ in scale but they differ very little in matters of principle.

It is, however, at the national level that the most significant developments have taken place. In Sweden (Andersson 1989; Ottoson and Rystedt 1991 in this volume) and in Australia (Sedunary 1988; O'Callaghan and Garner 1991 in this volume), on-line access to land registry records already exists. In England and Wales, there is already pressure to introduce on-line access to the local land charges registers. This pressure is likely to increase when Her Majesty's Land Registry (HMLR) provides more public access to land title data. Until the end of 1990, the records held by HMLR were officially secret and could not be divulged without the permission of the land owner – unlike, for example, the Registers of Scotland which have been open to public access. On-line access to the records held by HMLR is now expected by the year 1998; when implemented, it should bring significant changes to the handling of spatial information in the United Kingdom. Although technical problems and delays in the conversion of data into computer-readable form will continue, it seems likely that the main problems stemming from this and equivalent developments elsewhere will be institutional and organizational.

INSTITUTIONAL AND ORGANIZATIONAL ISSUES

The key to the success of LIS lies in the ability of the users to treat information as a corporate resource. At present, for instance in government-controlled LIS, data are usually compiled and held by different government ministries and departments. Data records are often duplicated and cooperation between governmental bodies is often very limited. Notionally at least, once the definition of the land parcel has been agreed, much land information can be compiled on a unified basis since – for administrative purposes – the land parcel is the spatial unit of human activity. Unfortunately, even within a single organization, there may be no agreement about a unique parcel referencing number. Each sub-department may use its own system – for instance a sequential number, a reference to the volume and folio on which the records are kept, a street reference, a geographical coordinate, and so forth. Within the United Kingdom, this has led one commercial company to produce files and software that link the postal address, the post code and the National Grid coordinates of each land parcel (Singh 1989).

That linkages such as this have been left to the private sector to develop is unusual. Much of the work in LIS has been controlled by central or local government agencies or is in the hands of quasi-governmental bodies, such as the public utilities and the Land Registry. Small private companies have had to operate either in consultancy or in the management of small LIS, such as those for complex buildings. The only other role for the private sector until recently has been in data gathering, for instance by licensed surveyors undertaking cadastral work, or by sub-contracting work such as digitizing maps for the national mapping agencies or for the utilities. Even where there are licensed cadastral surveyors, government may still be the guarantor of the work, taking responsibility for its overall reliability (Dale 1976).

Recently, however, there have been signs that some governments are willing to contract much more work out to the private sector. The land titling programme in St Lucia in the 1980s, for instance, was undertaken by private contractors. In the late 1980s in the United Kingdom, much privatization of government and quasi-government services took place while some organizations (such as the Ordnance Survey, the Hydrographic Department of the Admiralty and even Her Majesty's Land Registry) were made 'executive agencies' whereby they would be less constrained by central government restrictions and regulations. In 1989 in

New South Wales, Australia, tenders to bid to 'develop and operate a public enquiry service for land information' were opened to the private sector. The State Land Information Council had reached the point at which it was giving consideration to the provision of a state-wide on-line computerized enquiry system for the marketing to the general public of land information integrated from many government agencies. An advertisement by the New South Wales Government, working under the motto 'Putting people first by managing better', required the respondents to indicate the potential benefit of their proposed approach to the economy of New South Wales.

Elsewhere, the concepts of good spatial information management have not been so clearly understood. In many countries, national policies for handling spatial data have yet to be established. In the United Kingdom in 1990, in spite of three years of a central government initiative on tradeable information and the publication of the Chorley Report (Chorley and Buxton 1991 in this volume), there was little progress towards providing access for the public to government-held data. Though there is a Freedom of Information Act in the United States that allows any citizen to gain access to a wide range of government information, in very few other countries have governments been willing to release much of their basic spatial data. In many developing countries, maps and aerial photographs are treated as secret documents for reasons of national security. The Thailand Land Titling Project (Angus Leppan 1989), for instance, had to be modified to meet strategic military considerations.

The problems of data access are in part associated with scale and the extent of the mapping that is involved. Even in the United Kingdom, there are acceptable reasons why an individual may need to know where pipes are buried outside an individual house, but there are equally good reasons why the whole network should not be revealed – for instance, a terrorist in possession of a certain level of information would know where to destroy vital services with minimum effort. As a result, access to data may need to be restricted by attribute, location or spatial extent.

The use of spatial information as a corporate resource implies an understanding of who owns the data and what rights can and should be retained over their use. Not all countries have copyright laws while, in the United Kingdom, it was not until the Copyright, Designs and Patents Act of 1988 that effective control of intellectual property rights was extended to electronic media. Spatial data held electronically in the United Kingdom are now protected from unauthorized copying.

At present, the liability of a land information manager for the accuracy of the data held within a LIS is uncertain. If wrong decisions are made on the basis of incorrect information derived from a LIS, then there may be a case for suing the data provider for negligence (see also Epstein 1991 in this volume). Many land registration systems guarantee title to land and some claim to guarantee boundaries. Where owners of land are deprived of their rights through defects in the system, they may receive compensation – as happens on rare occasions in England and Wales. In such circumstances, it is irrelevant whether the data are held on paper or within a computer. Such guarantees may, as in parts of the United States, be offered through title insurance schemes. It is, however, more common (especially in developing countries) for the guarantees to be offered by governments themselves.

MANAGING LIS

The adoption of a computerized land information system usually follows a complex process of analysis and review. Thus the introduction and management of LIS must address the many issues that are highlighted in what follows (McLaren 1989). Clarke (1991 in this volume) and Dangermond (1991 in this volume) outline similar schemes.

Initial Appraisal

Many countries are in the early stages of planning and developing LIS (Dale 1990). The first phase in developing a computerized LIS is to undertake an analysis of existing procedures and to assess the difficulties being faced with present manual systems of record management. Existing inefficiencies are rarely costed (but see Buxton 1989) and hence investment in LIS is often initially perceived as an additional expenditure, rather than as a saving of resources. In practice, with better management techniques, many manual systems can be significantly improved, even without the application of computer technology. Computerization can, however, act as a catalyst for making essential changes in working practices. The investment appraisal should look at existing costs and benefits, as well as the levels of investments necessary to make the desired improvements in the overall running of the organization.

Organizational arrangements

Having identified a possible need for a computerized LIS, it is necessary to gather a team of individuals who will investigate in detail what is required and make appropriate recommendations. While this team may often be led by those already working in electronic data processing, it is essential to have as members some people who are experienced in analysing organizational structures. Because of the need to share data between departments and external agencies, including (in the case of government) other ministries, the study team must identify all the institutional implications behind its proposals. Often there are few, if any, clear policies within central and local governments about how to manage information as a resource. Hence new institutional arrangements have to be made and new policies developed and approved. In some countries (e.g. Australia), the importance of LIS is seen to be such that, in organizational terms, it is located close to top management and answerable in a government context at cabinet or council level (Fig. 41.3). Even where different and independent systems are networked together, there still needs to be a lead agency to set procedures and standards. Hence from the very beginning of implementing LIS, the issues of power, authority and responsibility must be addressed.

Feasibility study

Having established a LIS development team, the next stage is to undertake a detailed feasibility study to determine whether a computerized LIS is justifiable. A balance must be struck between individual departmental interests and the corporate view of all potential users of the system. Many

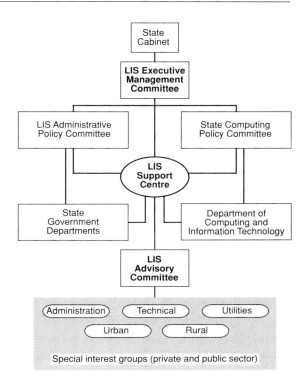

Figure 41.3 LIS organizational arrangements in Western Australia.

systems start by being 'producer-driven', that is they are dominated by one or two producers of data, such as surveying departments or land registries. Once the system is up and running, there is increasing pressure for further modification and development from the users of the system who want to develop different applications. The feasibility study must therefore identify, and if possible quantify, the potential costs and benefits to both producers and users of the system. Once the general philosophy has been worked out, a more detailed analysis of the system performance characteristics should be undertaken, known as the User Requirement Analysis (URA). Here, a detailed assessment is made of what is needed in terms of data and performance – for instance by estimating the probable number of users, the volumes and types of data that they will need and the response times that they will accept. The system must be designed to meet existing user needs and be capable of expansion to meet any projected further growth in demand.

System specification

From the URA, a detailed technical specification can be drawn up and tender documents produced indicating to potential suppliers what is needed, what form of benchmark tests will be carried out and which criteria will be used to determine whether their products are acceptable. The specification will be influenced by national or institutional information technology (IT) strategies relating to hardware and software acquisition since many, particularly less developed, countries are trying to standardize their procurement procedures. Early specifications tended to be either open-ended and, therefore, difficult to enforce when they reached legal contract stage, or else were unnecessarily restrictive.

Invitation to tender (ITT)

The system specification is normally sent to as many suppliers as is practical so that a wide choice of systems can be considered. From their responses, and having analysed what is on the market, a short list of possible vendors will be invited to tender for the supply of the system. They will be expected to undergo a benchmark test to determine the suitability of the system that is being offered. Since there is no standard LIS, there is no 'off the shelf' solution that will meet every organization's requirements. Hence every potential solution should be rigorously tested.

System selection and customization

An indirect benefit of the benchmark test is that the LIS team should have the opportunity to learn much about both the vendors whose products it is testing and the present 'state of the art' in LIS technology. Factors that will be considered in the selection of a system include the availability of the hardware and software and the ability of the supplier to maintain them and carry out repairs if anything goes wrong; the speed of operation of the system under load when many people are trying to gain access; the form of the data model; the ability of the system to integrate data and the possibility of developing multi-user applications; the security of the system, especially if the public is allowed access to any sensitive records such as those of land ownership; the ability to link into other databases run on different systems; the ease of using any query language and the overall human interface; the ease with which the system can be customized to meet individual user needs; and the overall extent of system support. If the decision is taken to computerize all the land records, there must be a fall-back position in case of catastrophic failure. Not only are back-up records essential, but an alternative system may need to be available so that, for example, dealings in land are not significantly delayed because of system failure.

Data conversion

As indicated earlier, the conversion and subsequent maintenance of digital maps and textual records is a matter of major importance and expense. Data conversion is a major task that on its own can account for 80 per cent or more of the cost of introducing a computerized system. The processes of data conversion take a long time since much of the work must presently be done by manual methods (Jackson and Woodsford 1991 in this volume).

While undertaking the data conversion, many records will need to be updated and this will tend to delay progress. Such updating is, however, essential if the records are not to become an historical archive before they are even complete. Contrary to the perceptions of many in the labour force, computerization poses little immediate threat to overall levels of employment although it does change the nature of the skills that are required.

The pilot study and its appraisal

It is common to undertake a pilot study before introducing a system. From the lessons learnt, techniques may be modified and new procedures adopted, or institutional weaknesses become apparent that will prove difficult to eliminate. If not all possible organizations are willing to cooperate, progress may still go ahead since some ministries and departments that were not willing to take part initially may well join the system at a later date.

Production

On completion of the pilot study and a review of the lessons learnt, the design of the full production flow-line can be clarified and then implemented. The four basic functions of a LIS are monitoring, planning, decision taking and project implementation. Such functions apply to the management of the LIS as well as to the service that it provides. It is important to monitor progress in both cost and benefit terms, to plan for future developments, to decide on alternative courses of action and then to implement them. LIS is not a static record-keeping process but a dynamic, evolving system that changes over time with new technology and new institutional arrangements.

System upgrade

The pace of change in technology means that, within a relatively short period of time (such as a few years), the system will need to be upgraded. In this respect, the problems of changing hardware and software are less significant than those of maintaining the integrity of the database. The data will have been subject to continual updating as an integral part of the system; but since much of the information may be of historical importance, for instance some land title data, reference may need to be made to old records dating back over long periods, even centuries. While it is possible to throw away old topographic maps and create new ones, with cadastral records each entry may have legal significance and be impossible to change without due processes of the law. Any systems upgrade must, therefore, be backwards compatible in terms of the existing data and forwards compatible in terms of new data types to be accommodated.

CONCLUSIONS

LIS have been identified as a response to existing or perceived user needs. The extent of the use of land-related information is considerable – in the United Kingdom, for example, the public and private sectors probably spend of the order of £1500 million (US$3000 million) per year, or £25 (US$50) per head of population, on handling land-related data; this is fairly close to estimates from Canada which suggest that $50 Canadian per head of population is spent each year on land information products and services (Dale and McLaughlin 1988). LIS are concerned with the efficient management of land-related data. This poses both technical and institutional problems, the technical ones being the easier to solve. If land information is to be treated as a corporate resource, then the institutional problems – and especially those concerned with the sharing of data – must be addressed. Progress towards a true information system rather than a data management system depends on the resolution of such institutional problems. Various claims have been made about the levels of benefits that can arise from investing in LIS, with a tentative consensus around a benefit to cost ratio of between 3:1 and 4:1. Such assessments however take little account of the costs that arise through inefficiencies in existing manual systems; nor have they in general been able to quantify 'public good'. They do suggest, however, that LIS can lead both to savings over existing procedures and to income generation from sales of new products and services (Dale 1988). Both factors make an investment in LIS worth while.

REFERENCES

Andersson S (1987) The Swedish Land Data Bank. *International Journal of Geographical Information Systems* **1** (3): 253–64

Andersson S (1989) Demand for access to the Swedish Land Data Bank System – a second wave. *Mapping Awareness* **3** (1): 9–12

Angus Leppan P (1989) The Thailand Land Titling Project -first steps in a parcel-based LIS. *International Journal of Geographical Information Systems* **3** (1): 59–68

Ardrey R (1966) *The Territorial Imperative*. Fontana/Collins, London

Bromley R D F, Coulson M G (1989) The value of corporate GIS to local authorities. *Mapping Awareness* **3** (5): 32–5

Buxton R (1989) Integrated spatial information systems in local government – is there a financial justification? *Mapping Awareness* **2** (6) 14–16

Chorley R, Buxton R (1991) The government setting of GIS in the United Kingdom. In: Maguire D J, Goodchild M F, Rhind D W (eds.) *Geographical Information*

Systems: principles and applications. Longman, London, pp. 67–79, Vol 1

Chrisman N R (1991) The error component in spatial data. In: Maguire D J, Goodchild M F, Rhind D W (eds.) *Geographical Information Systems: principles and applications*. Longman, London, pp. 165–74, Vol 1

Clarke A L (1991) GIS specification, evaluation and implementation. In: Maguire D J, Goodchild M F, Rhind D W (eds.) *Geographical Information Systems: principles and applications*. Longman, London, pp. 477–88, Vol 1

Coppock J T, Rhind D W (1991) The history of GIS. In: Maguire D J, Goodchild M F, Rhind D W (eds.) *Geographical Information Systems: principles and applications*. Longman, London, pp. 21–43, Vol 1

Crawley K J, Nitze R T (1989) One Hundred Million Connections. GIS/LIS for Public Utilities. *Proceedings of Surveying and Mapping '89*, Royal Institution of Chartered Surveyors, London, Paper F3

Dale P F (1976) *Cadastral Surveys within the Commonwealth*. Her Majesty's Stationery Office, London

Dale P F (1988) Economic considerations in the development of land information systems. *Proceedings from the FIG Land Information Systems Workshop, Bali, Indonesia*, pp. 75–83

Dale P F (1990) All the world's a stage – but where are all the players? *Proceedings of National Mapping Awareness Conference*. Miles Arnold, Oxford, pp. 12.1–12.3

Dale P F, McLaughlin J D (1988) *Land Information Management – an introduction with special reference to cadastral problems in Third World countries*. Oxford University Press, Oxford

Dangermond J (1991) The commercial setting of GIS. In: Maguire D J, Goodchild M F, Rhind D W (eds.) *Geographical Information Systems: principles and applications*. Longman, London, pp. 55–65, Vol 1

Department of the Environment (DoE) (1987) *Handling Geographic Information*. Her Majesty's Stationery Office, London

DOI (1989) *Managing Our Land Information Resources*. Bureau of Land Management, US Department of the Interior, Washington DC

Dowson E, Sheppard V L O (1952) *Land Registration*. Her Majesty's Stationery Office, London

Eichhorn G (1981) Das FIG-Symposium in Darmstadt – Eine Zusammenfassung. *Proceedings of FIG XVI Congress, Montreux*, pp. 304.1/1–9

Epstein E F (1991) Legal aspects of GIS. In: Maguire D J, Goodchild M F, Rhind D W (eds.) *Geographical Information Systems: principles and applications*. Longman, London, pp. 489–502, Vol 1

Hamilton A C, Williamson I P (1984) A critique of the FIG definition of a Land Information System. In: *The Decision Maker and Land Information Systems. Papers and Proceedings from the FIG International Symposium, Edmonton, Alberta*, pp. 28–34

Harris N (1989) Aid and urbanization – an overview. *Cities* **6** (3): 174–85

Her Majesty's Land Registry (1990) *Report on the work of HM Land Registry 1989–90*. Her Majesty's Stationery Office, London

Holstein L (1988) LIS problems and issues in urban areas. *Proceedings from the FIG Land Information Systems Workshop, Bali, Indonesia*, pp. 53–9

Jackson M J, Woodsford P A (1991) GIS data capture hardware and software. In: Maguire D J, Goodchild M F, Rhind D W (eds.) *Geographical Information Systems: principles and applications*. Longman, London, pp. 239–49, Vol 1

LAMSAC (1989) *An Approach to Evaluating GIS for Local Authorities (Requirements Study)*. LAMSAC, London

Leick A (ed.) (1982) Land information at the local level. *Proceedings of the International Symposium, Orono, Maine*

Lyons H G (1931) Land surveying in early times. *Proceedings of Conference of Empire Survey Officers* pp. 175–180

Maguire D J (1991) An overview and definition of GIS. In: Maguire D J, Goodchild M F, Rhind D W (eds.) *Geographical Information Systems: principles and applications*. Longman, London, pp. 9–20, Vol 1

Mahoney R P (1991) GIS and utilities. In: Maguire D J, Goodchild M F, Rhind D W (eds.) *Geographical Information Systems: principles and applications*. Longman, London, pp. 101–14, Vol 2

McLaren R A (1989) Choosing GIS/LIS. *FIG Newsletter No.3; Commission 3 Working Group on Land Information Systems in Developing Countries*

NRC (1980) *Need for a Multipurpose Cadastre*. National Research Council, Washington DC

NRC (1983) *Procedures and Standards for a Multipurpose Cadastre*. National Research Council, Washington DC

O'Callaghan J F, Garner B J (1991) Land and geographical information systems in Australia. In: Maguire D J, Goodchild M F, Rhind D W (eds.) *Geographical Information Systems: principles and applications*. Longman, London, pp. 57–70, Vol 2

Ottoson L, Rystedt B (1991) National GIS programmes in Sweden. In: Maguire D J, Goodchild M F, Rhind D W (eds.) *Geographical Information Systems: principles and applications*. Longman, London, pp. 39–46, Vol 2

Raper J F, Kelk B (1991) Three-dimensional GIS. In: Maguire D J, Goodchild M F, Rhind D W (eds.) *Geographical Information Systems: principles and applications*. Longman, London, pp. 299–317, Vol 1

Sedunary M E (1988) Land Information Systems – their reasons and rewards. *Proceedings from the FIG Land Information Systems Workshop, Bali, Indonesia*, pp. 66–74

Simpson S R (1976) *Land Law and Registration*. Cambridge University Press, Cambridge

Singh G (1989) Grid referenced data as a decision support system. *Proceedings of the 2nd National Mapping Awareness Conference*. Miles Arnold, Oxford, pp. 22.1–22.3

Taylor D R F (1991) GIS and developing nations. In: Maguire D J, Goodchild M F, Rhind D W (eds.) *Geographical Information Systems: principles and applications*. Longman, London, pp. 71–84, Vol 2

Trollegaard S (1985) *Land Information Systems in Denmark*. Ministry of Housing, Copenhagen

Yarrow G J (1989) Dudley – the lessons. *Proceedings of the National Joint Utilities' Conference*

42

GIS AND UTILITIES

R P MAHONEY

This chapter outlines the general principles behind GIS in the utilities, exploring the requirements and applications of each utility in turn and identifying many anomalies from the general case. It discusses the specific uses made by the utilities of digital maps and their plant records. While the examples chosen relate mainly to the United Kingdom, most conclusions apply more generally. Since hardware and software have been covered in detail in other chapters of this book, reference is only made to the specific needs of the utilities. Finally, the chapter examines the trials undertaken in the United Kingdom to establish principles of GIS record exchange and describes a GIS of joint utilities boards being established in the United States.

INTRODUCTION

The utilities have many uses for GIS, all of which focus on the need to provide a cost-effective service (supply) to the consumer. Across the world, codes of practice, government and federal legislation and the pressure from the regulatory bodies vary. Each of these factors has a direct bearing on the manner in which GIS is introduced, operated and integrated with other systems. In general, however, all utilities have the same requirements for map-based record keeping, that is to maintain a record of their transmission/distribution networks. This enables them to forecast demand, plan expansion, and locate plant for maintenance and the provision of service connections. GIS are both a means of providing up-to-date information for the planning and operational engineer and a means of ensuring that it is also readily accessible to enquiry personnel and field operatives. Management in turn benefits from such systems by the provision of up-to-date management information (Department of the Environment 1987).

THE NATURE, ROLE AND STRUCTURE OF THE UTILITIES

The ownership, size and commercial status of utilities vary considerably from country to country. These differences are the natural result of different historical developments and the intervention of politics. Utilities range from small, private and locally-based independent distribution companies, to state-owned national industries; some have a monopoly status while others are in direct commercial competition with one another. The geographical area covered by the utilities and the number of customers served therein are significant in GIS terms, since they dictate the cost of the map base. Customer numbers can be as few as 1000 or as large as several million. As one example, electricity supply was privatized in 1990 and goes to over 22 million consumers in England and Wales from an industry with a turnover in 1988 of £11 200 million. It is common practice in some parts of the world (e.g. Italy and the Netherlands) for cities to own and maintain all utilities in their area of responsibility; they may still, however, operate them as separate companies since they come under the jurisdiction of different regulatory authorities and the engineering skills required differ from one to the other. In principle, however, common ownership enables these organizations to work more closely together by sharing the same map base within a GIS context (Olson 1988).

The utilities are charged with providing a particular type of service to commercial and domestic consumers. To achieve this, they have traditionally used maps in some form to record their plant network. GIS have enabled them to link these geographical records to alphanumeric information associated with the plant, providing the ability to interrogate and analyse their whole operation more efficiently. In order to introduce GIS, an amalgamation of skills including those from engineering, cartography, surveying and computing has been required to ensure its successful implementation. The best of traditional practices have combined with computing techniques to provide a robust business solution which can be seen initially as asset management and which develops into an integrated arm of information technology.

The density of environmental development has some considerable bearing on the type of plant used, the complexity of the network and the degree of growth and modification undertaken upon it. This, in turn, affects the accuracy of recording, the volume of map and plant data held in the system and the frequency of update required. In addition, the type and location of the utilities are influential factors in determining the essential functionality required of GIS. To facilitate understanding of the industry's needs from GIS, it is helpful to consider the inherent characteristics of each type of utility in more detail, broadly subdivided into those utilizing pipes as a delivery mechanism and those using cables.

Pipe Utilities

These include gas and water. The attributes generally associated with a pipe network are pipe diameter, material of construction, age, joint type, depth, condition and the operational and test pressures. There are several methods of recording the position of pipes: tape measurements from fixed objects, tape triangulation, graphic survey and coordinate positioning from bearing and distance observation. The results are to differing levels of accuracy, depending not only on the method employed but also upon the quality of the 'control' data. In order to undertake any analysis of the pipe network, it is essential that there is connectivity between the network links within the GIS database.

Sewers

A special and important subcategory of pipe utilities is that dealing with sewers. The infrastructure of the underground systems of waste disposal, both surface water and foul waste, is fundamental to the well-being of society. The construction detail is different from those of the other utilities, mainly due to the greater physical size of the buried conduit. Furthermore, the requirement to analyse the system under various conditions and to predict failure is inevitably reliant on a number of interrelated data sets. As one example, the hazardous nature of the sewer's contents – chiefly poisonous and suffocating gases – can be monitored through a GIS in order that the safety of the personnel entering the system can be assured. In this chapter, the sewerage authorities are considered to be a subset of the water industry, though in practice they often function as a separate organization.

Cable Utilities

This can be further subdivided into three subcategories: electricity, telecom (PTT) and cable television. However, the complexity of the telecom networks and the additional requirement for them to record their individual cables, as well as the duct network, requires a further level of explanation.

Electricity

Engineering records are separated by voltage into transmission and distribution. The transmission section has a much smaller supply network. The normally associated attributes of the materials employed in these networks are: size and age of the conductor, its depth, insulation, phasing and the operational voltage. The networks generally are of greater length than those of the pipe utilities within the same geographical area – the ratio is 2 : 1 in the United Kingdom.

Telecom

The demands from GIS in telecommunication utilities tend to be greater than from the others since there is a need to record the physical duct route for underground plant and to maintain records so that lines can be traced from individual subscribers. In terms of planning, it is also necessary to know the amount and location of the 'free duct space'. There is, then, a four-fold information requirement – on the duct, cable, duct space and subscriber pairs (though the last is not applicable in some countries). Hence this adds substantially to the complexity of the GIS through increased data volumes and the sophistication of analytical software required.

While the complexity of the duct route and duct space record does not apply to the overhead sections of the network, connectivity and cable tracing do. There are differences in the European and North American systems which result in software written for the North American market being unsuitable for most European systems; the effect of this is that implementations in Europe are delayed while expensive customization is undertaken and the overall cost of projects is increased.

Cable television

These services can be a combination of overhead and underground networks. Ducts are generally smaller than those of telecom since, in normal circumstances, the consumer numbers are fewer and the cable volumes are correspondingly reduced.

Underground and overground networks

An alternative – though overlapping with the pipe/cable distinction used above – way of classifying the industry is to differentiate between overground and underground supplies. Again this has implications for operational GIS.

The asset value of underground plant is considerable. Total figures are not available for the United States but the United Kingdom's 1 650 000 km of utility plant was estimated to have a replacement value of £117 000 million (US$230 billion) at 1983 prices. Older plant in particular has rarely been located accurately on maps or other records. Thus, in order to manage the plant effectively, it is essential to be able to relocate it. A number of different methods and associated levels of accuracy are used to record the spatial location of plant. These include use of a data logger producing coordinates in a pre-defined system, position measurement relative to fixed geographical monuments, alphanumeric description with no position dimensions, or some combination of these methods. The particular method used will depend on several factors such as the required accuracy, the method and skill of the staff used to relocate the plant and (in some cases) legislation which may require certain criteria to be met. It is obvious that the method and accuracy used to record the plant's position manifestly influence the design and utility of the GIS module.

Overhead networks differ from underground ones in that (in general) their spatial position is not required to be as accurately defined, since the plant can be relocated visually on site. Some apparatus is pole mounted, with the cables strung between the poles, while the higher voltages used in electricity are normally suspended between pylons.

Irrespective of the position of the service in relation to the ground, the delivery point of the service may give rise to particular needs. The nature of the practice of recording individual consumer services – usually defined as the pipe or cable from the off-take point on the main supply to the consumer's in-house meter – is dependent upon several factors. These include legislation and the particular point at which the consumer becomes responsible for the internal apparatus (this varies between countries and between utilities).

THE DIGITAL MAP AS A SPATIAL FRAMEWORK

The geography of utility records can be considered to exist in two forms – the topographic base map which provides the spatial framework to which other data are 'snapped' and the location of the utility's pipeline or cables. These are treated separately below.

The base map

The cost of acquiring the digital map base generally ranges between 10 and 25 per cent of the overall project cost. Where the digital maps can be purchased from the national mapping organization, such as in the United Kingdom, and where the number of maps required is small, the percentage is at the lower end of the range. This cost range also depends very much upon pricing policy in circumstances where the maps are obtained from a non-commercial supplier. In the United States, where it may be necessary to compile a map base from aerial photography, the costs are normally higher, especially where high accuracy recording is necessary (Fisher 1991 in this volume; Jackson and Woodsford 1991 in this volume).

The use of digital maps by the utilities should be viewed against the background of building development. New development and infill of existing areas lead to expansion or reinforcement of the existing utility network and the laying of new plant. In many countries, a vast amount of utility work is in the expansion of the network due to such new developments. Where this occurs, there is a need for utility planners to obtain plans of the proposals to enable them to design the network prior to on-site construction. There can also be a requirement to identify those physical features in the environment that have been removed subsequent to the date of original survey. The position of plant is often recorded against (i.e. in relation to) them and, in order to re-establish their position, some comparison between other old and new topographic features may be necessary.

This need for historical information is not restricted to visible structures: the use of techniques that enable plant to be inserted into the ground without disturbing the road surface requires, ideally prior to the commencement of work, the identification of underground obstructions. Since many national mapping and other survey organizations do not make available historic data, it is necessary for software-based or manual comparisons to be made between existing and new data by the utilities themselves. This, together with the new developments, results in the need for some form of structuring or 'layering' of geographical features to enable them to be identified separately and displayed on the screen or output in physical form. Maps for utilities, therefore, should be envisaged as containing information about 'present', 'future' and 'historical' (immediate past) geographical features; a time dimension, which is sometimes referred to as a time structure or series, is essential in work in the industry (Mahoney 1985).

In general terms, as the user's geographical area of interest reduces in size, so the detail required on the map increases. The map must also satisfy the two distinct requirements of the operational and the detailed planning functions. The map required by the operational engineer, for instance, requires more detail than does that for the planner who – while needing detail in some instances – can work adequately with a schematic representation of the network since the exact geographical location of the plant is not required. In some respects, then, the digital map acts as a geographical 'backdrop' to a foreground consisting of the utility's own data. Vector-based mapping and topologically structured data may be important facilities in the system, especially as the system applications mature. But there are examples (such as in the South Western Electricity Board in England) where raster-based digital maps have been used to great advantage, particularly where there is little environmental change and the network is stable. In such circumstances, there may well be good justification for the introduction of raster mapping beyond its role as a means of providing 'backdrop geography', particularly where vector data are not currently available or are uneconomic to provide.

The maps used by most utilities are two dimensional (with position expressed in eastings and northings on the National Grid in the United Kingdom, state plane coordinates in the United States, etc). As altitude is related to pressure in the system of certain utilities, there is sometimes a requirement to maintain height information. This is normally achieved by holding the height as an attribute of the plant network, as opposed to holding the third (Z) coordinate in the map data. This reduces the cost of the map and saves the overhead of holding three-dimensional topography, normally unnecessary except where tunnelling operations are required (and which are usually so localized as to be treated in a different fashion).

Further types of spatial information may be held in digital map form. The type of soil and general geological conditions in which plant is buried can, for instance, be valuable information to engineers. In practice, the storage of this information is often by attributes attached to links or nodes but a raster image of a geological map can be provided to act as a 'backdrop'.

Source map scales

The scale of the map base used by the utilities varies with the density of development within the area of interest, becoming larger in urban areas. The map bases used in such areas typically range in scale from 1 : 200 to 1 : 10 000 (Gateaud 1988). Outside of the urban areas, the utility plant normally becomes less complex and, therefore, the smaller scale still shows sufficient detail for plant to be relocated. For overhead plant, still smaller scales may be acceptable. In Europe, the maps are often obtained from, and updated by, a national mapping organization or local government department; in the United States, the general tendency is for the utilities to provide their own map base. Digital maps can, of course, be enlarged easily using GIS software. Enlarging maps beyond their survey scale does not increase their accuracy commensurably (Muller 1991 in this volume). This apparently elementary point needs to be made clear to non-cartographic staff who are often unaware of the map data's limitations.

Up-to-date geography

Before the introduction of GIS, changes which occurred in the mapped environment often took so long to be added to the map that the field personnel were operating with out-of-date maps for an unacceptably long period. Such delays generated hazards to the health of contractors as well as adding to the costs of operation. The frequency with which digital maps need to be updated depends upon the volume and type of change to the topography and the particular tasks to be carried out. The majority of new plant is laid into new developments; the ability to have access to this development data at the earliest possible stage enables extensions to the network to be planned efficiently. When the plant is laid, its recorded position is available before the overlying built forms have been created, let alone surveyed: a form of interim recording is thus sometimes necessary. In Britain, this requirement is being addressed by collaboration between the National Joint Utilities Group (NJUG) and the Ordnance Survey. The use of GIS has enabled the utilities to determine and adhere to a suitable time-frame for these updates to be included without incurring unacceptable labour costs. But GIS also has other advantages because descriptions of the changes can come from several sources, including the national mapping organization, the local government or private survey. In principle, therefore, GIS can provide the mechanism for a coherent spatial framework. Where it is necessary for utilities to exchange information, it is essential that map updates are made at the same time and from the same source of update. This is essential as plant is often recorded by reference to geographical features, rather than through descriptions using absolute coordinates: thus the relative position of the utility's plant can be changed when it is overlaid on the revised topography if the coordinates of the two geographies are different. How long this practice will continue if costs of GPS receivers continue to fall in price is, however, unclear; movement to low cost fixing of absolute position has advantages if the topographic features as mapped 'match' their positions in the absolute positioning system (Goodchild 1991).

Time Series

As indicated earlier, the geography and plant records can both logically be structured in the GIS in a time structure or series. This is best described under the headings of present, past and forthcoming developments/changes (see Fig. 42.1). So far as the present is concerned, such records depict the environment and the network as it existed at the time of the last update. They are taken, therefore, as the record of the current situation and used accordingly, being required for a variety of operational and planning uses such as engineering enquiries and plant replacement. Retention of historical geographical information is also of value, particularly where the plant is buried. Plant is often recorded against features which have subsequently been demolished. In order to re-establish their location, some form of comparison will be necessary between the new and old topographic features. It is also important in the detection of now-buried obstructions, especially when laying pipes by 'no dig' methods (i.e. without disturbing the metalled road surfaces) as such complications cause additional expense when unexpectedly discovered. Finally, forthcoming developments/changes are normally the province of the planner. Such 'intelligence' enables anticipated environmental changes to be seen in relationship to the existing network and facilitates planning of modifications to the network. It also provides a datum for asking 'what if ?' enquiries, so that design proposals can be amended or modified to find the most cost-effective scenario. Most developments are the subject of frequent modifications and it is possible for the initial layout to be amended several times before construction starts.

Recording the Utility's Plant

The techniques used to record the position of utility plant vary considerably depending on tradition,

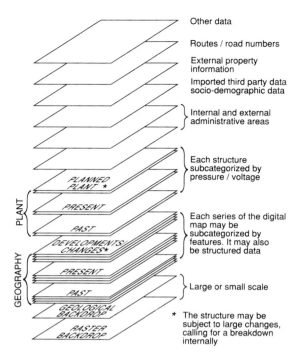

Fig. 42.1 The layers typical of a utility GIS.

legislation, the method of land registration, the required accuracy, the type of utility and the cost efficiency demands of relocating the plant for operational needs. The measurements used to record the position of plant can be tape distances, or instrumental or graphic survey, depending upon the required accuracy and the scale of the base map. The overwhelming reason for taking these measurements is the ability to re-establish the plant position at a later date. Where the plant is positioned relative to a physical feature, it should be one that is unlikely to change. The most common features used as reference points are road edges, boundary walls, buildings, lot boundaries and cadastral stations. In situations where the plant is some distance from any of these features, basic triangulation is used.

Accuracy of plant recording

There is no significant variation between the accuracies with which the position of pipe and cable networks are recorded. The position is taken from the centre line of the pipe or ductway. Depth, which is held as an attribute, is recorded as cover from ground level to the top of the plant. The average position of underground (buried) plant is recorded to +/- 0.1 m, while the range for overhead plant can be +/- 15 m. In extreme cases, no measurements are taken and the plant is drawn in the approximate position on the map. This large variation is due to the ability to relocate some plant visually, the assumption being made that, in remote areas, the pole or pylon can easily be seen whereas buried plant presents obvious difficulties.

Data security

The question of data security presents a conflict between the need to allow free exchange of information and the question of legal liability in the event of error or misuse of the information. Such misuse could involve severe structural damage and loss of life. The ability of GIS to make data more easily available is thus of concern to some users, particularly when data are imported, combined with other third party data and used for analysis and subsequent decision making. More prosaically, the question of internal data security is the same for GIS as any computer system and requires procedures to be adapted for data back-up and professional management of the data. A particular aspect of data security in the utilities relates to the maintenance of services. Emergencies do occur within the utilities themselves or nearby which – as usual – require plant records to be made available to field personnel; in these situations, there may be loss of power to the utility and so a microfilm back-up facility is often provided to ensure that the information is always available. Fortunately, the development of fault-tolerant computer systems and duplicate storage of data on other, network-accessible parts of a distributed computer system may reduce the need for running two parallel systems of records.

APPLICATIONS AREAS WITHIN THE UTILITIES

This section sets out details of the major GIS applications made by the utilities. Their usage of GIS can be broadly subdivided into enquiry and analysis, together with the function of general record maintenance (see Fig. 42.2).

GIS and Utilities

Application	Utility			
	Electricity	Gas	Telecom	Water
Map maintenance	1	1	1	1
Plant maintenance	1	1	1	1
System entry methods	1	1	1	1
Engineering enquiry	1	1	1	1
Plant replacement	2	1	2	1
Carriageway reinstatement	1●	1●	1●	1●
Microfiche production	1●	1●	2	2
Planning	2	2	2	2
Network analysis	1	1	1	1
Exchange of record	1●	1●	1●	1●
Point of sales enquiry	3●	3		3●
Wayleave / easement	2	2	2	2
Marketing analysis	3	3	3	3
On-line grid control	2	2		2
Leakage survey		1		
Fault location	2		2	
Free duct analysis			2	
Water resources management				2
Water quality				2
Emergency planning	3	3	3	3
Transport planning	3	3	3	3

1 Initial transport requirement
2 Intermediate phase requirement   ● Varies with country
3 Advanced stage requirement

Fig. 42.2 The requirements of typical utility applications.

Graphic and plant maintenance

In general, the basic needs of the utilities are the same. However, at a detailed technical level, the precise requirements vary due, in most cases, to the different operating conditions and engineering needs. The graphic maintenance application covers the maintenance of the map base and the line plant record. They can be seen as separate functions, although there is a tendency within the pipe utilities for both to be combined into a task for a single operator. Maintenance of the plant record is more complex for the cable utilities and often requires dedicated staff. The representation of plant on the map at first sight appears simple; intuitively, the complexity arises in the database representation and in subsequent graphic annotation. The pipe utilities are normally able to operate with a single representation of the network, whereas the electricity utility can require more than one such representation. Telecom's need is for multiple representations, ranging from a single line sharing the duct position to individual cable runs used for fault location, planning and operations. Classification of the data is necessary to ensure basic distinction between, low, medium or high pressure pipes, low or high voltage, etc. Separation of plant into time series of 'present,' 'past' and 'development/change' is also required.

Exploiting the database

In order to gain maximum productivity from a utility's GIS, it must be used for multiple purposes beyond those merely involving inspection of the whole of a map graphic. To facilitate this, simple and task-related methods of access to geographically related information are required. These are principally via the street name (via a street gazetteer), map number, town name, district, supervisor's area, administration areas and plant number, but other keys are also needed.

Engineering enquiry

The display of a property, which has been selected by typing the address or customer name and involving a search of a street gazetteer, allows clerical and engineering staff to gain instant access to geographically based information. There are many simple enquiries for which visual analysis is sufficient; for example, 'where is the plant outside the specified address?', 'how does this relate to the position of other plant outside this specified address?' or, 'is there any plant outside this specified address?' This enquiry method may well be the initial point of entry to the system. From it, access to software should be available which can issue job instructions or job vouchers, presenting the field operator with sufficient information to enable the task to be undertaken safely and expeditiously. These operational activities programs may be installed on the same machine as the GIS or run on a separate machine (typically a mainframe at present) with appropriate communications.

Plant replacement

The utilities have a requirement to replace plant on a cyclic basis prior to its failure. To accomplish this task, a whole series of criteria are used to implement the replacement policy. Sometimes these criteria apply not only to the plant itself but also to the surrounding environment, type of buildings, type of road surface, etc. When the environmental data are held on the system, it is possible to undertake analyses to ascertain the most economical schedules and – with more sophisticated systems – it should also be possible to ask where, within a specific area, situations or conditions exist similar to those in which the failure has occurred.

Carriageway re-instatement

In the United Kingdom, there is a requirement to maintain records of carriageway reinstatement. GIS allow these records to be maintained and therefore reduce the clerical maintenance effort; in addition, the condition of the environment should also be improved as a result – especially if operatives know that all such actions are logged and available for inspection.

Microfiche production

Many utilities issue operational personnel with information on the network during standby (out of normal hours) duty. For those vehicles without remote terminals, portable microfiche viewers are normally provided to enable staff to determine the location of plant. Production of microfiche directly from plot files from the GIS enables microfiche to be produced automatically. The principle is that plot files be created as automatic batch runs and dumped to tape. The software control has to ensure that the 'present' plant network and geography are automatically combined and included in the plot file.

Planning

The planning function in all utilities uses information drawn from a variety of sources. Through an iterative process, this information is analysed by engineers and planners to calculate the optimum, cost-effective solution to the expansion of the network. Each utility requires specific software to be written in order to address its own particular requirements. The US marketplace is larger than that in Europe and thus facilitates software houses' ability to address generic solutions to a number of industry-specific problems which should be capable of integration with existing GIS.

Network analysis

To undertake network analysis, database connectivity of the network links is obviously required. The other key requirements are details of the length of pipe or cable and specific details on pressure, flow, attenuation or voltage drop. Demand is defined at node points on the network where information can be collated from the metering systems. Other required components of the analytical capability are specific to each utility.

The most common tasks are to predict the reaction of the network under certain conditions – before that network becomes overloaded and unable to satisfy demand – and to define areas where reinforcements are required. Thus network analysis (NA) is a fundamental planning tool in the prediction of demand and in establishing a resource input when defining expansion policy. To achieve the highest productivity, computer links are necessary to the metering systems in order to model the loading patterns; at present, NA is used as a planning tool rather than a real time network monitoring device.

Exchange of records

In some countries (such as the United Kingdom), the exchange of records between utilities is controlled by legislation; in others (e.g. the United States), there are voluntary codes of practice on record exchange. In some other situations, all the utilities are maintained by the same local authority. Graphics are usually held in proprietary structures in GIS; hence where the exchange of records is required between different systems, a 'neutral' format is used to transfer data in and out of each system. In the United Kingdom, this neutral format is the National Transfer Format or NTF (see Sowton 1991 in this volume). In other countries, 'open formats' such as the Intermediate Standard Transfer Format (ISIF) are used (see also Guptill 1991 in this volume).

Point of sales enquiry

To 'sign up' a customer immediately is important in the sales environment; if the customer is asked to come back, a sale may be lost. It is, therefore, highly desirable for the point of sales personnel to have on-line access, through a form of GIS, to the appropriate data in order to avoid customer referral. Access to any geographical area data by address is particularly vital for this task. Other facilities required are those which enable the database to be questioned in order to establish the nearest apparatus for connection. Following successful closure of the sale, the GIS can also act as a 'front end' to job issue/note and customer billing.

Wayleaves/easements

Wayleaves or easements are legal agreements which grant, often subject to certain conditions, a utility access to private land for the purpose of laying and maintaining its plant. The depiction of wayleaves as a graphic overlay allows the operational engineer to determine instantly the legality of access to plant laid in or over private property. It also provides the utility's legal department with a method of record keeping if such details are included in the database. As with many GIS uses in the utilities, a prime requirement is to be able to turn on or turn off this information as required and to allow access to it only to specified users. This is not a complicated application but one which is essential to the day-to-day operations.

Marketing analysis

As marketing within the utilities becomes more sophisticated, so the requirement for display and analysis of socio-economic data becomes important. The location, probably in coordinate form, of each property centroid is required, together with data from the appropriate statistical sources such as market survey and national census. By a selection of the appropriate criteria, marketing/sales representatives are able to target their activities more productively (see Beaumont 1991 in this volume). It is also possible to direct mailshots more accurately using this approach.

On-line grid control

The water, gas and electricity industries have an on-line requirement to monitor and control the network. This is normally a separate function within the industry and has traditionally been monitored on a schematic representation of the network. Developments are taking place, however, to enable this to be based upon a realistic geographical representation, with direct links to the emergency planning procedures.

Leakage survey

Traverses of the carriageway by vehicles with equipment to detect small amounts of gas in the atmosphere are an essential part of the maintenance of the distribution system; planning of such traverses is a valuable GIS capability. In the initial stages, simply the production of plans that cover specific pipe criteria is essential; further sophistication allows the input of data describing the results of the survey and their classification. Subsequently, areas can be analysed for patterns of leakage and areas of specific concern identified by interrogation of data by then contained in the system.

Fault location

The telecom industry has a requirement to trace the geographical position of faults in the network and this is possible using GIS. The analysis of the trace is carried out automatically by software; however, since the telecom systems differ in detail in many parts of the world, software packages which perform these tasks are not readily transferred from one country to another.

Free duct analysis

The telecom industry also needs to record the position of cables within ductways and, in the planning stage, there is a requirement to find the free space in order to place new cables within the ductway. A GIS can search the records and display the free space record against appropriate ductways to enable the planner to perform this task. It is obvious that topological linkages are essential in the representation of both the cables and the ducts!

Water resource management

In several parts of the world, the water authority has the responsibility for rivers (Annand 1988); this can require monitoring of water catchment areas and pollution, plus responsibility for flood control, fisheries and sewage disposal and the provision of recreation amenities on rivers and reservoirs. In many respects, this can be summarized as water resource planning and requires specific software to address the multiplicity of interrelated applications where much of the information is geographically related.

Water quality

The quality of water attracts a great deal of comment from the consumer. Complaints may well have to be monitored in order that patterns can be determined, the trends established and sources of the problems eliminated. This is a database application with a spatial content, where visual analysis of patterns of complaints can help the engineer to identify and hence resolve the problems.

Emergency planning

The very nature of utilities means that they are required to maintain plans which can be enacted in the event of emergencies ranging from minor disasters to major catastrophes. The gas industry, for instance, must always have procedures ready for catastrophes such as gas explosions in urban areas. GIS can assist in simulating or monitoring an incident or even in the planning of responses to one; the majority of the information resulting from the planning process or the immediate on-site incident is geographically related. As the sophistication of GIS develops, so the incidence of emergency planning procedures being designed and operated through them will increase.

Transport planning

At present, this application is at an early stage of development. There are two principal uses for transport planning within the utilities: the scheduling of bulk supply delivery and route planning for regular delivery vehicles. Again, however, this is expected to develop greatly and will exploit GIS.

HARDWARE AND SOFTWARE

The workstation platform requirements of the utilities change as the systems mature and stabilize; the latter normally occurs when all data have been taken on to the system and it has become fully operational. Some utilities tend to describe GIS workstations by the type of activity undertaken by their operators; those capable of map management and analysis are described as fully operational while the enquiry terminal is described as a review station. The widespread use of digitizing, which has formed an essential component of many GIS installations in the 1980s, is broadly a function of the data conversion exercise and not a function of a fully integrated and operational GIS: thus the use of digitizing tables will in the future become substantially reduced if not eliminated. As paper output is also required, a plotter/screen dump device is associated with the installations but naturally there are many variations in the detail of these peripherals.

In the United States, as has been stressed earlier, the size of the potential marketplace has made it possible for vendors and some utilities to develop and market off-the-shelf packages designed to fulfil the requirements of individual utilities. These include full object-oriented databases and software written as a rules-based system. However, many such packages do not readily transfer to the European Market where regulations and legislation differ (often substantially) from those of the United States.

The demand by the regulatory authorities for more stringent standards and an improvement in the return on investor's capital in privatized utilities requires that geographically referenced information takes on a more strategic role within an organization's data architecture. The effect of all this is increased pressure for greater productivity and tighter investment criteria; as a result, more complex analytical software tools will be developed in the future. As the uses of GIS expand beyond the basic engineering function, the need for analysis of data within polygons, polygon within polygon and of lines within or overlapping polygons is becoming widespread.

CASE STUDIES OF GIS IN THE UTILITIES

However valuable are descriptions of existing or potential individual applications of GIS, it is much more convincing to have these associated with details of some major case studies. This section provides case studies in two of the leading countries.

GIS in utilities in the United Kingdom

The United Kingdom has a very dense and substantially urban environment: there is an average of over 200 people per square kilometre across the country as a whole and a maximum density of over 24 000 people in any one such square. There is a correspondingly complex and dense underground utility infrastructure. This infrastructure and the demands upon it has, over time, created specific requirements and a unique liaison between the utilities has emerged. Legislation and business pressures have catalysed the utilities to work together to ensure that their map-based plant records are interchangeable – to the benefit of the national interest and the profitability and safety of the utilities' operations.

In recent years, the utilities in the United Kingdom have either undergone or are undergoing major changes in their financing and organization. This is the result of privatization where financial control has passed from the state to the private sector, with a regulatory directorate overseeing the trading position. The variation in the size of the UK utilities is considerable; British Gas and British Telecom cover the whole country and are administered through a region structure (Cole and Voller 1988). In contrast, the water supply industry consists of 10 major companies and over 30 smaller ones together with the National Rivers Authority (Bolland 1986); the electricity supply industry, privatized in 1990 (Peacock and Rutherford 1989), has been divided into 12 distribution companies with others responsible for production and transmission. In Scotland, different legislation applies to the water and electricity industry and in Northern Ireland another set of legislation applies. Overall, however, two major pieces of legislation are relevant to GIS, the Public Utilities Street Works Act (often shortened to PUSWA) and the Health and Safety at Work Act. The major implications of the former are referred to later in this chapter; the latter, which is enforced by a government inspectorate (the Health and Safety Executive) covers the opening of the highway and all aspects of the utilities' technical operations.

A significant movement towards joint coordination of utility operation began in 1977 with the formation of the National Joint Utility Group (NJUG), whose general aims were to provide a better service to the community through minimizing inconvenience to the public, and to save money and improve safety for both the general public and the utilities' own operators. This group took the initiative to establish a digital records trial in the Metropolitan Borough of Dudley in the West Midlands in 1982 (Yarrow 1987). The aim was to build a joint data bank to serve both the local government and the utilities. All data were logged in one computer, with terminals at the offices of each utility and in the local government. One of the reasons for selecting this area was the availability at that time of large-scale Ordnance Survey digital maps in vector form covering the whole of the trial area (see Sowton 1991 in this volume). The Dudley installation is also being used to test an operational street works register, which is intended to overcome the logistical problems currently encountered using the manual system. Initial findings highlighted two related concerns. Artificial boundaries to the operational area had been created for the purposes of the trial; in practice, boundaries of operating units of different utilities are not coterminous and, even within one utility, adjacent operating centres occur. Standards for data exchange are, therefore, essential and the research carried out culminated in the publication of a standard format for the exchange of utility data (NJUG 1986a). In addition, the trial enabled much practical experience to be gained. The next phase is to investigate the automating of notices under PUSWA; under this legislation, each utility is required to inform the local highways authority and the other utilities of its intention to carry out work in the highway. This notification must be given 28 days (or three days for minor works) in advance and be accompanied by a plan.

In the south west of England, another trial was established in 1983 and is known as the Taunton Joint Utility Group (TJUG). This investigated the practical exchange of data when the boundaries of the utility and local government remain unaltered (Ives and Lovett 1986). In practice, this means that the utilities cover large geographical areas from one office and may find that they need to relate to more than one operational area of another organization in order to obtain information. Indeed, the effects of such boundary overlaps are a real handicap to data interchange in practice. The other practical part of the trial was to gain experience in operating a data exchange system when several different vendors' systems are being used – a realistic situation in the light of vendor sales in the United Kingdom.

Both of these trials are ongoing and interim reports are available from the NJUG (e.g. NJUG 1986a). Two other documents produced by NJUG have acted as stimulants to shortening the time scale for the availability of vectorized large-scale map data supplied by the Ordnance Survey. The utilities produced their own specification for digitized maps (NJUG 1986b), a much simplified version of the then existing Ordnance Survey specification, plus a quality assurance procedure (NJUG 1988) designed to automate the quality control of large scale digital maps (see also Sowton 1991 in this volume). An

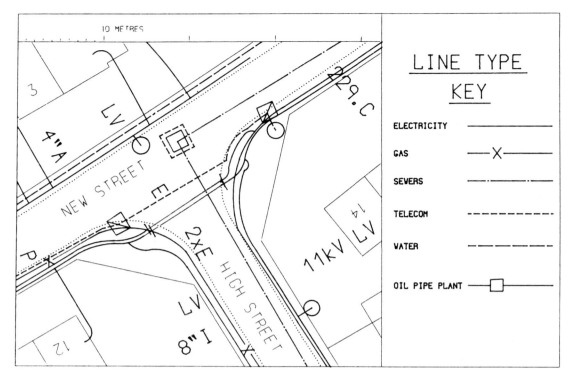

Fig. 42.3 An example of a typical UK National Joint Utilities Group vector map (courtesy Gordon Yarrow, Chairman of the NJUG Digital Record Trial, Dudley. Crown Copyright Reserved).

example of a typical joint utilities vector map is shown in Fig 42.3.

GIS in the utilities in the United States

The trading pattern of the utilities in the United States is governed by the federal deregulation legislation of the 1980s and is overseen by regulating bodies. Companies specialize in production, transmission or distribution, an arrangement designed to give customer choice between suppliers for the provision of certain services (Whelan 1983). Selecting a typical case study to represent the United States is difficult due to the variation in the size of the companies involved in GIS and the complexity of the systems being developed. None the less, the example cited is representative of companies that manage the utilities information systems through integrating their data with that of local government and administration.

The Knoxville Utilities Board (KUB) is a non-profit making public agency that operates with four separate engineering boards covering gas, water, waste water and electricity; the telephone service is provided by South Bell Central which is not part of the KUB. Information about the location of the utility's plant is provided to companies wishing to excavate the highway through a 'one-call' system. Following the identification of the site's location, details of the excavation area are passed to the KUB which is responsible then for physically marking the plant's position on-site.

Knox County, the City of Knoxville and the Knoxville Utilities Board developed a GIS in response to the findings of an initial research programme that started in 1984. This initial research was undertaken partly because of the problems inherent in the manual systems: the use of several map bases by different organizations; accidental damage to utility plant; and the fact that the maps could be up to six months out of date. The level of funding necessary was achieved by the Knox County Commissioners floating a $5.5 million general obligation bond with the City and with the

Knoxville Utilities Board. Each party took a one-third share in the investment with the agreement that the three parties would pay for the use of the system on a user basis, with income from outside defraying the operating costs. The payback period is estimated at seven to eight years. The Knoxville Utilities Board is an independent agency of the City, relying on the City to maintain the digital map base (which reduces the operating cost). The Board serves 138 000 electric customers, 60 000 water and waste water customers and 30 000 gas customers. The GIS will enable increased efficiency to be achieved in engineering design and work order processing. The utilization of the same map base and sharing of the cost of its production and maintenance will also minimize expenditure. A new planimetric map is being stereo-digitized together with tax maps for 515 square miles (1334 square kilometres) which incorporate 135 000 parcels, consisting of 96 levels of information. The map scale varies between 1 : 2400 and 1 : 1200; map updating will be achieved by re-flying the area every three years with intermediate updating being provided by the City. The GIS will contain three-dimensional digital terrain modelling with a contour separation of two feet (60 centimetres) within the City and four feet (120 centimetres) elsewhere. Database links have been made between road centre lines, parcel numbers, street names and addresses. An example of a Knoxville Utilities Board map is shown in Plate 42.1.

The objectives of the GIS extend beyond that of maintaining utility records into the area of planning and technology groups: the GIS is designed to include data relating to planimetry, topography, property, schools, transport and much else and to relate to the departments of health, fire, police, sheriff and highways. The system is, then, intended to be a large database covering the whole county and will eventually connect to the emergency services and communicate with a mainframe installation.

CONCLUSIONS

The use of GIS in the utilities has already had a significant impact upon the productivity levels of service and staffing. Although there are local variations, in general GIS in the utilities have a great many common features. The ability to display and manipulate maps on computers and the increased ability of electronic communications to handle the potentially large data volumes involved have created a major advance in the ability of the utilities to analyse, manipulate and maintain up-to-date records of their plant assets (Mahoney 1986). As well as providing economic advantages to the utilities, GIS also contribute substantially to the well-being of the environment by enabling the utilities to liaise and coordinate their activities, particularly in areas of highly developed conurbations.

In terms of the management and analytical facilities offered, GIS can therefore be considered as one of the fundamental advances in asset management, encompassing a wide spectrum of functions and used by every level of an organization from the executive to the operational spearhead.

REFERENCES

Annand K P (1988) A geographic information system for river management. *Proceedings of AM/FM Today. Nottingham Conference.* AM/FM European Division, PO Box 6, CH4005, Basel, Switzerland

Beaumont J R (1991) GIS and market analysis. In: Maguire D J, Goodchild M F, Rhind D W (eds.) *Geographical Information Systems: principles and applications.* Longman, London, pp. 139–51, Vol 2

Bolland J D (1986) Digital mapping and facilities management in a UK Water Authority. In: Blakemore M J (ed.) *Proceedings of AUTOCARTO London*, Volume 2. Royal Institution of Chartered Surveyors, London, pp. 162–70

Cole G, Voller J (1988) Introduction of FM into British Telecom. *Proceedings of AM/FM Today. Nottingham Conference.* AM/FM European Division, PO Box 6, CH4005, Basel, Switzerland

Department of the Environment (DoE) (1987) *Handling Geographic Information.* Report of the Committee of enquiry chaired by Lord Chorley. HMSO, London

Fisher P F (1991) Spatial data sources and data problems. In: Maguire D J, Goodchild M F, Rhind D W (eds.) *Geographical Information Systems: principles and applications.* Longman, London, pp. 175–89, Vol 1

Gateaud J (1988) The use of cartography databases in multi-purpose utility applications – an experience report. *Proceedings of AM/FM International – European Division*

Conference Montreux. AM/FM European Division, PO Box 6, CH4005, Basel, Switzerland, pp. 15–18

Goodchild M F (1991) The technological setting of GIS. In: Maguire D J, Goodchild M F, Rhind D W (eds.) *Geographical Information Systems: principles and applications*. Longman, London, pp. 45–54, Vol 1

Guptill S C (1991) Spatial data exchange and standardization. In: Maguire D J, Goodchild M F, Rhind D W (eds.) *Geographical Information Systems: principles and applications*. Longman, London, pp. 515–30, Vol 1

Ives M J, Lovett R (1986) Exchange of digital records between public utility digital mapping systems. In: Blakemore M J (ed.) *Proceedings of AUTOCARTO London*, Volume 2. Royal Institution of Chartered Surveyors, London, pp. 181–9

Jackson M J, Woodsford P A (1991) GIS data capture hardware and software. In: Maguire D J, Goodchild M F, Rhind D W (eds.) *Geographical Information Systems: principles and applications*. Longman, London, pp. 239–49, Vol 1

Mahoney R P (1985) Digital mapping in SEGAS. *Proceedings of AM/FM International – European Division Conference. Montreux*. AM/FM European Division, PO Box 6, CH4005, Basel, Switzerland, pp. 112–22

Mahoney R P (1986) Digital mapping – an information centre. In: Blakemore M (ed.) *Proceedings of AUTOCARTO London*, Volume 2. Royal Institution of Chartered Surveyors, pp. 190–9

Muller J-C (1991) Generalization of spatial databases. In: Maguire D J, Goodchild M F, Rhind D W (eds.) *Geographical Information Systems: principles and applications*. Longman, London, pp. 457–75, Vol 1

NJUG (1986a) *Proposed Data Exchange Format for Utility Map Data*. NJUG 11. National Joint Utilities Group, 30 Millbank, London, SW1P 4RD

NJUG (1986b) *NJUG Specification for the Digitisation of Large Scale OS Maps*. NJUG 12. National Joint Utilities Group, 30 Millbank, London, SW1P 4RD

NJUG (1988) *Quality Control Procedures for Large Scale OS Maps Digitised to OS 1988*. NJUG 13. National Joint Utilities Group, 30 Millbank, London, SW1P 4RD

Olsson L (1988) Automation of the pipeline register in the City of Stockholm. *Proceedings of AM/FM International – European Division Conference, Montreux*. AM/FM European Division, PO Box 6, CH4005, Basel, Switzerland, pp. 173–7

Peacock D, Rutherford I (1989) Concepts into reality – an account of a GIS implementation in SWEB. *Proceedings of AGI 89 Conference, Birmingham*. AGI, 12 Great George Street, London, SW1P 3AD, pp. 2.3.1–2.3.6

Sowton M (1991) Development of GIS-related activities at the Ordnance Survey. In: Maguire D J, Goodchild M F, Rhind D W (eds.) *Geographical Information Systems: principles and applications*. Longman, London, pp. 23–38, Vol 2

Whelan S D (1983) The MIDAS project: considerations for success. *Proceedings of AM/FM International, Keystone, USA*. AM/FM International, 8775 E. Orchard Rd, Suite 820, Englewood, CO80111

Yarrow G J (1987) Joint utility mapping. *Proceedings of NJUG 87 First National Conference, Birmingham*. National Joint Utilities Group, 30 Millbank, London, SW1P 4RD

CAR NAVIGATION SYSTEMS

M WHITE

Automobile navigation is a demanding application of digital maps and appears likely to become a common and economically important one. A few systems are commercially available and many prototypes exist. These systems determine location using wheel rotation sensors, solid state compasses, inertial devices (gyros and other novel devices), radio location or some combination of them. Requirements of the source maps depend on the methods used and the user interface, as well as on functions performed in addition to location determination (such as map display, verbal directions, pathfinding and destination finding by address or landmark). Typical map requirements for particular systems include positional accuracy to the order of a car length, detailed street classification, turn restriction data and topological encoding. Creating such digital maps to support navigation is a daunting task. At the time of writing, there are several pilot projects, just a few commercial operations and some fledgling consortia which have as their mission the production of digital maps for navigation or the promulgation of standards for such maps. All systems require faster retrieval than GIS systems have typically provided. Applications using navigation systems include experimental traffic systems, such as traffic congestion reporting and 'sign-post' transmitters and receivers for communicating with on-board navigation systems.

INTRODUCTION

The automobile is becoming a much richer electronic environment for the driver. On-board computers, cellular telephones and vehicle navigation are already available, and real-time traffic information and route guidance have been demonstrated. The market for factory-installed systems appears to be huge. In Japan, Nissan has been selling more than 1000 systems per month as an option on the Nissan Cedric. This option is a combination of navigation system and television (which can only be operated with the vehicle stopped). In Germany, Bosch began to sell the Travelpilot in 1989. In the United States, Etak sold 2000 Navigators over a period of two years. Because electronics are pervading the automobile, a factory-installed navigation option will probably become inexpensive, perhaps less than US $500. As a consequence, demand for and use of digital map data will grow. Market analysts have estimated that sales of navigation systems will grow from US $5 million in 1990 to US $100 million in 1994 (Frost & Sullivan 1989).

Car navigation uses maps intensively. The map must provide information for:

- determining and maintaining the location of the vehicle in relation to features represented on the map;
- displaying a map graphically or generating routing instructions in text or voice;
- linking effectively with infrastructure.

This chapter reviews the current 'state of the art' of digital mapping as regards vehicle navigation and, since it is still in its infancy, some speculations are made about likely future developments. The infancy of the technology is reflected in the meagre

Fig. 43.2 The Honda Gyrocator screen (courtesy author).

supply of prior research considering the subject and directly related cartography (Petchenik 1989). Marine navigation is not included in this discussion. It has similar requirements and applications and, indeed, was the origin and inspiration for much of the current vehicle navigation technology. However, it differs in many ways from land-based vehicle navigation and warrants separate discussion.

The following sections discuss vehicle navigation systems and methods already in use and how information is displayed graphically, reported textually or by voice. Then applications such as finding destinations and pathfinding are considered. Finally, there is a review of the essential characteristics of digital maps, in so far as navigation and its related functions are concerned. From this, it will become evident that navigation and related applications require a topologically encoded and seamless database, as well as very fast data retrieval.

NAVIGATION

There are only a few vehicle navigation systems commercially available at the time of writing (mid-1990). In the United States, the Etak Navigator has been available since 1985. The Bosch Travelpilot, a derivative of the Etak Navigator, became available in Germany in 1989. Both of these systems are 'after-market' devices, that is, they are installed after manufacture and usually after the end-user purchases the vehicle. In Japan, the Toyota Crown and the Nissan Cedric have offered factory-installed navigation options since 1987 and 1989 respectively. The Etak, Bosch and Nissan systems use dead reckoning and map matching (explained below) but the Toyota system uses only dead reckoning. The map matching systems require topologically encoded digital maps, whereas the Toyota system uses bit-mapped images of paper maps (see Plate 43.1 and Figs. 43.1 and 43.2)

Fig. 43.1 The Nissan Cedric screen (courtesy author).

In addition, there are several experimental systems and 'concept cars' either demonstrating or 'mocking up' navigation systems. In an auto show in Japan in early 1990, more than a dozen

Car Navigation Systems

Fig. 43.3 The Autoguide screen (courtesy Department of Transport).

manufacturers showed such concept cars. This indicates a strong interest in navigation and, by implication, maps for navigation. Examples of experimental systems include the Philips CARIN (Thoone 1987), Clarion NAVI and the UK Autoguide (Catling and Belcher 1989). CARIN and Autoguide present stylized graphic instructions representing the upcoming intersection to the driver (see Fig. 43.3). Only the general principles on which such systems work are known: all the current vendors of navigation systems regard their software and data storage methodology as proprietary and, accordingly, do not reveal details. This is unsurprising because navigation has pushed forward the frontier of map access technology: typically, on-board computers are much less powerful computationally and contain less copious RAM than 'normal' GIS require and, at the same time, demand a faster response rate than available GIS offer. In addition, navigation algorithms and their implementation have involved substantial expenditure. The commercial stakes are high and, accordingly, secrecy prevails on the internal details of each vendor's offerings.

POSITION DETERMINATION

Navigation includes determination of position as well as guidance toward a destination. There are three essentially different technologies used for position determination. These are dead reckoning, radio location and proximity beacon detection. They can be used alone or in combination. Destination finding and guidance towards the destination have various quite different user interfaces.

Dead reckoning and radio location

Dead Reckoning (DR) is the process of computing an updated position from three inputs: details of a prior position; the distance travelled from the prior position; and the heading travelled since that prior position. The Etak Navigator, Bosch Travelpilot and Nissan Cedric all use DR. Figure 43.4 illustrates dead reckoning. To measure the distance travelled, all three use sensors mounted on the wheels. Other systems have tried to use the vehicle's odometer but this is much less accurate.

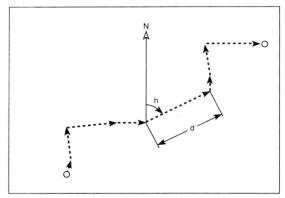

Fig. 43.4 Dead reckoning – computing a new position from heading (h) and distance (d).

For determining the heading, two measurements are taken. An absolute heading estimate is made using a solid-state compass (e.g. see Phillips 1987) and a relative heading is computed from the wheel sensor measurements. A solid state compass (i.e. a two-axis magnetometer) measures two components of the ambient magnetic field; from this the horizontal component of the earth's magnetic field is computed. There are many physical considerations involved such as the magnetic flux focusing effect of the steel in the vehicle and the local magnetic declination. However, all mapping considerations eventually come down to using the approximate position of the vehicle, a model of the earth's magnetic field and the measured magnetic field. An important consideration for in-vehicle applications is dip angle, the angle that the plane of the compass makes with the earth's magnetic field vector. The earth's magnetic field is horizontal only at the magnetic equator, which coincides approximately with the geographical equator. So the compass measures the magnetic field vector projected on to its own plane. While this is normally close to horizontal, local variations in ground slope caused by hills and the road crown may amount to several degrees and affect the compass/magnetic field relationship accordingly. Computation of the heading from compass measurements must take all these effects into consideration.

The difference in the distance travelled on two opposing wheels depends on the change in heading. When travelling straight ahead (i.e. without heading change), the two wheels travel the same distance. When turning, the outside wheel travels further than does that on the inside of the curve. Thus wheel sensor readings yield relative heading information. Again many physical considerations come into play, including wheel base, circumference, radius of curvature of the turn, steering geometry and wheel slip. Taking all these factors into account, however, a new heading can be computed from the prior heading and the difference in distance travelled by the two wheels.

Other sensors are under development or have been demonstrated in experimental systems. These include a gyro turning rate sensor, a vibrating rod turning rate sensor, an inclinometer, a GPS (Global Positioning System) receiver, a LORAN-C receiver and an optical speed sensor.

A gyroscope (more commonly a 'gyro') is a spinning mass and the vehicle's turning rate is measured indirectly by measuring forces resulting from the conservation of momentum; such forces can be experienced by holding a spinning bicycle wheel off the ground and turning it. Large gyros are used in inertial navigation systems common on board ships or aircraft. The vibrating rod sensors also operate on conservation of momentum. An inclinometer measures the angle of inclination of a stationary (or, more generally, a non-accelerating) vehicle and may be used to remove the effects of dip angle on the compass measurement as well as effects of hills on distance travelled. Any acceleration experienced affects the inclinometer so this must also be considered. As a group, the gyro, vibrating rod and inclinometer are all inertial sensors: they depend on the physics of momentum and inertia for their operation. For a survey of such inertial navigation sensors, see Smith (1986).

GPS and LORAN-C are radio location systems. These radio location sensors are not used in dead reckoning. Instead they provide position 'fixes' that are independent of the prior position. They both operate by an on-board receiver and computer comparing signals from multiple transmitters and determining receiver location from known transmitter positions and signal propagation times. The LORAN-C transmitters are based on the ground and the GPS are on a constellation of satellites in orbit. GPS will cover the entire globe when the satellite constellation is completed. French (1986) provides an overview of radio location systems.

Compass and radio location sensors are 'absolute' sensors; in contrast, wheel sensors and gyros are 'relative' sensors. Relative sensors give change information and absolute sensors provide information with respect to the earth itself. All sensors, however, suffer characteristic defects. Wheel sensors and gyros have noise and bias. Magnetic compasses measure magnetic anomalies as well as the earth's magnetic field. Radio location (GPS and LORAN) signals are distorted or blocked in highly urbanized areas. Manifestly, the sensor characteristics are important in assessing the accuracy of the estimated position. In addition, however, combining sensors can yield good results even when one sensor is noisy or fails entirely. The Etak method of computing heading, using both a compass and differential wheel sensor measurement, is an example in which the absolute sensor (the compass) suffers no accumulation of error and the relative sensor (the differential odometer) is unaffected by magnetic anomalies – yielding a combined result that is rarely erroneous (Honey, Milnes and Zavoli 1988).

Despite such accurate and resilient methods of deriving heading, the accuracy of a dead reckoned position still also depends on the accuracy of location of the prior position. The ineluctable errors in sensors lead to accumulated error in DR position. In practice, DR alone is insufficient for navigation since the accumulated error will eventually exceed a threshold of usefulness. So occasional fixes are needed, achieved either by human intervention, radio location or map matching. The first of these is tiresome and assumes accuracy on the part of the user; the third method is discussed in detail below. Radio location, however, has characteristic errors that are quite different to those already discussed. These errors do not accumulate over time or distance. Instead, signals are typically received clearly and the error level is the characteristic minimum or, alternatively, there is no position information available. It is, however, possible to dead reckon between radio fixes or, as Etak has done, use radio location (in this case LORAN-C) as just another sensor to be considered in location determination.

Map matching

Map matching is used to remove accumulated error from dead reckoning. The path travelled is determined by dead reckoning or radio location and integrating this with roads and intersections constitutes map matching (see Fig. 43.5). Dead reckoning with map matching is like navigation with absolute sensors in that the error in estimated position does not continue to grow (as it does with use of dead reckoning alone). It differs in that, once lost, the map matching algorithm is unlikely to recover; absolute sensors, on the other hand, may fail for a time or region but, outside that period or region, they have their usual error characteristics.

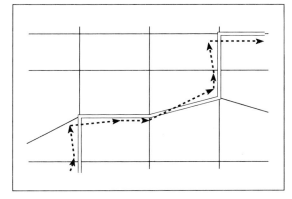

Fig. 43.5 Map matching – identifying a DR path (dashed line) with streets on the map.

By way of an example, one would eventually accumulate significant error using only DR while wandering along city streets. Through comparing the DR path to the map, however, the navigation algorithm can eliminate errors that accumulate from sensor noise. Etak pioneered the map matching approach (see Honey *et al.* 1989) for the Navigator. The Bosch Travelpilot uses the same approach and the Nissan Cedric uses a similar map matching method. Such map matching depends on the driver staying mainly on the roads; it is inappropriate for automatic guidance of a vehicle. In this approach, heading as well as position is determined as an output of map matching and is used for orienting the map displayed to the driver. Experience indicates that the impression given by a map display with a slightly 'wrong' orientation is that the computer is lost or will be soon – somewhat like the impression of a misaligned street name on a printed map. For this reason, map matching methods are used to orient and position the display even for absolute location methods, such as radio location.

Other navigation approaches that have been tried require extensive infrastructure, such as beacons mounted on traffic signal standards. ALI/ SCOUT and Autoguide (Catling and Belcher 1989) are examples of such systems. Such approaches can also be coupled with broadcast traffic information. In Japan, the Advanced Mobile Traffic Information and Communication System (AMTICS) project was a test of such a concept (Tsuzawa and Okamoto 1989). The PATHFINDER project in the Los Angeles region is intended to gather information about alternative routes drivers select when provided with traffic congestion information (Wasielewski 1988).

Display and report

All of the commercially available systems display map and vehicle location information graphically on a dash-mounted CRT. Some work has been done to present instructions by voice, but this approach is still in early development stages. Regardless of the method, safety is paramount. Map displays in this context are a dashboard instrument and must provide the needed information at a glance and must not distract the driver. When audio systems become available, they will also be required to facilitate driving, but not distract the driver's attention. As a result, the human interface must conform to dashboard instrumentation design guidelines. For visual displays, this includes letter and symbol sizes in terms of subtended angle for the driver and readability at a glance. In the case of audio output, sounds must be non-distracting and easily understood.

So far as map displays in cars are concerned, heading-up orientation (i.e. displaying the map so that 'up' on the display is 'ahead' on the ground and hence left and right on the display show features that are left and right of the vehicle respectively) makes the display much simpler to understand and read at a glance. In the Etak Navigator and Bosch Travelpilot, the display is heading up with some hysteresis in the heading adjustment to avoid a 'jumpy' display. The Nissan Cedric permits display at only the four cardinal headings and operates in a 'near heading up' mode. In addition, more generalized views provided through smaller scale map presentations are also quite helpful to a driver for choosing routes or just learning context. All commercially available systems provide generalized views. For a map to be readable at a glance, very

Fig. 43.6 Etak map displays at three scales showing few feature labels (courtesy author).

little annotation is possible. All three of the systems mentioned show only four or five feature labels at one time. Figure 43.6 shows three displays from the Travel pilot at various scales, each showing only a few labels. The labels shown were chosen by an algorithm that favours more important streets, the selected destination street and the street on which the car is currently placed.

GUIDANCE TOWARDS A DESTINATION

A primary use of navigation systems is in finding the location of destinations, usually specified by street address but also by street intersection or major landmark, and then finding a way to proceed to the destination.

Destination finding

To find a destination, the map database is searched via specially designed indexes and the destination is shown, for example, on the plot with a flashing star. The driver proceeds towards the star and his or her destination, as it was for the Biblical Star of Bethlehem! In-vehicle destination finding is interactive, may lack a keyboard and – because it is interactive – can take advantage of the user's ingenuity. In the Bosch Travelpilot and the Etak Navigator, for example, there are 12 buttons for input and the user only needs to enter a few characters before selecting from a list of possible cities or street names which match what has already been entered. Figure 43.7 shows a destination entry in progress. The user's ingenuity is exploited for recognizing spelling variants, in contrast to the common practice in geocoding software to search for sound-alike or otherwise similar words.

Fig. 43.7 Destination entry to the Etak Navigator.

In the future, business directories ('Yellow Pages') and other lists of destinations will be provided as part of the map. Finding the nearest hardware store or service station is an example of such applications. Detailed business information or advertising could also be provided: for example, restaurant menus may be included. Various experiments are under way to test technical aspects as well as market acceptance of in-vehicle business listings.

Path finding

At the time of writing, only experimental systems such as EVA and CARIN compute recommended paths from the current location to the destination. For pathfinding, the street network topology is required. Furthermore, for the recommended paths to be feasible, the pathfinding algorithm must use traffic flow and turn restriction information; this places a significantly larger burden on the map database. People often expect the guidance system to declare the best route and, ultimately, pathfinding is likely to be a required feature of all navigation systems.

The user interface for the pathfinding function can take many forms. Autoguide, for example, provides only an arrow indicating the action at the next intersection, or a more elaborate graphic for a roundabout. Highlighting the path on a map display is another approach. Two further approaches highlight the path on the map display and offer verbal instructions (Cass 1989).

DIGITAL MAP REQUIREMENTS AND CHARACTERISTICS

A digital map for navigation must meet demanding criteria. It must reside on rugged media, satisfy geometrical requirements imposed by the method of position determination, provide very fast retrieval and use an appropriate coordinate system.

Storage media

The storage medium for all available systems except the Etak Navigator is Compact Disk (CD) (Honey and White 1986). The Navigator uses compact cassette tape. The media and reading device must be sufficiently rugged for vehicle environments and these suffer wide temperature fluctuations and severe vibration. CD players meeting in-vehicle environmental specifications only became available in 1989 and, being designed some years earlier, the Etak cassette player was made specifically to meet in-vehicle requirements for the application. All such devices are relatively slow for random retrieval; typical average seek time for a CD is 1 second – over 30 times that of a typical hard disk. The Etak cassette tape, which operates at 80 inches per second, has typical seek times of 10 seconds. These relatively slow speeds impose noteworthy challenges and severe constraints for the retrieval software, which are discussed below.

Digital maps also consume considerable space. Each CD holds approximately 600 Mb. This is sufficient in EtakMap format to contain all of the streets, with their names and address ranges, in the United States. Etak's cassette tape holds 3.5 Mb, which is sufficient for approximately the same information as shown in two typical folded paper street maps. Inevitably, the current trend is towards Compact Disk because the speed is workable and the storage available is capacious.

Images, vectors, topology and geometry

The simplest digital map representation to acquire and display is the bit-mapped image. It is also the least informative to the navigation software and most voracious in memory requirements. Map matching systems cannot use such images nor are images useful for destination finding. They only support display and, in any event, only at one scale and in one or a very few orientations: thus an upside-down image would not be readable. This is a severe limitation since most systems display the map with the heading of the vehicle being towards the top of the display, the so-called 'heading-up' orientation described above.

A more useful form of map encoding for navigation software is the vector encoding, in which linear features are encoded as directed line segments (vectors) or sequences of segments (see Egenhofer and Herring 1991 in this volume). This encoding is far more compact but is much more costly to acquire. It can support rudimentary map matching and display as well as variations in scale and orientation. Simply coding vectors (i.e. storing the equivalent of plotter commands) is not, however, sufficient for pathfinding nor is it adequate for sophisticated map matching that uses the network topology in its calculations. On the other hand, a geometrical encoding which includes topology fully supports map matching and display. Map matching requires the geometry of the road network for comparing and matching the dead reckoned path with streets; it also requires the geometry for evaluating possible matches against paths permitted in the road network topology. For example, a road connected to the previously 'occupied' road is more likely to be the one currently occupied by the vehicle than one that is not connected but which is near by.

In addition to applications that directly use topological information from the map, the well-known advantages of topological encoding for error detection and control, consistency of feature attribute assignment and control of digital map maintenance all favour such a method of encoding. Furthermore, topological data can be used to improve retrieval speed, which is quite important and is discussed below. Etak uses a topological encoding that also includes generalized views; these are themselves topological encodings of generalized maps computed from the detailed digital map. These views are used for small scale displays and will be used in the future for pathfinding over large distances. In this case, topology in both the fully detailed map and the generalized maps is required for pathfinding.

Retrieval

There are three different types of map retrieval criteria used in vehicle navigation. The first is window retrieval, which is used to retrieve map data surrounding the vehicle or the destination; these data are used both for map matching and display. Second is retrieval by attributes, such as address or street intersection, for destination finding. The third criterion is topological, which is used in pathfinding.

Map retrieval while driving must keep pace with the vehicle. That is, regardless of the vehicle's speed, map data for all the streets surrounding the vehicle must be in RAM for use by the map matching algorithm. Depending on the scale of the display, all or a selection of streets and other features must be in RAM for display. This is a very difficult requirement to meet given the constraints of in-vehicle systems, particularly the slow speed of mass storage and limits on amount of RAM available. For the Etak Navigator, the mass storage is cassette tape and the CPU is an Intel 8088 with 256 Kb RAM. To make retrieval sufficiently fast, Etak organized data so that geographically neighbouring features were usually near by on tape. This reduced the number of searches and the seek time quite dramatically over many GIS implementations.

The constraints for attribute-based retrieval are determined by human factors considerations. The system must find a destination before the user tires of waiting. Typically this constrains the retrieval to 10 seconds or so. Similarly, pathfinding must be fast but probably need not be as fast as destination finding.

Seamless map and coordinate systems

Various coordinate systems have been proposed for use in navigation. Plane projected systems simplify distance and heading computations for dead reckoning and map matching, at least within single map sheets. Complications arise at the seams where projection parameters change. Geodetic coordinates involve more complicated calculations but have the advantage of being seamless, at least over the region that the same approximating ellipsoid is used. The WGS84 ellipsoid is the global reference for GPS (Global Positioning System) and appears likely to be adopted even for systems not using GPS.

For pathfinding, it is necessary to have a connected graph covering the origin, destination and environs. Having unrelated databases for adjacent countries prevents pathfinding from an origin in one country to a destination in another. This means that the map must be topologically seamless, at least at the application software level. Pathfinding software must be able to 'crawl' along the digital street network in a sequence of high level retrieval calls. Seamless topology also simplifies the task of map matching and display algorithms, but these are not quite so dependent on seamlessness.

Digital map production

Providing digital maps meeting the requirements set out above is a huge job and is out of the line of business of automotive electronics suppliers. This fact has impeded development and marketing of navigation systems. Providing electronics alone is not nearly sufficient and mounting a digital mapping effort is expensive and fraught with risk, particularly for companies unfamiliar with the business and technology. Even for companies with considerable experience in digital mapping, the coverage and other requirements for general navigation are daunting. On the other hand, the future navigation market could be huge and the navigation maps are valuable in a multitude of other applications – especially in those countries (like the United States) where provision of large scale and up-to-date mapping has hitherto been sparse.

In the private sector, Etak has produced digital maps for navigation for all major cities in the United States, all of The Netherlands, all of West Germany and various other cities in several countries, including Japan, Argentina, Saudi Arabia, France, England and Hong Kong. Etak sees its business as electronic publishing of digital maps and is building a commercial business accordingly. For source material, Etak uses topographic maps (usually at 1 : 25 000 scale or larger), digital map files, such as TIGER (see Rhind 1991 in this volume), aerial photography, plus various lists of addresses, street names and geographical names and codes. Etak has done some very limited data capture in the field. Navigation Technologies of Santa Clara, California has also produced digital maps for navigation, particularly to support pathfinding for a few metropolitan areas (notably San Francisco Bay and Los Angeles) but has relied much more than Etak on field data capture. TeleAtlas in The Netherlands has produced maps for The Netherlands and has done extensive data capture in the field with specially equipped vehicles. Also, Geographic Data Technologies of Lyme, New Hampshire has provided map data to navigation system developers for US cities. In Japan, Zenrin is providing digital maps containing only major roads to Mazda for its navigation system. Mazda then uses its own manuscripts as the basis for building digital maps.

In the public sector, the Japan Digital Road Map Association (JDRMA) has digitized all of Japan using topographic maps supplied by the government at 1 : 50 000 scale. The Ordnance Survey in Britain has produced the OSCAR data (see Sowton 1991 in this volume) and has provided data for Autoguide covering a corridor between London and Heathrow airport. Several consortia

STANDARDS

The blossoming of navigation research has given rise to several standards committees and prototyping projects, including the Society of Automotive Engineers (SAE) Committee on Vehicle Navigation, the JDRMA, DRIVE (Dedicated Road Infrastructure for Vehicle Safety), PANDORA (Prototyping a Navigation Database of Road Network Attributes) and GDF (Geographic Data File). Many of these groups have proposed database content and format standards. None of these standards however has enjoyed market acceptance or even market evaluation, since they are not related to commercially available systems. The interested reader should consult the most recent conference proceedings describing these efforts. At the time of writing, the *Vehicle Navigation & Information Systems Conference (VNIS)*, Toronto, 1989, Conference Record offers over 100 papers describing current projects and consortia and much additional material can be found in RIN (1990).

JDRMA has embarked on a ten-year programme of data collection and dissemination and has completed the first phase, digitizing Japanese major roads for urban areas of 200 000 population or greater at 1 : 25 000 scale and rural areas at 1 : 50 000 scale (Kamijo, Okumura and Kitamura 1989). GDF has defined a three-tiered standard for navigation-related map data, including a data exchange standard (Claussen *et al.* 1989). PANDORA is building a prototype database for a corridor between London and Birmingham (Smith 1989).

A different approach to standards is to agree on a software interface. This is analogous to agreeing to a Basic Input Output System (BIOS) interface for personal computers. Etak has adopted this approach in providing its maps and software for use by vendors of other navigation technology (Alegiani, Buxton and Honey 1989). A software interface standard permits flexibility and innovation in storage and retrieval of data just as BIOS permits flexibility and innovation in hardware design and improvement.

CONCLUSIONS

Vehicle navigation is in its infancy but promises to be a voracious consumer of digital maps and GIS technology. Already there are commercial systems available in the United States, Germany and Japan offering street network topology, destination finding by address, intersection and landmark, head up displays and moving map displays. Navigation by dead reckoning and map matching requires maps with a positional accuracy of a car length and street network topology. Radio location, such as LORAN-C and GPS, are alternatives that have not yet emerged as strong contenders for the consumer market and require maps with coordinate information related to the LORAN or GPS transmitters. In the future, it seems certain that the vehicle will contain facilities for providing a variety of information related to vehicle position, location of facilities and traffic. Digital maps and GIS will necessarily play an important role in bringing about that situation.

REFERENCES

Alegiani J B, Buxton J, Honey S (1989) An in-vehicle navigation and information system utilizing defined software services. In: Reekie D H M, Case E R, Tsai J (eds.) *Vehicle Navigation & Information Systems Conference, Toronto*, IEEE, Toronto, 156 pp.

Cass R (1989) Digital databases for vehicle navigation: review of the state of the art. *Proceedings of the 20th International Symposium on Automotive Technology and Automation, Florence*, IEEE, Toronto, pp. 1241–54

Catling I, Belcher P (1989) Autoguide – Route Guidance in the United Kingdom. In: Reekie D H M, Case E R, Tsai J (eds.) *Vehicle Navigation & Information Systems Conference, Toronto*, pp. 1127–44

Claussen H, Lichtner W, Siebold J, Heres L, Lahaije P (1989) GDF, a proposed standard for digital road maps to be used in car navigation system. In: Reekie D H M, Case E R, Tsai J (eds.) *Vehicle Navigation & Information Systems Conference, Toronto*, pp. 324–30

Egenhofer M J, Herring J R (1991) High-level spatial data structures for GIS. In: Maguire D J, Goodchild M F,

Rhind D W (eds.) *Geographical Information Systems, principles and applications*, Longman, London, pp. 227–37, Vol 1

French R (1986) Automobile navigation: where is it going? *IEEE Position Location and Navigation Symposium, Las Vegas*

Frost & Sullivan, Inc. (1989) *The U.S. Non-Entertainment Automotive Electronics Market*. Frost & Sullivan, New York

Honey S, Milnes K, Zavoli W (1988) *Apparatus for generating a heading signal for a land vehicle*. US Patent 4,734,863.

Honey S, White M (1986) Cartographic databases. In: Lambert S S, Ropiequet S (ed.) *CD/ROM The New Papyrus*. Microsoft Press, Redmond WA, pp. 563–72

Honey S, Zavoli W, Milnes K, Phillips A, White M, Loughmiller G (1989) *Vehicle navigational system and method*. US Patent 4,796,191.

Kamijo S, Okumura K, Kitamura A (1989) Digital road map data base for vehicle navigation and road information systems. In: Reekie D H M, Case E R, Tsai J (ed.) *Vehicle Navigation & Information Systems Conference, Toronto*, pp. 319–23

Petchenik B (1989) The road not taken. *The American Cartographer* 16 (1): 47–50

Phillips A (1987) *Flux gate sensor with improved sense winding gating*. US Patent 4,646,015.

Rhind D W (1991) Counting the people: the role of GIS. In: Maguire D J, Goodchild M F, Rhind D W (eds.) *Geographical Information Systems: principles and applications*, Longman, London, pp. 127–37, Vol 2

RIN (1990) NAV 90. Land Navigation and Information Systems. *Proceedings of the 1990 Conference of the Royal Institute of Navigation*. Royal Institute of Navigation, London

Smith A B (1986) Developments in inertial navigation. *The Journal of Navigation* 39 (3): 401–15

Smith A B (1989) Prototyping a navigation database of road network attributes (PANDORA), In: Reekie D H M, Case E R, Tsai J (ed.) *Vehicle Navigation & Information Systems Conference, Toronto*, pp. 331–6

Sowton M (1991) Development of GIS-related activities at the Ordnance Survey. In: Maguire D J, Goodchild M F and Rhind D W (eds.) *Geographical Information Systems: principles and applications*, Longman, London, pp. 23–38, Vol 2

Thoone M (1987) CARIN, a car information and navigation system, *Philips Technical Review* 43 (11/12): 317–29

Tsuzawa M, Okamoto H (1989) Advanced mobile traffic information and communication system (AMTICS). In: *Proceedings of the 20th International Symposium on Automotive Technology and Automation, Florence*, pp. 1145–60

Wasielewski P (1988) Overview of PATHFINDER. *Proceedings of Research and Development Conference, California Department of Transportation, Sacramento*, September 263–4

44

COUNTING THE PEOPLE: THE ROLE OF GIS

D W RHIND

The role of GIS in the official counting of population numbers has expanded substantially in recent years, even if the procedures are rarely described officially in GIS terms. Counting the people and ascertaining their characteristics is a non-trivial operation. This chapter sets out to describe the fundamental tasks involved in counting population, the alternative ways in which this is achieved in different social, economic and political circumstances, and how GIS can underpin both the pre-planning phase and the subsequent data compilation, analysis, dissemination and display. It uses case studies of censuses in Britain and the United States and population registers in Scandinavia to demonstrate the international variations. The chapter concludes by pointing out that, while the technology has facilitated the routine counting and monitoring of population numbers and movements, the privacy of personal information is now a major issue and may well constrain the obvious additional uses to which GIS can be put in tallying the citizenry.

INTRODUCTION

There are over 5000 million people in the world and the total number is growing at around 1.7 per cent per annum (UN 1989). It is widely accepted that such population growth is probably a more important and immediate problem than environmental factors such as global warming (and, indeed, contributes to them). Yet the variations in growth rates are immense: a few countries (e.g. both the Federal and Democratic Republics of Germany from 1980 to 1987) are actually suffering population decline while, in other countries (e.g. in India, Iran and Bangladesh), the population growth is spectacular; urban population, especially in the Third World, continues to grow relative to rural populations. Knowing about such population changes is of importance at the global and continental scale. But equivalent information – enhanced by a breakdown of population totals by age, sex or other characteristics – is also vital at the local level where it is required for planning, for example, of the number of school places needed, to assess the likely impact of new road systems and to predict the availability of new, potential customers. Indeed, these two levels are linked since (see below) the data collection procedures currently in use mostly operate 'bottom up'. Information about individuals or groups of them is aggregated into statistics for larger and larger areas. In practice, most censuses provide information used for different purposes at different levels of resolution. In the United States, for instance, where the decennial counting of the people is enshrined in the Constitution, it is used as the basis for determining the number of members for each state in the House of Representatives and for taxation, as well as for many more local purposes.

It is not, therefore, surprising that most countries devote considerable resources to ascertaining demographic and socio-economic statistics and have long done so. Indeed, as *The Times* of 6 April 1981 pointed out, the counting of people is long-established and has sometimes had unfortunate consequences:

> The first *Book of Chronicles* recounts how King David conducted a census, at a time when a

graver view was taken of such matters than today, and how a pestilence was visited upon Israel to punish him. The king and his inner cabinet donned sackcloth to a man and, by energetic displays of contrition and diplomacy, persuaded God to stay his hand. The chronicler records that as a result of the pestilence there fell of Israel 70 000 men.

METHODS FOR COUNTING PEOPLE

Where a comprehensive count of all the population is required and the results need to be accurate even at small area level, this can only be accomplished in one of two ways. The first is to carry out an exhaustive census, enumerating the characteristics of each household and the people within it. Since such an undertaking is expensive (the 1980 US Census is reckoned to have cost about $4.7 per head of the population), they are carried out infrequently: most censuses have been taken at 10-year intervals although some countries (such as Canada) have usually carried them out at five-year intervals. Moreover, the scale of the enterprise has normally ensured that it is economic to ask many other questions, typically relating to household characteristics (income, fuel use, access to amenities such as telephones, etc.) as well as the standard ones relating to numbers in each household and the age and sex composition of the household. In all cases, the objective is to obtain, from a previously unknown population, a response which can then be aggregated to form statistics for small areas; the statistics for each of these areas in turn may be aggregated to give equivalent figures for larger areas, culminating in national totals. The nature of the census process ensures that the statistics are usually out of date for much of the period for which they are used, yet they have a surprisingly long half-life because there are no direct alternatives in the bulk of countries. The characteristics of censuses vary greatly, however, and no greater contrast exists than between those for the United Kingdom and the United States (Dewdney and Rhind 1988).

The second approach is to have no decennial census or, at best, to hold one only to calibrate and extend data obtained from other sources. The best examples of this are the population registers held in mainland Europe, notably those long maintained in Scandinavia (Redfern 1989; see also Ottoson and Rystedt 1991 in this volume). Such registers provide essentially up-to-date statistics by aggregations of information on individuals located in space by postal address to areas of relevance to administration.

There is, however, a third way of obtaining population totals useful when no on-ground figures may be collected. This involves use of a surrogate or 'proxy' variable, normally the areal extent of the urban area. Thus Tobler (1969) and other authors have demonstrated relationships between readily measured areal extent and population; both satellite imagery (Ogrosky 1975; Lo and Welch 1977; Han 1985) and air photography (Collins and El-Beik 1971; Hsu 1971; Clayton and Estes 1980) have been used – especially for Third World cities – as the main source of information. Such studies have calibrated their findings in supposedly similar areas where both population figures and area measurements exist. A development of this has been described by Langford, Maguire and Unwin (1989) who used land cover information deduced from satellite imagery to convert total population statistics from one areal base to another – a frequent requirement of GIS. It is obvious that such procedures can give no socio-economic or demographic breakdown of totals; it is also obvious that they are liable to be significantly in error at local levels and to work ineffectively in rural areas. Yet they may well be the only possible procedures for obtaining even crude estimates of population totals for those countries in which no census is held or register is maintained.

The geographical dimension is clearly central to both census taking and creating and maintaining a register; it is patently vital in collecting population data by surrogate means from satellite imagery. But beyond the counting process itself, the procedures used to assemble the population data, the accuracy and 'explicitness' involved and the nature and number of the geographical 'hooks' contained in the data sets generated and made available all affect the extent and success of subsequent data use. It seems likely that, with the possible exception of a few global environmental data sets, census statistics are the most widely used of all; they are, for instance, typically used to standardize all mortality and morbidity statistics to remove the effects of population characteristics varying between different areas. (Beaumont 1991 in this volume has described some of the business 'targeting' applications of such data.)

For these reasons – and because GIS hardware and software have begun to play key roles in the gathering and use of demographic and socio-economic data – this chapter sets out to demonstrate current practice and what might well be possible in future.

COUNTING PEOPLE UNDER DIFFERENT SOCIAL AND TECHNICAL SYSTEMS

Current practice and future trends in population counting may be examined by considering three countries:

1. A technically and socially advanced country where population registers are in routine use (with the Nordic countries used as examples).

2. A technically advanced country where much up-to-date knowledge of the physical infrastructure (location of houses, roads, etc.) is already known to the census-taking agency from other sources (using Britain as the example).

3. A technically advanced country where relatively little detailed, consistent and up-to-date information on physical infrastructure is available to the census agency from other government sources (with the United States used as the example).

In the last two cases, separate consideration is given to pre-census planning and the post-census preparation of results. It will be evident that political factors also require consideration and these are touched upon in several places. Census taking is by no means limited to the developed countries: as Nag (1984) makes clear, many other countries have a long and distinguished tradition of census taking. None of these is considered here because, while China and some others have made intensive use of computers for checking and aggregating the results from their censuses, no use is yet known of GIS in their census activities beyond some choropleth mapping (Rhind 1983).

The population register in Europe

Table 44.1 shows the different types of registers in use in 15 countries of Western Europe. The greatest development of population registers has occurred in the Nordic countries (Denmark, Finland, Norway and Sweden). There the existing local population registers have been computerized and interrelated through a central population register; each citizen is assigned a permanent reference number at birth or on immigration, which is held in the population registers and used in a wide range of administrative dealings between the citizen and the state. In these countries the population census derives its data in part or whole from the central population register and linked administrative files. The extreme case is Denmark, where the traditional census has been abandoned and replaced by statistics generated from 37 registers of administrative agencies. These provide annual or more frequent statistics of population, employment, commuting, income, housing and construction for municipalities or (sometimes) smaller areas.

Almost all countries with a central register have local registers which act as the method of informing the national one of changes. These local population registers comprise continuously updated records of the people resident in a local area such as a parish or commune. It is a list of names and addresses with some basic information about each person, usually including sex, place and date of birth and marital status and possibly also items like parentage, citizenship and even occupation. Such registers in Finland and Sweden date from the seventeenth century, while those in Belgium, Germany, Italy and the Netherlands were set up in the nineteenth century and those in Denmark, Luxembourg and Spain were founded in the twentieth century.

The accuracy of registers is critical if they are to be of value: in the Swedish register, for instance, census data revealed that only 0.3 per cent of people recorded in the population registers are not living at the recorded address, including some 0.05 per cent unrecorded immigrants (Redfern 1989). To maintain such accuracy, updating of the registers must be efficient. The main sources of information for updating are vital registrations (births, marriages and deaths) and information that has to be supplied to the registering authorities in that country (usually a change of residence). In

Table 44.1 Different types of population register used in some Western European countries.

	Local population registers	Central register to coordinate administrative records	Personal reference number
A. With full system of population registration			
Belgium	x	x	x
Denmark	x	x	x
Finland	x	x	x
Luxembourg	x	x	x
Norway	x	x	x
Sweden	x	x	x
B. Intermediate group			
France		x	x
Netherlands	x		x
Portugal		x	x
Spain	x	(x)	x
C. With local population registers only			
Federal Republic of Germany	x		
Greece	x		
Italy	x		
D. Without population registers			
Ireland			
UK			
Number of countries with feature (out of 15)	11	8	10

Source: Redfern 1989.

countries where people are slow to notify such changes (such as in Italy and Spain) individual details from the census are used to update the registers. The primary role of the registers is administrative: in the most developed ones the personal reference numbers carried over into the files of administrative agencies facilitate checking on the *bona fides* of an applicant (e.g. for social security) and facilitate automated search for those people who need to be informed of rights or obligations (such as contacting women to tell them where and when to go to a clinic for cancer screening purposes). The geography on the record is the postal address and this is normally used as the means of contacting individuals; in Sweden, however, this facilitates linkage with property registers and – in principle at least – it would permit the creation of statistical tables for areas in a fashion identical to that used by the US Bureau of the Census (see below).

Not all countries have accurate registers. Those of Southern Europe, for instance, are less up to date and complete than those further north. The main shortcomings are failures or delays on the part of the public in reporting events such as change of address, failures to remove the names of those who have died or emigrated and duplicate registrations. In practice, the causes of such problems include the use of the register for too few administrative purposes (and hence little self-correcting mechanism exists), a lack of personal reference numbers or a central register to regulate the local ones and the disinclination of the citizens to cooperate with bureaucracy!

If the primary role of registers is administrative, they may prove extremely useful as sources of population statistics. In Sweden, for instance, the national end-of-year statistics analysed by sex, age and region are available in the fifth week of the new year with error levels normally below 1 part in 1000. In Britain, which has some of the better census-style statistics, migration is normally only known for a one year period every tenth year and official estimates of it for local government areas in the intervening period are sometimes as much as 10 per cent in error. It is also obvious that registers can support one type of research which is impossible from the cross-sectional statistics provided by the census: longitudinal studies, which obviate many of the problems arising from the Modifiable Areal Unit Problem (MAUP) and are described by Openshaw (1991 in this volume).

So far as GIS are concerned, population registers hold basic geographical information which can be exploited in aggregating information to provide summary statistics, including the ability to produce these at different levels of spatial resolution – a vital ability if the stability of the results of any geographically-based analysis is to be established. In addition, the postal address of residence can be used as an additional key (over and above the highly limited name and date-of-birth keys) for linkage between data files if no unique personal identity number is in use. Finally, a GIS may be used to facilitate planning of activities such as cancer screening: women deduced to be at risk by age or some other factor may be notified of the time and place to attend their nearest clinic and sophistications such as ensuring that they do not go the same day as others from their immediate area may be built in if required.

Census taking: some general considerations

To carry out a count of the population by census means it is necessary to locate all the population (or at least functionally coherent groups within it, i.e. households) so that these may each receive a census form and, if no response is forthcoming, for each to be contacted again to rectify the situation. In essence, therefore, part of the answer (the number of people and where they live) has to be known to the administration before the census is carried out in order to carry out an efficient and accurate census! Furthermore, as in any measurement process, post-censal checks must be put in place to provide an estimate of the accuracy of the tabulated results; this again involves returning to a sample of the population.

If the principle is clear, the *modus operandus* of a census agency is influenced above all by the availability of data on which to plan the entire exercise. In this respect, the US and the British censuses differ dramatically. It might be thought that the 30-fold difference in areal size of the two countries accounts for these differences. However, the immediate reason for the differences in approach (and probably the explanation for the much higher cost per person enumerated in the US case) is the vastly more up to date, nationally consistent and accurate knowledge of where people are likely to be found which is provided by the large scale topographic maps in Britain (compare Sowton, 1991 in this volume, with Starr and Anderson 1991 in this volume). In the absence of such mapping, the US Bureau of the Census has devised quite different procedures, based substantially upon mailing address lists and use of the US Postal Service. Of course, such differences go much deeper than simply the availability of data: they reflect long-standing and almost opposed (until the 1980s) views of the role of the state in information gathering. A paradox, however, is that while the British government believes it to be perfectly appropriate for the state to compile information on infrastructure (and hence of the location of dwellings) in great detail, the US Census is much more probing in the questions it asks (e.g. on income) of respondents.

The British Census procedures

The essence of the British census-taking procedure is the delivery of census forms to each and every household and their collection by an enumerator; use of the postal service is largely absent. Each of the 130 000 or so enumerators is responsible for delivering census forms to every household within his or her allocated Enumeration District (ED). On average, this area contains about 160 households but this varies considerably between urban areas (with an average of about 200 households) and rural ones (with an average of about 60). Since each census response is coded with an ED identifier, the data from individual responses are readily aggregated into statistics for EDs and for any area which can be built from these building blocks. Thus statistics for the standard administrative hierarchy of ED/Electoral Ward/Administrative District/County/Region/Country/UK as a whole can be produced as a matter of routine.

Enumeration Districts are, therefore (at least in England and Wales), the basis of census geography. In practice, they are planned so as to make the workload for each enumerator approximately constant but obvious physical divides (rivers, major highways, etc.) are taken into account in drawing boundaries. The procedure for defining such EDs is largely a manual and map-based one; it involves human judgement and would also be impossible without the up-to-date, nationally comprehensive and very large-scale maps produced by the national mapping agency, the Ordnance Survey (see Sowton 1991 in this volume). Copies of OS maps at 1 : 1250, 1 : 2500 and 1 : 10 000 scale (the last only for rural areas) and annotated with the boundaries and names of EDs and larger areas are sold after the census. For those interested in research, there are some shortcomings in the ED design process – for instance, the resulting areas are often heterogeneous in demographic and social characteristics and shape. Linkage to non-census data is difficult since the only geographical descriptions in the 1971 and 1981 census data were a National Grid reference (coordinate) at 100 metres resolution which related to the centroid of the ED.

None the less, the simplicity of this approach and the quality of mapped knowledge about the whole country enable the census agency to produce numerous tabulations and data tapes for all 140 000+ standard areas based upon both 100 per cent and 10 per cent samples within 19 months of the 1991 Census – and at a cost of about £1 per head of the population (compare the cost with that of the US Census – see below).

In Scotland in 1981 and 1991, a rather different procedure was used to create EDs. These were based upon aggregations of unit postcodes. The British postcode is increasingly used for purposes other than the delivery of mail: since there are 1.3 million such non-business unit postcodes, each includes an average of about 15 mail delivery points. The pseudo-area which enveloped each postcode was mapped in Scotland and became the basic areal 'building block'; EDs were created by amalgamation of contiguous unit postcodes. In addition, a file of the National Grid reference for each postcode was created. The advantage of this procedure is that it enforces a mechanism for simplifying linkage of census and much other socio-economic or business data which is now often aggregated by some combination of postcodes. Moreover, since each questionnaire is coded with the postcode, aggregations to areas of any desired size and shape can be produced for users more accurately than with data held only by EDs. The disadvantage is increased costs in the planning process – at least the first time it is done. Again it was only possible because of the availability of very large scale and up-to-date maps.

A procedure of this type was urged upon government for use in England and Wales in 1991 in the Chorley Report (see Chorley and Buxton 1991 in this volume). The response was to compromise: each household response will be coded with its postcode but no maps showing individual postcodes will be produced or used in the planning process. None the less, users will – in theory at least – have the ability to obtain data for any specified combination of postcodes.

Such a prospect has resulted in academic and commercial organizations using GIS to generate Dirichlet (or Thiessen or 'proximal') tiles around the centroids of each postcode; considerable ingenuity has been shown by researchers in constraining the tile boundaries to fit with centre lines of streets, and so on. Thus, to a reasonable level of approximation, exceedingly small areas are now defined which can be used to facilitate data linkage. (It should be noted that confidentiality constraints preclude the release of much detailed information at the postcode level.)

Traditionally, the role of GIS and related tools in the British Census has been at the post-processing stage where the data are analysed and mapped. Thus HMSO (1980) was perhaps the first very fine grain census-based atlas of a whole country, showing distributions of some 60 variables from the 1971 Census for 150 000 1 km areas; Rhind, Visvalingham and Evans (1980) describe how the maps were produced in a few seconds of computer time and how the economics were changed dramatically as a consequence. This and the ready availability of mapping software (Rhind 1983) caused a proliferation of computer-produced atlases from 1982 onwards. Beyond this and Openshaw's analytical work, relatively little spatial analysis was carried out from the 1981 Census data: the standard software for handling the 1981 Census data – SASPAC (Rhind 1984) – was created by geographers and was used by almost every local government in the country yet provided little by way of geographical analysis capabilities. There is every reason to think that the ready availability of GIS technology and the easier-to-use data sets will change the situation following the 1991 Census. A significant difficulty remains in that – unlike the situation in the United States – the census-taking agency does not provide digital boundaries of census areas; in the United Kingdom, some of these have been provided by the Department of the Environment and others by the Ordnance Survey but, as of the time of writing (mid-1990), no national scheme for digitizing ED boundaries had been agreed.

In the longer term, however, an increased role of GIS in census pre-planning as well as in post-census analysis is inevitable. Experiments in 1988 suggested that design of EDs using PC-based GIS products was not yet cost effective – in part because of the then incompleteness of OS digital maps (see Sowton 1991 in this volume) and the difficulties of handling the data volumes involved. These data will certainly be available long before the next census and, assuming no fundamental change in the principles on which British censuses have been carried out, GIS technology will be the most cost-effective procedures by then.

Finally, all of the above is predicated upon the initial, pre-census creation of a standard set of census areas founded upon the ED or the unit postcode. An alternative approach has been demonstrated by Rhind *et al.* (1990). This involves retaining the storage of data for each household and individual, and generating aggregate statistics for whichever cross-tabulation of census questions is required for any user-specified area on demand. On-line working with simulated data sets mimicking the 20 million census returns provides tables at the ED or higher level of aggregation in under 4 seconds CPU time on an Amdahl 5990 running the Model 204 database system. The advantage of this (unusual form of) GIS is that it provides only what the user really requires – as opposed to over 6000 cross-tabulated values for each and every area – and does this at negligible cost; its disadvantage is that the public are extremely suspicious of any computer system which is readily accessed and which holds confidential personal data – even if it contains rules and many other safeguards to prevent misuse of the initial data. GIS technology, then, has provided new ways of carrying out census planning and analysis but privacy and societal considerations ultimately determine what will be adopted.

The US Census procedures

That the US Census is posited on geographical knowledge and creates yet more of it is evidenced by the 8 million maps produced before and after the 1990 Census (Tomasi 1990). Yet the form in which the knowledge is obtained and the extent of the automated geographical data handling differ considerably from those in British censuses. Indeed, the 1990 US Census serves as an international landmark in the integration of pre-census and post-census data processing, much of it based upon digital representation of the geography of the United States.

Since 1960, return of census forms from the bulk of the population has been via the US mail; mail-out was introduced in 1970. By 1990, the mail-out/mail-back procedure had been extended to areas covering 95 per cent of the population. It is obvious that such a procedure is highly economical in a country of the size and shape of the United States. But, to be effective, it requires up-to-date and accurate address lists, an army of enumerators to follow up the 37 per cent non-responses and seek out previously 'unknown' people plus a map base which shows all known settlements. Moreover, the user requirements are for tabulations for an enormous variety of different areas: states, counties, incorporated places, minor civil divisions, census county divisions, census tracts, neighbourhoods, urbanized areas and tribal designated statistical areas are only a few of those now used. The basic 'building unit' of this aggregation is the block and production of statistics for any area is achieved by aggregation 'bottom up' from individual household responses or from block statistics. Hence the use of postal address as the 'distribution and collection key' also requires the pre-assignment of numerous area codes to each address, especially that of the block. The 1990 US Census tackled all these requirements in a way that broke substantially with tradition; the central element in their new approach was the TIGER (Topologically Integrated Geographic Encoding and Referencing) system.

It is impossible to understand the ambition and magnitude of the TIGER system program without being aware of the nature of public-sector mapping in the United States (compare Starr and Anderson 1991 in this volume with, for instance, Sowton, 1991 in this volume and Ottoson and Rystedt 1991 in this volume). In essence, the national mapping agency (the US Geological Survey) provides near-comprehensive map coverage only to scales as large as 1 : 24 000 and most of these sheets are significantly out-of-date. For larger scale mapping, essential for coping with many urban areas in the census, the Census Bureau created its own manually produced Metropolitan Map Series (MMS). Yet, by 1980, when there were 10 000 map sheets in the series, only 2 per cent of the land area was covered (Tomasi 1990). Moreover, the immense variety of source materials were not integrated in any way. These sources were used for several purposes, including: making pre- and post-census maps; updating the multiple address lists that were obtained from any available source; and for producing output tabulations and maps. The result was a multiplicity of systems, some automated, for planning, carrying out and reporting the census; duplication of effort and under-representation were the result. Tomasi (1990 : 25) has described the shortcomings of the 1980 mapping in graphic terms:

To prepare the numerous map copies the decennial census requires, staff reproduced the maps using the diazo process. To meet distribution deadlines, most maps eventually were shipped to the field without being reviewed for completeness or legibility. As a consequence, the maps had a variety of deficiencies. Boundaries to be used specifically for the 1980 census often could not be distinguished from other boundaries. Boundaries which ended on the border of one map sheet did not always resume at the same location on the border of the adjacent sheet. Maps often were illegible, had indistinguishable features, or were of insufficient size for use in supporting the 1980 field activities, and maps had features which were as much as 20 years out-of-date because there was no program for updating these maps outside the MMS coverage. The pressure imposed by rigid time schedules resulted in some maps being overexposed or underexposed, with very dark blurred images or images too light to see. These problems led the Census Bureau field staff to wander outside assigned areas, miscode information, and perform unnecessary work. Inconsistencies among the information contained in the three components of the geographical support system also created data tabulation problems, caused the Census Bureau's staff to spend time resolving questions posed by data users, and raised doubts in the minds of local officials about the accuracy of the 1980 census.

From 1983 onwards, the Census Bureau was engaged in planning a coherent system for integrating almost all of its activities in the census of housing and population. To facilitate this, the Bureau and the USGS signed an agreement that year to collaborate over the digitizing and coding of certain features from the latter's new 1 : 100 000 scale maps of the entire country. The Bureau added its own codes to this data and added more detail wherever necessary. As a result, the TIGER/Line™ files made generally available by the Bureau are the most detailed and up-to-date network (road, rail and hydrography) and boundary files in the United States.

The next section describes briefly the nature of the system that emerged; considerable additional detail is given in Volume 17, Part 1 of the journal *Cartography and Geographic Information Systems* which was devoted to TIGER. Marx (1990) has provided an overview of the rationale for TIGER, a history of its development and suggestions for future enhancements.

The TIGER system

The requirements of the TIGER system are:

- to provide an integrated, spatially cohesive and up-to-date description of the census geography of the entire United States;

- to provide an automated field mapping system;

- to provide a system for tabulating data by any of the standard administrative or statistical sets of areal units (comprising some 39 000 units in total);

- to provide a publication mapping system.

This has been achieved by designing a spatial database system (Broome and Meixler 1990) and, for the cartographic products, devising additional mapping application programs which act upon the database or on derived products from it (see Bishton 1990; Beard and Robbins 1990; Ebinger and Goulette 1990; Broome and Godwin 1990). Although other elements are contained within TIGER, notably the tools to assign the addresses of millions of housing units to blocks, the focus here is on the spatial aspects of the system.

The TIGER spatial database, though conceptually a single entity, in fact comprises four main types of files and, within them, partitioned sub-files. The four main file types are the national partition files, the county partition files, the geographical catalogue and temporary work files. Some 3287 county partition files exist, each containing all the geographical coordinates, codes and relationships within that area and all held as topologically consistent data sets (see Franklin 1991 in this volume; see also Egenhofer and Herring 1991 in this volume); these include street address ranges along sides of blocks. They comprise the largest fraction by far of the database. Central to the concept is that these are stored as points, lines (or chains) and areas; in the census terminology these are 0-cells, 1-cells and 2-cells (see Corbett 1979 and Fig. 44.1). Metric information in the form of coordinates is stored at the 0-cell level or as separate curvature records; this ensures that the many queries which can be answered on the basis of relationships need not access large coordinate files.

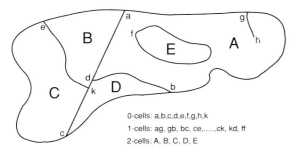

Fig. 44.1 Relationships of the TIGER spatial primitives.

All lines and areas are 'atomic fragments' in the sense that each is homogeneous in terms of all the codes and features within the mapped area. They are encoded after all the boundary lines of all types of areas of interest to the census are compiled on base maps and vertically integrated on a 'once and for all' basis. The national partition file comprises all the equivalent features for each of the county boundary areas. Finally, the catalogue file contains current and historical information on political and statistical entities above those of the individual (e.g. 2-cell or area) feature. It is the source of place, county and state names, information about the geographical codes for each entity and the relationships among the stored entities. As such, it serves as an index for accessing data when the search is based upon area name or geographical code.

There is now little of novelty in the basic principles of the TIGER spatial data structure, although many of the application programs break new ground. What is particularly impressive, however, is the magnitude of the task achieved, the demonstrable importance of 'provably consistent' entities achieved through the use of a topological structure and the variety of roles that can be played by one database. It is also noteworthy that the software was written within the Bureau rather than by the commercial sector. So far as GIS users are concerned, however, the sale of TIGER/Line™ files is of the greatest importance: these provide the most detailed feature network and administrative coverage of the country yet available and – despite costing $330 million to compile – are being sold at a very modest cost (Marx 1990). Moreover, the Bureau of the Census has encouraged software vendors to provide interfaces to the TIGER data so that they can be used for many other purposes. In reality, therefore, the Bureau has fostered an industry and has become in effect a national mapping organization, currently providing rather more detailed and up-to-date information than does the USGS. Plans have been laid to maintain the TIGER files throughout the next decade; their success will depend primarily on the levels of local cooperation and federal funding made available to the Bureau. A number of commercial organizations have also claimed that they will maintain the TIGER files in metropolitan areas but, as such, these operations total no more than 2 per cent of the land area.

CONCLUSIONS

From all that has been said above, it should be evident that GIS already play a significant role in the counting of population in many countries. Even if the obvious use of GIS in the inference of population numbers using satellite imagery, or the aggregation of statistics 'bottom up' from population registers is excluded, the role of such systems in census taking is significant and growing. The TIGER system in the United States is much the most comprehensive (and expensive) GIS yet used in this way; it seems likely that the benefits attributable to such a scheme will influence other census takers in years to come. Certainly the technology is improving and becoming less expensive faster than population numbers are growing and user demands are increasing! It should be noted, however, that direct transfer of the TIGER concepts would be difficult in those parts of the world which have very different forms of geocoding to the United States (e.g. Japanese and Arab street nomenclature is very different).

One of the more intriguing questions which arises from any comparison of the way in which the British and the Americans conduct censuses; is why they differ so much in cost: the 1980/81 censuses in the two countries cost about £1.30 and $4.7 per head respectively. There is a reasonable case that, despite the much larger size of the United States, economies of scale should have been achievable so the cost differential should have been negligible. One contributing factor is the availability of up-to-date, detailed and spatially comprehensive information on the location of infrastructure and on administrative boundaries. In Britain these are provided on a routine and continuing basis by the national mapping agency, funded directly by the tax payer or from commercial sales; the census agency pays very little for this information by comparison with that necessarily expended in the United States. The continuing availability of TIGER files (assuming they are continually updated after 1990) makes the United States much closer to the British situation than hitherto and will inevitably enforce a re-examination of the respective roles of the Bureau of the Census and of the US Geological Survey.

We live in a world where the use of credit cards is commonplace and where computer systems are ubiquitously employed to support administrative functions in both public and private services. Unsurprisingly, therefore, it is not now difficult to design GIS which link together census and administratively collected data of various kinds (Rhind 1985), thereby creating a hybrid register- and census-based method for counting population. It is also relatively easy to demonstrate that such systems, tailored to suit local circumstances, can be more economical and productive than massive decennial events on their own. Yet the availability of the technology to achieve all this is only a necessary – not a sufficient – condition. In the Western world, the perceived threats to civil liberties from computer storage of personal and precisely located information have already resulted in the cancellation of the Dutch Census in 1981 and a two-year postponement of the German one from 1981 to 1983 (Redfern 1987, 1989). Census agencies are, therefore, understandably cautious about introducing technology like GIS which, within one system, can search records for individuals and tabulate results in aggregate form. There are demonstrable benefits from providing more flexible, GIS-based facilities to the public. Yet the fear of disclosure of confidential information and the resulting impact on census responses may well constrain the level of use of GIS in analysis and reporting of census data to whatever can be achieved from pre-packaged area aggregate statistics. In the privacy of census taking within the authorized government agency, however, GIS are set to make an ever more critical contribution to counting the people.

REFERENCES

Beard C, Robbins A M (1990) Scale determination and inset selection within a totally automated map production system. *Cartography and Geographic Information Systems* **17** (1): 57–68

Beaumont J R (1991) GIS and market analysis. In: Maguire D J, Goodchild M F, Rhind D W (eds.) *Geographical Information Systems: principles and applications.* Longman, London, pp. 139–51, Vol 2

Bishton A (1990) Mapping from a cartographic extract. *Cartography and Geographic Information Systems* **17** (1): 49–56

Broome F R, Godwin L (1990) The Census Bureau's publication map system. *Cartography and Geographic Information Systems* **17** (1): 79–88

Broome F R, Meixler D B (1990) The TIGER database structure. *Cartography and Geographic Information Systems* **17** (1): 39–47

Chorley R, Buxton R (1991) The government setting of GIS in the United Kingdom. In: Maguire D J, Goodchild M F, Rhind D W (eds.) *Geographical Information Systems: principles and applications.* Longman, London, pp. 67–79, Vol 1

Clayton C, Estes J E (1980) Image analysis as a check on census enumeration accuracy. *Photogrammetric Engineering and Remote Sensing* **46**: 757–64

Collins W G, El-Beik A H A (1971) Population census with the aid of aerial photographs: an experiment in the city of Leeds. *Photogrammetric Record* **7**: 16–26

Corbett J P (1979) Topological principles in cartography. *Technical paper 48*, US Bureau of Census, Suitland, December 1979. (Also published in *Proceedings of AUTOCARTO4*, 1975. ASPRS, Falls Church Virginia)

Dewdney J C, Rhind D W (1988) The British and United States Censuses of Population. In: Pacione M (ed.) *Population Geography: progress and prospects.* Croom Helm, London, pp. 35–57

Ebinger L, Goulette A (1990) Noninteractive automated names placement for the 1990 decennial census. *Cartography and Geographic Information Systems* **17** (1): 69–78

Egenhofer M J, Herring J R (1991) High-level spatial data structures for GIS. In: Maguire D J, Goodchild M F, Rhind D W (eds.) *Geographical Information Systems: principles and applications.* Longman, London, pp. 227–37, Vol 1

Franklin Wm R (1991) Computer systems and low-level data structures for GIS. In: Maguire D J, Goodchild M F, Rhind D W (eds.) *Geographical Information Systems:*

principles and applications. Longman, London, pp. 215–25, Vol 1

Han K H (1985) *Estimation of Major City Population in Korea Using Landsat Imagery.* Unpublished PhD thesis, University of Utah

HMSO (1980) *People in Britain – a census atlas.* HMSO, London

Hsu S Y (1971) Population estimation. *Photogrammetric Engineering* **37**: 449–54

Langford M, Maguire D J, Unwin D J (1989) Modelling population distribution using remote sensing and GIS. *Research Report 3 Midlands Regional Research Laboratory.* MRRL, Leicester UK

Lo C P, Welch R (1977) Chinese urban population estimates. *Annals of the Association of American Geographers* **67**: 246–53

Marx R W (1990) The TIGER system: yesterday, today and tomorrow. *Cartography and Geographic Information Systems* **17** (1): 89–97

Nag P (1984) *Census Mapping Survey.* International Geographical Union Commission on Population Geography/Concept Publishing Company, New Delhi

Ogrosky C E (1975) Population estimates from satellite imagery. *Photogrammetric Engineering and Remote Sensing* **41**: 707–12

Openshaw S (1991) Developing appropriate spatial analysis methods for GIS. In: Maguire D J, Goodchild M F, Rhind D W (eds.) *Geographical Information Systems: principles and applications.* Longman, London, pp. 389–402, Vol 1

Ottoson L, Rystedt B (1991) National GIS programmes in Sweden. In: Maguire D J, Goodchild M F, Rhind D W (eds.) *Geographical Information Systems: principles and applications.* Longman, London, pp. 39–46, Vol 2

Redfern P (1987) *A Study on the Future of the Census of Population: alternative approaches.* EUROSTAT Report 3C, Luxembourg

Redfern P (1989) Population registers: some administrative and statistical pros and cons. *Journal of the Royal Statistical Society A* **152** (1): 1–41

Rhind D W (ed.) (1983) *A Census Users Handbook.* Methuen, London

Rhind D W (1984) The SASPAC story. *BURISA* **60**: 8–10

Rhind D W (1985) Successors to the Census of Population. *Journal of Economic and Social Measurement* **13** (1): 29–38

Rhind D W, Visvalingham M, Evans I S (1980) Making a national atlas of population by computer. *Cartographic Journal* **17** (1) 3–11

Rhind D W, Cole K, Armstrong M, Chow L, Openshaw S (1990) An on-line, secure and infinitely flexible database system for the national population census. *Working Report 14 South East Regional Research Laboratory.* SERRL, Birkbeck College, London

Sowton M (1991) Development of GIS-related activities at the Ordnance Survey. In: Maguire D J, Goodchild M F, Rhind D W (eds.) *Geographical Information Systems: principles and applications.* Longman, London, pp. 23–38, Vol 2

Starr L E, Anderson K E (1991) A USGS perspective on GIS. In: Maguire D J, Goodchild M F, Rhind D W (eds.) *Geographical Information Systems: principles and applications.* Longman, London, pp. 11–22, Vol 2

Tobler W R (1969) Satellite confirmation of settlement size coefficients. *Area* **3**: 30–3

Tomasi S G (1990) Why the nation needs a TIGER system. *Cartography and Geographic Information Systems* **17** (1): 21–6

UN (1989) *United Nations 1987 Demographic Yearbook.* UN, New York

GIS AND MARKET ANALYSIS

J R BEAUMONT

Market analysis is a pervasive characteristic of highly competitive capitalist societies. This chapter describes the needs of marketeers for detailed information for different decision categories and for GIS systems to provide this in the most assimilable form. The existing applications are summarized through a consideration of Marketing Information Systems, Branch Location Analysis and the use of Direct Mail. A final section examines the likely trends and concludes that there is some scope for evolution of GIS – notably in the provision of better spatial analytical tools – but that 'bundling' of software and data plus increasing ease of use (especially in conjunction with existing tools for financial analysis and investment appraisal) will be most important in future.

INTRODUCTION

At the end of the 1970s, GIS were not central to geographically-related research (e.g. Rhind 1981). Yet, at the beginning of the 1990s, GIS represent a significant and growing field of both fundamental and applied geographical research. There are many reasons for this development but they can be illustrated by reference to one application domain: marketing of goods and services. For marketing, the 1950s and 1960s were characterized by 'mass' marketing, but the 1970s and 1980s have been characterized increasingly by 'niche' marketing. Such marketing trends have required more spatially disaggregated information about both consumers and competitors. This trend will continue, particularly through the growing establishment of customer databases. For competitive advantage and business effectiveness, marketeers need to be able to handle geographical data efficiently. GIS are being recognized increasingly as useful and relevant tools in their armoury, especially if designed appropriately as Spatial Decision Support Systems (see Densham 1991 in this volume).

The application of GIS in market analysis involves both practitioners in public and private sector organizations and academics stimulated by applied and policy research; in some ways, this field illustrates many of the dimensions and interrelationships between 'fundamental' and 'applied' research in the social sciences. It also reflects the new academic era of greater specialization and accountability. While attention here focuses on private sector applications, the analyses have important parallels in the public sector (and such applications extend the policy paradigm being advocated by many researchers). The planning and evaluation of health care, for instance, involves estimation of the spatial pattern of needs to decide the location of hospitals, general practitioners and emergency services (see also Calkins, 1991 in this volume).

This specific discussion covers the distinctive industry of market analysis (sometimes referred to as 'geodemographics'). It is rapidly expanding, particularly in North America, Europe and Australia. While the industry has been established for over 15 years in the United States, the major orientation there remains the re-supply or re-packaging of census of population data. By contrast, there has been a stronger emphasis on analysis and on new product developments in the United Kingdom. However, as with GIS generally and in spite of enhanced data availability and quality, there is minimal incorporation of the methodological advances in spatial analysis of the

1960s and 1970s (which are well covered by Bennett and Wrigley 1981; see also Openshaw, 1991 in this volume). This chapter contains a broad overview of the current major applications areas of GIS in market analysis and this discussion provides the basis of a prediction of further developments over the next decade.

It is difficult to do justice to 'GIS and market analysis' in a short chapter. There is no intention here to provide a comprehensive listing of all possible GIS applications. The selection of topics – marketing information systems, branch location analysis and direct mail – necessarily ignores other applications such as advertising effectiveness, credit scoring and other forms of direct marketing. For a more thorough discussion of these and other topics in the context of marketing strategy and implementation, see Bonoma (1985), Kotler (1988) and Peters (1987). More comprehensive discussions of market analysis have become available recently which are aimed at different markets: for students and teachers, see Beaumont (1991); for researchers, see Beaumont (1989); and for practitioners, see Rothman (1989).

A short overview of market analysis is presented below to summarize the context of this discussion. A framework is also outlined to illustrate the explicit links with GIS principles. An applications perspective follows: it is stressed that GIS can provide useful and actionable information as an input to management's decision-making process. Then, in the main section of this chapter, there is a general discussion of three selected application areas. In the final section of this chapter, some personal interpretations are made about the future outlook, primarily with regard to GIS developments rather than to market analysis.

MARKET ANALYSIS

'Market analysis' covers a wide range of topics and, as organizations have become more strategic and externally orientated, there has been a tendency for it to be indistinguishable from 'marketing' and, indeed, from business (development) planning (see Kotler, 1988, for a 'classic' coverage of marketing). Conventionally, the 'marketing mix' is summarized as the 'four Ps': product; price; place; and promotion. The contribution of these dimensions constitutes the offering to satisfy customers' needs; the mix will be different for different market segments. Marketeers must manage this mix effectively and, increasingly (as Fig. 45.1 indicates) a fifth 'P' (data) processing should be acknowledged as being significant.

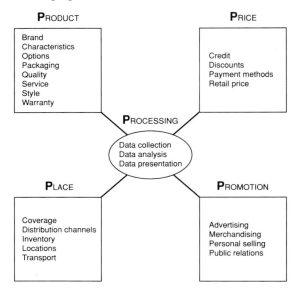

Fig. 45.1 The 'five Ps' of the marketing mix.

For market analysis, it is necessary for an organization to undertake both an external and an internal evaluation. It is necessary to define the market(s), describe and locate the target group(s) and to consider the purchasing process – all within the context of the (local) competitive position. This external evaluation should be complemented by an internal PANIC (Potential And Needs, Investments and Capabilities) audit. For marketing management, a range of fundamental questions must be answered, including:

- Who?
  - are our customers?
  - should our customers be?
  - are our competitors?
- What?
  - new/existing products and services should we develop?
  - new/existing markets should we enter?
- Where?
  - should we develop?

are our customers?
should we distribute our products and
 services?
are our competitors?

- When?
 should we launch new products and services?
 should we enter new/leave existing markets?

- How?
 should we promote our products and
  services?
 should we distribute our products and
  services?
 should we handle consumer
  reactions/expectations?
 should we compete?
 should we maximize our returns?
 should we monitor our performance and
  evaluate new opportunities?

- Why?
 should consumers buy our products and
  services?
 should we develop new products
  and services?
 should we remain in particular
  markets/businesses?

While reference is often made by practitioners to the importance of 'location, location and location', in practice the backcloth is multidimensional. Generally for business (development) planning, market analysis must take a broader perspective, incorporating not only products and services, consumers and competitors, but also marketing channels, order processing, distribution, financial transactions and the corporate organization. The marketing system's (multi-site) dimensions each have their own spatial components and it is becoming increasingly more complicated with interrelated flows. Moreover, advances in computing and communications technologies are changing many space–time relationships and, indeed, the way business is done. For example, Electronic Data Interchange (EDI) – where orders, invoices and other documentation are transferred directly between the computers of different companies – is becoming very important in a range of different industries (e.g. see some of the case studies developed for the Department of Trade and Industry 1990).

For market analysis, it is important to relate the different management planning and control activities with their different information requirements. Following the framework of Gorry and Scott Morton (1989), Fig. 45.2 summarizes the relationships between different types of decisions and their information characteristics. So far as operational control is concerned, for example, detailed (often real-time) data are required on stock levels for inventory control, to enable efficient replenishment via the warehousing/distribution system to satisfy customers' needs. In comparison, much less detailed and broader data are needed for strategic planning in order to assess alternative distribution channels and branch and warehouse locations, covering not only their general cost structures but also the new markets that could be covered.

Information characteristics	TYPE OF DECISION		
	Operational control	Management control	Strategic planning
Source	Largely internal ←	→	External
Scope	Well defined, narrow ←	→	Very wide
Level of aggregation	Detailed ←	→	Aggregate
Time horizon	Historical ←	→	Future
Currency	Highly current ←	→	Quite old
Required accuracy	High ←	→	Low
Frequency of use	Very frequent ←	→	Infrequent

Fig. 45.2 Information requirements for market analysis by decision category (after Gorry and Scott Morton 1989).

In the case of planning and control, a number of different marketing decisions can be recognized which relate to target marketing, resource allocation, sales force automation, performance evaluation, distribution channels, stock levels, promotional activity, sales forecasting and pricing. All these decisions can have an explicit spatial dimension and there is a basic requirement to be able to handle geographical data effectively. For example, how and where should a promotion budget be spent? In terms of discounting, a fundamental dimension is by channel or key account, and it is necessary to focus on marginal profitability by incorporating the different costs of distribution for each option.

COMPUTER-BASED INFORMATION SYSTEMS AND MANAGEMENT DECISION MAKING

In essence, the significance of GIS should be demonstrated through their applications. How does an organization benefit from its investment in GIS? The orientation must be on (spatial) information as an input into the decision-making process, rather than an examination of either Geographical Information Systems or Information Technology *per se*. However, more fundamentally, the design, specification and implementation of any information system must be driven by a comprehension of management's information needs. It is both very surprising and myopic that most discussions of GIS and their applications are devoid of any explicit decision-making orientation. Indeed it is essential to question and refute the implicit, if not explicit, conventional wisdom that GIS are *necessarily* useful and relevant for decision making (see Densham and Goodchild 1989; see also Densham 1991 in this volume).

Without becoming embroiled in a debate on alternative taxonomies for computer-based information systems (see Gray *et al.* 1989 for a discussion of the research issues in this field), there are GIS examples which can be 'located' in Data Processing Systems, Management Information Systems, Decision Support Systems, Expert Systems, and Value Added and Data Services. Although this list represents a chronological order of development, these computer-based information systems are complementary, with their own distinctive characteristics and applications. (Electronic) Data Processing (DP) systems, for instance, are operational – not merely transactional – systems, involving the computer processing of data. Examples include sales transactions and inventory systems. Additional computer processing, particularly analysis, is characteristic of Management Information Systems (MIS). Outputs from MIS are structured, scheduled and/or exception reports, which should be decision oriented. For example in retailing, regular weekly and monthly reports on branch sales by product line are provided with associated exception reports highlighting important conditions such as below-average branch sales.

Decision Support Systems (DSS) involve semi-structured and/or unstructured, simple and/or complex problems that can be explored in an interactive or recursive manner by decision makers (see Densham 1991 in this volume). Following Montgomery and Urban (1969), four elements of DSS can be recognized as the database, analysis tools, decision models and the interface. Individual DSS vary in the relative emphasis given to these capabilities (Fig. 45.3). In the business world, however, two particular types of DSS are especially important – spreadsheets and database management systems. Spreadsheets combine the 'decision models' and 'interface' capabilities; database management systems combine the 'database' and 'interface' capabilities. Within this framework of DSS capabilities, it is possible to view the majority of GIS as oriented towards the 'database' and 'interface' capabilities, although database management is strongly associated with automated cartography.

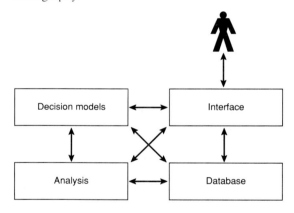

Fig. 45.3 The four elements of a Decision Support System recognized by Montgomery and Urban (1969).

Moreover, while a number of people have begun to argue strongly (and correctly) that the lack of analytic capabilities in GIS is a major shortcoming (e.g. see Dixon, Openshaw and Wymer 1987; see also Openshaw 1991 in this volume), this framework also suggests that insufficient attention has been given to 'decision models'. In market analysis, the applications domain has been confined to the conventional two main GIS capabilities; these capabilities must be extended in the future because marketeers cannot evolve their concepts and ideas through a current DSS in their usual learning pattern by performing increasingly complicated analyses as and when required for their decision making.

Expert Systems (ES) are the most exciting, practical application of Artificial Intelligence (see Smith and Ye Jiang 1991 in this volume). They incorporate knowledge of a specific application with an inference capability to generate decisions (that can or should be justified). In the business and management area, in which the detailed operational specification of problems is not straightforward, few ES have been introduced (see Silverman 1987). A notable exception, which incorporates spatial data, is in application credit scoring.

Value Added and Data Services (VADS) is a generic term that covers a range of information services, including electronic mail, on-line databases and Electronic Data Interchange. For instance, the majority of market analysis consultancies now offer clients on-line access to their various geographical databases. Credit referencing agents promote real-time decision taking through on-line database access and analysis via clients' terminals and/or computers (TRW Inc., for example, has credit rating files of 130 million Americans and over half a million businesses). In the future, some successful global organizations will exist entirely because of communications channels and data flows, controlling a network by an information centre. They will be structures that focus on marketing and financial control and planning; networks will permit effective collaborative links to both suppliers and customers or consumers. The Benetton company, for example, does not possess many assets for manufacturing clothes or selling them to consumers; contracts are given to small firms to manufacture the desired products and retailers are licensees.

SELECTED MARKETING APPLICATIONS

Every day marketeers are faced with real problems that require decisions. While some of the analyses termed 'market analysis' do not have strong theoretical underpinnings, they are proving relevant and useful to understand markets, customers and competitors. A current estimate of this specific industry's global size is over $150 million per annum.

The three selected application areas (marketing information systems, branch location analysis and direct mail) are now each considered in terms of database management, spatial analysis and information presentation; from this discussion, the role of GIS in market analysis can be demonstrated by example.

Marketing Information Systems

Marketing is about customers and satisfying their needs with appropriate products and services. To gain competitive advantages, Marketing Information Systems are being established and maintained by many organizations to assist their marketeers' decision making (see, for example, Piercy and Evans's (1983) introductory overview and Buzzell's (1985) and McKenna's (1988) discussions of marketing in the IT age). More specifically, for the last 20 years, the PIMS (Profit Impact of Market Strategy) programme has developed a set of principles and a methodology for business strategy founded on a database of nearly 500 companies and over 3000 business units (for more details see Buzzell and Gale 1987). Figure 45.4 summarizes the cumulatively evolving and growing applications importance of customer databases since the 1960s.

	1960s	1970s	1980s	1990s
MARKETING PURPOSE	Separate channel of distribution	Cost-effective, measurable communications	Cross-selling, maximum value of existing base	Maintain and increase customer loyalty
METHOD	Mail order	Direct mail	Direct mail to customers	Integrated communicating mail, telephone (in) sales staff
IMPACT ON DATABASE	Database essential basis for business	Database optional 'junk-mail'	Rationalise development for targeting and control	Database essential to manage customer relationships

Fig. 45.4 The growing importance of customer databases in market analysis.

Building on the three common blocks of the marketing process (reaching the prospect, making the sale and developing the relationship for repeat business), Rapp and Collins (1987) have suggested that 'Maxi Marketing' should be the new direction in promotion, advertising and marketing strategy.

Founded on a customer database, their model illustrates a sequence that can be followed to maximize business opportunities (see Fig. 45.5).

Handling geographical data, such as customers' addresses, and their linkage with other data, such as branch locations and sales territories, is therefore a necessary basic operation. From a database management perspective, it is essential that the opportunities for 'cross-selling' of new products and services to existing customers can be identified easily for pro-active marketing activity. Banks, for instance, which formerly stored their data by separate accounts to facilitate processing of transactions are beginning to arrange and explore their databases by customer to build up multi-account profiles.

Residential classification systems provide a consistent and meaningful base for the development of Marketing Information Systems. Geo-demographic discriminators, such as ACORN (A Classification of Residential Neighbourhoods), are used to provide summary descriptions of the neighbourhoods in which existing customers reside (for more details see Beaumont 1991; CACI 1983; Openshaw, Cullingford and Gillard 1980).

Not surprisingly, geodemographic discriminators have also become an integral component of survey design for market research. They are especially helpful for stratified sample designs, because the classifications are based on a large number of census variables; if single census variables – such as age, sex, social class and region – are used to stratify a sample, the design becomes impractical (see Baker 1989).

In terms of analysis, the profiling of existing customers by a geodemographic discriminator offers a marketing tool for extending the customer base. Moreover, as the discriminators are now used to reference different market research surveys, it is possible to derive estimates of (local) market shares for specific products and services, and to assess performance against target competitive positions. Figure 45.6 is an ACORN profile of Laura Ashley customers in Britain based on Target Group Index market research data.

Obviously, the data available from Marketing Information Systems are used for a range of purposes. The ability of GIS to map markets is becoming an increasingly important medium for information presentation (see Plate 45.1(a)) which maps an estimate of life assurance policies in part of

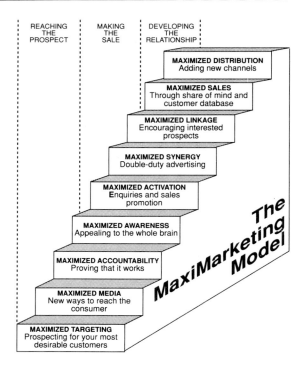

Fig. 45.5 The 'MaxiMarketing' model (after Rapp and Collins 1987).

France and Plate 45.1(b) which maps the percentage of the population aged over 65 in part of Sweden). The advantage of this medium over, say, even a sorted list of addresses for describing local market potential is obvious. In the United States, Blue Cross/Blue Shield, the non-profit health insurance association, uses geographical analysis and automated cartography as a management tool for both marketing and operations functions for its 75 regional licensees. For marketing, GIS support the sales efforts by generating specific maps of service areas for new business proposals; for operations, GIS generate maps indicating service areas covered by members of a national health maintenance organization or by a preferred provider organization. Generally two maps are provided: a general state map describing the association's service areas by county and a more detailed map assigning employees' locations with service areas. Other, actionable output formats are also important, particularly name and address extraction for personal direct mail campaigns.

While the advances in data capture technologies, such as Electronic Point of Sales

(EPoS) systems and Electronic Funds Transfer at the Point of Sales (EFTPoS) systems, can provide information for marketing based on customers' purchasing patterns, it must be stressed that there is also a real danger of 'data overload' which hinders decision making. As this potential problem is likely to increase, the need for improved analytical capabilities in Marketing Information Systems will become more urgent (see also Openshaw's 1991 discussion in this volume of the development of new types and styles of spatial analysis). Some retailers have opted already to store data only for a sample of branches in the network and by a sample of products or brands. However, with the changing patterns of consumer behaviour and of the local competitive position, can this sample be expected to be representative over time? The power of any management information system should grow over time as historical data series are expanded and as the system provides meaningful yet terse summaries of the data it holds.

Branch Location Analysis

Branch location analysis illustrates the essence of market analysis because the fundamental objective is to provide a dynamic equilibrium for the demand and supply of products and services over space; there is a geographically uneven demand for products and services which have to be supplied from a number of locations, with facilities of different sizes offering various ranges of products and services. Banks, for example, can range from the large city branches, which provide a comprehensive range of domestic and commercial services, to simple 'hole-in-the-wall' automatic teller machines (ATM), dispensing cash and permitting some customer information queries. Branch location analysis is not confined to selecting sites for new branches or to closing existing branches; the merchandise mix, the targeted customer groups, the competitive situation, advertising and distribution all have direct locational ramifications and, moreover, change over time requiring repeated analyses. Finally, branch location analysis also extends to space or shelf management within a branch. Software is now available to generate 'planograms' of the optimum distribution of products by shelves; this development is linked to retailers' broader interests in direct product profitability.

Branch location analyses are driven by catchment area definitions. While primary research in the form of customer origin surveys is often carried out to collect the necessary data, secondary sources – increasingly founded on travel times rather than straight-line distances – are also important (see Fig. 45.7 and Plate 45.2, which show travel time isochrones around Nottingham, England and the 'primary', 'secondary' and 'tertiary' retail catchments of Swansea in Wales, respectively). Such information is particularly important for an evaluation of a potential new, out-of-town site. Once a catchment area is defined, it is necessary to extract data on its household composition in order to make local market expenditure estimates for particular products and services. Most analyses are founded on spatial interactions between households' residential locations and the branch network; work-based, rather than home-based, trips are considered rarely although they are significant for some products and services. Moreover, in practice, little attention is given to the distorting effect of multi-purpose trips for a 'basket' of products and services.

Once an estimate is made of the local market demand of a catchment area for specific products and services, taking into account the competitive situation, an estimate is made of branch sales (or local market share) disaggregated by products and services. A variety of forecasting methods may be employed, ranging from the simple 'fair share' approach based on selling space through multiple regression techniques to gravity-based, spatial interaction models (see Wrigley 1988).

Maps have proved to be an important output medium in branch location analysis. In addition, this application has demonstrated the power of direct management–computer interaction through so-called Decision Support Systems, which usually have very good graphics capabilities. Based on calibrated models, 'what if . . .' simulations are undertaken in the safe environment of the GIS to explore the implications of alternative location decisions, such as:

- What sales by product and services would we expect?

- What would be the competitive effects

ANALYSIS BY ACORN FROM THE TARGET GROUP INDEX
PRODUCT: Shopped in Laura Ashley in last 12 mnths   BASE:

ACORN GROUP		PRODUCT (x1000)	%	BASE (x1000)	%
A	Agricultural Areas	67	3.3	1400	3.1
B	Modern Family Housing, Higher Incomes	336	16.6	7426	16.5
C	Older Housing of Intermediate Status	366	18.1	8027	17.8
D	Older Terraced Housing	70	3.5	1904	4.2
E	Council Estates - Category I	146	7.2	5858	13.0
F	Council Estates - Category II	75	3.7	4136	9.2
G	Council Estates - Category III	41	2.0	2912	6.5
H	Mixed Inner Metropolitan Areas	83	4.1	1598	3.5
I	High Status Non-family Areas	213	10.5	2068	4.6
J	Affluent Suburban Housing	500	24.7	7904	17.5
K	Better-off Retirement Areas	127	6.3	1888	4.2

ACORN TYPE	PRODUCT (x1000)	%	BASE (x1000)	%
A01 Agricultural Villages	60	3.0	1070	2.4
A02 Areas of Farms and Smallholdings	7	0.4	331	0.7
B03 Post-war Functional Private Housing	85	4.2	1946	4.3
B04 Modern Private Housing, Young Families	69	3.4	1373	3.0
B05 Established Private Family Housing	94	4.6	2689	6.0
B06 New Detached Houses, Young Families	86	4.2	1274	2.8
B07 Military Bases	3	0.2	143	0.3
C08 Mixed Owner-occupied & Council Estates	54	2.7	1620	3.6
C09 Small Town Centres & Flats above Shops	108	5.3	1738	3.9
C10 Villages with Non-farm Employment	127	6.3	2193	4.9
C11 Older Private Housing, Skilled Workers	77	3.8	2477	5.5
D12 Unmodernised Terraces, Older People	58	2.9	1211	2.7
D13 Older Terraces, Lower Income Families	4	0.2	531	1.2
D14 Tenement Flats Lacking Amenities	8	0.4	162	0.4
E15 Council Estates, Well-off Older Workers	43	2.1	1756	3.9
E16 Recent Council Estates	28	1.4	1158	2.6
E17 Better Council Estates, Younger Workers	53	2.6	2121	4.7
E18 Small Council Houses, often Scottish	22	1.1	823	1.8
F19 Low Rise Estates in Industrial Towns	34	1.7	2086	4.6
F20 Inter-war Council Estates, Older People	27	1.3	1340	3.0
F21 Council Housing, Elderly People	15	0.7	709	1.6
G22 New Council Estates in Inner Cities	20	1.0	795	1.8
G23 Overspill Estates, Higher Unemployment	11	0.6	1149	2.5
G24 Council Estates with Some Overcrowding	8	0.4	641	1.4
G25 Council Estates with Greatest Hardship	2	0.1	326	0.7
H26 Multi-occupied Older Housing	3	0.2	49	0.1
H27 Cosmopolitan Owner-occupied Terraces	13	0.6	464	1.0
H28 Multi-let Housing in Cosmopolitan Areas	14	0.7	325	0.7
H29 Better-off Cosmopolitan Areas	54	2.6	760	1.7
I30 High Status Non-family Areas	110	5.4	1037	2.3
I31 Multi-let Big Old Houses and Flats	90	4.4	803	1.8
I32 Furnished Flats, Mostly Single People	14	0.7	228	0.5
J33 Inter-war Semis, White Collar Workers	164	8.1	2938	6.5
J34 Spacious Inter-war Semis, Big Gardens	149	7.4	2529	5.6
J35 Villages with Wealthy Older Commuters	97	4.8	1359	3.0
J36 Detached Houses, Exclusive Suburbs	90	4.5	1077	2.4
K37 Private Houses, Well-off Older Resident	77	3.8	1117	2.5
K38 Private Flats, Older Single People	50	2.5	771	1.7
U39 Unclassified and Unmatched Respondents	0	0.0	0	0.0
TOTALS	2027	100.0	45122	100.0

CACI COPYRIGHT RESERVED   CACI MARKET ANALYSIS DIVISION
SURVEY PERIOD APR 1988 to MAR 1989

```
ADULTS

PENET.  INDEX    0           50          100         150         200   225+
   %                 :           :           :           :           :    >
 ------ -----
   4.8    107   AAAAAAAAAAAAAAAAAAAAAA
   4.5    101   BBBBBBBBBBBBBBBBBBBBB
   4.6    102   CCCCCCCCCCCCCCCCCCCCC
   3.7     82   DDDDDDDDDDDDDDDDD
   2.5     55   EEEEEEEEEEE
   1.8     41   FFFFFFFFF
   1.4     32   GGGGGGG
   5.2    116   HHHHHHHHHHHHHHHHHHHHHHH
  10.3    230   IIIIIIIIIIIIIIIIIIIIIIIIIIIIIIIIIIIIIIIIIIIIIIII
   6.3    141   JJJJJJJJJJJJJJJJJJJJJJJJJJJJJ
   6.7    150   KKKKKKKKKKKKKKKKKKKKKKKKKKKKKKK

PENET.  INDEX    0           50          100         150         200   225+
   %                 :           :           :           :           :    >
 ------ -----
   5.6    125   AAAAAAAAAAAAAAAAAAAAAAAAAA
   2.2     48   AAAAAAAAAA
   4.4     97   BBBBBBBBBBBBBBBBBBB
   5.0    111   BBBBBBBBBBBBBBBBBBBBBBB
   3.5     78   BBBBBBBBBBBBBBBB
   6.7    150   BBBBBBBBBBBBBBBBBBBBBBBBBBBBBBB
   2.2     49   BBBBBBBBBB
   3.4     75   CCCCCCCCCCCCCCC
   6.2    138   CCCCCCCCCCCCCCCCCCCCCCCCCCCC
   5.8    129   CCCCCCCCCCCCCCCCCCCCCCCCCCC
   3.1     69   CCCCCCCCCCCCCC
   4.8    107   DDDDDDDDDDDDDDDDDDDDDD
   0.7     16   DDDD
   5.2    117   DDDDDDDDDDDDDDDDDDDDDDD
   2.4     54   EEEEEEEEEEE
   2.4     53   EEEEEEEEEEE
   2.5     56   EEEEEEEEEEE
   2.6     59   EEEEEEEEEEEE
   1.6     36   FFFFFFFF
   2.0     45   FFFFFFFFFF
   2.1     46   FFFFFFFFFF
   2.5     55   GGGGGGGGGGGG
   1.0     22   GGGGG
   1.3     29   GGGGGGG
   0.6     14   GGGG
   6.4    142   HHHHHHHHHHHHHHHHHHHHHHHHHHHH
   2.8     63   HHHHHHHHHHHHH
   4.2     93   HHHHHHHHHHHHHHHHHH
   7.1    157   HHHHHHHHHHHHHHHHHHHHHHHHHHHHHHHH
  10.6    235   IIIIIIIIIIIIIIIIIIIIIIIIIIIIIIIIIIIIIIIIIIIIIIII
  11.2    250   IIIIIIIIIIIIIIIIIIIIIIIIIIIIIIIIIIIIIIIIIIIIIIIIII
   6.0    134   IIIIIIIIIIIIIIIIIIIIIIIIIII
   5.6    124   JJJJJJJJJJJJJJJJJJJJJJJJJ
   5.9    131   JJJJJJJJJJJJJJJJJJJJJJJJJJ
   7.1    159   JJJJJJJJJJJJJJJJJJJJJJJJJJJJJJJJ
   8.4    187   JJJJJJJJJJJJJJJJJJJJJJJJJJJJJJJJJJJJJ
   6.9    153   KKKKKKKKKKKKKKKKKKKKKKKKKKKKKKK
   6.5    146   KKKKKKKKKKKKKKKKKKKKKKKKKKKKK
   0.0      0   U

   4.5    100
```

Fig. 45.6 An ACORN profile of Laura Ashley customers in Britain based on Target Group Index market research data.

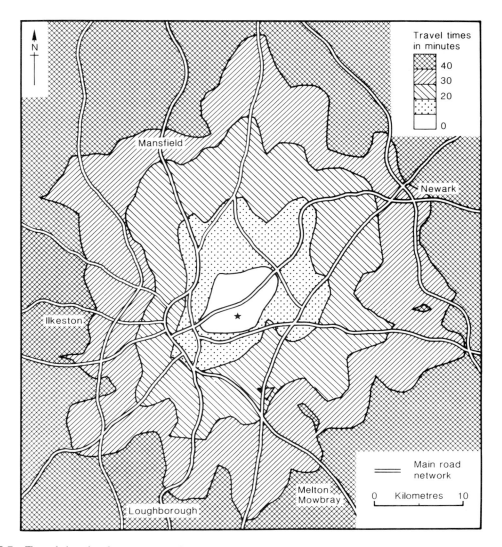

Fig. 45.7 Travel time isochrones around Nottingham, England, generated by GIS (redrawn from original).

(including 'cannibalization' of our existing branches)?

- What is the optimum sequence for development of the branch network?

As time progresses towards the twenty-first century, it should be remembered that the conventional shopping trips for particular products and services may well be replaced by new marketing channels. Teleshopping, which has been introduced successfully in some US cities using rather different technology infrastructures, offers new opportunities for marketeers; it reaches additional customers and also captures and permits analyses of data for the marketeers' decision making (see also Malone, Yates and Benjamin's 1989 discussion of electronic markets). Direct marketing, can generally be thought of as an information-driven activity; Bird (1989) provides a comprehensive and practical discussion of direct marketing.

Direct Mail

Direct mail is currently the most important direct marketing medium (e.g. see Fraser-Robinson

1989). Its rapid growth during the 1980s can be explained partly by the effective handling of (customer) databases and general developments in market analyses. It is operationalized through the derivation and use of geodemographic discriminators. While solicitation by direct mail is much lower in volume in Britain than in North America (and, indeed, lower than in Europe), there remains considerable scope to expand and improve this cost-effective form of marketing.

Direct mail campaigns can be used for cross-selling to existing customers or for expanding the customer base. With regard to the former, a company's Marketing Information System should be able to identify a mailing target group and offer a simple mechanism for a personalized mailshot. For the latter, once a target market is defined, it is straightforward to complete a direct mail campaign since every domestic address can be described by a geodemographic discriminator (through linkage of files using postal geography and census geography).

In the recent past, direct mail campaigns were often seen as 'one-off' exercises to promote a particular product or service. Any analysis was confined to the definition of the target market. However, in parallel with the establishment and maintenance of Marketing Information Systems, much more analysis is now undertaken. This frequently incorporates a customer's response/non-response to individual campaigns over time, with the database disaggregated to customer name (and address) level. Most mailshots are driven by a fixed budget and, therefore, the basic objective is to maximize the response rate within the limits of available resources, rather than reach every potential customer. It must not be forgotten, however, that market analysis will never be successful if the product or service, or the associated creative promotion material, does not appeal to the potential customer!

As indicated by direct mail, credit scoring and customer databases, the capabilities of today's computers to process and link data about individuals raises important issues of civil liberties and the need for protection to all. While it is true that IT developments and the laws have not necessarily kept pace with each other in the past, there are indications that, for instance with data privacy legislation, the law could come to be a controlling mechanism for the use of GIS in market analysis.

THE OUTLOOK FOR GIS IN MARKETING

For the future, viewed primarily in terms of GIS rather than market analysis, the prospects are likely to be of a need for development of existing schemes, rather than for new and fundamental research. The development avenues will include the following:

- Microcomputer GIS, marketed in a form with both suitable applications capabilities and relevant data.

- Enhanced availability of up-to-date data in different forms, especially on-line and on CD-ROM.

- Real-time and group Decision Support Systems (see Densham 1991 in this volume).

- Micro-level and longitudinal analyses of individual customers' lifestyles and purchasing patterns.

- Incorporation of more spatial and dynamic analytical capabilities, especially for simulation modelling.

- Enhanced presentation of outputs (not only maps), particularly as Executive Information Systems (e.g. see Bittlestone 1990; Davenport and Hammer 1989).

- Access through a file interface to standard routines for financial analysis and investment appraisal.

- More consideration of the accuracy levels required for decision making.

The intense competition and dynamics found in most markets will mean that GIS continue to be important tools for market analysis. But the emphasis of current applications on data status reporting with regard to (actual or forecast) sales, market shares and prices should be complemented by more analytical impact reporting on, say, price elasticity, advertising effectiveness, and on-site location and the merchandise mix. Moreover, the true promise of such systems can only be realized through significant education of both the technicians who design the systems and the marketeers who use the systems. This task should cover the possible nature of different applications through real demonstrations. Bespoke GIS for market analysis will be developed but they will need to be marketed much more professionally than hitherto!

For real progress and to ensure that the real potential of GIS is realized, much more explicit attention must be given to an organization's decision-making context and its marketing information requirements. Today's focus is on how GIS affect the marketeer and market analysis. For the future there is a need to know how the implementation and effectiveness of GIS are affected by the information culture of marketeers and their organizations – and how these are likely to change.

Finally, it is appropriate to explore the wider scope of GIS in terms of decision-making processes, organizational structures and competitive positions. Why should investments be made in GIS and what returns can be envisaged from them? The current emphasis is on efficiency or productivity gains, which are important and can be evaluated directly (although not easily) by conventional methods such as cost/benefit analysis. This 'automate' argument is unnecessarily restrictive. Zuboff (1988), in a significant contribution to management thinking, extends the traditional perspective by proposing an 'informate' argument, with an explicit emphasis on the importance of the information content of administrative and productive processes within an organization. Electronic Point of Sales (EPoS) systems, for example, have been introduced by retailers to automate checkout and stock control processes; such raw data can also be transformed into useful information for branch-level market analysis. Figure 45.8 takes this argument further by portraying two additional possible IT capabilities – 'communicate' and 'transformate'.

Information technologies have already enhanced the effectiveness of communications in terms of speed, capacity and accuracy. Traditional perspectives on organizations, hierarchies and bureaucracy are becoming obsolete in the IT age of networks and networking. Retailers, for example, are using this infrastructural 'communicate' capability to permit local branch-level action, while maintaining head office control. Group Decision Support Systems will become increasingly important. 'Transformate' is used to indicate the ways in which IT is affecting competitive and collaborative forces facing organizations. While no evidence exists to support the assertion that IT can be a source of sustainable competitive advantage, IT does impact directly on industrial structures and ways of doing business. For example, shared ATM (Automatic Teller Machines) networks have enhanced service provision and home shopping is opening up new geographical markets. GIS, as an extremely important part of IT, can be a significant strategic and operational tool for marketeers, who no longer need to be constrained by system capabilities and data availability and quality.

INFORMATION TECHNOLOGY

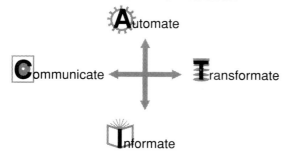

Fig. 45.8 Four aspects of Information Technology in the decision-making process (after Zuboff 1988).

REFERENCES

Baker K (1989) Using geodemographics in market research surveys. *Journal of the Market Research Society* **31**: 37–44

Beaumont J R (ed.) (1989) Market analysis. *Environment and Planning A* (Special Edition) **21** (5): 587–653

Beaumont J R (1991) An introduction to market analysis. *CATMOG 53*, Geo-Abstracts, Norwich.

Bennett, R J, Wrigley N (eds.) (1981) *Quantitative Geography: retrospect and prospect*. Routledge and Kegan Paul, London

Bird D (1989) *Commonsense Direct Marketing*. Kogan Page, London

Bittlestone R (1990) Financial control in the 1990s. *International Journal of Information Resource Management* **1** (1): 12–18

Bonoma T V (1985) *The Marketing Edge*. Free Press, New York

Buzzell R D (1985) *Marketing in an Electronic Age*. Harvard Business School Press, Boston

Buzzell R D, Gale B T (1987) *The PIMS Principles: linking strategy to performance*. Free Press, New York

CACI (1983) *1981 ACORN Classification*. CACI Market Analysis, 59/62 High Holborn, London.

Calkins H W (1991) GIS and public policy. In: Maguire

D J, Goodchild M F, Rhind D W (eds.) *Geographical Information Systems: principles and applications*, Longman, London, pp. 233–45, Vol 2

Davenport T H, Hammer M (1989) How executives can shape their company's information systems. *Harvard Business Review* **67** (2): 130–4

Densham P J (1991) Spatial decision support systems. In: Maguire D J, Goodchild M F, Rhind D W (eds.) *Geographical Information Systems: principles and applications*, Longman, London, pp. 403–12, Vol 1

Densham P J, Goodchild M F (1989) Spatial decision support systems: a research agenda. *Proceedings of GIS/LIS '89*, Vol. 2. ACSM/ASPRS, Falls Church Virginia, pp. 707–16

Department of Trade and Industry (1990) *Profiting from Electronic Trading: the case study package*. HMSO, London

Dixon J F, Openshaw S, Wymer C (1987) A proposal and specification for a geographical analysis sub-routine library. *Research Report 3 Northern Regional Research Laboratory*. NRRL, Department of Geography University of Newcastle, Newcastle-upon-Tyne

Fraser-Robinson J (1989) *The Secrets of Effective Direct Mail*. McGraw-Hill, New York

Gorry G A, Scott Morton M S (1989) A framework for management information systems. *Sloan Management Review* **30** (3): 49–61

Gray P, King W R, McLean E R, Watson E J (eds.) (1989) *Management of Information Systems*. Dryden Press, Chicago

Kotler P (1988) *Marketing Management: analysis, planning implementation and control*. Prentice-Hall, Englewood Cliffs

McKenna R (1988) Marketing in an age of diversity. *Harvard Business Review* **88** (5): 88–95

Malone T W, Yates J, Benjamin R I (1989) The logic of electronic markets. *Harvard Business Review* **67** (3): 166–72

Montgomery D, Urban G (1969) *Management Science in Marketing*. Prentice-Hall, Englewood Cliffs

Openshaw S (1991) Developing appropriate spatial analysis methods for GIS. In: Maguire D J, Goodchild M F, Rhind D W (eds.) *Geographical Information Systems: principles and applications*, Longman, London, pp. 389–402, Vol 1

Openshaw S, Cullingford D, Gillard A A (1980) A critique of the national census classifications of OPCS and PRAG. *Town Planning Review* **51**: 421–39

Peters T (1987) *Thriving on Chaos*. Macmillan, London

Piercy N, Evans M (1983) *Managing Marketing Information*. Croom Helm, London

Rapp S, Collins T (1987) *Maxi Marketing*. McGraw-Hill, New York

Rhind D W (1981) Geographical Information Systems in Britain. In: Bennett R J, Wrigley N (eds.) *Quantitative Geography: retrospect and prospect*. Routledge and Kegan Paul, London, pp. 17–35

Rothman J (ed.) (1989) Geodemographics. *Journal of the Market Research Society* (Special Edition) **31** (1): 1–131

Silverman B G (ed.) (1987) *Expert Systems for Business*. Addison-Wesley, Reading Massachusetts

Smith T R, Ye Jiang (1991) Knowledge-based approaches in GIS. In: Maguire D J, Goodchild M F, Rhind D W (eds.) *Geographical Information Systems: principles and applications*, Longman, London, pp. 413–25, Vol 1

Wrigley N (ed.) (1988) *Store Choice, Store Location and Market Analysis*. Routledge and Kegan Paul, London

Zuboff S (1988) *In the Age of the Smart Machine*. Heinemann, London

SOIL INFORMATION SYSTEMS

P A BURROUGH

The history of the introduction of automated information systems and GIS in soil survey, from the automation of map production to the quantitative modelling of soil and land resources, is reviewed. The methods used for collecting data from soil profiles and about the spatial distribution of soil are described. Soil profile data and the attributes of soil map units are often stored in relational databases, whereas the spatial distribution of soil mapping units (polygons) is often stored in topological arc-node (vector) form or in grid cell (raster) form depending on the software and application. The use of optimal interpolation methods in soil survey is reviewed, including extensions such as co-kriging and disjunctive kriging. The general principles of a range of applications are discussed and illustrated by examples. GIS are now firmly established in modern soil survey practice and are used for map production, deriving suitability maps to meet users' requests for special-purpose information and for modelling environmental processes.

DEVELOPMENTS IN SOIL INFORMATION SYSTEMS AND IDEAS ABOUT THE NATURE OF SOIL

The first international scientific meeting on soil information systems was held in Wageningen in the Netherlands in September 1975. The meeting was organized by the newly formed Working Group on Soil Information Systems set up under Commission V of the International Society of Soil Science, as had been proposed at the Tenth International Congress of the Society in Moscow in 1974. The 55 scientists from 18 countries who attended the meeting hoped that their activities would be the first steps towards a revolution in soil research methodology and the problems of soil science. Professor Ciric, then Chairman of Commission V of the International Society of Soil Science, wrote in his Foreword to the Proceedings of the meeting (Bie 1975), that the high cost of collecting and analysing soil samples fully justifies the inclusion of all indices (attributes) in a soil information system, and he noted that 'the adaptation of methodology to the requirements of the information system will result in a definitive break with the old descriptive, largely subjective, methods of our field research. The logic of the information system cannot tolerate any vague or undefined notions'.

The first phase of development

The Working Group on Soil Information Systems was extremely active and the Wageningen meeting was followed in rapid succession by others. Meetings were held in Canberra, Australia in 1976 (Moore and Bie 1977), Bulgaria in 1977 (Sadovski and Bie 1978), Canberra again in 1980 (Moore, Cook and Lynch 1981), Paris 1981 (Girard 1981) and Bolkesjø, Norway in 1983 (Burrough and Bie 1984). The papers presented at these meetings represent the first phase in quantifying soil survey data. As might be expected, they concentrate on the problems of recording and storing data from soil profiles in the computer. Brought up on the philosophy of strict hierarchical classification (cf. *Soil Taxonomy* – Soil Survey Staff 1976) and lacking the modern insights of relational database structures, soil scientists first wrestled with the problems of obtaining data that contained both qualitative and quantitative characteristics in variable length fields into the readily available hierarchical and network database structures of the time (Mackenzie and Smith 1977). Soil profiles are difficult to record because data are usually collected for those naturally occurring horizons which can be seen when the soil is exposed in a pit or cutting. Unfortunately, these horizons are not always clear or easy to see and define unambiguously, with the result that the number of horizons – and hence the number of data items to be recorded – can vary greatly, even between profiles belonging to the same soil landscape unit. The positive benefit of this early work was that soil survey organizations were forced to think very carefully about the way in which soil data should be collected and organized, which brought a considerable amount of standardization and improved the ways in which data were recorded in the field. Standard computer forms were developed for field recording and (somewhat later) portable field computers were used. These developments of national standards were particularly vigorous in Canada, The Netherlands, the United States and France (Bie 1975; Dumanski, Kloosterman and Brandon 1975; Girard 1981; Mausbach and Reybold 1987).

One aim of the early soil information systems was to provide viable alternatives to the rigid, bureaucratic, hierarchical soil classification systems that are still in use. The work in the 1970s on using the methods of numerical taxonomy as an alternative to established soil classification (cf. Webster and Burrough 1972a, 1972b, 1974; de Gruijter 1977; Webster 1977; Lamp 1983) stimulated much academic research but did not lead to general acceptance of the methods in regular soil surveys. This was largely because of the difficulties associated with interpreting the classes that were so constructed and in dealing with the problems of spatial variation.

Soil survey applications were among the first uses of GIS. Both the US Department of Agriculture (Johnson 1975) and the Dutch Soil Survey STIBOKA (van Kuilenburg *et al.* 1981) were first to automate the production of soil survey maps. The methods of digital cartography developed by the United States Geological Survey were used for soil mapping and irrigation studies in Kentucky (Loveland and Ramey 1986). In the case of STIBOKA, the technology for producing the 1 : 50 000-scale digital soil survey map base was considerably enhanced by the parallel development of a GIS for landscape mapping (Burrough 1980; Burrough and de Veer 1980, 1984) which dealt not only with point and polygon data, but also with complex line attributes, spatial searches and adjacencies. Burrough (1982) gives a review of these first developments.

The second phase

The second phase in the automated handling of soil information came as soil scientists attempted to bring in rigorous methods for mapping. Before automation, the spatial variation of soils in the landscape had been mapped by interpretation of the relationships between the kind of soil recorded at a soil profile pit or boring and the external features of the landscape in which the profile was situated. In reconnaissance surveys, few observations of the soil were made and maps showing the distribution of different kinds of soil were made almost exclusively by the informed interpretation of external features as seen on aerial photographs. This kind of mapping is a complex, subjective art which resists quantification and it was, therefore, extremely difficult to assess the intrinsic value of the documents produced (Burrough and Beckett 1971a, 1971b; Burrough, Beckett and Jarvis 1971; Beckett and Burrough 1971a, 1971b). The ability to record, store and retrieve data from many soil observations, including their exact location and elevation on the ground (the exact location of a soil profile observation was rarely recorded in many early surveys) paved the way for studies of the spatial variation of soil properties within the subjectively delineated landscape units.

Although the phenomenon of the continuous, but noisy, spatial variation of soil property values had been recognized earlier (Wilding, Jones and Schafer 1965; Beckett and Webster 1971), it was not until the late 1970s and the 1980s that soil scientists began to pay much attention to methods for interpolating soil attribute values directly from point observations. Much work was done both by soil physicists (e.g. Nielsen and Bouma 1985) and field soil scientists (Webster 1985) to apply the methods of geostatistics to interpolation, to the analysis of spatial structures, to the problem of optimizing sampling networks and to simulating the spatial variation of soil properties (McBratney and

Webster 1981, 1983a; McBratney, Webster and Burgess 1981; Webster and Burgess 1984; Burrough 1990). The study of how geostatistical methods can assist soil survey has been a subject of international soil survey meetings since 1983 (e.g. Giltrap 1984; Nielsen and Bouma 1985; Mausbach and Wilding 1991) and remains a theme of current interest even though the basic technology is now available to all (Englund and Sparks 1988).

The third phase

The third phase in the quantification of soil information has taken four largely separate paths:

- consolidation and implementation;
- the use of digital soil information for analysis and modelling;
- the basic data models used in soil survey;
- the use of expert systems.

Consolidation and implementation

The first path represents the consolidation of the research of the 1970s and 1980s in the form of local, national and indeed international soil profile and soil map databases. For the most part, these are standard applications of existing commercial relational database and automated thematic mapping technology. The question facing national and international soil information organizations is no longer how to build original systems nor how to adapt commercial systems to meet specifications, but rather how to choose between the wide range of commercial options that is now available. The problem of building a very large database of soil information has now shifted from the technology to the ways in which data from different areas or lands are modelled, recorded and stored. These problems of data standardization are more acute than any technology problem when building an international database (e.g. van Reeuwijk 1982, 1984; Baumgardner and Oldeman 1986; Pleijsier 1986, 1989; Baumgardner and Van der Weg 1989). There has also been increasing attention paid to the problems of data quality and loss of information when soil data are converted from one format to another (Marsman and de Gruijter 1984; Burrough 1986; Marsman and de Gruijter 1986; Bregt 1989; Bregt and Beemster 1989).

The use of digital soil information for analysis and modelling

The second path concerns the use of digital soil information. The problems when using the earlier, non-digital, databases to answer queries about land evaluation were twofold. In the first instance, the data were only held in a generalized, classified form, under the assumption that the class model was a sufficient carrier of information for all applications that could be envisaged. In the second case, it cost much time and money to redraw a reclassified soil map every time a different interpretation map was made. Standard GIS software, with its ability to reclassify soil polygons or pixels according to the attributes held in order to make a new map, has solved the latter problem. The costs of producing derived maps have been replaced by the challenge of working out how the information on the new maps should be derived in a logical, systematic way from the original data.

The largely qualitative land evaluation wisdom developed during the 1970s (FAO 1976) is still being used in many countries for deriving maps showing complex land qualities or land suitabilities but, in recent years, there have been very strong moves towards quantifying the land evaluation process (Bouma *et al.* 1986; Burrough 1986, 1989a, 1990; Beek, Burrough and McCormack 1987; Bouma and Bregt 1989; Driessen 1989). This quantification involves linking the soil information base (profiles and map polygons) to models of crop yield (van Diepen *et al.* 1989; Dumanski and Onofrei 1989), simulating regional and local soil moisture regimes (Bouma *et al.* 1980; Busoni, Sanesi and Torri 1986; King *et al.* 1986), nitrate leaching, pesticide redistribution, erosion and runoff (Herndon and Schertz 1989; de Roo, Hazelhoff and Burrough 1989), to remote sensing of soil moisture regimes (Olsson 1989) and assessing woody biomass (Helldén 1987). Associated with this trend towards linking of the largely static soil database to process models has come an awareness of the problems of change in soil resources (Bouma 1989a, 1989b). One important result of this phase was the decision at the 13th International Congress in Hamburg in 1986 to terminate the purely technically-oriented International Soil Science Society (ISSS) Working Group on Soil Information

Systems and to replace it by a new ISSS Working Group on Quantitative Land Evaluation. The role of the ISSS Working Group in soil variability studies was taken over by the Commission I Working Group on Soil Moisture Variability, and a new Working Group was set up to concentrate activities on the problems of creating a world soil map database at a scale of 1 : 1 000 000 (Baumgardner and Oldeman 1986; Baumgardner and van der Weg 1989).

Data models for soil survey

The third path in the latest phase of work in soil information systems, which has to do with the nature of the basic data models used for recording data, is the least followed. None the less, it is beginning to attract attention, largely through the work on spatial variation and modelling. Much work on modelling, for example of crop yields, has ignored the spatial component entirely. The modellers have often implicitly assumed that the results of their calculations can be directly applied to the spatial units identified in the field, that is to whole soil polygons – irrespective of the scale of mapping. It is now being realized that, as with many soil properties, the results of models can (and very possibly should) be interpolated from the fixed data points in order to describe better the spatial variation within the major landscape units (Stein, Hoogerwert and Bouma 1988). This work is challenging the old ideas that the landscape is built from basic, homogeneous entities – the units of the choropleth (or at least chorochromatic) map model that can be characterized completely in terms of a small number of 'representative profiles' (cf. Bregt 1989; Bregt and Beemster 1989). In its place is coming a realization that all soil information and all interpretations of that information need to be related to the resolution of the survey and to the uses to which that information is being put (Wösten, Bannink and Bouma 1989). Although it now seems clear that the original concepts of fractals as put forward by Mandelbrot (1982) are not completely applicable to soil, the ideas of scaling and multiple-scale variation that they imply are seen as being important aspects of the soil data model (Miller 1980; Burrough 1983a, 1983b, Burrough 1989b; Hopmans and Stricker 1989).

The problems of how to fit the 'messy' data units of soil survey into exactly defined classes has engaged the minds of soil scientists for decades. As noted by Professor Ćirić in 1975, the logic of the information system cannot tolerate any vague or undefined notions. Unfortunately, the soil itself has not become more susceptible to exact description as a result of nearly 20 years of applied computer science; it is a phenomenon for which the provision of exact, crisp data models is bedevilled by overlap, complexity, ambiguity and uncertainty. The implications of these complicating factors for soil classification had been foreseen in the 1960s (Webster 1968) and the 1970s (Webster and Burrough 1974) but these problems have received little attention until recently. The importance of these complicating factors has been clearly revealed by retrospective, objective tests of soil map quality. In these, it has often been found that very few soil profiles in a soil mapping unit actually meet all the specifications of the classification unit or mapping unit in which they occur (cf. Marsman and de Gruijter 1984, 1986). The consequences of this dichotomy are that standard Boolean retrieval (SQL) sequences may fail to retrieve soil data adequately, thereby losing information (cf. Burrough 1987, 1989c), and that soil information systems, including soil maps, may appear to outsiders to be less valuable than they really are. The solution to this problem appears to lie in adopting either the geostatistical approach to mapping data quantitatively (which requires large numbers of observations) or in using the methods of fuzzy set theory in order to handle the conundrums of class overlap, complexity and ambiguity (Burrough 1989c).

Expert systems

To date, there seems to have been little concerted effort by soil survey agencies to incorporate their expertise in knowledge-based systems that could be used with GIS. Exploratory work on expert systems and soil classification has been done by Dale, McBratney and Russell (1989), and on land evaluation by Maes, Vereecken and Darius (1987). The most practical expert system to date is probably the ALES system (Rossiter 1989). This is an independent personal computer program that allows farmers to explore the effects of price changes and variations in inputs on expected yields and gross returns in the context of the soil–climatic ecosystem of their farm or region.

RECORDING DATA ABOUT SOIL AND STORING THEM IN THE COMPUTER

Data about soil profiles are recorded from auger borings and soil pits (Hodgson 1978). Field data are usually recorded directly on prepared forms for computer input or may be collected directly using portable field computers. The data collected include qualitative and quantitative descriptions of the location (X,Y,Z coordinates if possible) including the general and local landform, the geological formation, land use and vegetation data. The morphological aspects of the soil profile, including thickness, colour (Munsell Hue, Value and Chroma), texture (per cent sand, silt and clay), structure, consistence, porosity, organic matter and roots, and other attributes of interest such as the presence of indurated material, will be recorded for each soil horizon. The nature of the transition from one horizon to the next will also be recorded. Soil samples weighing between 1 and 2 kilograms may be taken from each horizon for chemical analysis. By using stainless steel cylinders pushed into the soil, undisturbed samples can be collected for determining physical characteristics of the soil such as bulk density, porosity and its hydrological properties. For special-purpose surveys in agricultural experimental stations and for surveying particular problems such as soil pollution, the samples may be taken at fixed depth intervals and not according to any perceived horizonation. When it is known that short-range spatial variation is large, this can be compensated for by taking bulk samples made up of many sub-samples drawn from within a given radius (say 5 metres) from the chosen location.

Standard soil maps are made by drawing boundaries around areas of land that appear to contain similar soil. The boundaries are usually interpreted from the external aspects of the landscape as seen in the field or on stereo aerial photographs. Remote sensing has not proved to be sufficiently useful for directly delineating different kinds of soil but may be valuable for providing information about time-dependent aspects of the soil such as moisture status and erosion. Only rarely are soil boundaries mapped directly by 'eyeball interpolation' between field observations of the soil profile. When field observations are made to locate boundaries, they are almost always quick auger borings that are not fully recorded. The smaller the map scale, the fewer the field observations and the less often that the position of boundaries is checked in the field.

The data from the detailed pit and profile observations are used to create a central concept (a sort of average or 'representative') soil profile with which each delineated map unit can be characterized. A set of central concepts can become formalized in a hierarchical classification system (cf. Soil Survey Staff 1976). According to this concept, the classification unit becomes the sole carrier of information about all soil profiles that are identified as being of that type. The soil map unit shows the spatial distribution of single types or sets of spatially related types of soil.

In recent years, it has become clear that it is not sensible to work only in terms of the central class concepts and their expression on choropleth thematic maps. The main reason for reducing all soil observations to central class concepts was because humans could not handle all the detail provided by large numbers of soil profile descriptions and analyses. Today, however, it is realized that classification is but one use of the expensively collected soil data and that it is also worth storing all data collected in the soil information system. A data model for soil survey is given in Fig. 46.1. Each soil mapping unit (legend unit) will be supported by a single set of records containing general information about the kinds of soil found therein, their relative abundances and position in the landscape, and the central concepts underlying their definition together with attribute values that describe them. Because a single mapping unit may consist of many separate delineations (polygons) all carrying the same soil information, the relational data structure for the soil will have the form shown in Fig. 46.2. The polygon boundary data will be held as vectors in an arc-node structure or as compact rasters depending on the type of GIS used.

The data from the soil profiles will also be held in a series of tables. For example, there may be tables for the classification name, the field site and the morphological, chemical and physical properties, all of which can be retrieved without reference to the soil map. In order to facilitate the use of the profile data to support crop modelling, spatial interpolation and computations of means and standard deviations of important soil properties for each separate delineation, it is also sensible to

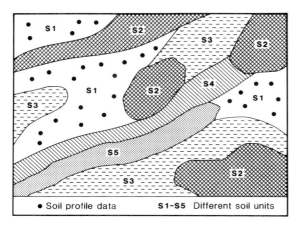

Fig. 46.1 Mapped soil units, polygons and soil profiles are the basic elements of a soil information system.

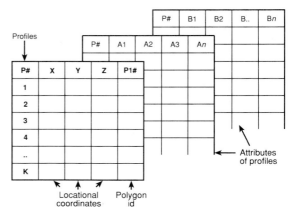

Fig. 46.3 Relational structure for the soil profiles. Profiles are identified by a serial number (P); the tables contain data on location (X, Y and Z coordinates), the soil polygon in which they occur and attribute values ($A1 \ldots, An, B1 \ldots, Bn$).

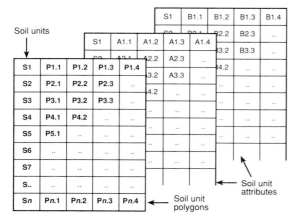

Fig. 46.2 Relational structure of a soil polygon map: S1–Sn refer to the kinds of soil (mapping units); P1.1 ... refer to the polygons representing the location of each kind of soil; the property values held by each kind of soil for all polygons are given by the attribute tables $A1.1 \ldots, B1.1 \ldots$.

cross-link each profile with the polygon in which it falls (Fig. 46.3). This could be done 'on the fly' by point-in-polygon search but it is probably quicker to do it once as a batch process and store the results in the database. It is also possible to make the reverse linkages and, for each polygon, to store a list of all profiles occurring within its boundaries. In this way, access to either the spatial data or the profile data can be made quickly and easily either directly or through the other.

TREATING SOIL VARIATION AS CONTINUOUS VARIATION: OPTIMAL INTERPOLATION

When soil profile data have been stored in a relational database they can be used in several ways. One is to use them simply to characterize the mapping units in which they occur, by performing either logical, numerical or statistical analysis (see the next section on page 163). Although spatial data on soil are most frequently stored in a form linked to clearly delineated soil map units (polygons), there are many instances where the simple choropleth (or chorochromatic) map model is inadequate. This may be the case when the soil boundaries are vague and diffuse (see Burrough 1986:121 for a discussion of the different kinds of lateral change in soil that may occur at 'boundaries') or when the properties of interest show strong spatial variation within the polygons.

Therefore, an alternative to using profile data merely to characterize the soil polygons is to use the data from the profiles to interpolate single-attribute surfaces that can be displayed individually or used as separate layers in a GIS. There are many interpolation methods that can be used (see Burrough 1986 for a review) but, when sufficient data are available, it is sensible to consider using geostatistical methods to aid interpolation. This is because soil properties only rarely vary in a smooth and continuous way over space. Besides the abrupt changes (usually called soil boundaries), there is often much short-range variation in the values of soil attributes that cannot be modelled by a smoothly changing function such as a trend surface. The short-range variations can be split into two components: a spatially correlated but irregularly varying component; and a random component (or 'noise') that arises from measurement and sampling errors and very short-range variations that cannot be detected with the resolution of the chosen sample spacing. The spatially correlated but irregular variation can be characterized in terms of a spatial correlation function known as the variogram. The variogram contains information that can be used for optimal interpolation, for optimizing sample spacing and for simulating the spatial variation of soil. This interpolation method is known as 'kriging', after the South African mining engineer D G Krige who first used it. The methodology has been put on a firm theoretical foundation by the French geomathematician Georges Matheron (1971) and, in recent years, it has found many applications in soil science.

A brief introduction to kriging and regionalized variable theory

The kriging technique assumes that the spatial variation of the soil attribute under study can be modelled by a stochastic surface. Attributes that vary in this way are called *regionalized variables* and they satisfy the intrinsic hypothesis (Journel and Huijbregts 1978).

The theory of regionalized variables is now well known, so only the most important aspects will be summarized here (see Journel and Huijbregts 1978; Burgess and Webster 1980a, 1980b; Webster 1985; Burrough 1986; Webster and Oliver 1990). Regionalized variable theory assumes that the spatial variation of any variable can be expressed as the sum of three major components. These are:

- a structural component, associated with a constant mean value or a polynomial trend;
- a spatially correlated random component; and
- a 'white noise' or residual error term that is spatially uncorrelated.

Let x be a position in one, two or three dimensions. Then the spatial variable Z_i at x is given by

$$Z_i(x) = m(x) + \epsilon'(x) + \epsilon'' \quad [46.1]$$

where $m(x)$ is a deterministic function describing the structural component of Z_i at x, $\epsilon'(x)$ is the term denoting the stochastic, locally varying spatially dependent residuals from $m(x)$ and ϵ'' is a residual, spatially independent noise term having zero mean and variance σ^2. To simplify matters, it is assumed here that $m(x)$ is constant. The variation of the random function $\epsilon'(x)$ over space is summarized by the semivariance which, for a lag (sample separation) of h, is given by:

$$\gamma(h) = \tfrac{1}{2} E[Z_{x+h} - Z_x]^2 \quad [46.2]$$

For a one-dimensional transect, the semivariance at lag h is estimated by

$$\gamma(h) = \frac{1}{2(n-h)} \cdot \sum_{i=1}^{n-h} [Z_{xi+h} - Z_{xi}]^2 \quad [46.3]$$

where h is the distance between $(n - h)$ pairs of sample sites Z_i, Z_{i-h}. The function can also be estimated for sample sites in two and three dimensions and for different directions to determine possible anisotropy. A plot of $\gamma(h)$ versus h is called an experimental variogram. Various theoretical models (spherical, linear, exponential, Gaussian, De Wijssian, Bessel functions – see Journel and Huijbregts 1978 or Webster 1985 for details) can be fitted through the experimental variogram in order to describe how the semivariance attribute values vary with sample spacing.

Features of the variogram

The variogram summarizes the way in which the values of the attribute being sampled covary in space. Variograms may take many forms but they can be summarized in the terms of non-transitional and transitional variograms.

With non-transitional variograms, the semivariance increases monotonically with increasing sample spacing (Fig. 46.4(a)). With transitional variograms (Fig. 46.4(b)), the semivariance increases with sample spacing up to a critical distance called the *range* at which it levels out. The value of semivariance beyond the range is termed the *sill*. Beyond the range, there is no spatial covariance between sample sites. Up to the range, the semivariance increases with sample spacing as in the non-transitional case. Both kinds of variogram may show a positive intersection with the Y-axis, which estimates the *nugget* variance. This nugget estimates the non-spatially correlated noise term ϵ'' in eq [46.1] which is caused by measurement errors and very short-range spatial variation below the resolution of the sampling net. Transitional variograms can be modelled by spherical, circular, exponential, Bessel functions or Gaussian models (Journel and Huijbregts 1978).

Besides these simple models, variograms may show a variety of more complex forms. Anisotropy in the underlying spatial pattern will be revealed by the experimental variograms having different slopes, ranges and possibly sills and nuggets when determined from samples laid out in different directions. When several spatial patterns have been superimposed upon each other (cf. Journel and Huijbregts 1978; Burrough 1983a, 1983b), the variogram will be a composite embodying variation at all the scales sampled. Periodic variation yields variograms with a periodic form. Complex experimental variograms can be modelled by sets of the variogram models given above (e.g. a double spherical model in which the ranges of the models match two distinctly separate scales of spatial variation).

Using the variogram to optimize sampling for mapping

Once the variogram is known, the value of an attribute at any point in a mapping unit can be predicted from the data points in that mapping unit which are located nearest to it. The error of the prediction depends only on the variogram, the number and configuration of the data points and the size of the block for which the prediction is made. Knowledge of the variogram can substantially reduce the number of samples required to make predictions of mean values (or location-specific point or block predictions) for a given prediction error as compared with the classical model (see Burgess, Webster and McBratney 1981; Burrough 1990).

Using the variogram for interpolation of point predictions

The fitted variogram can be used to determine the weights λ_i needed for predicting the value of an attribute Z at any unsampled point x_0 from measurements of Z at points x_i. The prediction is a linear weighted sum:

$$\hat{Z}(x_0) = \sum_{i=1}^{n} \lambda_i \cdot Z(x_i) \qquad [46.4]$$

with

$$\sum_{i=1}^{n} \lambda_i = 1$$

The weights λ_i are chosen so that the prediction

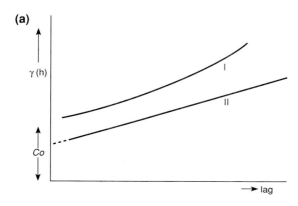

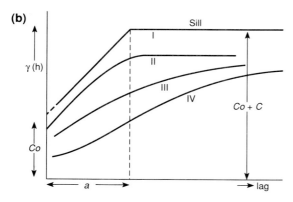

Fig. 46.4 (a) Non-transitional variogram models. Curve I is indicative of a trend in the data. Curve II indicates that spatial dependence occurs for all scales covered by the variogram. (b) Transitional variogram models. I. Linear with sill; II Spherical model; III Exponential model; IV Gaussian model. All models indicate that once the sample spacing exceeds a certain value, then there is no spatial dependence between the sample sites.

$\hat{Z}(x_0)$ is unbiased, and the prediction variance σ^2_e is less than for any other linear combination of the observed values.

The minimum variance of $Z(x_0)$ is obtained when

$$\sum_{j=1}^{n} \lambda j \cdot \gamma(x_i, x_j) + \varphi = \gamma(x_i, x_0) \text{ for all } i, \quad [46.5]$$

and is

$$\sigma^2_e = \sum_{j=1}^{n} \lambda j \cdot \gamma(x_j, x_0) + \varphi \quad [46.6]$$

The quantity $\gamma(x_i, x_j)$ is the semivariance of Z between the sampling points x_i and x_j; $\gamma(x_i, x_0)$ is the semivariance between the sampling point x_i and the unvisited point x_0. Both these quantities are obtained from the fitted variogram. The quantity φ is a Lagrange multiplier required for the minimalization.

Using the variogram for interpolation of block predictions

Equations [46.4] and [46.6] give predictions of the attribute and its prediction variance at unvisited sites for areas or volumes of soil that are the same size as that of the original sampling support. Very often there is a requirement to predict local average values for areas that are larger than units that can be practically sampled, such as the area under an experimental plot or that covered by a remotely sensed pixel or equivalent grid cell in a raster GIS. This can be achieved by modifying the kriging equations to predict an average value of Z over a block B, given by

$$Z(x_B) = \int_B \frac{Z(x) \, dx}{\text{area } B} \quad [46.7]$$

is predicted by

$$Z(x_B) = \sum_{i=1}^{n} \lambda_i \cdot Z(x_i)$$

with $\sum_{i=1}^{n} \lambda_i = 1$, as before, but the weights are calculated using average semivariances between the data points and all points in the block (Burgess and Webster 1980b). The minimum variance is now

$$\sigma^2_B = \sum_{j=1}^{n} \lambda_j \gamma(x_j, x_B) + \varphi_B - \gamma(x_B, x_B) \quad [46.8]$$

and is obtained when

$$\sum_{i=1}^{n} \lambda_j \gamma(x_i, x_B) + \varphi_B = \gamma(x_i, x_B) \text{ for all } i \quad [46.9]$$

Figure 46.5 is an example of a spherical variogram fitted to experimental semivariances computed for the sand content of the 0–20 cm layer at 69 soil sites located on a regular 75 m grid in Turen, Venezuela (Mateos et al. 1987). Figures 46.6(a) and 46.6(b) display the interpolated surface and the associated kriging error surface for 15 × 15 m blocks. GIS display techniques can enhance the presentation of interpolated data (see Plate 46.1).

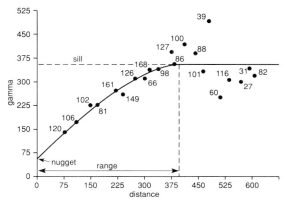

Fig. 46.5 Experimental variogram of per cent sand (0–20 cm) from an experimental field in Turen, Venezuela with a fitted spherical model: sill 355.09 per cent squared, nugget 57.20 per cent squared, range 410.5 m.

Given the variogram (or other estimate of the covariance function), eqs [46.4], [46.5], [46.7] and [46.8] permit the prediction of the value of an attribute Z at any location within the map unit for blocks of land having a minimum area of the sample support or larger. By predicting the value of Z at points on a regular grid, the attribute can be mapped within the map unit and a map of the associated prediction errors can be made. Note that, because the error of these predictions depends only on the covariance function and the configuration of the data points, we have a way in which – once the variogram is known – sampling strategies can be designed to give any required minimum interpolation error (Burrough 1991).

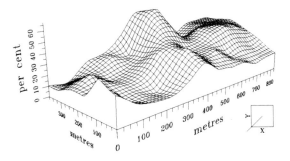

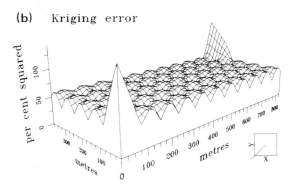

Fig. 46.6 (a) Interpolated surface of sand content for the topsoil of an experimental field in Turen, Venezuela. The surface has been constructed by interpolating from a data grid spacing of 75 m to blocks of 15 × 15 m. (b) Kriging error surface of surface in Fig. 46.6(a). The errors are lower for the 15 × 15 m blocks that are centred over data points, except at the two corners where errors increase markedly because of missing values.

Extensions of kriging in soil science

Choosing the correct spatial domains

The first attempts to use kriging in soil science compared the results of interpolation with the results of classical mapping (van Kuilenburg et al. 1982). They suggested that kriging did not always produce results that were better than those obtained by treating each mapping unit (set of soil polygons) as a homogeneous unit characterized by a mean and standard deviation. Further work showed that the relative success of the interpolation depended greatly on the type of soil and the processes that had controlled its development. Work by Stein et al. (1988) and Burrough (1986) has shown that an average variogram for a whole area is often insufficient for distinguishing between the kinds of spatial covariation that may occur in different landscape units. Consequently, it may be sensible to divide the landscape up into major soil units before selecting the soil profiles for interpolation (see Fig. 46.7). There is a possibility that, when a soil mapping unit has multiple occurrences (as is often the case), the spatial variation of any given natural attribute within all occurrences may be characterized by a single variogram. If this were so – and it has yet to be demonstrated – then the parameters of the variograms for each important property could be stored as new attributes in relational tables that are linked to each soil polygon.

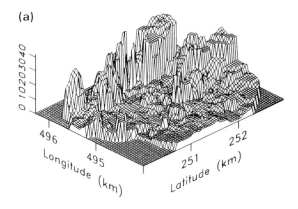

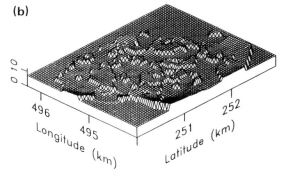

Fig. 46.7 (a) Co-kriged map of 30–year average moisture deficit (MD30) based on stratification according to soil type; (b) Standard deviation of the prediction error. (From Stein et al. 1988, Geoderma, Elsevier Science Publishers B. V.)

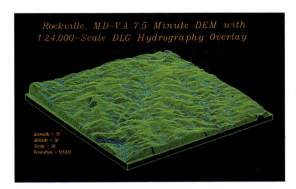

Plate 35.1 Digital isometric plot of a 7.5 minute Digital Elevation Model superimposed with Digital Line Graph hydrology data (Rockville, MD-VA).

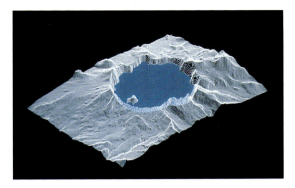

Plate 35.2 Digital isometric plot of two merged 7.5 minute Digital Elevation Models (Crater Lake East and Crater Lake West, Oregon).

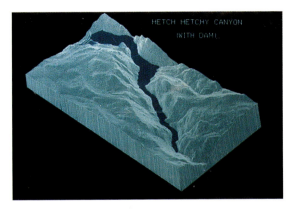

Plate 35.3 Digital isometric plot of a 7.5 minute Digital Elevation Model, with dam and reservoir superimposed.

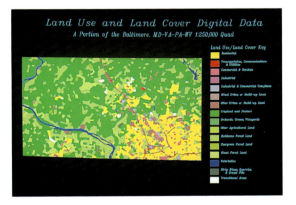

Plate 35.4 Digital plot showing a portion of the Baltimore, MD-VA-PA-WV 1:250 000-scale Land Use and Land Cover digital data.

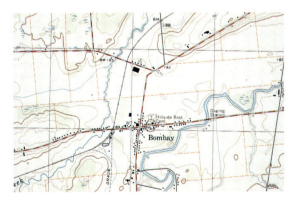

Plate 35.5 A portion of the experimental Bombay, NY-Que. 1:24 000-scale topographic map, produced from digital line graph data using automated cartographic methods and GIS technology.

Plate 35.6 Dane County, Wisconsin – Digital Orthophoto displayed on cartographic editing workstation with a scanning resolution of 50 microns.

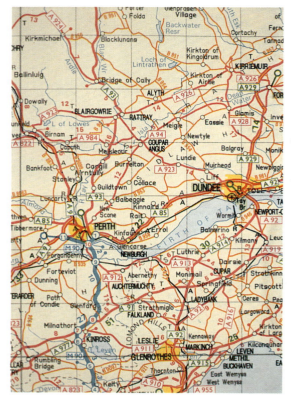

Plate 36.1 Plot from Ordnance Survey 1:625 000 digital data. Crown copyright reserved.

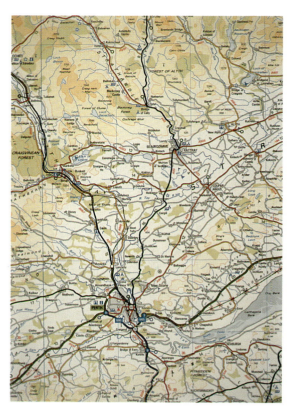

Plate 36.2 Plot from Ordnance Survey 1:250 000 digital data available for the whole of Britain. Crown copyright reserved.

Plate 36.3 Plot from Ordnance Survey 1:10 000 digital data. This is an experimental map derived by generalization from structured 1:2500 data. Crown copyright reserved.

Plate 36.4 Plot from Ordnance Survey 1:1250 digital data. This is a monochrome Superplan from unstructured ('spaghetti') data. Crown copyright reserved.

Plate 36.5 Plot from Ordnance Survey 1:1250 digital data. This is a colour Superplan from structured data. Crown copyright reserved.

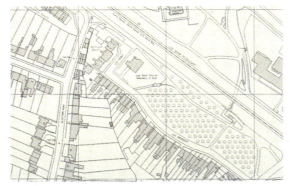

Plate 36.6 Plot from Ordnance Survey 1:1250 digital data. This is a monochrome Superplan from structured data. Crown copyright reserved.

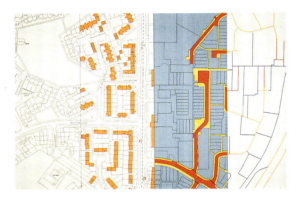

Plate 36.7 Plot from Ordnance Survey 1:1250 digital data. This is a composite map showing unstructured data, OSBASE, OSLAND and OSCAR data. Crown copyright reserved.

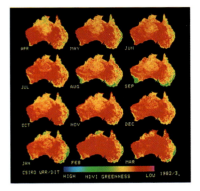

Plate 39.1 Series of images depicting monthly vegetative conditions in Australia from April 1982 to March 1983. The data were produced by NASA Goddard Space Flight Center from NOAA meteorological satellite images, and were used in a national image-based GIS developed by the CSIRO Divisions of Information Technology and Wildlife and Ecology.

Plate 42.1 An example of output from the Knoxville Utilities Board GIS (courtesy David A Reece, Manager, Information Services, Knoxville Utilities Board).

Plate 43.1 The Bosch Travelpilot screen (courtesy author).

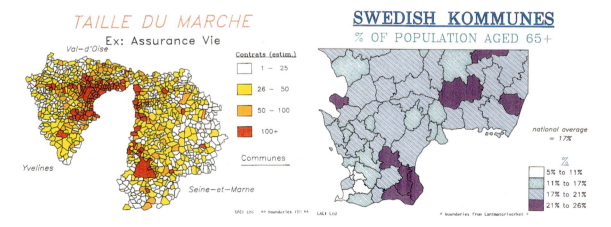

Plate 45.1 Market maps produced by GIS: (a) Estimate of life assurance policies in part of France; (b) Percentage of the population aged over 65 in part of Sweden.

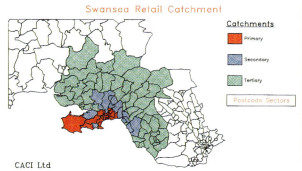

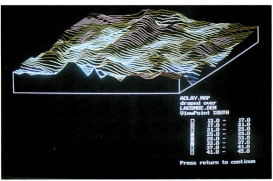

Plate 45.2 The 'primary', 'secondary' and 'tertiary' retail catchments of Swansea in Wales produced by GIS.

Plate 46.1 Variation of surface clay content interpolated by block kriging displayed over a digital elevation model of the site (courtesy R A MacMillan and W van Deursen).

(a)

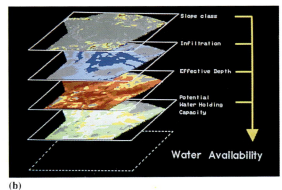

(b)

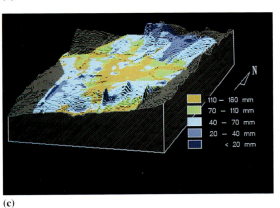

(c)

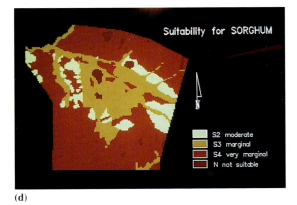

(d)

Plate 46.2 Land evaluation by map overlay and transfer functions: (a) model factors; (b) GIS layers; (c) water availability; (d) suitability of land for Sorghum according to the model (courtesy V Jetten, S de Jong and E-J Henkens).

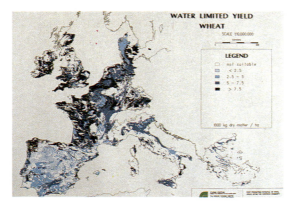

Plate 46.3 Results of computer simulation of water-limited wheat yield for the European Community as computed for the soil mapping units of the CORINE European Data Base. The potential yield is estimated from climatic data and is then modified to take account of soil moisture supply (deficits and excesses). Other factors may result in actual yields being much lower than those shown here. (courtesy A K Bregt, Winand Staring Centre for Integrated Land, Soil and Water Research, Wageningen).

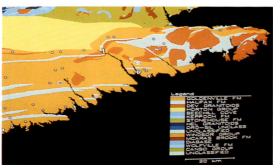

Plate 47.1 Map showing geology and gold occurrences, Meguma Terrane, Nova Scotia.

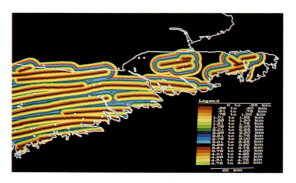

Plate 47.2 Map showing proximity to Devonian anticlinal axes generated from vectors by multiple corridor buffering.

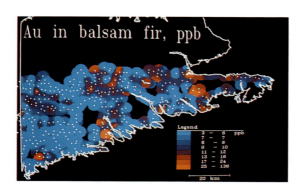

Plate 47.3 Gold in balsam fir twigs, showing sample locations (ppb = parts per billion).

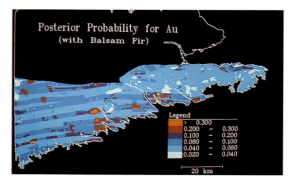

Plate 47.4 Posterior probability of gold (Au) occurrence per $1\ km^2$, estimated by weights of evidence.

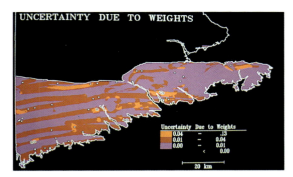

Plate 47.5 Standard deviation of posterior probability for gold, based on standard deviation of weights.

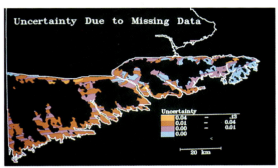

Plate 47.6 Standard deviation of posterior probability for gold, based on missing information. The lake sediment geochemistry map has areas of missing data, outside catchment basins.

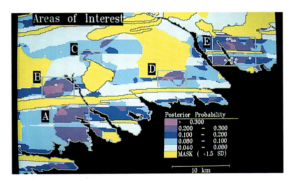

Plate 47.7 Part of Plate 47.4 showing areas of exploration interest. The combined effects of uncertainty due to weights and missing information are shown by masking out those areas with P(post)/total standard deviation less than 1.5, suggesting that P(post) is not significantly different from zero.

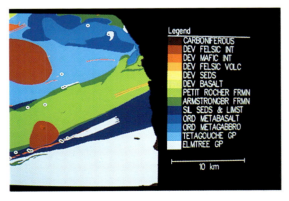

Plate 47.8 Geology map for New Brunswick study area, from Watson *et al.* (1989). The city of Bathurst is just outside the SE corner of the map.

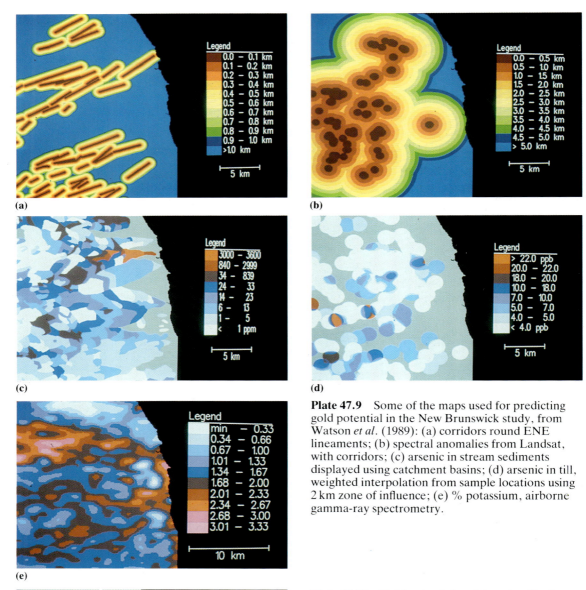

Plate 47.9 Some of the maps used for predicting gold potential in the New Brunswick study, from Watson *et al.* (1989): (a) corridors round ENE lineaments; (b) spectral anomalies from Landsat, with corridors; (c) arsenic in stream sediments displayed using catchment basins; (d) arsenic in till, weighted interpolation from sample locations using 2 km zone of influence; (e) % potassium, airborne gamma-ray spectrometry.

Plate 47.10 Gold potential as determined in the New Brunswick study.

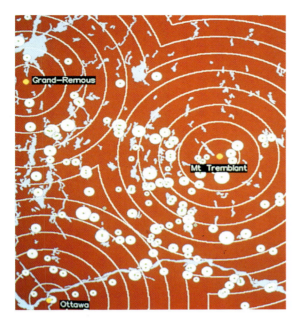

Plate 47.11 Map showing location and magnitude of seismic epicentres in an area of west Quebec for the period 1982–88. The circular contours show distance in 10 km intervals round three seismometer stations. Notice the location of Ottawa in the SW corner of the map, on the Ottawa River.

Plate 47.12 Interpreted stream lineaments, superimposed on base map showing lakes and main rivers.

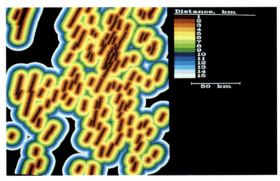

Plate 47.13 Proximity map showing distance to streams in the 9–27 degree azimuth class, generated by buffering a subset of the lines in Plate 47.12.

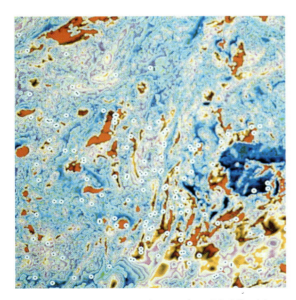

Plate 47.14 Aeromagnetic map (total field) with epicentres superimposed for west Quebec study area. The red areas are magnetic highs.

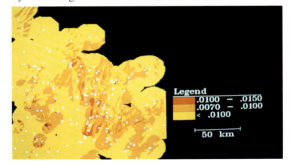

Plate 47.15 Posterior probability of an epicentre occurring per 1 km², based on 147 epicentres recorded in the 1982–88 period and using three binary maps for prediction (geology, drainage and magnetics).

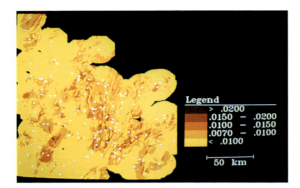

Plate 47.16 Similar to Plate 47.15, but using multi-state ordinal maps for deriving the distance to streams and magnetics.

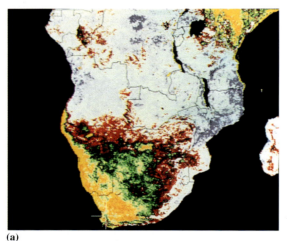

Plate 49.1 Estimation of fuelwood supplies in southern Africa using remotely sensed data (Millington *et al.* 1989). Images of the normalized difference vegetation index (NDVI) for southern Africa for three different periods: (a) April 1984; (b) June 1984; (c) July 1984. The index is sensitive to vegetation greenness: the changing response of the vegetation to seasonal variations in rainfall can be clearly seen. The data are derived from the US National Oceanographic and Atmospheric Administration's (NOAA) satellites' sensors known as the Advanced Very High Resolution Radiometer (AVHRR). These multitemporal images were used to identify woody biomass classes (see plate 49.2) (Justice *et al.* 1985).

(a)

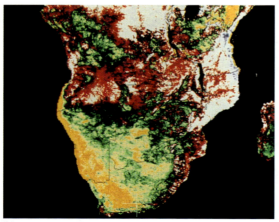

(b)

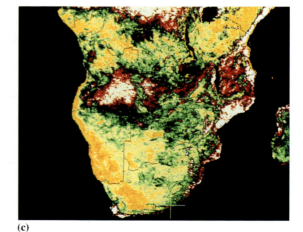

(c)

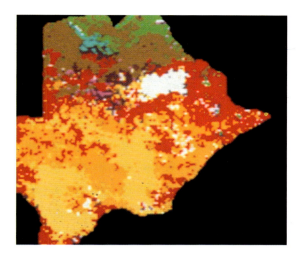

Plate 49.2 Subdivision of Botswana into woody biomass classes using automated classification of multi-date NDVI data (see Plate 49.1a). Cover classes are defined using the magnitude and seasonal variations of the NDVI (Millington *et al.* 1989).

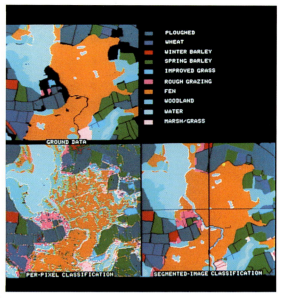

Plate 49.3 Comparison of the results of land cover classification of remotely sensed data using a classifier relying on a rule-base applied to topographic data (bottom right) and a classifier relying on remotely sensed data alone (bottom left) (Mason *et al.* 1988).

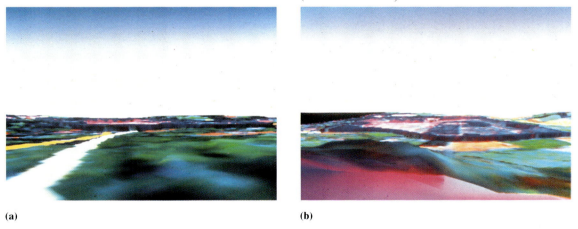

(a) (b)

Plate 49.4 Perspective views derived by overlaying SPOT satellite data on a digital elevation data for the Foxley Wood development, Hampshire, UK. The dark strip in the middle background is a belt of trees 'grown' on top of the DEM. From the perspective in (a) this appears to be adequate to hide development in the area behind, whereas from the position shown in (b) it has little effect in ameliorating the impact on the rural landscape (Quarmby and Saull 1989).

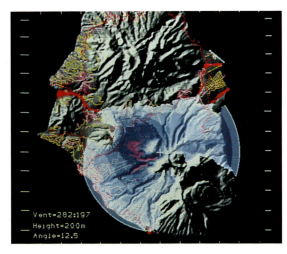

Plate 49.5 Deposit map of Montserrat pyroclastic deposits derived from the model illustrated in Figure 49.4 (Wadge and Isaacs 1988).

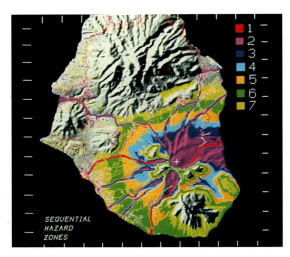

Plate 49.6 Hazard map of Montserrat generated using the model illustrated in Figure 49.4.

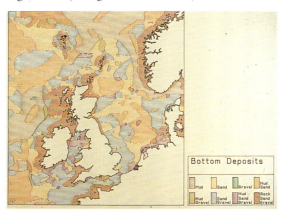

Plate 49.7 Example of a map from the NERC Marine Atlas (see fig. 49.5) (after Mason and Townshend 1988, Robinson 1991).

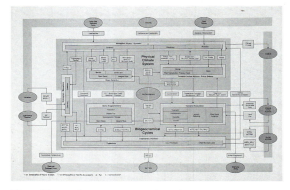

Plate 50.1 Conceptual model of the Earth system process operating on time scales of decades to centuries (*Source*: Earth System Science Committee 1988).

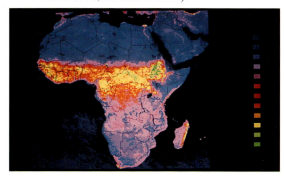

Plate 50.2 NOAA normalized vegetation index for Africa for September 1985 (*Source*: Kineman 1989).

Plate 50.3 Global ecosystems (*Source*: Olson *et al.* 1989).

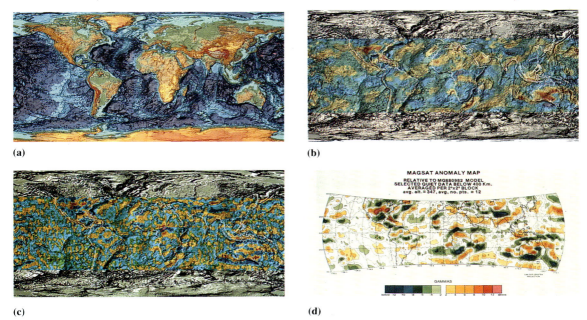

Plate 50.4 Global databases: (a) Global elevations and bathymetry, shaded relief base. Stereo pair (*Source*: Hastings 1986a) and digital data available from NOAA National Geophysical Data Center; (b) Total-field magnetic anomalies from NASA's MAGSAT, plotted on shaded relief base from NOAA National Geophysical Data Center archives (*Source*: Hastings 1986b); (c) As Plate 50.4(b), with MAGSAT anomalies filtered to emphasize short wavelength features, apparently better related to large-scale geological features (at the cost of showing more noise from the data compilation) (*Source*: Hastings 1986b); (d) Original NASA MAGSAT total-field anomaly map (*Source*: Langel, Phillips and Horner 1982).

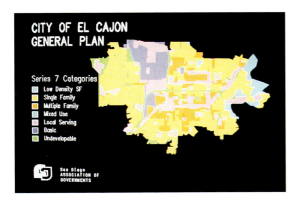

Plate 52.1(a) General plan of the city of El Cajon.

Plate 52.1(b) Land use in El Cajon in 1986.

Plate 52.1(c) Land constrained from development.

Plate 52.1(d) Developable land in El Cajon.

Plate 53.1 USGS LUDA map of A/P Study area.

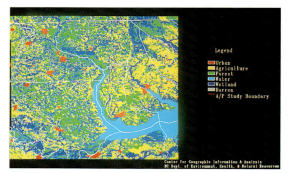

Plate 53.2 TM Image of A/P Study area.

Plate 53.3 Water zones and regions of influence.

Plate 53.4 Water tracts and T values.

Plate 53.5 Water area use classification – alternative 1.

Plate 53.6 Areas excluded in step 1 screening for a hazardous waste site.

Plate 53.7 Parcels formed for evaluation of remaining suitable areas.

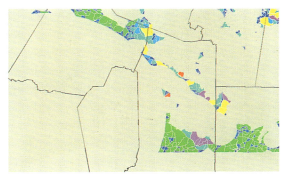

Plate 53.8 Areas excluded in further evaluation of hazardous waste site.

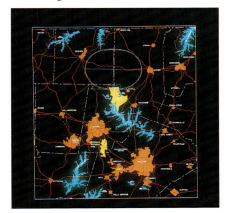

Plate 53.9 Proposed SSC location in North Carolina.

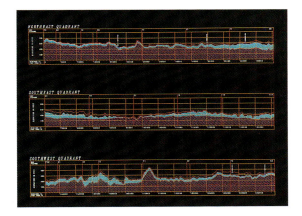

Plate 53.10 Profile of the SSC collider ring.

Plate 53.11 Geology of SSC proposed site.

Plate 53.12 Block Diagram of proposed SSC site.

Plate 54.1 Aquatic and terrestrial acid rain sensitivity in Minnesota in 1987 (courtesy of Minnesota Pollution Control Agency and Land Management Information Center (LMIC)).

Plate 54.2 Critical erosion areas in Minnesota (courtesy of Minnesota Board of Water and Soil Resources and LMIC).

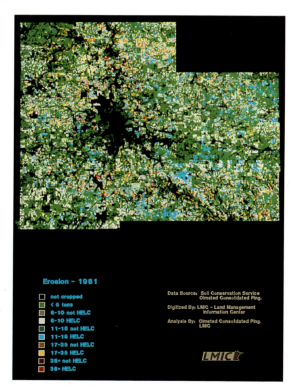

Plate 54.3 Erosion classes in Olmsted County, Minnesota in 1981 (courtesy of Rochester-Olmstead County Planning & LMIC).

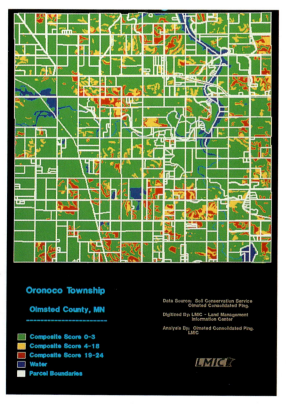

Plate 54.4 Oronoco Township, Minnesota erosion ranking for 1986 (courtesy of Rochester-Olmstead County Planning & LMIC).

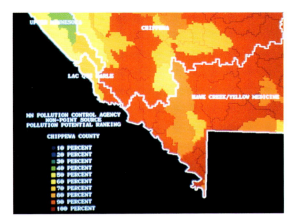

Plate 54.5 Non-Point source pollution potential in Chippewa County, Minnesota (courtesy of Minnesota Pollution Control Agency and LMIC).

Plate 54.6 Minnesota Water Systems monitoring stations (courtesy LMIC).

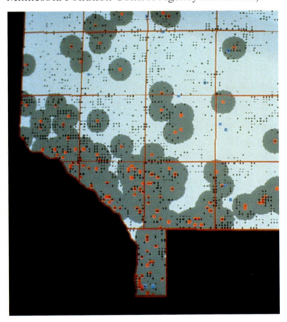

Plate 54.7 Water well distribution and observation well network in Anoka County, Minnesota, April 1989 (courtesy of Minnesota Department of Natural Resources).

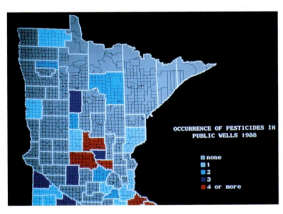

Plate 54.8 Occurrence of pesticides in public wells in Minnesota in 1988 (courtesy DATANET Plus Mapping, LMIC).

Plate 54.9 Groundwater contamination susceptibility in Minnesota in 1988 (courtesy of Minnesota Pollution Control Agency and LMIC).

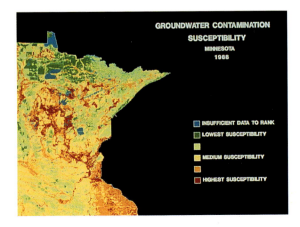

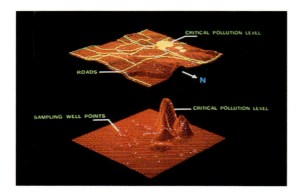

Plate 54.10 Site level groundwater assessment in Minnesota (courtesy LMIC).

Plate 54.11 Potential economic timber management model with 1983 assumptions; colours indicate different recommended management classes (courtesy Minnesota Department of Natural Resources).

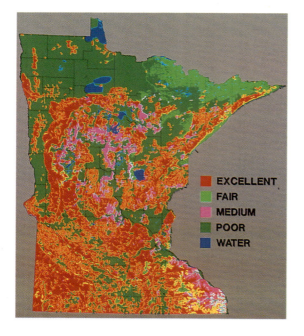

Plate 54.12 Potential Red Oak sites in Minnesota (courtesy Minnesota Department of Natural Resources and LMIC).

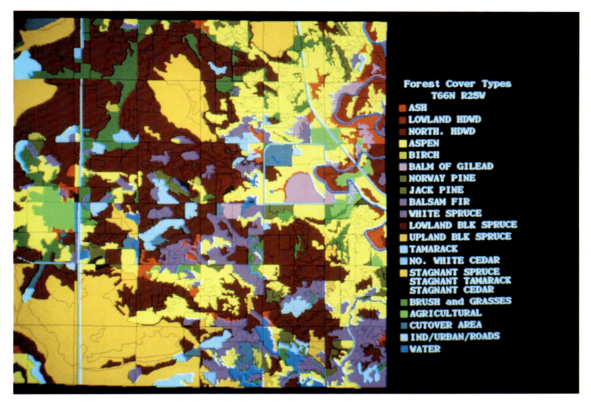

Plate 54.13 Minnesota Department of Natural Resources Phase II forest inventory (courtesy Minnesota Department of Natural Resources).

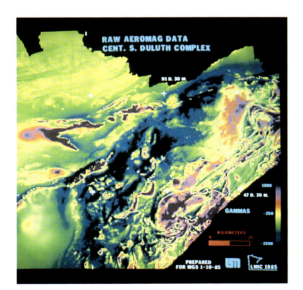 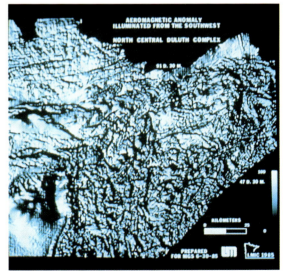

Plate 54.14 Aeromagnetic Survey – Duluth Complex. (a) Raw aeromagnetic data. (b) Aeromagnetic data illuminated from the southwest (courtesy Minnesota Geological Survey, funded by the Minnesota Legislative Commission on Natural Resources).

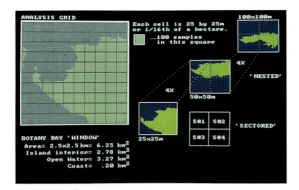

Plate 55.1 Botany Bay study area and database configuration.

Plate 55.2 Areas of recreation, limited use and preservation.

Plate 55.3 Watershed areas delineated and evaluated for ecological research potential.

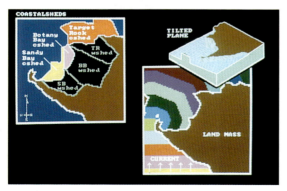

Plate 55.4 Delineated coastalsheds corresponding to the three terrestrial watersheds identified in Plate 53.3.

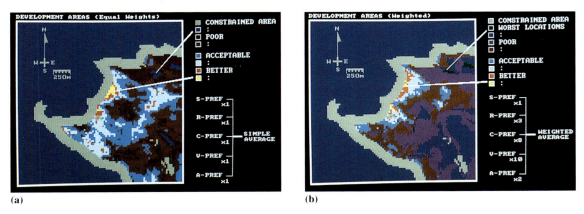

Plate 55.5 Development suitability derived from combining five preference maps.

Plate 55.6 Hierarchical Land Use Allocation map.

(a)

(b)

Plate 55.7 Land Use Conflict maps: (a) all land use combinations; (b) one interpretation of the 'best' allocation of land uses.

Plate 56.1 Example of pin map created by address matching a set of addresses. Based on TIGER file for Richland County, South Carolina.

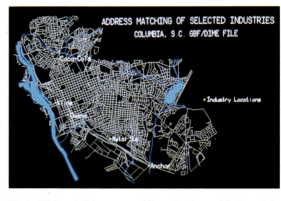

Plate 56.2 Address matching of selected industrial sites in Columbia SC based on GBF/DIME file.

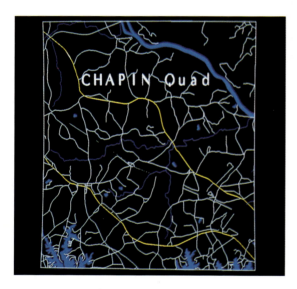

Plate 56.3 Chapin SC 7.5 minute quadrangle generated from the USGS 1 : 100 000 scale digital line graphs.

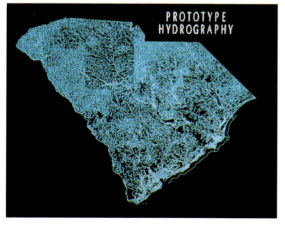

Plate 56.4 Hydrological features for South Carolina extracted from the 1 : 100 000 scale digital line graphs.

Plate 56.5 State-wide representation of all water supply lines of 6 or more inches in diameter.

Plate 56.6 Map of Lexington County SC generated entirely from the Bureau of Census TIGER file.

Plate 56.7 Location of industrial sites in Orangeburg SC. This Plate demonstrates how point locations such as industrial sites can be added to the TIGER line files.

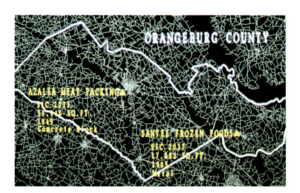

Plate 56.8 SPOT scene of part of Columbia SC metropolitan area overlayed with TIGER representation of interstate highways, the Congaree River and Columbia Airport. © 1989 CNES, provided courtesy of SPOT Image Corporation.

Plate 56.9 Enlargement of SPOT scene shown in Plate 56.8. Notice the mis-registration of the TIGER representation of the large interchange in the southeastern portion of the image. © 1989 CNES, provided courtesy of SPOT Image Corporation.

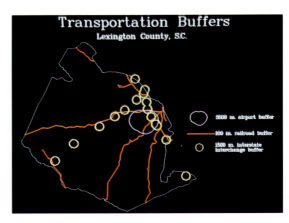

Plate 56.10 Initial overlay of transportation buffers for the industrial site selection model.

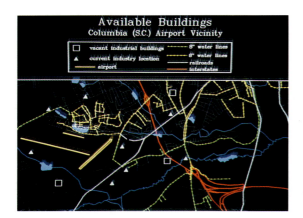

Plate 56.11 Enlargement of the site selection model centred on the Columbia SC metropolitan airport.

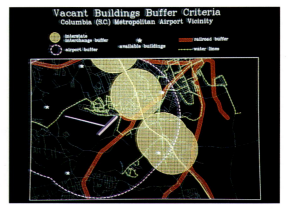

Plate 56.12 Final map used to make the site selection based on location of available buildings and water supply lines.

Co-kriging

Very often data are available on cheap-to-measure attributes but it is necessary to make reliable statements about expensive or difficult-to-measure attributes – for which there are fewer observations available. If there are sufficient data then the expensive-to-measure attributes can be estimated and mapped using one of four approaches : transfer models (i.e. empirical relations between cheap-to-measure and expensive-to-measure soil properties – see Bouma and van Lanen 1987), regression equations, numerical models and co-kriging. Co-kriging is a multivariate analogue of kriging in which the spatial variation of two or more attributes and their joint spatial variation is used to guide interpolation. This is done by estimating the variograms for both attributes and their joint co-variogram (McBratney and Webster 1983b; Alemi, Shariari and Nielsen 1988; Stein et al. 1988; Leenaers, Burrough and Okx 1989; Leenaers, Okx and Burrough 1989).

Disjunctive kriging

Many applications in soil survey and environmental assessment do not require that the actual value of a soil property at a point be known with a given confidence level. Often it is sufficient only to know if the value exceeds a given threshold with a known probability. This information can be valuable for management decisions, such as those taken for adding lime (Webster and Oliver 1989), or for evaluating decisions to install septic tanks (Yates and Yates 1988). The use of disjunctive kriging requires point data from sample sites, knowledge of critical levels of the attribute in question and the conditional probability distribution of the attribute. Disjunctive kriging is particularly useful in situations where data are non-normally distributed.

APPLICATIONS

Many national soil survey agencies, such as the USDA Soil Conservation Service, the Canadian National and Provincial Agencies and the Dutch Soil Survey Institute (now part of the Staring Institute for Integrated Land, Water and Rural Survey) use GIS, as described above, as general tools for mapping and providing soils information to users. In many cases, the use of GIS has become standard rather than innovative and many regular products of these organizations could not be produced without automation; the latter ranges from the electronic collection of data to the production of digital maps. The wide range of applications can be illustrated by examining some of the ways in which soil data are now being analysed.

Soil data in a GIS can be manipulated in several ways even when only the digital soil map and associated attributes are used. A greater range of manipulations is possible if the data from the soil profiles are also used to create new single or multiple property overlays (e.g. by interpolation or modelling). Non-spatial applications (where, for example, only the soil profile data are used as happened in many earlier soil information systems) will not be mentioned.

Using the soil polygon map and associated attributes

Regardless of its scale, the soil polygon map can be used to create derived maps in the ways shown below.

Renaming, reclassifying and recolouring of the polygons

These actions are based upon a logical evaluation of the associated attributes. One example is the creation of a map of the major soil texture classes by renaming all the individual soil units in terms of the texture classes of the map units. Note that there is no difference here whether the graphics data are held in raster or vector form. These kinds of empirical functions are sometimes called transfer functions (see Bouma and van Lanen 1987). Plate 46.2 shows a typical land evaluation procedure using a GIS.

Logical overlays of the soil polygons with other coverages

Soil polygons are frequently overlaid with other 'coverages' such as climatic zones, soil parent material or land use to yield new composite overlays indicating various grades of soil suitability. These overlays can be computed when the graphics data are held in either raster or vector form. Typical applications are in natural resource management

(Walsh 1985), rangeland management (Best and Westin 1984) or land evaluation (see Plate 46.2).

Calculation of new attribute values from those for the soil polygons

For example, estimates might be computed of annual soil loss (A) from the Universal Soil Loss Equation

$$A = R \times E \times S \times L \times C \times P$$

from annual rainfall (R), the erodibility of the soil (E), slope angle (S) and length of slope (L) computed from a digital elevation model, and land cover (C) and protection indices (P) from land use and cropping overlays (Wischmeier and Smith 1978). The model can be applied in two ways. For vector overlays, the model can be applied once to the set of attributes for each individual polygon; the polygon network then shows the distribution of the results of the calculation. For raster overlays, the model can be applied to each pixel position separately. This requires much more computing but permits a better spatial resolution to be used because single pixel estimates of slope and slope length can be used instead of polygon-lumped averages. The same approach can be used with other models, such as crop yield models and simple land evaluation models (cf. Bouma and van Lanen 1987; Dumanski and Onofrei 1989). Heuvelink, Burrough and Stein (1989) have studied the use of geostatistics for understanding error propagation through these kinds of models.

Retrieval of profiles within polygons and generation of new polygon attributes

One such example is the computation of the average clay content of the topsoil and its variance for a given class of soil. The computed attributes can then be added to the list of soil mapping unit attributes in the relational database. An instance of this approach is a recent Dutch Soil Survey study to analyse the phosphate loads of soils in a small catchment in The Netherlands (Breeusma et al. 1989).

Using the profile data

Estimation of quantitative descriptors of soil properties

This includes means, modes, variances and semivariances of all quantitative soil properties. As described earlier, the semivariances give an estimate of the spatial autocovariance structure of the attributes (which is often expressed as the variogram); they can be used for interpolation, for designing sampling schemes and for simulating the spatial variation of soil attributes both within polygons and over the landscape at large. Statistical tests can reveal how meaningful the division of the landscape into soil polygons has been. If profile data have been collected using a nested sampling strategy, then useful estimates of the appropriate sampling spacing can be made (Webster 1977; Oliver and Webster 1986; Riezebos 1989; Webster and Oliver 1990).

Production of single-attribute maps by interpolation from the profile data

These maps can be made by standard non-statistical interpolation methods but if possible should be made using geostatistical methods (e.g. kriging). Co-kriging may allow expensive-to-sample attributes to be mapped more reliably from observations on cheap-to-measure attributes. Multi-attribute maps can be made by first submitting the profile data to principal components or principal coordinates analysis and then mapping the principal component scores. If the results of these interpolations are mapped as blocks on a regular grid (block kriging), the resulting overlays can be used with other coverages as indicated above. These methods are finding increasing use, particularly for soil pollution studies (see Leenaers, Burrough and Okx 1989; Leenaers, Okx and Burrough 1989) and erosion studies (Beurden and Riezebos 1988).

Creation of crop yield or other quantitative models from soil profile and other data

The results of these models can then be interpolated to give new coverages – see, for example, van Diepen et al. (1989); van Lanen et al. (1990) or Petach and Wagenet (1989). There are many different kinds of crop model, most of which have been reviewed by Dumanski and Onofrei (1989). Plate 46.3 is an example of crop yield modelling using a large soil database (van Lanen et al. 1990).

All these different ways of manipulating soil data in GIS are currently used in projects ranging from international scales (e.g. SOTER – Baumgardner and van der Weg 1989 and the European Community CORINE Project – Verhey 1986) through national soil advisory systems in large countries (e.g. Mausbach and Reybold 1987) to land evaluation in developed countries (e.g. Meijerink, Valenzuela and Stewart 1988; Batjes and Bouwman 1989) where soil data are often used in combination with remotely sensed data (Helldén 1987; Olsson 1989). Soil information systems are not just limited to large national soil inventories but are currently also used for local studies on agricultural experimental farms, for real-time control of fertilizer placement in the tractor cab (Robert and Anderson 1987; Robert 1989) and for soil pollution studies (e.g. Leenaers, Burrough and Okx 1989; Leenaers, Okx and Burrough 1989).

CONCLUSIONS

GIS are not new to soil science, but have been introduced into the profession during the last 15 years. Although the original soil information systems were limited to soil profile data, the recent developments in mapping technology, interpolation methods, remote sensing and modelling have provided soil survey and environmental agencies with useful tools that are used for standard production of maps and reports and for research. The impact on soil science has been gentle but profound as soil scientists have gradually moved from a descriptive to a quantitative science. As a result of being able to handle much larger volumes of data, soil scientists have come to grips with the difficult problems of describing the spatial variation of soil and they are now providing useful information services to a wide range of different kinds of land user, ranging from urban planners in western countries to land resource experts in developing lands.

REFERENCES

Alemi M H, Shariari M R, Nielsen D R (1988) Kriging and co-kriging of soil water properties. *Soil Technology* **1**: 117–32

Batjes N H, Bouwman A F (1989) JAMPLES: a computerized land evaluation system for Jamaica. In: Bouma J, Bregt A K (eds.) *Land Qualities in Space and Time. Proceedings of the Symposium organised by the International Society of Soil Science (ISSS)*, Wageningen, The Netherlands, 22–26 August 1988. PUDOC, Wageningen, pp. 257–60

Baumgardner M F, Oldeman L R (eds.) (1986) *Proceedings of an international workshop on the structure of a digital international soil resources map annex database, held 20–24 January 1986 at the International Soil Reference and Information Centre, Wageningen, The Netherlands.* International Soil Science Society, Wageningen, 138 pp.

Baumgardner M F, Weg R F Van der (1989) Space and time dimensions of a world soils and terrain digital database. In: Bouma J, Bregt A K (eds.) *Land Qualities in Space and Time. Proceedings of a Symposium organised by the International Society of Soil Science (ISSS)*, Wageningen, The Netherlands, 22–26 August 1988. PUDOC, Wageningen, 356 pp

Beckett P H T, Burrough P A (1971a) The relations between cost and utility in soil survey. IV. Comparisons of the utilities of soil maps produced by different survey procedures and to different scales. *Journal of Soil Science* **22**: 466–80

Beckett P H T, Burrough P A (1971b) The relations between cost and utility in soil survey. V. The cost effectiveness of different soil survey procedures. *Journal of Soil Science* **22**: 481–9

Beckett P H T, Webster R (1971) Soil variability – a review. *Soils and Fertilizers* **34**: 1–15

Beek K-J, Burrough P A, McCormack D E (1987) Quantified land evaluation procedures. *Proceedings of a Joint Meeting of ISSS Working Groups on Land Evaluation and Soil Information Systems, Washington 25 April–2 May 1986.* ITC Publication No 6, Enschede, 165 pp

Best R G, Westin F C (1984) GIS for soils and rangeland management. *IEEE Pecora 9 Proceedings Spatial Information Technologies for Remote Sensing Today and Tomorrow, 2–4 October 1984, Sioux Falls.* IEEE, Sioux Falls, pp. 70–4

Beurden S A H A van, Riezebos H Th. (1988) The application of geostatistics in erosion hazard mapping. *Soil Technology* **1**: 349–64

Bie S W (1975) Soil information systems. *Proceedings of the meeting of the ISSS Working Group on Soil Information Systems, Wageningen, The Netherlands, 1–4 Sept. 1975*, PUDOC, Wageningen, 87 pp

Bouma J (1989a) Land qualities in space and time. In: Bouma J, Bregt A K (eds.) *Land Qualities in Space and Time. Proceedings of a Symposium organised by the International Society of Soil Science (ISSS)*, Wageningen, The Netherlands, 22–26 August 1988. PUDOC, Wageningen, pp. 3–14

Bouma J (1989b) Using soil survey data for quantitative land evaluation. *Advances in Soil Science*. Volume 9. Springer-Verlag, New York, pp. 177–213

Bouma J, Bregt A K (eds.) (1989) *Land Qualities in Space and Time. Proceedings of a Symposium organised by the International Society of Soil Science (ISSS)*, Wageningen, The Netherlands, 22–26 August 1988. PUDOC, Wageningen, 356 pp.

Bouma J, Lanen H A J van (1987) Transfer functions and threshold values: from soil characteristics to land qualities. In: Beek K J, Burrough P A, McCormack D E (eds.) *Quantified Land Evaluation Procedures*. ITC Publication No 6, Enschede, pp. 106–10

Bouma J, Laat P J M de, Awater R H C M, Heesen H C van, Holst A F van, Nes Th. J van de (1980) Use of soil survey data in a model for simulating regional soil moisture regimes. *Soil Science Society of America Journal* **44**: 808–14

Bouma J, Lanen H A J van, Breeuwsma A, Wösten H J M, Kooistra M J (1986) Soil survey data needs when studying modern land use problems. *Soil Use and Management* **2**: 125–29

Breeusma A, Reijerink J G A, Schoumans O F, Brus D J H van het Loo (1989) *Fosfaatbelasting van bodem, grond- en oppervlaktewater in het stroomgebied van de Schuitenbeek. Rapport 10*. Instituut voor Onderzoek van het Landelijk Gebied, Wageningen, The Netherlands, 95 pp.

Bregt A K (1989) Quality of representative profile descriptions for predicting the land quality moisture deficit at different scales. In: Bouma J, Bregt A K (eds.) *Land Qualities in Space and Time. Proceedings of a Symposium organised by the International Society of Soil Science (ISSS), Wageningen, The Netherlands, 22–26 August 1988*. PUDOC, Wageningen, pp. 169–72

Bregt A K, Beemster J G R (1989) Accuracy in predicting moisture deficits and changes in yield from soil maps. *Geoderma* **43**: 301–10

Burgess T M, Webster R (1980a) Optimal interpolation and isarithmic mapping of soil properties: 1. The semi-variogram and punctual kriging. *Journal of Soil Science* **31**: 315–31

Burgess T M, Webster R (1980b) Optimal interpolation and isarithmic mapping of soil properties: 2. Block kriging. *Journal of Soil Science* **31**: 333–41

Burgess T M, Webster R, McBratney A B (1981) Optimal interpolation and isarithmic mapping of soil properties: 4. Sampling strategy. *Journal of Soil Science* **32**: 643–59

Burrough P A (1980) The development of a landscape information system in the Netherlands, based on a turn-key graphics system. *GeoProcessing* **1** (3): 257–74

Burrough P A (1982) Computer assistance for soil survey and land evaluation. *Soil Survey and Land Evaluation* **2**: 25–36

Burrough P A (1983a) Multi-scale sources of spatial variation in soil. I. The application of Fractal concepts to nested levels of soil variation. *Journal of Soil Science* **34**: 577–97

Burrough P A (1983b) Multi-scale sources of spatial variation in soil II. A non-Brownian Fractal model and its application to soil survey. *Journal of Soil Science* **34**: 599–620

Burrough P A (1986) *Principles of Geographical Information Systems for Land Resources Assessment*. Clarendon Press, Oxford, 194 pp.

Burrough P A (1987) Natural resources databases: conceptual units, data structures and natural variation. In: Beek K J, Burrough P A, McCormack D (eds.) *Quantified Land Evaluation. Proceedings of a Joint Meeting of ISSS Working Groups on Land Evaluation and Soil Information Systems, Washington 25 April–2 May 1986*. ITC, Enschede, pp. 60–5

Burrough P A (1989a) Matching spatial databases and quantitative models in land resource assessment. *Soil Use and Management* **5**: 3–8

Burrough P A (1989b) Fractals and geochemistry. In: Avnir D (ed.) *The Fractal Approach to Heterogeneous Chemistry*. Wiley, Chichester, pp. 383–406

Burrough P A (1989c) Fuzzy mathematical methods for soil survey and land evaluation. *Journal of Soil Science* **40**: 477–92

Burrough P A (1990) Sampling designs for quantifying map unit composition. In: Mausbach M J, Wilding L (eds.) *Spatial Variability and Map Units for Soil Surveys*. International Soil Science Society Working Group of Soil and Moisture Variability in Time and Space/ American Society of Agronomy, the Crop Science Society of America and the Soil Science Society of America (in press)

Burrough P A, Beckett P H T (1971a) The relations between cost and utility in soil survey. I. The design of the experiment. *Journal of Soil Science* **22**: 359–68

Burrough P A, Beckett P H T (1971b) The relations between cost and utility in soil survey. III. The costs of soil survey. *Journal of Soil Science* **22**: 382–94

Burrough P A, Beckett P H T, Jarvis M (1971) The relations between cost and utility in soil survey. II. Conventional or free survey. *Journal of Soil Science* **22**: 369–81

Burrough P A, Bie S W (eds.) (1984) *Soil Information Systems Technology*. PUDOC, Wageningen, 178 pp.

Burrough P A, Veer A A de (1980) Cartographic processes. In: Machover C, Blauth R E (ed.) *The CAD/CAM Handbook*. Computervision Corporation, Massachusetts, pp. 97–120

Burrough P A, Veer A A de (1984) Automated production of landscape maps for physical planning in the Netherlands. *Landscape Planning* **11**: 205–26

Busoni E, Sanesi G, Torri D (1986) Soil moisture regimes and erodibility in the assessment of soil suitability for crops in Tuscany. *Soil Use and Management* **2**: 130–3

Dale M B, McBratney A B, Russell J S (1989) On the role of expert systems and numerical taxonomy in soil classification. *Journal of Soil Science* **40**: 223–34

Diepen C van, Wolf J, Keulen H van, Rappolt C (1989) WOFOST: a simulation model of crop production. *Soil Use and Management* **5**: 16–24

Driessen P M (1989) Quantified land evaluation: consistency in time and space. In: Bouma J, Bregt A K (eds.) *Land Qualities in Space and Time. Proceedings of a Symposium organised by the International Society of Soil Science (ISSS), Wageningen, The Netherlands, 22–26 August 1988*. PUDOC, Wageningen, pp. 3–14

Dumanski J B, Kloosterman B, Brandon S E (1975)

Concepts, objectives and structure of the Canadian Soil Information System. *Canadian Journal of Soil Science* **55**: 181–7

Dumanski J B, Onofrei C (1989) Crop yield models for agricultural land evaluation. *Soil Use and Management* **5**: 9–15

Englund E, Sparks A (1988) *GEO-EAS User's Guide*. Environmental Monitoring Systems Laboratory, Office of Research and Development, Environmental Protection Agency, Las Vegas, Nevada

FAO (1976) *A Framework for Land Evaluation*. FAO Soils Bulletin 32, Rome

Giltrap D J (1984) MIDGE – a microcomputer soil information system. In: Burrough P A, Bie S W (eds.) *Soil Information Systems Technology*. PUDOC, Wageningen, pp. 112–19

Girard M-C (ed.) (1981) *Proceedings of the International Society of Soil Science Working Group on Soil Information Systems Colloquium, 14–17 Sept. 1981, Paris*. Institut National Agronomique, Paris, Grignon (3 volumes). Departement des Sols Nos 4, 5, 6

Gruijter J J de (1977) *Numerical Classification of Soils and its Application in Survey*. PUDOC, Wageningen, 117 pp.

Helldén U (1987) An assessment of woody biomass, community forests, land use and soil erosion in Ethiopia. *Lund Studies in Geography, Ser C General, Mathematical and Regional Geography No. 14*. Lund University Press, Lund, 75 pp.

Herndon L, Schertz D L (1989) The Water Erosion Prediction Project (WEPP) – SCS Implementation. *Poster Paper in 1989 ASA-CSSA-SSSA Annual Meetings, Las Vegas, Nevada, 16 October 1989*

Heuvelink G B M, Burrough P A, Stein A (1989) Propagation of error in spatial modelling with GIS. *International Journal of Geographical Information Systems* **3**: 303–22

Hodgson J M (1978) *Soil Sampling and Description*. Oxford University Press, Oxford

Hopmans J W, Stricker J N M (1989) Applications of scaling techniques at a watershed scale. In: Bouma J, Bregt A K (eds.) *Land Qualities in Space and Time. Proceedings of a Symposium organised by the International Society of Soil Science (ISSS), Wageningen, The Netherlands, 22–26 August 1988*. PUDOC, Wageningen, pp. 181–4

Johnson C G (1975) The role of automated cartography in soil survey. In: Bie S W (Ed.) *Soil Information Systems. Proceedings of the meeting of the ISSS Working Group on Soil Information Systems, Wageningen, The Netherlands, 1–4 Sept 1975*. PUDOC, Wageningen, pp. 48–51

Journel A G, Huijbregts C J (1978) *Mining Geostatistics*. Academic Press, London

King D, Daroussin J, Bonneton P, Nicoullaud J (1986) An improved method for combining map data. *Soil Use and Management* **2**: 140–5

Kuilenburg J van, Bunschoten B, Burrough P A, Schelling J (1981) The digital soil map, scale 1 : 50 000 of The Netherlands. *Proceedings of the International Society of Soil Science Working Group on Soil Information Systems Colloquium, 14–17 Sept 1981, Paris*. Institut National Agronomique, Paris, Grignon Departement des Sols No. 4 pp. 73–86

Kuilenburg J van, Gruijter J J de, Marsman B A, Bouma J (1982) Accuracy of spatial interpolation between point data on soil moisture capacity, compared with estimates from mapping units. *Geoderma* **27**: 311–25

Lamp J (1983) Habilitation thesis. Christian-Albrecht University of Kiel, West Germany

Lanen H A J van, Bregt A K, Bulens J D, van Diepen C A, Hendriks C M A, de Koning G H J, Reinds G J (1989) *Crop Production potential of Rural Areas Within the European Community*. Dutch Scientific Council for Government Policy, The Hague

Leenaers H, Burrough P A, Okx J P (1989) Efficient mapping of heavy metal pollution on floodplains by co-kriging from elevation data. In: Raper J F (ed.) *Three dimensional applications in Geographic Information Systems*. Taylor & Francis, London, pp. 37–50

Leenaers H, Okx J P, Burrough P A (1989) Co-kriging: an accurate and inexpensive means of mapping floodplain soil pollution by using elevation data. In: Armstrong M (ed.) *Geostatistics. Proceedings of the third Geostatistics Congress, Avignon, October 1988*. Kluwer, pp. 371–82

Loveland T R, Ramey B (1986) Applications of US Geological Survey Digital Cartographic Products, 1979–1983. *US Geological Survey Bulletin 1583*, United States Government Printing Office, Washington

McBratney A B, Webster R (1981) The design of optimal sampling schemes for local estimation and mapping of regionalized variables: 2 Program and examples. *Computers & Geosciences* **7**: 335–65

McBratney A B, Webster R (1983a) How many observations are needed for regional estimation of soil properties? *Soil Science* **135**: 177–83

McBratney A B, Webster R (1983b) Optimal interpolation and isarithmic mapping of soil properties. V. Co-regionalisation and multiple sampling strategy. *Journal of Soil Science* **34**: 137–62

McBratney A B, Webster R, Burgess T M (1981) The design of optimal sampling schemes for local estimation and mapping of regionalised variables. 1. Theory and method. *Computers & Geosciences* **7**: 331–4

Mackenzie H G, Smith J L (1977) Data storage and retrieval. In: Moore A W and Bie S W (eds.) *Uses of Soil Information Systems. Proceedings of the Australian Meeting of the ISSS Working Group on Soil Information Systems, Canberra, Australia, 2–4 March 1976*. PUDOC, Wageningen, pp. 19–36

Maes J, Vereecken H, Darius P (1987) Knowledge processing in Land Evaluation. In: Beek K-J, Burrough P A, McCormack D E (eds.) *Quantified Land Evaluation Procedures. Proceedings of the Joint Meeting of the ISSS*

Working Groups on Land Evaluation and Soil Information Systems, Washington 25 April–2 May 1986; ITC Publication No. 6. ITC, Enschede, pp. 66–73

Mandelbrot B B (1982) *The Fractal Geometry of Nature.* Freeman, New York

Marsman B, Gruijter J J de (1984) Dutch soil survey goes into quality control. In: Burrough P A, Bie S W (eds.) *Soil Information Systems Technology.* PUDOC, Wageningen, pp. 127–34

Marsman B, Gruijter J J de (1986) Quality of soil maps. A comparison of survey methods in a sandy area. *Soil Survey Papers No. 15.* Netherlands Soil Survey Institute, Wageningen, 103 pp

Mateo A, Burrough P A, Comerma J (1987) Analysis espacial de propiedadas de suelo para estudios de modelacion de cultivos en Venezuela. *Proceedings First Latin American GIS Conference, Costa Rica.* Ed. Lyen M, October 1987, Universidad Estatal a Distancia, San José, Costa Rica. pp. 164–78

Matheron G (1971) *The Theory of Regionalised Variables and its Applications.* Les Cahiers du Centre de Morphologie Mathématique de Fontainebleau. Ecole Nationale Superieure des Mines de Paris

Mausbach M J, Reybold W U (1987) In support of GIS in the SCS: SIS. In: Beek K-J, Burrough P A, McCormack D E (eds.) *Quantified Land Evaluation Procedures. Proceeedings of the Joint Meeting of the ISSS Working Groups on Land Evaluation and Soil Information Systems, Washington 25 April–2 May 1986. ITC Publication No. 6.* ITC, Enschede, pp. 77–80

Mausbach M, Wilding L (eds.) (1990) *Spatial Variability and Map Units for Soil Surveys.* International Soil Science Society Working Group of Soil and Moisture Variability in Time and Space/American Society of Agronomy, the Crop Science Society of America and the Soil Science Society of America

Meijerink A M J, Valenzuela C R, Stewart A (1988) ILWIS: the Integrated Land and Watershed Management Information System. *ITC Publication No. 7.* International Institute for Aerospace Survey and Earth Sciences (ITC), Enschede, The Netherlands, 115 pp

Miller E E (1980) Similitude and scaling of soil-water phenomena. In: Hillel D (ed.) *Applications of Soil Physics.* Academic Press, New York

Moore A W, Bie S W (1977) Uses of soil information systems. *Proceedings of the Australian Meeting of the ISSS Working Group on Soil Information Systems, Canberra, Australia, 2–4 March 1976.* PUDOC, Wageningen, 103 pp

Moore A W, Cook B G, Lynch L G (1981) Information systems for soil and related data. *Proceedings of the Second Australian Meeting of the ISSS Working Group on Soil Information Systems, Canberra, Australia, 19–21 February 1980.* PUDOC, Wageningen, 1–10

Nielsen D R, Bouma J (1985) *Spatial Analysis of Soil Data.* PUDOC, Wageningen

Oliver M A, Webster R (1986) Combining nested and linear sampling for determining the scale and form of spatial variation of regionalised variables. *Geographical Analysis* **18**: 227–42

Olsson L (1989) Integrated resource monitoring by means of remote sensing, GIS and spatial modelling in arid environments. *Soil Use and Management* **5**: 30–7

Petach M, Wagenet R J (1989) Integrating and analyzing spatially variable soil properties for land evaluation. In: Bouma J, Bregt A K (eds.) *Land Qualities in Space and Time. Proceedings of a Symposium organised by the International Society of Soil Science (ISSS), Wageningen, The Netherlands, 22–26 August 1988.* PUDOC, Wageningen, pp. 145–54

Pleijsier L K (1986) The laboratory methods and data exchange programme. *Interim Report on the Exchange Round 85–2.* International Soil Reference and Information Centre, Wageningen

Pleijsier L K (1989) Variability in soil data. In: Bouma J, Bregt A K (eds.) *Land Qualities in Space and Time. Proceedings of a Symposium organised by the International Society of Soil Science (ISSS), Wageningen, The Netherlands, 22–26 August 1988.* PUDOC, Wageningen, pp. 3–14

Reeuwijk L P van (1982) *Laboratory methods and data quality. Program for soil characterisation: a report on the pilot round. Part I. CEC and texture. Proceedings of the 5th International Classification Workshop.* Khartoum, Sudan, 58 pp

Reeuwijk L P van (1984) *Laboratory methods and data quality. Program for soil characterisation: a report on the pilot round. Part II. Exchangeable bases, base saturation and pH.* International Soil Reference and Information Centre, Wageningen, 28 pp.

Riezebos H Th. (1989) Application of nested analysis of variance in mapping procedures for land evaluation. *Soil Use and Management* **5**: 25–9

Robert P (1989) Land evaluation at farm level using soil survey information systems. In: Bouma J, Bregt A K (eds.) *Land Qualities in Space and Time. Proceedings of a Symposium organised by the International Society of Soil Science (ISSS), Wageningen, The Netherlands, 22–26 August 1988.* PUDOC, Wageningen, pp. 289–98

Robert P, Anderson J (1987) Use of computerised soil survey reports in county extension offices. In: Beek K-J, Burrough P A, McCormack D E (eds.) *Quantified Land Evaluation Procedures. Proceedings of the Joint Meeting ISSS Working Groups on Land Evaluation and Soil Information Systems, Washington 25 April–2 May 1986. ITC Publication No. 6.* ITC, Enschede, 165 pp.

Roo A de, Hazelhoff L, Burrough P A (1989) Soil erosion modelling using ANSWERS and Geographical Information Systems. *Earth Surface Processes and Landforms* **14**: 517–32

Rossiter D (1989) ALES: a microcomputer program to assist in land evaluation. In: Bouma J, Bregt A K (eds.) *Land Qualities in Space and Time. Proceedings of a Symposium organised by the International Society of Soil Science (ISSS), Wageningen, The Netherlands, 22–26 August 1988.* PUDOC, Wageningen, pp. 113–16

Sadovski A, Bie S W (1978) Developments in soil information systems. *Proceedings of the Second Meeting of the ISSS Working Group on Soil Information Systems, Varna/Sofia, Bulgaria, 30 May–June 1977.* PUDOC, Wageningen, 113 pp

Soil Survey Staff (1976) *Soil Taxonomy.* US Government Printing Office, Washington DC

Stein A, Hoogerwerf M, Bouma J (1988) Use of soil map delineations to improve (co)kriging of point data on moisture deficits. *Geoderma* **43**: 163–77

Verhey W H (1986) Principles of land appraisal and land use planning within the European Community. *Soil Use and Management* **2**: 120–4

Walsh S J (1985) Geographic information systems for natural resource management. *Journal of Soil and Water Conservation* **40**: 202–5

Webster R (1968) Fundamental objections to the 7th Approximation. *Journal of Soil Science* **19**: 354–66

Webster R (1977) *Quantitative and Numerical Methods in Soil Classification and Survey.* Oxford University Press, Oxford

Webster R (1985) Quantitative spatial analysis of soil in the field. *Advances in Soil Science* **3**: 2–70

Webster R, Burgess T M (1984) Sampling and bulking strategies for estimating soil properties in small regions. Journal of Soil Science **5**: 127–40

Webster R, Burrough P A (1972a) Computer-based soil mapping of small areas from sample data: I. Multivariate classification and ordination. *Journal of Soil Science* **23**: 210–21

Webster R, Burrough P A (1972b) Computer-based soil mapping of small areas from sample data: II Classification smoothing. *Journal of Soil Science* **23**: 222–34

Webster R, Burrough P A (1974) Multiple discriminant analysis in soil survey. *Journal of Soil Science* **25**: 120–34

Webster R, Oliver M (1989) Optimal interpolation and isarithmic mapping of soil properties: VI. Disjunctive Kriging and mapping the conditional probability. *Journal of Soil Science* **40**: 497–512

Webster R, Oliver M (1990) *Statistical Methods in Soil and Land Resource Survey. Spatial Information Series.* Oxford University Press, Oxford

Wilding L P, Jones R B, Schafer G M (1965) Variation of soil morphological properties within Miami, Celina and Crosby mapping units in West-Central Ohio. *Proceedings of the Soil Science Society of America* **29**: 711–17

Wischmeier W H, Smith D D (1978) *Predicting Rainfall Erosion Losses. Agricultural Handbook 537.* USDA, Washington DC

Wösten J H M, Bannink M H, Bouma J (1989) Relation between the questions being asked and the sales and costs at which land evaluation is performed. In: Bouma J, Bregt A K (eds.) *Land Qualities in Space and Time. Proceedings of a Symposium organised by the International Society of Soil Science (ISSS), Wageningen, The Netherlands, 22–26 August 1988.* PUDOC, Wageningen, pp. 213–5

Yates S R, Yates M V (1988) Disjunctive kriging as an approach to management decision making. *Soil Science Society of America Journal* **62**: 1554–58

INTEGRATION OF GEOSCIENTIFIC DATA USING GIS

G F BONHAM-CARTER

A model based on Bayes Rule and an assumption of conditional independence is used to predict point patterns (mineral occurrences and seismic epicentres) from a combination of geological, geophysical and geochemical maps. In applying this model, a GIS is used to build a spatial database from diverse map inputs; to provide measurements necessary for determining the spatial association between a known set of points and each map layer; to create a multi-map overlay and associated unique conditions file; to make model calculations for each unique condition; to generate new maps showing posterior probabilities and associated uncertainties; and to visualize and interactively probe the results. Three applications of this methodology are described: the assessment of gold potential in eastern shore Nova Scotia, assessment of gold potential in northeastern New Brunswick and analysis of seismic epicentres in western Quebec. The mathematical model is summarized in an appendix.

INTRODUCTION

At a regional scale, a number of geological phenomena can be regarded as points on a map. Examples include the locations of mineral deposits or occurrences, oil pools and seismic epicentres. The spatial distributions of these point-like phenomena can often be partly explained and predicted from maps and images showing geological, geophysical and geochemical variables. For example, mineral occurrences are often spatially associated with geochemical anomalies, structures such as faults or contacts, geophysical features such as steep gradients on the magnetic map, and other variables. Usually there is not a direct correlation with any one mapped variable; more often, many variables will show a weak association individually but, combined, they can provide a useful tool for prediction.

Mineral occurrences and other geological point-like phenomena are difficult to predict for numerous reasons. Some important ones are:

- the observed sample of points may be poorly representative of the population, both because of undiscovered points and sampling bias;

- the mapped variables used for prediction may be inadequately sampled and/or fail to provide diagnostic signatures because they are unrelated to the points; and

- models used to integrate mapped variables may provide erroneous predictions.

Furthermore, quantitative studies for spatial data integration have often been hampered by the difficulty of digitally capturing, manipulating and overlaying map data.

Traditionally, geoscientists have used a manual approach for registering, enhancing, reclassifying and overlaying multiple maps on a light table. Since the 1970s, image processing systems have been quite widely employed for graphical overlay of remote sensing and geophysical images (Davis and Simonett 1991 in this volume; Townshend 1991 in this volume) and, in some cases, have used raster forms of geochemical and geological maps. Because they are raster based, image processing systems fail to provide efficient data structures for point, line and polygon data and for associated attributes; yet much of the map information of interest to the geoscientist is of these types. Conversely, CAD systems and vector GIS provide inadequate tools for handling raster images; yet remote sensing images and most geophysical data are available only in raster formats. Thus those GIS which support a variety of spatial data structures, including raster, vector and attribute data, are proving to be powerful and versatile tools for geological data integration. They are also being widely adopted for building and maintaining large spatial databases by numerous geological organizations, although this custodial aspect of GIS is not discussed here.

This chapter reviews some recent work carried out at the Geological Survey of Canada on the use of GIS for map integration. The work is based on a methodology for statistical prediction of point distributions on maps. The methodology is implemented on a PC-based GIS called SPANS (TYDAC 1989), which supports a variety of spatial data structures, including linear quadtrees. Three applications are illustrated, two on the mapping of mineral potential and the third on the analysis of the distribution of seismic epicentres.

DATA INTEGRATION MODELLING

The digital integration of geoscientific maps, particularly in the field of mineral resource estimation, has been practised for about 25 years. Much of this work has involved multivariate statistical analysis (e.g. Harris 1984; Agterberg 1988; Gaal 1988). In most cases, these studies have subdivided the region of interest using a coarse rectilinear sampling grid. Each cell in the grid provides an areal sample of each layer of a spatial database. Various methods have been successfully employed to develop multivariable signatures which identify those cells with an elevated mineral potential. Agterberg (1989b) has discussed some recent approaches, including the use of expert systems and Bayesian methods.

A major drawback to the use of a coarse sampling grid has been the difficulty of representing objects that are either smaller than the cell size, or have a shape that is lost in the gridded approximation. For example, proximity to linear features such as formation contacts or lineaments is difficult to characterize in a coarse raster yet may be of prime importance in modelling mineral deposits. Moreover, the presence of thin stratigraphic units, sometimes folded and faulted, is also difficult to represent in a coarse grid. Point observations, such as geochemical sample locations, are often logically associated with irregularly shaped polygons that are poorly captured with a rectilinear grid. For example, if a stream sediment sample is to be associated with its catchment area on a map, a coarse raster is a poor means of representing it. Fortunately, technological developments have improved the situation: with inexpensive mass storage devices and efficient data structures such as area quadtrees, large raster images are practical and provide adequate spatial resolution for most problems (Egenhofer and Herring 1991 in this volume). However, to use every pixel in a large multi-image database for statistical modelling becomes computationally expensive and highly redundant.

To circumvent this redundancy problem, 'unique conditions' mapping can provide a useful solution. Unique conditions is here used (in SPANS terminology) to describe a map produced by an overlay operation of two or more maps; the resulting new polygons are labelled according to a set of unique conditions classes. The classes are defined in the rows of a unique conditions table, whose columns are the attributes of the maps involved in the overlay. Each class is compositionally unique and many polygons may belong to the same class. Where the input maps have relatively few classes, the number of unique conditions is often relatively small. Unique conditions is a natural construct in vector GIS; in raster systems, the idea of building a unique conditions map and associated table may seem redundant, but it can significantly increase the efficiency of modelling. In some cases, where the input maps have a large number of classes (e.g. remote-sensing images), the number of unique conditions may approach the number of pixels in the image, with no resulting benefit. However, for cases with several compositionally-simple input maps (as is the case with 'weights of evidence' modelling which uses binary maps – see below) the computational benefits can be dramatic. For example, if the pixel resolution of the working universe is that of an image with 1000 rows by 1000 columns, model computations would need to be carried out 1 million times on the full raster; typically the number of unique conditions for weights of evidence is less than 1000 and model calculations need only be carried out once per condition, thereby reducing the computing time by three orders of magnitude. Furthermore, the same unique conditions map can be used repeatedly with different models. New attribute columns can be added to the unique conditions table, these simply being used to re-classify the same unique conditions map. A similar principle is involved in using 'look up' tables in image processing systems (Mather 1987).

Weights of Evidence Modelling

This overlay concept of GIS has been particularly useful for implementing 'weights of evidence' modelling, which uses Bayesian principles for combining multiple maps (Agterberg 1989a; Agterberg, Bonham-Carter and Wright 1990; Bonham-Carter, Agterberg and Wright 1988). The goal is to combine the input maps to produce an output map which predicts a point distribution, such as mineral occurrences. Each map in the overlay is associated with weights determined by the spatial association of the map with the known points. The mathematical model for weights of evidence is summarized in the appendix to this chapter.

The points, sometimes referred to in this chapter as occurrences, are not themselves classified or weighted and each point is treated as equally important. It is assumed that the points represent a sample of some population and that the sample is large enough to provide an estimate of the spatial association of the points with each input map. By combining input maps, an estimated point density map is produced which should be a reasonable approximation to the known points; it will also indicate areas where more points are expected than are known. Each point is associated with a small unit area, so that point density is expressed as the number of occurrences per unit area.

The maps to be used for predicting the points are normally binary, although this is not a necessary condition. In the binary case, each map can be treated as a map pattern. The first step in weights of evidence modelling is to calculate a pair of weights for each binary pattern, W^+ for pattern present, W^- for pattern not present (as distinct from unknown). The equations for the weights are given in the appendix to this chapter and depend on the ratio of the occurrences that fall on the pattern to the total occurrences versus the ratio of the binary pattern area to the total map area. Where these ratios are equal, W^+ and W^- are both zero and no spatial association between the map pattern and points exists. If more points occur on the map pattern than would be expected due to chance, W^+ is positive and W^- is negative. The contrast, C, is equal to the difference $W^+ - W^-$ and provides a useful measure of spatial association. The variances of the weights and contrast can also be estimated, providing a guide to the significance of a particular association (see the appendix to this chapter). A systematic analysis of map patterns with respect to a particular distribution of occurrences is valuable for revealing or confirming spatial associations.

In order to combine map patterns for predicting points, a prior probability is assumed, normally taken as a constant over the whole map. Each map layer is treated as a new piece of evidence and can either be added one at a time or altogether to yield a posterior probability map (Fig. 47.1). In the weights of evidence model, probabilities are expressed as logits, or log odds, which make the model linear and additive. Equation [47A.14] is evaluated for each sampling unit on the map. In a full raster-based system, the equation would be evaluated for each pixel, yielding the posterior logit, which is simply converted to a posterior probability of an occurrence per unit area. For a 1000×1000 pixel image, 1 million evaluations of the equation would be needed. On the other hand, using a unique conditions table, the number of evaluations is often reduced to a few hundred and hence leads to rapid map calculation. Even on a PC, a new posterior probability map can often be produced in less than 5 minutes. For unique conditions characterized by overlap of map patterns with positive weights, the posterior probability will be larger than the prior; conversely, unique conditions with few or no binary patterns present will have posterior probabilities lower than the prior.

The uncertainty of the posterior probability map can also be calculated. The uncertainty due to variances of the weights can easily be estimated, as shown in the appendix to this chapter. Bonham-

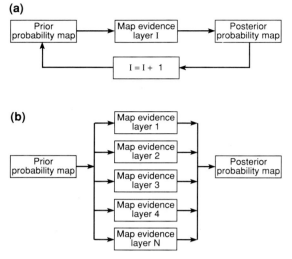

Fig. 47.1 Block diagram to illustrate (a) sequential or (b) simultaneous combination of evidence from multiple map layers.

Carter, Agterberg and Wright (1990) and Agterberg et al. (1990) also show how uncertainty due to missing information – such as a geochemical or geophysical survey covering only part of the total study area – can be modelled. These uncertainties can be mapped using the same unique conditions as for the probabilities. The uncertainty map and the probability map can be displayed separately or combined together. For example, those regions with a relatively large uncertainty can be masked out on the probability map.

An important assumption is made in using the model, namely that of conditional independence. Although this assumption is never completely adhered to, clear violations can be recognized using pair-wise tests. Maps can be correlated with one another but must be conditionally independent with respect to the points, as defined in the appendix to this chapter. For example, if exactly the same points were occurring on the black parts of two different binary map patterns, as would happen if a binary map was simply duplicated, the test for conditional independence would fail because the model would predict too many points in the black area. If the conditional independence assumption is rejected according to a pair-wise test, one of the maps can be omitted altogether or the two maps can be combined to form a new joint map. This assumption can also be tested by using an overall goodness-of-fit test, which compares the pdf (probability density function) of the posterior probability estimated for the actual points with that based on the posterior probability map. These tests are illustrated in Bonham-Carter and Agterberg (1990).

The key to a successful application of the weights of evidence method is to create useful predictive maps from the raw data input and to avoid gross abuses of the conditional independence assumption. In the next section, some aspects of building a spatial database and extracting critical and diagnostic map patterns with a GIS are discussed. The discussion is centred on data structures and operations used in the SPANS GIS. This system is particularly suited for modelling and is an excellent computing platform for developing applications like weights of evidence. However, it should be stressed that weights of evidence methodology is independent of the GIS and could be implemented on systems other than SPANS. The latter, however, offers a number of advantages since it makes extensive use of quadtrees. Such hierarchical data structures are efficient for many raster algorithms (Samet 1989; Egenhofer and Herring 1991 in this volume) and are often effective for data compression.

GENERATING BINARY PREDICTOR MAPS

Building a database with the SPANS GIS for the problems discussed here involves:

- establishing a project universe;
- digitizing or importing geological, geophysical, geochemical and other maps to a common quadtree base;
- extracting binary signature maps to be used for modelling.

Mineral occurrence point data are also imported as an ASCII file containing geographical coordinates and other attributes, and are left in point form. This point attribute file is used extensively for appending the classes of quadtree maps as new columns, these being obtained by sampling the maps at the coordinates of the points (as indicated in Action 9 on Fig. 47.2); they are used subsequently for calculating weights of evidence.

The geological map

A geological map is usually digitized or imported in digital format as vectors (Fig. 47.2, Input 5) but sometimes as a raster (Fig. 47.2, Input 1). Map units (e.g. geological formations) are converted to quadtree format (Fig. 47.2, Action 1 or 5). The map unit associated with each mineral occurrence is appended to the occurrence point file (Fig. 47.2, Action 9) and the area of each map unit is calculated with an area analysis operation.

Weights of evidence, W^+, W^- and C, are determined for each map unit (see Eqns [47A.15] and [47A.16] of the appendix). The variances of these quantities are also calculated using Eqns [47A.17] and [47A.18]. If the ratio $C/\sigma(C)$ is larger than about 2, it suggests that the process which generated the points is not independent of the process that generated the map unit; that is more (or fewer) points occur in that unit than would be expected due to chance. The weights are calculated for each map unit in turn. On the basis of these results, it may be useful to reclassify the map and group some units together if they are not predictively useful. The resulting map may be binary, or can be a multi-state categorical map.

The contact areas between geological units are often important zones for some types of mineralization. Such a relationship can be tested statistically. For example, suppose that a particular granite contact is to be tested. First the vector boundary of the granite is extracted (Fig. 47.2, Action 2) and a new quadtree map is generated by buffering the contact at successive distances (e.g. 0.25 km, 0.5 km, . . .). The distance between each point and the contact is then estimated by sampling the distance map at the point locations (Fig. 47.2, Action 9). The areas of the distance corridors are measured by area analysis and the weights and contrast values are calculated as before.

However, instead of treating each distance corridor as an independent map class, the number of points and corridor area are used cumulatively for each distance interval. The value of C can then be plotted against distance (see Fig. 47.3) to determine whether the contact zone has any spatial association with the points; if one exists, this will

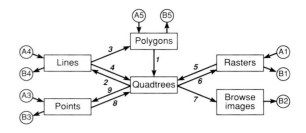

Number on arrow	Action
1	Build quadtree from vector polygons
2	Extract vector boundary from quadtree classes
3	Build topology
4	Build quadtree generating corridors round lines
5	Build quadtree from raster
6	Expand quadtree to raster
7	Build run length encoded browse image
8	Build quadtree from points using: a) buffer round points b) Voronoi polygons c) interpolation methods
9	Sample quadtrees at point locations, appending resulting map classes to point attribute file

Number in circle	A - input B - output
1	Raster interchange formats (e.g. image analysis systems)
2	Display monitor, hardcopy devices
3	ASCII files, shareable with other software
4	Vector interchange formats (e.g. CAD)
5	Vector interchange formats (e.g. vector GIS, with topology)

Fig. 47.2 Inputs, outputs and internal transformations between spatial data structures in the SPANS GIS.

help in deciding a suitable distance for thresholding the multi-state distance map to produce a binary map. If a simple maximum of C occurs, this decision is straightforward but, in less clear cases, some subjective judgement may be required. For a geological map with a large number of map units, it may be impractical to test each type of contact for spatial association with the points. In such circumstances, the opinion of an expert can be used to reduce the number of contacts using prior geological knowledge.

Other types of spatial data on the geological map may also be important. For example, proximity to faults, lineaments or fold axes may be significant guides to mineral deposits. Lines can be selected on the basis of orientation, age or other attributes before testing for spatial association with points.

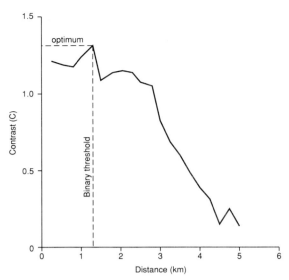

Fig. 47.3 Graph showing value of contrast, C, versus distance to anticlinal axes. C is a measure of the spatial association between gold occurrences and the anticlines shown in Plate 47.2.

Geophysical data

For mineral deposit studies, a knowledge of the regional patterns of gravity, magnetic susceptibility, gamma radioactivity, electromagnetic response and other variables may be direct or indirect guides for locating mineral deposits. Derived map quantities such as vertical or horizontal derivatives and upward or downward continuation maps are also valuable. Geophysical observations are made at points either on the ground or (more often) from the air at successive locations along flight lines, and (sometimes) below ground in boreholes. Digital geophysical data are usually obtainable in a gridded format, after various levelling and interpolation procedures. Gridded data can be imported as 8-bit or 16-bit raster images to the GIS (Fig. 47.2, Input 1).

Geophysical images can be tested for spatial association with point distributions as before, but the testing is not only for associations with positive and negative anomalies: it is also with particular contour intervals. Mid-range intervals will sometimes be characteristic of particular buried contacts. If significant spatial associations result, maps are reclassified to binary form following the same steps employed for the 'distance to contact' maps. In cases where too much information is lost by binary conversion, multi-state ordinal-scale maps are generated with a weight calculated for each class.

Geochemical data

Most geochemical surveys are available as digital ASCII files, with each record being described by geographical coordinates and chemical and other attributes. Sample density is often too sparse for reliable estimation of geochemical surfaces; point data are often converted to an image either by using 'representative polygons' or by interpolation. For stream and lake sediment data, catchment basins upstream from sample sites are a logical means of representing samples as polygons (Bonham-Carter, Rogers and Ellwood 1987; Wright, Bonham-Carter and Rogers 1988). For bedrock, till or biogeochemical sampling, simple buffer zones round points (Fig. 47.2, Action 8(a)) or Thiessen polygons can be effective. Alternatively, a host of interpolation methods can be used, either internal to the GIS (Fig. 47.2, Action 8(c)) or using external software followed by re-importation of the resulting data.

After generating a quadtree map for each geochemical element, the weights and contrast are calculated as for the 'distance to contact' map, except that C is evaluated as a function of element concentration rather than distance. If significant spatial associations occur between the areas with elevated geochemical values and the points, the map is reclassified to binary form. In cases where a large number of chemical elements have been analysed, elements can be grouped together. For example, Wright *et al.* (1988) combined elements associated with gold mineralization using a regression method before making a binary geochemical anomaly map. This also helps to reduce the likelihood of violating the conditional independence assumption made in the weights of evidence model.

EXAMPLES OF APPLICATIONS

Three applications are briefly described, mainly focusing on summary tables and images. The colour plates were made from photographs of a 19-inch

Table 47.1 Weights of evidence, contrast values and their standard deviations for the maps used in the Nova Scotia gold study (from Bonham-Carter et al. (1990)).

Map Layers	$W+$	$\sigma(W^+)$	W^-	$\sigma(W^-)$	C	$\sigma(C)$	$C/\sigma(C)$
Goldenville Fm	0.31	0.13	−1.47	0.45	1.78	0.47	3.81
Anticline axes	0.55	0.14	−0.77	0.24	1.32	0.28	4.75
Au biogeochem	0.90	0.21	−0.28	0.15	1.19	0.26	4.57
Lake sed. chem.	1.00	0.33	−0.10	0.13	1.11	0.35	3.15
Golden-Hal contact	0.37	0.17	−0.27	0.17	0.64	0.25	2.59
Granite contact	0.34	0.29	−0.06	0.14	0.40	0.32	1.23
NW lineaments	−0.02	0.25	0.01	0.14	−0.03	0.28	0.09
Halifax Fm.	−1.24	0.58	0.12	0.13	−1.46	0.56	2.47
Devonian granite	−1.74	0.71	0.15	0.13	−1.89	0.72	2.63

(48 cm) colour monitor. All work was carried out with SPANS on an 80386 PC using a Number Nine PRO-1280 graphics card, which has 1280 × 1000 pixel resolution and 8 bits for colour display.

Gold potential on the eastern shore of Nova Scotia

Gold occurs in quartz veins in the Meguma Terrane of Nova Scotia. Sixty-eight gold occurrences have been recorded in the study area (Plate 47.1), about half of which have been mined. Agterberg et al. (1990) and Bonham-Carter et al. (1988) calculated a gold potential map using weights of evidence applied to six predictor maps. Bonham-Carter and Agterberg (1990) calculated maps showing uncertainty of the potential. Later, a biogeochemical map of gold in balsam fir was added as an additional predictor by Bonham-Carter et al. (1990). Table 47.1 summarizes the maps used, their weights of evidence and associated variances.

Of the three principal lithologic units shown in Plate 47.1, the Goldenville Fm is the primary host for gold veins in this part of Nova Scotia, as reflected in the W^+ value of 0.31; the W^+ values for the Halifax Fm and Devonian granites are −1.24 and −1.74 respectively. Distance to the surface traces of Devonian anticlinal axes is a strong predictor, with a contrast of 1.32. The binary map for anticlines was constructed by the following process:

- digitizing the anticlines as lines on the geological map and importing these into the GIS;
- creation of a quadtree map on which the lines were dilated with twenty 0.25 km corridors (Plate 47.2);
- the appending of an attribute column to the gold occurrence attribute file showing distance of each point to the nearest anticline;
- calculation of the area and cumulative area of each corridor;
- computation of the weights and contrast values for each cumulative corridor;
- selection of a distance of 1.25 km for thresholding, where C reaches a maximum (Fig. 47.3) and;
- reclassifying the distance map as a binary map.

The map of gold in balsam fir (Plate 47.3) was created from the original sample points by interpolation using kriging (Burrough 1991 in this volume). A threshold of 12 parts per thousand million was used to separate anomaly from background, established by evaluating the contrast for successive levels (see Fig. 47.4). Note that some areas on the balsam fir map are left as 'unknown' because they are too far from a sample point, as determined by the kriging variance.

The lake sediment anomaly map was created using catchment basins as the zone of influence around sample points. Using a regression method, Wright et al. (1988) found the linear combination of 12 elements which best predicted basins with known mineralization. A regression score map was created and thresholded to binary form by optimizing the contrast, as before. Note that, in this map, the areas outside the catchment basins are unknown.

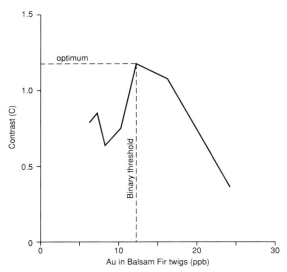

Fig. 47.4 Graph showing spatial association of gold in balsam fir with known gold occurrences.

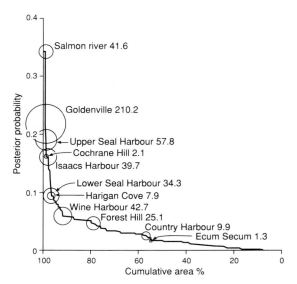

Fig. 47.5 Graph showing modelled gold potential versus area, with the predictions for known occurrences superimposed; from Bonham-Carter *et al.* (1990). The size of the circles is proportional to gold production and the values are specified in thousand ounces.

The three remaining maps (see Table 47.1) were each based on optimizing the contrast for distance to linear structures. The Goldenville–Halifax contact is weakly predictive; the granite contact has a positive value of C but the standard deviation is large and the association is of doubtful significance; and the NW-trending lineaments have a contrast not significantly different from zero.

The SPANS modelling language and unique conditions mapping were used to predict the posterior probability of a gold occurrence per square kilometre area, combining the weights of evidence from seven maps (see Plate 47.4). The uncertainties due to the weights and due to missing information (in the lake sediment and biogeochemical maps) are shown in Plates 47.5 and 47.6. Plate 47.7 displays a smaller sub-area of the gold (Au) probability potential map, with those areas masked out where the ratio of posterior probability to its standard deviation is less than 1.5. The 11 largest gold producers have predicted posterior probabilities in the 90th percentile by area (Fig. 47.5) except for Forest Hill (which is at the 78th percentile) and two smaller deposits at the 57th percentile. The prior probability is 0.02. Several areas have many of the same characteristics as the known gold areas yet no mineralization has been reported. These are prime areas for follow-up exploration with detailed surveys.

Gold potential in northeast New Brunswick

A 30 × 30 km area just west and north of Bathurst, New Brunswick has a number of small gold occurrences, many of them lying close to fault structures with an ENE orientation (Plate 47.8). In a preliminary study, Watson, Rencz and Bonham-Carter (1989) used weights of evidence to combine maps showing proximity to structures, stream and till geochemical surveys, airborne geophysical data and spectral anomalies from satellite imagery (see Table 47.2 and Plate 47.9). The spectral anomalies were determined using an image analysis system to classify pixels from a Landsat Thematic Mapper image which had spectral characteristics similar to the area round the Elmtree deposit, the most promising gold property in the study area. An image showing spectral anomalies was imported to the GIS and, because these anomalies comprised only scattered pixels, distance corridors were generated around them; 12 out of the 18 occurrences were found to lie within 1.5 km of these anomalies, yielding a strong value for the contrast, C.

Generally, areas of elevated potential on the posterior probability map (Plate 47.10) reflect

Table 47.2 Weights of evidence and contrasts for the maps used in the New Brunswick gold study (from Watson et al. (1989)).

Map	Threshold	Occurrences	W^+	W^-	C
As, Streams	34 ppm	7	1.68	−0.45	2.14
Au, Till	6 ppb	14	0.79	−1.27	2.06
As, Till	40 ppb	14	0.73	−1.23	1.96
K, Radiometric	1.25%	16	0.37	−1.24	1.61
Spectral Anomaly	1.5 km	12	0.82	−0.75	1.56
Lineaments (ENE–WSW)	0.7 km	13	0.88	−0.77	1.34
Sb, Till	3.2 ppm	11	0.65	−0.63	1.27
Lineaments (WNW–ESE)	0.5 km	13	0.63	−0.01	0.65
TOTAL		18			

As = arsenic
Au = gold
K = potassium
Sb = antimony
ppm = parts per million
ppb = parts per billion (thousand million)

known gold-bearing mineral occurrences or can be explained as contamination effects from past mining activity. The graph of potential versus area (Fig. 47.6) shows that the Elmtree occurrence has a higher predicted potential than have any other known occurrences and 10 out of the 18 are found in the 93rd probability percentile by area. Other areas of high potential (Plate 47.10), not linked to known mineralization or contamination, could be viable exploration targets, although they are as yet untested.

Seismic epicentres in western Quebec

Goodacre and colleagues have used weights of evidence to search for spatial associations between seismic epicentres and geological, drainage and geophysical maps and also to calculate a map of epicentre probability for an area in west Quebec (Plate 47.11). Earthquakes in this region are relatively weak, usually with Richter magnitudes less than four. The 147 epicentres used as points were recorded between 1982 and 1988, of which 96 were of magnitude two or greater. Epicentre locations are known imprecisely – usually to within 3 km – so that spatial associations are difficult to see visually. For calculation purposes, the study area was confined to a region lying within 15 km of the nearest epicentre.

The drainage network was digitized, together with a lineament interpretation (Plate 47.12) made

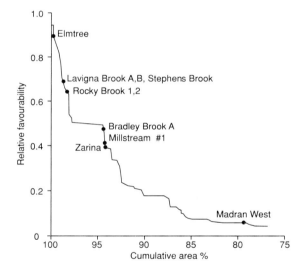

Fig. 47.6 Graph showing gold potential versus area from the New Brunswick study, with the major gold occurrences superimposed. From Watson et al. (1989).

by hand on the stream map. Stream lineaments were divided into ten azimuth classes of 18 degrees and each class was converted to a quadtree map, using 1 km buffer zones out to a distance of 15 km (e.g. Plate 47.13). At a fixed radius of 5 km, the contrast was compared for each stream orientation (Fig. 47.7). The comparison shows that streams in the azimuth interval 9–27 degrees are spatially associated with epicentres; streams in the azimuth interval 117–135 degrees also show a weak association. The NNE direction parallels the principal structural trends in the area, as shown by the geology and total magnetic field map.

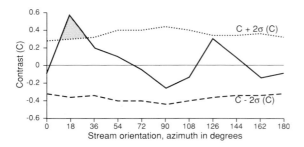

Fig. 47.7 Graph showing variation in spatial association of epicentres with streams in different orientations. The contrast was measured using a 5 km buffer zone round stream lineaments.

The magnetic map shows an interesting spatial association between epicentres and positive anomalies (Plate 47.14). Out of 20 map units on a 1 : 250 000-scale geological map, a Helikian paragneiss is the site of more epicentres than would be expected if the epicentres were independent of map unit, as is shown by the strong contrast value. A simple three-map binary model (Table 47.3) produced the predicted epicentre probability map shown in Plate 47.15. The complete unique conditions attribute file (Table 47.4) shows that the observed and predicted number of epicentres in the eight classes compare well, indicating conditional independence of the binary maps with respect to the epicentres. The prior probability is 0.006 07, so that classes 1 to 4 (Table 47.4) which occupy 6170 km^2 and contain 76 of the 147 epicentres have posterior probabilities larger than the prior; classes 5 to 8 occupy 15 996 km^2, contain 71 epicentres and have posterior probabilities lower than the prior. Thus, although the model identifies areas with differing degrees of epicentre risk which accord quite well with observations, it fails to put about half of the epicentres into probability classes with posterior greater than prior values. In order to model the distance to NNE streams and magnetic intensity values more closely, weights of evidence were estimated for multi-class ordinal scale maps to create a second model, the results of which are shown in Plate 47.16. In fact, the main features of the posterior probability map differ little from the binary model; this is confirmed by the summary plot of epicentres versus posterior probability (Fig. 47.8). Epicentre prediction is, therefore, only moderately successful. However, this is not altogether surprising since so few factors are considered, the stream lineament map was highly subjective and the locational imprecision of the epicentres was considerable.

CONCLUSIONS

The PC-based GIS used for this work improved productivity. It brought together on a single computing platform many of the tools needed for integrating geoscientific maps. Easy access to locally developed software and other software packages, using shared ASCII files as the medium of exchange, allows the user to carry out development work in a toolbox environment.

This chapter has shown the utility of GIS for a particular data integration model. Yet GIS would be equally useful for applying other types of modelling. For example, multivariate statistical modelling using standard packages can readily be carried out on point or polygon attribute files generated by the GIS, with new attributes such as regression scores re-imported for further analysis and display. In particular, the attributes associated with unique conditions classes created by map overlay provide a data file which can be exploited in a number of ways, such as in decision tree analysis (Walker and Moore 1988), in forward chaining expert systems using inference nets or in general exploratory spatial data analysis.

Like many data analysis methods, weights of evidence modelling is open to abuse. In particular, the conditional independence assumption should be tested and selection of the domain of interest is critical; for example, the weight calculations are sensitive to the extent of the map area and care should be used in defining the points to reduce the risk of mixing types that should be modelled separately. Despite these operational difficulties, readily implemented analytical techniques which exploit standard GIS capabilities demonstrably have much to offer the earth scientist.

Table 47.3 Weights of evidence, contrast values and their standard deviations for the three binary maps used in the epicentre study.

Map	W^+	$\sigma(W^+)$	W^-	$\sigma(W^-)$	C	$\sigma(C)$
Dist. to NNE streams (<7 km, ≥ 7 km)	0.26	0.10	−0.54	0.17	0.80	0.19
Total mag. field (≥ 156 nT, <156 nT)	0.23	0.12	−0.16	0.11	0.39	0.17
Helikian paragneiss (present, absent)	0.35	0.15	−0.12	0.10	0.47	0.18

Table 47.4 Unique conditions table for binary epicentre model, including the area, posterior probability, predicted and observed number of epicentres for each unique condition.

Class	Streams	Magnetics	Geology	P_{post}	A (km²)	Predicted epicentres	Observed epicentres
1	+	+	+	0.01399	714	9.99	13
2	+	−	+	0.00953	230	21.85	16
3	+	+	−	0.00881	4791	42.21	43
4	−	+	+	0.00631	435	2.75	4
5	+	−	−	0.00599	6280	37.62	39
6	−	−	+	0.00429	1555	6.67	10
7	−	+	−	0.00396	2928	11.60	7
8	−	−	−	0.00269	5233	14.08	15

+ indicates pattern present
− indicates pattern absent

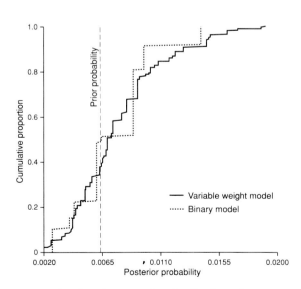

Fig. 47.8 Graph comparing distribution of posterior probability with map area for the binary and multi-state models. Note the value of prior probability.

REFERENCES

Agterberg F P (1988) Application of recent developments of regression analysis in regional mineral resource evaluation. In: Chung C F, Fabbri A, Sinding-Larsen G R (eds.) *Quantitative Analysis of Mineral and Energy Resources*. D. Reidel Publishing, Dordrecht, pp. 1–28

Agterberg F P (1989a) Systematic approach to dealing with uncertainty of geoscience information in mineral exploration. *Proceedings of the 21st APCOM Symposium*. Las Vegas, March 1989, Chapter 18, pp. 165–78

Agterberg F P (1989b) Computer programs for mineral exploration. *Science* **245**: 76–81

Agterberg F P, Bonham-Carter G F, Wright D F (1990) Statistical pattern integration for mineral exploration. In: Gaal G (ed.) *Computer Applications in Resource Exploration*. Pergamon Press, Oxford, pp. 1–22

Bishop M M, Fienberg S E, Holland P W (1975) *Discrete Multi-variate Analysis: theory and analysis*. MIT Press, Cambridge Massachusetts

Bonham-Carter G F, Agterberg F P (1990) Application of a micro-computer based geographic information system to mineral potential mapping. In: Hanley T, Merriam D F (eds.) *Microcomputers in Geology*, Volume 2. Pergamon Press, Oxford, pp. 49–74

Bonham-Carter G F, Agterberg F P, Wright D F (1988) Integration of geological data sets for gold exploration in

Nova Scotia. *Photogrammetric Engineering and Remote Sensing* **54** (11): 1585–92

Bonham-Carter G F, Agterberg F P, Wright D F (1990) Weights of evidence modelling: a new approach to mapping mineral potential. *Geological Survey of Canada Paper* **89–9**, pp. 171–83

Bonham-Carter G F, Rogers P J, Ellwood D J (1987) Catchment basin analysis applied to surficial geochemical data, Cobequid Highlands, Nova Scotia. *Journal of Geochemical Exploration* **29**: 259–78

Burrough P A (1991) Soil information systems. In: Maguire D J, Goodchild M F, Rhind D W (eds.) *Geographical Information Systems: principles and applications.* Longman, London, pp. 153–69, Vol 2

Cohen P R (1985) *Heuristic Reasoning About Uncertainty: an artificial intelligence approach.* Pitman, London

Davis F W, Simonett D S (1991) GIS and remote sensing. In: Maguire D J, Goodchild M F, Rhind D W (eds.) *Geographical Information Systems: principles and applications.* Longman, London, pp. 191–213, Vol 1

Egenhofer M J, Herring J R (1991) High-level spatial data structures for GIS. In: Maguire D J, Goodchild M F, Rhind D W (eds.) *Geographical Information Systems: principles and applications.* Longman, London, pp. 227–37, Vol 1

Gaal G (1988) Exploration target selection by integration of geodata using statistical and image processing techniques: an example from Central Finland. *Geological Survey of Finland, Report of Investigation* **80**: 156 pp.

Harris D P (1984) *Mineral Resource Appraisal.* Clarendon Press, Oxford

Mather P M (1987) *Computer Processing of Remotely-sensed Images.* Wiley, Chichester

Moon W M (1989) Application of evidential belief theory in geological, geophysical and remote sensing data integration. *Proceedings of IGARRS '89*, pp. 838–41

Samet H (1989) *The Design and Analysis of Spatial Data Structures.* Addison-Wesley, Reading Massachusetts

Spiegelhalter D J, Knill-Jones R P (1984) Statistical and knowledge-based approaches to clinical decision-support systems, with an application to gastro-enterology. *Journal of the Royal Statistical Society* **A 147** (1): 35–77

Townshend J R G (1991) Environmental databases and GIS. In: Maguire D J, Goodchild M F, Rhind D W (eds.) *Geographical Information Systems: principles and applications.* Longman, London, pp. 201–16, Vol 2

TYDAC (1989) *SPANS User Guide, Version 4.3.* Tydac Technologies Inc., 1600 Carling Ave., Ottawa, Ontario, Canada

Walker P A, Moore D M (1988) SIMPLE An inductive modelling and mapping tool for spatially-oriented data. *International Journal of Geographical Information Systems* **2**: 347–63

Watson G P, Rencz A N, Bonham-Carter G F (1989) Computers assist prospecting. *GEOS* **18** (1): 8–15

Wright D F, Bonham-Carter G F, Rogers P J (1988) Spatial data integration of lake-sediment geochemistry, geology and gold occurrences, Meguma Terrane, Nova Scotia. In: MacDonald D R, Mills K A (eds.) *Prospecting in Areas of Glaciated Terrain – 1988.* Canadian Institute of Mining and Metallurgy, pp. 501–15

APPENDIX

Weights of evidence model for binary maps

Weights of evidence have been used in medical decision making for diagnosing disease from evidence of symptoms (e.g. Spiegelhalter and Knill-Jones 1984). An alternative approach for combining evidence uses Dempster–Schafer theory (Cohen 1985); Moon (1989) has described an application of this to geoscientific map integration. The Dempster–Schafer method differs from the weights of evidence one in that the uncertainty of evidence is modelled as an 'evidential interval'. Weights of evidence formulated for maps was described by Agterberg (1989a) and this summary is drawn mainly from that paper, Cohen (1985) and Agterberg et al. (1990).

Suppose that a number of points (such as mineral occurrences or earthquake epicentres) are known on the map, and that each one is associated with a small unit cell of area u km^2. Let D be the number of unit cells containing a point, equal to the number of points if u is small enough. Let the area of the study region be t km^2, or $T = t/u$ unit cells in total.

In addition, assume that $j = 1, 2, \ldots, N$ binary maps are known, to be used as predictors for the points D. For the jth binary map, let the area of the binary pattern be b_j km^2, or $B_j = \frac{b_j}{u}$ unit cells. Then the area $\bar{B}_j = T - B_j$ is the number of unit cells of the jth map not occupied by the binary pattern.

If the prior probability that a unit cell contains a point is assumed to be $P(D) = D/T$ and constant over the study region, Bayes Rule can be used to calculate the posterior probability that a unit cell will contain a point, given the presence of the jth binary pattern:

$$P(D|B_j) = \frac{P(B_j|D) \, P(D)}{P(B_j|D) \, P(D) + P(B_j|\bar{D}) \, P(\bar{D})}, \quad [47A.1]$$

where $P(B_j|D)$ is the conditional probability of B_j given the presence of a point, and $\bar{D} = T - D$, the number of unit cells containing no point. Alternatively, the probability that a cell contains a point given the absence of pattern j is

$$P(D|\bar{B}_j) = \frac{P(\bar{B}_j|D) \, P(D)}{P(\bar{B}_j|D) \, P(D) + P(\bar{B}_j|\bar{D}) \, P(\bar{D})}. \quad [47A.2]$$

47A.1 and 47A.2 can be conveniently re-cast using a log odds formulation, where odds, O, are defined as $O = P/(1-P)$. Then

$$\ln O(D|B_j) = \ln O(D) + W_j^+ \quad [47A.3]$$

and

$$\ln O(D|\bar{B}_j) = \ln O(D) + W_j^-, \quad [47A.4]$$

$$W_j^+ = \ln \frac{P(B_j|D)}{P(B_j|\bar{D})} \quad [47A.5]$$

and

$$W_j^- = \ln \frac{P(\bar{B}_j|D)}{P(\bar{B}_j|\bar{D})} \quad [47A.6]$$

are the positive and negative weights of evidence associated with the presence and absence of the jth binary pattern. It is assumed that there are only two mutually exclusive hypotheses, either that a cell contains a point or it does not contain a point so that $P(D|B_j) = 1 - P(\bar{D}|B_j)$

If evidence is pooled from two binary maps, $j = 1$ and 2, Bayes Rule can be used to state that if both binary patterns are present, then the posterior probability that a unit cell contains an occurrence is

$$P(D|B_1 \cap B_2) = \frac{P(B_1 \cap B_2|D) \, P(D)}{P(B_1 \cap B_2|D) \, P(D) + P(B_1 \cap B_2|\bar{D}) \, P(\bar{D})} \quad [47A.7]$$

Further, if an assumption of conditional independence is made such that

$$P(B_1 \cap B_2|D) = P(B_1|D) \, P(B_2|D) \quad [47A.8]$$

then

$$P(D|B_1 \cap B_2)$$

$$= \frac{P(B_1|D) \, P(B_2|D) \, P(D)}{P(B_1|D) \, P(B_2|D) \, P(D) + P(B_1|\bar{D}) P(B_2|\bar{D}) P(\bar{D})} \quad [47A.9]$$

with comparable expressions for $P(D|B_1 \cap \bar{B}_2)$, $P(D|\bar{B}_1 \cap B_2)$ and $P(D|\bar{B}_1 \cap \bar{B}_2)$. Using the log odds formulation, these reduce to

$$\ln(O|B_1 \cap B_2) = \ln O(D) + W_1^+ + W_2^+ \quad [47A.10]$$

$$\ln(O|B_1 \cap \bar{B}_2) = \ln O(D) + W_1^+ + W_2^- \quad [47A.11]$$

$$\ln(O|\bar{B}_1 \cap B_2) = \ln O(D) + W_1^- + W_2^+ \quad [47A.12]$$

and

$$\ln(O|\bar{B}_1 \cap \bar{B}_2) = \ln O(D) + W_1^- + W_2^- \quad [47A.13]$$

where the weights are defined for each binary map as before.

For pooling more than two binary maps, a general expression can be written as

$$\ln O(D|B_1^{k(1)} B_2^{k(2)} \ldots B_N^{k(N)}) = \ln O(D) + \sum_{j=1}^{N} W_j^{k(j)} \quad [47A.14]$$

where $k(j)$ is $+$ for presence or $-$ for absence of the jth binary pattern.

The weights for the jth map are calculated from the overlap relationships measured between the binary map and the points:

$$W_j^+ = \ln \frac{(B_j \cap D/D)}{(B_j \cap \bar{D}/\bar{D})} \quad [47A.15]$$

and

$$W_j^- = \ln \frac{(\bar{B}_j \cap D/D)}{(\bar{B}_j \cap \bar{D}/\bar{D})} \qquad [47A.16]$$

The contrast for the jth map with respect to the points is given by $C_j = W_j^+ - W_j^-$.

Uncertainty Estimation

The values for the weights are estimates whose uncertainty varies with the magnitude of the four overlap regions used for calculating W^+ and W^-. If the number of unit cells containing an occurrence is large, an asymptotic result (Bishop, Fienberg and Holland 1975) can be used to calculate the variances of the weights:

$$\sigma^2(W_j^+) = \frac{1}{B_j \cap D} + \frac{1}{B_j \cap \bar{D}} \qquad [47A.17]$$

$$\sigma^2(W_j^-) = \frac{1}{\bar{B}_j \cap D} + \frac{1}{\bar{B}_j \cap \bar{D}} \qquad [47A.18]$$

If $P(D) = D/T$, then it can be shown that the variance of the prior log odds is $1/D$. The variance of the posterior probability where evidence arises from N maps is modelled as

$$\sigma^2(P_{\text{post}}) = \frac{1}{D} + \sum_{j=1}^{N} \sigma^2(W_j^{k(j)}) \, P^2_{\text{post}} \qquad [47A.19]$$

where $k(j)$ is $+$ or $-$ and refers to the presence or absence of the jth binary map as before.

If one or more of the binary maps being used as evidence is incomplete, Agterberg *et al.* (1990) have shown how an uncertainty component can be calculated in areas of missing data. They also discussed the pair-wise tests for conditional independence of the binary maps and an overall goodness-of-fit test of conditional independence.

48

MULTISOURCE, MULTINATIONAL ENVIRONMENTAL GIS: LESSONS LEARNT FROM CORINE

H M MOUNSEY

This chapter complements those by Clark, Hastings and Kineman and by Townshend in discussing the design and creation of environmental databases covering large areas. It differs, however, in describing the problems associated with databases created largely from existing data sets, many derived from map and on-ground sample sources. The problems of defining user needs in multinational projects and the consequent difficulties of system design – best approached by prototyping – are outlined. Throughout, the arguments are illustrated by examples drawn from the European Commission's CORINE programme: this multinational environmental monitoring and assessment tool was set up from 1985 onwards and was predicated entirely upon the availability of a comprehensive database and GIS for the 12 countries in the Community. Experience gained in this programme has fostered moves to harmonize the collection of much environmental data and hence minimize the variations in parameters encountered across national frontiers because of differences in the collection methodology. A key factor in the programme was the requirement to meet the changing needs of the bureaucracy in Brussels: the paramount need for system designers, environmentalists and bureaucrats to understand each other is stressed. The project's success has led to agreement to set up a European Environment Agency.

INTRODUCTION

Rising concern over the degradation of the environment has resulted in an increase in research on the identification and study of environmental problems. Unfortunately, much of this work has been speculative and theoretical and, at least until recently, not supported to any great extent by adequate databases. This situation is changing: in parallel to a rapid rise in the volumes and quantity of data collected, massive changes in technical capability have facilitated the development of GIS to handle the diversity of information involved. Moreover, since environmental planning and management is inherently cross-disciplinary, the use of GIS technology to build environmental databases from disparate sources of information to study problems of some commonality is highly appropriate.

The forerunner of much work in the development of national environmental databases was the now well-known Canada Land Inventory (Canada Department of Forestry and Rural Development 1965; Tomlinson, Calkins and Marble 1976), since followed by the developmental work of the US Environmental Protection Agency (EPA 1987) and the proposed development of an Australian federal resources database (Mott 1990). Environmental problems, however, are not only a matter for national concern; they also have profound social and economic consequences at a continental and global scale. Examples of this include the widespread effects of environmental disasters like the Chernobyl explosion, famine throughout the African sub-continent and the late-1980s drought in the American Midwest. Further, although their effects are not as well understood, processes operating at a global scale (e.g. those leading to the greenhouse effect and the ozone hole) are now also recognized as having significant local impacts; the development of environmental databases which allow further study of such complex real- and whole-world problems is now both possible and necessary.

Environmental databases are being developed by a number of organizations to address a wide range of issues (Clark, Hastings and Kineman 1991 in this volume; Townshend 1991 in this volume); there is much diversity in scale and spatial coverage, in technological implementation, in the range of data holdings and in the organizational background supporting the development and use of the databases. However, some features common to all operational environmental databases covering large areas can be identified:

- They typically draw on a wide range of spatial data sources (i.e. data with some type of locational reference).

- They provide software for data retrieval, modelling and output by a wide range of users of varying abilities.

- They normally operate centrally within a corporate organization – generally as a spin-off from other activities (indeed, it is often doubtful whether it would be economic to develop such a database solely for environmental monitoring purposes).

What then are the major issues behind, and the challenges facing, the development of environmental databases? One way to examine these is within the context of an existing continental-scale environmental database, the CORINE (CO-ordinated INformation on the European environment) Programme. The development of this programme has been supported by the European Community (the EC) since 1984 and, in nearing the conclusion of its development phase, it provides a good example of the development of a database from initial idea to working prototype (CEC 1990). Many of the issues which had to be resolved over the early period of the Programme are now well understood and even pedestrian; moreover, developments in hardware have transformed some problems from daunting to trivial. None the less, the early stages of CORINE remain a good example of GIS implementation because of four factors: the continuing need for pragmatism in building databases near the limits of contemporary technology; the commonplace need to sew together data from many sources; the essential requirement to provide a database useful to the bureaucracy; and – at the same time – the desirability of ensuring that the host of pragmatic decisions did not render the results of analyses meaningless in scientific terms. Finally, by way of introduction, this chapter differs from those by Clark *et al.* (1991 in this volume) and Townshend (1991 in this volume) because they concentrate on the use of global or continental environmental databases assembled largely from remote sensing imagery; relatively little of CORINE data has been obtained from such sources to date. Despite this, the reader is urged to read all three chapters to obtain a comprehensive picture of environmental GIS applications.

DEVELOPMENT OF THE DATABASE

The establishment of a database to meet the requirements of a user community normally follows a well-defined series of steps irrespective of the subject matter of the database (Tschritzis and Lochovsky 1982; Benyon 1990). Simplified, these include:

- identification and documentation of the user requirements;

- definition of the data requirements which will address the user requirements;

- establishment of an information technology (IT) solution which offers facilities for data handling to meet the user requirements;

- an assessment of the costs and benefits of such a solution; and

- if the above are favourable, installation and implementation of the selected solution.

In building databases to meet business requirements in the government, commercial and utilities sectors, such steps are usually reasonably easy to define and follow. However, in the establishment of environmental databases (and in this the CORINE Programme is no exception), the path is not as clear for a number of reasons. For example, it is often difficult to delimit the range and number of user requirements and to rank them in order of importance. The CORINE Programme in particular is broad in scope and its outer boundaries hard to define; ultimately, the database will serve a much wider range of applications than those defined at the outset. While these original foci may serve as a starting point from which to define data requirements, it seems likely that – as in the case of many environmental databases – it is the availability of existing data which (initially at least) dictates the range of applications rather than *vice versa*; the first two stages above are thus effectively reversed. Nevertheless, it is convenient to discuss each stage in turn and this is done below.

Definition of user requirements

The origins of the CORINE Programme lie in studies during the late 1970s towards the establishment of an environmental database for the European Community (Rhind *et al.* 1986). The Programme itself was formally established by the Directorate General of the Environment (DG XI) in June 1985 and was aimed at 'gathering, coordinating and ensuring the consistency of information on the state of the environment and natural resources' as an aid to Community environmental policy (Official Journal of the European Community 1985). Such aims are rather broad in scope; thus two more specific tasks were targeted for study. The first of these was seen as the improvement of data availability and compatibility both within the European Community itself and in the member states, to be achieved through the development of appropriate techniques for the collection, storage, manipulation and output of environmental data. Secondly, in order to focus data collection policies and to avoid the random assimilation of data, three specific topics of environmental importance were identified as initial targets for study. These include:

- biotopes (through the setting up of an inventory of sites of scientific importance for nature conservation);
- acid deposition (through provision of information on emissions and on risks of damage to flora and fauna, etc.);
- protection of the environment in the Mediterranean region (through the supply of information on land cover, quality and use, on water resources and on coastal problems).

Several of working groups of national experts were established to address these and related topics; these groups included those on air pollution, on coastal erosion, on water resources, on land use in the Mediterranean region and on biotopes. Each group defined the nature of the problems to be solved and the data requirements to address them, organized the acquisition of data from pre-existing sources and fed the data sets to a centralized database for analysis and output to other users. The user community for these data was seen in the first instance as being limited to DG XI but with subsequent expansion to other DGs within the European Commission, to international organizations such as the UN Environment Programme and the UN's Food and Agriculture Organization, and eventually to *bona fide* users within the member states such as government institutes and individual researchers.

Definition of data requirements

The range of data to be included in an environmental database depends naturally on the objectives of the system. In the case of the CORINE database, the three specific topics of environmental importance listed in the original communiqué (see above) should have defined, at least in part, the range of data for inclusion. However, these were broad in scope and left much room for interpretation. Thus, in practice, data collection has been governed by pragmatic considerations: the constraints of resources and time, of data availability and consistency, and of data volumes. These practical limitations should not be underestimated, especially when designing an environmental database to meet the many and diverse requirements of the European Community; its land area is 2.25 million square kilometres and attempts to cover this in fine detail would have generated quantities of data which were unmanageable – at least when the programme began. In the development system at least, such detailed data would have been both unwieldy to use and costly to administer. Furthermore, time and resource availability precluded the primary collection of data by ground survey to any great extent. Thus, at the outset of the Programme, four basic principles were defined for data collection (Wiggins et al. 1987):

- that raw data (as opposed to aggregated or interpreted data) should be included as far as possible, allowing for maximum use by researchers wishing to carry out their own classifications and aggregations to meet their specific needs;

- that existing data should be used wherever possible;

- that data input from maps should be restricted to small scales (1 : 250 000 or less) in order to reduce data volumes to manageable levels, at least during the early stages of the Programme, and to minimize international compatibility issues and to keep the data conversion costs within acceptable bounds;

- that only data already in machine-readable format should be used as far as possible, to minimize the need for encoding and digitizing.

Clearly these constraints reduced the amount of data available and are not wholly attainable; in order to obtain any data whatsoever on some topics, some encoding and digitizing had to be undertaken and undesirably aggregated data had to be included in the database. It is also unrealistic to study other environmental issues (for instance, coastal erosion) at such low resolution; hence, in practice, data collection at map scales as large as 1 : 25 000 has been undertaken – in rare circumstances and with consequential difficulties, as discussed below.

It is inappropriate to consider the holdings of the CORINE database in detail, not least because they are constantly under review. However, Table 48.1 provides an overall view of the holdings and Whimbrel (1989) and CEC (1990) document the holdings in greater detail. A fundamental requirement of any environmental database is a sound topographic framework, to which all other data can be related; in effect, it acts as a spatial template or control mechanism ensuring spatial consistency. Ideally, this should include, as a minimum, the coastal outline for display purposes. For environmental modelling, however, there is normally an additional requirement for information pertaining to the hydrological network, to ground altitude and to slope. Unfortunately, the CORINE Programme encountered significant difficulties in obtaining such data for the European Community. These did not arise from a simple lack of information; indeed, some digital topographic data exist for most of the member states of the Community at national level. But the characteristics of the data sources from which these were derived (the map scales and projections), the data contents (which features have been included, the contour intervals used, etc.) and the degree of topological structuring all differ so markedly that integration into a common, small-scale database, at least in the short term, would have been an impossible task. Furthermore, there is no common official map series across the European Community at a scale greater than 1 : 1 million (and, for areas of Greece, no topographical maps are available at all for reasons of military confidentiality); thus the digitizing of a topographic base would have been a considerable, if not an impossible, undertaking.

The solution adopted is, in many ways, less than ideal but at least it has provided a topographic base for the CORINE Programme. A 1 : 1 million scale digital database for the European Community, but excluding Greece and originally digitized from the ONC (Operational Navigation Charts) series, was obtained from the German national mapping agency, the Institut fur Angewandte Geodasie (IfAG). Received in 'spaghetti' form, this was topologically structured at Birkbeck College, University of London and had several hundred digitizing errors removed; with the addition of data for Greece (digitized in-house from the ONC series), this forms the initial CORINE topographical framework. Primarily designed for use in air navigation, the topographic base of the ONC series is not of the highest quality (see Rhind and Clarke 1988 for some examples of its internal inconsistencies) but nevertheless it formed the best single, consistent data set available. A number of additional layers of thematic data have been added to this base; these include a digital representation of the European Community's soils map of Europe compiled at 1 : 1 million scale, climatic data compiled from national meteorological organizations and information on biotopes, coastal erosion, land cover and water resources, compiled from local sources by groups of national experts.

The IT solution

The wide variety of tasks to be addressed within the CORINE Programme and the potentially enormous volumes of data suggested at the outset the need for a powerful GIS. The requirements for other software and for hardware were less well defined although some were identifiable in outline; these included the requirement to:

- be easy to use and maintain;

- be a relatively low-cost solution;

- be flexible enough to handle large volumes of data from many sources, at a wide range of scales and in many projections; and

- offer full GIS functionality to perform the many routine tasks required of an environmental database.

The selection of any IT system, including a GIS, would usually be subject to full testing and bench-marking procedures in order to establish the optimum from various possible alternatives. However, in order to launch the experimental programme in a short time period and to permit evaluation of different options, it was thought appropriate to use an existing system and expertise. Thus a pilot system was established, based on ARC/INFO at Birkbeck College in the University of London, UK; although not necessarily intended as a long-term solution, this prototyping has indeed provided invaluable pointers towards the long-term requirements as well as supporting the short-term needs. The same software was later implemented in DG XI in Brussels.

Functional requirements of a GIS

Data input

Data were generally input to the CORINE database from two sources: third-party data already in digital format or through digitizing maps by EC staff or a sub-contractor. In either case, data capture – and subsequent validation and editing – is time consuming but generally provides little technical challenge. On the other hand, data input frequently includes the process of data conversion, notably projection conversion and generalization. These are necessary because source maps often vary in their scale and projection, while data from existing databases are often provided in a wide range of geographical forms; unless data are converted onto a consistent spatial base, accurate data integration is not possible (Flowerdew 1991 in this volume). As well as algebraically-based projection facilities, provision for the 'rubber sheeting' of input data has proved essential; in a number of cases, the projection of the input map or data was unclear, unknown or even specified incorrectly; in such circumstances, local transformations were applied to give a 'best fit' to other data sets using large numbers of control points as a spatial template. It follows that detailed documentation of the procedures applied to each data set was essential.

Some databases are considered by the end user to be 'scale free' (in that they can be output at any scale within the constraints of the user's hardware). In practice, however, the storage of 'scale free' databases is still at a research stage (Muller 1991 in this volume). Thus within the CORINE Programme, data are stored in one of two forms appropriate to the scales most usually required by the end user, one at a notional scale of 1 : 1 million and another at 1 : 3 million. Moreover, in order to avoid massive storage volumes and long processing times, generalization procedures form an important feature of the exploitation of GIS software both in pre-archiving processing and at run-time.

Data analysis

It is self-evident that, if the data stored within an environmental database are to be of any use, the software must offer a capability to analyse them according to the user's requirements; the degree of matching between the analytical requirements of the user and the facilities offered by the system is often the most important criterion in the selection

Table 48.1 Overview and contents of the CORINE GIS.

Theme	Nature of information	Characteristics of digital data	Mbyte	Resolution/scale
Biotopes	Location and description of biotopes of major importance for nature conservation in the Community	5600 biotopes described on about 20 characteristics. Boundaries of 440 biotopes in Belgium and Portugal	20.0 2.0	Location of the centre of the site
Designated areas	Location and description of areas classified under various types of protection	13 000 areas with 11 attributes. Computerised boundaries of areas designated in compliance with article 4 of EEC/409/79 directive on the conservation of wild birds	6.5	Location of the centre of the site 1/100 000
Emissions into the air	Tons of pollutants (SO2, NOx, VOC emitted in 1985 per source category: power stations, industry, transport, nature, oil refineries, combustion	1 value per pollutant, per category of source and per region, plus data for 1400 point sources i.e. +/−200 000 values in total	2.5	Regional (NUTS III) and location of large emission sources
Water resources	Location of gauging station. Drainage basin area, mean and minimum discharge 1970–85 for southern part of EC	Data recorded for 1061 gauging stations for 12 variables	3.2	Location of gauging stations
Coastal erosion	Morpho-sedimentological characteristics (4 categories), presence of constructions, coastal evolution characteristics, erosion, accretion, stability	17 500 coastal segments described	25.0	Base file 1/100 000 generalized version 1/1 million
Soil erosion risk	Assessment of potential and actual soil erosion risk by combining 4 sets of factors: soil, climate, slopes, vegetation	180 000 homogeneous areas (southern part of Community)	4000.0	1/1 million
Important land resources	Assessment of land quality by combining 4 sets of factors: soil, climate, slopes, land improvements	170 000 homogeneous (southern part of Community)	300.0	1/1 million
Natural potential vegetation	Mapping of 140 classes of potential vegetation	2288 homogeneous areas	2.0	1/3 million
Land cover	Inventory of biophysical land cover in 44 classes	Vectorized database for Portugal, Luxembourg	51.0	1/100 000
Water pattern	Navigability, categories (river, canals, lake, reservoirs)	49 141 digitized river segments	13.8 0.3	1/1 million 1/3 million
Bathing water quality	Annual values for up to 18 parameters, 113 stations for 1976–86, supplied in compliance with EEC/76/160 directive	2650 values	0.2	Location of station
Soil types	320 soil classes mapped	15 498 homogeneous areas	9.8	1/1 million

Table 48.1 *Continued*

Theme	Nature of information	Characteristics of digital data	Mbyte	Resolution/scale
Climate	Precipitation and temperature (+incomplete data for other variables)	Mean monthly values for 4773 stations	7.4	Location of station
Slopes	Mean slopes per square km (southern regions of Community)	1 value per km^2 i.e. 800 000 values	150.0	1/100 000
Administrative units	EC NUTS (Nomenclature of Territorial Units for Statistics); 4 hierarchial levels	470 NUTS digitized	0.7	1/3 million
Coasts and countries	Coastline and national boundaries (Community and adjacent territories)	62 734 km	0.3 3.2	1/3 million 1/1 million
Coasts and countries	Coastline and boundaries (planet)	196 countries	1.5	1/25 million
ERDF regions	Eligibility for the Structural Funds	309 regions classified	0.01	Eligible regions
Settlements	Name, location, population of urban centres >20 000 people	1542 centres	0.1	Location of centre
Socio-economic data	Statistical series extracted from the SOEG-REGIO database	Population, transport, agriculture, etc	40.0	Statistical Units NUTS III
Air traffic	Name, location of airports, type and volume of traffic (1985–87)	254 airports	0.1	Location of airport
Nuclear power stations	Capacity, type of reactor, energy production	97 stations, up-date 1985	0.03	Location of station

(Source: CEC 1990).

of a GIS (Clarke 1991 in this volume). Only its use ultimately justifies the development of the system! Although the requirements of the end-user of the CORINE Programme were initially ill-defined, it is nevertheless possible to identify some basic requirements of such a GIS. These include facilities for feature selection and display, and for statistical analysis and modelling of single and multiple data sets (see Maguire and Dangermond, 1991 in this volume for further discussion of the functionality of GIS).

Feature selection and display includes selection both by geographical area and by thematic attribute. Where appropriate, this may also include generalization for mapping at smaller scales, including the generalization of attributes (e.g. the merging of classes or of individual features with specific attributes for clarity) according to pre-determined rules. The overlay of separate data sets to produce a single data set with a combination of attributes is often important in environmental modelling, as is the construction of 'buffer zones' or 'corridors' of user-selected width around features of a defined type within data sets.

Data output

The results of any analysis must also be available in a form selected by the user. Typically, these might include tables and tabular reports but also a wide variety of graphics, produced either on a terminal or as hard copy. The production of a well-designed and balanced map is a much neglected area of GIS, given the importance of these in the communication of the results of an analysis to the end-user and the problems arising from a lack of cartographic skills among many GIS users (Blatchford and Rhind 1989). The situation is a delicate one; on the one hand, a poorly designed map may fail to convey the results to the user and may also inadequately represent the effort involved in the establishment of the database and carrying out of the analysis. On the other hand, it is often easy to convince end-users on the basis of inadequate evidence – a highly effective map may well be used to mask inadequacies in the original data from the decision maker. Facilities must of course be available within the GIS to enable the production of well-designed maps, but the responsibility ultimately rests with both the producer and the user to ensure proper interpretation; there is, then, a moral and professional element to the use of GIS.

Costs versus benefits

The balance of costs and benefits is an extremely difficult one to establish for geographical databases of all kinds (Didier 1990; Calkins 1991 in this volume; Clarke 1991 in this volume). It is especially so for environmental databases (and was never undertaken formally for the CORINE Programme). The costs of the IT hardware and software will be the easiest to establish and data costs will be governed by data availability and hence are (usually) quantifiable. However, a major component in the costs of any programme are those of staff, the requirements for which are governed, at least in part, by the volume of use of the database and by the skills of the end-user. In addition, training and documentation needs often form a significant proportion of the total costs.

Benefits are even harder to quantify; the usual ones of improvements in service and productivity or exploitation of new business opportunities may be inappropriate measures in the creation of multinational databases. In such circumstances, the usual criteria are replaced by more intangible concepts such as 'better management of information and assessment of risk'. The implementation of a commercial strategy (and, therefore, the acceptance of the burden of cost) by one organization for the benefit of a wider user community requires that well defined cost recovery procedures are agreed beforehand. If not (as in the case of the CORINE Programme), the establishment of an environmental database is likely to be an act of faith investment legitimated for the greater good of the world's population, with largely intangible (or at least unquantifiable) benefits.

IMPLEMENTATION — THE REALITIES

Detailed planning of the construction of an environmental database is an idea which is excellent in theory (and in hindsight), but in reality is unrealistic; it is difficult to gauge the full measure of the user requirements and thus the data requirements that underpin these. In such circumstances, investment appraisal becomes a matter of academic speculation. The CORINE Programme has grown thus far through the enthusiasm of a small group of people and through the availability of appropriate technology, rather than through a well-thought-out development plan to meet the end-user requirements; it has also benefited from external shifts in policy and in public opinion. It is not unique in this approach.

The lack of a development plan aside, it is still possible to draw a number of lessons from the implementation of the Programme thus far; principally that the constraints on the development of environmental databases are not at present technology based, but relate to the availability of data and to aspects of access and use of the database. Areas of technical development on the research agenda for environmental databases include:

- the development of scale-free databases such that environmental issues should be addressed at local, regional, national, continental and global scale;

- the efficient and well-integrated handling of raster and vector information to ensure best use of all sources of environmental data;

- the recognition and handling of error conditions in analysis and modelling, especially in the light of the 'fuzzy' nature of much environmental data; and

- the development of icon-based interfaces to GIS

to enable the wider use by an increasingly non-specialist audience.

Data limitations

Although few system limitations have been encountered in the development of the CORINE database, the same cannot be said of the data. In a 'perfect' database, all layers of data would be spatially and temporally complete and consistent in terms of units of measurement, definitional, spatial and temporal characteristics (Briggs and Mounsey 1989). Even though the CORINE Programme is still under development, it is possible to highlight a number of problems which are representative of environmental databases in general. These include data availability and access, data quality, data maintenance and update, data volumes and data documentation.

Data availability and access

There are still many deficiencies in the CORINE database, both regional (e.g. the lack of adequate topographical data for Greece) or thematic (e.g. only limited data are available on atmospheric emissions for the whole Community). In addition (and not surprisingly in a database designed only to cover part of a continent), there are substantial edge-effects where data end at national borders. As an example of the latter problem, the lack of data for areas outside, but adjacent to, the EC prevented much work on either the Chernobyl explosion or on the consequences of a Swiss toxic spill into the Rhine. Both these and internal gaps in the data are a serious constraint which may take much time and resources before they can be overcome; experience in CORINE suggests that the '80 : 20 rule' may well apply (i.e. the last 20 per cent of the data required costs 80 per cent of the total effort). Even if the effort is discounted, the extension of a data set to cover adjoining countries represents a major policy decision and may have political ramifications.

Notwithstanding such deficiencies, the progressive 'bottom-up' development of an environmental database has the advantage that it may be a sensitive indicator of which data are already available and what else is required; if the data sets are available, but are not to be integrated in the database, it is still advantageous simply to know of their existence. Thus one valuable product of the CORINE Programme is an ongoing inventory of environmental data sources (CEC 1990), which is of use in its own right. An extreme example of such data 'signposting' or cataloguing (Department of the Environment 1987) is the Australian National Resources Information Centre, which is presently under development: it aims to hold no data at all, merely acting as a source of information on data holdings at state and federal level (Mott 1990).

Acquisition of data sets that are available in digital form is not always straightforward. In common with many other environmental databases, the CORINE Programme has never had a large budget with which to purchase data. Consequently, some available data sets were simply too expensive to be funded by viring from other funds. A related problem is that of transfer formats; the CORINE database draws upon data from a wide range of sources and thus international developments in data transfer formats are of particular concern to it. However, notwithstanding the existence of a number of national standards, it is difficult to force 'data donors', who may be contributing data on a very low or no-cost basis, to reformat data from their own method of organization to that requested by the builders of another database. Thus, notwithstanding the evolution of various standards (see, for instance, Guptill 1991 in this volume), at least in the foreseeable future staff involved in building any multi-contributor database will need to be adept at writing short 'one off' programs to reformat data from the many and varied formats in which they are received.

Data quality

By far the greatest problem in the development of any environmental database is that of data quality – are the data an accurate representation of the real world? Because the CORINE Programme, in common with many other environmental databases, draws on a wide variety of sources, the potential for variation in data quality and character is great. Variations in timeliness, spatial coverage, density and measurement method may all be hidden behind imprecise definitions and inconsistent use of terminology; alone or in combination, these all present a real danger to the end-user. More seriously, but even less considered, it is unclear how much liability rests with which party should unfortunate consequences arise from the use of such data (Epstein 1991 in this volume). It is only through the understanding of the totality of these issues that the user can judge whether the data are appropriate and should be applied to his or her task.

There are two major components of data quality – accuracy and completeness (Chrisman 1991 in this volume). Within any one data set, these components must be known for both the position of the features and for their attributes. Positional accuracy is a measure of the proximity of the coordinates of any feature in the database to their true position on the ground and is a function, at least in part, of the method for data collection. Many of the data within the interim CORINE database are derived from digitizing paper maps; while positional accuracy is partly a reflection of the quality of data compilation, it is thus primarily dependent on the original map scale and the quality of the generalization carried out by a cartographer. Maps are usually held to be accurate to one line width (typically drawn at about 0.5 mm: Fisher 1991 in this volume); as source material used within the interim database was compiled within the range 1 : 500 000 to 1 : 1 million scales, this is equivalent to a maximum positional error of 250 m. However, while national standards laying down acceptable levels of generalization and accuracy frequently exist for topographical map compilation at medium scales (e.g. 1 : 50 000 scale), this is not often the case for small-scale mapping which is drawn from multiple sources and often not for thematic mapping at any scale. Certainly there are no published standards of accuracy for many of the maps used in the CORINE Programme, and it is doubtful whether they would meet the US standards for map accuracy (see Rhind and Clark 1988). Thus the user may find it difficult to judge the relationship between a line on the map and a line on the ground; in practice, it is doubtful whether the positional accuracy of much of the material within the development database is greater than 1 km. The representation of 'fuzzy features' such as soil boundaries is inherently less accurate than is that of physically discrete ones like railways (see Burrough 1991 in this volume).

Distortions in the position of features stored in the database can also be introduced inadvertently through data processing. This may be extremely obvious (for instance, digitizing spikes), or alternatively very subtle and not immediately apparent. A good example of the latter is provided by the soils data within the interim CORINE database, derived from the already published paper EC soils map (Tavernier 1985). This original map was compiled from a set of national soil map sheets which, although each was on a known projection, were only minimally transformed in conversion to the whole EC map. Perhaps the most severe effects of this method of compilation were the distortions in soil boundaries along the edges of the original, national sheets in order that a continent-wide continuous paper map could be assembled for wall display purposes. Worse still, the map was then partitioned into other map sheets for publication purposes. Described thus, the compilation process seems to have been inept but it must be remembered that no thought whatever had been given to the final map being anything other than a free-standing pictorial display when its production began in the late 1970s.

The digital representation of the EC map was produced through scanning and subsequent vectorization of the final, published (and internally distorted) map sheets, thus embodying the original map's significant distortions along original (but, by then, unrecognizable and unrecorded) sheet edges. These distortions were only discovered when the soils and other data sets – supposedly derived from the same ONC topographic map base (Rhind and Clark 1988) – were overlayed. To allow integration with other data sets, the distortions had to be removed. The first attempt to solve the problem involved the use of 'rubber sheeting' with over 7000 control points. Unhappily, this proved unsuccessful because of the lack of control points available on both the spatial template (the ONC map) and the soils database in certain critical areas, allied to the nature of the errors. To achieve the desired result, substantial 'detective work' had to be carried out to discover the processes through which the maps had been. After that, the digital data were divided into the original sheets and reprojected to their known projections. The distortion introduced through the original edge-matching had then to be removed by 'rubber-sheeting' techniques; the data set now overlays the topographic coverage, but cannot be compared directly with the source document from which the digitizing was carried out.

Attribute accuracy is a separate issue, and defines the closeness of the attribute values to their true values. Gross errors (such as miscoded polygons) may become obvious through use of the data and familiarity with the area or comparison against other sources; if so, these are easily fixed. Other errors are more subtle. Problems in categorizing what are in reality continuous variables (e.g. soil properties) may be compounded by the difficulty in defining the position of the polygon on the ground. Finally, although the interim CORINE database aims to avoid the storage of derived data, in some cases this is unavoidable. This can give rise to the derivation of indices by differing methodologies (e.g. five different formulae were found to be in use between the 12 national climatological organizations for the derivation of the monthly maximum daily temperature, and eight for the calculation of potential evapo-transpiration statistics).

The second component of data quality is that of completeness. This can also be expressed in terms of position and attributes. In the former, parts of the data set may be missing; for instance, when the CORINE project began, a digital cartographic database of topography at a scale of 1 : 500 000 was made available by the Ministry of Defence in the United Kingdom. This data set avoids many of the difficulties with the IfAG data set referred to above and also contains contour information. Unhappily, it is complete only as far south as 46° N, thus excluding much of the Mediterranean area – one of the key areas for study in the Programme. The mismatch between data extent and the area of EC needs reflected the differing responsibilities of the two organizations involved.

In the case of point-sampled data sets, the concept of positional completeness is more difficult to determine; there is a need to ensure consistent and representative density of sites across the study area. There are no invariable rules for determining this; Burrough (1986) shows that the sampling density for boulder clay (which varies widely across short distances) should be much higher than that for sandstone (which is generally far more consistent in its properties). In climatic data sets, more sites are needed to represent rainfall accurately (which is locally distributed) than solar radiation (which is more regional in character). In essence, therefore, sampling should be related to autocorrelation in the data set. In practice, this is rarely known before data are collected and sampling strategies are often complicated by pragmatic and even political considerations.

Such problems in data collection also determine the completeness of attributes, both through space and time. Many data sets within the interim CORINE database are temporally incomplete, due either to failure of recording equipment or to disruption to the monitoring systems (for instance during the period 1939 to 1945). Positional information is recorded for some data sets (for instance, that on biotopes), but sometimes lacks a full range of attribute information (e.g. species at that site). As indicated earlier, problems of data quality become particularly acute (indeed, they may only be recognized) when data sets are overlaid during environmental modelling. Users should be aware of the limitations that map source scale places on this process; data derived from small-scale sources cannot realistically be used in conjunction with that collected at larger scales because of the effect of scale on accuracy and spatial precision. For example, the CORINE database contains data on land cover compiled at a scale of 1 : 100 000 and derived from the interpretation of Landsat MSS satellite imagery. For studies on land use in the Mediterranean region, this needs to be overlaid on to the soils map derived from manual compilations of pre-existing national soils maps at 1 : 1 million scale. Clearly, the former should be generalized before this operation can take place. While a tenfold linear generalization will lead to a (possibly unacceptable) loss of information in the land cover data set, the alternative of expanding the soils data set to 1 : 100 000 is unacceptable as it would simply magnify the distortion already inherent in that data set.

A related problem is that of the spatial relationships between different data sets. Often these are hidden or implied but, unless they are known, then the user is at risk of drawing conclusions from the analysis which are at best tautologous or, at worst, nonsense. The problem is particularly acute where data sets are thought to share common boundaries (e.g. soil and vegetation which may terminate along river banks). If the two data sets are derived from different sources (e.g. maps of differing projections and scales) then, when overlaid, the boundaries may no longer be coincident and sliver polygons will occur. The problem for the user is to decide whether these are real or whether they are simply a reflection of variations in data quality. To answer this, the user requires specialist knowledge of the data sets, including the history of their derivation; without this, they may collapse polygons which in reality are discrete and real and thus force a spurious correlation between the data sets.

Database volume and update

Because the CORINE database is still under development, a range of problems have been identified which have still to be addressed. These include the question of handling large data volumes as the spatial resolution increases and the maintenance and update of the database. The CORINE database, at the time of writing, totals about 750 megabytes when held in ARC/INFO format. While small by global standards (especially in comparison with those derived from remote sensing imagery; see Clark *et al.*, 1991; Townshend 1991 in this volume), it is expected to increase considerably in the future. Many environmental processes operate at resolutions considerably finer than 1 km^2 (the best attainable resolution on the ground of the existing database at a scale of 1 : 1 million and very unlikely to be attained consistently). Thus an increase in resolution is clearly desirable and, indeed, essential if the database is to be put to routine practical use for many purposes. Indeed, such an increase in resolution is already reflected in data holdings on both land cover and coastal erosion which were compiled at larger scales. The NATO requirements for digital topographical cover across Europe at 1 : 50 000 scale ensure that, even in the medium term, the potential size of the EC database is measured in terms of gigabytes rather than megabytes.

Databases of this size require careful design and structuring if the information within them is to be readily accessible to the user; it is already clear that some form of spatial partitioning ('tiling') of the CORINE database is required, whether achieved by system designer or internally by the system itself. Originally stored as one seamless whole, this has the advantage of simplicity of database design but increases processing time for user access to only part of the area of the European Community. Some early experiments to identify an optimum tiling strategy using ARC/INFO suggested that partitioning by country would be most appropriate and readily understandable by the end-user (Wiggins 1986); many queries arose on a country-by-country basis. However, data volumes by tile were still too large to give acceptable access times. An alternative series of tiles of 2 degrees longitude by 1 degree latitude (which happened to be the 'building blocks' of one of the sets of map sheets used) were constructed; while improving the access times, the pattern was not readily identifiable by the user. It is now clear that patterns of user access to data should determine the tiling structure; irrevocable decisions on partitioning have been deferred until there is more extensive use of the database by a variety of different users and until selection is made of the final system to be used.

The problem of updating the CORINE database has yet to be put to the practical test; clearly there should be procedures for any database to ensure that its contents are accurate and up to date. The currency of data and the frequency of their update are a function of the type of data and of the uses of them. In the case of environmental databases, many update cycles are quite long; geology and soils, for instance, change most rapidly through re-interpretation rather than through natural processes! Hence replacement of a whole data set or aggregation or disaggregation of classes in the data are normally required with such data. Meteorological data, at least when stored as 30 year means, are also fairly stable. In contrast, both biological populations and patterns of land use and cover may change extremely rapidly; their update cycles are thus much shorter. Procedures for updating have yet to be determined for the CORINE database; what is already clear is that revision will be as resource-intensive as was compilation of the original data. A further complication is that the responsibility for revision of primary data will rest with the data suppliers (many of whom are national agencies in the member states of the EC) rather than the users or the data holders (the EC). In practice, therefore, updating of such a multinational database as CORINE is likely to require much collaboration at the political as well as technical levels and may require EC directives.

Database documentation

Standard procedures for database documentation must be established if the user is to know the history of each data set and thus have some understanding of its quality and potential for use. There are several levels of documentation: of individual features or of classes of features (or variables) within data sets, and of the data sets themselves. Chrisman (1984,

1991) has argued for the inclusion of information on data quality and reliability within each data set by individual feature. Further, the system should be intelligent enough to act upon this information, in order to guard against misuse. While obviously this is one ultimate aim of the CORINE database, the information on which to judge data quality at present is often unavailable, is often only in freetext form where it does exist and its inclusion would have some implications for data volumes.

Documentation of standards for data collection and definition will go some way to ensuring an increase in data quality and attribute accuracy. The CORINE Programme team is presently compiling a catalogue of data definitions. It would be advantageous to construct and disseminate these before data collection takes place, in order to ensure more rigorous selection and thus increase data quality. In practice, many are at present established either during or after data collection, but are still useful in identifying errors in the database (for instance the inconsistencies of definition within the climate data sets noted earlier). Standard procedures for the documentation of the history of each data set have also been established for the CORINE database. In this way, users are able to determine the source of each data set and follow its history of processing and assimilation into the database. The history files and audit trail facilities available in some GIS are invaluable in this respect.

ISSUES OF USER ACCESS TO ENVIRONMENTAL DATABASES

Underlying the various issues concerning environmental data and GIS technology to handle it are questions concerning the organizational background: where should the database be sited, to whom should it be accessible and for what purposes?

Centralized versus distributed database

The CORINE database is presently centralized at one site, but this need not be a model for other environmental databases or even for CORINE in the longer term. There are three possible scenarios: all data at a central site; all data at many sites; or some data across a range of sites with a greater or lesser degree of transparency in access to the user.

Significant improvements in networking and communications technology over the past decade have provided direct access for users to many centralized databases. The idea of many users having access to environmental data distributed across many databases is not yet, however, as realistic for a number of reasons. The requirement for multiple variables across large geographical areas can result in massive volumes of data for file transfer, and this may be complicated by the difficulties in processing some typical GIS operations over a network (particularly when complex graphics are involved) and the inexperience of many users in use of network technology. An alternative is to distribute the database on optical storage media for local access but this in turn raises problems of database update. The ever-decreasing cost of storage of data on CD-ROM and the economic possibility of repeat pressing at intervals may resolve this issue. Another alternative is that developments in data broadcast offer realistic longer-term prospects.

User access

Free and uncontrolled access to a centralized CORINE database is a technical possibility. In reality, however, it is at present neither feasible nor desirable. Many users have only limited knowledge of the operation of a GIS and, without significant improvements in the user interface and/or user education, this is likely to pose a practical barrier to free access to the data. Other users, while technically capable of accessing the database, have only limited understanding of some of the issues of data quality noted above. Though it may be argued that it is not the duty of the database builder to prevent *bona fide* users from misusing the data, there are strong scientific, ethical and political reasons for doing so. For instance, many environmental issues are scientifically and politically very sensitive; misinterpretation of the data and results of analyses could lead either to the establishment of inappropriate policies or to the discrediting of the whole information system, providing a justification for suspending its implementation.

The CORINE database is accessed at present through a user service; access to the data is via in-house, 'expert' users only. This allows use of the data to be carefully regulated and inappropriate uses filtered out. It also offers the opportunity for education through discussion with users of the design of any data analysis or output, and the provision of advice on the most appropriate analytical techniques. A disadvantage is that it may deter use of the database or slow down access. More seriously, if not sensitively and openly implemented, it may amount to a form of data censorship, filtering out politically or administratively undesirable queries.

In the long term, more open use of environmental databases may be achieved through the use of expert systems, with their own built-in rules for data use. Unfortunately, while examples of such systems have been demonstrated (see, e.g. Smith and Ye Jiang (1991 in this volume) and Smith, MacKenzie and Stanton (1988) on the development of an expert system to support zoning of the Australian Great Barrier Reef), they are still some way from widespread operation and the rules which they can apply are only as good as the people who devise them. In the case of the CORINE system, this presents serious difficulties for the database is not yet in a sufficiently stable state nor is the management science yet sufficiently advanced to permit the application of the 'hard and fast' rules required of most expert systems. In particular, the user needs are not yet sufficiently understood to define the rules and the complex interaction between environmental variables remains inadequately understood.

FUTURE DEVELOPMENT

Although still in its formative stages, the CORINE database already represents one of the most substantial fully integrated systems in the world – certainly if those comprised wholly of remote sensing imagery are excluded. Already, there have been three positive achievements (Wyatt, Briggs and Mounsey 1988):

- some harmonization in existing practices and the acceptance of standards for recording environmental data;

- a demonstration of the feasibility of establishing one centralized database to meet the requirements of a diverse variety of end-users; and

- the development of similar integrative activities at national level which, in themselves, reinforce the improvement in data collection practices.

But there are also some lessons which should be taken forward into the next stage. First, it should be noted that the issues behind the development of environmental databases are largely non-technological; indeed the rate of development of technology is (at least at present) outstripping both data quality improvements and the ability of the user to operate it. Substantial efforts in user education are needed to resolve this issue.

Secondly, the development of an environmental database needs to be well resourced. Four years of data collection and integration merely confirms that such database creation is an expensive process, principally because tasks which appear conceptually simple are either highly labour intensive or more complex (and thus time consuming) than originally envisaged. This is especially the case when judged by those without practical GIS experience.

Thirdly, the CORINE database was developed as a reaction to existing problems of nature conservation, acid deposition and conflicts of land use in the Mediterranean. But, to be most effective, the creation of environmental databases should be pro-active, backed up with sufficient resources to involve modellers as well as database builders. The gestation period for assembling environmental databases is such that only by early – and, ideally, prior – identification of the key processes which govern environmental change can databases be developed which make real contributions at the most apposite moment in the battle against environmental degradation.

Fourthly, environmental databases should be built through better efforts on overall system design and basic data requirements, rather than through the random provision of information by disparate policy themes. Although three specific topics for study were defined at the outset of the CORINE Programme, little initial thought was given to definition of the fundamental data requirements which should ideally underpin an environmental database. The *ad hoc* approach adopted by the CORINE Programme is probably not untypical of 'first-generation' systems driven by enthusiasm and a need to demonstrate results, rather than having a commitment to longevity and sound principles of design. This should not be a long-term policy.

Finally, the development of any environmental database requires full and substantial organizational support by all interested parties. In the case of CORINE, these include directorates within the European Community itself, national governments and their agencies and international organizations. The international dimension of environmental problems requires reliable information and rigorous analysis. But, as Wyatt *et al.* (1988) have noted, the balancing of political objectives and financial commitment against technical reality and scientific rigour is one of the most elusive goals in policy making. It would be unrealistic to assume that science alone will ever dictate how, when and why environmental GIS and their databases are created and used.

REFERENCES

Benyon D (1990) *Information and Data Modelling*. Blackwell Scientific Publications, Oxford
Blatchford R P, Rhind D W (1989) The ideal mapping system. In: Rhind D W, Taylor D R F (eds.) *Cartography Past, Present and Future*. Elsevier, London, pp. 157–68
Briggs D J, Mounsey H M (1989) Integrating land resource data into a European geographical information system. *Applied Geography* **9** (1): 5–20
Burrough P A (1986) *Principles of Geographical Information Systems for Land Resource Assessment*. Clarendon Press, Oxford
Burrough P A (1991) Soil information systems. In: Maguire D J, Goodchild M F, Rhind D W (eds.) *Geographical Information Systems: principles and applications*. Longman, London, pp. 153–69, Vol 2
Calkins H W (1991) GIS and public policy. In: Maguire D J, Goodchild M F, Rhind D W (eds.) *Geographical Information Systems: principles and applications*. Longman, London, pp. 233–45, Vol 2
Canada Department of Forestry and Rural Development (1965) *The Canada Land Inventory: objectives, scope and organisation*. Report No. 1. Ottawa, Canada Land Inventory
Chrisman N R (1984) The role of information quality in a GIS. *Cartographica* **21** (2/3): 79–87

Chrisman N R (1991) The error component in spatial data. In: Maguire D J, Goodchild M F, Rhind D W (eds.) *Geographical Information Systems: principles and applications*. Longman, London, pp. 165–74, Vol 1
Clark D M, Hastings D A, Kineman J J (1991) Global databases and their implications for GIS. In: Maguire D J, Goodchild M F, Rhind D W (eds.) *Geographical Information Systems: principles and applications*. Longman, London, pp. 217–31, Vol 2
Clarke A L (1991) GIS specification, evaluation and implementation. In: Maguire D J, Goodchild M F, Rhind D W (eds.) *Geographical Information Systems: principles and applications*. Longman, London, pp. 477–88, Vol 1
CEC (1990) *CORINE: Examples of the Use of the Results of the Programme 1985–90*. Directorate General of the Environment, Nuclear Safety and Civil Protection, Commission of the European Communities, Brussels

Department of the Environment (DoE) (1987) *Handling Geographic Information. Report of the Committee of Inquiry chaired by Lord Chorley*. HMSO, London
Didier M (1990) *Utilité et valeur de l'Information Géographique*. CNIG Economica, Paris

EPA (1987) *Sharing Data for Environmental Results*. State/EPA Data Management Program Project Report 1987. United States Environmental Protection Agency, Washington
Epstein E F (1991) Legal aspects of GIS. In: Maguire D J, Goodchild M F, Rhind D W (eds.) *Geographical Information Systems: principles and applications*. Longman, London, pp. 489–502, Vol 1

Fisher P F (1991) Spatial data sources and data problems. In: Maguire D J, Goodchild M F, Rhind D W (eds.) *Geographical Information Systems: principles and applications*. Longman, London, pp. 175–89, Vol 1
Flowerdew R (1991) Spatial data integration. In: Maguire D J, Goodchild M F, Rhind D W (eds.) *Geographical Information Systems: principles and applications*. Longman, London, pp. 375–87, Vol 1

Guptill S C (1991) Spatial data exchange and standardization. In: Maguire D J, Goodchild M F, Rhind D W (eds.) *Geographical Information Systems: principles and applications*. Longman, London, pp. 515–30, Vol 1

Maguire D J, Dangermond J (1991) The functionality of GIS. In: Maguire D J, Goodchild M F, Rhind D W (eds.) *Geographical Information Systems: principles and applications*. Longman, London, pp. 319–35, Vol 1
Mott J (1990) The National Resource Information Centre – data directory, data broker. In: Parvey C, Grainger K (eds.) *A national Geographic Information System – an achievable objective?* AURISA Monograph 4. AURISA, Eastwood New South Wales, pp. 57–60
Muller J-C (1991) Generalization of spatial databases. In: Maguire D J, Goodchild M F, Rhind D W (eds.) *Geographical Information Systems: principles and applications*. Longman, London, pp. 457–75, Vol 1

Official Journal of the European Community (1985) Council Decision on 27 June 1985 on the adoption of the Commission work programme concerning an experimental project for gathering, coordinating and ensuring the consistency of information on the state of the environment and natural resources in the Community. OJ L 176, 6 July 1985

Rhind D W, Clarke P K (1988) Cartographic inputs to global databases. In: Mounsey H M (ed.) *Building Databases for Global Science*. Taylor & Francis, London, pp. 79–104

Rhind D W, Wyatt B K, Briggs D J, Wiggins J C (1986) The creation of an environmental information system for the European Community. *Nachrichten aus dem Karten und Vermessungswesen Series 2*, **44**: 147–57

Smith J L, Mackenzie H G, Stanton R B (1988) A knowledge-based decision support for environmental planning. *Proceedings of the 3rd International Symposium on Spatial Data Handling*. International Geographical Union, Columbus Ohio, pp. 307–20

Smith T R, Ye Jiang (1991) Knowledge-based approaches in GIS. In: Maguire D J, Goodchild M F, Rhind D W (eds.) *Geographical Information Systems: principles and applications*. Longman, London, pp. 413–25, Vol 1

Tavernier R (1985) *Soil Map of the European Communities. 1 : 1 000 000*. Office for Official Publications of the European Communities, Luxembourg

Tomlinson R F, Calkins H W, Marble D F (1976) *Computer Handling of Geographical Data*. UNESCO, Paris

Townshend J R G (1991) Environmental databases and GIS. In: Maguire D J, Goodchild M F, Rhind D W (eds.) *Geographical Information Systems: principles and applications*. Longman, London, pp. 201–16, Vol 2

Tsichritzis D C, Lochovsky F H (1982) *Data Models*. Prentice-Hall, New York

Whimbrel Consultants Ltd (1989) *CORINE Database Manual, Version 2.1*. Brussels

Wiggins J C (1986) Performance considerations in the design of a map library: a user perspective. *Proceedings of the ARC/INFO Users' Conference*. ESRI, Redlands California

Wiggins J C, Hartley R P, Higgins M J, Whittaker R J (1987) Computing aspects of a large geographic information system for the European Community. *International Journal of Geographical Information Systems* **1** (1): 77–87

Wyatt B K, Briggs D J, Mounsey H M (1988) CORINE: An information system on the state of the environment in the European Community. In: Mounsey H M, Tomlinson R F (eds.) *Building Databases for Global Science*. Taylor & Francis, London, pp. 378–96

49

ENVIRONMENTAL DATABASES AND GIS

J R G TOWNSHEND

An enormous variety of environmental data is found within existing databases, which are growing rapidly. As yet a relatively small proportion of such data have benefited from the application of GIS technology. This arises because of the high investment needed to convert existing archival data into digital format, because of a lack of awareness of the value of these techniques and because traditional GIS is often unsatisfactory for many of these data, which are inherently three and four dimensional. The diversity of environmental databases also hinders their integration, which is an activity essential for exploiting the full value of their data. The benefits of integrating data sets through GIS is illustrated in five examples: in estimating the availability of natural resources, in improving data capture, in assisting the visualization of changes, in applying physical models and in extrapolating and modelling environmental parameters through the use of sample data. This chapter complements those by Clark, Hastings and Kineman (1991) and Mounsey (1991).

INTRODUCTION

Environmental databases contain an enormous diversity of types of data (Table 49.1), most of which are spatially located either explicitly or implicitly. Consequently the capture, analysis, management and display of environmental data are all activities that can greatly benefit from the application of GIS. Moreover, inherent in the solution of many environmental problems is the need to bring together disparate data sets. Another characteristic of many environmental data sets is that they are often extremely large in volume, arising in part because their collection and maintenance is carried out on a national or even international basis. The size and complexity of these databases makes the requirement for the application of GIS technology all the more necessary. But, perversely, this is also a hindrance to their introduction because of the high investment necessary to convert data in existing archives into digital format.

The benefits of handling environmental data sets within GIS does not mean that all environmental data sets are likely to be stored and handled in a single uniform manner. The establishment of international formats within specific disciplines, coupled with the very different space and time scales of the phenomena being depicted, militate strongly against such standardization.

Despite the high potential of GIS technology for environmental applications, its penetration remains modest in this field in the early 1990s. This relates in part to a lack of awareness of the potential of the technology and in part to the expense in achieving its full operational usage. Many potential users regard GIS as little more than automated map-editing systems. Although this is a mistaken idea, it is undoubtedly true that currently available commercial GIS are most effective when dealing with two-dimensional spatial data (Smith and Paradis 1989; Raper and Kelk 1991 in this volume), whereas many environmental data sets are inherently three dimensional, as in the case of solid geology, or even four dimensional, in the case of

Table 49.1 Examples of geographically referenced environmental data holdings (NERC 1988).

Geological data sets
1. Borehole logs
2. Geochemical records (including stream geochemistry)
3. Geophysical survey data
4. Gravity data
5. Geomagnetic survey
6. Hydrogeological well records

Marine data sets
1. Sea surface temperature
2. Current meter data
3. Wave height/period data records
4. Ocean geophysics
5. Salinity data
6. Side scan sonar data

Ecological data sets
1. Species location data
2. Terrain/land characteristics
3. Location of conservation sites
4. Soil types distribution
5. Biomass data

Hydrological data sets
1. Rainfall data
2. Soil moisture
3. Evapotranspiration
4. River discharge
5. Location of river networks

Atmospheric data sets
1. Air temperature at various heights
2. Air pressure at various heights
3. Atmospheric chemistry
4. Wind speed
5. Humidity

Important ancillary vector data sets
1. Coastlines and political boundaries
2. Digital terrain models
3. Topographic maps.

Important ancillary remote sensing data sets
1. Data from Meteosat/NOAA (National Oceanographic and Atmospheric Administration) AVHRR (Advanced Very High Resolution Radiometer)/DMSP (Defense Meteorological Satellite Program) for climate and meteorological applications.
2. Landsat Thematic Mapper and MSS (Multispectral Scanner System) data, SPOT-HRV (Système Probatoire pour l'Observation de la Terre) and AVHRR data for land survey and monitoring.
3. AVHRR, CZCS (Coastal Zone Color Scanning System) and ERS-1 data for oceanic monitoring.

most atmospheric, marine, and geophysical data sets. Finally – and notwithstanding the low level of awareness of the contribution of GIS *per se* – many users of environmental data have independently developed very sophisticated procedures for the capture, handling and analysis of environmental data. Nowhere is this more apparent than in the field of meteorology where the demands for continuously updated and frequent forecasts have spurred the development and application of highly effective four dimensional data handling systems.

CHARACTERISTICS OF ENVIRONMENTAL DATA SETS

In order to demonstrate the characteristics and diversity of environmental data sets, each one of four main natural science areas will be discussed in turn, followed by an analysis of their differences and similarities (NERC 1988).

Earth science data

Almost all data that are used in the earth sciences are spatially referenced to a point on or below the earth's surface, location being described in terms of the three dimensions of geographical space. Frequently, such data are aggregated into areas defined as polygons or into volumes for the purposes of analysis and visualization. Earth science databases contain a wide variety of geological, geotechnical, geophysical and geochemical parameters, and increasingly include detailed chemical and biological descriptions. Some geophysical data, such as those concerned with seismology and geomagnetism, also have a time dimension. The spatial referencing system used is normally either that of the national topographic mapping agency if on land or latitude and longitude (or UTM grid) if off-shore. Heights and depths variously refer either to a national datum, such as the National Geodetic Vertical Datum of the United States, or to mean sea level. The former is fixed and the latter varies through time and space due to the various local and regional environmental factors that affect sea level (Ellis 1978).

Data are increasingly captured in digital form but, in most national surveys, there is an enormous backlog of analogue data requiring digitizing. Some data are inordinately expensive to digitize such as field notebooks or hand-annotated field maps: others, such as rock specimens, fossil collections and borehole materials, are impossible to digitize though measurements of many of their parameters can of course be collected and stored in digital form. National geological surveys or their equivalent are usually the main repository of systematically stored geological information and, in some countries such as the United Kingdom, some borehole logs and specimens are deposited as a statutory requirement. Smaller collections are also found in universities, museums, industry and local government organizations. Collaboration on a global scale is provided under the World Data Center system (Table 49.2; see also Clark *et al.* 1991 in this volume) for several types of earth science data. These include seismology at the US Geological Survey in Golden, Colorado; recent crustal movements at the International Centre for Recent Crustal Movements in Prague, Czechoslovakia; and Geomagnetism at the British Geological Survey in Edinburgh. Regional collaborations are also under consideration, such as that for the North Sea under the auspices of WEGS (Western European Geological Surveys).

Marine data

Marine data typically refer to the sea surface, the body of the water beneath it, the seabed and the sub-seabed: they include physical, chemical, biological, geological and geophysical parameters (Table 49.3); clearly there is overlap with earth science interests with respect to the latter two categories though separate sets of databases are usually maintained. Marine data are geographically located in three dimensions and are usually referenced by latitude and longitude and depth below the sea surface. For more precise measurements in the vertical dimension, such as sea level itself, a geoidal reference is required. Many of the data sets have an additional time dimension, especially those concerned'with the characteristics of the sea itself. The time scales vary enormously, ranging from the high frequencies of sea surface waves, through phenological variations of many biological phenomena to much longer term variations associated with climate change.

Marine data are often stored in the form of summary descriptors, such as averages, in order to characterize an area of the sea surface or volume of the sea body. For example, data are commonly aggregated into 1 degree squares, FAO fisheries squares or Marsden squares (NERC 1988). Some data with a time dimension are presented in a processed form, such as wave spectra. Data such as temperature, salinity, current and wave measurements are readily captured in, or can be converted to, digital form. Other data, such as photographs or sonar and seismic records, can be digitized using raster scanning, but with much greater effort. Biological specimens and geological materials are impossible to digitize.

Capture of marine data sets is carried out in many contrasting ways. Some are collected from commercial shipping whereas others are derived primarily from specific scientific or commercial survey cruises, as in the case of many collections of geological samples of seabed rocks and marine geophysical data.

As a consequence of the diversity of data sets and the underlying requirements for their creation, there are local, national, regional and international organizational frameworks and agreements to ensure the maintenance of data sets and their standards. Table 49.4 illustrates some of the organizations that have responsibilities for marine data. The collection and dissemination of marine data forms an important part of the World Data Center System (Table 49.2).

Terrestrial ecological data

Ecological data sets often include both attributes (e.g. species name, vegetation class and growth stage) along with numerical measurements (e.g. temperature, pH and nutrient levels). Many such ecological measurements are recorded with reference to only two spatial dimensions, usually by means of the locational referencing system of the country within which the data are collected through use of local topographical maps to define location. In international data sets, however, latitude and longitude or the UTM grid are normally used. The vertical dimension (specified in terms of elevation above sea level) is often explicitly recorded or is readily derivable from topographic maps. Measurements made within a soil profile will also

Table 49.2 The World Data Center System (from Allen, 1988 and ICSU 1989).

Type of data serviced	Sponsoring Institution	Location
World Data Center – A		
Coordination Office: US National Academy of Sciences.		
Glaciology (Snow and Ice)	University of Colorado and NOAA/NGDC	Boulder, Colorado
Meteorology	NOAA, National Climate Data Center	Asheville, N. Carolina
Oceanography	NOAA, National Oceanographic Data Center	Washington DC,
Rockets and Satellites	NASA, National Space Science Data Center	Greenbelt, Maryland
Rotation of the Earth	US Naval Observatory	Washington DC
Seismology	US Geological Survey	Golden, Colorado
Marine Geology/Geophysics, Solar-Terrestrial Physics, and Solid Earth Geophysics	NOAA, National Geophysical Data Center	Boulder, Colorado
World Data Center – B		
Operated under the Soviet Geophysical Committee of the Academy of Sciences of the USSR		
World Data Center – B1		
Meteorology, Oceanography, Marine Geology/ Geophysics, Glaciology, Tsunamis, Rockets and Satellites, Rotation of the Earth, Mean Sea Level and Ocean Tides.	USSR State Committee for Hydro-meteorology and Control of the Environment.	Obninsk, USSR
World Data Center-B2		
Solar-Terrestrial Physics and Solid Earth Geophysics	Soviet Geophysical Committee, Academy of Sciences, USSR.	Moscow, USSR
World Data Center – C		
World Data Center – C1		
Earth Tides & Sunspot Index	Royal Observatory of Belgium	Brussels, Belgium
Geomagnetism	Danish Meteorological Institute	Copenhagen, Denmark
	and British Geological Survey	Edinburgh, UK
Glaciology	Scott Polar Research Institute	Cambridge, UK
Recent Crustal Movements	International Centre for Recent Crustal Movements	Prague, Czechoslovakia
Soil Geography and Classification	International Soil Reference and Information Center	Wageningen, The Netherlands
Solar Activity	Observatoire de Paris	Meudon, France
Solar-Terrestrial Physics	Science and Engineering Research Laboratory	Chilton, UK
World Data Center – C2		
Airglow	Tokyo Astronomical Observatory	Tokyo, Japan
Aurora	National Institute of Polar Research	Kaga, Japan
Cosmic Rays	Institute of Physical and Chemical Research	Tokyo, Japan
Geomagnetism	Kyoto University, Ministry of Education	Kyoto, Japan
Ionosphere	Ministry of Posts and Telecommunications	Tokyo, Japan
Nuclear Radiation	Japan Meteorological Agency	Tokyo, Japan
Solar Radio Emissions	Nagoya University, Ministry of Education	Toyokawa, Japan
Solar-Terrestrial Activity	Institute of Space and Aeronautical Research, Ministry of Education	Tokyo, Japan
World Data Center – D		
Astronomy	Beijing Astronomical Observatory	Beijing, China
Geophysics	Institute for Geophysics	Beijing, China
Geology	Chinese Academy of Geological Sciences	Beijing, China
Glaciology and Geocryology	Lanzhou Institute of Glaciology and Geocryology	Lanzhou, China

Table 49.2 *Continued*

Type of data serviced	Sponsoring Institution	Location
World Data Center – D (continued)		
Meteorology	National Meteorological Center	Beijing, China
Oceanography	National Oceanographic and Information Centre	Tianjin, China
Renewable Resources and Environment	Commission for Integrated Survey of Natural Resources	Beijing, China
Seismology	Department of Science Programming and Earthquake Monitoring	Beijing, China
Space Sciences	Chinese Academy of Sciences	Beijing, China

Table 49.3 Types of marine data sets.

1. Ocean biological samples
2. Geological collections of seabed rocks and sediments
3. Current measurements
4. Echo sounding profiles
5. Seismic records
6. Sidescan sonar records
7. Magnetic records
8. Gravity records
9. Earth tide data
10. Plankton records
11. Inter-tidal biological records
12. Sea surface temperature
13. Frequency and location of sea mammals
14. Fisheries data
15. Wind data
16. Bathymetric data
17. Conductivity data
18. Salinity

require a depth dimension, but this is recorded with much greater resolution. The time of data acquisition will usually be recorded but continuously recorded time series outside climatological and hydrological data sets are uncommon. Data sets may be made available in highly aggregated forms, such as the presence or absence of species within grid cells of a specified size, origin and orientation.

However, many types of attribute data are difficult, if not impossible, to manage in digital form. These include actual samples, such as biological reference specimens and soil samples, as well as many paper records. International collaboration with respect to such matters as compilation of global databases, agreement on standards and exchange formats, is apparently not well developed compared with most other environmental disciplines. There are, however, already efforts to coordinate certain types of ecological data such as the global databases on the Status of Biological Diversity, compiled by the Conservation Monitoring Centre under the aegis of the International Union for Conservation of Nature and Natural Resources (Pellew and Harrison 1988); World Data Center-C2 has been extended to include a new centre for Soil Geography and Classification and a centre for Renewable Resources and Environment has been set up in the newly constituted World Data Center-D (Table 49.2). As part of the International Geosphere Biosphere Programme, considerable efforts are being directed towards setting up a global information system for land cover (Rasool and Ojima 1989). Also, as part of the Global Environmental Monitoring System (GEMS) of the United Nations Environmental Programme (UNEP), the Global Resource Information Database (GRID) project has been set up to bring together environmental databases on a common geographical base at both global and more local scales (Mooneyhan 1988).

Atmospheric sciences

Enormous quantities of atmospheric data are collected, processed and managed on a regular daily basis to meet the requirements of operational meteorology, although climate monitoring and modelling are increasingly important users of atmospheric data. Data are referenced to all three spatial dimensions as well as time. The spatial and temporal frequencies of data collection are very variable, especially between land and sea and between developed and developing countries, though satellite data are bringing greater uniformity for some parameters such as sea surface

Table 49.4 Examples of organizations responsible for marine data (NERC 1988).

1. National organizations such as NOAA (National Oceanographic and Atmospheric Administration of the USA) and NERC (the Natural Environment Research Council of the UK).
2. International Oceanographic Commission's (IOC) Working Committee on International Oceanographic Data Exchange (IODE)* which has set up:
   (a) a group on format development leading to a general Formatting System for Geo-referenced Data (GF3)
   (b) National Oceanographic Data Centres (NODC) including Responsible NODC's (RNODC) with responsibilities for specific data sets for the international community. For example, the UK NODC is called MIAS (Marine Information Advisory Service) and has particular responsibility for world waves.
3. International Gravity Bureau at Toulouse.
4. General Bathymetric Chart of the Oceans (GEBCO) under the International Oceanographic Commission and the IHO.
5. FAO Fishery Data Centre in Rome.
6. Major international programmes such as WOCE (World Ocean Climate Experiment), JASIN, IGY.
7. Regional organizations such as the International Council for the Exploration of the Sea (ICES).

* Subsequently renamed the IOC Technical Committee on International Oceanographic Data and Information Exchange (though retaining the same acronym).

---

temperature and cloud cover. One of the first requirements after data capture is to convert sparse, irregular sets of observations to smooth continuous displays of spatially and temporally referenced meteorological variables for use in numerical weather prediction (NERC 1988).

The strategic and economic requirements for international information on weather conditions, and the need for data for very large areas in producing effective weather forecasting, have led to establishment of the Global Telecommunications System (GTS) under the World Meteorological Organization (WMO). This organization distributes large volumes of atmospheric data in internationally agreed formats to most countries in the world, several times every day. Meteorological data are the responsibilities in World Data Center A of the National Climate Data Center in Asheville, North Carolina and in World Data Centre B they are the responsibility of the USSR State Committee for Hydrometeorology and Control of the Environment at a facility in Obninsk, USSR (Table 49.2).

Overview of the characteristics of environmental databases

The foregoing summary overview has demonstrated the considerable range of environmental data sets. Among the most diverse aspects are the following:

- *Locational referencing.* Although all data are collected in time and space, for some data sets two spatial dimensions provide sufficient locational referencing whereas for many others, especially in the marine and atmospheric areas, three spatial dimensions and the time dimension are required.

- *Longevity of databases.* The longevity of the usefulness of data sets varies from the immediate requirements of weather forecasting, where data become essentially valueless in a few hours, to some geological data banks where observations made in the nineteenth century remain important.

- *Types and formats of data.* Many environmental databases typically contain data in many different forms, including raster and vector, digital and analogue types (the latter, in particular, being manifested in many different forms). Data sets may also often consist of tangible materials such as type examples of biological, soil, or rock specimens.

- *Availability of digital data.* In some fields, such as meteorology and climatology, the majority of data are in digital form but in others this is not the case. In the latter situation, the inherent diversity of data types and the lack of resources for digitizing data ensure that implementation of a modern GIS capability is considerably curtailed.

- *Degree of integration of data sets.* For meteorology, a highly sophisticated global system of continuous data collection and distribution exists though major weather systems can be well characterized for the purposes of forecasting by a relatively coarse spatial sample of observations, at least as compared with many other environmental phenomena. At a national level, there is often a considerable degree of central management of geological information, though their different data sets are typically imperfectly linked. For ecological information, local and poorly integrated data sets are often the norm.

Some similarities can also be recognized:

- *Growth in size of environmental data sets.* This trend continues because of the addition of new contemporary data and the impact of new, more spatially and temporally comprehensive, methods of data capture – notably remote sensing (Fig. 49.1; see also Davis and Simonett 1991 in this volume). Another factor has been the requirements for creating longer time series of environmental characteristics at global scales associated with growing interest in longer term climate changes and their impacts on the biosphere.

- *Increasing digitizing of data holdings, catalogues and indices.* In all environmental disciplines there is an increasing drive towards digitizing data holdings wherever possible and to improve digital methods of data cataloguing and indexing.

- *Mismatches between requirements for use of environmental data sets and current GIS technology.* In all environmental areas, currently available commercial GIS have substantial limitations: among the most important are their inability easily to deal with hybrid data sets containing both raster and vector data and their failure to handle three- and four-dimensional data sets fully, though techniques are being developed to ameliorate these problems (e.g. Langran 1989; Raper and Kelk 1991 in this volume).

- *Increased inter-linking and spatial integration of data sets.* Environmental data sets are increasingly being linked due to the needs of the environmental sciences and the applications to which they are put (as discussed in the next section), and because of technology-driven improvements in information handling technology. Inter-linking is being facilitated in part through the adoption of common formats and, in particular, through agreements on national and international exchange formats. The latter are especially important in producing spatially more comprehensive data sets. One of the most important of these exchange formats in the environmental field is GF3 (General Format 3) used by the marine community which was formally accepted by the international community over 10 years ago. As Fig. 49.2 indicates, achieving acceptance of the format and maintaining it has involved a considerable amount of international collaboration and organization.

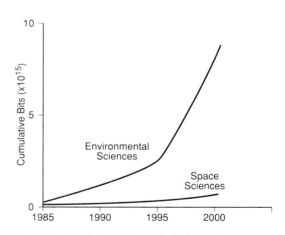

Fig. 49.1 Anticipated growth in data volumes arising from the use of space-borne remote sensing instruments for the environmental sciences compared with the space sciences (Earth System Sciences Committee 1988).

LINKING ENVIRONMENTAL DATA SETS

In all environmental fields, there is increasing interest in problems which by their very nature

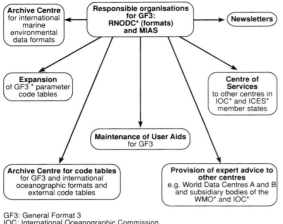

GF3: General Format 3
IOC: International Oceanographic Commission
ICES: International Council for Exploration of the Sea
MIAS: Marine Information Advisory Service
NODC: National Oceanographic Data Centre
RNODC: Responsible NODC for formats
(Service Hydrographique of ICES)
WMO: World Meteorological Organisation

Fig. 49.2 The various functions associated with GF3, the widely used international system for the exchange of marine data (Intergovernmental Oceanographic Commission 1987).

require the integrated use of several different data sets. Three examples can be used to illustrate this point. First, the integrated use of environmental parameters (e.g. surface roughness and soil and vegetation characteristics) with atmospheric parameters is increasingly common within global climate models (GCMs) in order to improve estimates of the partitioning of energy and mass transport at the land surface. Secondly, investigations of environmental geochemistry require integration of geological, stream chemistry and human disease data sets. Thirdly, comprehension of the human impact of climate change requires not only an integration of climatic and vegetation data sets, but also a wide range of socio-economic characteristics as well.

Despite the widely recognized benefits of linking environmental data sets, there are major hindrances which inhibit this activity. Some of those impacting most strongly are discussed below.

Varied procedures of data capture

Generation of spatially comprehensive databases often requires linking many more local data sets. The latter may well frequently use different definitions of attributes and different procedures of data gathering and sampling making the creation of internally consistent data sets difficult (see Mounsey 1991 in this volume). Notable examples where this occurs include the generation of rainfall fields across national frontiers, because of the different ways in which rainfall is measured (Bull 1960), and problems in the creation of globally consistent vegetation maps assembled from numerous local surveys. In the latter example, difficulties arise through variations in the type of classification used (the main types being floristic, physiognomic and ecological), as well as variations in the definition of classes within a given classificatory scheme. This undoubtedly contributes to the considerable variations in both local and global estimates of vegetation types (Table 49.5). An additional cause of error arises from different times of data acquisition. For some geological phenomena, this is relatively unimportant because they change so little. However, in the case of land cover or land use, the phenomena often change rapidly and, moreover, data collection for large areas can extend over several years: consequently, some of the spatial variations within the resultant data set may be spurious.

Table 49.5 Variations in estimates of the global areal extent of major vegetation types.

| Vegetation type | Sources | | | |
| | 1 | 2 | 3 | 4 |
	(Area in km^2 × 10^6)			
Forest	48.5	37.4	39.3	49.3
Tundra	8.0	11.7	7.3	11.9
Desert	8.5	4.8	15.6	20.8
Marshland	2.0	3.0	*	2.5
Cultivated	14.0	56.6	17.6	15.9

* Category absent

Sources: 1, Lieth (1975); 2, Hummel and Reck (1979); 3, Matthews (1983); 4, Olson, Watts and Allison (1983).

Lack of compatibility of co-registered data sets

The simple physical co-registration of environmental data sets, through the use of common or linked spatial referencing systems, does not of itself ensure that the interrelationships of phenomena themselves are sensibly described. Data sets may have very different sampling densities or the errors inherent in one data set may be unacceptably high to allow their integrated use – due, for example, to errors introduced during measurement or by generalization. One specific example of this problem is the inadequacy of current USGS digital elevation models for the correction of relief effects in high resolution remotely sensed data (Topographic Science Working Group 1988) because the DEMs have errors sufficiently large to prevent the slope and azimuth of individual Thematic Mapper 30 m pixels to be estimated accurately. However these DEMs would be much more satisfactory for coarse resolution data such as that from the AVHRR with a resolution of 1 km.

Use of polygons to represent heterogeneous phenomena

Polygonal representations of environmental characteristics are common, notably in traditional, geological soils and vegetation maps: a relatively small number of class labels relative to the number of polygons is typically used. Such representations can pose substantial problems, even when used singly, because of the considerable internal variability of the units. In geological maps, the lithological description of a rock unit almost always hides considerable vertical and horizontal variability and, in the case of soil mapping units, the within-class variability is often comparable with (and may even greatly exceed) the between-class variability for some parameters (Webster 1978; Webster and Butler 1976; Burrough 1991 in this volume). In environmental maps, the use of polygons often poses particular problems because of the use of a single set of units to represent multiple environmental parameters and attributes. Thus, in the case of soil maps, each mapped class has to represent a complex three-dimensional combination of physical and chemical soil characteristics. The use of a single set of polygons to represent the variation of multiple attributes and parameters exacerbates substantially the problems associated with polygon overlay. Probably the most extreme case of a single set of polygons being forced to represent a set of heterogeneous environmental properties is found in the 'land system' approach of mapping where the pedological, geological, geomorphological and hydrological properties are all purported to be summarized in a single hierarchical set of areal units (Mitchell 1973).

Diversity of data formats and data types

This is a very common characteristic of environmental data sets and has already been alluded to: it can place a substantial overhead on use of multiple data sets where they have not already been linked.

Maintaining the integrity of data sets through time

The creation of linked data sets depicting changes through time is central to many studies of environmental change. Their creation requires not only the maintenance of consistent measurement and sampling procedures – often accompanied by careful calibration – but should also demand the maintenance of audit trails. One recent example where this was not done occurred in the widely used Global Vegetation Index product of NOAA which depicts vegetation 'greenness' at a global scale (e.g. Justice *et al.* 1986). Subsequent analysis by Goward *et al.* (1991) has revealed considerable unrecorded changes in the specification of this image product; these can introduce considerable errors if used to create longer term time series.

Unlinking data sets

Not only do data sets often need to be linked but, conversely, it is also necessary to ensure that data sets do not suffer from the reverse process and diverge. Specifically, the creation of split systems – involving dual maintenance of copy databases without a clearly established central database manager – can lead to a substantial effort in re-creating a single data set. For example in the United Kingdom, the Water Resources Board produced a copy of the National Well Record Collection and separately maintained it; subsequently the Department of the Environment had to fund the merging of the two databases which had substantially diverged (NERC 1988).

APPLICATIONS OF GIS IN THE ENVIRONMENTAL SCIENCES

Many of the uses of GIS in the environmental sciences will continue to be prosaic, involving more efficient capture, manipulation and display of data in conventional formats. However, the use of GIS opens up a variety of additional analytical opportunities and five case studies are presented in order to demonstrate the contribution of GIS. The role of GIS methods is described successively in estimation of the availability of natural resources, in improving the quality of data capture, in assisting visualization of changes, in applying physical models, in extrapolating and modelling changing environmental parameters through use of sample data, and in providing better access to environmental data.

Use of coarse resolution satellite data for estimating the availability of natural resources

For several years, remotely sensed data have been used for the provision of information concerning the physical environment. More recently, the value of coarse resolution data derived from weather satellites for monitoring the vegetation cover of very large areas has been recognized (e.g. Justice *et al.* 1986; Tucker, Townshend and Goff 1985). The value of these data can be illustrated by a study reported in Millington *et al.* (1989) in which coarse resolution sampled images were used to characterize vegetation types of several countries in southern Africa, using the variation of a spectral vegetation index throughout the year to stratify vegetation types in terms of their woody biomass. Plate 49.1 shows three such images, obtained at different times of year. The pattern of vegetation activity shown by these images is clearly related to the spatial pattern and temporal sequence of rainfall. Using automated classification procedures applied to the multi-temporal data sets, it was possible to separate the area into cover classes (Plate 49.2) and the areas occupied by each class were estimated (Fig. 49.3(a)). Ground survey and previously published results were then used to assign woody biomass values to these classes; statistical estimates of the growing stock (Fig. 49.3(b)) and the mean annual increment were estimated (Fig. 49.3(c)) for the biomass classes of each country. Using an overlay of regional boundaries, estimates were made of the fraction of the growing stock and the mean annual increment in each sub-national region (Fig. 49.3(d)). Figure 49.3(e) outlines the procedures used in making these estimates.

Combining data sets to improve the quality of data capture

The integration of different data sets can greatly assist the data capture process. Work by Mason *et al.* (1988) shows the benefit of incorporating data from topographical maps with remotely sensed data in order to improve the capture of land cover information (Plate 49.3). Specifically, land unit boundaries were linked with remotely sensed data using a knowledge-based approach. The basic system first involved an initial segmentation into polygons using boundaries derived from the topographical map. The segmentation was then revised using information from the remotely sensed data, together with external knowledge embodied as rules in a rule base. This allowed a preliminary identification of the broad classes to which each polygon belonged and this information was then used to guide the classification of the remotely sensed data. Three types of rules were used:

- *Domain consistency rules*. These were concerned with knowledge of a region's characteristics and are used to increase or decrease confidence in the broad classes to which each polygon is assigned.

- *Split rules*. These were used to assess whether a polygon should be split. One rule found to be very important was whether a polygon was homogeneous in terms of its combined spectral and textural properties.

- *Merge rules*. Conversely, these rules were used to assess where congruent regions should be merged. For example, if one region was already assigned to the 'field' class then it was merged with an adjacent class if the merged region was more like a field as measured by a reduction in concavity.

Classification using the remotely sensed data was carried out using a region or polygon-based

Environmental Databases and GIS

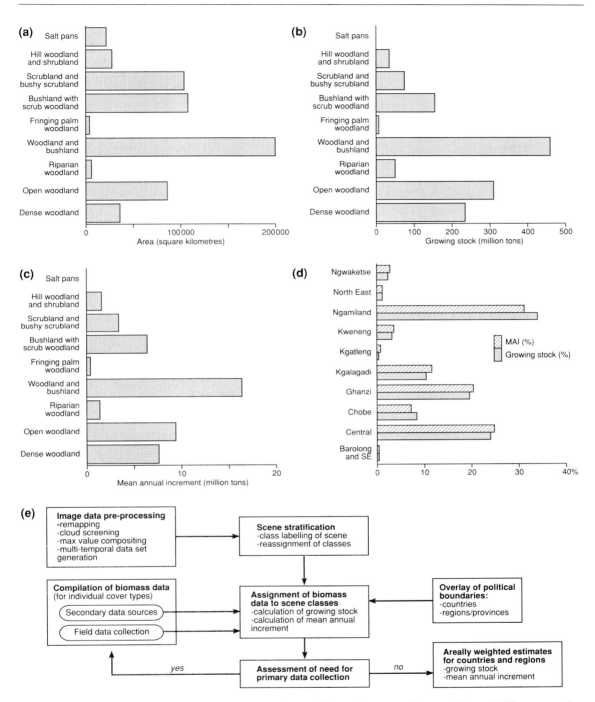

Fig. 49.3 Estimation of fuelwood supplies in southern Africa using remotely sensed data (Millington *et al.* 1989): (a) areal estimates of the extent of biomass classes in Botswana; (b) growing stock of biomass classes for Botswana; (c) mean annual increment for each of the biomass classes for Botswana; (d) biomass attributes by province for Botswana. The percentage of the country's mean annual increment and the percentage of the national growing stock are depicted for each province; (e) overall procedures for estimating fuelwood supplies.

approach rather than a conventional pixel-based approach. Moreover, the class to which a polygon could be allocated was restricted by the broad class to which it had been previously assigned using the rule base. Thus, if a polygon was classified as a field, the class could only be one of the agricultural classes. As a result of applying this approach, areal errors of land cover classification were reduced from 24–29 per cent to 8–9 per cent within the test areas investigated. In Plate 49.3, the benefits of using this approach can be appreciated by comparing the reference data collected on the ground with the results of classification using the per-pixel data and the segmented image. An important methodological point to make about this approach is that the successful integrated use of data sets was achieved through external knowledge and modelling of the phenomena depicted – and not merely by a simple overlay of the data.

Assessment of the visual impacts on the physical environment

In the previous example, remotely sensed data and topographic data were used in an integrated manner to improve the capture of derived land cover information. An alternative benefit of such integration which has become increasingly common is for the visualization of terrain, where remotely sensed data are draped over digital elevation models. This technique not only permits the current appearance of landscape to be depicted but also allows the impact of various changes to be simulated. For example, Quarmby and Saull (1990) carried out an assessment of the impact of residential building on part of rural north Hampshire in the United Kingdom (Plate 49.4). Perspective views were generated from a number of locations and then the impact of screening by trees was investigated by 'growing' belts of trees vertically on top of the digital elevation model. The results showed that, from some viewpoints, this had a significant ameliorating effect but that, from several others, little of the development was obscured.

Incorporation of physical models in a GIS framework

The previous example showed how 'what if' questions could be posed in an informal way in the context of visual impact. However, predictive questions in the environmental sciences often require the use of explicit quantitative models. One example where this has been carried out successfully is in the field of gravitationally induced sediment transport, especially in the cases of pyroclastic surges (Malin and Sheridan 1982), large-scale landslides and small-scale mudflows (Wadge 1988). As one example, Wadge and Isaacs (1988) have developed a procedure based on the integration of digital elevation models with a model for pyroclastic eruptions and have applied it to the Soufriere Hills Volcano on Montserrat in the West Indies. The model has essentially three variables, namely the site of the vent (which is locatable approximately using geophysical observations of pre-eruption activity), the height of the eruption column and an energy decay function. A conceptual representation of this model is given in Fig. 49.4.

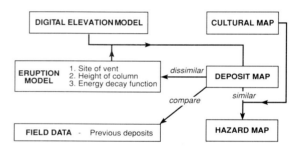

Fig. 49.4 Flow diagram of hazard modelling process (from Wadge and Isaacs 1988).

Application of this model allowed a variety of maps of geological deposits to be generated over the terrain model (Plate 49.5). Comparison of these maps with field data of previous deposits showed good agreement. Constraining the eruption model in terms of parameters (such as the height of the column and the angle which the collapse makes with the horizontal) and using values typical of such conditions allows production of a map showing the resultant expansion of pyroclastic deposits, along with pre-eruption hazards from fumarolic areas. This was used to generate a hazard map (Plate 49.6), which can be used not only as a basis for land use planning but also for planning the sequential evacuation of threatened areas. Wadge (1988) has applied this approach to a number of other gravity flows and slope instabilities and has shown how the use of raster-based GIS operations, combined with

Table 49.6 Examples of GIS operations which can be used for modelling of mass movements within a raster-based GIS (from Wadge 1988).

Class of operation	Specific operation	Example of application
Connectivity	Optimal path identification	Steepest downhill gradient path for the flow paths of debris flows
Characterizing neighbourhoods	Slope determination	First derivative of DEM for landslide stability and dynamic flow models
Overlay	Arithmetic	Calculate deposit thickness in energy balance model (e.g., cone height-original DEM height)
Pixel re-classification	(a) Isolating	Locate and display unstable pixels in landslide potential map
	(b) Contouring	Display thickness of deposit in energy balance models.
Region re-classification	Edge definition	Comparison of boundaries derived from models with those obtained from other sources (e.g. remotely sensed images and/or field work)

appropriate physical equations, can be used to model their various types of behaviour (Table 49.6).

B. Use of stratified sampling system for predictive purposes

Prediction of the behaviour of the environment is often dependent on spatially comprehensive sets of data; these are often not available and limitations in resources or time may preclude collection of new, census-type data. An alternative approach is to use a scheme of land and ecological characterization based on a relatively small sample of the total area. One such scheme is the land classification scheme of the UK's Institute of Terrestrial Ecology (Bunce, Barr and Whittaker 1982), which involves three main phases:

- *Land classification*. In this phase, classes were determined by analysis of 282 attributes recorded from 1228 1 km^2 sample areas drawn from a grid over the whole of the United Kingdom at 15 km by 15 km intersections of the National Grid. The attributes describe the climate, topography, geology and features of human occupancy which were used to define 32 land classes. The procedure allows the identification of indicators which can then be used to assign any other sample 1 km^2 to the appropriate class.

- *Ecological characterization*. In this second phase, field data are added to the initial classification to improve their characterization. The patterns of land use throughout the 1 km squares are mapped, along with ecological information such as hedgerow length and woodland composition.

- *Predictive phase*. Since the numbers of squares in the country belonging to each class are already known, it is possible to estimate any given factor for the whole country based on the conditions within a small sample of squares.

Among the many applications of this approach are the environmental assessment of changes in the farming industry in response to changes in the European Community's Common Agricultural Policy and, consequently, the prediction of impacts on the rural environment (Harvey 1986). Similarly, the area of land which could be available for energy crops was estimated for the Department of Energy and this was combined with existing land use information to determine an optimal allocation of land for wood energy production (Mitchell *et al.* 1983). In more local surveys in South-West England, the land classification scheme was used to provide input for forestry and agricultural models in order to assess the scope for economic integration of wood production in agriculture (Dartington Institute 1986). These various applications have demonstrated that survey, monitoring and modelling in the rural environment can be carried out effectively by combining limited amounts of sampled field survey data with a classification based on readily available environmental characteristics.

IMPROVING THE ACCESSIBILITY OF ENVIRONMENTAL DATABASES

The existence of environmental databases does not guarantee their easy access or availability. This is in part because of questions of confidentiality, cost and inappropriate physical storage mechanisms. It also arises, however, because of the highly dispersed character of many environmental data sets and the varying formats of available digital data. To solve the latter problem, considerable effort has been expended in defining and setting up exchange formats for digital data (see Guptill 1991 in this volume): in some environmental fields, there is now widespread national and even international agreement on such formats. In the field of cataloguing and indexing of data there is much less agreement on standards but recent work, as described below, has done much to demonstrate the potential of an automated graphic approach.

Because of the size and diversity of environmental data sets in terms of their formats, heterogeneity and coverage, users often face major hindrances in simply finding what data are available. Machine-readable catalogues form one partial solution to this problem but these do not necessarily provide easily accessible information on which data are available within a particular area. This problem is particularly acute when information is required from more than one particular data set. One possible solution to this is graphics-based spatial data retrieval, associated with automated graphic indexing. Typically, such experiments include the display at small scale of the environmental attributes, along with information on the availability of more detailed data together with their physical location.

One such indexing facility is the Natural Environment Research Council's Marine Atlas project of the seas around the British Isles (Mason and Townshend 1988; Robinson 1991). Figure 49.5 shows the main components of the system. Data and information from the data holders flow into a central Marine Information System data bank via a process of selection and processing carried out at the discretion of the data holders themselves. There is also a common data bank holding widely used data sets such as coastlines. Only a small sample of data will be included, since the main intent is not to provide a large comprehensive geo-referenced data bank but to provide meta-information (information about information) concerning the availability and quality of environmental data. Graphical display is via VDU displays or may take a number of other forms, such as catalogue lists or traditional atlas displays (Plate 49.7). This particular system is not intended to provide a completely comprehensive catalogue but is intended in part to act as a 'shop window' to make the user community more aware of the various marine data sets that are available. A similar approach has been proposed by Adlam, Clayton and Kelk (1988) in the development of a prototype of a central geosciences data index with a graphics interface. A much more general model and flexible approach for the explicit management of data sets, rather than just their cataloguing, has been suggested by Abel (1989). An interchange format has already been proposed for the exchange of directory-level information about data sets among information systems by NSSDC (1989).

CONCLUSIONS

The examples discussed in the previous section demonstrate the power of GIS for improving the quality of environmental databases and expanding their applications. It is important to restate, however, that the mere existence of these benefits does not in itself ensure the widespread adoption of GIS. Some large and valuable data sets and complex systems for their management already exist to support environmental science and its applications. Converting existing data sets to forms appropriate to GIS and achieving the transition from traditional to modern methods of spatial information handling will be a complex, expensive and time-consuming process: moreover, it will have to compete for resources with many other more glamorous activities. However, without the

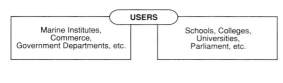

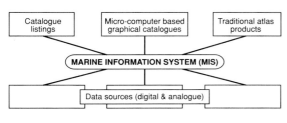

Figure 49.5 Proposed schematic outline of the NERC Marine Atlas (Robinson 1991; Mason and Townshend 1988).

necessary investment in the infrastructure of information handling, our ability to make best use of our data in addressing fundamental environmental questions will be profoundly damaged.

REFERENCES

Abel D J (1989) A model for data set management in large spatial information systems. *International Journal of Geographical Information Systems* **3**: 291–302

Adlam K H, Clayton A R, Kelk B (1988) A demonstrator for the National Sciences Geodata Index. *International Journal of Geographical Information Systems* **2**: 161–70

Allen J H (1988) The World Data Center System, international data exchange and global change. In: Mounsey H M (ed.) *Building Databases for Global Science*. Taylor & Francis, London, pp. 138–53

Bull G A (1960) Comparison of rain-gauges. *Nature* **185**: 437–38

Bunce R G H, Barr C J, Whittaker H A (1982) A stratification system for ecological sampling. In: Fuller R M (ed.) *Ecological Mapping from, Ground, Air and Space*. Institute of Terrestrial Ecology Symposium No. 10. Monk's Wood, Cambridgeshire, pp. 39–46

Burrough P A (1991) Soil information systems. In: Maguire D J, Goodchild M F and Rhind D W (eds.) *Geographical Information Systems: principles and applications*. Longman, London, pp. 153–69, Vol 2

Clark D M, Hastings D A, Kineman J J (1991) Global databases and their implications for GIS. In: Maguire D J, Goodchild M F, Rhind D W (eds.) *Geographical Information Systems: principles and applications*. Longman, London, pp. 217–31, Vol 2

Dartington Institute (1986) *The Potential for Forestry on the Culm Measures Farms of south west England*. Dartington Institute, Dartington Devon

Davis F W, Simonett D S (1991) GIS and remote sensing. In: Maguire D J, Goodchild M F, Rhind D W (eds.) *Geographical Information Systems: principles and applications*. Longman, London, pp. 191–213, Vol 1

Earth System Sciences Committee (1988) *Earth System Science: a closer view*. NASA, Washington DC.

Ellis M Y (1978) *Coastal Mapping Handbook*. United States Government Printing Office, Washington DC

Goward S N, Markham B, Dye D G, Dulaney W, Yang J (1991) Normalized difference vegetation index measurements from the Advanced Very High Resolution Radiometer. *Remote Sensing of Environment* **35**: 257–78

Guptill S C (1991) Spatial data exchange and standardization. In: Maguire D J, Goodchild M F, Rhind D W (eds.) *Geographical Information Systems: principles and applications*. Longman, London, pp. 515–30, Vol 1

Harvey D R (1986) *Countryside Implications for England and Wales of Possible Changes in the Common Agricultural Policy*. Centre for Agricultural Strategy, University of Reading UK

Hummel J, Reck R (1979) A global surface albedo model. *Journal of Applied Meteorology* **18**: 239–53

ICSU (International Council for Scientific Unions) (1989) *Guide to the World Data Center System: part I(a) Updates, Corrections and Additions to Part 1*. ICSU, Boulder Colorado Intergovernmental Oceanographic Commission (1987) GF3, A general formatting system for geo-referenced data, vol 2, Technical description of the GF3 Format and code tables. *Intergovernmental Oceanographic Commission, Manuals and Guides* **17**: UNESCO, Paris

Justice C O, Townshend J R G, Holben B N, Tucker C J (1986) Analysis of the phenology of global vegetation using meteorological satellite data. *International Journal of Remote Sensing* **6**: 1271–318

Langran G (1989) Accessing spatio-temporal data in a temporal GIS. *Proceedings of AUTOCARTO9*. ACSM/ASPRS, Falls Church Virginia, pp. 191–98

Lieth H (1975) Primary production of the major vegetation units of the world. In: Lieth H, Whittaker R H (eds.) *Primary productivity of the Biosphere* (Ecological Studies 14). Springer-Verlag, New York, pp. 203–15

Malin M C, Sheridan M F (1982) Computer-assisted mapping of pyroclastic surges. *Science* **217**: 637

Mason D C, Townshend J R G (1988) Research related to

geographical information systems at the Natural Environment Research Council's Unit for Thematic Information System. *International Journal of Geographical Information Systems* **2**: 121–41

Mason D C, Corr D G, Cross A, Hogg D C, Lawrence D H, Petrou M, Tailor A M (1988) The use of digital map data in the segmentation and classification of remotely sensed images. *International Journal of Geographical Information Systems* **2**: 195–218

Matthews E (1983) Global vegetation and land use: new high resolution databases for climate studies. *Journal of Climatology and Applied Meteorology* **22**: 474–87

Millington A C, Townshend J R G, Kennedy P, Saull R, Prince S, Madams R (1989) *Biomass Assessment in the SADCC Region*. Earthscan Publications, London

Mitchell C W (1973) *Terrain Evaluation*. Longman, London

Mitchell C P, Brandon O H, Bunce R G H, Barr C J, Tranter R B, Downing P, Pearce M L, Whittaker H A (1983) Land availability for production of wood energy in Great Britain. In: Strub A, Cartier P, Scleser G (eds.) *Energy from Biomass. Proceedings 2nd European Community Conference, Berlin*. Applied Science, London, pp. 159–63

Mooneyhan D W (1988) Applications of Geographic Information Systems within the United Nations Environmental Programme. In: Mounsey H M, Tomlinson R F (eds.) *Building Databases for Global Science*. Taylor & Francis, London, pp. 315–29

Mounsey H M (1991) Multisource, multinational environmental GIS: lessons learnt from CORINE. In: Maguire D J, Goodchild M F, Rhind D W (eds.) *Geographical Information Systems: principles and applications*. Longman, London, pp. 185–200, Vol 2

NERC (1988) *Geographical Information in the Environmental Sciences*. (Report of the Working Group on Geographic Information), Natural Environment Research Council, Swindon

NSSDC (National Space Science Data Center) (1989) *Directory Interchange Format Manual, Version 1.0*. NASA Goddard Space Flight Center, Greenbelt Maryland

Olson J S, Watts J, Allison L (1983) *Carbon in Live Vegetation of Major World Ecosystems*. US Department of Energy contract No. W-7405–ENG-26. Oak Ridge Laboratory, Oak Ridge Tennessee

Pellew R A, Harrison J D (1988) A global database on the status of biological diversity: the IUCN perspective. In: Mounsey H M, Tomlinson R F (eds.) *Building Databases for Global Science*. Taylor & Francis, London, pp. 330–9

Quarmby N A, Saull R J (1990) The use of perspective views in local planning. *International Journal of Remote Sensing* **11**: 1329–30

Raper J F, Kelk B (1991) Three-dimensional GIS. In: Maguire D J, Goodchild M F, Rhind D W (eds.) *Geographical Information Systems: principles and applications*. Longman, London, pp. 299–317, Vol 1

Rasool S I, Ojima D S (1989) Pilot studies for remote sensing and data management. *International Geosphere Biosphere Program, Global Change Report No. 8.*

Robinson G R (1991) The UK digital Marine Atlas Project: an evolutionary approach towards a Marine Information System. *International Hydrographic Review*, Monaco. **68**: 39–51

Smith D R, Paradis A R (1989) Three-dimensional GIS for the Earth Sciences. *Proceedings of AUTOCARTO9*. ACSM/ASPRS, Falls Church Virginia, pp. 324–35

Topographic Science Working Group (1988) *Topographic Science Working Group Report to the Land Processes Branch, Earth Science and Applications Division*. NASA Headquarters Lunar and Planetary Institute, Houston

Tucker C J, Townshend J R G, Goff T E (1985) African land-cover classification using satellite data. *Science* **227**: 369–75

Wadge G (1988) The potential of GIS modelling of gravity flows and slope instabilities. *International Journal of Geographic Information Systems* **2**: 143–52

Wadge G, Isaacs M C (1988) Mapping the volcanic hazards from Soufriere Hills Volcano, Montserrat, West Indies using an image processor. *Journal of the Geological Society* **145**: 541–52

Webster R (1978) Mathematical treatment of soil information. *Proceedings of the 11th International Congress of Soil Science, Edmonton, Canada*, Volume 3. pp. 161–90

Webster R, Butler B E (1976) Soil classification and survey studies at Ginninderra. *Australian Journal of Soil Science* **14**: 1–24

GLOBAL DATABASES AND THEIR IMPLICATIONS FOR GIS

D M CLARK, D A HASTINGS AND J J KINEMAN

Interdisciplinary study of the Earth as a global system has revolutionized the thinking of earth scientists. Multidisciplinary databases of global thematic data are currently being collected, developed and integrated for use in such studies. The tools needed for this new area of research will include GIS. Many of the early applications of GIS were originally for small-area urban planning and assessments and, because of this, GIS are not currently optimized for the much more sophisticated and greatly expanded applications currently emerging from various global research programmes. These programmes are described and the implications for GIS examined in relation to global science. A few case studies of GIS applications employing global databases are reviewed. Examples of possible future developments in GIS to optimize global studies are discussed.

CREATING A GLOBAL INTERDISCIPLINARY SCIENCE

The study of the Earth is undergoing a revolution. Historically, the Earth was studied separately by biologists, ecologists, geologists, geophysicists and other scientists. Specialists traditionally concentrate on their own discipline and research topic, largely refraining from truly cross-disciplinary studies. Despite this, it has long been recognized that if the study of a single facet of the Earth system (e.g. ecological systems' response to drought) was made without knowing something about what was causing the effect (e.g. secular variation of rainfall patterns), then it was not possible to have a comprehensive understanding of the entire problem. Besides limiting the scientific breadth of a study, such specialization tends to limit the approach. For example, the physicist and chemist often try to idealize their experiments, forever influenced by the frictionless pulleys, massless springs and idealized substances of theory. This is of limited value in the real world. On the other hand, applied scientists may become so involved in the complexities of their laboratory (the Earth) and the unique aspects of one system as to forgo theoretical rigour. Interdisciplinary global science now calls for a balance between theoretical and applied approaches.

Until recently, much of the research effort was tied up in the definition and research of each discipline-specific problem. It is now realized that research in the earth sciences has progressed to a point where all of the many parts of the Earth system must be studied together and integrated if a reasonable attempt is to be made to understand fully the problem under study and to predict the nature of the processes involved. This concept has been called Earth System Science (Earth System Sciences Committee 1988) or, simply known by the phrase which describes its predictive goal, Global Change (IGBP Special Committee 1988). To make this a reality, there are three necessary links to be forged: between narrowly focused disciplines and interdisciplinary studies; between theoretical and applied research; and between local and global scales.

The means, methods and tools to perform these interdisciplinary studies have only come to be available to researchers for the last 10 or 20 years.

Of course, computers are the most fundamental tool because of the large volumes of data necessary and, in some cases, the huge computational capabilities required. While supercomputer-based modelling systems are often needed to handle theoretical studies, GIS – an extension of computerized data handling and analysis – are a natural tool for observationally-based studies.

THE NECESSARY DATA

In addition to having the computer tools for studying global change, perhaps the most critical aspect is the data. Many of the databases which are used currently are regional or, if global, are of non-uniform coverage, usually due to sampling inconsistencies or varying needs in different areas. Nevertheless, many global databases already exist (Kineman, Hastings and Colby 1986) and efforts are under way to identify and catalogue them. It is obvious that accurate and comprehensive global databases must be available to the global change researcher for use in GIS if any real progress is going to be made in understanding earth processes; an untenable procedure, in this field at least, is for individuals to collect all their own data.

Unninayar (1988) divided global databases into three categories. The first of these, Global Reference Data Sets, are those which represent 'normal' or long-term averages (e.g. climate parameters, soils, population density). The main consideration in this category is that there is some type of long-duration invariance which may be on the scale of decades to centuries. He terms this the 'mean state'. The second category is Global Monitoring Data Sets (Synoptic), which reflect the Earth 'change' on a temporal and spatial scale. These are variable in temporal resolution (months to years) and are snapshots of Earth conditions such as snow cover, wind and precipitation. His third category is the Global Monitoring Data Sets (Time Series) which consist of a time series of data or indices measured at points or averaged for cells. Examples of these are surface heat flux, vegetation index and sea surface temperature.

For all of the above types of global databases, satellite remote sensing provides perhaps the most powerful tool to study the Earth as a system since, for the first time, the entire Earth can be seen as an entity (see Townshend 1991 in this volume). However, remotely sensed Earth imagery and corresponding digital data pose a challenge to GIS implementation for global studies in that the data quantities are large and most GIS are not optimized for this large-scale implementation. In addition, the data are often in unusual formats and in combinations of raster and vector form at different scales; few present-day GIS can handle such data without considerable pre-processing. On the other hand, there will continue to be a need for reliable field measurements made *in situ*. Finally, many historical records of past Earth conditions will be invaluable to global change research. To unite these types of data, the way in which local data are linked with global studies must be improved and, to do this, GIS will be required.

THE NEED FOR GIS IN GLOBAL STUDIES

It has been suggested by many (e.g. the IGBP Special Committee 1988) that GIS functionality will be needed, even required, for any study of global change. In many cases, the digital databases involved will be global in nature, multispatial, multitemporal and multidisciplinary. Regardless of the form and format, many of the databases will be large. However, GIS were originally developed for local or regional-scale applications, such as urban planning (Smith *et al.* 1987). With these new interdisciplinary studies which view the Earth as a complete system, there is a need to improve methods of handling global databases for analysis. In particular, there is a need to improve the specialized GIS functions that would support analysis of patterns, trends and associations and to add the means for linking GIS analysis with theoretical modelling systems. This raises a multitude of issues ranging from simple cartographic projection and representational problems to conceptual issues in modelling global systems.

GLOBAL PROGRAMMES

The Earth has been studied on a global basis from the earliest times. The first global programme may have been in the third century BC when Eratosthenes estimated the Earth's circumference by using shadows cast by the sun! With the advent of modern technology in the twentieth century, many truly global programmes were conducted which ultimately led to new ways of thinking about the Earth system. Programmes of the 1950s, 1960s and 1970s, such as the International Geophysical Year and the Global Atmospheric Research Programme, laid the groundwork for many of the current global equivalents and initiated the development of many global databases, some of which are still used today. The need for new and large global databases to support global science is becoming much more common, in part due to advancing technology and in part due to the increasing complexity of a global society. For example, the advent of supercomputers has given rise to vastly more sophisticated numerical climate models which, in turn, drive the need for improved digital thematic global databases such as topography and land cover. Moreover, the routine availability of remotely sensed data has encouraged the development of different types of derived global databases.

Many national- and international-scale programmes to study the Earth system and global change have been proposed or implemented in the 1980s and early 1990s. Numerous global databases will be required to support them. Each programme description identifies GIS as critical to the success of the enterprise. Some examples of these programmes are given below to illustrate their scope and the need for GIS involvement.

The ICSU International Geosphere–Biosphere Programme

In September 1986, the International Council of Scientific Unions or ICSU established the International Geosphere–Biosphere Programme (IGBP): A Study of Global Change. The IGBP is a 10- to 20-year programme of monitoring and research on the global system. Its objective is 'to describe and understand the interactive, physical and biological processes that regulate the Earth system, the unique environment that provides for life, the changes that are occurring in this system, and the manner in which they are influenced by human actions' (IGBP Special Committee 1988).

Many nations have established national committees and have begun actively to plan and implement their respective programmes. The major themes of the IGBP are:

- documenting and predicting global change;

- observing and improving our understanding of dominant global forcing functions;

- improving our understanding of interactive phenomena in the total Earth system; and

- assessing the effects of global change that will cause large scale and important modifications in the availability of renewable and non-renewable resources.

The IGBP has formed a Working Group on Data and Information Systems. It has defined broad categories of environmental data required for global change studies while also noting that GIS will be a 'powerful tool for integrating and making accessible Earth land-based data of diverse types' (IGBP Special Committee 1988). The initial data 'categories', or areas of the environmental spectrum, identified as critical to global change research by the Working Group pertain to the solar flux, stratosphere (and above), clouds and the Earth radiation budget, tropospheric chemistry, vegetation in the hydrological cycle, the land surface, oceans, sea level and snow and ice. It is realized that, to address fully the issues in the IGBP objectives, other types of global data will eventually be needed, especially socio-economic databases (e.g. population and industrial productivity). It is readily apparent from the IGBP plans that GIS will have to evolve to satisfy fully the needs of global change studies.

In order to begin to address the 'data and systems' issues of the IGBP, the Working Group has begun four projects. These are the Land Cover Change Pilot Project, the Global Change Diskette Project (now called the Global Change Database Project), the End-to-End Systems Study on Surface Temperature Data and an IGBP Data Directory Project. These are described in detail in IGBP Special Committee (1989). The Global Change Database Project (GCDP), for example, is aimed at regional applications of a global database analysis using a GIS (which is discussed in more detail later). The GCDP is an effort to assemble various global environmental databases on floppy disks (and eventually on more advanced computer media like CD-ROM); to integrate the data with a sophisticated but widely available GIS; and to disseminate the package to global change scientists world-wide for evaluation and experimentation in actual global change problems. Phase I of the project is for Africa. The next phases may include South America and Asia. The databases contain satellite-derived NOAA vegetation indices for 1985–88, plus topography, soils, ecosystems and other thematic and cartographic data. A popular personal-computer-based GIS accompanies the databases, along with training materials. Eventually, this project will evolve from floppy-disk-based regional databases to CD-ROM-based global databases with a GIS capable of addressing various aspects of global change studies (Kineman, Clark and Croze 1990).

The GCDP has highlighted awareness that existing global databases, many of which were compiled from scientific literature in isolated laboratories, contain numerous errors and the data are sometimes very misleading. Some of the problems include inappropriate definition of classes, inaccurate (or worse!) classification of specific areas, less (or more) spatial detail in the derived data sets than is justified by the original data, registration and projection errors, and (typically) no information on data quality. Interest in forming international cooperative groups to compile, analyse and test global environmental data has been stimulated by the GCDP. This is a necessary precursor to having truly useful GIS systems with highly usable global databases.

US Global Change Research Programme

Partly in response to IGBP, but also because a better understanding of the Earth system is critical to improving our ability to predict Earth processes (including weather prediction, a very important public service), various US government agencies have begun a programme of global change research. The US national goal is very similar to that of the IGBP, that is 'to gain an adequate predictive understanding of the interactive physical, geological, chemical, biological and social processes that regulate the total Earth system, and hence establish the scientific basis for national and international policy formulation and decisions related to natural and human-induced changes in the global environment and their regional impacts' (Committee on Earth Sciences 1989). This programme closely follows and complements the similar plan developed by the US National Academy of Sciences' Committee for the IGBP (Committee on Global Change 1988).

Numerous US government agencies are participating in the US national programme, as well as many academic institutions. Each agency's programme has been described in detail in Committee on Earth Sciences (1989) but two are described in more detail below.

NASA Earth System Science Programme

The NASA programme of earth system science may be the widest ranging and most comprehensive global programme ever envisaged. Its goal is 'to obtain a scientific understanding of the entire Earth system on a global scale by describing how its component parts and their interactions have evolved, how they function, and how they may be expected to continue to evolve on all time scales' (Earth System Sciences Committee 1988).

The complexity of this task is evident from the conceptual model of the Earth system processes as applicable to time scale of decades to centuries shown graphically in Plate 50.1. The diagram relates the physical climate system to biogeochemical cycles. Though not shown, there is a similar model developed for the time scale of thousands to billions of years. Figure 50.1 depicts the climate system portion of the model in an easier-to-visualize schematic form. Close examination of the conceptual model reveals that traditional GIS applications are applicable only to portions of the model (e.g. land use, terrestrial ecosystems) for which empirical studies are most needed. Many global databases will be required for each aspect of this model; an extensive list of potential databases was derived for it. Table 50.1 lists the global variables required for a long-term study of global change. Based upon present understanding of the processes and interactions involved, these

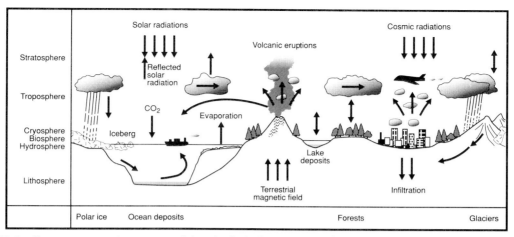

Fig. 50.1 Components and processes of the physical climate system (*Source*: Unninayar 1988).

Table 50.1 The variables of which measurements are required for a long-term study of global change as recommended by the Earth System Science Committee (1988).

External forcing	Palaeoclimate	Land surface properties
solar irradiance	atmospheric composition	surface temperature
ultraviolet flux	land and sea temperature	incident solar flux
volcanic emissions	vegetation	snow cover
	ice volume and extent	snow water equivalent
Trace gases	sea level	ice sheet volume (changes)
carbon dioxide	lake levels	river runoff
nitrous oxide		surface characteristics
methane	**Ocean variables**	land use
chlorofluoromethanes	sea surface temperature	surface wetness
ozone	sea ice extent	soil moisture
carbon monoxide	sea ice motion	biomes
water vapour	ocean wind stress	topography
nitric acid	sea level	surface structure
hydrogen chloride	incident solar flux	lithology
stratospheric aerosols	subsurface circulation	mineral composition
	ocean chlorophyll	ice sheet elevation
Atmospheric response variables	biogeochemical fluxes	surficial deposits
surface air temperature	ocean carbon dioxide	soils
tropospheric temperature		
surface pressure		**Geophysical variables**
winds		plate motions
tropospheric water vapour		plate deformations
precipitation		polar motion
Earth radiation budget		Earth rotation
clouds		secular magnetic field
tropospheric aerosols		gravity and geoid
		seismic properties
		crustal magnetism

parameters are generally considered as the main priority global change databases for the 1990s. Yet these data sets, even when properly integrated and made available to scientists, will not answer scientific questions directly. It will be essential to develop adequate analytical tools and ways of interfacing empirically-derived results with predictive models. It thus becomes clear that GIS will need to develop in sophistication if they are to be used as an integral part of the programme. New GIS technology will be required to compile the integrated global databases as well as to investigate the relationships between the Earth system processes.

NOAA Climate and Global Change Programme

In contrast to the NASA programme described above, the NOAA Climate and Global Change Programme focuses primarily on the short-term predictive theme of the overall global change programme. Its goal is 'to provide reliable predictions of global climate change and assorted regional implications on time scales ranging from seasons to a century or more' (NOAA 1987).

This predictive goal cannot be realized without an adequate understanding of the causes and the nature of climate variability in terms of global processes. Many of the global databases identified in Table 50.1 will be needed as inputs, for development and validation of the new long-term climate and short-term weather prediction models in the NOAA programme. Fortunately, NOAA operates environmental observation and monitoring networks ranging from the US weather satellite system to *in situ* weather stations world-wide. Because of its global mission for oceanic and atmospheric monitoring and prediction, NOAA has been using GIS-like applications for global studies since its foundation in the early 1970s. All of these early systems were heavily customized and, since large quantities of human and fiscal resources were invested in them, many still survive today. But, with the many orders of magnitude increase in the amount of data needed to study these complex Earth processes on a truly global scale, new GIS technology will certainly be needed within NOAA.

The staff of NOAA's National Geophysical Data Center (NGDC) have used GIS for scientific data management, analysis and (static) spatial modelling since 1980. Some image processing and raster GIS systems have analytical and display tools to depict and assess errors (and other characteristics) of spatial data sets, and to apply such data to scientific modelling. Vector GIS technology is useful for digitizing and editing paper maps (represented originally in vector-like points, lines and polygons), for conversion to raster for more complete and sophisticated analysis and for storing vector boundary data for overlay in hybrid systems.

The IGBP Global Change Database Project, mentioned earlier, is an extension of NGDC efforts to compile global-scale, multivariate spatial databases. Several examples of such databases are shown in Plates 50.2, 50.3 and 50.4. Plate 50.2 was derived at NGDC from the NOAA AVHRR vegetation index and shows the African portion of the global database of monthly composites for September 1985. Plate 50.3 is a re-sampled version of the 30-minute gridded ecosystems classifications database which has been enhanced at NGDC. Plate 50.4 depicts global data including elevations, bathymetry and satellite magnetic anomalies from NASA's MAGSAT. In Plate 50.4(a), colour level-slicing shows different value ranges of elevation and bathymetry; shaded relief shows details of the global terrain as well as artifacts of the database, which contains several estimates of elevation in areas lacking actual elevation measurements; it is part of a stereo pair which has computer-generated parallax allowing the Earth to be viewed in three dimensions. Plate 50.4(b) has satellite anomalies from MAGSAT superimposed on the shaded relief base from Plate 50.4(a) to enhance data interpretation. Plate 50.4(c) shows the same MAGSAT anomalies, filtered to enhance the shorter wavelengths; this appears to correlate better with crustal geology on land (and, in some cases, with systematic noise in the data compilation in some areas at sea; note the north–south oriented stripes caused by varying orbital heights used in the data compilation). Plate 50.4(d) shows the original MAGSAT anomaly map for comparison.

Other National and International Programmes

Several other national and international programmes have been implemented for the general improvement of global databases or to fulfil a specific need of the scientific community. In almost all cases, these programmes are being implemented to support global change studies or at least will greatly facilitate the study of global processes.

ICA World Digital Database for Environmental Science

The World Digital Database for Environmental Science (WDDES) started as a joint effort of the International Cartographic Association and the International Geographical Union to develop a standard global digital database of cartographic 'base' map data for use in global studies (Bickmore 1987). The types of data to be incorporated into this database include Earth relief (topography and bathymetry), coastlines, hydrology and cultural information. The project plan noted that there were several global map series that could be suitable for digitizing to produce the proposed database. An analysis was carried out by the ICA as well as by others (e.g. Rhind and Clark 1988) on the suitability of the different map series to fulfil the programme objectives. As a result, the best consistent resolution was determined to be that provided by the 1:1 million Operational Navigational Charts (ONC) map series of the US Defense Mapping Agency (DMA) and its collaborators.

DMA has started the process of digitizing the ONCs and these will become generally available by 1992. The resultant database will be in all-vector format (e.g. the topography will be in vector contours). The size will be enormous (about 5 Gb), so the 'next generation' of GIS will be needed to use these data on a global basis. The ICA WDDES Commission has recommended that, in addition to the information shown on the maps, supplemental data could be included in the digital database, which would improve the usefulness for global change studies. These data include spot elevations, missing topographic contours and first, second, and third order administrative boundaries (country, state or province and county respectively) where available. Incorporating these enhancements to the ONC database in an efficient manner would require a GIS with global functionality, especially for enhancing the database through rigorous quality control procedures.

Global Topography Data Base

In the late 1980s, NASA sponsored a study on the status of global topographic data. The result was a report (Burke and Dixon 1988) that noted the need for Digital Elevation Models (DEMs) of sufficient quality for sophisticated quantitative analysis. The first formal response to the report was the convening of a Topography Workshop held in 1990 at the University of California, Santa Barbara, to discuss possible options for a dedicated space mission to map the Earth topographically. A phased development was tentatively agreed upon:

- *Phase I*, to edit and improve existing global DEMs. The most-used global DEMs are distributed by the NOAA. The data are available on 10- and 5-minute latitude–longitude grids and based on a collection of data sets derived by several US agencies. This level of resolution exceeds that of most global modelling at present, though recent attempts to use GIS for global modelling (Kineman, Hastings and Colby 1986; Kineman, Clark and Croze 1990) are introducing a need for higher resolution. Despite its popularity, there is room for considerable improvement in this data set, especially if used for continental or sub-continental studies.

- *Phase II*, using existing sources to develop a new DEM. AVHRR data can be used stereoscopically (Hastings 1987) to view large areas and may be useful for developing a global DEM on about 1 km pixel size. SPOT data have greater engineering challenges than was first envisaged for developing DEMs, but may be a practical source of global high resolution DEMs (Muller 1989; Muller *et al.* 1988) if costs of data acquisition and processing can be made manageable.

- *Phase III*, to adapt laser altimetric technology for terrestrial applications. This technology has been used to map the topography of the Earth's oceans and is being developed to map the surface of Mars. The Mars mission will have backup hardware that, under favourable conditions, could be placed in orbit about Earth to measure the topography of this planet.

- *Phase IV*, to develop embryonic technology in radar interferometry into a new satellite mission to map the Earth's topography. Radar technology would have advantages in cloud penetration and rapid collection of a detailed global database unattainable with the other methods noted above. However, it is untried technology, requires the longest lead time of the methods discussed above and there are several other engineering and administrative hurdles to be overcome.

It is now almost universally accepted that a research quality, digital topographic database is an essential part of almost any global study. The Santa Barbara Topography Workshop was the start of the effort that will create such a database.

ISSS Soil and Terrain Database Project

The Soil and Terrain Database (SOTER) project is an effort of the International Soil Science Society to create a 1 km resolution database of global soils and corresponding terrain data (Baumgardner 1988; Burrough 1991 in this volume). The database will consist of three types of data: soil types classed as vector polygons; a terrain file; and a point or sampled soil layer file. SOTER is intended to be compatible with other global databases being developed. The data would be compiled on a common base, perhaps the digitized ONCs noted above. A GIS will be necessary to achieve the goals of easy updating and ease of use. Also, the database is intended for decision makers and policy makers so 'usability' is critical and a natural-language GIS (yet to be designed and developed) may well be the ideal choice for SOTER. It is hoped that SOTER will readily be transportable to various countries (especially developing countries) so that it will encourage local quality checking of the existing data and the compilation of higher resolution data.

UNEP/GEMS Global Resources Information Database (GRID)

GRID, part of the UNEP Global Environment Monitoring System, is a system for compiling and analysing environmental data, performing environmental assessments and training scientists in the use of data systems and databases (Fanshawe 1985). GRID's overall mission is to establish a global network for environmental and resource data. Project staff have compiled various global databases of thematic and cartographic data; its pilot phase focused on Africa, where it has acquired additional higher resolution databases. The largely successful pilot phase finished in 1988 and GRID has embarked on the operational phase during the 1990s (UNEP Global Resource Information Database 1988).

GRID will particularly serve the needs of developing countries and, to facilitate this, is currently establishing regional 'nodes' in Bangkok (Thailand), Norway, Sioux Falls (United States), and Mexico City (Mexico) in addition to the two headquarters in Geneva (Switzerland) and Nairobi (Kenya). Its staff are currently engaged in a major GIS training effort for African countries, with the assistance of the UN Institute for Training and Research (UNITAR) and with donations from IBM UK Ltd. A series of GIS training courses and workshops are being conducted whereby governmental groups, acting as a national (and in some cases regional) focus, will receive training, equipment, and long-term assistance to establish GIS capabilities. In 1989, GRID and UNITAR became joint participants in the IGBP Global Change Database Project and conversely the GCDP has joined the GRID/UNITAR workshops.

ICSU World Data Center System

While the World Data Center System is not a database nor really a programme, it is nevertheless a significant mechanism for the compilation of global databases. The WDC system was established by ICSU to provide data archival and dissemination points for data collected during the International Geophysical Year (ICSU Panel on World Data Centers 1987). Currently, there are WDCs in the United States, the Soviet Union, the People's Republic of China, Europe and Japan (see Table 49.2 in Townshend 1991 in this volume). The WDC disciplines address much of the environmental spectrum and include meteorology, oceanography, soils, geophysics, glaciology (snow and ice), solar-terrestrial physics, space science, geology and renewable resources. For over 30 years, databases have been compiled at the WDCs. They have instituted several projects designed to compile data from numerous diverse world-wide sources. All that is usually needed to assemble a global database through the WDC is a special project or programme. Currently, the emphasis on global change is beginning to motivate the WDCs to focus on compilation of global databases. In particular, the new study of global change and the IGBP may cause the expansion of the WDC system to include biological and ecological data centres.

GLOBAL DATABASES IN GIS

As applied to global databases, GIS can be thought of as having two philosophies of implementation. The one of most interest to scientists is the implementation of truly global applications, that is using global databases as an entire entity in the application, not merely using pieces of a global database. This concept will be developed in more detail below. The other concept, which is currently much more common, is a regional application drawn from global databases.

Pre-existing regional data sets may be sources for global compilations. Indeed, they have helped the development of several currently used global data sets. However, there are inherent problems in such an approach, for example rectifying legends designed for regional study to global contexts and filling in gaps in coverage between existing regional compilations. At the very least, regional data sets (and an analysis of their strong and weak points) can be used to help design and implement global compilations.

Regional database systems

There are numerous examples of large regional applications of global databases used for multi-thematic studies (see, for instance, Mounsey 1991 in this volume). Most of these applications have a requirement to perform regional assessments or research, but also have a broader requirement to address an issue on a global basis. Therefore, the user must have both a set of global databases to draw from and a GIS which will handle global aspects such as scale and projection. Generally, projections become a less critical consideration for site-specific mapping of small areas. However, for larger areas of a regional or continental scale, specialized projections become desirable for preserving distance and area values. There are no two-dimensional projections which can preserve both distances and areas on a global scale and so, for data storage reasons, the question becomes more one of providing a reasonable way of defining sample units (i.e. a tessellation). Presently, the latitude/longitude grid is the most common and simplest scheme to work with, although other more complex and efficient methods are being developed.

The CORINE project (Mounsey 1991 in this volume) is a good example of a regional application (although it is not intended for world-wide applications). CORINE was a project to assemble a large amount of multi-thematic environmental data for the Commission of the European Communities. A commercial GIS was adapted and enhanced with custom software to help with environmental policy formulation from the compiled databases. A similar example is the environmental database and GIS developed for Australia (Cocks, Walker and Parvey 1988). In that case, the GIS software consists of various commercial and in-house packages. Again, this system is intended only for continental scale applications. However, both of these systems use geographical subsections from their larger continental-scale databases and systems for the local-scale applications.

Perhaps the best example of the regional database concept is UNEP's Global Resources Information Database, noted earlier. Many parts of the Earth will be studied using GRID, from the South American rain forests to the African savannah to the Arctic tundra. GRID requirements for regional assessments are wide ranging, variable and – as yet – loosely defined. The GIS used by GRID is a combination of commercial and public software.

Global database systems

GIS that utilize completely global databases are few but, as we have seen in the above descriptions of global programmes, the requirements for these types of systems are growing. At NOAA's National Geophysical Data Center, two systems were developed to utilize a global database as a unit. These initial efforts involved inventory systems to describe and query a large global database of geophysical data. The first system is described in detail in Hittelman and Metzger (1983). Known as the Geophysical Data System (GEODAS), it was developed from 1977 onwards. The main database consists of three gigabytes of underway (trackline) marine geophysical data (see Fig. 50.2). GEODAS is an automated data assimilation, inventory, quality control, selection and retrieval system based on customized software. It is a graphics-based system that provides procedures to assimilate data while automatically building a directory and detailed inventory of the database. In addition, the

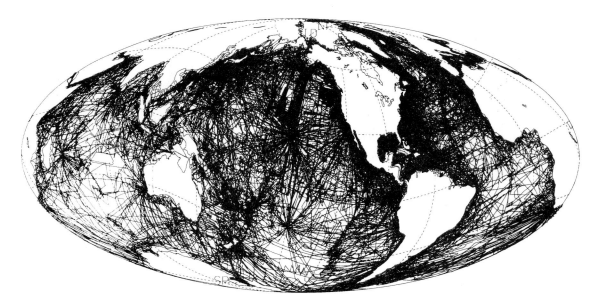

Fig. 50.2 Map output for GEODAS showing global coverage of marine geophysical data (courtesy of D. Metzger, NOAA).

inventory allows selection and retrieval by spatial or temporal criteria. Selection can also be performed by cruise identifier, institution, survey parameter, etc. After selection of the data from the 20 Mb inventory, a graphical and tabular representation of the data is generated for perusal; then the data are selected from the magnetic tape-based archive.

While not a true GIS *sensu stricto* (Maguire 1991 in this volume), GEODAS has many of the functions of a vector GIS and is still used today. Because of this, it was decided to try to adapt a contemporary GIS to a similar application. NOAA archives a large majority of the publicly available aeromagnetic data. The global database consists of 7 gigabytes of data (about 50 million observations or 6 million miles of aeromagnetic survey lines). The GIS selected for the experimental implementation was the non-copyrighted US Map Overlay and Statistical System (MOSS). Just as GEODAS created an inventory file from the actual trackline data, this application sampled about every 100th point from the flightline data using a flight line approximation algorithm. In this way a 'metadata' file was derived which contained multiple attributes including latitude, longitude, survey number, flight line identifier, aircraft altitude and observed magnetic field. The GIS functions could then be applied to derive required inventory information, such as quantity of data within a geographical area and number of flight line miles for a specific search criterion. Overlay functions were used to provide geographical reference information in the output. Figure 50.3 is a sample output from this system.

This experimental prototype implementation of a GIS for a global application was successful in theory but not in practice. Most, if not all, of the GEODAS-type functions could be duplicated using combinations of GIS functions. However, the run-time execution was often very slow or the software had to be modified by re-writing the source code (access to the source code was one of the reasons a public domain GIS was selected). Other problems included the need for software patches to enable the system to handle 360 degree longitude, the International Date Line, and multiple overlays of many flight segments. More recent GIS have, of course, resolved many of the problems encountered in this implementation; other problems now serve as some of the challenges and research topics for the future. Ironically, the NGDC aeromagnetic database is now successfully being implemented in the GEODAS system.

Another application of GIS to global databases is shown by the development of a global relief

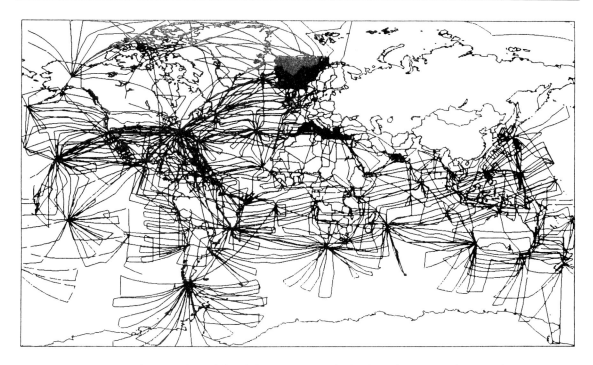

Fig. 50.3 Map output for a portion of the global aeromagnetic database (courtesy of Ron Buhmann, NOAA).

database. In this compilation (shown in Plate 50.4(a)), a combination of 10-minute and 5-minute latitude–longitude gridded data was used; some of the data were based on actual measurements, other data on inference. This provided several challenges to the data compilation effort. For example, the bathymetric model included the generation of surfaces which, where poorly controlled by available data, could rise above sea level. Since this is physically impossible, the developers of the data set truncated these values to zero (sea level). Close inspection of Plate 50.4(a) shows shaded-relief representations of fictitious submarine plateaux off the coast of Argentina that were created in this manner. Early published maps (National Geophysical Data Center 1985) from these data actually had these 'plateaux' coloured as low islands, since the level-slicing technique used was too simple to trap the erroneous data.

Many authors have delved into the requirements of what is needed in a GIS for global interdisciplinary studies (e.g. Billingsley and Urena 1984; Smith *et al.* 1987; Clark and Kineman 1988; Kineman and Clark 1988; Steyaert 1989). From these investigations, it is possible to begin to compile what is needed to utilize GIS for global database applications such as the study of global patterns and change. Table 50.2 represents a list of the functions and utilities required, but is not all-encompassing and will evolve as global studies begin to be implemented in the 1990s.

Finally, as an example of one of the functions needed by a GIS for global applications, a review of the various scales currently being used is appropriate. Global environmental studies will require databases from remotely sensed and *in situ* observing systems, in addition to historical and retrospective data. The GIS systems will ultimately serve as the integration tool for these studies and will need to be designed to integrate data from multiple levels of remote sensing and direct observations (e.g. satellite, aerial, and low-altitude sampling and conventional data gathered on the ground). To provide this capability, the GIS will have to permit data to be stored and manipulated in a hierarchy of grid scales as seen in Table 50.3.

Table 50.2 GIS functions and utilities needed for global applications.

1. Integrated raster and vector functionality
2. Vector-to-raster and raster-to-vector conversions
3. Multiple cartographic (forward and inverse) projection capability
4. GIS functionality with hierarchical directory/catalogue/inventory (metadata representations of the global database) for data manipulation and database access
5. Gridding in various projections
6. Contouring from gridded data
7. Ability to work with global (360 degree) latitude–longitude coordinates as well as projected coordinates
8. Ability to integrate temporal (time series) with spatial data
9. Ability to imput random and gridded point data for large geographical areas (up to global)
10. Ability to convert random or gridded data to different grids using a variety of algorithms (in various projections) and to export them as new data sets
11. Ability to interpolate, abstract or re-sample data using user-specified algorithms
12. Ability to edit vector and raster data using DBMS/spreadsheet algorithms and/or AI procedures
13. Full functionality of standard GIS functions, such as overlay, merge, statistical reports and search by attributes
14. Cartographic output, include shade and fill, attribute placement, contour labelling, legends, annotation, scaling
15. Conversions for all major standard data formats, both input and output, such asDLG and Landsat
16. Integration with full function image processing systems
17. Integration with state-of-the-art Data Base Management System
18. Integration with statistical systems and statistical graphics systems
19. Integration with expert systems and artificial intelligence
20. High efficiency database access using new and innovative database indexing techniques
21. Ability to handle different scales (e.g. raster cell sizes) conveniently
22. Ability to handle 8-bit (byte) integer and real data values in ASCII or binary forms, with conversion and editing capabilities
23. Ability to handle input/output directly (by self-contained tape drives) or indirectly (through a LAN) for ease of large database manipulation
24. Integration with Exploratory Data Analysis (EDA) tools

Table 50.3 Hierarchy of grid scales.

- 1 degree (most global environmental databases at present)
- 1/2 degree (best resolution of majority of available global environmental data)
- 10 arc-minute (approximately matching 16 km global vegetation index coverage)
- 5 arc-minute (9 km at equator, matching topography data for part of world)
- 2 arc-minute (approximately matching extent of 4 km AVHRR Global Area Coverage)
- 30 second (approximately 1 km, matching AVHRR Local Area Coverage data and reference databases under development; also matching existing data for parts of the world)
- 3 second (90 m at equator; matching the DMA Digital Terrain Elevation Data)
- 1 second (approximately 30 m; matching Landsat Thematic Mapper data)
- 1/2 second (15 m at equator; approximately matching SPOT data)

Source: Clark and Kineman (1988).

FUTURE CONSIDERATIONS

The future of GIS in global applications for Earth system studies and global change can be summed up as evolutionary. The greatly increased magnitude and the widely varying scope of the global databases required for these studies will cause the next generation of GIS to have many of the functions described above. Current research is already addressing many of the problems such as integrated raster–vector functionality and variable scale utilization. Some problems will be resolved by the continuously advancing hardware technology.

Artificial intelligence

The real challenge for the 1990s and the next millennium will be the sheer volume of data which GIS will need to handle to derive usable information. This is especially evident for the proposed NASA Earth Observation System (EOS). It has been estimated that 1–10 terabytes (i.e. 10^{12} bytes) of data per day will flow from EOS. Aside from the very serious archival question of the raw data, a perhaps more critical and difficult one will be the methods and procedures of deriving information from the data. Some scientists are of the opinion that GIS-based systems coupled with Artificial Intelligence tools might be the answer (Hastings and Moll 1986). Such Artificial Intelligence (AI) holds promise for improving our ability to do many things, including GIS activity for global applications (Barr and Feigenbaum 1981). AI is often divided into three areas: natural languages, expert systems and machine vision (see Smith and Ye Jiang 1991 in this volume). Each of these offers something to the GIS community. Natural language interfaces on a GIS would allow the resource scientist to use the power of GIS and associated software more effectively, reducing the need for a go-between who is an expert on the software but not on the scientific application. Expert systems contain querying capabilities based partly on knowledge acquired from experts in the scientific field under study. When coupled with GIS systems and databases, the expert system of the future may be able to ask some questions directly of the GIS rather than of the human user. Machine vision involves the detection and identification of patterns in images. Pattern detection in global environmental science is very difficult. However, many environmental features can be described well enough to be retrieved by an image processing system, with the results transferred to a database.

This may be one method of deriving easily used information from global databases.

Environmental modelling

Finally, as the descendants of today's GIS become better adapted for global change studies, they will need to be interfaced more effectively with various mathematical simulation and process models currently being developed. As this interface evolves, GIS methods will provide the observationally based modelling and analysis activities required for both ends of the overall modelling process. The first need is support of observational analysis and exploration with inputs to process models; the second is support for data inter-comparison and model testing.

Considerable research and development is required to meet these challenges. Having emerged from the two specific needs of resource management and image processing, many of today's GIS are still bound by their past. In the early days of GIS development, both computer power and storage space were limiting factors in developing and using sophisticated algorithms. As a consequence, GIS have been largely ignored by the environmental research community until very recently. But, as the possibilities for development of advanced GIS functions are realized, it is to be expected that the descendants of current systems will have vastly different and more numerous applications. For example, many of the GIS elements that have been described earlier will find a place in the integrated software environment. This may well include the use of AI, the use of 'intelligent' enquiry via a spatial equivalent of Exploratory Data Analysis; the use of integral database management (DBMS) software for tracking attribute information; interfaces which track session histories, map lineage and error propagation; animation software for exploring temporal phenomena and certainly other capabilities which are only now being researched. This vision of systems integration is limited by present technical complexities, but mostly by the lack of standard methods in a new and developing Earth systems science which has yet to define itself fully.

CONCLUSIONS

Clearly, the desire for and potential of global GIS and databases are great. However, even global scientists may have little idea of what to ask for in GIS and GIS developers are not currently well informed as to what are the requirements for global science. Pilot projects are needed which will test both applications and innovations and will initiate communication links and cooperative mechanisms so that GIS developers and application scientists can function in concert. The specifications for future systems will probably come from such experimentation and will be evolving continuously. This, coupled with cooperative programmes and information exchange, may be able to facilitate peer review of data, software and methods and thereby develop specifications for a future design of a truly global GIS application.

REFERENCES

Barr A, Feigenbaum E A (eds.) (1981) *The Handbook of Artificial Intelligence*. William Kaufmann Inc., Los Altos

Baumgardner M F (1988) A global soils and terrain digital database. In: Mounsey H M, Tomlinson R F (eds.) *Building Databases for Global Science*. Taylor & Francis, London, pp. 172–80

Environmental Science – An ICA/IGU Project. ICA/IGU Joint Working Group on Atlases and Maps, Oxford

Billingsley F C, Urena J L (1984) Concepts for a global resources information system. *Proceedings of the Ninth Pecora Symposium: spatial information technologies for remote sensing today and tomorrow*. IEEE Computer Society Press, Silver Spring, pp. 123–31

Burke K C, Dixon T M (eds.) (1988) *Topographic Science Working Group, Final Report*. National Aeronautics and Space Administration, Washington DC

Burrough P A (1991) Soil information systems. In: Maguire D J, Goodchild M F, Rhind D W (eds.) *Geographical Information Systems: principles and applications*, Longman, London, pp. 153–69, Vol 2

Clark D M, Kineman J J (1988) Global databases: a NOAA experience. In: Mounsey H M (ed.) *Building Databases for Global Science*. Taylor & Francis, London, pp. 216–33

Cocks K D, Walker P A, Parvey C A (1988) Evolution of a continental-scale geographical information system. *International Journal of Geographical Information Systems* **2** (3): 263–80

Committee on Earth Sciences (1989) *Our Changing planet: the FY90 research plan – the US global change research program*. Office of Science and Technology Policy, Washington DC

Committee on Global Change (1988) *Toward an Understanding of Global Change: Initial priorities for US contributions to the International Geosphere-Biosphere Program*. National Academy Press, Washington DC

Earth System Sciences Committee (1988) *Earth System Science, a closer view*. NASA, Washington DC

Fanshawe J (1985) *Global Resource Information Database*. UNEP Global Environment Monitoring System, Nairobi

Hastings D A (1986a) *Stereo-pair World Map*. NOAA National Geophysical Data Center, Boulder Colorado

Hastings D A (1986b) *Global MAGSAT Scalar Anomaly Maps*. NOAA National Geophysical Data Center, Boulder Colorado

Hastings D A (1987) AVHRR Stereography. *Proceedings of the North American NOAA Polar Orbiter Users Group First Meeting*. NOAA National Geophysical Data Center, Boulder Colorado (USA), pp. 121–4. Reprinted in *Photogrammetric Engineering and Remote Sensing* **54**: cover and p. 105

Hastings D A, Moll S H (1986) Using Geographic Information Systems as an initial approach to Artificial Intelligence in the geological sciences. *Proceedings of the 1st Annual Rocky Mountain Conference on Artificial Intelligence*. BREIT International Inc, Boulder, pp. 191–200

Hittelman A M, Metzger D R (1983) Marine geophysics: database management and supportive graphics. *Computers and Geosciences* **9** (1): 27–33

ICSU Panel on World Data Centers (1987) *Guide to the World Data Center System*. International Council of Scientific Unions, Boulder Colorado

IGBP Special Committee (1988) *The International Geosphere–Biosphere Programme: a study of global change – a plan for action*. Report No. 4. IGBP Secretariat, Stockholm

IGBP Special Committee (1989) *Pilot Studies for Remote Sensing and Data Management*. Report No. 8. IGBP Secretariat, Stockholm

Kineman J J (1989) *Monthly composites of the NOAA Vegetation Index from April 1985 through December 1988 on a 10' grid*. National Geophysical Data Center, Boulder, Colorado

Kineman J J, Clark D M (1988) Connecting global science through spatial data and information technology. In: Aangeenbrug R T, Schiffman Y E (eds.) *Proceedings of the International GIS Symposium: the research agenda*, Volume 1. American Association of Geographers, Falls Church, pp. 209–27

Kineman J J, Clark D M, Croze H (1990 in press) Data integration and modelling for global change: an international experiment. *Proceedings of the International Conference and Workshop on Global Natural Resource Monitoring and Assessments: preparing for the 21st*

Century. Volume 2 American Society of Photogrammetry and Remote Sensing, Falls Church, pp. 660–9

Kineman J J, Hastings D A, Colby J D (1986) Developments in global databases for the environmental sciences: discussion and review. *Proceedings of the 12th International Symposium on Remote Sensing of the Environment*. Volume 2. Environmental Research Institute of Michigan, Ann Arbor, pp. 471–82

Langel R A, Phillips J D, Horner R G (1982) Initial scalar anomaly map from MAGSAT. *Geophysical Research Letters* **9**: 269–72

Maguire D J (1991) An overview and definition of GIS. In: Maguire D J, Goodchild M F, Rhind D W (eds.) *Geographical Information Systems: principles and applications*. Longman, London: pp. 9–20, Vol 1

Mounsey H M (1991) Multisource, multinational environmental GIS: lessons learnt from CORINE. In: Maguire D J, Goodchild M F, Rhind D W (eds.) *Geographical Information Systems: principles and applications*, Longman, London, pp. 185–200, Vol 2

Muller J-P (1989) Real-time stereo matching and its role in future mapping systems. *Proceedings of Surveying and Mapping 89*. Royal Institution of Chartered.Surveyors, London, Paper C5, 15 pp

Muller J-P, Anthony A, Brown A T, Deacon A T, Kennedy S A, Montgomery P M, Robertson G W, Watson D M (1988) Real-time stereo matching using transputer arrays for close-range applications. *Proceedings of the Joint IAPR Workshop on 'Computer vision – Special Hardware and Industrial Applications'*. Tokyo, Japan. 12–14 October 1988, pp. 45–9

National Geophysical Data Center (1985) *Relief of the Surface of the Earth (maps, scale approximately 1 : 39 000 000)*. Report MGG-2. National Geophysical Data Center, Boulder Colorado

NOAA (1987) *Climate and Global Change: An integrated NOAA program in Earth System Science*. NOAA, Washington DC

Olson J S (1989) *World Ecosystems* (WE2.0) NOAA/ National Geophysical Data Center, Boulder, Colorado

Rhind D W, Clark P (1988) Cartographic data inputs to global databases. In: Mounsey H M, Tomlinson R F (eds.) *Building Databases for Global Science*. Taylor & Francis, London, pp. 79–104

Smith T R, Ye Jiang (1991) Knowledge-based approaches in GIS. In: Maguire D J, Goodchild M F, Rhind D W (eds.) *Geographical Information Systems: principles and applications*, Longman, London, pp. 413–25, Vol 1

Smith T R, Menon S, Star J L, Estes J E (1987) Requirements and principles for the implementation and construction of large scale geographic information systems. *International Journal of Geographical Information Systems* **1** (1): 13–31

Steyaert L T (1989) Investigating the use of geographic information systems technology in the computer workstation environment for global change research. *Proceedings of the ASPRS/ACSM 1989 annual meeting*, April 1989, Volume 4. American Society of Photogrammetry and Remote Sensing, Falls Church, pp. 46–53

Townshend J R G (1991) Environmental databases and GIS. In: Maguire D J, Goodchild M F, Rhind D W (eds.) *Geographical Information Systems: principles and applications*, Longman, London, pp. 201–16, Vol 2

UNEP Global Resource Information Database (1988) *Report on the meeting of the GRID Scientific and Technical Management Advisory Committee, Jan. 1988*. Report No. 15. UNEP/GEMS/GRID, Nairobi

Unninayar S (1988) The global system: observing and monitoring change, data problems, data management and databases. In: Mounsey H M, Tomlinson R F (eds.) *Building Databases for Global Science*. Taylor & Francis, London, pp. 357–77

51

GIS AND PUBLIC POLICY

H W CALKINS

A rational approach to policy decisions (as opposed to incrementalism) will be assumed in order to facilitate understanding of how GIS can be used in public policy decision making. In the GIS context, public policy making is supported by policy analysis based on the application of scientific or systematic methods. Such an approach leads to an idealized view of the public policy decision-making process, which is acknowledged to exist only rarely. However, rather than providing all the reasons and conditions arguing against the rational model in every section of this chapter, the reader is directed to the literature on public policy analysis, most notably Quade (1982). He has suggested that it never has been and never will be possible to make policy analysis a purely rational, coldly objective, scientific aid to decision making that will neatly lay bare the solution to every problem to which it is applied. The focus of this chapter then is on the potential for GIS to play a significant role in 'real world' public policy analysis as it supports public decision making.

PUBLIC POLICY

Public policies are made by elected officials or (sometimes) by their appointed representatives; they are aimed at 'setting the stage' for the development of public programmes or influencing private decisions. Public policies reflect the goals and objectives of the public authority, even though there may not be an explicit policy statement. Typically, the policies are intended to influence both public and private sector actions in a manner to accomplish these goals and objectives. As such, policy decisions made by public authorities may have significant impact on individuals and organizations other than those who make the policies. Moreover (and ideally), all actions taken by the public authority would be consistent with the policies of that authority.

The process of setting public policies within a rational planning framework involves problem identification, analysis, review (including extensive public hearings in some countries) and final decisions by the appropriate decision-making authority. The requirement for public involvement in the review process and the appropriate scope of the review varies between countries. The role of GIS in this process will also vary. For example, in the United States, the combination of open access to virtually all information used in reaching a public decision and acceptance of reasonable analysis procedures by the court system give GIS a potentially predominant role in the entire process.

The total set of public policies form a statement of intent and principles that guide other action-oriented decisions in the particular area of concern (e.g. suburban growth). Actions by public agencies (both policy setters and others), private organizations and private citizens drive change in various areas. The intent of a set of public policies is to direct these actions in the desired directions, as indicated by the goals and objectives. Policies may have implementing mechanisms which require conformance (e.g. by statute); however, the general case is that such mechanisms do not exist or are not directly equitable to the policy decisions. Thus most decision makers have some freedom of choice. They may also be affected by other forces which play a role in the specific actions taken, or not taken, as the case may be. Public policy statements are often very general in nature, a characteristic which makes direct comparison of the policy with other more specific decisions difficult. Further, in considering a set of public policies which cover a large geographical area, multiple organizations or even departments within organizations, a set of policy statements can often be internally contradictory (e.g. an aggressive economic development policy could be in conflict with a residential growth management policy or an environmental preservation/conservation policy).

Three major categories of GIS use in policy analysis will be discussed in this chapter:

1. The use of GIS to determine where and when public policies are needed.
2. Analysis to assist in the formulation of public policies.
3. Analysis to determine the extent to which public policies are successful and have achieved the goals and objectives intended.

The examples used to illustrate these uses will be an integrated scenario of possible GIS use, but one which does not represent a real situation. This scenario approach has been adopted rather than to draw real, but partial, examples from a number of jurisdictions to provide a coherent and extensive example for this chapter. Although all of the components of the scenario are real and exist in some local government authority, they do not all exist in a single place. Therefore, the example is a composite of activities at several places and is presented as a scenario. It is, however, certainly possible that all components *could* exist at one place!

The topic of the example scenario will be urban growth management. This topic has been a particular concern to a certain set of local governments in the United States and elsewhere for about the last 20 years. Local land use ordinances have been created to manage urban growth; some have been the result of policy analysis and direct public decision, others have not. The ordinances have been subjected to the legal system where some have been upheld and others overturned. The use of analysis and geographical information (with or without a GIS) has not been commonplace in these situations, but it could well have been had the technology and knowledge of how to use it existed at the time.

Policy analysis paradigm

A three-level policy analysis paradigm, based on systems analysis principles and containing the necessary characteristics of verification, iteration and feedback, would perform the following functions (adapted from Meyerson 1956 : 60):

- an intelligence function, aimed at facilitating market operations;
- a problem-sensing function to alert decision makers to potential problems through periodic reports or an exception reporting process;
- a problem clarification function to help frame and/or revise specific objectives of the organization;
- a detailed plan development function for specific private and public programmes as part of a comprehensive course of action; and
- a monitoring, evaluation and feedback function for comparison of results with the goals and objectives of the organization.

Such a three-level paradigm including all five Meyerson functions is shown in Fig. 51.1. Problems or concerns which are discovered during the intelligence or problem-sensing functions (Level 1) which are deemed by policy makers to require specific actions or programmes – whether public or private – are then the topics for public action (Level 2). A planning activity (Level 3) is then executed for those problems or situations for which the policy makers require analysis and information support. The results from the planning level (Level 3) are returned to the decision maker for consideration. The recommendations can be accepted for implementation or referred back for further study. Upon acceptance of the recommendations, the expected results from implementation would be the subject of future monitoring at Level 1.

Thus, Level 1 is an ongoing monitoring of significant attributes of the urban (or other) system, capable of detecting the effects of past public policies and government programmes and capable of revealing situations that may call for new policies or actions. Level 2 consists of seven activities encompassing problem identification, the definition of specific objectives, specification of decision criteria relevant to the problem, a process of validating assumptions, and a search for additional

GIS and Public Policy

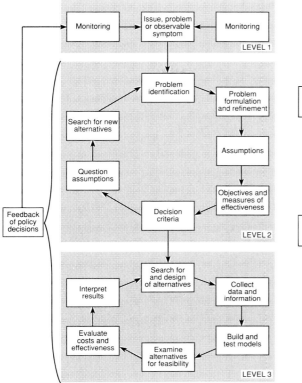

Fig. 51.1 A paradigm for policy analysis using GIS.

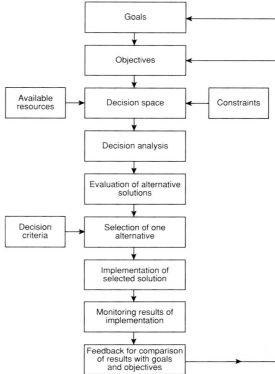

Fig. 51.2 The public decision-making systems model.

alternative solutions. Finally, Level 3 is the detailed specification and analysis of all (or some) of the alternative solutions identified for the problem in question. This multi-stage process is driven by the ongoing observations in Level 1: these constitute a continuing process of monitoring of significant measures or indicators. Both Levels 2 and 3 are internally structured as iterative processes, with Level 3 providing feedback to Level 2, and Level 2 providing feedback to Level 1, in order to facilitate the continuing operation of Level 1.

Systems approach applied to public policy

As implied above, the link between GIS and public policy analysis is best viewed as a systems analysis model. A general systems model for public decision making is shown in Fig. 51.2. This model assumes one or more issues, problems or conditions have been recognized and that remedial actions are necessary. The model starts with a definite set of goals and objectives, proceeds to a decision space bounded by resources and constraints and this leads in turn to a set of alternatives for evaluation. Possible solutions are considered in sequence, the evaluation of each proceeding on the decision criteria which have previously been defined. This part of the model corresponds to a general systems model (GSM), as described by Churchman (1968 : 29).

The remaining two components of the GSM, monitoring the results and evaluating performance for the purpose of adjusting the implementing mechanisms, are normally part of systems models of physical systems (process control). However, these are not usually part of the less well-defined social and economic systems which are frequently the subject of policy analysis. This is due to the long time period involved in the implementation of social and economic policies and to the difficulty of defining appropriate measures of effectiveness. Not only must good measures of effectiveness be defined, but an information collection activity must be implemented to support the monitoring and evaluation activities. In fact, *all* stages of the systems model in a social or economic application require a higher level of quantification for the whole to function. As a generality, GIS can potentially make a very substantial contribution in the policy analysis area but a long-term commitment is required and the GIS must be integrated into the entire system of policy analysis.

THE URBAN GROWTH MANAGEMENT EXAMPLE

In the urban growth management example used to illustrate the application of GIS in public policy analysis, a simple implementation of the systems model for a suburban town will be presented. The hypothetical town is a suburban community within a large metropolitan area. After a long period of moderate residential growth, the town has recently experienced very rapid growth which is changing the character of the community. This rate of growth is placing a major strain on the provision of municipal services, such as water, streets and other community services. It has been viewed as a problem, or issue, which requires action by the elected town officials. It components of the general systems model would thus be as follows:

Goal. Manage growth to maintain the character of the community and to match the provision of infrastructure facilities with the financial resources of the town.

Objective. Limit the size of the town to 47 500 residential units (with an estimated population of 147 500 inhabitants).

Decision space
The options are:

- set a 'cap' – an arbitrary limit and stop permits for residential units when the cap is reached;
- issue a fixed number of building permits for residential units each year until the limit is reached;
- place a moratorium on all development until a new plan to provide the needed facilities can be provided;
- plan for proportional growth as a function of regional growth.

Analysis. The analysis associated with the above options could be the determination of some form of residential carrying capacity to assess the maximum number of new residential units (either per year or total), the creation of a regional growth model to calculate the community's 'fair share' of the region's new growth, and a population prediction model for the town.

Evaluation. Criteria appropriate in this example could be the fiscal impact of each option in the provision of community services (streets, water, sewer, social, educational, etc.) and an evaluation of the changes in town character that might result from any one option. The latter is a very subjective evaluation, but has been used as justification for limiting growth in several North American communities.

Selected solution. One option is selected, based on the decision criteria which will have been specified earlier, and should be a function of the goals, objectives, available resources and constraints. Such factors as available land for development, planned urban density, access to community services and facilities, the tax base and the capital improvements programme are examples of criteria used in reaching a decision of this type.

Implementation. In this case this is a joint activity between the local authority, which would provide roads and other elements of the infrastructure, and local builders providing housing units.

Monitoring results. This activity compares the actual residential development (probably measured in terms of the number of building permits issued) as it occurs over one or more time periods with the expected or planned growth. This comparison can be made for the community as a whole or on the basis of geographical subsections of the community.

Feedback. The comparison conducted as part of the monitoring activity will indicate what adjustments, if any, need to be made in the policy for growth management. Depending on the nature of the adjustments, the appropriate part of this entire process can be repeated.

Thus, the composite public policy of the community would be:

- to retain the character of the community;
- to limit residential growth to a fixed amount per year by restricting the number of building permits issued;
- to restrict (or encourage) growth in only selected parts of the community (such as adjacent to existing residential development):
- to limit growth to the community's fair share of the total regional growth.

All aspects of this urban growth management policy could be followed and monitored using GIS. In practice, other policy statements would be included in a comprehensive growth management plan. The four listed above, however, are sufficient to illustrate the role of a GIS in the formulation and implementation of public policies.

GIS FOR PUBLIC POLICY ANALYSIS – THE THEORY

The ability to use a GIS effectively to assist in the public policy area requires two conditions to be met. These are a rational (or at least partially rational) process for the formulation of the public policies and the quantification of the significant attributes of the policy.

The rational planning model

The process of growth management in the example is assumed to follow the rational planning model. While at least one option in the 'decision space' of the example could simply be arbitrarily set, the courts in the United States have tended to invalidate policies formulated without an analytical base. Conversely, even in contentious cases, policies formulated as a result of structured analysis have been upheld by the courts. Clearly, then, the establishment of public policies through the use of the rational planning process is one approach which could link GIS to public policies. Various versions of this planning process exist (most based on all or part of the general systems model concept). One such version (Harris 1965 : 91; Calkins 1979 : 757) describes the actions of the public authority as including:

- the projections of the most probable pattern of future development;
- the identification of objectionable or undesirable features of this development pattern;
- the identification of desirable alternative patterns and directions of development;
- the creation of policies and public actions which may influence development in desired directions;
- the generation of plans reflecting various combinations of these policies and actions;
- testing these plans for effectiveness, feasibility and costs;
- choosing among alternative sets of policies;
- activating the public policies and programmes to implement the plan;
- monitoring changes in the community to measure the effectiveness of policies and programmes; and
- evaluating the policies and programmes by comparison of the expected with the actual results.

Assuming this, a GIS can be used in the rational planning process to:

- project and display the probable patterns of future development in order to permit decision makers to visualize the direction of community growth;
- generate and test alternative plans to provide information to the decision makers; and
- monitor changes in the community resulting from plan implementation. The importance of such a monitoring function has been described as follows:

'... government programs rarely have an automatic regulator that tells us when an activity has ceased to be productive or could be made more efficient, or should be displaced by another activity. In private business, society relies upon profits and competition to furnish the needed incentives and discipline and to provide feedback on the quality of decisions. The system is imperfect, but basically sound in the private sector – it is virtually non-existent in the government sector. In government, we must find another tool for making the choices which resource scarcity forces upon us'.

(Schultze 1970, cited in Quade 1982 : 4)

Quantification of attributes

The second condition, the quantification of attributes relevant to the policy issues, is a necessary step if a GIS is to be useful as a decision support tool for public policy. Ideally, the quantification of goals, objectives and specific targets for policies or programmes would be defined. For example, the following might be defined as consistent with the public policies in urban growth management already noted:

General policy statement	Quantification
1. Retain character of community	Limit multi-family units to 20% of all new residential construction per year
2. Limit new residential construction	Issue only 400 building permits per year
3. Limit (or encourage) growth in selected areas	All multi-family units and 50% of single family units must be adjacent to existing development
4. Accommodate fair share of regional growth	Limit all new residential construction to 8% of regional growth (8% being the proportional area of the community)

Several items are implicit in the above quantification of goals, objectives and targets. First, a detailed level of analysis of the existing housing situation would be needed. Second, the analysis would include the region, however defined, as well as the local community. Third, the quantified targets may not be internally consistent. For example, the policy to issue only 400 building permits per year may conflict with the 8 per cent fair share of regional growth.

The rational planning process and the quantification of goals or objectives set the stage for the ongoing use of GIS. These systems can support the initial analysis leading up to the establishment of a set of public policies; can be used to determine if conflict exists between specific objectives; and, lastly, can be used as a tool to monitor the achievement of the objectives. The example shows the detail necessary to use a GIS for policy analysis, including the need to work at different levels of spatial resolution (region, local community and sub-areas in the example). Moreover, urban growth management is usually implemented over several time periods and would also involve data related to several time periods.

The degree to which such a public policy support system can be established will depend on the willingness of policy-makers to commit themselves to specific, quantified targets for important policy issues. Generally, policy statements lack specificity and only describe conditions that it is hoped will evolve at some future date. Also, the achievement of public policy usually relies on a combination of government-funded programmes and private actions. The government authorities have at best only indirect control over the private actions.

The successful use of GIS will depend, then, on the ability to define attributes related to those government programmes and private actions which are considered adequate measures of the success or failure of any public policy. In addition, where possible, these measurable attributes should be associated with specific policy objectives, rather than with more general measures concerning public policy as a whole. As will be discussed in the next section, the evaluation of public policies can only be carried out in a meaningful way if a causal relationship between policies and change can be demonstrated.

GIS FOR POLICY ANALYSIS AND MONITORING – THE PRACTICE

1The three uses of GIS in the rational planning model have been identified as to:

- project the future pattern of development;
- model or analyse alternative plans; and
- monitor changes in the community.

The first two would use various projection/analysis models, in this case land use growth and allocation models. These models can be incorporated into the GIS or linked to it through a program or data interface. The initial database and the monitoring of change in attribute values within the database provide the information needed for policy evaluation.

Five general questions need to be answered in an evaluation of public policy statements (Calkins 1979 : 748):

1. What is the initial condition of the environment (where 'environment' is used in the broadest sense)?
2. What are the subsequent conditions of the environment at the end of each planning time increment?
3. What change has occurred during the relevant time period?
4. Are the changes attributable to public policies, to government programmes or to undefined exogenous factors?
5. How does the present state of the environment compare to what was planned or forecast?

Answers to these questions will only be obtainable if the public policies and government programmes have specific performance targets attached to them. The contribution of each individual policy and programme and the extent of their interactions must also be measurable if the presence and contribution of undefined exogenous factors is to be isolated.

A structure to answer these questions using GIS was proposed by Calkins (1979). The scenario based on the urban growth management problem and described earlier will be used by way of example; it assumes a suburban community of a fixed size with a current (1990) population of 137 000 and a growth pattern shown in Fig. 51.3(a). This community is becoming overcrowded and does not feel that much more residential growth can be accepted. Existing community facilities are becoming overtaxed and the current residents desire to retain the prevailing character of the community. The population projection shown would result from a regional and/or population projection model (step 1 of the rational planning process). After careful study and due debate, the town council sets the following policies:

- The community population will be 'capped' at 147 500 residents (based on the ability to provide facilities and the amount of developable land remaining).
- Growth will proceed at the maximum rate of 950 persons per year (only 400 residential building permits will be issued each year, assuming an average of 2.4 persons per residential unit).

Other factors, which play an important part in setting the residential growth policy are the distribution of housing units in 1980 (Fig. 51.3(c)), and the sub-areas which have experienced rapid growth between 1980 and 1989 (Figs. 51.3(c) and 51.3(d)). By 1980, the southwest portion of the town was almost completely developed and growth spread north and east during the 1980–89 period. Development pressure in the 1990s will be mostly in the northwest and northeast quadrants of the town. The maps showing these trends (Figs. 51.3(c) and 51.3(d)) result from the analysis of existing population and housing data within a GIS.

Further analysis of the town's sub-areas (operationalized as census tracts) indicates where population growth can be expected to take place in the coming decade (Tables 51.1 and 51.2). Columns 1 to 6 of Table 51.1 show the population and housing statistics for the 23 census tracts of the town for the time period 1980 to 1990. Table 51.2 shows the expected growth by census tract for the period 1990 to 2000 (columns 7 and 8), the total projected population and dwelling units by census tract for the year 2000 (columns 9 and 10) and, finally, the amount by which each census tract can grow and

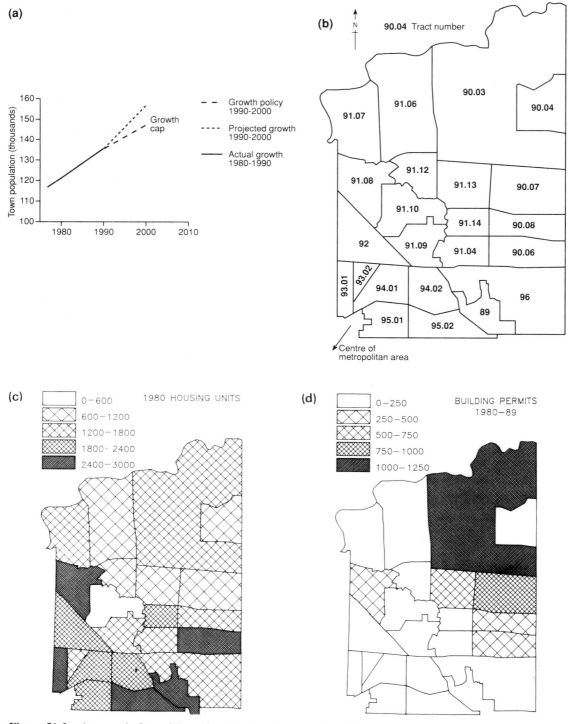

Figure 51.3 A scenario for public policy planning based on the urban growth management problem. (a) Town growth graph; (b) Census tract outline map; (c) 1980 housing unit map; (d) 1980–89 building permit map.

still stay within the policy objectives of the town (columns 11 and 12). The population and dwelling unit policy targets by census tract reflect land capability for development in the northern portions of the town and were set by a process of negotiation within the planning process. Additional information from the GIS, in this case a map of wetlands and desirable open space, indicated that limiting growth in census tracts 90.04 and 90.06 would assist in achieving the town's growth management objectives and, at the same time, meet other objectives for open space conservation. The final policy in this case is expressed in terms of population growth, number of dwelling units and the anticipated average household size. The resulting quantified policy statement is the number of building permits to be issued by census tract in the 1990–2000 time period. To determine the success of the growth policy, the town will need to monitor the issue of building permits over the next decade. The other factors used during the analysis, specifically the average household size, will also need to be monitored to evaluate the effectiveness of the policy. Additionally, further sub-objectives based on annual growth targets could be incorporated into this analysis.

The above example takes a single goal, three attributes and 23 spatial units to analyse and present a public policy. Even this simple example is difficult to construct without the support of automated tools. The application of GIS to public policies in a broader context will quickly involve many more objectives, attributes, temporal units and spatial units. This results in a substantial accounting task (in addition to the analytical task within the planning activities) which virtually requires a GIS to accomplish. Attempts to carry out such policy analysis otherwise will involve the analyst in an overwhelming amount of geographical data containing many relationships between attributes. This leads to the conclusion that not only will GIS be required, but additional spatial data handling functions will need to be added to standard GIS software to support the policy analyst in all of the policy analysis tasks – monitoring to determine when and where policies are needed, analysing specific situations or conditions and structuring the policy decisions in a form which permits further monitoring and the subsequent evaluation of the policies.

GIS SUPPORT FOR PUBLIC POLICY ANALYSIS

In all of the previous discussion of GIS and public policy, including the example given, it has been assumed that all important and necessary factors can be described as quantified attributes. Clearly, not all public policy issues can be reduced to a consistent set of measurable factors. However, GIS support for public policy making will probably be limited to those situations where most, if not all, of the issues can be structured in such a manner. The remaining portions of a policy issue will have to be left to the decision makers and the negotiation process that takes place in public decision-making situations. From a GIS perspective, the objective should be to present as much high quality information to the decision maker as is needed, to be able to describe important relationships within the information, to predict the impacts of selected decisions and to follow up by evaluating the results of decisions. Thus, for each quantified or measurable attribute that contributes to the attainment of a goal or objective, a GIS should be able to answer the following questions:

- What was the value of the attribute for one or more previous points in time?

- What is the current value of the attribute?

- What is the projected value of the attribute for one or more future time periods?

- What is the planned change in the attribute value (where planned change equals the sum of public-funded and private actions)?

- What is the value of the attribute at time $(t+1)$ and subsequent time periods, as appropriate?

- What is the difference between the planned change in the attribute value and its value at time $(t+1)$?

- What is the difference between the projected value of the attribute and its value at time $(t+1)$?

- What amount of change is the result of specific policies and can be related to either public and/or private actions intended to implement the policy?

Table 51.1 Population and Housing Policy Worksheet – actual statistics

Total Tracts	1980 Census		1980–90 Growth		1990 Census	
	Population (1) 121 696	Dwel units (2) 38 030	Population (3) 16 285	Dwel units (4) 5089	Population (5) 137 981	Dwel units (6) 43 119
89	8560	2675	0	0	8650	2675
90.03	5018	1568	3862	1207	8880	2775
90.04	3277	1024	678	212	3955	1236
90.06	8051	2516	1555	486	9606	3002
90.07	2960	925	563	176	3523	1101
90.08	3117	974	3942	1232	7059	1166
91.04	5005	1564	221	69	5226	1633
91.06	3642	1138	128	40	3770	1178
91.07	5472	1710	166	52	5638	1762
91.08	8339	2606	1530	478	9869	3082
91.09	4107	1303	42	13	4212	1316
91.10	25	2	0	0	25	2
91.12	2115	661	554	173	2669	834
91.13	6259	1956	1853	579	8112	2535
91.14	3341	1044	250	78	3591	1122
92.00	7178	2246	150	47	7337	2293
93.01	7917	2474	10	3	7927	2477
93.02	3853	1204	0	0	3853	1204
94.01	7302	1282	106	33	7408	2315
94.02	5936	1855	102	32	6038	1887
95.01	6915	2161	26	8	6941	2169
95.02	9133	2854	26	8	9159	2862
96.00	4102	1282	521	163	4623	1445

Note: As different assumptions and methods were used to calculate the values in this table, not all rows and columns sum exactly. These minor differences are not significant in this type of application. Dwel units = Dwelling units.

- What change has occurred that cannot be related to the expected change (projections)?

A full implementation of these concepts in a GIS would require that public policies be linked to a set of public and/or private actions where the amount of change from each action can be estimated. The total expected change, then, would be the sum of the results of all public and private actions. Of course, all future change cannot be anticipated. There will, therefore, always be an element of unanticipated change included in each measured attribute value at times $(t+n)$. The identification of this unanticipated change, including the reasons for it, are of considerable importance in the evaluation of public policies. The unanticipated change can either contribute to the achievement of the policy or it may be counter-productive. This change and its effect on goal achievement can only be recognized and measured if the results of all public and private actions are quantified and monitored. Inevitably, such quantification of all actions related to public policies becomes very complex in practice. A significant contribution of the GIS in public policy analysis will thus be to perform the data management function necessary to carry out the policy evaluations. A more detailed discussion of the representation of public policy goals and objectives in a GIS is contained in Calkins (1979).

If all public policies and government programmes produced the intended results, the role of analysis and of the supporting GIS would end at this stage. However, most policies and programmes extend over long time periods where, if nothing else, expectations change. In addition, results do

GIS and Public Policy

Table 51.2 Population and Housing Policy Worksheet – projections and policy objectives

Total Tracts	1990–2000 Growth		Estimated 2000		Within-Policy Growth	
	Population (7)	Dwel units (8)	Population (9)	Dwel units (10)	Population (11)	Dwel units (12)
	18 445	6142	156 426	49 261	147 500	47 500
89	0	0	8 560	2675	0	0
90.03	4260	1540	13 500	4315	2149	977
90.04	1100	366	5 055	1601	550	250
90.06	750	250	10 356	3252	550	250
90.07	1800	600	5 323	1701	1320	600
90.08	3500	1166	10 559	3371	1716	833
91.04	100	33	5 326	1666	72	33
91.06	1450	483	5 220	1661	110	50
91.07	1250	416	6 888	3178	220	100
91.08	800	266	10 669	3350	585	266
91.09	100	33	4 312	1349	72	33
91.10	0	0	25	2	0	0
91.12	1100	366	3 769	1200	805	366
91.13	900	300	9 012	2835	660	300
91.14	50	16	3 641	1138	35	16
92.00	50	16	7 387	2309	35	16
93.01	0	0	7 927	2477	0	0
93.02	0	0	3 853	1204	0	0
94.01	50	16	7 458	2331	35	16
94.02	75	25	6 113	1912	55	25
95.01	0	0	6 941	2169	0	0
95.02	0	0	9 159	2862	0	0
96.00	750	250	5 373	1695	550	250
TOTAL PROGRAMME TARGETS					9519	4381

Note: As different assumptions and methods were used to calculate the values in this table, not all rows and columns sum exactly. These minor differences are not significant in this type of application. Dwel units = Dwelling units.

not always match expectations nor do the original problems remain constant. In the field of urban management, for instance, there are many examples of well-intentioned programmes solving one problem, but creating additional problems of equal severity. Thus the concept of monitoring both the changes in the urban environment and the performance of public policies and government programmes must be part of a general systems approach. As emphasized earlier, the significant features of the systems approach in this instance are verification, iteration and feedback. The monitoring concept presented accomplishes verification but not iterative analysis or feedback. To provide continuous monitoring and evaluation (Level 1 in Fig. 51.1) necessarily leads to a consideration of a fully integrated GIS containing all relevant information and operating continuously. This leads, in turn, to a detailed consideration of the process of GIS planning and implementation which is covered in other chapters of this book.

CONCLUSIONS

This chapter has presented GIS as a tool for supporting the conduct of public policy through analysis. A paradigm of public policy analysis has been described, within which a systems view of public decision making can be embedded.

Furthermore, a rational planning process was envisaged to support the decision-making model. If such a well integrated decision-making mechanism actually existed, using GIS would be relatively simple. However, as stated earlier in this chapter, it is not often that such a rational decision-making process exists. This does not mean, however, that a GIS is not useful in less structured situations. Selected geographical data can be presented for specific issues at specific times and still be very valuable in the decision-making process (Densham 1991 in this volume). The value of the GIS will, however, increase substantially with a more structured decision-making environment. Moreover, the development of the GIS for policy implementation – which is a lengthy process in itself – can be made much easier if the nature of its anticipated use can be specified in some detail. Even where this was not initially possible some systems have still been successful (see, for instance, Blakemore 1991 in this volume).

Given the other chapters in this book, the process of planning and developing a GIS (formerly termed 'GIS design') is not the object of this discussion. There is, however, one aspect of this process which needs identification here – specifically, the benefits and associated costs of developing and maintaining a GIS. Dickinson and Calkins (1988) identified three categories of benefit from a GIS. These are accomplishing current (or existing) tasks more efficiently; accommodating a higher volume of current tasks; and facilitating the development of new tasks or applications. Using GIS for public policy analysis falls into the third category, that is using the GIS for new purposes. The normal procedure for justifying a GIS is to conduct a cost/benefit analysis where all benefits are defined and the associated costs are calculated. Benefits are generally divided into two categories – tangible and intangible. Tangible benefits usually involve cost savings related to personnel time and other measurable resources of the organization. Estimates of future workloads for existing, known tasks are also added to the tangible benefit list. Unfortunately, the benefits arising from new applications are very difficult to identify and describe in sufficient detail for inclusion into cost–benefit analysis. Yet almost all GIS proposals identify intangible benefits including better quality data, more timely and accurate information and better decision making. While a listing of these intangible benefits expected from a GIS may be helpful, the quantified cost/benefit ratio becomes a significant factor in the decision to develop a GIS. This may well create a situation where the potential of the GIS is vastly underestimated. Assuming the GIS is actually implemented, the resulting system may not be capable of providing the level of support required.

The results expected from using GIS in public policy analysis all fall into the category of intangible benefits. It is not known, at this time, how valuable may be the use of GIS in much public policy making. It is known, partly from the example presented in this chapter, that a public policy GIS is likely to be large and costly. Thus the justification for funding development of such a system will need to consider better ways of anticipating and expressing the value of the GIS. It may be that the most valuable use of GIS will come from highly critical policy analysis areas where every effort has to be made to ensure the best decision is made. In these – and probably many more – circumstances, the application of GIS to public policy may be too important to be made solely on a basis of traditional cost-effectiveness estimates.

REFERENCES

Blakemore M J (1991) Managing an operational GIS: the UK National On-line Manpower Information System (NOMIS). In: Maguire D J, Goodchild M F, Rhind D W (eds.) *Geographical Information Systems: principles and applications.* Longman, London, pp. 503–13, Vol 1

Calkins, H W (1979) The planning monitor: an accountability theory of plan evaluation. *Environment and Planning* A **11**: 745–58

Churchman C W (1968) *The Systems Approach.* Dell Publishing Co. Inc., New York

Densham P J (1991) Spatial decision support systems. In: Maguire D J, Goodchild M F, Rhind D W (eds.) *Geographical Information Systems: principles and applications.* Longman, London, pp. 403–12, Vol 1

Dickinson H J, Calkins H W (1988) The economic evaluation of implementing a GIS. *International Journal of Geographical Information Systems* **2**: 307–27

Harris B (1965) New tools for planning. *Journal of the American Institute of Planners* **31** (2): 90–5

Meyerson M (1956) Building the middle-range bridge for

comprehensive planning. *Journal of the American Institute of Planners* **22** (2): 58–64

Quade E S (1982) *Analysis of Public Decisions*, 2nd edn. North-Holland, New York

Schultze C L (1970) Director, Bureau of the Budget, Statement in *Planning, Programming, Budgeting*, 91st Congress, 2nd Session, Subcommittee on National Security and International Operations. US Government Publications Office, Washington DC. pp. 172–3

52

URBAN GIS APPLICATIONS

R PARROTT AND F P STUTZ

This chapter illustrates the role of GIS in urban planning through the example of its use in the San Diego Association of Governments (SANDAG). Though the detailed uses of GIS for urban areas will vary between (and even within) countries because of legal, fiscal and administrative differences in the roles of local government, the SANDAG example is one in which information-based planning strategies covering both the long and the short term have been used. The principles underlying it are thus relevant to the situation in many other urban environments. A primary use of GIS has been for modelling purposes: four example applications described illustrate the use of GIS in finding land for development; emergency planning; determining the ideal location for fire stations; and assistance in crime control and documentation.

INTRODUCTION

The uses of GIS for urban applications are, not surprisingly, many and varied. Recent examples from just one conference include applications as disparate as: industrial location modelling (Cowen, Mitchell and Meyer 1990); supply and demand forecasting in real estate markets (Gurd 1990); dynamic vehicle routing (Lee and Russell 1990); and redistricting (Sullivan and Chow 1990). Other chapters of this book deal with utility applications (Mahoney 1991) and land suitability and facility siting (Siderelis 1991; Berry 1991; Cowen and Shirley 1991). More general reviews of urban GIS applications are to be found in Newkirk (1987), Sommers (1987) and Dueker (1988). This chapter therefore concentrates on an in-depth analysis of urban applications in a single urban area, namely San Diego.

The population of the San Diego region increased by over half a million people between 1979 and 1988, making it one of the fastest growing metropolitan areas in the United States. In 1984, the San Diego region reached 2 million residents. During 1987, the region experienced a growth rate of 3.6 per cent bringing the total population to 2 328 328 residents by the end of the year and 2.5 million by 1990. San Diego County is currently the fifteenth largest metropolitan area in the nation in terms of population and the fifth largest legal city. It is the fourth largest county in the nation (behind Los Angeles, California; Cook, Illinois; and Harris, Texas). Overall, the county also experienced the third largest numeric increase in population between 1980 and 1988, behind Los Angeles, California and Maricopa County in Arizona. It is evident that such rapid development creates many problems in the provision of physical and social infrastructure at acceptable cost, in preserving the quality of the environment, in safeguarding the safety of the populace and much else.

The San Diego Association of Governments (SANDAG) is a quasi-government agency consisting of the County of San Diego in the southwestern corner of California as well as 18 cities located therein. It has a Board of Directors comprised of elected officials from each local jurisdiction and has three main functions:

- To promote regional planning among local governments.

- To maintain a regional information system.

- To provide technical planning assistance to the 19 member government agencies.

A key input to these functions is SANDAG's long-range forecast of population, housing and economic activities for the entire San Diego region and for the smaller geographical areas within it. Locally, this product is known as the Regional Growth Forecast (RGF). The RGF has a wide variety of uses and applications and is based on a large GIS. It helps determine the need for transportation systems and the size and location of public facilities such as fire stations, schools, hospitals and sewage and water treatment plants. The RGF is also used to assess water and energy demands for county agencies and geographical areas and can help predict the future quality of the region's air based on developmental aspects of land uses and population growth. Local governments which do not have a large planning and GIS capacity make use of the RGF and other products of local technical assistance from SANDAG as they evaluate housing needs for their constituencies and update their general and community plans. Uses of the RGF are summarized in Fig. 52.1.

Fig. 52.1 How SANDAG uses the forecast data for Regional Growth Forecasts (RGFs).

This chapter describes the urban development modelling system of SANDAG used for San Diego County in southern California. Four applications of the use of urban information systems as a solution to geographic problems are described. Some more general points about urban information systems are made in various places in this chapter.

THE URBAN DEVELOPMENT GIS MODELLING SYSTEM

There are two phases to the Regional Growth Forecasting process and four major models are used to obtain the projected population and land use values. The first phase uses the Demographic and Economic Forecasting Model (DEFM) which produces a forecast for the San Diego region as a whole. The second phase employs three allocation models to disaggregate the RGF tabulations to each of the sub-areas in the county. Figure 52.2 presents the overall relationships between the various models, databases and GIS for the Regional Growth Forecasting system.

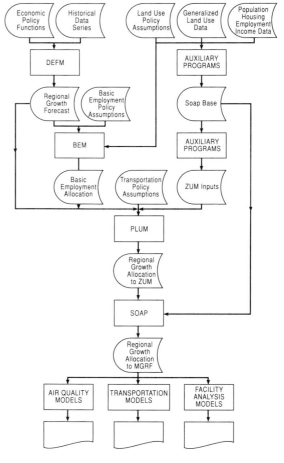

Fig. 52.2 SANDAG's urban development modelling system flowchart.

The first of the allocation models is the Basic Employment Allocation Model (BEM). It provides the future distribution of basic employment in the region, primarily on the basis of the policies of the local jurisdictions on industrial development and on the present split between industrial and service employment. This distribution then becomes the input to the Projective Land Use Model (PLUM). PLUM allocates other activities such as population, housing units, persons per household and local serving (or non-basic employment) to sub-areas based on the location of the basic employment, the availability of usable land, physical accessibility to major activity centres, residential locations in the region and land use policies of the local jurisdictions. This allocation is made for Zones for Urban Modelling (ZUM), which are collections of census tracts and traffic analysis zones within a local jurisdiction. The last regional model involved is the SOphisticated Allocation Process (SOAP). It allocates population, housing and employment activities to the smallest geographical level, the Master Geographical Reference Area (MGRA). The principal aim of this chapter however is not to discuss the population growth models and the land use allocation models used by SANDAG nor the GIS architecture itself. The bulk of this effort will be spent demonstrating, in a non-technical manner, four of the many uses of such a GIS modelling system.

SANDAG'S GIS

Two key elements comprise the SANDAG GIS: the geographical database and the tools available. Both are described below.

The area units in the geographical database

SANDAG uses two geographical reference systems. The first of these is a multi-level nested system in which the census tract is the basis of the hierarchy of spatial units. There are four levels of aggregation and the boundaries at one level do not cross over the other. Smaller subdivisions and larger aggregations are created from the census tract system. The Traffic Analysis Zones (TAZ) are the smallest areas of reference. Geographical aggregations of census tracts form the larger Sub-Regional Areas (SRA) and Major Statistical Areas (MSA). Thus there are 759 TAZs, 380 census tracts, 41 SRAs and 7 MSAs covering the San Diego region in a nested system. In addition to these four basic levels, others are generated by aggregation: the PLUM zonal system, for instance, is composed of 161 Zones for Urban Modelling (ZUM), which are shown in Fig. 52.3. The zones are groups of census tracts within each city's corporate boundaries. For the City of San Diego, ZUM conforms to community planning area boundaries. Projection of population, housing or land use can be retrieved for any user-defined region for 10, 20 or 25 years hence.

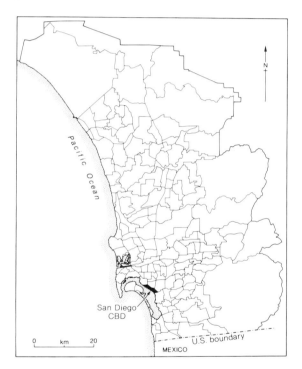

Fig. 52.3 San Diego County Zones for Urban Modelling (ZUM).

The second geographical referencing system is a non-nested one and its basis is the grid cell. It is independent of the nested system mentioned above. The grid cells form a matrix of 2000 ft by 2000 ft (610 × 610 m) squares, each containing approximately 90 acres (220 ha). There are roughly 15 000 such land-based grid cells covering the county. A Sub-Regional Forecast, however, is needed for geographical areas and jurisdictions in addition to those mentioned above. Data must be prepared by the coarsest geographical units that will support the detailed needs. As a consequence, account must be taken of grid cells split by boundaries of government jurisdictions, traffic analysis zones and the city and county of San Diego community planning areas. There are approximately 25 000 split grid cells within the county and these comprise the Master Geographical Reference Areas (MGRA).

The files generated by the SOAP program allow forecast data to be retrieved in one of several ways, depending on the needs of each city within the county. SANDAG has developed report programs to display data either for a single variable or as a complete profile. Table 52.1 is an example report: it gives sub-regional forecast model outputs. This information can be retrieved and printed out for standard geographical areas such as TAZ, census tracts or entire cities or for any user-defined geographical area. Results for the last of these are accomplished by a program which aggregates MGRA-level data to approximate to the non-standard shape of the user-defined polygons. Forecast data can also be retrieved for any radial distance, driving distance or driving time from a given point (such as particular land parcel, street intersection or major activity centre such as shopping centre, stadium or employment node). An example of output from the projection programs is Fig. 52.4 which shows total change in population by grid cell between 1986 and the year 2010.

The software and hardware tools

The software component of SANDAG's GIS is ARC/INFO, a product from Environmental Systems Research Institute of Redlands, California. For urban and regional planners this provides the important capabilities to automate mapped information, overlay different types of map information, perform network routing and allocation analysis, and produce maps at any level of aggregation. The hardware used for running SANDAG's regional forecasting model system and GIS includes a Prime 9955 and peripherals such as a digitizer, plotter and various Tektronix colour graphics display terminals.

APPLICATIONS OF GIS IN URBAN PLANNING WITHIN SAN DIEGO COUNTY

Four applications are considered in turn. These are finding land for development, emergency planning, determining the ideal location for fire stations and assistance in crime control and documentation.

Finding land for development

The location of land suitable for new land use activities is a well known and widely practised GIS application. Typical applications include suitability of land for locating waste disposal sites (e.g. Estes *et al.* 1987; Stewart 1987; Maguire *et al.* 1991; Siderelis 1991 in this volume), large processing plants (e.g. Siderelis 1991 in this volume) and resource planning (e.g. Berry 1991 in this volume; Cowen and Shirley 1991 in this volume).

San Diego County is composed of 18 incorporated cities and the unincorporated county area. Each city maintains a general plan which identifies land use classification for the areas it governs. Land use classifications differ between cities. SANDAG reviewed the general and community classifications used in each jurisdiction and developed a generic coding system to apply to all jurisdictions. Classifications from each city's plan were converted to the new SANDAG system and overlaid. The resulting database is shown in Fig. 52.5. Calculations of the gross extent allotted for different land use types and the number of vacant developable acres remaining were then created under the new coding system. With this overlay system, SANDAG has the capability to examine the development quality of any area within the county. In addition, vacant land for a particular type of development can be identified and located. Demographic profiles, expenditure patterns of residents and employment levels for surrounding areas can even be examined and land use suitability modelling can be performed.

Through digitizing, the general or community plan for each city in San Diego County was entered into the SANDAG GIS database. The general plan database was analysed in conjunction with other information. Land already developed was identified using the 1986 generalized land use inventory. Lands constrained from private development through general plan policy, public ownership or

Table 52.1 SANDAG sub-regional forecast model outputs.

Population	Occupied housing units
Total population	Total occupied units
Household	Single family
Group quarters	Multiple family
Civilian	Mobile homes
Military	Persons per household

Employment

Land use

Employment	Land use
Total employment	Total acres
Civilian	Developed
Basic	Single family
Agriculture (SIC 1–9)	Multiple family
Mining (SIC 10–14)	Mobile homes
Manufacturing (SIC 20–39)	Basic
Transportation (SIC 40, 42, 44–47)	Local serving
Wholesale (SIC 50, 51)	1986 Freeway
State and federal government (SIC 90, 91, 92)	Vacant developable
Hotel (SIC 70)	Low density single family
Basic military[1]	Single family
Local serving	Multiple family
Retail trade (SIC 52–59)	Mixed use
Retail services (SIC 72, 74–88)	Local serving
Business services (SIC 73, 89)	Industrial
Construction (SIC 15–17)	Unusable
Finance, insurance and real estate (SIC 60–67)	Redevelopment/infill acres
Local government (SIC 93, 94)	Single family to multiple family
Local serving transportation (SIC 41, 48–49)	Single family to mixed use
Uniformed military[2]	Single family to local serving
	Multiple family to mixed use
	Multiple family to local serving
	Single family intensification
	Multiple family intensification

[1] All military persons at their place of work, excluding persons living on-base in barracks or on-board ships. Civilian persons working on military bases are included in the State and federal government category.

[2] Basic military + military group quarters.

SIC: Standard Industrial Classification.

because of environmental reasons were also identified for the GIS. Flood areas, steep slopes, publicly owned lands, areas of endangered species, riparian habitats, transmission line easements, airport noise contours and land set aside for future freeways all limit the type and amount of land development which may occur in a given area. The 19 study areas defined were each given 17 generic land use designations as follows:

- Low Density Single Family Residential
- Single Family Residential
- Multiple Family Residential
- Mobile Home Parks
- Mixed Use Commercial and Multi-Family Residential
- Commercial and Office Shopping Centre Business Parks
- Tourist, Commercial, Motel, Recreation
- Schools, Colleges, Universities
- Government, City Halls, Federal Facilities
- Hospitals, Health Services, Medical Centres
- Other Services, Churches, Cemeteries, Civic Centres

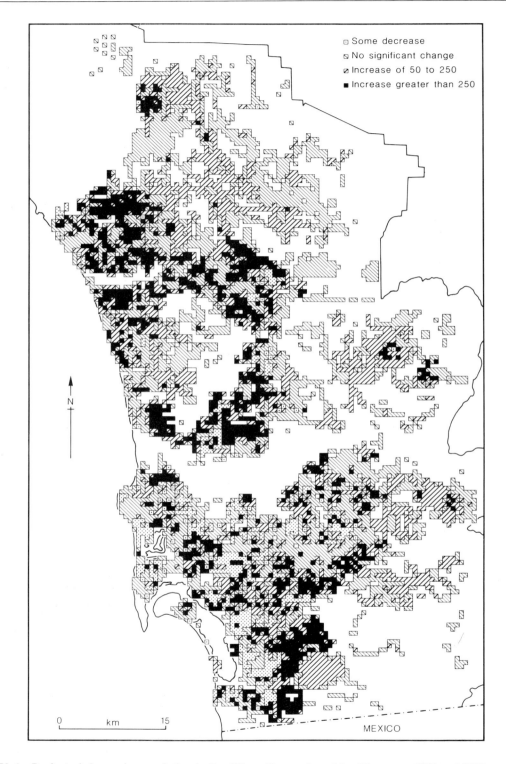

Fig. 52.4 Projected change in population in San Diego County by grid cell between 1986 and 2010.

Urban GIS Applications

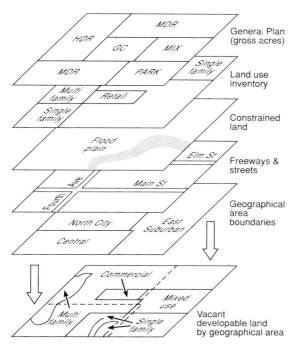

Fig. 52.5 The use of geographical overlay to isolate vacant developable land.

- Industrial Manufacturing and Research
- Transportation, Public Utilities, Airports, Broadcasting
- Electrical Power Plants, Sewage, Freeways
- Open Space, Parks, Recreational, Non-commercial
- Reserve Land, Open Space
- Agricultural, Dairies, Orchards
- Public/Semi-Public
- Solid Waste

Figure 52.5 shows the process used to calculate the vacant land acreage. Once the plan classifications for the 19 study areas were reassigned with the new generic land use system described above, the resulting file was overlaid on files of land use inventories and constrained lands. The resulting file was then overlaid on land set aside for freeways and traffic circulation. Through this process, the total number of vacant lands available for prior development for the 17 private land use designations was determined. SANDAG's geographical area boundary files were then overlaid and the information was aggregated for Major Statistical Areas (MSA). The land available for urban development as indicated by this overlay process is shown for 1986 in Fig. 52.6. With such a map, planning for new major public and private facilities such as a new regional and international airport – which San Diego desperately needs – can proceed. Moreover, since one key determinant underlying the sub-area forecast of the SOAP model is the amount of land available for development, this overlay process is also a key component of the Regional Growth Forecasting System.

A further example of this process is given by the Municipality of El Cajon, a city in eastern San Diego County comprising 80 000 people. Plate 52.1(a) depicts the general plan for El Cajon. Community plan land use codes were placed into seven categories for consistency in the computer model. The seven vertical and horizontal green lines represent unusable land designated for freeways in the city plan. Plate 52.1(b) shows existing land use in El Cajon. These data were obtained from aerial photographs derived from low altitude aircraft flown in 1986. The process included identifying 39 separate land uses on 90 maps at 1 : 24 000 scale. This information was translated to a mylar base and entered into the computer. Plate 52.1(c) shows land constrained from development because of flood areas, steep slopes, publicly owned lands, airport noise contours and future freeways. This plate also includes areas identified on El Cajon's general plan as undevelopable. To these, planners added new constraints such as riparian habitats and transmission line easements.

A vital requirement in order to prepare the RGF sub-regional SOAP forecast for El Cajon is the amount and type of land available for development, referred to as 'developable land'. This information is produced by a computer matching of the existing information shown in the three figures just described; the general plan, existing land uses and constrained and private lands. Beginning with the general plan, areas of existing development were subtracted. From the remaining vacant acreage, constrained land was removed as well as areas designated in the plan as undevelopable. The result is a computer file of developable land with associated general plan

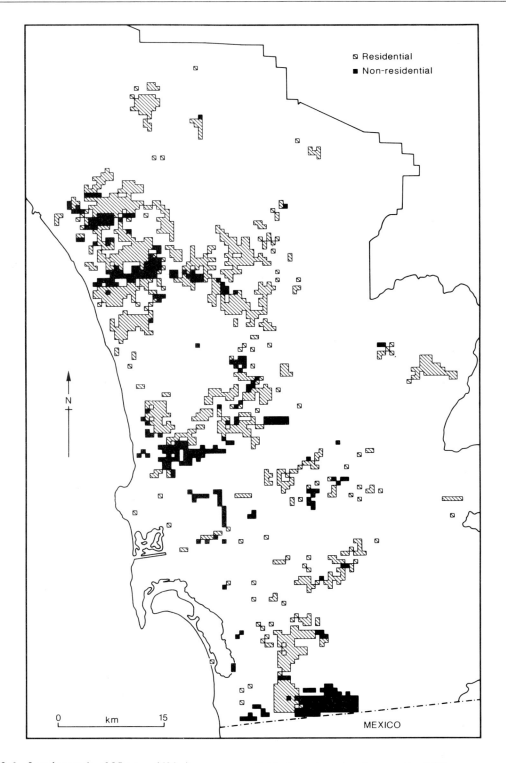

Fig. 52.6 Land parcels of 25 acres (62 ha) or more available for urban development in 1986.

designations and the generalized land use codes used in the forecast. This is shown in Plate 52.1(d).

Emergency planning and population shifts between day and night

Planning for emergencies has to take account of where people are at the relevant moment of time (Gatrell and Vincent 1990). The night-time location and distribution of a region's population is easy to identify. Many sources, from the federal census (see Rhind 1991 in this volume) to the local telephone directory, indicate where people live during the evening hours. The day-time population distribution, on the other hand, is equally important but almost impossible to ascertain. Exactly where people work, where people shop, where they go to school and – as a result – the location and the magnitude of the highest population densities taxing transportation and local community services are elusive. Sport stadia, employment centres and emergency evacuation bottlenecks are but a few of the places and infrastructures that must be considered in planning a wide variety of public uses and emergencies. For example, the routing of hazardous wastes should be done as far away from large day-time population clusters as is possible – but where are those clusters? Again, earthquakes and civil defence preparedness measures must also account for variations in day-time and resident population and should be based ideally on a knowledge of population shifts by each hour of the day; evacuation routes and emergency services are greatly affected depending on the time of day at which a disaster occurs.

A methodology for establishing the day-time population

During 1986, SANDAG produced a comprehensive travel behaviour survey of the region's residents to update transportation models, thus permitting an estimate of day-time population. For each regional grid cell, information on the number and type of trips and land use at origin and destination, vehicular categories and the times of trips made was stored. Forty demographic characteristics of the surveyed respondents were also made.

Trip generation was one of the aspects included in the transportation models. The number of daily person trips leaving or entering each of the 753 Traffic Analysis Zones (TAZ) was calculated by hour of day, day of week, type of trip and demographic characteristics of the traveller. Rates of trip generation were computed for the population to determine the amount and type of daily trips that will be made. These rates vary according to the zone's population and employment characteristics. For example, the number of trips generated at TAZ with relatively small income households are lower than TAZ with higher incomes, everything else being equal.

Day-time population by hour of day at each TAZ throughout the county and the reasons for trips by time of day and type of trip (i.e. home-to-work, work-to-shop, etc.) were calculated using the travel behaviour survey. These reasons were converted to proportions of all trips and applied to daily trip productions and attractions obtained from the transportation models. In the terminology used, factored trip productions refer to the number of trips leaving a zone: these are related to population and income data. Factored trip attractions refer to the number of trips entering a zone: they are dependent upon the type and amount of employment and land use in the zone. Therefore, a zone with high employment and low residential levels would have more attractions than productions. To calculate the locations of the population throughout San Diego County for every hour of the day, the number of factored trip productions was subtracted from the zone's resident population. Visitors and tourists residing in hotels and motels were included in the resident population values. Factored trip attractions were then added to the resulting values to produce the day-time population estimate by hour of day.

Day-time population shifts

The results for San Diego County are shown in Fig. 52.7. Of the 37 sub-regional areas in San Diego, 28 had net losses of population during the day-time and nine gained population for the time period shown in the figure (11 a.m. on an average weekday). The areas of largest gain correspond to areas of central San Diego which house major employment centres and the military bases. The areas of net numerical loss are primarily residential territories.

'Maximum population' refers to the distribution of non-typical accumulations of people. These estimates include productions and attractions

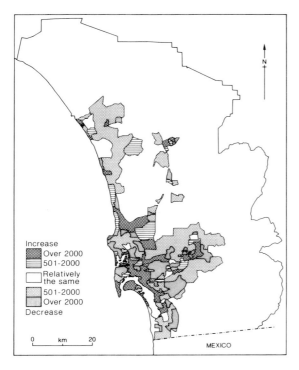

Fig. 52.7 Estimated changes from night-time to average 11 am population within census tracts in San Diego County.

for each zone, including special or unusual events. One such example is an event at San Diego Stadium which may add up to 70 000 people to a single zone. A warm summer day may add hundreds of thousands of people to zones along the Pacific Ocean beaches. The result is not necessarily 'typical': the value of such calculations produced from the GIS is to target localized worst-case scenarios which can be helpful in warding off traffic jams and emergency situations. 'Maximum population densities' within census tracts represent the maximum populations that would be likely to occur throughout the course of the year during the most crowded times and for which appropriate levels of emergency services, transportation facilities, water, sewer and fire protection should be provided.

Public facilities modelling: determining the optimal locations for fire stations

SANDAG has regularly provided support for decision making on the location of public facilities for the 18 incorporated cities within San Diego County. The City of La Mesa, for instance, requested SANDAG's assistance in determining the optimum number and location of fire stations for their city which is located adjacent to El Cajon in eastern San Diego County. One of the three existing fire stations is in the path of a planned freeway extension and will be closed in the early 1990s. Major changes in travel patterns will also result from a ramp construction to produce a service interchange between two other freeways. The city wanted to know how alternative fire station configurations would affect fire response times, given these anticipated changes. SANDAG's Public Facilities Model, the ARC/INFO Allocate program, the San Diego DIME File and the RGF were used to provide information on the impacts of service area response times as a consequence of proposed new site locations and closure of other sites.

The DIME file

The study area road network was determined from the regional Dual Independent Map Encoding (or DIME) file. This is a computerized street network originally developed by the US Bureau of Census and later supplanted by TIGER files (see Rhind 1991 in this volume). It contains geographical coordinates defining the location of street segments and information about each street, including the street name, address ranges and census tract codes. Attributes added to the network file of existing road systems included maximum speeds possible on each link. Other input included SANDAG's 'circulation element' or traffic on existing and future planned major roads. Each street segment was assigned an impedance value representing travel time in seconds for fire equipment to drive from one end to the other. The impedance value is based on the segment length and assigned speed. These values were calculated from travel speeds reviewed and adjusted by the La Mesa Fire Department and from street segment lengths. According to the RGF described earlier, the 1995 La Mesa population will be 53 794 people and the detailed forecasts of population dwelling units and employment levels were allocated to road networks from Master Geographical Referencing Area data (MGRA). In this case, MGRA data were derived from the intersections of incorporated city limits, the city's sphere of influence boundaries, community planning areas, census tracts and traffic analysis zone boundaries, all overlaid on a matrix of the 2000 by 2000 ft square (610 × 610 m) grid cells. Finally, the MGRA data were allocated to street segments based on the proportion of each segment's length to the total MGRA street length.

Evaluation of alternative fire station locations

Response times were calculated for alternative station configurations. The ARC/INFO Allocate model performs competitive allocations wherein each street segment is allocated to the closest site based on travel time. For each alternative, tables of 1995 population at place of residence, the occupied dwelling units and employment at place of work by two minute response time bands were produced. Table 52.2 shows the city of La Mesa's population, housing units and places of employment within two minute response time bands for six of the eleven alternatives that were calculated. Tabulations of high priority sites designated by the fire department by two minute time bands were also produced. High priority sites included commercial shopping centres, schools, rest homes and hospitals. According to Fig. 52.8, which shows model comparison of average response time, Model 3B has the most favourable response time for total population averaging just less than two minutes.

This study was restricted to the analysis of fire station response times involving existing and relocated stations in relation to La Mesa's population, employment locations and high priority response sites. The study did not consider other factors important in siting fire stations, such as acquisition costs, compatibility with adjacent land uses, physical site size and suitability and driveway access. None the less, the city of La Mesa is currently acquiring new space in order to bring its response times into line with model values presented in this study.

Crime reporting and crime prevention planning

The Crime Reporting and Interactive Mapping Environment (CRIME) was developed from the City of Tacoma, Washington, Crime Analysis Mapping System. It is a reporting and planning device for the Regional Urban Information System (RUIS). CRIME is a menu-driven system with which law enforcement personnel can analyse criminal data and plan for emergency enforcement and prevention. It also utilizes ARC/INFO and ESRI's Network software; indeed, it is written using the ARC Macro Language (AML) and other interface tools. CRIME provides the user with the capability of point mapping of crime occurrences or polygon-shaded (or choropleth) mapping of crime statistics; it can create reports on individual crimes or on aggregations of crimes by various geographical areas. The user of CRIME can also perform small area analysis by entering individual territories of law enforcement (Beats), entering radii of search areas around an address or interactively creating a polygonal area. The crime data used in this system were developed from the Automated Regional Justice Information System (ARJIS) of San Diego County and the Crime Analysis Statistical System (CASS). The street data are from the DIME file maintained and updated by SANDAG (see above). Land use data are from SANDAG's 1986 generalized land use inventory and population data are from the Series 7 RGF and housing allocation estimation described earlier. Polygon files were also digitized by SANDAG.

The necessary inputs

These included two CASS files – an incident file and a violation file – for each time period to be analysed. Both of these files contain data for crime cases and arrest incident types by dates and street address. Citation, field interview and traffic accident incident types may also be incorporated. Address matching was completed by the ARJIS with x,y coordinates in California State plane feet included on each record. Address information is included in the incidents file. All other geocodes except county community plan areas and supervisorial districts are in the violations file. The two files have a common incident number, facilitating the establishment of relationships.

Geographical units digitized as ARC/INFO coverages and available for analysis purposes are police beats (and sheriff territories), community planning areas, common census tracts and districts and divisions. These districts are either council or supervisorial districts. Each division is either a police division or a sheriff's command area.

The function CALK DATA calculates the above-average number of crimes, the number of crimes per square mile (2.59 km^2), the crimes per 1000 population and the property crimes and crimes against persons for every beat, community planning

Table 52.2 Comparisons of model runs – total population, housing units and employment served within specified response times (all model runs include automatic AID).

Model La Mesa Stations	Response	Popn.	Housing units	Employment
EXISTING CONDITION				
Model 1–A				
11, 12, 13	<2 min	23 132	9 968	19 103
	2–4 min	29 749	13 102	8 896
	4–6 min	913	417	25
	TOTAL	53 794	23 487	28 024
CONSOLIDATION				
RUNS				
Model 2–A				
11 & 13	<2 min	19 904	8 669	18 404
	2–4 min	32 918	14 375	9 586
	4–6 min	972	443	34
	TOTAL	53 794	23 487	28 024
Model 2–B				
11 & alternative A	<2 min	20 786	8 926	15 956
Fletcher	2–4 min	31 982	14 095	12 027
Parkway	4–6 min	1 026	466	41
	TOTAL	53 794	23 487	28 024
Model 2–C				
11 & alternative C				
Brier Patch	<2 min	17 438	7 595	16 403
	2–4 min	35 171	15 360	11 562
	4–6 min	1 185	532	59
	TOTAL	53 794	23 487	28 024
Model 2–D				
11 & alternative B	<2 min	20 981	9 282	10 963
Sunset Park	2–4 min	31 633	13 678	16 963
	4–6 min	1 180	527	98
	TOTAL	53 794	23 487	28 024
Model 2–E				
11	<2 min	14 712	6 555	9 762
	2–4 min	37 645	16 292	18 147
	4–6 min	1 436	640	115
	TOTAL	53 794	23 487	28 024
Model 2–F				
No La Mesa	<2 min	2 268	968	569
stations	2–4 min	17 060	6 995	10 486
	4–6 min	31 807	14 279	16 397
	6–8 min	2 562	1 200	569
	8–10 min	97	46	3
	TOTAL	53 794	23 487	28 024

area, census tract, council or supervisorial district and division or command area. The function AGCBATA generates aggregated data of incidents and violations by the same areas. The data are stored in ARC/INFO data files.

Point mapping and reporting of crime incidents

A simple point mapping option is available to CRIME users. Selecting the 'Beats' box on a menu sets the geographical area to beats and requests user

Urban GIS Applications

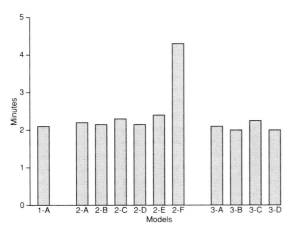

Fig. 52.8 Average response time to service population with different models of fire station provision.

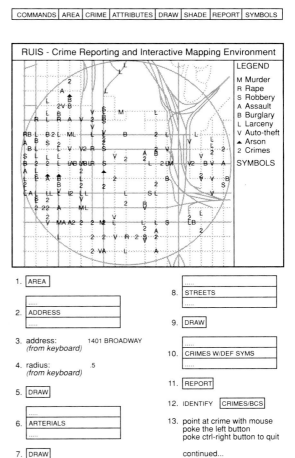

Fig. 52.9 Interactive mapping and analysis of crimes within 0.5 mile (0.8 km) of a specified point using RUIS.

input for the beat number to be entered from the keyboard. Entering 113 from the keyboard causes the system to select all crimes geocoded to that beat. Messages will be displayed in the dialogue area describing the procedure the system is performing. The mapping area will be cleared and beat boundaries drawn. The last message displayed in the dialogue area is the number of points currently selected. By selecting the 'Crimes' box, the system draws currently selected crimes and their level of occurrence. By selecting 'arterials', the freeways, ramps and other roads are drawn in various colours.

Figure 52.9 displays the point reporting option. Choice of 'Address' sets the area to the address given and requests user input from the keyboard concerning crimes. For this figure, the street address 1401 Broadway has been chosen as the centre of the radius search. The radius has been set at 0.5 mile (0.8 km). 'Draw' displays the draw menu. 'Arterials' will draw freeways and ramps in red and major roads in green. By touching 'Crimes', the system draws the currently selected crimes with default symbols. Positioning the mouse on the crime symbol and clicking the left button displays the code and descriptions of the code for that particular crime. Thus the system is easy to use even by those unskilled in GIS operations.

CONCLUSIONS

Because of the myriad of geographical reporting regions in San Diego County and because of the burgeoning population growth in the region, planning for a wide variety of facilities and programmes requires the use of a large-scale GIS. SANDAG has streamlined the GIS in San Diego County so that 18 cities, the County of San Diego's unincorporated area plus a large number of private commercial groups, can use standardized information to provide compatible results and planning activities. A regional information system is the responsibility of each large regional area in order to meet the increasing economic, environmental and public facility needs and analysis. In this rapidly developing county at least, GIS has proved a major boon in urban and regional planning.

The example case studies chosen here illustrate graphically the range of urban GIS applications. Already much of the potential of GIS in urban environments is being realized in San Diego, in other US cities and, indeed, throughout the world. There are extremely large urban GIS projects well underway in cities as diverse as Baghdad, Glasgow, Mexico City and Stockholm (Gault and Peuther 1990; Yeh 1990). Each of these has its own particular problems and utilize GIS in different ways. Nevertheless, the requirement of managing large quantities of disparate spatial referenced data is common to them all.

REFERENCES

Berry J K (1991) GIS in island resource planning: a case study in map analysis. In: Maguire D J, Goodchild M F, Rhind D W (eds.) *Geographical Information Systems: principles and applications*. Longman, London, pp. 285–95, Vol 2

Cowen D J, Mitchell L, Meyer W (1990) Industrial modeling using a Geographic Information System: the first step in developing an expert system for industrial site selection. *Proceedings of GIS/LIS '90*, Volume 1. ASPRS/ACSM/AAG/URISA/AM-FM, Bethesda Maryland, pp. 1–10

Cowen D J, Shirley W L (1991) Integrated planning information systems. In: Maguire D J, Goodchild M F, Rhind D W (eds.) *Geographical Information Systems: principles and applications*. Longman, London, pp. 297–310, Vol 2

Dueker K J (1988) Urban applications of geographical information systems: a grouping into three levels of resolution. *URISA Proceedings*, Volume 2, pp. 104–9

Estes J E, McGwire K E, Fletcher G E, Foresman T W (1987) Coordinating hazardous waste management activities using GIS *International Journal of Geographical Information Systems* 1: 359–77

Gatrell A C, Vincent P (1990) Managing natural and technological hazards: the role of GIS. *Regional Research Laboratory Initiative Discussion Paper 7*. RRL Initiative, Sheffield University

Gault I, Peutherer D (1990) Developing geographical information systems in local government in the UK: case studies from Birmingham City Council and Strathclyde Regional Council. In: Worrell L (ed.) *Geographic Information Systems: developments and applications*. Belhaven, London, pp. 109–32

Gurd F B (1990) Requirements of Geographic Information Systems used for supply/demand analysis of real estate markets. *Proceedings of GIS/LIS '90* **1**: ASPRS/ACSM/AAG/URISA/AM-FM, Bethesda Maryland, pp. 21–5

Lee T S, Russell J S (1990) Potential applications of Geographic Information Systems to the construction industry. *Proceedings of GIS/LIS '90*, Volume 1. ASPRS/ACSM/AAG/URISA/AM-FM, Bethesda Maryland, pp. 11–20

Maguire D J, Hickin B W, Longley I, Mesev T (1991) Waste disposal site selection using raster and vector GIS. *Mapping Awareness* **5** (1): 24–7

Mahoney R P (1991) GIS and utilities. In: Maguire D J, Goodchild M F, Rhind D W (eds.) *Geographical Information Systems: principles and applications*. Longman, London, pp. 101–14, Vol 2

Newkirk P (1987) Municipal information systems: challenges and opportunities. *Plan Canada* **27**: 94–100

Rhind D W (1991) Counting the people: the role of GIS. In: Maguire D J, Goodchild M F, Rhind D W (eds.) *Geographical Information Systems: principles and applications*. Longman, London, pp. 127–37, Vol 2

Siderelis K C (1991) Land resource information systems. In: Maguire D J, Goodchild M F, Rhind D W (eds.) *Geographical Information Systems: principles and applications*. Longman, London, pp. 261–73, Vol 2

Sommers R (1987) Geographic information systems in local government: a commentary. *Photogrammetric Engineering and Remote Sensing* **53**: 1379–82

Stewart J C (1987) Geographic criteria for the siting of low level waste disposal sites. *Proceedings of the International Geographic Information Systems (IGIS) Symposium: the research agenda*, Volume 3. AAG, Washington, pp. 87–101

Sullivan J G, Chow A L K (1990) The Wisconsin legislative redistricting project: design interface, training, and policy issues. *Proceedings of GIS/LIS '90*, Volume 1. ASPRS/ACSM/AAG/URISA/AM-FM, Bethesda Maryland, pp. 26–41

Yeh A G (1990) A land information system for the monitoring of land supply in the urban development of Hong Kong. In: Worrell L (ed.) *Geographic information systems: developments and applications*. Belhaven, London, pp. 163–87

53

LAND RESOURCE INFORMATION SYSTEMS

K C SIDERELIS

This chapter examines the realm of GIS applications which involve information on land resources. It draws extensively on the work of North Carolina's Center for Geographic Information and Analysis. Land resource information systems are first defined and the features which distinguish them from other application areas of GIS are described. The chapter also defines the various user groups of such systems and describes the types and characteristics of data that the systems handle. The bulk of the chapter, however, comprises a description of three very major case studies illustrating the value of LRIS in a variety of practical ways: these are the Albemarle–Pamlico estuarine study, state-wide screening for a hazardous waste management facility and the location of an optimal proposed site for the Superconducting Super Collider.

THE SCOPE OF LAND RESOURCE INFORMATION SYSTEMS

For the purposes of this chapter, Land Resource Information Systems (LRIS) are defined as an application area of GIS which involves the use of spatial information for the broad purpose of managing land. In this context, the land resource includes water, air, soil and biota. Examples of disciplines which utilize GIS as land resource information systems include hydrology, soil science, forestry, environmental management, fish and wildlife management, planning, geology and archaeology.

The contents of a LRIS typically include a wide range of data, such as those describing the character and distribution of the resources themselves (including resources associated with the marine environment and the subsurface). Other data present may well include environmental parameters that reflect human activities and programmes affecting the land resources, census and demographic data describing the human environment and its potential impact on resources, and data about the physical, man-made infrastructure. Cadastral data, not for the purpose of registry and taxation but rather for assessing the relationship of land ownership to the use of resources, is often a key component of the LRIS databases.

Most applications of LRIS typically involve utilization of large volumes of data. Traditionally, the use of polygonal data has dominated the applications. This has been due partially to a fascination with polygon overlay capabilities and partially to a lack of robust software for dealing with linear (e.g. network) data. Perhaps most fundamentally, it has been due to the fact that soils, land use, land cover and many natural resources data are usually conceived and mapped as sets of internally homogeneous polygons – even though that is sometimes a gross approximation (see Burrough 1991 in this volume).

Land resource managers usually (but not invariably – see Robinette 1991 in this volume) deal with data in GIS that are relatively small scale. In general, survey data of engineering accuracy are not a requirement for effective land management. Other characteristics of data in LRIS are that the data may represent rapidly changing phenomena, they are often derived from disparate sources and they may involve uncertainty – thereby limiting their comparability and reliability. Finally, the attribute or tabular data associated with cartographic features – as well as those features themselves – are normally very significant so far as the analyses associated with land management are concerned.

The importance of data integration capabilities and spatial analysis tools in LRIS cannot be overstated. Few applications are possible solely with data retrieval and display tools; most demand the capacity to link diverse data together using spatial keys (see Flowerdew 1991 in this volume). Therefore, the systems make widespread use of polygon overlay, buffer (or corridor) generation and the development of structured spatial models.

In practice, the uses of LRIS range from automated cartography to support of policy formulation and management. They serve to underpin routine operations, such as making inventories and monitoring change, but also support policy reviews and the planning process. In other cases, they aid the completion of special 'one off' projects and support research and scientific studies. It will be obvious that some overlap exists between the role envisaged for GIS by Robinette (1991 in this volume) and that espoused here; the case studies used in both chapters are, however, highly complementary and – in totality – serve to demonstrate the range and importance of GIS in dealings with land by governments, such as the states in North America.

LRIS CASE STUDIES AND THE CENTER FOR GEOGRAPHIC INFORMATION AND ANALYSIS

Three case studies have been selected to illustrate use of the LRIS that is managed by the Center for Geographic Information and Analysis (CGIA) in North Carolina. The projects are the Albemarle–Pamlico (A/P) Estuarine Study, a project involving state-wide site screening for a hazardous waste management facility, and the preparation of a site proposal for the Superconducting Super Collider (SSC). This particular set of projects is an assortment of different kinds of GIS applications which were conducted for a variety of purposes.

The state-wide screening of suitable areas for a hazardous waste facility and the siting of the Superconducting Super Collider, for example, were special 'one off' projects performed on behalf of the state. The Albemarle–Pamlico Estuarine Study is an ongoing programme that provides an opportunity for multiple agencies in the state to utilize GIS in support of daily operations and, at the same time, employ GIS as a tool in policy formulation and administration. All three applications involved the development or utilization of complex databases and each case study illustrates the use of evaluative spatial models to solve problems. Thus the screening of suitable areas for a hazardous waste facility incorporated a suitability model based on successive elimination of unsuitable areas. The SSC siting involved a comparative analysis of alternative sites and the A/P Study tested a model for water area classification as a component of water use planning. All of the applications utilized vector-based GIS software. Raster data processing was also used in the Superconducting Super Collider project for surface modelling and in the Albemarle–Pamlico Study for image processing.

All of the work described was carried out by the North Carolina Center for Geographic Information and Analysis. This was established in 1977, at that time under the name of the Land Resources Information Service. The agency is in the state's Department of Environment, Health and Natural Resources. The mission of CGIA is to develop a state-wide geographical database and to operate a GIS service bureau for other agencies in the state. CGIA has conducted literally hundreds of projects using GIS over the last decade. This variety of experience has provided important lessons on how best to meet customer needs and on how to build long-term capabilities from short-term, 'one-off' support. No state funding has been provided for the development and maintenance of the database at CGIA, nor for the operation of the system. Consequently, the database has developed as a by-product of projects which are performed on a cost recovery basis. Nevertheless, substantial data holdings now exist in the system which are available for users. Typically, a user who bears the cost to enter or update a component of the database also enjoys the benefits of data entered by another user.

At the time of writing and for much of the period covered by the case studies, CGIA utilized the following software: ESRI's ARC/INFO GIS software, the ERDAS image analysis system and Dynamic Graphics' ISM (Interactive Surface Modeling). All the software runs on a network of SUN Microsystems workstations and server in the UNIX environment, though earlier work was carried out on a Data General minicomputer.

THE ALBEMARLE–PAMLICO ESTUARINE STUDY

The Albemarle–Pamlico Estuarine system in North Carolina is the second largest estuarine complex in the United States and the third largest system in North America. It has been designated as an estuary of national concern under the Environmental Protection Agency's National Estuary Program. The A/P Study is jointly funded by the Environmental Protection Agency (EPA) and the state. It includes numerous cooperators from federal and state government, as well as research institutions in North Carolina. The ambitious goals of the Study are to:

- collect, characterize and assess data to identify the causes of environmental problems;
- assess status and trends in water quality, natural resources and uses of the estuary;
- develop a comprehensive management plan to restore and maintain the chemical, physical and biological integrity of the estuary.

The A/P Study Office and the oversight committees identified information management as one of the major components of the study. They selected CGIA to provide data management support, thereby recognizing the importance of GIS in attaining the goals of the overall study. The GIS has been used in the collection and characterization of data, in assessing the status and trends of the area's resources and to support and assess various resource management alternatives (Clark 1990; Copeland 1989).

Data collection and characterization

CGIA conducted a 'data needs' assessment for the A/P Study in order to identify the existing data resources about the area and to determine the data requirements of resource managers, the research community and other likely users of a database. Although numerous existing data holdings and special studies were documented, the focus of the A/P Study data collection effort has been to assemble a database in the GIS consisting of data layers that have clear relevance to effective resource management. The information and information needs were separated into four general categories: 'resource-critical' areas, water quality, fisheries dynamics and the human environment. The data layers in the 'resource-critical' area include information on sensitive estuarine habitats. The water quality layers include data related to non-point and point source pollution, as well as data describing in-stream relationships. The fisheries dynamics layers consist of information about fish and shellfish stocks and the possible causes of declines in fish catches. The human environment category includes data that describe the human uses of the estuarine area and the institutional setting in which management plans must function.

The A/P Study area includes the drainage basins of both Albemarle Sound and Pamlico Sound. The region includes 4 million hectares in North Carolina and another 0.8 million hectares of Virginia. Consequently, the volume of data that has accumulated is extremely large. Upon completion, the database will contain over 60 layers of cartographic data, covering nearly 400 US Geological Survey 7.5 minute quadrangle maps. The abundant tabular data that are being collected will consist of approximately 60 data sets. Another factor contributing to the volume of data is the multi-temporal nature of many of the data sets.

Status and trends assessment

A rigorous and quantitative assessment of trends in the Albemarle–Pamlico area has been problematic. Although a considerable amount of historical data exist from the monitoring efforts of environmental regulatory programmes and from demographic censuses and surveys, their condition often limits or precludes reliable integration and analysis. This situation, combined with the initial dearth of data about the ambient environment, resulted in the gathering of new baseline data. These have provided an increased understanding of the status of the estuarine area and fortunately should enable robust analysis of trends in the future.

Land use/land cover information is one of numerous data sets of baseline data being developed for the Albemarle–Pamlico area. It is in many ways representative of the problems and the potential value of data in a GIS for trend analysis. A number of land use/land cover inventories have been conducted for portions of the study area over the years. The data, however, are not readily comparable due to differences in geographical coverage, scale, date of collection, classification scheme and mapping technique used. In recognition of the critical need for current, uniform land use data for the entire study area, the A/P Study has funded the acquisition and analysis of Landsat Thematic Mapper (TM) data to produce a land use and land cover inventory. This is being stored as image data and the classified version of it is also being converted to a vector format. The classification scheme used for the project is a modification of the Level II classification described by Anderson et al. (1976).

Plates 53.1 and 53.2, portraying a US Geological Survey Land Use Data Analysis (LUDA) map of a portion of the study area and a corresponding TM image respectively, illustrate the differences in the two data sets and the potential for misleading comparisons. However, with appropriate aggregation of categories, use of the two data sets may reveal general trends in changing land use and land cover. Perhaps the most promising prospect for the future is the ability to integrate the vector database with the image data. For example, the TM image in Plate 53.2 is superimposed with county boundary data held in vector form.

Support of Management Strategies

The comprehensive management plan being developed for the A/P Study will identify and recommend specific strategies to preserve and maintain the estuarine environment. One such management strategy under consideration is a comprehensive water use planning and zoning programme which is consistent with the land use planning requirements of the state's Coastal Area Management Act (CAMA). A Water Area Use Classification System that incorporates a GIS model has been designed as a component of the planning and zoning programme. A project team, consisting of representatives of the North Carolina Sea Grant College Program and CGIA, along with a planning consultant and a local county planning official, was assembled to design and test the Classification System. This System designates estuarine waters as one of three area classification types: Preservation Water Area, Conservation Water Area or Developed Water Area. The first of these will be established to assure the protection of significant fish and wildlife habitats, to assure continued biological productivity and to provide for scientific, research and educational needs. Conservation Water Areas will be designated for long-term uses of renewable resources that do not require alteration of the estuary except for the purposes of restoration. Finally, Developed Water Areas will be designated for navigation and other public, commercial and industrial water-dependent uses.

The GIS model developed for implementing the Water Area Use Classification System was tested in an area of Carteret County where uses of the estuarine waters are fraught with conflict. The GIS was used to assess the determining and non-determining factors associated with the classification and to classify the estuarine waters. Application of the system consisted of the following five steps: identification of the factors that govern water area use classification; segmentation of the estuarine waters into water tracts; evaluation of non-determining factors; assignment of factor values to water tracts; and classification of water tracts (Nagy and Siderelis 1990). The process is described in more detail below.

Identification of Factors

CGIA prepared a series of data layers for Carteret County, each representing a factor used in the Water Area Use Classification. For this test, four data layers were developed to represent determining factors or areas where use is established by legal or legislative mandate. Seven layers were used to represent non-determining factors; four of the factors involved are land features and three are water features. Table 53.1 lists the factor data layers created for use in the model.

Segmentation of the Estuarine Area

The waters of the study area were geographically segmented using the GIS. The first step in this

Table 53.1 Determining and non-determining factor data layers.

Determining factor data layers
  Fisheries nursery areas
  Outstanding resource waters
  Crab spawning sanctuaries
  Maintained channels/turning basins

Non-determining land factor data layers
  Land use and land cover
  Coastal Area Management Act (CAMA) permits
  Marinas
  Point source dischargers

Non-determining water factor data layers
  Submerged aquatic vegetation
  Shellfish evaluation areas
  Tidal salt water quality classifications

process was to separate water areas containing determining factors from other waters; this was accomplished using overlay techniques. The remaining water areas were divided into water zones, all of similar size and hydrographic properties. These areas were delineated on a study area map and incorporated into the GIS as a data layer.

As a further step in segmenting the estuarine area, regions of influence were outlined for each water zone to facilitate assessment of the land factors. The project team decided that land activities within 1000 feet (305 m) of the estuarine waters would influence the water use area classification. The GIS was used to generate a 1000-foot buffer to each of the 13 water zones. The regions of influence were also stored as a data layer and coded with the identification number of the associated water zone. Plate 52.3 illustrates the 13 water zones created for this application and the corresponding regions of influence.

Evaluation of Non-Determining Factor Data Layers

To assess the influence of land-related factors on the adjacent water areas, a series of overlays was performed. Each region of influence was overlaid with the land factor data layers. The percentage of urban land in each region was calculated from the overlay of land use and land cover data. In a similar fashion, the concentrations of several point features were tallied on a 'number per unit area' or area density basis. These features include marinas, major coastal developments requiring CAMA permits and facilities with environmental permits to discharge waste water into surface waters (point source dischargers). These raw data values were stored as attributes of the water zone data layer.

The evaluation of water factors was conducted in a manner similar to the evaluation of land factors and was an extension of that process. The water zone data layer (now encoded with raw data values from the land factor assessment) was overlaid with each of the data layers representing the water factors. The resultant data layer contained hundreds of water tracts encoded with the original water zone number, raw land factor data values and raw water factor data values. For instance, codes from the Submerged Aquatic Vegetation (SAV) data layer indicated the presence or absence of that resource. Codes from the Shellfish Evaluation Area data layer indicated whether an area is open or closed for shell fishing. Codes from the Water Quality Classification data layer indicated one of three values: SA waters are suitable for shell fishing; SB waters are suitable for swimming; and SC waters are suitable for fish propagation. The classifications, which are shown in Table 53.2, are assigned to tidal salt waters and indicate the existing or contemplated 'best usage' for which they must be protected.

Assignment of Factor Values to Water Tracts

The next step in the model was to assign numerical factor values to the raw data values for each water tract, thereby normalizing the diversity of raw data types. Percentages, area density values and text descriptions were all translated to integers ranging between one and four. In this case, the ranges of data groupings were selected by the project team on the basis of a qualitative evaluation of the data distribution and the factor values were chosen to reflect the overall policy direction of the County. Of course, a different assignment of factor values potentially could yield significantly different final results. The groupings and possible factor values used in this application of the model are shown in Table 53.2.

Classification of Water Tracts

Water areas containing determining factors were readily classified. Areas classified as Preservation Water Area included Fisheries Nursery Areas, Outstanding Resource Waters and Crab Spawning Sanctuaries. Areas classified as Developed Water Areas included Maintained Channels and Turning

Table 53.2 Land and water factor values

Factor	Raw data value	Description	Factor value
Land use	76%–100% urban	Very high influence	1
	51%– 75% urban	High influence	2
	26%– 50% urban	Moderate influence	3
	0%– 25% urban	Low influence	4
CAMA permits	> 4 square miles (10 km^2)	High concentration	1
	2–4 square miles (5–10 km^2)	Moderate concentration	2
	< 2 square miles (<5 km^2)	Low concentration	3
Marinas	> 1.5 square miles (4 km^2)	High concentration	1
	0.5–1.5 square miles (1.3–4 km^2)	Moderate concentration	2
	< 0.5 square miles (1.3 km^2)	Low concentration	3
Dischargers	> 2.0 square miles (5 km^2)	High concentration	1
	1.5–2.0 square miles (4–5 km^2)	Moderate concentration	2
	< 1.5 square miles (4 km^2)	Low concentration	3
Submerged vegetation	no	SAV absent	1
	yes	SAV present	3
Shellfish evaluation	closed	Area closed to shell fishing	1
	open	Area open to shell fishing	3
Water quality class	SA	Suitable for shell fishing	2
	SB	Suitable for swimming	3
	SC	Suitable for fish propagation	1

SAV: Submerged Aquatic Vegetation.
SA: Salt Water Class A
SB: Salt Water Class B
SC: Salt Water Class C

Basins. GIS overlays were used to determine if intersections of Preservation Water Areas with Developed Water Areas occurred. Areas of overlap were appropriately reclassified.

The classification of water tracts containing non-determining factors began by establishing a weight or multiplier to reflect the relative importance of one factor as compared to other factors. A simple equation was applied to evaluate the weighted values for each water tract. The equation is:

$$T = \sum_{i=1}^{n} F_i W_i$$

where: T is the total weighted sum of factor values;
F_i is the value of each respective factor;
W_i is the weight of each respective factor;
and
n is the total number of factors (seven).

In the test case, all of the weights were given a value of 1. The lowest possible value of T for any water tract (see Plate 53.4 and Table 53.2) was 7 and the highest possible score 22. The T values were used to group water tracts and classify them as a Preservation Water Area, Conservation Water Area or Developed Water Area. The ranges of data values for each class were once again determined by a qualitative evaluation of the distribution of values. Two alternative groupings were performed. Plate 53.5 is a map of the study area classified according to the first option.

The application of the model for the test area in Carteret County was intended only to illustrate the Water Area Use Classification System. Although the results are not actual recommendations for the County and the classification system is not yet (at the time of writing) formally endorsed as a management option by the A/P Study, the value of GIS in helping to formulate and administer policy was clearly demonstrated. Upon review of the project, members of the Policy Committee that guides the A/P Study enthusiastically initiated plans for a workshop to refine the water area classification model and to explore the use of similar GIS techniques in developing a simulation model for the study area.

Significant Findings of the Case Study

In many ways, the data management efforts made in the Albemarle–Pamlico Estuarine Study seem to be fulfilling the expectations of GIS predicted by its pioneers over at least two decades. A common database is being used to support technicians, scientists, managers and decision makers alike. The use and integration of allied technologies, such as image processing, are being incorporated into a production setting. Moreover, through this project GIS is enabling and fostering institutional change. For example, new working relationships have been forged between agencies to collect data, share systems, train users and accomplish projects. Perhaps most important of all in the longer term, GIS has caught the attention of key decision makers in the state who are, as a consequence, likely to continue to utilize GIS in making policies and instituting programmes to manage the fragile estuarine environment.

STATE-WIDE SCREENING FOR A HAZARDOUS WASTE SITE

The North Carolina Hazardous Waste Management Commission was created to make recommendations on the siting, design, construction and operation of hazardous waste management facilities authorized by the governor of the state. The Commission implemented a state-wide screening process in 1989 to identify a suitable site for a waste management facility. In so doing, it enlisted the aid of CGIA to conduct the state-wide screening, requiring a search of the entire state accomplished by successive elimination of unsuitable areas. The GIS was employed to identify, map and then measure areas excluded from consideration for a hazardous waste facility. The purpose of the project was to identify all acceptable areas from which a specific site could be selected.

A three-step process was employed to eliminate unsuitable areas from consideration as a site for such a facility. First, a preliminary screening was conducted by considering a number of criteria that were set forth in rules or by statute. This step excluded 89 per cent of the state from consideration. The second step in the process was the formation of parcels from the residual potentially suitable areas: this step identified 2851 parcels. Finally, a further screening of the parcels was accomplished by application of a set of evaluation procedures. These three steps are described in more detail below.

Application of Rules and Statutes

The Commission's site selection criteria were based on factors established by North Carolina General Statutes, North Carolina Administrative Code and the Code of Federal Regulations. They formed three groups, termed Rule Sets (Table 53.3). These criteria, paraphrased from the rules and statutes and grouped by Rule Set, excluded from consideration all those areas which meet one or more of the conditions shown in Table 53.3.

The application of these criteria in the GIS environment was straightforward and the general approach involved sequential use of the following measures for each of the criteria:

- *Extraction of relevant data from the database.* For application of the three Rule Sets, the data used were of state-wide coverage and were derived from small-scale mapping that ranged from 1 : 100 000 to 1 : 250 000 scale. Although the existing database at CGIA was used extensively for this project, it was also necessary to enhance it. Several layers and a number of items were added to the attribute data describing geographical features. Many of the attribute data were compiled specifically for this project.

- *Application of unique analyses and interpretations to the data.* The determination of unsuitability of an area was accomplished by selecting features based on attribute values or by performing buffer analysis on geographical features.

- *Addition of results to the composite inventory of*

Table 53.3 Rule sets used in the site selection process.

	Acreage excluded on this criterion
Rule Set 1:	
• upon an inland lake;	
• upon an upland bog or pocosin, or upon marsh or swamp;	6 331 530
• in a coastal hurricane storm surge or inundation area;	2 055 400
• within 25 miles (40 km) of an existing polychlorinated biphenyl (PCB) landfill;	1 058 950
• greater than 60 miles (100 km), measured in a straight line, from the Interstate Highway System in North Carolina;	4 832 150
• within 0.25 miles (0.4 km) of the epicentre of a seismic event of a magnitude greater than three, as measured by the Modified Mercalli Intensity Scale of 1931;	5110
• in or on an Indian reservation or federal military reservation;	320 330
• in or on state and national parks or forests, federal wildlife refuges, state-owned gamelands, and designated wilderness areas.	3 818 670
Rule Set 2:	
• within 5 miles of the state boundary (figures for buffer zone only);	3 957 810
• within 10 miles from the centre line of the Blue Ridge National Parkway;	2 538 060
• upon the geological formations of Castle Hayne; Shady Dolomite; and Murphy Marble, Andrews Formation and Nottely Quartzite, Undivided;	703 200
• upon a general soils association type that floods in more than 10% of the area;	7 072 450
• within the corporate limits of a municipality.	1 285 960
Rule Set 3:	
• upon a general soils association type that has a surface slope greater than 15% for more than 70% of the area;	3 732 470
• within a drainage area of fresh waters or tidal salt waters that are protected by regulation as water supplies;	
• within two miles (3 km) of a surface water intake that provides water for human or animal consumption, unless it is downstream of the intake;	5 210 610
• within the drainage area of the head waters of state-designated Outstanding Resources Waters or High Quality Waters, or within two miles (3 km) of a stream segment below the head waters area;	
• greater than 15 miles (25 km) to the Interstate Highway System or to a four lane highway that directly connects to the Interstate Highway System;	12 916 700
• upon a general soils association type in which 50% of the soils have less than 35% clay.	9 973 450

unsuitable areas. A data layer was maintained as a composite of all unsuitable areas. This data layer was updated each time a criterion was evaluated.

• *Resolution of areas of overlap within the composite inventory*. The unsuitable areas identified in application of one criterion often overlapped areas identified by previous criteria. For example, many upland bogs and pocosins are also located in hurricane storm surge areas and some areas within the boundaries of a municipality are also greater than 60 miles (100 km) from an interstate highway. GIS overlays were used to resolve these areas of overlap within the composite file.

• *Production of maps and reports of results*. Maps were produced to illustrate the areas in the state that were excluded from consideration and reports were printed to summarize the acreage excluded by criterion, by Rule Set and in total. Application of the criteria in Rule Set 1 eliminated 29 per cent of the state; Rule Set 2 excluded another 26 per cent; and a total of 89 per cent of the state was excluded from consideration after application of Rule Set 3. Table 53.3 is a list of each criterion in each Rule Set and a summary of the acreage eliminated by the individual criteria while Plate 53.6 provides a series of maps displaying the result of application of each Rule Set and the resulting composite of unsuitable areas.

Formation of Parcels

The North Carolina Hazardous Waste Management Commission wished to identify discernible tracts of land, based on physical features, to aid further evaluation. Using the GIS, parcels were formed from the suitable areas remaining after the preliminary screening. First, the composite data layer of unsuitable areas was used to create a layer of residual potentially suitable areas. Arcs representing primary roads from the transportation data layer and perennial streams from the hydrography layer (linear data types) were combined with arcs from the data layer of suitable areas and used to build a polygon data layer of parcels. The parcels were created where either roads, streams or boundaries of a suitable area fully enclosed a suitable area. This technique produced parcels which, in some cases, enclosed non-intersecting roads or streams. Plate 53.7 is a map of parcels that were created. As a final step, parcels less than 350 acres (140 ha) in size were eliminated. Through this process 2851 parcels were formed.

Application of Evaluation Procedures

Because the site-screening criteria of the three Rule Sets failed to exclude almost 300 000 acres (120 000 ha) of land, evaluation procedures were applied to reduce still further the area being considered for a hazardous waste management facility. In this case, the procedures were used to identify parcels with acceptable characteristics. The GIS was used to apply three procedures, reducing the list of priority parcels to 1512 or about 2 per cent of the land area of the state. The following areas were deemed by the Commission to be more acceptable than others:

- areas within a 75 mile (120 km) radius around the state's measured centre of hazardous waste generation and off-site shipment;
- areas within a 45 mile (72 km) radius around meteorological stations (for air modelling purposes); and
- areas within a 15 mile (24 km) zone around the interstate highways.

Plate 53.8 is a map showing the effect of the application of these three factors. Further evaluations were conducted outside the GIS environment but results of the evaluations were incorporated into the system. Evaluations of parcel shape and configuration, presence of streams on parcels, geological considerations and a detailed verification process reduced the number of priority parcels to 18. After deliberation, the Commission selected two finalist sites and will eventually recommend a single site.

Significant Findings of the Case Study

Three significant findings surfaced from this project. The first was that GIS can demonstrably be effective in a public forum. The Hazardous Waste Management Commission conducted a series of public meetings during the course of this project, the purpose of which was to review each Rule Set in draft form and to convey the results of applying the previous Rule Set. Representatives of CGIA attended the meetings and conducted real-time demonstrations of the application of the three Rule Sets in the screening process using a workstation and graphic projection system. The response to the demonstrations on the part of local citizens was largely favourable and the demonstrations served to convey the objectivity and equity of a rather distrusted process.

The second finding was that the GIS-supported solution could endure intense scrutiny. When the Commission selected the two finalist sites for a hazardous waste management facility, there was ferocious opposition to all aspects of the site screening and a vigorous attempt was made to scrutinize the process for fatal flaws. Doubt was cast on the appropriateness of the rules and statutes, on the motives of the Commission members, on the need for a facility and on the ability of the state to manage and regulate a facility. In spite of queries from hired consultants about the processes employed by the GIS and a court subpoena to a CGIA staff member, very few attempts have been made to discredit the GIS effort and all scepticism has been satisfactorily answered thus far (though in part this may be a reflection of the intimidating nature of the technology to non-specialists).

The final significant finding was that GIS did not overcome the 'not in my back yard' (NIMBY) attitude. Although the site-screening process employed by the Commission was applied in an objective and efficient manner, citizens of the two local areas are still not convinced that their communities are suitable for the hazardous waste facility. Perhaps in the future GIS techniques can be integrated with decision analysis and public participation techniques to gain greater acceptance of undesirable but necessary projects. Unfortunately, there are still citizens in North Carolina who are very displeased with a decision that was reached through thoughtful and effective use of GIS but, assuming the need for such a facility, such a result is inevitable.

SITING THE SUPERCONDUCTING SUPER COLLIDER

The Superconducting Super Collider (SSC) is an advanced particle accelerator which is currently under design and construction (SSC Central Design Group 1986; Universities Research Association 1987). It will be used to explore the origins and basic structure of matter. When complete, the SSC will be the world's foremost facility for high energy physics research and will be the largest and one of the costliest scientific instruments ever constructed. The Super Collider will be located in an elliptical, underground tunnel 53 miles (85 km) in circumference, 10 feet (3 m) in cross-section diameter and situated at least 35 feet (11 m) underground. The object of the SSC is to accelerate two counter-rotating beams of high energy protons to near the speed of light. The beams will be guided around the tunnel, also called the ring, by superconducting magnets and made to collide head-on. The collisions will generate showers of sub-nuclear particles that will be detected and analysed and thereby enhance the understanding of the ultimate forces and particles that constitute our world.

The US Department of Energy (DOE) conducted a site-selection process that commenced in 1987 with an invitation to the states to provide land on which to build and operate the SSC (United States Department of Energy, Office of Energy Research, Superconducting Super Collider Site Task Force 1987). The State of North Carolina submitted a site proposal and was selected as one of seven best qualified sites (State of North Carolina 1987). The GIS at CGIA was used extensively in the proposal preparation process (Westcott and Reiman 1987; Siderelis and Tribble 1988). One of the most challenging requirements of the project was to find an optimal orientation and placement of the SSC facilities within a pre-determined region of the state. This work is described below.

Objective of the Siting

The primary objective of the siting exercise was to place the SSC to meet in an efficient manner the technical evaluation criteria used by DOE in selecting the final site. These criteria included:

- *Geology and tunnelling.* The land should be suitable for efficient construction of underground structures. Stable geological conditions are desirable, as are shallow depths of tunnels and access shafts to the tunnels.

- *Regional resources.* Nearby communities should be capable of supporting the increased population with adequate housing, schools, cultural amenities and transportation.

- *Environment.* Construction and operation of the SSC should not impose significant environmental impacts on the area.

- *Setting.* The government must be given title to the land on which permanent surface structures will be built, to areas where the tunnels are below ground and for rights-of-way, utility corridors, etc.

- *Regional conditions.* There should be minimal natural or man-made disturbances that could adversely affect the SSC, such as extreme vibration, noise or climatic conditions.

- *Utilities.* The SSC requires ample, specified supplies of electricity (average 120 MW), water (2200 gallons per minute), fuel and waste disposal facilities.

The GIS was used to evaluate alternative positions and layouts for the SSC that maximized the positive features of the proposed region. The goal was to place the above-ground facilities in satisfactory geology and topography. There was also a need to minimize their overlap with urban areas, roads, railroads, water bodies and environmental features such as wetland, rare species habitats and archaeological sites. At the same time, attempts were made to locate the SSC facilities close to an airport, major road systems, universities and urban areas.

The orientation of underground structures was also evaluated. Ideally, the tunnel of the collider ring should rest in a horizontal plane. However, the SSC design permits tilting the tunnel up to 0.5 degrees to accommodate slope and geological conditions. The goal of the underground evaluations was to locate tunnels near the surface and in geological material suitable for cost-effective tunnel construction. Attempts were also made to minimize the depths of tunnel access shafts.

The SSC Data Base

A specialized database was developed for the SSC project. It contained over 40 data layers including transportation, hydrography, political boundaries, land use/land cover, wetland, elevation and surface geological units. Numerous other geographical data and related attribute information were added to the SSC database including river basin boundaries, census tract and enumeration district boundaries, county and municipal boundaries, detailed soils characteristics, locations of archaeological and historical sites and of threatened and endangered plant and animal species, plus data about water quality, air quality and background radiation.

Multi-surface modelling software was used to create grid models of the subsurface geology based on locations and measurements from geophysical investigations. Surfaces were developed to model the overburden (soil and saprolite), weathered rock and unweathered rock. A data layer representing the SSC was also stored in the GIS. It contained the campus area, the tunnels, access shafts and experimental areas. Coordinates of the SSC were mathematically generated from dimensions and formulae provided by DOE and moved and rotated to the proposed location in the state.

The Siting Process

The GIS was used to evaluate alternative locations and orientations of the SSC. The process generally involved selecting a configuration, evaluating it against a set of tests and then comparing the results with those from previous configurations. Numerous alternatives were evaluated and compared. In general, the steps of the process included the following:

- *Determination of a surface location.* A possible location of the collider ring and associated facilities on the surface was determined manually, using small-scale maps produced by the GIS. The ring was placed to minimize overlap of the SSC with major roads, railroads, streams, water bodies, urban areas, municipalities and areas of extremely low or high elevation. The ring was also placed to coincide with areas where geological conditions were expected to be favourable for tunnelling. The SSC was generally oriented with the campus and injector complex nearest to the airport and urban areas.

- *Adjustment of the SSC facility data layer.* The angle of rotation of the axis of the SSC from grid north and the offset from the Cartesian coordinates provided by the Department of Energy were measured. The data layer stored in the GIS containing the SSC facilities was interactively adjusted to the specified horizontal position. Plate 53.9 is a map of the final proposed location of the SSC and the surrounding region.

- *Overlay of environmental and cultural features.* The GIS file containing SSC estates was overlaid with the digital files of environmental features such as wetland, rare species habitats and archaeological sites to determine if intersections occurred and, if so, to measure the extent of the overlaps. Small-scale maps were plotted to illustrate the location of the SSC in relation to major surface features.

- *Determination of tilt.* X,Y coordinates and elevation values were determined for stations spaced around the collider ring. The X,Y values were determined in the GIS environment by interactively selecting locations and reading the corresponding coordinates. These X,Y coordinates were then used with the grid model of topography to estimate ground elevation values. The data were used in Fortran programs to identify an optimal tilt for the tunnel plane which located the tunnel in shallow unweathered rock but at least 35 feet (11 m) underground; the programs also minimized the depths of access shafts. The final proposal was for a tilted collider ring in a plane 0.054 degrees from horizontal and rotated about an axis 284.5 degrees counter-clockwise from grid north.

- *Creation of a surface to represent the underground tunnel.* Two sets of X, Y and Z (depth) values representing the tilted tunnel plane were used to generate a grid model of the tunnel. Proposed land and tunnel elevations and tunnel depths at access shaft locations and at three low elevation points were derived from the surface models.

- *Plot graphics.* A detailed profile, or cross-section, around the proposed collider ring was produced and is shown in Plate 53.10. It shows the land above the tunnel and the approximate boundaries between overburden, weathered rock and unweathered rock.

This process was repeated in an iterative manner until the preferred configuration of the SSC was determined. After a final placement was agreed, the GIS was used to produce many other maps and graphic products to illustrate the site. Plate 53.11 shows a 2.5D ARC/INFO plot of geological units draped over a terrain model. Plate 53.12 is a block diagram of the SSC campus area, showing the subsurface geology with the land use draped over topography.

Significant Findings of the Case Study

The SSC project was significant to CGIA because it involved an authentic application of GIS for which the analytical requirements were challenging, the stakes were high and in which the GIS could (and did) meet expectations. The system was relied upon throughout the project and was thus an integral part of the proposal preparation process. GIS was instrumental in North Carolina's selection as one of the seven best qualified sites.

Although the project occurred ten years after the inception of CGIA and the finally chosen site was in another state, this study marked a turning point in the acceptance of GIS technology by executive level managers in state government. The recognition gained from this effort led to numerous other projects, including the two case studies mentioned above, and to the rapid uptake of GIS to support decision making at the state level.

CONCLUSIONS

What has been described above is not unique to North Carolina: the use of GIS to support land resource management is now among the more established application areas. It is clear both from this chapter and from Robinette (1991 in this volume) that the requirement for internal efficiency, plus the need to obtain competitive advantage over competitor governments ensure that a state cannot now be without some GIS tools and the skilled staff to drive them. The State of North Carolina, through the Center for Geographic Information and Analysis, has operated a GIS for more than a decade with the primary focus of aiding in management of the state's land resource. Perhaps the single most important conclusion which may be drawn from this experience is that such systems have to pay their way from the outset: few governments are prepared to commit themselves to long-term data compilation without short-term benefits. State databases are, almost inevitably then, grown 'bottom up'. This places considerable emphasis upon the need for management to anticipate other uses of the data and compromise its value as little as possible in the pressure to complete any individual project. 'Adding value' is often only possible with prior planning and a commitment to long-term enterprise even from short-term financing.

REFERENCES

Anderson J R, Hardy E E, Roach J T, Witmer R E (1976) A land use and land cover classification system for use with remote sensor data. *US Geological Survey Professional Paper 964.* USGS, Washington DC

Burrough P A (1991) Soil information systems. In:

Maguire D J, Goodchild M F, Rhind D W (eds.) *Geographical Information Systems: principles and applications*. Longman, London, pp. 153–69, Vol 2

Clark W F (1990) *North Carolina's Estuaries: a pilot study for managing multiple use in the State's public trust waters*. Albemarle-Pamlico Study Report 90–10. Albemarle-Pamlico Study Program, Raleigh North Carolina

Copeland B J (1989) *Albemarle-Pamlico Esturine System: Preliminary Technical Analysis of Status and Trends*. Albemarle-Pamlico Study Report 89–13A. Albemarle-Pamlico Study Program, Raleigh North Carolina

Flowerdew R (1991) Spatial data integration. In: Maguire D J, Goodchild M F, Rhind D W (eds.) *Geographical Information Systems: principles and applications*. Longman, London, pp. 375–87, Vol 1

Nagy Z, Siderelis K C (1990) A GIS model for local water use planning and zoning. *Proceedings of the Tenth Annual ESRI User Conference, Volume 2*. Environmental Systems Research Institute, Redlands California

Robinette A (1991) Land management applications of GIS in the state of Minnesota. In: Maguire D J, Goodchild M F, Rhind D W (eds.) *Geographical Information Systems: principles and applications*. Longman, London, pp. 275–83, Vol 2

Siderelis K C, Tribble T N (1988) Using a Geographic Information System to prepare a site proposal for the Superconducting Super Collider. *Proceedings of GIS/LIS '88 Volume 1*. ACSM/ASPRS/AAG/URISA, Falls Church Virginia, pp. 459–68

SSC Central Design Group (1986) *SSC Conceptual Design of the Superconducting Super Collider*. Universities Research Association, SSC-SR-2020C, Washington DC

State of North Carolina (1987) *North Carolina Site Proposal for the Superconducting Super Collider (SSC)*, Volumes 1–8. State of North Carolina, Raleigh NC

United States Department of Energy, Office of Energy Research, Superconducting Super Collider Site Task Force (1987) *Invitation for Site Proposals for the Superconducting Super Collider (SSC)*. DOE/ER-0315 US Department of Energy, Washington DC

Universities Research Association (1987) *To The Heart of Matter – The Superconducting Super Collider*. Universities Research Association, Washington DC

Westcott T, Reiman R (1987) Siting the Superconducting Super Collider: a case study of the role of Geographic Information Systems in macro site analysis. *Paper presented at the 42nd Annual Meeting of the Southeast Division of the Association of American Geographers, Charlotte, NC*

54

LAND MANAGEMENT APPLICATIONS OF GIS IN THE STATE OF MINNESOTA

A ROBINETTE

Minnesota is a large state with over 20 years of experience in the application of GIS to environmental management. It has been necessary to grapple with the conflict between breadth and depth in the inventory and analysis of cultural and natural resources. Decisions are needed on issues ranging from state-wide land suitability to clean-up of pollution at an individual site. A GIS has been employed, together with a reconnaissance level database, to address a wide range of such topical issues. The chapter describes a conceptual hierarchy of planning decisions and the appropriate scale and resolution of data required to support these decisions. Case studies in five topical areas are described which exemplify the concept of 'telescoping' to the appropriate levels of decision and geography.

INTRODUCTION

Minnesota is a state with 22 million hectares of diverse landscape, ranging from rich agricultural plains, urban corridors and productive timber and mineral lands to wilderness conservation areas. This complex landscape is a large and difficult setting in which to accommodate new land uses while protecting valuable natural resources.

Over the past 20 years, the Minnesota GIS has provided application services to many government agencies. In so doing, it has been necessary to grapple with the conflict between breadth and depth in the inventory and analysis of cultural and natural resources. The challenge has been both to obtain data with sufficient detail to serve decision making and to provide uniform state-wide coverage. The various GIS applications have had differing needs, ranging from description of a state-wide picture to location of specific sites. Some experts advocate a 'bottom-up' approach, that is compiling data at the most detailed level required and then summarizing them to less detailed scales. This approach has not been possible within a reasonable budget or timeframe in Minnesota. The need for state-wide decisions has prompted Minnesota to apply a 'top-down' approach, one of developing reconnaissance level data first and later establishing a programme to compile more detailed data for selected areas. The principal objective is to apply as much knowledge, data and technology as is necessary to influence a decision. It is essential to use the tool effectively – to deal with the correct planning level, to match the right level of geography, to apply the most appropriate analytical model and to display the map results at the best scale. What follows, then, is a discussion of this dilemma in terms of decision making, data resolution and technology.

Minnesota is not the only government to have exploited GIS successfully but it is one of those with the longest experience. It will be obvious that some overlap exists between the role envisaged for GIS by Siderelis (1991 in this volume) and that espoused here; the case studies used in both chapters are, however, highly complementary and – in totality – serve to demonstrate the range and importance of

GIS in dealings with land by governments such as the states in North America.

DECISION MAKING

GIS can serve as a decision support tool at all levels of planning. Different ways exist of classifying the planning levels (see Calkins 1991 in this volume; Densham 1991 in this volume). In Minnesota, planning decisions are made at the following four levels:

- *Strategic planning* – 'whether to do it': identification and trend analysis.

- *Tactical planning* – 'what to do': assessing alternatives and targeting the issue.

- *Operational planning* – 'how to do it': managing facilities or resources to meet an objective function.

- *Project planning* – 'doing it': design and physical placement of facilities or resources.

Data resolution

Each of these decision levels requires appropriately scaled data in order to make informed judgements. For instance, project-scale data (such as road type) are irrelevant for strategic decisions, but a summary of project data (such as traffic congestion) displayed as a trend or overall pattern would be informative. The data levels that correspond to these decision levels are:

- *Strategic data* – summary statistical data aggregated to data collection units such as political or physical subdivisions (e.g. housing density) which could be mapped at a small scale on a single page, generally at scales ranging from 1 : 4 million to 1 : 500 000.

- *Tactical data* – reconnaissance inventory data compiled by general classification units (e.g. Level 1 land cover as defined by the USGS in Anderson *et al.* 1976), which can be mapped at scales ranging from 1 : 500 000 to 1 : 50 000.

- *Operational data* – management inventory data compiled by higher classification units (e.g. Level 2 land cover), which can be mapped at scales ranging from 1 : 50 000 to 1 : 10 000.

- *Project data* – engineering design data compiled by physical description units (e.g. residential structure type), which can be mapped at scales ranging from 1 : 10 000 to 1 : 500.

Although this progression is generalized, it illustrates – with possible exceptions – the value of conceptualizing GIS as a hierarchy of decisions and data.

Technology

In the recent past, the hardware and software for individual GIS applications have evolved to a sophisticated level. Although this evolution will continue, the focus of attention has shifted towards developing comprehensive databases. Lack of sufficient data currently inhibits the optimum use of GIS for most users. This limitation will also pass as data capture technology improves and more effort is spent on data entry (see Jackson and Woodsford 1991 in this volume).

The next barrier, acquiring the knowledge necessary to simulate environmental conditions, is not as easily overcome. While much of the application of GIS is currently to produce simple thematic maps or to answer simple data queries, expectations that complex models will be able to describe and predict environmental impacts of development options are rising. These expectations can be met through professionals from the academic, scientific, and political communities addressing environmental issues collectively.

CASE STUDIES

The following case studies demonstrate the range of scope (or breadth) and depth described earlier. They also involve the concept of 'telescoping' between general, small-scale investigations and detailed, large-scale studies using the same or similar data. The projects deal with acid rain sensitivity, critical erosion targeting, water resource assessment, forest resource management and mineral exploration.

Acid rain sensitivity

The Minnesota Pollution Control Agency, together with the Land Management Information Center (Anderson and Thornton 1985) and acting in response to a 1980 state statute, has developed an assessment of the potential geographical sensitivity of Minnesota's aquatic and terrestrial resources to acid rain. There are over 15 000 lakes in Minnesota so that comprehensive monitoring is not feasible. In order to understand state-wide conditions, it was necessary to measure the status of selected lakes and drainage basins and then extrapolate equivalent values for the rest. This project was done in two phases over the period 1982–87.

In 1982, the study started with the measurement of chemical characteristics, such as lake alkalinity, for 1300 lakes plus the compilation of GIS data for four drainage basins, each over 200 000 hectares in area. Through statistical correlation of lake water quality and drainage basin resource profiles derived from 1 : 250 000 scale mapping, it was possible to identify lake basins that were vulnerable to acidification. The profiles involved data on soils, geology, land use, vegetation, drainage basin size and the ratio of land to water area. Other models were developed for sensitivity of peat lands and terrestrial resources. Results from localized investigations were extrapolated state-wide to identify other potentially sensitive areas. Hence this is an example of detailed operational data at sample sites contributing to a state-wide tactical plan.

Additional field work was done on this project in 1985 and 1987 which added water quality data measures to an increased number of sampled lakes. This improved the accuracy of the sensitivity predictions. Refinements were also made to the models as additional predictive indicators were isolated. As a consequence, more precise and reliable maps were produced identifying aquatic, terrestrial and peat sensitivity to acid rain (Plate 54.1).

Critical erosion targeting

A 1982 Minnesota statute required the Soil and Water Conservation Board to target state cost-share funding on high priority areas of erosion and sedimentation. This targeting approach is designed to direct funds to areas of critical concern. Land owners in these critical areas were then encouraged to apply corrective land practice measures. A tactical GIS approach was used to identify critical small areas rather than using a more general statistical approach which could only define critically important counties (Muessig, Robinette and Rowekamp 1983).

An inter-governmental task force developed a definition of critical areas as 'areas with erosion from wind and/or water occurring on Class I–IV (high to moderately productive) cropland in excess of 2 times the tolerable soil loss (T) per hectare per year; or any land within 100 m of a stream or 330 m of a lake losing in excess of 8.2 metric tonnes per hectare per year'. The state-wide GIS database was used to model erosion using the Universal Soil Loss Equation (USLE) and the Wind Erosion Equation (WEE). The result of this analysis is a state-wide map (Plate 54.2) showing critical areas, together with statistics by county. These statistics were used to allocate the state's annual $1.3 million cost-share funds. County maps were used by soil conservation officers to contact land operators about preparing land management plans. About 12 200 out of 22 million hectares in Minnesota were identified as critical.

This tactical approach was adequate for state-wide fund allocation and critical area targeting but was too coarse for implementation of local erosion ordinances and farm planning. For these applications, it was necessary to shift to an operational planning level with data compiled on 1 : 15 840-scale mapping. This has been done for selected areas of the state, including Olmsted County in southeastern Minnesota. Olmsted County's planning office (Wheeler 1988) has successfully implemented an erosion zoning ordinance. Prior to a county GIS, the county commissioners were reluctant to adopt an erosion amendment to their zoning ordinance because it was unclear how non-complying sites could be identified consistently and how much of the county was affected. The process used allowed sites as small as 400 square metres to be evaluated for water and wind erosion loss. The resulting maps (Plate 54.3) and statistics gave the elected officials the evidence they needed to adopt and implement the erosion ordinance. In addition, the planners have digitized the ownership parcel boundaries in the county and matched land owners to parcels through the tax assessors' records. This allows the planners to identify the fraction of farmsteads which does not comply and allows notification of landowners (Plate 54.4). The zoning ordinance contains a series of progressive penalties for such a failure to comply.

This use of GIS allows planners and elected officials to target their funds, effort and controls in the areas that have the highest priority. In Olmsted County, for instance, 6 per cent of the land area accounts for 40 per cent of the total erosion. Correcting these problems will not affect a large number of farmers but will substantially reduce the loss of productivity and the pollution of surface water.

Water resource assessment

Minnesota is a water-rich state with its 15 000 lakes, pothole wetlands, headwaters, stream network and abundant groundwater aquifers. Because of this, there is considerable research, policy planning and GIS activity in this topical area.

Surface water assessment

As headwaters to the Mississippi River, the Red River and the Great Lakes chain, Minnesota has 11 river basins, 83 major drainage basins, and 5700 minor drainage basins. For the Relative Nonpoint Source Pollution Potential study (Fandrei 1989), an assessment was done for each of the seven eco-regions, as defined by the US Environmental Protection Agency (EPA). Potential problem areas were defined by correlating water quality records with geographical characteristics of minor drainage basins (Maeder and Tessar 1988). Profiles were developed for each drainage basin based on GIS inventories of the extent of forest lands, cultivated land, urban areas, stream shore, lake shore, silt soil, sand soil, areas of 3–6 per cent slope, those where the slope was greater than 6 per cent and on other parameters. Through regression analysis, it was determined that the extent of forests and sand soils showed a negative correlation to water quality and all others were positive. The non-point pollution potential for each minor drainage basin was then scored by summing the rank values of the water quality predictors. The extent of shore land in a drainage basin had by far the highest correlation with water quality so the weighting of its score was doubled. Special factors, such as high wind erosion, were included for some eco-regions. A series of 1 : 500 000-scale eco-region maps was produced which displayed the final scores in decile classes (Plate 54.5).

This type of study is intended to target those areas requiring the most attention and is a form of tactical planning. The map describes the geographical extent of the problem, the areas of highest priority and the overall geographical pattern. Once this is done, the next step is to address those high priority minor drainage basins at an operational planning level by applying a dynamic stormwater simulation program. The Agricultural Nonpoint Source Pollution Model (AGNPS) is such a model and was developed by the US Department of Agriculture's Agricultural Research Service in Morris, Minnesota, in cooperation with the Minnesota Pollution Control Agency. It is an enhancement of the CREAMS model. The two objectives of the model are to obtain uniform and accurate estimates of runoff quality for large drainage basins ranging from 200 to 10 000 hectares, with primary emphasis laid on sediment and nutrients, and to compare the effects of various conservation alternatives and management practices in the drainage basin.

The model simulates single storm events defined in terms of frequency and duration. For the defined storm event, the model simulates the transport of sediment, nutrients and stream flow from the headwaters to the outlet in a step-wise manner. The data must be in a raster file and can be at any grid resolution, though under 4 hectares in size is preferable. The model is data intensive and provides progressively better results as the data become more refined in resolution and classification. The results are, as already stated, in the form of runoff statistics for flow, sediment and nutrients at the outfall point or at any selected point in the drainage basin. A series of maps (such as Fig. 54.1) can be produced which describe the degree of contribution from each of the grid cells. The effects of alternative land management practices can be compared. This level of field-specific, operational planning and management is now being applied by local water planners on a case-by-case basis. Throughout the state, there is a network of surface water monitoring stations; these can be shown on a map in relation to the streams, the drainage basin

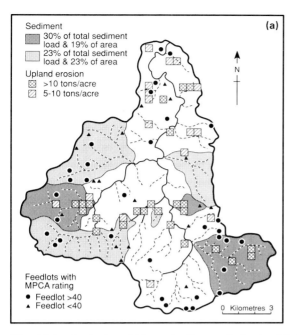 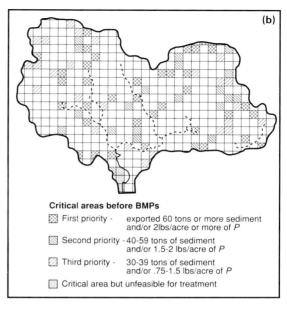

Fig. 54.1 Agricultural Nonpoint Source Pollution Model (AGNPS). (a) Estimated sediment discharge from Garvin Brook watershed, Winona County, Minnesota. (b) Estimated discharge in Salmonson Creek watershed, Big Stone County, Minnesota (courtesy USDA, ARS, North Central Soil Conservation Research Laboratory).

system and each other. The stations provide climate recording, river gauging and water quality monitoring facilities. With these stations plotted on a map, it is possible to relate them to areas of surface water problems and to correlate the monitoring records they produce with the modelling results (Plate 54.6).

Groundwater assessment

For groundwater data, there is a similar network of monitoring sites throughout the state. Observations from a network of wells are stored in a series of databases covering water levels, water quality, water appropriations, stratigraphy, etc. Plate 54.7 illustrates the distribution of water well locations by type for a county. From monitoring data, issues can be diagnosed and mapped. For instance, a review of water quality reports from public wells in 1988 by the Department of Health identified eight counties with four or more wells containing pesticides. A map of these areas can serve as an early warning that requires further site-level investigation (Plate 54.8). This is an example of displaying detailed case-level data as aggregated, summary-level data state-wide.

Another approach possible with GIS is to predict areas that are susceptible to groundwater contamination through mapping and modelling the factors involved. The selected approach is called DRASTIC and was developed by the National Water Well Association under contract to the US EPA. It is one of the few approaches designed to predict hydrogeological sensitivity to surface-derived contaminants in areas larger than 40 hectares. This system is based on major geological and hydrogeological parameters including depth to water, net recharge, aquifer media, soil media, topography, influence of the radose zone and hydraulic conductivity of the aquifer in question. Each of the above DRASTIC parameters is weighted and each individual factor (within a given parameter) is assigned a rating on a scale of 1 to 10. A map of the area to be rated is developed for each of the respective parameters using available data. A numerical score is assigned to each different factor on a given parameter map. To obtain the final

DRASTIC rating, all of the factors are multiplied by their respective parameter weights and then summed to obtain a relative score.

The study was carried out by the Minnesota Pollution Control Agency, together with the Land Management Information Center (Porcher 1989). A series of seven (DRASTIC) parameter maps was developed from available data inventories. Ratings of susceptibility were developed for each class on the maps and weights were developed for each map. Final scores ranging from 7 to 32 were divided into five susceptibility classes from lowest to highest. Well over 1000 unique combinations of the seven input parameters occur in Minnesota. This state-wide map (Plate 54.9) provides a context for concern about groundwater pollution. It represents a geographically disaggregated description of the land's ability to alternate or restrict the downward migration of contaminants to the saturated zone. It also serves as a targeting map for regulatory action and further investigation.

Sometimes the groundwater contamination problem results from a single localized source. In the case of US EPA-funded Superfund Site clean-ups, it is necessary to assess the extent of the contamination in terms of concentrations and geographical dispersion. This requires a three-dimensional approach to data display. In the vicinity of the site, historic data are sought for existing water wells and, in addition, new wells are placed to complete the monitoring needs. Water samples are tested and the results are shown in three-dimensional space in relation to surface and subsurface conditions (Plate 54.10). Readings over time can produce an animation of the contamination plume as it changes in concentration and location. These results are used in clean-up negotiation and, if necessary, in court proceedings. They provide a clear communication of facts to both scientists and lay persons. This, then, is an example of a project-level issue.

Forest resource management

Minnesota's forest resource is primarily second growth pulp wood that is used for waferboard and paper products. The state does not have a sustained yield of large saw timber like other regions. There are 5.5 million hectares of commercial timberland in Minnesota, 20 per cent of which is on state land. In order for the state to maximize the value of its forests, it must manage some of the land more intensively than it does now and with more reliance on an effective information system. A study has been carried out of state lands and their suitability to meet natural resource objectives (Minnesota Department of Natural Resources, Office of Planning 1986). In that study, a resource assessment for timber production was made using an economic timber model (Minnesota Department of Natural Resources, Division of Forestry and Office of Planning 1984). The forestry data used in this model were stand specific although the results were expressed for sections (square miles). Several factors were applied at different levels of resolution:

- forest productivity by stand;
- timber prices by area;
- management cost by region;
- distance to mill by township;
- soil expectations value by 40 acre (16 hectare) parcel.

The model resulted in assignment of sections into one of three timber management classes:

- intensive management (28 per cent);
- extensive management (33 per cent);
- custodial management (39 per cent).

Plate 54.11 shows the pattern of recommended timber management zones. This analysis demonstrates the effective use of variable resolution data. It also demonstrates that state-wide analysis can yield a result in map form with well-defined locational specification.

Another of the applications for forestry management is an assessment of land for hardwood production. Oak timber is particularly valuable for veneer products. Oak stands are scattered throughout the savanna transition zone in the state but there is potential for the management of even more. The Department of Natural Resources, Division of Forestry conducted an assessment of land suitability for oak management. This was a state-wide study using resource data compiled at a map scale of 1 : 250 000. The current pattern of oak and northern hardwoods forests is known from a reconnaissance survey by the US Forest Service. To determine what other sites are suitable for oak production, ratings were developed for soils and landform maps using their site index for oak. Those areas with high site indices should be considered (Plate 54.12). Of course, this map can be modified by overlaying higher value land uses and the extent of public lands. Even so, there are considerable opportunities for increasing the value of forest lands through improved species selection and management within 'eligible' areas identified by the GIS analysis.

Since the Minnesota forest inventory is compiled at a scale of 1 : 15 840, with stands as small as half a hectare, it is possible to use it to conduct site-level management. A mapping module is one township or 36 square miles. For each forest stand, up to 91 attributes (e.g. type, size, density) are compiled through field survey; a sample portion of an inventory map of these parameters is shown in Plate 54.13. The GIS allows a field forester to interrogate the data by asking such questions as 'Where are the mature aspen stands within one mile of road but beyond 300 feet from a stream?' This query conflates size and age, species, accessibility and regulatory setback of the woodland. The answer is provided both in map and tabular form for each area. Further assessments can be conducted to eliminate isolated parcels or areas that have higher suitability for other uses. In this way, GIS becomes a natural extension of a forester's daily tasks and serves to improve both staff productivity and the quality of decisions.

Mineral exploration

Minnesota's major mineral resource was formerly iron ore. Foreign competition and reduced ore grades have diminished mining activity in the state. In 1978, an initiative was begun by the Minnesota Geological Survey to increase the exploration activity through remote sensing for reserves. An eight-year survey measured the magnetic and gravity anomalies which are indicators of mineralization. This is done through remote sensing with flight line data on a 213-metre grid. The GIS processing includes correcting the geometry, registering the image, classifying the signals, smoothing the data and displaying them in map form. The most effective display for geologists to interpret transforms the readings into a false 3-D image, as if the readings were topographic values. A light source is then shown on the 3-D surface resulting in reflective levels with colour added to show elevation (Plate 54.14). These maps are used to target high probability mineral sites. Largely as a result of this mapping effort, exploration leases have increased from 4000 hectares in 1980 to 36 000 hectares in 1986. Many formations are being found which are similar to Canadian areas yielding gold, copper, nickel, silver, platinum and titanium. As a result of the use of this advanced information technology, it is expected that these minerals will be found and mined much sooner than otherwise would have been the case.

More detailed exploration is undertaken in areas with high mineral probability. This is usually done by assessing samples derived from drill cores, lake sediments, vegetation and rock outcrops. A GIS is an effective means of displaying and correlating the data. This has been done with the regional geochemical reconnaissance programme (Minnesota Department of Natural Resources, Division of Minerals 1989), together with the Land Management Information Center. From this sampling effort, it was possible to identify unique geochemical signatures at both the area and site levels. The resulting 10 000 hectare area was shown to have three distinctly anomalous localities based on geochemical signatures. Each of these sub-areas is shown to have many localized signatures, indicating concentrations of heavy minerals. Figure 54.2 shows the pattern of localized signatures. This type of localized operational investigation is clearly aided by the analytical and graphical capabilities of GIS.

CONCLUSIONS

These case studies demonstrate the principles described earlier. The objective of using GIS is to apply as much knowledge, data and technology as necessary to make an informed decision. It is essential to select the correct planning level, to match the appropriate level of geography, to apply the most appropriate analytical model and to display the map results at the best scale. In making these judgements, it is important to involve a

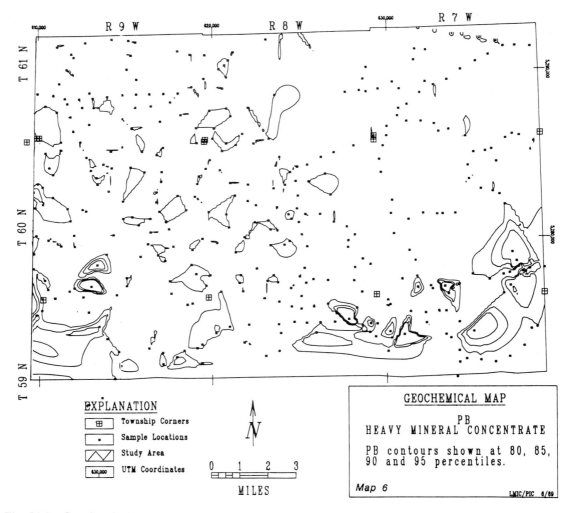

Fig. 54.2 Geochemical contour map of heavy lead heavy metal concentrate in June 1989 (courtesy Minnesota Department of Natural Resources).

variety of professionals since each will bring a bias from his or her own background. Elected officials will tend to seek more strategic and tactical answers while technicians will tend to seek a more operational direction.

In the past, the hardware/software technology of GIS was the challenge. For most systems, the database is the current challenge and the primary limitation in conducting studies. In the future, however, the limiting factor in applying GIS will be the knowledge of how to simulate environmental conditions. In pursuing these models, it is important to view them in more than scientific terms, as administrative tools to implement policies and programmes. The four levels of planning specified at the outset become a context for action, the details of which depend on what level of understanding exists for an issue and what level of geography is in question. The choice of data scale and resolution should naturally result from the needs of the scope and depth of the decision to be made. Increasingly, the technology issues will be more knowledge based than cost based as low-cost hardware/software systems become available. In the future, then, the challenge will be to apply technology appropriately to a correctly defined problem and to empower all employees to incorporate GIS technology – together with their other tools – in managing environmental problems and resources.

REFERENCES

Anderson D R, Thornton J D (1985) *Application of a Geographic Information System (GIS): identification of resources sensitive to acid deposition.* State of Minnesota, St Paul

Anderson J R, Hardy E E, Roach J T, Witmer R E (1976) A land use and land cover classification system for use with remote sensor data. *US Geological Survey Professional Paper 964*, Washington DC

Calkins H W (1991) GIS and public policy. In: Maguire D J, Goodchild M F, Rhind D W (eds.) *Geographical Information Systems: principles and applications.* Longman, London, pp. 233–45, Vol 2

Densham P J (1991) Spatial decision support systems. In: Maguire D J, Goodchild M F, Rhind D W (eds.) *Geographical Information Systems: principles and applications.* Longman, London, pp. 403–12, Vol 1

Fandrei G (1989) *Descriptive Characteristics of the Seven Eco-regions in Minnesota.* Minnesota Pollution Control Agency. Draft Report, State of Minnesota, St Paul

Jackson M J, Woodsford P A (1991) GIS data capture hardware and software. In: Maguire D J, Goodchild M F, Rhind D W (eds.) *Geographical Information Systems: principles and applications.* Longman, London, pp. 239–49, Vol 1

Maeder S R, Tessar P A (1988) *The Use of Geographic Information Systems for Lake Management in Minnesota.* Minnesota State Planning Agency, Minneapolis

Minnesota Department of Natural Resources, Division of Forestry and Office of Planning (1984) *Modelling Direct Economic Returns to Timber Management as a Component of a Comprehensive, Multiple-Use Forest Management Model.* State of Minnesota, St Paul

Minnesota Department of Natural Resources, Division of Minerals (1989) *Glacial Drift Geochemistry for Strategic Minerals; Duluth Complex, Lake County, Minnesota. Report 262.* State of Minnesota, St Paul

Minnesota Department of Natural Resources, Office of Planning (1986) *DNR-Administered Public Lands: their suitability to meet natural resource management objectives.* State of Minnesota, St Paul

Muessig L F, Robinette A, Rowekamp T (1983) *Application of the USLE to define critical erosion and sedimentation in Minnesota.* Paper given at 38th Annual Meeting of the Soil Conservation Society of America, 31 July–3 August. Hartford, Connetiut.

Porcher E (1989) *Ground Water Contamination Susceptibility in Minnesota.* Minnesota Pollution Control Agency, St Paul

Siderelis K C (1991) Land resource information systems. In: Maguire D J, Goodchild M F, Rhind D W (eds.) *Geographical Information Systems: principles and applications.* Longman, London, pp. 261–73, Vol 2

Wheeler P H (1988) *Olmsted County's Farmland Soil Loss Controls.* Rochester–Olmsted Consolidated Planning Department.

55

GIS IN ISLAND RESOURCE PLANNING: A CASE STUDY IN MAP ANALYSIS

J K BERRY

This chapter demonstrates the important concepts and practical considerations in map analysis using GIS. The case study presents three separate spatial models for allocating conservation, research and development land uses in planning island resources. A fourth model addresses conflict resolution in determining the best combination among the competing uses.

INTRODUCTION

Historically, maps have been used for navigation through unfamiliar terrain and seas. Within this context, the preparation of maps accurately locating physical features is the primary focus of attention. More recently, however, analysis of mapped data for decision making has become an important part of resource planning. During the 1960s, manual analytical procedures for overlaying maps were popularized. These techniques mark an important turning point in the use of maps – from one emphasizing physical description of geographical space to another spatially prescribing appropriate management actions. This movement from *descriptive* to *prescriptive* mapping has set the stage for revolutionary concepts of map structure, content and use. GIS provide the means for effecting such a transition. In one sense, this aspect of GIS is similar to conventional map processing involving map sheets and drafting aids such as pens, rub-on shading, rulers, planimeters, dot grids and acetate sheets for light-table overlays. In another sense, these systems provide a vast array of analytical capabilities enabling managers to address complex issues in entirely new ways.

GIS have several roles in spatial information processing. First, GIS can be viewed as a tool for 'computer mapping', emphasizing the creation and updating of traditional map products. From this perspective, the term GIS is purely descriptive – graphical output of information provided by the user. GIS then became viewed as a technology for 'spatial database management', providing a linkage between descriptive attributes and geographical locations. From this perspective, GIS are still purely descriptive, providing graphical summaries of the results from spatial data queries.

More recently, the roles of GIS as map production tools and as a database technology have evolved to include the capabilities for interpretation – as well as presentation – of mapped data. Within this context, the interrelationships among mapped data become the focus of attention. In such work, entirely new spatial information is created as users derive and interpret landscape factors for specific management activities. The application described in this chapter is one example of this revolution in map analysis, as applied to the planning of island resources. The history and theory of map analysis is covered extensively by Tomlin 1991 (in this volume).

MAPS AS DATA

Spatial analysis often involves large volumes of data. These data are characterized by maps describing both the 'where' (the locational attribute) and the 'what' (the thematic attribute). Map scale and projection determine the form of coordinates locating landscape features in geographical space. The features indicate the theme of the map, such as a soil map or a road map. Traditionally, this information is identified by lines and shadings carefully drawn on paper sheets. In a GIS, this information is computerized and stored as numbers. It is this digital nature of maps that fuels the revolution in map analysis.

Manual cartographic techniques allow simple manipulation of maps, but are limited for the most part to qualitative, rather than numerical processing. Such procedures are severely handicapped and often do not provide the numerical input demanded by modern decision-making models. Traditional quantitative approaches, on the other hand, enable numerical analysis of the data but the sheer magnitude of mapped data becomes prohibitive for practical processing. Most often, decisions are made based on the 'average' slope or 'dominant' soil type occurring over large geographical areas. These simplifying values are easily manipulated with a calculator but gloss over the actual spatial complexity of a landscape. For example (see Berry 1987a), a study area may have a gentle average slope most often containing very stable soil. Under these typical conditions, traditional analysis using the spatially aggregated averages would be free to allocate a land use generating high surface water runoff. However, scattered throughout the area may be pockets of very steep slopes with highly erodible soils. In these instances, the results could be environmentally devastating – a condition missed by assuming that the averages pertain everywhere.

The ability of GIS technology to retain detailed geographical information in characterizing space, termed locational specificity, is a major advantage over traditional numerical analysis, especially when allied to analytical procedures. For example (see Berry and Berry 1988), a set of maps indicating a town's suitability for residential development considering soil types, slopes, wetlands, farmland preservation, proximity to existing residential areas, schools, parks and numerous other factors could be drawn in various colours on to clear plastic sheets and overlaid on a light-table or office window. The resulting composite colours and subtle hues could be interpreted as a measure of overall suitability for development for all locations within the town (locational specificity). However, the manual approach does not allow for different weights being assigned to the various factors (a very realistic decision-making condition requiring thematic specificity), such as considering soil type as being twice as important as proximity to existing development and four times as important as the farmland classification. Even more frustrating is that the composites most often result in an undifferentiated deep magenta almost everywhere when more than just a few maps are used!

SPATIAL MODELLING

GIS systems store information as numbers, rather than colours, shadings, lines or discrete symbols. When overlaying a set of maps the values can be summed, averaged, weight-averaged, minimized, or any of a host of other appropriate statistical or mathematical operations. The result is a new number assigned to each location which is a numerical summary or mathematical function of the conditions occurring at that location on the 'input' maps. Such procedures greatly extend traditional map processing capabilities and provide a sort of 'map-ematics' (see Berry 1987b, 1987c).

As an example (see Berry 1987d), the spatial relationship between roads and timber resources can be rigorously modelled. Traditional timber supply analysis generalizes resource accessibility into a few broad groupings, such as the proportion of trees near roads, set back, and distant. The timber supply is calculated from values describing the typical timber composition within each broad accessibility zone. A serious limitation in this approach is that all trees are assumed to be transported straight to the nearest road. This concept of distance as the 'shortest straight line between two points' is the result of our traditional tool, the ruler – not reality. A straight line may indicate the distance 'as the crow flies' but offers little information about the complex pattern of spatial barriers in the real world: such a straight line from a stand of trees to the road might cross a pond or steep slopes (very realistic obstacles that must be circumvented by the harvesting machinery), effectively making the distance much greater. In fact, the actual route may be so much further that the trees are economically inaccessible.

Advanced GIS procedures can consider obstacles in computing effective distance and express this distance in decision-making terms, such as dollars or gallons of fuel, instead of static geographical units of metres or miles. The result is a more useful map of effective distance, indicating harvesting cost at each location throughout a study area as a function of landscape characteristics and harvesting equipment capabilities. Such timber access information can be combined with a map of forest cover for a new map indicating the forest type and harvesting cost combinations throughout a study area – the principal input to traditional supply models, yet now spatially specific *and* realistic.

It is the combined factors of digital format, spatial and thematic specificity and advanced analytical procedures which form the foundation of computer-assisted map analysis. The case study presented in this chapter demonstrates these points. Three separate spatial models allocating different land uses are presented. A fourth model addresses conflict resolution in determining the best combination among the competing uses.

DATABASE DEVELOPMENT

Since the 1970s, an ever-increasing quantity of mapped data are being collected and processed in digital format. Early use of GIS technology required users to become experts in the emerging field and develop their own systems and databases. Their efforts also required large mainframe computers costing hundreds of thousands of dollars, environmentally controlled buildings and a staff of computer technicians. These conditions made GIS non-viable for most potential users. More recently, GIS systems have become available for personal computers with a total investment of less than US $5000, with the familiar office desktop as the computing environment.

As a means of demonstrating GIS technology in resource planning, a demonstration database and example analyses are presented. The Professional Map Analysis Package (pMAP) by Spatial Information Systems (SIS 1986) and its optional modules were used for all data encoding, processing and map output. The total cost of the complete package is under US $1500. Processing and map displays were done with an IBM PC-AT 'clone' computer and a standard dot matrix printer. All of the accompanying figures were photographed from a standard EGA colour monitor. An inexpensive digitizer was used for encoding maps. The total cost of this general-purpose hardware in 1990 was about US$3000. The database was prepared in one man-week. The analyses were completed in three days. The finished report took nearly two weeks to prepare, with final map graphics for slides and figures requiring the greatest time (Berry *et al.* 1989).

The western portion of St Thomas, US Virgin Islands, comprises the demonstration site. A nested database centred on Botany Bay and consisting of three windows held at different resolutions was developed (Plate 55.1). Five primary data planes were digitized from two adjacent USGS topographic map sheets: island boundaries, elevation, roads, geographical points and cultural features. Ocean depth was digitized from a combination of US-NOAA and locally-produced navigational charts. A data plane indicating neighbourhood districts was obtained from a tourist map published by the local Merchants' Association. The digitized data were then converted to the three windows and stored as separate databases. These encoded data were used to derive maps of slope, aspect, proximity to road, proximity to coast, watersheds, 'coastalsheds' and visual exposure to coastline; these were used in the demonstration analyses determining the best locations for recreation, research and residential development.

MAP ANALYSIS

Four analyses were performed using the high resolution (25×25 m analysis grid) Botany Bay vicinity database. The first investigates the best areas for conservation uses including recreation, limited use and preservation. The rankings are based on relative accessibility to both existing roads and the coastline. The second model identifies the best areas for ecological research by characterizing watershed conditions and the 'coastalsheds' they influence. The third analysis determines the best locations for residential development considering several engineering and aesthetic factors. The final model addresses the best allocation of land, simultaneously considering all three landscape uses.

The analyses presented are hypothetical and do not represent actual plans under consideration. Field-verified data and considerable advice from local individuals would be required to transform these demonstrations into actual land use recommendations.

Defining Conservation Areas

A map of accessibility to existing roads and the coastline forms the basis of the conservation areas model. In determining access, the slope of the intervening terrain was considered. The following assumptions were used in characterizing off-road movement:

- 0 to 20 per cent slope, easiest to cross.
- 21 to 40 per cent slope, twice as difficult to cross as the easiest.
- 41 per cent slope or more, three times as difficult to cross as the easiest.

In implementing these criteria, a map of slope was first generated from the encoded map of elevation, then interpreted for relative ease of movement using the criteria described above. The 'weighted' distances first from the roads, then from the coastline, to all other locations in the study area were calculated. In these calculations, areas that appear geographically near a road may actually be much less accessible. Similarly, the coastline may be a 'stone's throw away', but if it is at the foot of a cliff it may be effectively inaccessible for recreation. The two maps of weighted proximity from both the roads and the coast were combined into an overall map of accessibility. The final step of the analysis involved interpreting relative access into conservation uses (Plate 55.2). Recreation was identified for those areas near both roads and the coast. Intermediate access areas were designated for limited use. Areas effectively 0.5 km or more away from both were designated as preservation areas. In determining accessibility, weighted distance is calculated in which areas with steep intervening slopes (lower right inset) are considered further away than their simple geographical distance would imply.

The ability of the GIS to calculate weighted distance provides a much more realistic interpretation of accessibility than do traditional methods involving rulers. However, the access map generated in this analysis is limited by data availability. In addition to slope, land cover type and density could be considered in characterizing the intervening terrain. If these data were available, they could be easily incorporated in the 'friction' map, with areas of steep, dense cover being the most difficult to cross. Similarly, if trails are known, they should be digitized and used to update the relative ease of movement implied by the slope, cover type and density maps. Another extension to the model would use aerial photos to identify beaches or other unique attractions along the coastline. These special areas can be incorporated in the distance calculations so they have more influence – things are effectively more accessible if they are more attractive. An intrepid recreationalist will travel much further, even over rough terrain and dense cover, for a unique experience.

Defining Ecological Research Areas

The characterization of the Botany Bay area for ecological research involved several sub-models. The first used the elevation map to identify individual watersheds. 'Nodes' defining the bays are identified where ridges meet the shore. The steepest uphill path from each node identifies the lateral ridge forming the sides between watersheds. The upper boundaries are more difficult to determine. In this process, each map location identifies its steepest downhill path over the elevation map – like water running down the surface after a storm. The result is a map that contains the number of 'paths' passing through each location. Those areas with only one path identify upper ridges with water running off, but no uphill neighbours. The approach works well in areas of considerable relief or highly resolved elevation data. Flat areas or inconsistent elevation values yield unreliable results. For the Botany Bay study area, the procedure identified about 80 per cent of the boundaries. Interactive human intervention was necessary to fill in the boundaries through the areas in which the computer failed.

Once all of the watersheds were identified, three major ones were isolated as best for research (Plate 55.3). These included the Target Rock, Botany Bay and Sandy Bay watersheds, selected because of the scientists' requirements that they be relatively large, wholly contained areas, with a diversity of landscape conditions. The second sub-model develops a summary table of watershed characteristics such as ownership, accessibility and terrain conditions, useful in planning ecological experiments and control areas. This process treats each watershed as a 'cookie-cutter' placed over another map and stores the data summarized, for example, as the average of all elevation values occurring within the Target Rock watershed. In general, the Target Rock watershed was found to be intermediate in size, divided between two administrative districts, the most remote watershed with intermediate elevations forming relatively steep, rough, northerly sloping terrain. The Botany Bay watershed is much larger, almost entirely within one district, relatively accessible and has terrain similar to Target Rock but is oriented to the west. The Sandy Bay watershed is much smaller, is wholly contained in one district and is easily accessible, with a similar westerly oriented terrain but much lower in elevation.

The final sub-model identifies and then summarizes the 'coastalshed' influenced by each of the three watersheds. The delineation of the coastal areas influenced by the landscape required the simulation of the prevailing southerly current. This process can be visualized as creating a three-dimensional surface forming a plane tilted from south to north over the ocean portion of the study area (right portion of Plate 55.4). The steepness of the plane corresponds to the rate of flow – the steeper it is, the faster the current. In this case, current flow was assumed to be the same throughout the area. However, detailed oceanographic charts show a similar map as blue arrows whose orientation and length indicate direction and rate of current flow. Such information, if available, could be used to refine the plane used in this analysis. The coastal portions of each of the watersheds formed the starting locations for delineating the corresponding coastalsheds. Like water flowing down a roof, areas down-current are identified by moving downhill along the tilted plane. It was assumed that thorough mixing among the watersheds' inputs would occur within 0.5 km, thereby defining the extent of the down-current movement.

Plate 55.4 shows the three coastalsheds corresponding to the three research watersheds.

There are several limitations in the procedure used in delineating these coastalsheds. Most notable is the lack of detailed information on current flow and depth, tides and thermal incline. Indeed, the interaction among these variables is complex and not fully understood in a modelling context. Although the coastalsheds delineated appear to be reasonable approximations, an empirical study involving dye and buoy releases would be necessary for detailed research on the land–water interface.

Defining Areas for Development

To determine the 'best' locations for development, several maps describing aesthetic, engineering and environmental factors were considered. These included:

- Engineering
  gentle slopes
  close to roads
- Aesthetics
  close to coast
  good view of coast
  westerly aspect
- Environmental constraints
  100 m set-back from coast
  no slopes over 50 per cent

The engineering and aesthetic considerations were treated as gradients. This approach interprets the data as relative rankings, or preferences, for development. For example, an area viewing twice as long a section of shoreline as another location is ranked twice as desirable. The environmental constraints, on the other hand, were treated as critical factors. For example, an area within the 100 m set-back is considered unacceptable, regardless of its aesthetic or engineering rankings.

Figure 55.1 is a flowchart of the Development Areas Model. The 'boxes' represent maps and the 'lines' represent processing operations. The schematic maps on the left identify encoded data, termed Primary maps. These data are transformed into Derived maps which are physical and could be measured, but are more easily calculated. The Interpreted maps are an abstraction of the physical ones indicating the relative preference of conditions for an intended use – residential development in this

case. The final level of abstraction is the
Prescriptive map, created by combining the
individual preference expressions into a single map.
This general approach of moving from encoded data
through increasing levels of abstraction is common
to all prescriptive models. The user conceptualizes
the important relationships involved in a spatial
decision, then uses GIS analytical tools to express
them.

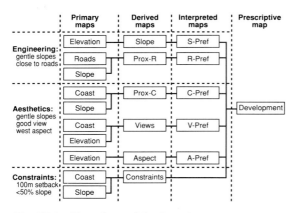

Fig. 55.1 Flowchart of the Development Areas Model.

To incorporate the engineering considerations,
a slope map was created from the encoded map of
elevation. The slope map was interpreted on a scale
of 0 (terrible) to 10 (best), as

10 – Best (0–5 per cent slope)
8 – (6–15 per cent slope)
6 – (16–25 per cent slope)
3 – (26–40 per cent slope)
1 – Worst (>40 per cent slope)

These criteria recognize the increased site
preparation and building costs on steeper slopes. A
related concern characterizes the preference for
proximity to existing roads, in recognition of the
increased cost of driveway construction as a
function of distance. In the same manner as used in
the Conservation Model, distance was weighted by
intervening slopes. The map of effective proximity
to roads was interpreted on the same '0 to 10
goodness scale' as:

10 – Best (0–50 effective units away)
8 – (51–100 effective units away)
6 – (101–200 effective units away)
3 – (201–400 effective units away)
1 – Worst (>400 effective units away)

The aesthetics consideration for siting
development used in this model favoured being
near the coast and having a good view. A slope-
weighted proximity to coast map was created, then
interpreted as:

10 – Best (0–100 effective units away)
9 – (101–150 effective units away)
8 – (151–200 effective units away)
6 – (201–300 effective units away)
4 – (301–400 effective units away)
3 – (401–600 effective units away)
1 – Worst (>600 effective units away)

To determine the visual aesthetics, the
'viewshed' of the shoreline was generated by
computing the lines of sight in all directions over the
elevation map from all of the shoreline locations.
This procedure is analogous to standing on the
shore and noting all the locations you can see, then
moving down the beach 25 m and again noting the
visual connections. When all shore locations have
been considered, a 'visual exposure' map is formed,
with each inland location assigned a value equal to
the number of times it was seen. The locations with
high visual exposure values are interpreted as
having the best views. In this analysis, vegetative
cover was not considered as an additional visual
barrier on top of the elevation, but could have been
if a map indicating canopy height were available.
The composite visual exposure map was interpreted
for view preference as:

10 – Best (>90 connections)
8 – (80–90 connections)
6 – (60–79 connections)
4 – (11–59 connections)
1 – Worst (0–10 connections)

The last consideration indicates the preference
for westerly facing slopes. Such orientation allows a
greater chance to view the setting sun. Easterly
orientations were ranked as next best as they
provide inspiring sunrises for energetic individuals.
An aspect map was created from the encoded map
of elevation, then interpreted as:

10 – Best (West)
9 – (Southwest)
8 – (Northwest; flat)
7 – (East; Southeast)
5 – (North; Northeast; South)

To determine environmental constraints to development, simple proximity to coast and steepness were considered. Maps of distance to coast and slope were interpreted as:

0 – Unsuitable (<100 metres from coast)
0 – Unsuitable (>50 per cent slope)

Plate 55.5(a) shows a composite containing the simple arithmetic average of the five separate preference maps. Environmentally constrained locations masked these results (values within constrained areas being forced to 0) and are light grey. Note that approximately half of the land area is ranked as 'Acceptable' or better (warmer tones). In averaging the five preference maps, all criteria were considered equally important.

The analysis was extended to generate a weighted suitability map preferentially favouring certain criteria as:

- view preference times 10 (most important)
- coast proximity times 8
- road proximity times 3
- aspect preference times 2
- slope preference times 1 (least important)

The resulting map of the weighted composite is presented in Plate 55.5(b). Note that a much smaller portion of the land is ranked as 'Acceptable' or better. Also note the spatial distribution of these prime areas is localized to three distinct clusters.

Three important aspects of cartographic modelling are illustrated in the Development Areas Model: dynamic simulation, concise expression and flexibility. By changing parameters of the model (preference values for slope, proximity, visual exposure, and orientation), a user can simulate numerous alternatives and gain insight into the sensitivity of the planned activity to the actual spatial patterns of the various factors. It is important to note that the decision maker is interactively interrogating the model as new maps are progressively generated. This approach contrasts sharply with manual techniques requiring tedious preparation of a separate set of overlays for each enquiry. Most often in such a manual approach, the patience of both the draftsperson and the decision maker ebbs after just a couple of iterations and a choice of one of the alternatives is made. The ease in simulating numerous scenarios using GIS encourages the decision maker to become an active ingredient in the analysis process and to develop a set of potential alternatives.

The quantitative nature of GIS technology also provides an effective framework for concise expression of complex spatial relationships. The flowchart of processing shown in Fig. 55.1 is an example. In a manner similar to a simple equation, this process uses a series of map operations successively to derive intermediate maps and ultimately leads to a final map of development suitability. Thus the flowchart establishes a succinct format for communicating the logic, assumptions and relationships embodied in the analysis.

Finally, the GIS approach encourages decision makers to change the model as new conditions or insights are developed. For example, the effect of a proposed road could be incorporated. The proposed route would be digitized and added to the existing road map. The model would be re-run and a new suitability map generated. The new suitability map could be compared to the previous one without the proposed road simply by subtracting the two maps. Differences equal to zero identify areas that did not change their suitability ranking. Non-zero differences indicate both the type of change (positive for increased suitability rating) and the magnitude of change (larger values indicate more change). Other factors, such as remoteness from existing or proposed utility lines, could be similarly incorporated.

In the pMAP system, the flowchart shown in Fig. 55.1 is implemented by entering a series of sentences. Changes may be made simply by editing the 'narrative' of a command file with a word processor and re-running the analysis. The 'preference weighting' sub-model takes less than two minutes to run on an inexpensive IBM PC-AT compatible computer. Running the model requires no more technical skills than those used in running database management and spreadsheet packages now commonplace in most offices. A decision maker could simulate several preference scenarios and compare the results in less than 30 minutes. Within this context, individual map products are no longer the focus; rather it is how maps change under various scenarios which provide information. In this approach, a decision maker becomes an active participant in the analysis rather than a 'choice chooser' among a few alternatives provided by the analyst.

A CONFLICT RESOLUTION MODEL

The previous three analyses determined the best use of the Botany Bay area considering conservation, research or development criteria in a unilateral or independent manner. However, most land use decisions require resolution of competing uses. Three basic approaches in resolving conflicts include 'hierarchical dominance', 'multiple use' and 'trade-off'. Hierarchical dominance assumes certain land uses are more important and, therefore, supersede all other potential uses. Multiple use, on the other hand, identifies compatible uses and assigns several uses to a single location. Trade-off recognizes conflicting uses at individual locations and attempts to develop the best mix of uses by choosing one over the others on a parcel-by-parcel basis. Effective land use decisions involve elements of each of these approaches.

From a map processing perspective, the hierarchical approach is easily expressed in a quantitative manner and results in a deterministic solution. Once the political system has identified a superseding use, it is relatively easy to map these areas and assign a suitable value indicating the desire to protect them from other uses. Multiple use also is technically simple from a map analysis context, although often difficult from a policy context. Once compatible uses are identified, a unique value is simply assigned to all areas with this joint condition.

Conflict arises when the uses are not entirely compatible or, as with many uses, completely incompatible. In these instances, quantitative solutions to the allocation of land use are difficult, if not impossible, to implement. So far, optimization models, such as linear or goal planning, have not been successfully extended to geographical space. The complex interaction of the frequency and juxtapositioning of several competing uses is still most effectively dealt with by human intervention. GIS technology assists in decision making under these conditions by deriving a 'conflict' map which indicates the set of alternative uses for each location. Once in this visual form, the decision maker can assess the patterns of conflicting uses and determine land use allocations. GIS can also assist by comparing different allocation scenarios and identifying areas of difference.

Hierarchical consideration of all three uses for the Botany Bay vicinity was performed. A map identifying just the 'recreation' areas was isolated from the Conservation Areas map. Similarly, a map of just the 'best' development areas was isolated from the Development Areas map; and a map isolating the 'Botany Bay watershed' was derived from the Research Areas map. Plate 55.6 shows the result of a hierarchical combination of these data. For this composite, development was least favoured, recreation next with the Botany Bay watershed taking final precedence. This process is similar to overlaying a set of maps delineated on transparencies. The information on each successive map layer obscures information on the preceding maps, while transparent areas allow information to show through. Note that the resultant map in Plate 55.6 contains very little area for development that is not fragmented into disjointed parcels, that is, non-feasible conditions. The hierarchical approach often results in such non-feasible solutions. What is clarified in 'policy space' is frequently muddled in the complex reality of geographical space.

An alternative approach is to create a map indicating all of the potential land uses for each location in a project area – a comprehensive 'conflicts' map. Plate 55.7(a) is such a map considering the Conservation Areas, Research Areas and Development Areas maps. Note that most of the Botany Bay area does not have competing uses (dark green). In most applications, this counter-intuitive condition exists. However, vested interest parties and decision makers alike assume conflict is everywhere. In the absence of the spatial guidance in a conflicts map, proponents attempt to convince others that their opinion is universally best. In the presence of a conflicts map, attention is quickly focused on the unique patterns and possible trade-offs and affording enlightened compromise.

Plate 55.7(b) presents one interpretation of the information on the Botany Bay conflict map (Plate

55.7(a)). This 'best' allocation involved several individuals' subjective trade-offs among areas of conflict, with research receiving the greatest consideration. Dialogue and group dynamics were involved in this process. As in all discussions, individual personalities, persuasiveness, rational arguments and facts resulted in the collective opinion. It was agreed that the Target Rock and Sandy Bay watersheds should remain intact. These watersheds have less conflict with other uses than does the Botany Bay watershed. They also have significant differences in their characteristics which would be useful in designing research experiments.

The remaining good development areas were set aside, ensuring that all development was contained within the Botany Bay watershed. In fact, this constraint would provide a third research setting to investigate development, with the other two watersheds serving as control. Structures would be constrained to the approximately 20 contiguous hectares identified as best for development, consistent with the island's policy to encourage 'cluster' development. The 'limited use' area between the development cluster and the coast would be for the exclusive use of the residents. The Sandy Bay and Target Rock research areas would provide additional buffering and open space. Conservation uses then received the group's attention. This step was easy as the large area extending from little St Thomas Point along the southern coast was identified for recreation with minimal conflict. Finally, the remaining small 'salt and pepper' parcels were absorbed by their surrounding 'limited or preservation use' areas. In all, this provides a fairly rational land use allocation result and one that is readily explained and justified. Although the decision group represented several diverse opinions, this final map achieved consensus. In addition, each person felt as though he or she had actively participated and, by using the interactive process, better understood both the area's spatial complexity and the perspectives of others. The result then is acceptable but not necessarily so in all such studies!

This last step in the analysis may seem anticlimactic. After a great deal of 'smoke and dust raising' about computer processing, the final assignment of land uses involved a large amount of subjective interpretation. This point, however, highlights GIS capabilities and limitations. GIS provide significant advances in data management and analysis and rapidly and tirelessly allow detailed spatial information to be assembled. They also allow much more sophisticated and realistic interpretations of the landscape to be incorporated, such as visual exposure and weighted distance. They do not, however, provide artificial intelligence for land use decision making. GIS greatly enhance decision-making capabilities but do not replace them.

CONCLUSIONS

The preceding discussion and demonstrations have established the important concepts in map analysis using GIS. Fundamental to this is the digital map – storing information as numbers, rather than as colours, shadings, lines or discrete symbols. This format enables maps to be rapidly updated and searched for a variety of spatial relationships. Within this context, the computer can be used to automate the manual cartographic process. From another perspective, the digital map may be treated as quantitative data and analysed in a manner analogous to traditional mathematics and statistics. Models can be constructed by logically sequencing basic map analysis operations on spatial data to solve specific application 'equations'. However, the unknowns of these equations are represented as entire maps, defined by thousands of numbers. This 'map-ematics' forms a conceptual framework for spatial modelling, easily adapted to a wide variety of applications in a familiar and intuitive manner.

Yet GIS is more than a cold, calculating science. It enables decision makers to propose scenario after scenario and to assess the spatial impacts of each one, as demonstrated in the two Development Areas maps. It also provides new analytical procedures that make analyses more realistic, as demonstrated in the Conservation Areas map's effective distance and the Development Areas map of visual exposure. The step-by-step process forms a concise expression of the assumptions and relationships used in the analysis, as demonstrated in the Development Areas flowchart. Most important of all, it provides a medium for consensus building that stimulates constructive discussion, as demonstrated in the interpretation of the Conflicts map. The fact that all of the demonstrations were completed on a personal computer confirms that GIS are coming within both the fiscal and technical reach of most resource professionals.

Readers might conclude that GIS application to island planning is an exacting science, or that the approach is nothing more than a handle-cranking exercise which can be carried out without much thought. It could also be suggested that it is entirely whimsical and unscrupulous planners may simply substitute 'weighting factors' that ensure their desired result. All three of these conclusions are partly right and partly wrong. The old adage of 'garbage in, garbage out' is particularly appropriate in GIS modelling. Inadequate topographic maps, for instance, will generate nonsense slope values, especially if the sampling is coarse. The mathematical solution to 1 per cent change in slope, unless the data are both accurate and highly resolved, can provide a false impression of exactness.

Another pitfall of planning models, whether GIS based or not, is that they are almost canonized. Implementation becomes merely a task of specifying the inputs and waiting for the 'black box' to transform them into a decision. The complexity and uniqueness of each decision situation becomes subordinate to standardization and ease of implementation. At the other extreme, no standards exist and each model is a subjective interpretation. In these instances, GIS are vulnerable to misuse as merely a means to 'prove' a point. The models are designed and calibrated to support a particular position – analogous to the adage 'statistics don't lie, statisticians do'.

These potential pitfalls are overcome only by informed end-users. In the application presented here, a group of interested individuals were involved from model development through to implementation. This integrative decision-making approach brings together a variety of disciplines to address a specific project. Under this open approach, the focus of deliberation becomes the analysis process and each participant is involved in the development of all aspects of the model. Manual map analysis, on the other hand, is so tedious that it is left to the technician; the decision makers enter the process after a few alternatives have been identified. They attempt to assess quickly both the analysis process and the relative merits of each alternative. They then become 'choice choosers' by selecting one of the limited set of alternatives assembled in the manual analysis.

Management of land has always required spatial information as its cornerstone. However, purely descriptive maps of the landscape are not enough. They must be translated into prescriptive maps expressing the interrelationships among mapped data in terms of the decision at hand. GIS technology provides the means to integrate these mapped data fully into resource and land use decision making.

NOTE

This chapter is based on an application sponsored by MacArthur Foundation under the direction of the Tropical Resources Institute, Yale University. The report demonstrates the important concepts in the development and analysis of a spatial database for the Botany Bay vicinity, St Thomas, US Virgin Islands. Its objective is to familiarize readers with the practical considerations and potential capabilities of computer-assisted map analysis in resource planning and management. The encoded and derived maps presented have not been field checked for accuracy. The maps should not be used in actual planning activities without extensive field verification. All of the analyses presented are academic and do not represent actual plans under consideration – the material is presented for demonstration purposes only.

REFERENCES

Berry J K (1987a) The use of a Geographic Information System for storm runoff prediction from small urban watersheds. *Environmental Management Journal* **11** (1): 21–7

Berry J K (1987b) Fundamental operations in computer-assisted map analysis. *International Journal of Geographical Information Systems* **1** (2): 119–36

Berry J K (1987c) Computer-assisted map analysis: potential and pitfalls. *Photogrammetric Engineering and Remote Sensing Journal* **53** (10): 1405–10

Berry J K (1987d) A spatial analysis of timber analysis. In: Ripple W J (ed.) *Geographical Information Systems: a compendium*. Falls Church Virginia, pp. 206–11

Berry J K, Berry J K (1988) Assessing spatial impacts of land use plans. *International Journal of Environmental Management* **27**: 1–9

Berry J K et al. (1989) Development and analysis of a spatial database for the Botany Bay vicinity, Volume 2, final report entitled *Natural and Cultural Resources in the United States Virgin Islands: research, education and management needs.* Tropical Resources Institute, Yale University, New Haven Connecticut

SIS (1986) *pMAP User's Guide and Technical Reference, Professional Map Analysis Package (pMAP).* Spatial Information Systems, Springfield Virginia

Tomlin C D (1991) Cartographic modelling. In: Maguire D J, Goodchild M F, Rhind D W (eds.) *Geographical Information Systems: principles and applications.* Longman, London, pp. 361–74, Vol 1

INTEGRATED PLANNING INFORMATION SYSTEMS

D J COWEN AND W L SHIRLEY

This chapter addresses the use of GIS within planning. It examines the tasks typically performed by planners which involve spatial data handling and the consequences in terms of data sets and GIS functionality. An objective of the chapter is to assess, in a critical way, the GIS resources currently available and the needs for a spatial decision support system. The final part of the chapter utilizes a case study of a major GIS project in the United States to demonstrate how Digital Line Graphs, TIGER files and remotely sensed data can be integrated into a single system that successfully addresses many of the obstacles normally associated with the use of GIS in planning.

INTRODUCTION

A decade – and a GIS lifetime – ago, Edgar Horwood (1980:12) stated that '... to be credible, planning must be cast in an information system context'. Donald Cooke (1980:12) went as far as to say that 'urban and regional planning is a data business. The nature of the data distinguishes planning from other data business because virtually all planning data is intimately related to geography or spatial location'. Since these concepts and beliefs became widely rooted in the community, it is not surprising that the planning profession has been greatly influenced by developments in GIS.

It will be obvious that the concerns of this chapter cut across those of other chapters in this book – notably those by Calkins (1991), Densham (1991), Robinette (1991), Siderelis (1991) and Parrott and Stutz (1991) – all in this volume. These chapters form a set covering a variety of aspects of planning and emphasizing the heterogeneity of the tasks faced by planners: at the very least, the terminology used differs and the type of planning functions involved are also disparate.

However, before proceeding to more detailed matters of planning in relation to GIS, a generic description of the planning process is established. This is essential for, without a shared understanding of planning objectives, concepts and terminology, no understanding of the role of GIS is possible.

THE NATURE OF PLANNING

On a daily basis, planners are confronted with a myriad of *ad hoc* decisions which require accurate and current spatial data. In fact, planners in New York City estimate that 85 per cent of all information handled is associated with geographical entities (Stiefel 1987) and comparable estimates have been made elsewhere in the world (e.g. DoE 1987; Bromley and Coulson 1989). The details of the planning process, the legal basis under which it operates and hence the information demands differ considerably across the world: while a *Plan d'Occupation du Sol* is mandatory in France, the legal requirement for local government to collect detailed land use data in Britain was abolished by the 1968 Town and Country Planning Act. Despite such differences, there are more similarities than differences and, based on an evaluation of activities performed by several local governments, Dangermond and Freedman (1986) developed a list of 21 common procedural and 12 managerial tasks. These include such functions as site planning, vehicle routing, traffic analysis, facility siting, school and political districting, land use planning, facility management, provision of public information and simply handling enquiries from the public. These tasks can be collapsed into a broader set of planning functions such as the one developed by Meyerson (1956) in his classic work:

- Central intelligence
- Pulse taking
- Policy clarification
- Detailed development planning
- Feedback and review.

Each of these functions requires a set of procedures which enable the planner to convert a diverse amount of spatial data into the type of information needed to support the decision-making process.

The 'central intelligence' function requires that a planning organization maintains a comprehensive repository of socio-economic and land use information as varied as housing provision, office space and census information. Unfortunately, this information normally consists of a wide variety of maps, aerial photographs, reports and digital data. The promise of GIS is to provide the tools to assemble these diverse forms of spatial information into an integrated format that will improve the ability of planners to see (and, where possible, anticipate) the major trends that are occurring within the community. By the nature of this function, the information needs are sometimes difficult to predict.

'Pulse-taking' functions serve as early warning systems. These activities often require in-depth analysis of existing conditions. To support these functions, planners must be able to convert miscellaneous transactions into meaningful interpretations of patterns and trends. For example, the sites of crimes and other occurrences – traditionally delineated by 'pin maps' – must be aggregated into meaningful statistical areas. Once this is done, the counts for each area can be converted into rates that can be analysed across the community. For many of these functions, simple statistical mapping and analysis is very useful.

'Policy clarification' results from the comparison of alternative scenarios arising from public issues. For example, it may be very important that planners have the ability to develop and compare various suitability models. Kindleberger (1988) has suggested that the essence of planning is understanding the implications of policy alternatives and recommending those alternatives most likely to achieve community goals and objectives. For instance, the development of new school districts or zoning changes often use a type of recursive process that incorporates group decision making (see Calkins 1991 in this volume). An effective GIS would enable the planner to assemble the data needed to measure and portray the relevant information and also to generate the various scenarios expeditiously.

'Development planning' also takes into account a wide variety of spatial and tabular information pertaining to the land use pattern of a community. As part of this process, policy makers prepare zoning maps that direct land development and substantially influence property values. These policies also include the siting of public facilities such as schools, hospitals, police and fire stations. This aspect of the planning process often requires that public officials mediate the delicate balance between the economic development needs of the community and the need for social services. Planners thus need to rely upon systems which can present 'objective resolutions' to (or at least which follow replicatable and explicit procedures in dealing with) disputes that may arise with respect to the location of noxious facilities or when faced by the classic 'Not in My Back Yard' (or NIMBY) attitudes. The ideal GIS would enable the planner to model the process and to generate a scenario that aids in finding common ground among competing factions (e.g. see Berry 1991 in this volume).

'Feedback and review' functions are essential in a public arena within a democracy. Citizens have a right to review the information that is being used to zone their property as well as to question how public officials are spending their tax money (Chrisman 1987). Historically, the control of information has also been the basis of political power. However, modern information system technology, coupled with the legal rights of citizens to access information, has changed the entire process (Archer and Croswell 1989). In those countries where data access is guaranteed to the citizenry, it is certain that decision making will no longer be controlled by a few public officials. It will thus be impossible for planners to ignore the views of citizens who come to public meetings with different solutions derived from the same information sources.

This review of basic planning functions demonstrates that planning is inherently a spatially oriented profession which involves a great deal of *ad hoc* decision making based on the evaluation of alternatives. Accepting this generality, Dueker (1980) characterized the ideal planning process as one that involves the following steps:

- Defining the problem
- Determining objectives
- Inventing alternative solutions
- Evaluating alternatives
- Selecting the best alternative
- Implementing the systems or plan
- Monitoring the results.

In summary, the nature of the planning process would appear to be a perfect setting for GIS to demonstrate their ability to manage a diverse set of spatial information and to form the information infrastructure of more efficiently and equitably operated communities. At a minimum, a set of GIS tools linked to an integrated database of the basic socio-economic and land use information enable the planners to conduct exploratory spatial analysis (Goodchild 1989; Openshaw 1991 in this volume). In an optimal setting, GIS offers the possibility of supporting a sophisticated decision support system. Densham and Rushton (1988) consider planning in a public service setting to be a process-oriented activity that not only attempts to identify optimal location patterns but also is one with intrinsic values that can generate 'a just pattern, justly arrived at'.

PLANNING INFORMATION SYSTEMS

The goal of an information system is to convert a magnitude of data into meaningful information. Successful information systems for planning have long been discussed and anticipated. The technology has rarely been held to be the problem. Thus, in a prescient (if slightly premature) comment, Cooke (1980:14) suggested that, even then, there was '"excess technology" with no pressing unsolved geoprocessing needs'. At the same time, Horwood (1980:11) forecast that, 'The 1980s will be a decade of database and data management development for multi-purpose use'. He likened the situation in 1980 to 'having a high-powered locomotive available but few railroad tracks'. Kindleberger (1988) has divided the history of database creation, management and use in planning into three categories: the 1960s as a time of high information systems excitement; the 1970s as a time of some disappointment, despite considerable government investment; and the 1980s as a time of explosive change.

An obvious example of how GIS should be able to aid decision making – and one which will be recalled several times later in the chapter – is in the location of new industrial sites which meet specified criteria. Once the basic infrastructure data layers are created, the analytical functions of the GIS can generate automatically many of the variables required. For example, distance measures can be generated to calculate a number of accessibility measures. Other factors, such as labour force measures, can be aggregated by relevant census areas. In practice, the key problem is not one of combining the data sets but one of selecting and weighting of the relevant layers. Yet this is not a new problem nor even one specific to GIS: Sweet (1970) proposed a solution through the development of industrial screening matrices. A screening matrix attempts to match target industrial groups with the locational criteria that are judged to be most important to the industry. Candidate industries are selected and evaluated on the basis of factors such as wages, materials, linkages, markets and labour factors. Weights are assigned to the locational factors and industries are then selected in terms of their compatibility with local objectives.

Analytical functions needed to support planning activities

Access to a current and appropriate set of map layers at a usable scale (see below) is only part of the problem facing planners who wish to utilize GIS. A successful system must integrate the appropriate set of retrieval, analysis and display functions with the database. Over the past decade,

major advances have included the ability to query and display ever-increasing amounts of spatial information (Croswell and Clark 1988). While these are not new facilities, they have been packaged into increasingly affordable, colourful and powerful computer systems. Thus these advances have resulted in better data management (providing electronic filing cabinets) and more mapping capabilities (electronic drafting); but they should not be mistaken for better decision-making tools. As Goodchild (1987:334) argued, 'in reality, most contemporary GIS place far more emphasis on efficient data input and retrieval than on sophisticated analysis'. The unhappy experience with the Decision Information Display System (DIDS) clearly demonstrated that GIS intended as decision support systems must be more than 'magical map-making systems' (see below). An atlas, even in electronic form, is not capable of providing the planner with the ability to evaluate alternatives, to deal with land use conflicts or even to handle simple routing or politically sensitive districting functions.

Data integration tools

Dangermond and Freedman (1986) suggested that the set of basic tools needed to support planning functions include the following:

- *Graphic overlay*: to produce a variety of maps.

- *Topological overlay*: to integrate two or more files to generate site suitability models and other forms of locational analysis.

- *Address geocoding*: to assign automatically a coordinate point or district to an address.

- *Polygonization*: to form new districts from the set of existing maps.

- *Relational matching*: the ability to relate two entities for functional purposes, such as parcels to tabular data or census data to census polygons.

At the technical level, the most important tools are those which permit the overlay and integration of different forms of geographical entities. Muller (1985:42) emphasized that the power of such tools is related to their ability to transform a map into 'a logical entity whose elements are subject to various combinatorial operations with other sub-sets of information'. Further, White (1984) emphasized that a multipurpose geographical data handling system must be able to perform true map overlay so that it can determine 'which regions cover a given region'. The importance of such map overlay was of course demonstrated long ago by Ian McHarg and has been widely used in a manual or photographic fashion by planners to create suitability and capability models (McHarg 1971). A fundamental question is whether these same analyses can now be performed economically on 'real world'-sized data sets by digital processing (McHarg 1987).

Some remaining problems

Goodchild (1987) claimed that the set of commercially available spatial analysis tools extant at the time he wrote still fell short of users' needs for combining spatial integration facilities, optimal location/allocation routines and statistical analysis capabilities within a common operating environment. It is obvious that these tools are of particular value to planners. Although he acknowledged that the interface between GIS and analytical modelling systems needs to improve, Dangermond (1987) responded by claiming that such a linkage was already beginning to emerge. This evolution is reflected in the appearance of location and allocation procedures in the standard set of functions included in some commercial GIS (Lupian, Moreland and Dangermond 1987).

But, despite recent developments (and as with any evolutionary process), there remain several barriers to the successful implementation of information system technology in general and GIS specifically. Dueker (1980:8) has argued that:

'... the systems approach has severe limitations and is rarely applied successfully especially in long-range planning where the system is open-ended and the purpose of the plan is general and vaguely identified ... The planning process itself is constantly shifting and, given the complexity and/or controversies in the planning decision, the scale of analysis is subject to considerable debate and change. Thus the design of information systems for planning cannot be considered a well-structured process'.

The complexity of these problems has led the

Urban and Regional Information Systems Association (URISA) to develop a research agenda which addresses 28 problems faced by planners and other professionals in attempts to implement GIS successfully (Craig 1989). Their list is divided into the following set of social and technical concerns:

- System adoption
- Social and legal impacts
- Management issues
- Economic factors
- Database development
- User interface and empowerment
- Software critique.

This list, assembled substantially by those active in some aspect or other of the planning profession, clearly indicates that a successful GIS involves a complex interrelationship between information, technology and human beings. More important still, it suggests that severe gaps currently exist between the ideal model that is often portrayed by the vendors and developers of GIS and those who are responsible for the daily operation of these systems.

Spatial Decision Support Systems (SDSS) in planning

An interesting parallel exists between the set of concerns that URISA has identified and the emerging debate on the adequacy of GIS to meet the needs for a Spatial Decision Support System (or SDSS). Specifically, the issues confronting SDSS are closely associated with the needs and obstacles that planners face in successfully implementing a GIS. Densham and Goodchild (1989:710) suggested that a SDSS can be viewed as 'spatial analogues of decision support systems (DSS) developed in operations research and management science to address business problems ... [They] provide a framework for integration of analytical modelling capabilities, database management systems and graphical display capabilities to improve decision-making processes' (see also Densham 1991 in this volume). According to the definition provided by Geoffrion (1983), there are six distinguishing characteristics of a DSS:

1. They are designed to handle ill- or semi-structured problems.
2. They have an interface that is easy to use.
3. They enable the user to have full access to the database.
4. They are able to generate a number of alternative scenarios.
5. They support a range of decision-making styles.
6. They support interactive and recursive decision-making processes.

Given these characteristics, it would seem that the 'ideal' SDSS would overcome many of the specific problems identified by URISA. For example, a good SDSS should address the URISA objective of making GIS software accessible to users with different levels of technical expertise through the use of Artificial Intelligence, help screens, relational databases and software layering (Craig 1989). In other words, the ultimate success of GIS in planning is closely related to how well it can succeed as a SDSS in being incorporated in the decision-making process. The limiting factors presently relate most directly to data problems, inadequacy of the analytical functions and an inability to support the type of decision-making process that characterizes the planning environment.

The creation of Spatial Decision Support Systems

Later in this chapter, a specific project will be described as a worked example of an integrated approach to the use of GIS in planning. The goal of that project is to develop a SDSS which will be used in the highly visible and politically sensitive area of economic development. Decisions made in this context must consider the interrelationships between land use factors, economic growth, water and waste water facilities, and major transportation networks. The ultimate challenge will be to forecast the economic impact of infrastructure projects and to recruit new industry into the state. This requires a sophisticated SDSS that can support different styles of decision making (Calkins 1991 in this volume). In such situations – according to Densham and Goodchild (1989:714) – a SDSS 'should incorporate knowledge used by expert analysts to guide the formulation of the problem, the articulation of the desired characteristics of the solution and the design and execution of a solution process'. Yet the development of expert systems for such applications is relatively new territory and not all experts are convinced it is worth while. Kindleberger (1988:12), for instance, expressed his pessimism about expert systems in saying, '... local government issues tend to be complex to the degree that it would be foolish to expect major progress'.

The decision-making context

The meaningful interpretation and use of large scale GIS databases demands that the users of the system have the theoretical background required to develop conceptual models which incorporate the relevant dimensions of the problem. Therefore, the first step in creating a useful decision-making context for any project is to develop an analytical framework to select and weight the various layers of the GIS database. A research initiative by the US National Center for Geographic Information and Analysis (NCGIA) has begun to attack this problem by developing a taxonomy of users of spatial information. For example, Beard (1989) maintained that there are only six generic uses for spatial data (see also Maguire 1991 in this volume):

1. Siting of location
2. Logistics or allocation
3. Routing
4. Navigation
5. Inventory of spatial objects
6. Monitoring and analysis.

Obermeyer (1989) suggested that each of these generic uses needs a spatial theory or model as well as a database that can support the analysis. For example, the siting of an agricultural activity should be guided by agricultural location theory. The SDSS for locating such an activity would incorporate transportation costs, environmental factors, crop characteristics, etc. Each of these factors would be represented by specific data elements such as soil conditions, slope and length of the growing season.
  One example where such theory-based approaches are guiding the use of GIS is in the South Carolina Infrastructure and Economic Planning Project (Cowen, Mitchell and Meyer 1990; see also below). In this, the selection of a suitable site for a prospective industry in the state is guided by industrial location theory: the decision-making process starts with a minimum transportation cost site and then compares that site with others which may offer savings in terms of labour costs, agglomeration factors or other variables. An interesting attempt to develop an expert system (ESMAN) to handle such decisions was also reported by Suh, Kim and Kim (1988). In their prototype, the authors used 13 components to develop a site suitability index for three hypothetical sites. The components included suitable plant site, availability of skilled and unskilled labour, wage rates, nearness to the market, accessibility to transportation, climate, utilities and tax rates. Each component was operationally defined. For example, accessibility to markets was measured by the distance to major cities, accessibility to transportation as distance to interchanges, airports and 'piggyback' services. Although this was only a prototype, the study provides a useful starting point for a SDSS to address industrial site selection problems.

SPATIAL DATABASES TO SUPPORT PLANNING

The simplest and fastest way to reach a decision is to use the minimum amount of information and to evaluate the fewest alternatives. Indeed, Horwood (1980) suggested that information systems often tend to make decision making more difficult. Simplistic analysis, however, often leads to simplistic and erroneous conclusions. Therefore, the overriding challenge to those creating a geographical database within a GIS is to combine the appropriate information in a format that can be easily queried, analysed and displayed – irrespective of the fact that detailed needs of the user may not emerge for some time after the system has been designed (see Mounsey 1991 in this volume)! The fundamental building block of a planning GIS must be an appropriate database.
  A classic SDSS example of the importance of an appropriate database was the Decision

Information Display System (DIDS). This was a 'state of the art' system developed at the beginning of the 1980s by the federal government in the US (Cowen 1983). With the backing of the Executive Office of the President, DIDS was designed to serve as a central repository and display system for geographical information collected by all federal agencies. Using the (then) latest in colour image processing workstation technology, NASA created the system and assembled a large variety of statistical information for all the US counties. Unfortunately, the Bureau of the Census, the most extensive source of these data, was simultaneously in the process of conducting a new decennial census of population and housing; most of the DIDS data were therefore almost obsolete when it was made available. In addition, the system also was limited severely in terms of the data structure used and hence the analytical capabilities. For example, it was not possible to incorporate point or linear features, interstate highways being represented simply by an attribute 'miles of road passing through the county' while topography was denoted by average elevation within a county. In effect, a decade ago the 'state of the art' decision support system was nothing more than an expensive county-level map-making machine. Despite its technological sophistication in other ways, DIDS was doomed to failure because it did not contain relevant and up-to-date information to support decision making.

The fundamental database for planning

For a GIS to meet the needs of local government successfully, planners must have access to the databases that can describe the urban system in abstract physical, social and economic terms (see Parrott and Stutz 1991). Only if the database is designed to model the functioning, 'real-world' system can it be used for multiple purposes. A 1989 study of the ACSM–ASPRS Geographical Information Management System Committee suggested that, when building such a multipurpose geographical database, an organization should always 'future proof' the database as much as possible by following a fixed sequence of stages:

- Identify potential users.
- Identify output product requirements.
- Define spatial data categories.
- Establish required levels of accuracy.
- Evaluate data sources and quality.

In practice, of course, any process involving the expenditure of public funds will involve a compromise between the requirements of the perfect database and practical solutions. Building databases is all about making trade-offs between present needs and future opportunities, even though the level of costs involved may preclude some players. As Kindleberger (1988:11) stated 'The . . . question has to do with economics and the extent to which entrepreneurs, either for profit or non-profit, will be able to build and support comprehensive databases. Local government has little discretionary funding to pay for such services.' Thus – in the United States at least – planning databases may be too expensive for the public sector to create except for those which are created 'bottom-up' from transaction-based data.

This uncertainty over costs has led to many governments starting in GIS with project-based schemes, rather than the creation of comprehensive databases (Robinette 1991 in this volume; Siderelis 1991 in this volume). Such projects are inevitably diverse in nature. If this is accepted as a necessity for the start-up phase, what data do planners need to exploit GIS in the bulk of their everyday work? The analysis by Dangermond and Freedman (1986) suggested that commonality *did* occur in the needs of planners for spatial data. They claimed that the spatial database needed for local government planning purposes consists of the following components:

- A base map   Environmental overlays
- Engineering overlays   Plan/profile drawings
- Parcel maps   Parcel/street address data
- Area tabular data   Area boundary maps (administrative boundaries)
- Street tabular data   Street network file (geographical base file).

The collection of these layers of spatially registered

information is actually a decision to establish a dynamic repository which, in principle at least, is capable of supporting all planning functions. The accuracy, timeliness, accessibility and flexibility of this 'digital atlas' will ultimately determine the success or failure of the system. The construction and maintenance process is an expensive one that involves the integration of a diverse variety of spatial information sources that normally include maps, aerial photography, surveys, census information and, increasingly, remotely sensed data (Ehlers, Edwards and Bedard 1989).

Scales of mapping

The survey by the ACSM–ASPRS committee found that there are about six different map scales, ranging from 1 : 600 to 1 : 24 000, which are commonly used in local government applications in the US. However, an application-oriented viewpoint would suggest that three levels of detail and representation of features are often employed in a planning context (Dueker 1988). The most generalized level is based on partitioning the region into a set of polygons which serve as geographical zones for aggregation of individual transactions or occurrences. These areal systems usually consist of census tracts, postal zones or traffic zones encoded from a scale of approximately 1 : 100 000, thereby confining much of the analysis to statistical analysis and mapping of socio-economic data.

An intermediate level of representation, at a map scale of about 1 : 10 000, is necessary to support locational analysis. Such applications are comprised of tasks which can be handled with an accurate representation of transportation networks, hydrological features and administrative boundaries. Many of the map layers identified by Dangermond and Freedman (1986) can be created at this level of resolution, in which an address can safely be represented as a single X, Y coordinate point. This level of analysis supports geocoding (typically, in North America, through address matching) which leads directly to point mapping, statistical analysis and network analysis (Plate 56.1). With an address matching capability, it is possible to convert any thematic information labelled with an address into a spatially registered layer. This approach is obviously useful for analysis of specific occurrences such as housing starts, registered voters, students, traffic accidents, emergency calls and criminal activities. Using such a GIS database, a planning organization can maintain a comprehensive and topologically correct base map for almost any size of planning region. Dueker has suggested that, for this level of analysis, a positional accuracy of 10 to 50 feet (3 to 15 m) is sufficient. In the United States it is common practice, however, to use 1 : 24 000 scale 7.5 minute US Geological Survey quadrangles for such applications. It is also striking that the US Bureau of Census used 1 : 100 000-scale maps as the base for the 1990 Census (see Starr and Anderson 1991 in this volume; Rhind 1991 in this volume).

In an urban setting, the finest level of spatial detail is required for facility management (Mahoney 1991 in this volume), maintenance of a multipurpose cadastre (Dale 1991 in this volume) and engineering design. For these applications, it is necessary to have geographical entities encoded at a scale of about 1 : 1000 with a positional accuracy of about 1 foot (0.3 m). This level of detail is required for tasks such as tax assessment which demand that geographical entities be represented as areas, not just as point features. Generally, compiling information at this level of detail costs two orders of magnitude more than the intermediate level database for the same geographical area. Therefore the decision to create and maintain such a database must be made with great care and the realization that a stable source of funding must exist. Such a financial requirement usually places this level of spatial detail beyond the scope of local planning departments and into the domain of tax assessors or utility companies. The situation differs, of course, in countries where national mapping agencies map at very large scales (e.g. see Sowton 1991 in this volume).

A SPATIAL DECISION SUPPORT SYSTEM FOR ECONOMIC DEVELOPMENT PLANNING IN SOUTH CAROLINA

Many planning activities are dedicated to fostering the prosperity of an area and of the people therein. Though they have only indirect influence on some factors which attract new industry or services (e.g. a pool of labour and its unit cost), planners can influence development in other ways. Commonly, they attempt to ensure that the area for which they operate has adequate infrastructure, an attractive environment, etc. For this reason, the remainder of this chapter forms a worked example: it describes a GIS project designed to support decisions on infrastructure improvement and industrial site selection. The South Carolina Infrastructure and Economic Planning Project is a collaborative one between the state, local government and university researchers (Cowen et al. 1990). It represents one of the first 'real world' implementations of GIS designed to support decision making in the economic development arena (Cowen and Shinar 1989).

One important aspect in the success of this project is the technological ability to share information. The system uses an existing federal digital database that can be accessed through a network of high performance workstations, enabling the partners in the project to share responsibilities and jointly participate in the processes of data gathering and use. For example, state officials have contracted directly with regional planning councils to create one of the most complex data layers. In turn, the ten regional planning councils contracted with nearly 600 water and waste water system administrators to gather their data in both spatial and tabular form. As Dueker (1988:104) suggested 'the technology provides the means by which economic constraints are relaxed, which reduces institutional barriers. Organizations can still maintain their institutionally independent layer of data and their control over it. But this increases incentives to share that data layer with others, which is leading to organizational innovation.'

Intermediate scale data from the federal government

The availability of intermediate scale digital data from the federal government was essential in this project since it provided a topographic framework on which many other data were 'draped'. The Bureau of Census GBF/DIME system represented an early (1967–71) attempt to develop a nation-wide geocoding system (Coppock and Rhind 1991 in this volume). These geographical base files, which represented skeletons of street centre lines, railroads, administrative boundaries and hydrological features, provided some address matching capabilities. However, they provided a poor cartographic representation of the geographical features and were limited to the 275 largest urban areas in the United States (Tomasi 1990). The needs of the Bureau of the Census to expand its geocoding coverage and to improve its cartographic capabilities prompted a joint effort with the USGS to create the 1 : 100 000 scale Digital Line Graphs or DLG (Starr and Anderson 1991 in this volume). In effect, this new database provides a reasonable cartographic and a good topological representation of the planimetric features on the standard USGS 7.5 minute quadrangles (Plate 56.2). The Bureau of the Census has converted these files into the TIGER database used to conduct the 1990 Census (Marx 1990).

Creation of the South Carolina database

The 1 : 100 000-scale DLG data provided a complete and unbiased representation of the basic transportation and hydrological networks of the state (Plates 56.3 and 56.4). The data were used to represent several important components of the state's infrastructure and as a template for the creation of other layers (Table 56.1) – just as in the CORINE project (see Mounsey 1991 in this volume).

Using the DLG base as a template to create other layers

The transportation layers in the DLG files were edge-matched between adjacent map sheets and reformatted into state-wide coverages. In conjunction with commercially available county boundaries, zip codes, census tracts and census county divisions, these transportation layers formed the basis of the 'molecules' from which other layers were created. One specific example is the way in which graphic DLG data were used as a template for the creation of the water and waste water networks. The procedure adopted required that a large variety of state-wide reference maps be plotted at various scales for local areas. In order to meet this need, a generalized mapping system was developed (Cowen and White 1989). This mapping system reads the original DLG files for any bounding rectangle and plots a base map of the highways, hydrography and miscellaneous transportation networks on an electrostatic plotter. For example, the map in Fig. 56.1 displays the

Table 56.1 Data layers to be included in the South Carolina system. ((DLG) represents those data that are derived from USGS 1 : 100 000 scale Digital Line Graphs and (SPOT) represents those that are derived from SPOT data.)

(a) Transportation
1. Highway location (DLG)
2. Traffic (count and type)
3. Railroad location (DLG)
4. Rail terminals and cargo loading sites (DLG)
5. Airport location (DLG)
6. Port location (DLG)

(b) Water supply systems
1. System extent and location
2. System capacities
3. System output (use)
4. Hydrology (DLG)
5. Stream capacities

(c) Waste water systems
1. System extent and location
2. System capacities
3. System output (use)
4. Stream discharge limits

(d) Air quality

(e) Land cover/land use (SPOT data)

(f) Flood plains

(g) Demographics and economics

(h) Business and industry
1. Directory of business and industry
2. Available buildings
3. Available 'developable' sites

various DLG layers for a section of the Columbia, South Carolina metropolitan area. Using this mapping system, it was possible to generate – as a matter of routine – a base map at 1 : 20 000 or 1 : 15 000 scale of the existing transportation and hydrography for each one of the 575 water and sewerage districts throughout the state. Local planners were used to transfer the contents of the water and sewerage lines engineering and standard maps on to the computer-generated base maps. The GIS coverages were created simply by selecting the relevant arcs from the transportation layer displayed on the workstation. Using this template approach, it was possible to create the complete water and waste water networks for the entire state in about nine months without ever touching a digitizing tablet (Plate 56.5).

Use of TIGER and remotely sensed data

The next stage of database development is focusing on the use of TIGER files to build complete census geographical area coverages for the state. The TIGER files provide a good county-oriented digital base (Plate 56.6). These files are superior to the DLG base for most applications because they contain street names for most roads and address ranges within the urbanized areas. Therefore, the TIGER data were used to create certain other layers, such as industrial locations, vacant buildings and commercial sites (Plate 56.7).

Another aspect of the project is focusing on land cover information from SPOT 20 metre multi-spectral satellite data (Plate 56.8). The creation of this coverage involves the integration of raster and vector data sources. The SPOT data are being handled in two different computing environments. A state agency is using standard remote sensing techniques to classify the data into a generalized land cover classification that will be converted into vector form for integration with the other layers. The data are also being used as raster graphic 'back planes' within the standard vector-based GIS workstation environment. In the second approach, the image-based data provide a basis for map edit and update. They also provide a quick overview of the basic land cover without going through the classification process (Plate 56.9).

Use of the system as an analytical tool

The South Carolina infrastructure GIS database is now beginning to be put into use for industrial site selection. The following scenario demonstrates how the data are being combined with GIS functions to determine quickly those areas which meet specific requirements for prospective industrial clients. For this example, it was assumed that the client has decided to locate a plant in the metropolitan Columbia SC area and needs to find an available building that meets specific infrastructure requirements. In particular, it has been assumed that the site should have good access to a major airport, interstate highway interchange, rail connection and be linked to a public water supply. In a GIS environment, each of the accessibility measures must be translated into a specific buffer

Integrated Planning Information Systems

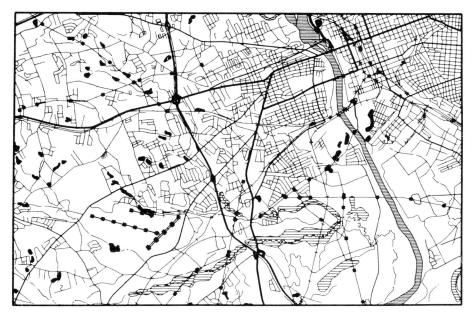

Fig. 56.1 Electrostatic plot of the 1 : 100 000 scale USGS Digital Line Graphs for a portion of the Columbia SC metropolitan area.

zone. The problem is then reduced to finding the Boolean combinations of the resultant proximity zones. For this example, the buffer zones for the airport, railroad and interstate interchange were set at 3500 m, 100 m and 1500 m respectively. Each of the layers was easily extracted from the TIGER base map and the zones automatically generated (Plate 56.10). From the resultant map, it was clear that accessibility to the airport was the most restrictive criterion. By examining the area around the airport more closely, it was possible to identify those areas that have good access to the interstate highway interchanges (Plate 56.11). An examination of the map also indicated there are only a few areas that would meet the narrowly defined railroad buffer criterion. Therefore, some compromise had to be made and the system had to be able to respond to the changes. In an interactive mode it was possible to display the three available buildings in the area and to examine the existing water supply lines to arrive speedily at a final site decision (Plate 56.12).

Although this is a somewhat simplistic example, it clearly demonstrates how TIGER files can be combined with locally generated information relating to water lines and industrial sites to create an extremely valuable GIS database for a wide range of planning activities. The interactive use of GIS analytical and display capabilities enables decision makers to retrieve and combine the relevant spatial information needed to arrive at the appropriate decision within acceptable time-frames. Given the performance of current graphic workstations, the type of scenario used in this example can be completed for the entire state in just a matter of minutes. Furthermore, unlike the situation where a static atlas of maps forms the information base, the decision maker in this environment can pick and choose the information that is relevant to the particular problem and can easily modify the proximity zones or other requirements. The next stage of this project is addressing the specific site requirements for different types of industries. For example, it has been empirically determined that major industrial water users in the state need to be located within 400 m of an existing waterline (see Cowen *et al.* 1990). This type of empirical work will result in a set of rules that can be built into an expert system to guide the initial determination of feasible sites throughout the state. The availability of 1990 Census of Population and Housing will provide the important labour market data needed to complete the model.

CONCLUSIONS

The objective of this chapter has been to examine the current status of GIS within the planning environment. It is apparent that planning is a form of spatial decision making which involves the detailed analysis of a complex set of geographical information. These activities require the creation of interrelated spatial databases and are perfect candidates for use of GIS technology. At the same time, there are several obstacles that have prevented GIS from gaining wide-scale acceptance within the planning profession to date. Many of these obstacles are related to the current limitations of GIS to fulfil its potential as a Spatial Decision Support System and to become an integrated part of the management and data processing systems within government. But the solution may partly lie outside GIS. Sommers (1987) maintained that local governments have to consider reorganizing the basic way they perform their responsibilities and cannot simply view the GIS as a substitute for manual processes. She recognized that it may be difficult for the GIS and the organization to adapt to each other yet this is the only way that the GIS can reach its full potential.

It is also increasingly evident that any public agency must address the complex legal issues relating to data ownership, accuracy, access, security and costs. For example, it may not be possible for an agency (at least in the US) to charge citizens for information that was compiled at taxpayers' expense. Any organization must also be aware that the development of a comprehensive GIS database is a long-term proposition. In particular, it must consider the cost and time associated with the inevitable migration to a higher resolution and more current base map.

In summary, then, GIS offers the potential to be the dynamic core for almost every aspect of planning. A truly successful planning-oriented GIS would be able to address a unified and current view of a community. This view would be maintained and updated on the basis of the transactions in which local government is already involved, thereby eliminating any redundant data collection and mapping. It seems clear that the ultimate success of GIS in planning depends on how well it serves the daily needs of the entire governmental arena and how well it is integrated into the entire realm of daily record keeping and data management. It is obvious that many difficulties still remain in bringing about this happy state. Yet the South Carolina Infrastructure and Economic Development Project demonstrates that, by using federally supplied databases and setting up local collaboration between autonomous agencies, it is possible to combine diverse information into an intermediate scale GIS database and exploit it successfully. Even more important, it also demonstrates that planning use of GIS cannot simply be a pragmatic exercise based on 'data crunching': industrial and other location theories must be used to inform economic development planning if the latter is to be successful.

REFERENCES

ACSM–ASPRS Geographic Information Management Committee (1989) Multi-purpose geographic database guidelines for local governments. *ACSM Bulletin* **121**: 1357–65

Archer H, Croswell P L (1989) Public access to public information systems: an emerging legal issue. *Photogrammetric Engineering and Remote Sensing* **15** (11): 1575–81

Beard M K (1989) Dimensions of use and value of geographic information. In: Onsrud H J, Calkins H W, Obermeyer N J (eds.) *Use and Value of Geographic Information*. Initiative Four Specialist Meeting Report and Proceedings *NCGIA Technical Paper 89–7*. University of California at Santa Barbara, Santa Barbara

Berry J K (1991) GIS in island resource planning: a case study in map analysis. In: Maguire D J, Goodchild M F, Rhind D W (eds.) *Geographical Information Systems: principles and applications*. Longman, London, pp. 285–95, Vol 2

Bromley R, Coulson M G (1989) *Geographical Information Systems and the Work of a Local Authority: the case of Swansea City Council*. Department of Geography University College Swansea, Swansea

Calkins H W (1991) GIS and public policy. In: Maguire D J, Goodchild M F, Rhind D W (eds.) *Geographical Information Systems: principles and applications*. Longman, London, pp. 233–45, Vol 2

Chrisman N R (1987) Design of geographic information systems based on social and cultural goals.

Photogrammetric Engineering and Remote Sensing **53** (10): 1367–70

Cooke D F (1980) A review of geoprocessing systems and a look at their future. In: Krammer K, King J (eds.) *Computers in Local Government Urban and Regional Planning*. Auerbach Publishers Inc., Pennsauken, pp. (2.4.1) 1–16

Coppock J T, Rhind D W (1991) The history of GIS. In: Maguire D J, Goodchild M F, Rhind D W (eds.) *Geographical Information Systems: principles and applications*. Longman, London, pp. 21–43, Vol 1

Cowen D J (1983) Rethinking DIDS: the next generation of interactive colour mapping systems *Cartographica* **21**: 89–92

Cowen D J, Mitchell L, Meyer W (1990) Industrial modelling using a GIS: the first step in developing an expert system for industrial site selection. *Proceedings of GIS/LIS '90*. ASPRS/ACSM/AAG/URISA/AM-FM, Bethesda, pp. 1–10

Cowen D J, Shinar W (1989) A GIS-based support system for economic development. *URISA Proceedings* **2**: 138–48

Cowen D J, White T (1989) A versatile mapping system for the USGS 1:100 000 DLGs. *Proceedings of AUTOCARTO9*. ACSM/ASPRS, Falls Church Virginia, pp. 705–14

Craig W (1989) URISA's research agenda and the NCGIA. *Journal of the Urban and Regional Information Systems Association* **1** (1): 7–16

Croswell P L, Clark S R (1988) Trends in automated mapping and geographic information systems. *Photogrammetric Engineering and Remote Sensing* **54**: 1571–6

Dale P F (1991) Land Information Systems. In: Maguire D J, Goodchild M F, Rhind D W (eds.) *Geographical Information Systems: principles and applications*. Longman, London, pp. 85–99, Vol 2

Dangermond J (1987) The maturing of GIS and a new age for geographic information modeling (GIMS). In: Aangeenbrug R T, Schiffman Y M (eds.) *International Geographic Information Systems (IGIS) Symposium, Arlington, Virginia*, Volume 2. ASPRS, Falls Church, pp. 55–67

Dangermond J, Freedman C (1986) Findings regarding a conceptual model of a municipal database and implications for software design. *Geo-Processing* **3**: 31–49

Densham P J (1991) Spatial decision support systems. In: Maguire D J, Goodchild M F, Rhind D W (eds.) *Geographical Information Systems: principles and applications*. Longman, London, pp. 403–12, Vol 1

Densham P J, Goodchild M F (1989) Spatial decision support systems: a research agenda. *Proceedings of GIS/LIS '89*, Volume 2. ACSM/ASPRS/AAG, Falls Church Virginia, pp. 707–16

Densham P J, Rushton G (1988) Decision support systems for locational planning. In: Golledge R, Timmermans H (eds.) *Behavioral Modelling in Geography and Planning*. Croom-Helm, London, pp. 56–90

Department of the Environment (DoE) (1987) *Handling Geographic Information: the report of the Committee of Inquiry chaired by Lord Chorley*. HMSO, London

Dueker K J (1980) An approach to integrated information systems for planning. In: Krammer K, King J (eds.) *Computers in Local Government Urban and Regional Planning*. Auerbach Publishers Inc., Pennsauken, pp.(2.1.2) 1–12

Dueker K J (1988) Urban applications of geographical information systems: a grouping into three levels of resolution. *URISA Proceedings*, Volume 2. pp. 104–9

Ehlers M, Edwards G, Bedard Y (1989) Integration of remote sensing with geographic information systems: a necessary evolution. *Photogrammetric Engineering and Remote Sensing* **55** (11): 1619–27

Geoffrion A M (1983) Can or/ms evolve fast enough? *Interfaces* **13**: 10–25

Goodchild M F (1987) A spatial analytical perspective on geographical information systems. *International Journal of Geographical Information Systems* **1** (4): 327–34

Goodchild M F (1989) Geographic information systems and market research. *Papers and Proceedings of Applied Geography Conferences*, Volume 12. 1–8

Horwood E M (1980) Planning information systems: functional approaches, evolution and pitfalls. In: Krammer K, King J (eds.) *Computers in Local Government Urban and Regional Planning*. Auerbach Publishers Inc., Pennsauken, pp. (2.1.1) 1–12

Kindleberger C (1988) Planning support systems for the 1990s: local government information processing challenges and opportunities. *URISA Proceedings* **3**: 1–21

Lupian A E, Moreland W H, Dangermond J (1987) Network analysis in geographic information systems. *Photogrammetric Engineering and Remote Sensing* **53** (10): 1417–21

Maguire D J (1991) An overview and definition of GIS. In: Maguire D J, Goodchild M F, Rhind D W (eds.) *Geographical Information Systems: principles and applications*. Longman, London, pp. 9–20, Vol 1

Mahoney R P (1991) GIS and utilities. In: Maguire D J, Goodchild M F, Rhind D W (eds.) *Geographical Information Systems: principles and applications*. Longman, London, pp. 101–14, Vol 2

Marx R W (1990) The TIGER system: yesterday, today and tomorrow. *Cartography and Geographic Information Systems* **17** (1): 89–97

McHarg I (1971) *Design with Nature*. Doubleday, Garden City New York

McHarg I (1987) Keynote speech. *Proceedings of GIS '87*. ACSM/ASPRS, Falls Church Virginia

Meyerson M (1956) Building the middle range bridge for comprehensive planning. *Journal of the American Institute of Planners* **22**

Mounsey H M (1991) Multisource, multinational environmental GIS: lessons learnt from CORINE. In: Maguire D J, Goodchild M F, Rhind D W (eds.)

Geographical Information Systems: principles and applications. Longman, London, pp. 185–200, Vol 2

Muller J-C (1985) Geographic information systems: a unifying force for geography. *The Operational Geographer* **8**: 41–3

Obermeyer N J (1989) A systematic approach to the taxonomy of geographic information use. *Proceedings GIS/LIS '89*, Volume 2. ASPRS/ACSM/AAG/URISA/AM-FM, Bethesda, pp. 421–9

Openshaw S (1991) Developing appropriate spatial analysis methods for GIS. In: Maguire D J, Goodchild M F, Rhind D W (eds.) *Geographical Information Systems: principles and applications*. Longman, London, pp. 389–402, Vol 1

Parrott R, Stutz F P (1991) Urban GIS applications. In: Maguire D J, Goodchild M F, Rhind D W (eds.) *Geographical Information Systems: principles and applications*. Longman, London, pp. 247–60, Vol 2

Rhind D W (1991) Counting the people: the role of GIS. In: Maguire D J, Goodchild M F, Rhind D W (eds.) *Geographical Information Systems: principles and applications*. Longman, London, pp. 127–37, Vol 2

Robinette A (1991) Land management applications of GIS in the state of Minnesota. In: Maguire D J, Goodchild M F, Rhind D W (eds.) *Geographical Information Systems: principles and applications*. Longman, London, pp. 275–83, Vol 2

Siderelis K C (1991) Land resource information systems. In: Maguire D J, Goodchild M F, Rhind D W (eds.) *Geographical Information Systems: principles and applications*. Longman, London, pp. 261–73, Vol 2

Sommers R (1987) Geographic information systems in local government: a commentary. *Photogrammetric Engineering and Remote Sensing* **53**: 1379–82

Sowton M (1991) Development of GIS-related activities at the Ordnance Survey. In: Maguire D J, Goodchild M F, Rhind D W (eds.) *Geographical Information Systems: principles and applications*. Longman, London, pp. 23–38, Vol 2

Starr L E, Anderson K E (1991) A USGS perspective on GIS. In: Maguire D J, Goodchild M F, Rhind D W (eds.) *Geographical Information Systems: principles and applications*. Longman, London, pp. 11–22, Vol 2

Stiefel M (1987) Mapping out the differences among geographic information systems *The S. Klein Computer Graphics Review*, Fall: 73–87

Suh S, Kim M P, Kim T J (1988) ESMAN: an expert system for manufacturing selection. *Computers, Environment and Urban Systems* **12**: 239–52

Sweet D C (1970) An industrial development screening matrix. *The Professional Geographer* **22**: 124–7

Tomasi S G (1990) Why the nation needs a TIGER system. *Cartography and Geographic Information Systems* **17** (1): 21–6

White M S (1984) Technical requirements and standards for a multi-purpose geographic data system. The *American Cartographer* **11**: 15–26

SECTION IV

EPILOGUE

Epilogue 313–27
D W Rhind, M F Goodchild and D J Maguire

EPILOGUE

D W RHIND, M F GOODCHILD AND D J MAGUIRE

The enormous growth in GIS over the past decade or so has left the industry in a buoyant state. To date GIS have been driven largely by technical considerations, although recently the importance of applying the technology has been widely demonstrated. As a consequence, the significance of geographical information science rather than geographical information systems has emerged. It is clear that in the early 1990s GIS have reached a level of maturity such that the 'GIS society' can properly be called a discipline in its own right. The basic principles on which GIS are predicated can be listed, at least in outline terms, and disciplinary trappings such as conferences, journals, textbooks and degree courses exist in abundance.

Future projections, based on current trends, suggest that the number of GIS systems installed will pass the 0.5 million mark before the end of this millennium. Substantial technical developments can also be anticipated, along with a diversification of applications and much-needed advances in understanding the introduction of GIS into organizations. Together, these should assist us in our corporate goal of describing, explaining and predicting Earth patterns and processes with a view to managing the environment, improving human welfare and sustaining our existence in general.

INTRODUCTION

The GIS boom that began in the early 1980s is still accelerating. New vendors are entering the market with new and exciting products, education and training programmes are proliferating, the GIS software industry is reporting rapid growth rates, new textbooks and magazines are appearing, and GIS technology continues to find new applications and new acceptance.

The 1980s were years of unprecedented economic growth, both in Western economies generally and in GIS, and it is clear that the resources that were available to fund this growth in the 1980s will be much harder to find in the future. The 1980s also saw unprecedented changes in computing hardware with the development of personal computing and the workstation. What have we learnt so far – and particularly from the intensive activity in GIS that characterized the 1980s? Where do we stand in GIS research, and what are the important items in the research agenda that remain to be investigated before GIS can really fulfil their promise? What are the prognoses for the future – where will GIS stand in the year 2000?

As we stated at the outset, our objective in this book has been to present a picture of the state of GIS thinking, and the condition of the GIS body politic. This epilogue reflects on that condition in four ways. The first section looks at GIS to date, and reflects on the short history of the field. The second looks at outstanding issues and the research agenda. The third looks into the crystal ball and presents a view of the condition of the field in the year 2000, based on current trends in the GIS market, and predictions about hardware and software. The final section considers the bigger picture, and looks at the social, economic, business and political context for GIS.

LOOKING BACK: THE STORY SO FAR

The technological drive

The roots of GIS go back well into the 1960s (Coppock and Rhind 1991 in this volume) and the field owes a great amount to early efforts at that time by the Canadian federal government, IBM Canada and individuals such as Roger Tomlinson who developed the Canada Geographic Information System (Tomlinson 1989; Tomlinson, Calkins and Marble 1976). In fact the system made a remarkable number of technical breakthroughs, including the use of a scanner and raster/vector conversion; the separation of attributes and spatial data; representation of polygons by arcs; use of chain codes; and the use of Morton order for indexing. It was not, however, until the late 1970s that GIS really began the period of rapid growth that continues today. Several technological developments allowed this to happen (Goodchild 1991 in this volume). On the hardware side, 1980 saw the introduction of the super-mini, a multi-user system with virtual memory management for around $200,000 and a useful platform for a stand-alone, turn-key GIS. On the software side, 1980 saw development of the first GIS to take advantage of a relational DBMS, providing enormous flexibility in the handling of relationships between spatial entities. Finally, 1980 saw the beginnings of the trend towards personal computing and the mass popularization of word processing and desktop publishing.

Today GIS incorporate a remarkably diverse set of interests. GIS applications range from resource management (Robinette 1991 in this volume), through urban infrastructure (Parrott and Stutz 1991 in this volume) to route finding (White 1991 in this volume), from political districting to forestry. GIS run on platforms from the PC to the large mainframe, including an enormous range of software architectures, from the simple, self-contained raster systems such as GRASS and IDRISI to the large database managers such as IBM's GFIS. Some vendors focus on a single platform, while others (notably ESRI) offer a single product over the full range of platforms and operating systems from DOS to VM/CMS. The GIS community includes an extraordinary range of disciplines, from archaeology and landscape ecology through forestry to civil engineering and computer science. Not surprisingly,'there is as much variety in the definitions of the field (Maguire 1991 in this volume). GIS are variously described as spatial decision support systems; systems for input, storage, analysis and output of geographical data; or geographically referenced information systems (to cite only three of the competing definitions).

Looking at the development of the field and its current condition raises curiosity about the glue that holds it all together. One major part of that glue is clearly the technology itself, and another is the widespread fascination with processing geographical data. Maps and graphics are interesting in their own right and a computer system that analyses and displays them is doubly interesting. There has been a steady and accelerating improvement over the past three decades in the cost and availability of graphical computing (see below), and this has had an undeniable impact on the growth of GIS. Peter Taylor, in an editorial in *Political Geography Quarterly*, characterized GIS as 'geography's own little bit of the "high-tech" revolution' (Taylor 1990: 212).

It would be grossly unfair to characterize GIS as a technology in search of applications, as this would largely ignore its enormous value to a wide range of its current users. While there may still be some doubt about the exact cost/benefit ratio, the old joke about dividing by zero is clearly inappropriate today in applications ranging from facilities management to forestry, at local and global scales. All the same, reference has been made at several points in this volume (e.g. Aangeenbrug 1991 in this volume; Openshaw 1991 in this volume) to a widely held sense that GIS have not yet found their full potential as tools for exploring and analysing the world, and for supporting human decisions. Instead, GIS seem too often limited to mapping, information management and simple inventory.

The importance of science

The current range of GIS software and hardware products incorporates an impressive range of technological breakthroughs. Concepts such as the TIN (Weibel and Heller 1991 in this volume) and quadtree (Egenhofer and Herring 1991 in this volume) are the direct result of GIS research, and are only two among the many innovative ideas to have emerged over the past three decades. Any technologically-based field must be constantly supplied with new ideas if it is to thrive and needs to be supported by an active research and development community.

However, there is a strong feeling at the present time in the GIS community that the most important issues confronting the field are not necessarily technological. The GIS community seems to be converging not around a single, uniform software product (a standard GIS) or a single application, or around the technology itself, but around a set of generic issues that emerge from using the technology. Whatever the application or data processing solution, every user of GIS faces the same set of problems in dealing effectively with digital geographical data; these problems in turn form the agenda for discussion at GIS meetings – the true glue of the GIS community. Some of the more prominent are:

- *Data capture*: how to convert data from raw to digital form in an efficient, cost-effective manner.

- *Data modelling*: how to represent the infinite complexity of the real world in a discrete, digital machine (e.g. whether to use raster or vector, layers or objects and how to model complex objects).

- *Accuracy*: how to cope with the uncertainty present to varying degrees in all geographical data.

- *Volume*: how to deal with the fact that demands for geographical data will often exceed the space available for storage or the access time which is acceptable (e.g. designing data structures, indexes and algorithms to provide rapid access to large volumes of geographical data).

- *Analysis*: how to link GIS databases with advanced modelling capabilities.

- *User interfaces*: how to present the GIS database to the user in a friendly, comprehensible, readily used fashion.

- *Costs and benefits*: how to measure the benefits of GIS information and compare them to the costs.

- *Impact on organizations*: how to introduce GIS successfully into a complex organization.

All of these issues transcend the technology itself and all of them in one way or another affect the technology's usefulness, whatever the application and whatever the platform. In recent years they have emerged in various guises as the basis of the research agenda of the National Center for Geographic Information and Analysis (NCGIA 1989), the Urban and Regional Information Systems Association (URISA: Craig 1989) and the UK Regional Research Laboratories (Masser 1990; Maguire 1990), as well as in independent assessments (Rhind 1988). Goodchild (1990) has argued that together they constitute a science of geographical information and that the future of the GIS community lies in recognizing a common interest in geographical information science rather than the technology of geographical information systems.

Once the generic issues that underlie GIS are highlighted, and it can be seen that GIS transcend the particulars of the technology and its applications, it is possible to begin to understand how GIS can affect people's view of the world. Traditionally, information about places on the Earth's surface has been stored and transmitted in the form of maps, images, text and to some degree sound. The focus of early GIS was on the digital database as a store of maps which were the input, output and metaphor of GIS applications. Increasingly, GIS are now seen as a means of access not to maps, but to the real world that those maps represent. The purpose of the database must be to inform the user accurately about the contents of the real world, not about the contents of a source document. A DEM, for example, should be assessed on its ability to return the elevation of any point on the Earth's surface, not the position of an abstract contour line.

GIS have also affected the role of geographical information within organizations. They encourage the notion that geographical information is a commodity that flows through the organization, and that has a value determined by its accuracy, currency, accessibility, etc. In fact it may be the central commodity in some organizations such as forest resource management agencies. Collecting and updating geographical data need careful planning and budgeting if they are to be undertaken on a regular basis and are to be accessible to an organization's analysts and decision makers. Finally, if information *is* important, then it is rational to use different types of information as the basis for the organization of departments and systems.

In summary, GIS are a diverse collection of interests, software and hardware solutions, and applications. Two software products applied to the same problem (e.g. ESRI's ARC/INFO and IBM's GFIS applied to management of a utility company's facilities) would produce entirely different solutions. Similarly, the needs of forest resource management and school bus routing appear to have very little in common. There is a growing sense, however, that the issues that hold the GIS community together and produce convergence rather than divergence, are the generic issues of dealing with geographical information, representing it in a digital computer and working effectively with it to produce answers to problems.

The case for GIS as the science of geographical information will probably be debated for many years to come. The complementary argument that GIS are a technological tool for the support of science is presently more widely accepted and is reflected in applications from archaeology to epidemiology. Geography provides a very powerful way of organizing and exploring data, but the map has lagged far behind the statistical table and graph because early generations of scientific computing tools made it so difficult to handle. GIS technology has finally provided the breakthrough, although it remains far from perfect. If we were to draw an analogy between GIS and the statistical software which began to emerge in the 1960s, then the current state of GIS development is probably equivalent to the state of the statistical packages around 1970. But GIS and statistics are ultimately very complementary sets of tools, both capable of supporting an enormous range of scientific enquiry.

To date, the major success of GIS has been in the capture and inventory of features of the Earth's surface, particularly as represented on maps, and in supporting simple queries. There has been much less success in making effective use of GIS capabilities for more sophisticated analysis and modelling (Maguire 1991 in this volume). It is hard to find examples of insights gained through the use of GIS, or discoveries made about the real world. GIS have not yet found widespread application in the solution of major social problems – disaster management, environmental quality, global issues or health. In part this comment is unfair, because such insights would be almost impossible to document. In part the reason is commercial – the market for GIS as information management tools is currently far larger than that for spatial analysis so vendors have invested relatively little in developing and promoting analytical and modelling capabilities. Although current GIS technology is a major improvement on that of a decade ago, it is still difficult to collect, display and analyse data in geographical perspective. Finally, Couclelis (1989) has made the point that the current generation of GIS concentrate on a static view of space occupied by passive objects, offering little in support of a more humanistic view of dynamic interactions.

GIS as a discipline

The current growth of GIS shows no signs of abating and will likely continue for some time into the 1990s. New magazines are appearing, and existing ones, such as *GISWorld and Mapping Awareness*, are growing and increasing their circulation. Conferences are numerous and successful, offering workshops on increasingly specialized topics and access to the latest vendor products. New software vendors are entering the market with exciting and innovative products. GIS are finding new applications and strengthening their penetration into existing markets. GIS courses are proliferating at universities and colleges, and are finding increasing interest from students anxious to acquire useful skills.

On the other hand, there are increasing signs of diversification and this trend is likely to continue to strengthen in the next few years. GIS applications such as facilities management fall under the spatial information paradigm, whereas scientific and resource analysis applications fall under the spatial analysis paradigm. The former emphasizes the database and query aspects of GIS, whereas the latter tends to focus on modelling. The split is illustrated by the case of two Canadian companies – TYDAC and GeoVision – the former marketing 'spatial analysis systems' with the very successful SPANS product, the latter marketing 'geographical information systems'. Within the PC marketplace, there is increasing divergence between products aimed at GIS applications such as resource management, facilities management and market research (compare, e.g. PAMAP, TYDAC's

SPANS, Facility Mapping Systems' FMS/AC and Strategic Mapping's ATLAS*GIS).

This trend to diversification is appropriate and rational, as it matches software and platforms with different functions and applications. The complex modelling and analysis of resource management requires a very different solution from intensive digitizing or the management of large facility inventories. In time, we can expect this trend to lead to more and more specialization within the GIS industry, as it becomes less and less possible to offer a single software solution for all platforms and all applications. One vendor may specialize in digitizing stations using PCs, another in database maintenance using large mainframes and terminals, another in spatial analysis using advanced personal workstations, and another in 3-D applications.

There is an interesting analogy between the development of GIS and the history of communication. The written letter, an analogue format, was first replaced by the digital telegraph, then by the analogue telephone. Electronic mail, a digital format for transmitting text as a string of characters, is now in competition with FAX which transmits an uninterpreted image of text. Having spent the past three decades working to replace the analogue map with the digital GIS database, we are only now beginning to realize that there can be great value in combining other types of information, particularly images, text and even sound, with GIS. The multimedia GIS is already functioning in many highway maintenance organizations, where digital or video-format images are linked with GPS-determined locations in a digital database, and multimedia GIS are also finding applications in resource management and marketing. In part this is a technical problem, as the software and hardware tools to manage multiple media have only recently become available, most prevalantly in the Macintosh world. But it is also a conceptual problem, having to do with the role of the symbolic map in GIS thinking. If GIS are a window on the world, then it makes sense to combine the view provided by the highly structured and interpreted database with other media, whether digital or analogue. We tend to see the structured GIS database as exclusive, and to know little about the relative value of other media.

Despite this sense of growing diversity in the GIS community, there is evidence of convergence. The past few years have seen the emergence of several series of conferences aimed at the full GIS community. In the United States, the annual GIS/LIS series sponsored by a consortium of five societies (AAG, ASPRS, ACSM, AM/FM and URISA) has grown quickly to over 3000 attendees (Morrison 1991 in this volume). In Canada, the Ottawa meetings in early March have been similarly successful. The lone textbook of 1986 by Burrough (*Principles of Geographical Information Systems for Land Resources Assessment*) has now been joined by several others (e.g. Aronoff (1989) *Geographic Information Systems: a management perspective*; Star and Estes (1990) *Geographic Information Systems: an introduction*) and many more are on the way. (See Maguire 1991 in this volume for a list of GIS textbooks.) New organizations have appeared and the Association for Geographic Information (AGI) in the United Kingdom seems to be a particularly successful example; and GIS technology now has its own journals. A large number of higher education institutions now offer Masters' courses and several even have undergraduate courses in GIS (e.g. Kingston and North East London Polytechnics in the United Kingdom).

All of these would be recognized in the sociology of science as symbols of an emerging scientific community – in short, a discipline. But unlike physics or biology, GIS have no fundamental problems to solve of the magnitude of the origins of the universe or the basis of life. One view holds that GIS are merely a tool, and that the GIS research community must wither away as the tool reaches perfection. Another, presented at some length above and amply illustrated in the chapters of this book, holds that there are fundamental issues in GIS – not so much in the tools any more as in the use of the tools. Alternatively, perhaps GIS are like statistics – a tool to most scientists, but a set of fundamental research problems to the parent discipline.

If GIS technology is a discipline, then it is clearly not 'owned' by any traditional one. Geography, cartography, surveying, photogrammetry and engineering have all been accused from time to time of trying to dominate GIS – but with little success as GIS are fundamentally an interdisciplinary field. Whether GIS develop the institutional structures of a discipline in its own right, like statistics, or remain an interdisciplinary consortium of interests like remote sensing remains to be seen.

LOOKING AROUND: WHAT REMAINS TO BE DONE

It is becoming increasingly impossible for any one vendor to be all things to all GIS users – to offer one product on all platforms, under all operating systems, as a solution to all applications. One way to view specialization in the GIS industry is in terms of three measures: functionality, capacity, and accessibility. Ideally, a GIS should offer a wide range of forms of spatial analysis and manipulation on a large and accurate database, and provide responses immediately. In practice, these objectives conflict. Fast access to large databases is feasible only if the number of possible operations is severely limited and systems that offer complex modelling and analysis often restrict capacity. In GIS there can be no limit either to functionality or to capacity, since users will always find reasons for more.

If the future of GIS lies in specialization, then the key to success will be standards. Encouraging progress is being made in data exchange formats (e.g. USGS's SDTS, DMA's DIGEST and the UK NTF) and in standardizing terminology (DCDSTF 1988; Guptill 1991 in this volume). But terminology is notoriously difficult to standardize. For example, there is little indication to date that the proposed term for the common boundary between two polygons ('chain') will replace those in current usage ('arc', 'segment', 'edge', '1 cell', etc.). It is also difficult to standardize when the central concepts of GIS are so poorly articulated. Key terms such as 'raster' and 'vector', 'object' and 'layer' need to be standardized if we are to develop a well-defined set of data models. Standards are needed for data sources, particularly in describing quality, and for user interfaces. However, the diversity of the GIS community makes the development of standards difficult. For example, the needs of the US Bureau of the Census in a street network database are very different from those of the vehicle navigation industry, or the emergency response community, or the highway maintenance authorities.

Despite their importance, standards will do little to solve many of the more pressing problems of GIS. The field is only now beginning to come to grips with the issues of uncertainty and accuracy (Fisher 1991 in this volume; Chrisman 1991 in this volume) and, while recent research has led to significant advances in understanding how uncertainty propagates through a GIS (Goodchild and Gopal 1989), it will be a long time before the accuracy requirements of GIS have significant impact on the process of geographical data collection and compilation. New and exciting concepts in data modelling, such as object orientation, are only now beginning to influence the field and much remains to be done in exploiting the ideas emerging from current research on user interfaces (Frank and Mark 1991 in this volume). If GIS research of the 1960s and 1970s was primarily directed at solving the technical problems of geographical data handling, allowing a significant industry to emerge in the 1980s, then the 1990s will be the decade in which the cycle reverses itself – when new concepts emerge from the application of the technology to affect conventional ways of thinking about geography. GIS are only now beginning to impact on the organizational structures of public agencies, the traditional providers of geographical data, conventions of map making, or the urban planning process.

Among the larger research issues still to be resolved are the following:

- How does GIS complement other technologies for handling geographical data, such as maps, atlases, text descriptions, or images? Should all of these be implemented in a digital environment, or can digital and analogue technologies complement each other?

- How will GIS, GPS and other novel technologies affect traditional methods of geographical data collection and compilation? Will the role of mapping agencies increase or diminish in the coming decades?

- How will the flexibility of digital geographical databases affect the role of geographical data in everyday life, which is now so closely geared to the paper map?

- How will the rigorous, objective perspective of GIS be adapted to the imprecise, subjective world of human reasoning and decision making? Will it be through the development of spatial decision support systems, knowledge-based or expert systems, or will the two paradigms find themselves incompatible?

Much also remains to be done in education and

training. Vendors and institutions have already responded to the critical shortage of staff by adding courses and programmes and the US NCGIA has developed and published a one-year course sequence (Goodchild and Kemp 1990). But GIS is still a novel field, and courses are often treated as add-ons to existing programmes, and rarely integrated into full curricula. There has been some discussion of integrated curriculum requirements in the literature (Nyerges and Chrisman 1989; Unwin and Dale 1990) and vendors are increasingly willing to offer more than simple training programmes. But GIS education remains an issue, intimately linked with the previous discussion of the nature of GIS as a discipline.

Much also remains to be done at the organizational and institutional level. The potential for sharing data between agencies remains unrealized in most countries because of traditional interdepartmental barriers. The development of standards is similarly impeded by a lack of coordination and leadership. The organizational structure of many public agencies continues to be dominated by the needs of traditional methods of map making and geographical data handling. In the new digital environment it is vital that the public agencies adopt a lead role in coordinating research and education programmes, in ensuring the health and vitality of the GIS industry, and in defining standards of data quality, data formats, etc. This is particularly important at a time when public sector funds for traditional map making are steadily diminishing.

In many areas the future of GIS will continue to be determined by developments in hardware – technological innovation will continue to influence GIS as long as new ideas continue to drive the computer industry. The cost per cycle will continue to drop in the next few years, as will the cost per megabyte of RAM. The 1990s will see the proliferation of 3-D technology, as high performance graphics adaptors become available for mass-produced workstations from vendors such as Silicon Graphics. The recent generation of workstations, typified by the IBM RS/6000, include 3-D adaptor options with display rates as high as one million 3-D vectors per second, with polyhedral rendering capabilities, in a platform running at 25–45 MIPS (Million Instructions Per Second). GIS will no longer be confined to the plane, and the DEM display capabilities of today will seem very primitive in a few years. It will become possible to model and visualize subsurface conditions, and to analyse distributions over the surface of the earth without the distortions and interruptions produced by conventional map projections. In 3-D, the map metaphor is completely inadequate and the user interfaces for these systems will have to explore entirely new territory. How, for example, should a system allow the user to build knowledge of subsurface conditions from a variety of different types of evidence? In 2-D, this task of map compilation takes place on paper but in 3-D it can only take place in the abstract domain of the digital database. What tools does a user need to explore a model of the subsurface once it has been built? What icons should be provided in an appropriate user interface?

If GIS have been dominated thus far by the map, then fundamental changes now occurring in mapping will have significant effects in the coming decade. Low-cost GPS receivers are already available with higher accuracy than the base mapping available over most of North America (1 : 100 000, 1 : 24 000 in continental United States) and many areas of the rest of the world. GPS also provide a significantly cheaper method of primary data collection for many mapping activities. This system is already being used to map road and rail networks, and to track vehicle movements. At the same time the funds available to support large, public-sector mapping programmes are diminishing.

Current prospects for the future

There seem to be two contrasting views of the prospects for GIS in the coming decade. The first is negative and the second positive, and it seems more likely that the second will prevail. However, there are actions that can be taken to strengthen the odds.

In the negative view, GIS will fragment and disappear, and by the end of the decade will be nothing but a memory. Geographers often draw a parallel between GIS and the introduction of quantitative methods to geography in the late 1960s (Taylor 1990), and comment on the lack of interest in quantification, at least in human geography, in the 1980s. On this view GIS will fragment because the system is too loose to hold together and because the glue is too weak and abstract. Users of IBM's GFIS, ESRI's ARC/INFO and Map/Info will cease to see any reason to attend the same conferences. The consortium of five organizations responsible for the North American GIS/LIS conference series will break up and each will concentrate on its own agenda. GIS will be seen as the Edsel of EDP, too awkward, complex and expensive except in some specialized applications.

In the positive view, the GIS consortium will continue to converge. A constant supply of better tools seems assured, particularly in computing speed, software integration, network communication, graphics and storage capacity. The infrastructure of the GIS community will continue to improve, with better magazines, organizations, textbooks, meetings, and all of the symbols of an emerging speciality. Less assured but essential is a constant supply of new players in the industry, since the pattern has been that new players are the source of a disproportionate share of technological innovation. New players such as Prime/Wild with System/9, SmallWorld, or Strategic Mapping with ATLAS*GIS bring new ideas to the industry.

In the positive view, the public agencies will promote and develop standards for data exchange formats, structures, models and data quality. Training and education programmes will develop through cooperation between vendors and institutions, and lead to the emergence of a strong set of core concepts. Funds will be available through cooperative agreements to support the development of teaching facilities, and to ensure that these keep pace with developments in the technology.

The results of research currently under way will emerge in improved products. Of particular significance will be:

- data models to handle 3-D and time dependence, and complex interactions between objects;

- support for complex analytical applications, including tracking of data lineage, tools for visual interaction with the stages in the analysis process, propagation of uncertainty;

- support for quality assurance and quality control (QA/QC) especially in GIS applications where litigation is a constant problem;

- support for multiple media – unstructured images, both digital and NTSC, text and sound;

- integration of GIS with the capabilities of GPS for data collection and compilation;

- tools for visualizing 3-D and time-dependent data;

- tools for data compilation, particularly in 3-D;

- improved techniques for conducting functional requirements studies, evaluating costs and benefits, benchmarking and other aspects of the GIS acquisition and project management process.

Finally, the GIS community will converge around a common concern not only for the technology of GIS, but more importantly for the common issues that transcend the technology and pervade all applications. GIS can survive by constantly developing new and exciting capabilities, or by constantly finding new applications. The really fundamental issues in GIS, however, are those that are common to all users of geographical information – how to capture a complex and dynamic world in a digital database and provide access to it in a useful, accurate and cost-effective manner.

LOOKING FORWARD: GIS 2000

All of the above is based upon our (considerable) collective experience in GIS and discussion with many colleagues. But it is also sensible to attempt to quantify some of our predictions: such forecasting is, for instance, central to all business planning and resource allocation. Inevitably, though, all such forecasts become less precise as the time period becomes more extended, but two basic techniques exist for predicting the future. The first is to project existing trends within the subject area and this is normally a sensible strategy in the short term, say for two years. The second is to analyse and understand what underlying changes are taking place in society or the environment as a whole, then to assess how long the effects of these will take to work through to individual sectors such as GIS. In this section, we attempt – briefly because of the paucity of the evidence – to use both methods in order to understand what is likely to happen to the future of GIS. In so doing, we avoid (wherever possible) technical and other details. It is all too easy to write about the subject at the 'nuts and bolts' level of detail; indeed, that is where the great bulk of applications work thus far has been carried out and where most of the technical work seems to be directed. Moreover, dealing with detail is often immensely satisfying: the possibility of error is reduced to minute levels if the topic is reduced to the mechanical and the specific! But we need to deal with broad issues involving many intangibles; inevitably, then, we will get some of them wrong.

Trend projections

The simplest and probably the most reliable trend to project is that of hardware performance. Figure E.1, produced by the British consultants Price Waterhouse, shows the rapid diminution in cost of one measure of computer power – MIPS or million instructions per second. In practice, this is often a most misleading statistic, but its trend parallels that of most other measures of performance. Over the last 30 years, there has been about an order of magnitude decrease in cost of computing power every six years. What cost $1 or £1 to compute with state-of-the-art equipment in 1990 cost about $100 000 or £100 000 to compute when Tobler (1959) wrote his famous seminal paper on automated cartography. More recently, things have been changing even more rapidly. A simple way of describing the current growth in computer power is to consider a Digital Equipment Vax 11/780 of 1984 with 1 MIPS power; the growth in power for the same cost since then can be approximated by the expression:

$$\text{MIPS}_{\text{year}} = 2^{(\text{year}-1984)}$$

Hence, for 1991, MIPS = 128

Moreover, data storage with similar characteristics (such as direct access capabilities) has decreased in cost at similar rates. The bulk of computers has diminished as rapidly as has their reliability increased. The drawing speed and resolution of output displays has changed from the slow, coarse and relatively expensive storage cathode ray tubes of the 1970s to the million colour, 300 000+ vectors per second and modestly priced workstations of today (Goodchild 1991 in this volume). If this trend is spectacular, it shows no signs of conclusion: all the indications are that even

'traditional' computing engines may be made to go substantially faster and will become still cheaper. Moreover, it is evident that parallel processing (see, for instance, Dowers *et al.* 1990) will provide further increases in performance once the myriad of algorithmic and software problems have been resolved (Franklin 1991 in this volume). Finally, perhaps the most important development in hardware other than general-purpose computing engines is the rapid improvement in performance/cost ratio for Global Positioning Systems (or GPS); to be able to establish absolute position in three dimensions anywhere on the Earth's surface with an accuracy of metres, all achieved within a few seconds, is likely to revolutionize surveying practice, generate many more GIS-type applications and improve existing embryonic ones like vehicle navigation (see White 1991 in this volume).

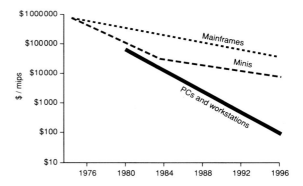

Fig. E.1 Hardware price performance trends. (*Source*: Price Waterhouse (1991).)

Costs of software can only be traced from the early 1980s since only then were the first commercial GIS available (Coppock and Rhind 1991 in this volume). Over that period, we have seen a decline in costs, accelerating as more and more systems arrive on the market. Thus the list price for a minicomputer version of ARC/INFO in 1983 was about $100 000 (or about $200 000 at 1990 prices); in 1990, a first copy for a 386-based computer of like performance (but with much more software functionality) was about $10 000, with heavy discounts for multiple copies. In practice, such list prices are rarely paid; most vendors will discount to many classes of customers and some have given GIS software to organizations purchasing hardware; it is thus difficult to quantify the trend precisely but dramatic price reductions and increase in quality of the product have occurred simultaneously. The extent to which this can go on is unknown, except in the mass market where GIS are sold for PCs and low cost workstations in a manner analogous to dBASE, Lotus 1-2-3, Excel or even word processing packages like Word and WordPerfect. If this occurs, we should expect to be able to buy fully functional GIS for about $500 in the mid-1990s.

All of the market surveys carried out in Europe and North America at the time of writing this book paint a story of increasing use of GIS and related data sets. Unhappily, little comparable evidence is available for other areas of the world. The surveys show global sales of between $500 million and $4000 million per annum for GIS software, hardware, services and data, the sum varying with information source, with the definition of GIS adopted and with the base year taken (see Maguire 1991 in this volume). All surveys are unanimous that growth in the total expenditure by users is of the order of 20 to 30 per cent per annum. Some individual vendors such as ESRI report growths of income of over 40 per cent per annum. This and the ubiquitous nature of GIS applications has led organizations such as IBM to identify GIS as an area on which to concentrate (see Dangermond 1991 in this volume).

The immensely broad spectrum of what different individuals consider as a GIS complicates establishing a benchmark of the number of systems now in operation. Based, however, on sales of systems of known capabilities, there were not less than about 20 000 installations world-wide in 1990 with at least significant claims to being a GIS. In early to mid-1990, annual sales seemed to be running at about 6000 systems per annum, including PC products. The advent of new low price systems such as Atlas*GIS later in that year made the forecasting of sales very much more difficult. Assuming, however, a 20 per cent per annum growth rate in GIS-related expenditure by users and a 40 per cent growth rate in the number of systems (because of the much faster growth in the number of small-machine than large-machine systems), the figures for sales and system numbers at different dates would be as indicated in Table E.1. It should be stressed that this is nothing more than projection of trends, assumed to be constant in proportional terms (i.e. exponential), from an uncertain base and over a time horizon during which the market will certainly change both qualitatively and quantitatively. None the less, even if these trends only hold up for a short period, the implications are enormous.

Table E.1 GIS trends 1990–2000

Year	1990	1993	1996	2000
Sales ($million)	1000	1750	3000	6200
Number of systems ('000s)	20	55	150	580

It is also entirely possible that these figures may be achieved despite apparent saturation in certain markets and in particular areas. Thus, for instance, we might expect the market for GIS in utility organizations within developed countries to be saturated by the late 1990s but for growth of that market to expand in other currently less developed countries. In addition, all the current indications suggest that growth in use of systems for environmental, health and other purposes will more than compensate for any 'flattening off' in demand for systems within the 'early adopter' sectors. Overall, most GIS applications thus far have been at the inventory or monitoring level – computing taxes, routing vehicles and assessing the extent of change in the natural environment. This is really little more than transaction processing and periodic reporting on the overall level of some activity. Such functions are often critical: the very life of cities may break down if taxes are not collected, if assets are not managed properly and resources allocated effectively. But it is at least arguable that the use of GIS in modelling, in prediction and in supporting high-level decision makers, policy makers and politicians is as important as inventory tasks, if not more important, and that the former will come of age before the end of the millennium.

LOOKING TO THE WIDER SCENE: THE SOCIAL, ECONOMIC, BUSINESS AND POLITICAL CONTEXT TO THE YEAR 2000

Irrespective of the means employed, prediction of the future is highly error-prone, as the substantially unexpected collapse of Communism in the nations of Eastern Europe in 1989 and the Gulf War of 1991 within six months of the Iraq invasion of Kuwait have demonstrated. In particular, trend projections never anticipate the broad patterns of change through history. While acknowledging the dangers involved, it is appropriate in this Epilogue to stand back and to examine the societal context in which GIS operates; from this, and an attempt to predict how this context will change, we can at least surmise how the use and form of GIS will be effected up to the end of the twentieth century.

We take the following societal changes at least to be likely:

- The 'internationalization' of national economies will continue to the extent that the economies of few, if any, countries will be unaffected by the state of global trade.

- There will be increasing levels of activity by multinational corporations and, as a proportion of the global market, a diminishing share will be held by national-only suppliers.

- Increasing levels of competition between states and between individual vendors will be the norm. Yet, despite free-trade agreements, multinational trading blocs such as the European Community will still attempt to foster indigenous developments and products.

- The acceptance and implementation of international standards will lead to increasing convergence of products, at least within individual market sectors.

- The need to maintain economic operations in a highly competitive market may ensure that only major vendors capable of financing new products, packaging and maintaining them and advertising appropriately will survive (except in niche markets). Set against this need for massive resources, of course, is the fact that small firms have thus far always been the source of innovation in the computing industry and that large firms not only become ossified but suffer the burden of having to support earlier systems in an upward-compatible manner. While the 'big and old' versus 'small and new' battle is unlikely always to be resolved one way, big and sclerotic firms will go out of business as well as those small ones unable to fund (by today's standards) very well packaged and reliable products.

- Labour-intensive operations will increasingly be exported to areas of low labour costs.

- The level of global prosperity as a whole will continue to increase, but may continue to decrease in some areas such as Africa (see Taylor 1991 in this volume).

- Societies are going to become increasingly protective over the confidentiality of data relating to individuals.

- Individuals, corporations and governments are increasingly going to take the use of computerized databases for granted and, as a consequence, more are going to be created.

- Information in general (and geographical or spatial information in particular) is going to become more and more of a commodity in most parts of the world and be treated as a valuable resource – with obvious commercial consequences.

The implications for GIS of societal changes

From all of the above, we can conjecture the following:

- We will see a convergence in general-purpose GIS, with most systems running under UNIX, and functionality (though not necessarily the ways of providing it) becoming more and more similar between different products. Interfaces will also come to share more common properties, whether through a standard spatial language (perhaps applied *post hoc*, via a universal dashboard which can be applied to any system – see Raper and Rhind 1990) or simply through use of similar menus, or because of the widespread use of the X-Windows Graphical User Interface (GUI).

- Notwithstanding such convergence, sector-specific products will probably appear. In part this will arise because the concept of an all-embracing GIS may well become impractical and in part because of market differentiation (see below).

- Vendors will attempt to differentiate their products in a number of ways. These will include: the efficiency of coding; the adaptation of their toolboxes to operate as 'self-contained and friendly' systems in important core markets such as the utilities; the production of spin-off products (such as ARCView); the transparent linkage of the GIS code with other functions such as modelling, accounting (e.g. spreadsheet), statistical and presentation graphics packages; the production of better training and documentation than their rivals; the production of 'national-specific' versions (see below); and through support of a variety of 'friendship' schemes such as user clubs.

- The market for GIS will attain the stage already reached by the Information Technology market as a whole so far as the world's biggest players – IBM and DEC – are concerned: the bulk of the market will lie outside the United States.

- Challenges to the US supremacy in software may well come from sources such as Japan and Europe.

- Political factors will ensure that software and system creation will need to be carried out in multiple locations. By analogy with car manufacturing in the 1980s, system creation will need, for instance, to be carried out by US and Japanese firms within Europe if they hope to be treated on equal terms with indigenous producers. Since there is a real possibility that the European Community by the year 2000 may include 20 countries and a population of nearly 500 million relatively affluent consumers (or almost twice that of the United States), this seems a matter of importance for all non-European-based vendors.

- Even ignoring the political case for local system creation, users will increasingly wish to see local customization in global products, such as the use of the local language – with all that implies for user interfaces, for the use of diacritical marks, etc.

- Digitizing, to accepted *de facto* standards, will be done wherever it is cheapest. Thus, manual digitizing contracts may well be carried out in China or elsewhere in South East Asia or in Eastern Europe. Mass digitizing may well die out in North America and Western Europe unless scanning and subsequent feature recognition and vectorization can be made routine and cheaper than the manual, 'offshore' digitizing.

- In any event, the peak of the mass digitizing will be just past in the United States, and long past in the United Kingdom and several other countries by the year 2000. The topographic base maps and the utilities' networks will by then mostly be digitized (at least on all current projections). Thus the source of material for mass digitizing will increasingly come from areas outside that of the pioneers.

- This decline in mass digitizing will be accompanied by a growth in the routine use of direct position-fixing by use of GPS receivers. This may cause significant problems because the readings obtained may be more accurate than maps to which the data can be compared. Map revision by national mapping agencies will, therefore, be necessary though some of this may be achieved by use of 'rubber sheet' transformations using enough control points.

- GIS technology may well have disappeared as a 'free-standing' activity in many organizations as its functionality becomes encompassed by business-oriented systems, such as those for market analysis, and it becomes part of wider Management Information Systems.

- The data volume problem will have disappeared so far as certain applications are concerned, but will remain acute for others. In dealing with population and other censuses, for instance, storage technology is improving much faster than population growth! Given reasonable data compaction routines, it should be possible to hold about 30 items of information for every person in the United States or in Britain, France, Italy and Germany on a single CD-ROM disk whose current reproduction costs are about $1 if produced in reasonable numbers. Even this storage capacity, however, palls into insignificance when contrasted with the need to hold the volumes of data produced from satellite imagery of the natural environment; global applications in particular seem likely to extend the range of hardware and software for decades to come.

- Much the greatest threat to widespread use of GIS comes from the data supply policies of those governments which require commercial returns to be made to the state for information already collected for the purposes of state administration. The ownership of data seems inevitably destined to become part of the competitive process and, as such, to affect the abilities of those in education in particular to carry out research and teaching relevant to the needs of the outside world except by forging intimate and individual links with data suppliers.

- Given all this and diminishing real costs of computing power, we expect to see a dramatic growth in 'value-added services'. These will include the use of GIS to combine data sets to meet the needs of specific customers, the use of skilled personnel in 'information literate' organizations to provide expert (and legally defensible) interpretations of geographical data sets for customer organizations and the provision of services for 'end-to-end' data compilation, analysis and interpretation when required.

- We suspect that the degree of concern over privacy and confidentiality of data will continue to be much greater for socio-economic data than for that pertaining to the natural environment (though emissions of pollution and like measures are obvious anomalies). In practice, GIS technology will have to grow much improved security facilities, but it also offers one major advantage: by offering the possibility of working at the area aggregate level and still permitting the linkage of different data sets, GIS can carry out analyses without infringing confidentiality restrictions on individual level data. The price to be paid for this is the set of problems which Openshaw (1991 in this volume) and others have described in this volume. Answers to analyses – at least using conventional statistical analysis tools – differ depending on what type and size of areal units are used. Clearly systems must be able to cope with such problems, or at least warn the unsuspecting users of the danger of data-induced artefacts.

- At the end of the day, the success of many applications of GIS will depend for the foreseeable future upon the skills and professionalism of the individuals involved – irrespective of the success of expert systems. Indeed, because of the fuzzy nature of 'rules' currently followed in manually based analyses, the success of artificial intelligence (AI) in GIS may yet turn out to be small. It is essential, therefore, that GIS operators have access to proper training, carried out to certified standards, and to chartered status. In practice, the latter may most easily be achieved by adding GIS to the training of engineers, planners and surveyors, rather than creating a new chartered, professional institute. However it is done, something of this sort is essential if GIS is to become an accepted part of professional judgement and risk taking, and if insurance of new schemes is to be obtainable. Education and training in future, then, will have to concentrate as much upon setting and demonstrating standards as on the curriculum content.

CONCLUSIONS

As we write this book, many already think of GIS as a mature discipline. Yet, as we have shown in the previous pages, there are still major shortcomings when GIS are used for certain purposes. Current research in progress will solve many of these yet, as the demands and range of users grow, presumably other problems will appear. While we expect many fundamental changes to occur in GIS – notably the decline of the 'map processing model' on which much early work and training were based – we are also clear that the best guide to the future is the recent past. We confidently expect, therefore:

- the further expansion of GIS concepts, tools and practice into a steadily widening range of roles;

- major technical developments and reductions in the price of hardware and software;

- the almost ubiquitous use of GIS in local and central government, in much business and in research and education;

- the rise of global applications and the

recognition that GIS are crucial components of Management Information Systems.

All of these developments will assist us greatly in achieving our corporate goal of describing, explaining and predicting the Earth's patterns and processes with a view to managing the environment and sustaining our existence.

REFERENCES

Aangeenbrug R T (1991) A critique of GIS. In: Maguire D J, Goodchild M F and Rhind D W (eds.) *Geographical Information Systems: principles and applications*. Longman, London, pp. 101–7, Vol 1

Aronoff S (1989) *Geographic Information Systems: a management perspective*. WDL Publications, Ottawa Canada

Burrough P A (1986) *Principles of Geographical Information Systems for Land Resources Assessment*. Oxford, Clarendon Press

Chrisman N R (1991) The error component in spatial data. In: Maguire D J, Goodchild M F, Rhind D W (eds.) *Geographical Information Systems: principles and applications*. London, Longman, pp. 165–74, Vol 1

Coppock J T, Rhind D W (1991) The history of GIS. In: Maguire D J, Goodchild M F, Rhind D W (eds.) *Geographical Information Systems: principles and applications*. London, Longman, pp. 21–43, Vol 1

Couclelis H (1989) Geographically informed planning: requirements for a planning-relevant GIS. Presented to the North American meetings of the Regional Science Association, Santa Barbara, November

Craig W J (1989) URISA's research agenda and the NCGIA. *Journal of the Urban and Regional Information Systems Association* **1** (1): 7–16

Dangermond J (1991) The commercial setting of GIS. In: Maguire D J, Goodchild M F, Rhind D W (eds.) *Geographical Information Systems: principles and applications*. Longman, London, pp. 55–65, Vol 1

DCDSTF (Digital Cartographic Data Standards Task Force) (1988) The proposed standard for digital cartographic data. *The American Cartographer* **15** (1)

Dowers S, Gittings B M, Sloan T M, Waugh T C, Healey R G (1990) Analysis of GIS performance on parallel architectures and workstation-server systems. *Proceedings of GIS/LIS '90*. ASPRS/ACSM/AAG/URISA/AM-FM, Bethesda, pp. 555–61

Egenhofer M J, Herring J R (1991) High-level spatial data structures for GIS. In: Maguire D J, Goodchild M F, Rhind D W (eds.) *Geographical Information Systems: principles and applications*. Longman, London, pp. 227–37, Vol 1

Fisher P F (1991) Spatial data sources and data problems. In: Maguire D J, Goodchild M F, Rhind D W (eds.) *Geographical Information Systems: principles and applications*. Longman, London, pp. 175–89, Vol 1

Frank A U, Mark D M (1991) Language issues for GIS. In: Maguire D J, Goodchild M F, Rhind D W (eds.) *Geographical Information Systems: principles and applications*. Longman, London, pp. 147–63, Vol 1

Franklin Wm R (1991) Computer systems and low-level data structures for GIS. In: Maguire D J, Goodchild M F, Rhind D W (eds.) *Geographical Information Systems: principles and applications*. Longman, London, pp. 215–25, Vol 1

Goodchild M F (1990) Keynote address: spatial information science. *Proceedings of the 4th International Symposium on Spatial Data Handling*, Vol 1. International Geographical Union, Columbus Ohio, pp. 3–14

Goodchild M F (1991) The technological setting of GIS. In: Maguire D J, Goodchild M F, Rhind D W (eds.) *Geographical Information Systems: principles and applications*. Longman, London, pp. 45–54, Vol 1

Goodchild M F, Gopal S (eds.) (1989) *Accuracy of Spatial Databases*. Taylor & Francis, London

Goodchild M F, Kemp K K (eds.) (1990) *Core Curriculum in GIS*. National Center for Geographic Information and Analysis, Santa Barbara

Guptill S C (1991) Spatial data exchange and standardization. In: Maguire D J, Goodchild M F, Rhind D W (eds.) *Geographical Information Systems: principles and applications*. Longman, London, pp. 515–30, Vol 1

Maguire D J (1990) A research plan for GIS in the 1990s. In: Foster M J, Shand P J (eds.) *The Association for Geographic Information Yearbook 1990*. Taylor & Francis and Miles Arnold, London, pp. 267–77

Maguire D J (1991) An overview and definition of GIS. In: Maguire D J, Goodchild M F and Rhind D W (eds.) *Geographical Information Systems: principles and applications*. Longman, London, pp. 9–20, Vol 1

Masser I (1990) The Regional Research Laboratory initiative: an update. In: Foster M J, Shand P J (eds.) *The Association for Geographic Information Yearbook 1990*. Taylor & Francis and Miles Arnold, London, pp. 259–63

Morrison J L (1991) The organizational home for GIS in the scientific professional community. In: Maguire D J, Goodchild M F and Rhind D W (eds.) *Geographical Information Systems: principles and applications*. Longman, London, pp. 91–100, Vol 1

Mounsey H M (1991) Multisource, multinational environmental GIS: lessons learnt from CORINE. In: Maguire D J, Goodchild M F, Rhind D W (eds.) *Geographical Information Systems: principles and applications*. Longman, London, pp. 185–200, Vol 2

NCGIA (1989) The research plan of the National Center for Geographic Information and Analysis. *International*

Journal of Geographical Information Systems **3** (2): 117–36

Nyerges T L, Chrisman N R (1989) A framework for model curricula development in cartography and geographic information systems. *Professional Geographer* **41** (3): 283–93

Openshaw S (1991) Developing appropriate spatial analysis methods for GIS. In: Maguire D J, Goodchild M F, Rhind D W (eds.) *Geographical Information Systems: principles and applications*. Longman, London, pp. 389–402, Vol 1

Parrott R, Stutz F P (1991) Urban GIS applications. In: Maguire D J, Goodchild M F, Rhind D W (eds.) *Geographical Information Systems: principles and applications*. Longman, London, pp. 247–60, Vol 2

Price Waterhouse (1991) Price performance trends. *Computer Weekly* 17 January: 1

Raper J F, Rhind D W (1990) UGIX (A): the design of a spatial language interface to a topological vector GIS. *Proceedings of the 4th International Conference on Spatial Data Handling*. International Geographical Union, Columbus Ohio, pp. 405–12

Rhind D W (1988) A GIS research agenda. *International Journal of Geographical Information Systems* **2**: 23–8

Star J, Estes J E (1990) *Geographic Information Systems*. Prentice Hall, Englewood Cliffs New Jersey

Taylor D R F (1991) GIS and developing nations. In: Maguire D J, Goodchild M F, Rhind D W (eds.) *Geographical Information Systems: principles and applications*. Longman, London, pp. 71–84, Vol 2

Taylor P J (1990) Editorial comment: GKS. *Political Geography Quarterly* **9** (3): 211–12

Tobler W R (1959) Automation and cartography. *Geographical Review* **49**: 526–34

Tomlinson R F (1989) Current and potential uses for geographical information systems. The North American experience. *International Journal of Geographical Information Systems* **1** (3): 203–18

Tomlinson R F, Calkins H W, Marble D F (1976) *Computer Handling of Geographical Data*. UNESCO Press, Paris

Townshend J G R (1991) Environmental databases and GIS. In: Maguire D J, Goodchild M F, Rhind D W (eds.) *Geographical Information Systems: principles and applications*. Longman, London, pp. 201–16, Vol 2

Unwin D, Dale P (1990) An educationalist's view of GIS. In: Foster M J, Shand P J (eds.) *The Association for Geographic Information Yearbook*. Taylor & Francis, London, pp. 304–12

Unwin D J *et al.* (1990) A syllabus for teaching geographical information systems. *International Journal of Geographical Information Systems* **4**: 475–65

Weibel R, Heller M (1991) Digital terrain modelling. In: Maguire D J, Goodchild M F, Rhind D W (eds.) *Geographical Information Systems: principles and applications*. Longman, London, pp. 269–97, Vol 1

White M (1991) Car navigation systems. In: Maguire D J, Goodchild M F, Rhind D W (eds.) *Geographical Information Systems: principles and applications*. Longman, London, pp. 115–25, Vol 2

CONSOLIDATED BIBLIOGRAPHY

Aangeenbrug R T (1982) The future of Geographic Information Systems. *Computer Graphics News* **2** (2): 4

Aangeenbrug R T (1991) A critique of GIS. In: Maguire D J, Goodchild M F and Rhind D W (eds.) *Geographical Information Systems: principles and applications*. Longman, London, pp. 101–7, Vol 1

Aanstoos R, Weitzel L (1988) Tracking oil and gas wells in Texas. *Proceedings of the Ninth Annual IASU Conference. Harnessing the hidden power of your system: maximizing your return-on-investment*. International Association of Synercom Users, Houston

Abel D J (1988) Relational data management facilities for spatial information systems. *Proceedings of the 3rd International Symposium on Spatial Data Handling*. International Geographical Union, Columbus Ohio, pp. 9–18

Abel D J (1989) A model for data set management in large spatial information systems. *International Journal of Geographical Information Systems* **3**: 291–302

Abel D J (1989) SIRO-DBMS: a database tool-kit for geographical information systems. *International Journal of Geographical Information Systems* **3**: 103–16

Abel D J, Smith J L (1986) A relational GIS database accommodating independent partitionings of the region. *Proceedings of the 2nd International Symposium on Spatial Data Handling*. International Geographical Union, Columbus Ohio, pp. 213–24

Abler R F (1987) The National Science Foundation Center for Geographic Information and Analysis. *International Journal of Geographical Information Systems* **1** (4): 303–26

Abler R F, Adams J, Gould P R (1971) *Spatial Organization: the geographer's view of the world*. Prentice-Hall, Englewood Cliffs New Jersey

Acquista C (1986) GENESSIS computer code reference manual. *Photon Research Associates Report R-135–86*. PRA Inc, La Jolla California

ACSM–ASPRS Geographic Information Management Committee (1989) Multi-purpose geographic database guidelines for local governments. *ACSM Bulletin* **121**: 1357–65

Adedeji A (1989) *The African Alternate Framework to Structural Adjustment*. Public Lecture, University of Ottawa, Canada, 23 October 1989

Adlam K H, Clayton A R, Kelk B (1988) A demonstrator for the National Sciences Geodata Index. *International Journal of Geographical Information Systems* **2**: 161–70

Aerospatiale Direction Technique (1984) *Système d'Echange et de Transfer (SET) Specification Rev. 1.1*. IGN, Paris

Aetna Casualty & Security Co. v. Jeppeson & Co. [1981] 642 F. 2nd 339 (9th Circuit)

Aglinfou (1986) *Program för forskning och utveckling inom landskapsinformationsområdet*. LMV-rapport 1986:13 ISSN 0280–5731. Gävle, Sweden

Agterberg F P (1988) Application of recent developments of regression analysis in regional mineral resource evaluation. In: Chung C F, Fabbri A, Sinding-Larsen G R (eds.) *Quantitative Analysis of Mineral and Energy Resources*. D. Reidel Publishing, Dordrecht, pp. 1–28

Agterberg F P (1989) Systematic approach to dealing with uncertainty of geoscience information in mineral exploration. *Proceedings of the 21st APCOM Symposium*. Las Vegas, March 1989, Chapter 18, pp. 165–78

Agterberg F P (1989) Computer programs for mineral exploration. *Science* **245**: 76–81

Agterberg F P, Bonham-Carter G F, Wright D F (1990) Statistical pattern integration for mineral exploration. In: Gaal G (ed.) *Computer Applications in Resource Exploration*. Pergamon Press, Oxford, pp. 1–22

Ahn J, Freeman H (1983) A program for automatic name placement. *Proceedings of AUTOCARTO 6*. ASPRS, Falls Church Virginia, pp. 444–53

Aho A V, Hopcroft J E, Ullman J D (1983) *Data Structures and Algorithms*. Addison-Wesley, Reading Massachusetts

Akima H (1978) A method of bivariate interpolation and smooth surface fitting for irregularly distributed data points. *ACM Transactions on Mathematical Software* **4** (2): 148–59

Aldersey-Williams H (1989) A Bauhaus for the media age. *New Scientist* **1655**: 54–60

Aldus Corporation (1988) *TIFF – Tag Image File Format Specification Revision 5.0 (Final)*

Alegiani J B, Buxton J, Honey S (1989) An in-vehicle navigation and information system utilizing defined software services. In: Reekie D H M, Case E R, Tsai J (eds.) *Vehicle Navigation & Information Systems Conference, Toronto*, IEEE, Toronto, 156 pp.

Alemi M H, Shariari M R, Nielsen D R (1988) Kriging and co-kriging of soil water properties. *Soil Technology* **1**: 117–32

Alexander F E, Ricketts T J, Williams J (forthcoming) Methods of mapping small clusters of rare diseases with applications to geographical epidemiology. *Geographical Analysis*

Alexandroff P (1961) *Elementary Concepts of Topology*. Dover Publications, New York

ALIC (1987) *National Strategy for Land Information Management*. Australian Land Information Council Secretariat, Canberra

ALIC (1988ff.) *Annual Report*. Australian Land Information Council, Canberra

Allen J H (1988) The World Data Center System, international data exchange and global change. In: Mounsey H M, Tomlinson R F (eds.) *Building Databases for Global Science*. Taylor & Francis, London, pp. 138–53

Alter S L (1977) A taxonomy of decision support systems. *Sloan Management Review* **19**: 39–56

Alter S L (1980) *Decision Support Systems: current practice and continuing challenges*. Addison-Wesley, Reading Massachusetts

Ambron S, Hooper C (1988) *Interactive Multi-media*. Microsoft Press, Redmond, WA

American Bar Association (1989) The year in review. *Natural Resources, Energy and Environmental Law Review*, American Bar Association, Chicago Illinois

American Society for Photogrammetry and Remote Sensing (1989) Interim accuracy standards for large scale line maps. *Photogrammetric Engineering and Remote Sensing* **55**: 1038–40

Amin S (1973) *Neo-Colonialism in West Africa*. Penguin Books, London

Amos L L et al. (1987) *Primary Mapping Economic Analysis, Phase One*, Internal report. US Geological Survey, Reston Virginia

Amos L L et al. (1988) *Primary Mapping Economic Analysis, Phase Two*, Internal report. US Geological Survey, Reston Virginia

Anderson D E, Angel J C, Gurney A J (1978) World Data Bank II. In: Dutton G (ed.) *Harvard Papers on Geographical Information Systems 2*. Laboratory for Computer Graphics and Spatial Analysis, Harvard University, Cambridge Massachusetts

Anderson D R, Thornton J D (1985) *Application of a Geographic Information System (GIS): identification of resources sensitive to acid deposition*. State of Minnesota, St Paul

Anderson J J, Sigmund J M, Cunningham C G, Steven T A, Lanigan J C, Rowley P D (1980) Geologic map of the Delano Peak SW Quadrangle, Beaver County, Utah. *Miscellaneous Field Studies Map, MF-1225*. USGS, Reston

Anderson J R, Hardy E E, Roach J T, Witmer R E (1976) A land use and land cover classification system for use with remote sensor data. *US Geological Survey Professional Paper 964*. USGS, Washington DC

Anderson K E, Callahan G M (1990) The modernization program of the US Geological Survey's National Mapping Division. *Cartography and Geographic Informations Systems* **17** (3): 243–8

Andersson S (1987) The Swedish Land Data Bank. *International Journal of Geographical Information Systems* **1** (3): 253–63

Andersson S (1989) Demand for access to the Swedish Land Data Bank System – a second wave. *Mapping Awareness* **3** (1): 9–12

Angus-Leppan P (1989) The Thailand Land Titling Project: first steps in a parcel-based LIS. *International Journal of Geographical Information Systems* **3** (1): 59–68

Annand K P (1988) A geographic information system for river management. *Proceedings of AM/FM Today. Nottingham Conference*. AM/FM European Division, PO Box 6, CH4005, Basel, Switzerland

Annoni A, Ventura A D, Mozzi E, Schettini R (1990) Towards the integration of remote sensing images within a cartographic system. *Computer Aided Design* **22** (3): 160–6

Anon (1990) The French Revolution of 1989. *Mapping Awareness* **4** (9): 48–9

Anselin L (1988) *Spatial Econometrics: methods and models*. Kluwer Academic Publishers, Dordrecht

Anselin L (1989) What is special about spatial data? Alternative perspectives on spatial data analysis. *Technical Paper 89-4*. National Center for Geographic Information and Analysis, Santa Barbara California

Anselin L, Griffith D (1988) Do spatial effects really matter in regression analysis? *Papers of the Regional Science Association* **65**: 11–34

ANSI Study Group on Database Management Systems (1975) Interim report. *SIGMOD 7*

ANSI X3H2 (1985) *American National Standard Database Language SQL*. American National Standards Institute, Washington DC

ANSI Y14.26M (1987) *Initial Graphic Exchange Specification (IGES), Version 3.0*. ANSI, Washington DC

Apple Computer Inc. (1986) *Human Interface Guidelines: the Apple desktop interface*. Apple Computer Inc., Cupertino California

Applegate L M, Konsynski B R, Nunamaker J F (1986) Model management systems: design for decision support. *Decision Support Systems* **2**: 81–91

Arbia G (1989) Statistical effect of spatial data transformations: a proposed general framework. In: Goodchild M F, Gopal S (eds.) *Accuracy of Spatial Databases*. Taylor & Francis, London, pp. 249–60

Archer H, Croswell P L (1989) Public access to public information systems: an emerging legal issue. *Photogrammetric Engineering and Remote Sensing* **15** (11): 1575–81

Archibald P D (1987) GIS and remote sensing data integration. *Geocarto International* **3**: 67–73

Ardrey R (1966) *The Territorial Imperative*. Fontana/Collins, London

Armstrong M P, De S, Densham P J, Lolonis P, Rushton G, Tewari V K (1990) A knowledge-based approach for supporting locational decision-making. *Environment and Planning B* **17**: 341–64

Armstrong M P (1988) Distance imprecision and error in spatial decision support systems. In: Aangeenbrug R T, Schiffman Y M (eds.) *International Geographic Information Systems (IGIS) Symposium, Arlington, Virginia*, Vol 2. NASA, Washington DC, pp. 23–34

Armstrong M P, Densham P J (1990) Database organization alternatives for spatial decision support systems. *International Journal of Geographical Information Systems* **4**: 3–20

Armstrong M P, Densham P J, Rushton G (1986) Architecture for a microcomputer-based decision support system. *Proceedings of the 2nd International Symposium on Spatial Data Handling*. International Geographical Union, Williamsville New York, pp. 120–31

Arnheim R (1974) *Art and Visual Perception*. University of California Press, Berkeley

Aronoff S (1989) *Geographic Information Systems: a management perspective*. WDL Publications, Ottawa Canada

Aronson P (1985) Applying software engineering to a general purpose geographic information system. *Proceedings of AUTOCARTO 7*. ASPRS, Falls Church Virginia, pp. 23–31

Aronson P (1987) Attribute handling for geographic information systems. *Proceedings of AUTOCARTO 8*. ASPRS/ACSM, Falls Church Virginia, pp. 346–55

Arthur D W G (1978) Orthogonal transformations. *The American Cartographer* **5**: 72–4

Artin E, Brown H (1969) *Introduction to Algebraic Topology*. Charles E Merrill Publishing Company, Columbus

Arur M G, Narayan L R A, Gopalan N (1989) Challenges of the 90's for Digital Cartography in India. *IX INCA International Seminar on Digital Cartography and Potential Users*. Pre-session Proceedings. Survey of India, Dehra Dun, pp. 7–14

Asrar G (ed.) (1989) *Theory and Applications of Optical Remote Sensing*. Wiley, New York

Association for Geographic Information (1988) *AGI NEWS* **1** (1): 1–8

Association for Promotion of Electronic Industries (1989) *Cartographic database standard*, Tokyo

Atkey R G, Gibson R J (1975) Progress in automated cartography. *Proceedings of the Conference of Commonwealth Survey Officers*. Cambridge, August 1975. Ministry of Overseas Development. Paper J3

AT&T Bell Laboratories (1978) *Bell System Technical Journal* **57** (6)

AT&T Bell Laboratories (1984) *Bell System Technical Journal* **63** (8)

Auerbach S, Schaeben H (1990) Computer-aided geometric design of geologic surfaces and bodies. *Mathematical Geology* **22**: 723–42

AURISA (1976ff.) *URPIS – Proceedings of the Urban and Regional Planning Information Systems Annual Conferences*. Australasian Urban and Regional Information Systems Association Inc., Sydney

AURISA (1985) *Report of the Working Group on Statewide Parcel-based Land Information Systems in Australasia*. Australasian Urban and Regional Information Systems Association Inc., Sydney

AURISA (1989) *Towards the Implementation of a National Strategy for Education and Research in Land and Geographic Information Systems*. Australasian Urban and Regional Information Systems Association Inc., Sydney

AUSLIG (1985) *LANDSEARCH 1: Directory of Commonwealth Land Related Data*. Commonwealth Department of Local Government and Administrative Services, Canberra

Aybet J (1990) Integrated mapping systems – data conversion and integration. *Mapping Awareness* **4** (6): 18–23

Babbage R (1989) Planning the future of defence geographic information systems. In: Ball D, Babbage R (eds.) *Geographical Information Systems: defence applications*. Pergamon Press, Sydney, pp. 232–42

Bachi R (1968) *Graphical Rational Patterns*. Universities Press, Jerusalem, Israel

Baerwald T J (1989) Fostering cooperation among academia, industry, and government – the establishment of the National Center for Geographic Information and Analysis in the USA. In: Grant N G (ed.) *Proceedings of National Conference Challenge for the 1990s GIS*. Canadian Institute of Surveying and Mapping, Ottawa, pp. 4–10

Bak P, Mill A (1989) Three dimensional representation in a Geoscientific Resource Management System for the minerals industry. In: Raper J F (ed.) *Three Dimensional Applications in Geographical Information Systems*. Taylor & Francis, London

Baker H H (1990) Scene structure from a moving camera. In: Blake A, Troscianko T (eds.) *AI and the Eye*. John Wiley, Chichester England, pp. 229–60

Baker K (1989) Using geodemographics in market research surveys. *Journal of the Market Research Society* **31**: 37–44

Ballard D H, Brown C M (1981) *Computer Vision*. Prentice-Hall, Englewood Cliffs New Jersey

Balodis M (1983) Positioning typography on maps. *Proceedings, ACSM Fall Convention, Salt Lake City*. ACSM, Falls Church Virginia, pp. 28–44

Band L E (1986) Topographic partition of watersheds with digital elevation models. *Water Resources Research* **22** (1): 15–24

Band L E (1989) A terrain-based watershed information system. *Hydrological Processes* **3**: 151–62

Band L E, Wood E F (1988) Strategies for large-scale

distributed hydrologic simulation. *Applied Mathematics and Computation* **27**: 23–37

Banting D (1988) Using GFIS for teaching GIS concepts. *Proceedings of GIS/LIS '88*. American Society for Photogrammetry and Remote Sensing, Falls Church, pp. 678–84

Barker G R (1988) Remote sensing: the unheralded component of geographic information systems. *Photogrammetric Engineering and Remote Sensing* **54**: 195–9

Barnard S T, Fischler M A (1982) Computational stereo. *ACM Computing Surveys* **14** (4): 553–72

Barr A, Feigenbaum E A (eds.) (1981) *The Handbook of Artificial Intelligence*, Vol. I. HeurisTech Press and William Kaufmann, Stanford

Barr A, Feigenbaum E A (eds.) (1982) *The Handbook of Artificial Intelligence*, Vol. II. HeurisTech Press and William Kaufmann, Stanford

Barton B A (1976) A note on the transformation of spherical coordinates. *The American Cartographer* **3**: 161–8

Barwinski K, Brüggemann H (1986) Development of digital cadastral and topographic maps – Requirements, goals, and basic concept. In: Blakemore M J (ed.) *Proceedings of AUTOCARTO London*, Vol. 2. Royal Institution of Chartered Surveyors, London, pp. 76–85

Basoglu U (1982) A new approach to automated name placement. *Proceedings of AUTOCARTO 5*. ASPRS, Falls Church Virginia, pp. 103–12

Bates M, Moser M G, Stallard D (1984) The IRUS transportable natural language database interface. *Technical Report*. Bolt, Beranek and Newman

Batjes N H, Bouwman A F (1989) JAMPLES: a computerized land evaluation system for Jamaica. In: Bouma J, Bregt A K (eds.) *Land Qualities in Space and Time. Proceedings of the Symposium organised by the International Society of Soil Science (ISSS), Wageningen, The Netherlands, 22–26 August 1988*. PUDOC, Wageningen, pp. 257–60

Batten L G (1989) National capital urban planning project: development of a 3-D GIS. *Proceedings of GIS/LIS '89*. ACSM/ASPRS, Falls Church Virginia, pp. 781–6

Batty M, Longley P, Fotheringham A S (1989) Urban growth and form: scaling, fractal geometry and diffusion-limited aggregation. *Environment and Planning A* **21**:1447–72

Baumgardner M F (1988) A global soils and terrain digital database. In: Mounsey H M, Tomlinson R F (eds.) *Building Databases for Global Science*. Taylor & Francis, London, pp. 172–80

Baumgardner M F, Oldeman L R (eds.) (1986) *Proceedings of an international workshop on the structure of a digital international soil resources map annex database, held 20–24 January 1986 at the International Soil Reference and Information Centre, Wageningen, The Netherlands*. International Soil Science Society, Wageningen, 138 pp.

Baumgardner M F, Weg R F Van der (1989) Space and time dimensions of a world soils and terrain digital database. In: Bouma J, Bregt A K (eds.) *Land Qualities in Space and Time. Proceedings of a Symposium organised by the International Society of Soil Science (ISSS), Wageningen, The Netherlands, 22–26 August 1988*. PUDOC, Wageningen, 356 pp

Bayard-White C (1985) *An Introduction to Interactive Video*. National Interactive Video Centre, and Council for Educational Technology, London

Beard C, Robbins A M (1990) Scale determination and inset selection within a totally automated map production system. *Cartography and Geographic Information Systems* **17** (1): 57–68

Beard M K (1987) How to survive on a single detailed database. *Proceedings of AUTOCARTO 8*. ASPRS/ACSM, Falls Church, pp. 211–20

Beard M K (1989) Design criteria for automated generalization. *Paper presented at International Cartographic Association*, Budapest, August 1989

Beard M K (1989) Dimensions of use and value of geographic information. In: Onsrud H J, Calkins H W, Obermeyer N J (eds.) *Use and Value of Geographic Information*. Initiative Four Specialist Meeting Report and Proceedings *NCGIA Technical Paper 89–7*. University of California at Santa Barbara, Santa Barbara

Beard M K, Chrisman N R (1986) Zipping: new software for merging map sheets. *Proceedings ACSM (vol 1)* ACSM, Falls Church Virginia **1**: 153

Beard M K, Chrisman N R (1988) Zipping: a localized approach to edgematching. *The American Cartographer* **15** (2): 163–72

Beaumont J R (ed.) (1989) Market analysis. *Environment and Planning A* (Special Edition) **21** (5): 587–653

Beaumont J R (1991) An introduction to market analysis. *CATMOG 53*, Geo-Abstracts, Norwich.

Beaumont J R (1991) GIS and market analysis. In: Maguire D J, Goodchild M F, Rhind D W (eds.) *Geographical Information Systems: principles and applications*. Longman, London, pp. 139–51, Vol 2

Beckett P H T, Burrough P A (1971) The relations between cost and utility in soil survey. IV. Comparisons of the utilities of soil maps produced by different survey procedures and to different scales. *Journal of Soil Science* **22**: 466–80

Beckett P H T, Burrough P A (1971) The relations between cost and utility in soil survey. V. The cost effectiveness of different soil survey procedures. *Journal of Soil Science* **22**: 481–9

Beckett P H T, Webster R (1971) Soil variability – a review. *Soils and Fertilizers* **34**: 1–15

Bedard Y, Epstein E F (1984) Spatial data integration in the information era. *Proceedings of the Federation Internationale des Geometres (FIG) Symposium on the Decisionmaker and Land Information Systems*. Canadian Institute of Surveying and Mapping, Ottawa Ontario, pp. 104–113

Bedell R (1988) *WARP: a program to warp computer drawings, maps and plans*. Terra Investigations and Imaging Ltd, Guildford Surrey

Beek K-J, Burrough P A, McCormack D E (1987) Quantified land evaluation procedures. *Proceedings of a Joint Meeting of ISSS Working Groups on Land Evaluation and Soil Information Systems, Washington 25 April–2 May 1986*. ITC Publication No 6, Enschede, 165 pp

Bell S B M, Diaz B M, Holroyd F, Jackson M J (1983) Spatially referenced methods of processing raster and vector data. *Image and Vision Computing* **1**: 211–20

Bennett J L (ed.) (1983) *Building Decision Support Systems*. Addison-Wesley, Reading

Bennett, R J, Wrigley N (eds.) (1981) *Quantitative Geography: retrospect and prospect*. Routledge and Kegan Paul, London

Bentley J L, Ottmann T A (1979) Algorithms for reporting and counting geometric intersections. *IEEE Transactions on Computing* **C-28** (9): 643–7

Bentley T J (1981) *Making Information Systems Work*. The Macmillan Press, London

Benyon D (1990) *Information and Data Modelling*. Blackwell Scientific Publications, Oxford

Berry B J L (1964) Approaches to regional analysis: a synthesis. *Annals of the Association of American Geographers* **54**: 2–11

Berry B J L, Baker A M (1968) Geographic sampling. In: Berry B J L, Marble D F (eds.) *Spatial Analysis*. Prentice Hall, Englewood Cliffs New Jersey, pp. 91–100

Berry B J L, Marble D F (eds.) (1968) *Spatial Analysis: A reader in statistical geography*. Prentice-Hall, Englewood Cliffs New Jersey

Berry J K (1985) Computer-assisted map analysis: fundamental techniques. *Proceedings of the 6th Annual NCGA Conference*, Volume 2, pp. 369–86

Berry J K (1987) Fundamental operations in computer-assisted map analysis. *International Journal of Geographical Information Systems* **1** (2): 119–36

Berry J K (1987) The use of a Geographic Information System for storm runoff prediction from small urban watersheds. *Environmental Management Journal* **11** (1): 21–7

Berry J K (1987) Computer-assisted map analysis: potential and pitfalls. *Photogrammetric Engineering and Remote Sensing Journal* **53** (10): 1405–10

Berry J K (1987) A spatial analysis of timber analysis. In: Ripple W J (ed.) *Geographical Information Systems: a compendium*. Falls Church Virginia, pp. 206–11

Berry J K (1988) Computer-based map analysis: characterizing proximity and connectivity. In: Aangeenbrug R T, Schiffman Y M (eds.) *International Geographic Information Systems (IGIS) Symposium*, Arlington, Virginia, Vol 2. NASA, Washington DC, pp. 11–22

Berry J K (1991) GIS in island resource planning: a case study in map analysis. In: Maguire D J, Goodchild M F, Rhind D W (eds.) *Geographical Information Systems: principles and applications*. Longman, London, pp. 285–95, Vol 2

Berry J K, Berry J K (1988) Assessing spatial impacts of land use plans. *International Journal of Environmental Management* **27**: 1–9

Berry J K et al. (1989) Development and analysis of a spatial database for the Botany Bay vicinity, Volume 2, final report entitled *Natural and Cultural Resources in the United States Virgin Islands: research, education and management needs*. Tropical Resources Institute, Yale University, New Haven Connecticut

Bertin J (1967) *Semiologie Graphique*. Gauthier-Villars and Co., Paris

Bertin J (1973) *Semiologie Graphique*. (Tr. Berg W J). University of Wisconsin Press, Madison Wisconsin

Besag J E (1986) On the statistical analysis of dirty pictures. *Journal of the Royal Statistical Society B* **48**: 192–236

Besag J E, Clifford P (1989) Generalised Monte Carlo significance tests. *Biometrika* **76**: 633–42

Besag J E, Newell J (forthcoming) The detection of clusters in rare diseases. *Journal of the Royal Statistical Society B*

Best R G, Westin F C (1984) GIS for soils and rangeland management. *IEEE Pecora 9 Proceedings Spatial Information Technologies for Remote Sensing Today and Tomorrow, 2–4 October 1984, Sioux Falls*. IEEE, Sioux Falls, pp. 70–4

Beurden S A H A van, Riezebos H Th. (1988) The application of geostatistics in erosion hazard mapping. *Soil Technology* **1**: 349–64

Bhatnagar S C, Jajoo B H (1987) A DSS generator for district planning. *Information and Management* **13**: 43–9

Bickmore D P (1971) Experimental maps of the Bideford area. *Proceedings of the Conference of Commonwealth Survey Officers*. Cambridge, August 1971. Foreign and Commonwealth Office. Paper E1, pp. 217–23

Bickmore D P (1987) *World Digital Database for Environmental Science – An ICA/IGU Project*. ICA/IGU Joint Working Group on Atlases and Maps, Oxford

Bickmore D P, Shaw M A (1963) *Atlas of Great Britain and Northern Ireland*. Clarendon Press, Oxford

Bie S W (1975) Soil information systems. *Proceedings of the meeting of the ISSS Working Group on Soil Information Systems, Wageningen, The Netherlands, 1–4 Sept. 1975*, PUDOC, Wageningen, 87 pp

Billingsley F C, Anuta P E, Carr J L, McGillem C D, Smith D M, Strand T C (1983) Data processing and reprocessing. In: Colwell R N (ed.) *Manual of Remote Sensing*. American Society of Photogrammetry, Falls Church Virginia, pp. 719–88

Billingsley F C, Urena J L (1984) Concepts for a global resources information system. *Proceedings of the Ninth Pecora Symposium: spatial information technologies for remote sensing today and tomorrow*. IEEE Computer Society Press, Silver Spring, pp. 123–31

Bird D (1989) *Commonsense Direct Marketing*. Kogan Page, London

Birkhoff G, Mansfield L (1974) Compatible triangular finite elements. *Journal of Mathematical Analysis and Applications* **47** (3): 531–53

Birugawa S, Yamamoto S, Okuno T, Kinto Y, Asano Y (1964) Distribution patterns of agricultural land use intensity and crop types. *Tokyo Geography Papers* **8**: 153–86

Bishop M M, Fienberg S E, Holland P W (1975) *Discrete Multi-variate Analysis: theory and analysis.* MIT Press, Cambridge Massachusetts

Bishton A (1990) Mapping from a cartographic extract. *Cartography and Geographic Information Systems* **17** (1): 49–56

Bittlestone R (1990) Financial control in the 1990s. *International Journal of Information Resource Management* **1** (1): 12–18

Black J, Sambura A, Salijevic R (1986) The conceptual and technological framework for the New South Wales Land Information System. *URPIS – Proceedings of the Urban and Regional Planning Information Systems Annual Conferences*, Volume 14. Australasian Urban and Regional Information Systems Association Inc., Sydney, pp. 356–67

Black Report (1984) *Investigation of the Possible Incidence of Cancer in West Cumbria. Report of the Independent Advisory Group.* HMSO, London

Blais, J A R, Chapman M A, Lam W K (1986) Optimal interval sampling in theory and practice. *Proceedings of the 2nd International Symposium on Spatial Data Handling.* International Geographical Union, Columbus Ohio, pp. 185–92

Blakemore M J (1984) Generalization and error in spatial databases. *Cartographica* **21**: 131–9

Blakemore M J (1991) Managing an operational GIS: the UK National On-line Manpower Information System (NOMIS). In: Maguire D J, Goodchild M F, Rhind D W (eds.) *Geographical Information Systems: principles and applications.* Longman, London, pp. 503–13, Vol 1

Blalock H M (1979) *Social Statistics*, 2nd edn. McGraw-Hill, New York

Blanning R W (1986) An entity–relationship approach to model management. *Decision Support Systems* **2**: 65–72

Blatchford R P, Rhind D W (1989) The ideal mapping system. In: Rhind D W, Taylor D R F (eds.) *Cartography Past, Present and Future.* Elsevier, London, pp. 157–68

Blum H (1967) A transformation for extracting new descriptors of shape. In: Wathen-Dunn W (ed.) *Models for the Perception of Speech and Visual Form.* MIT Press, Cambridge Massachusetts, pp. 362–80

Board C (1967) Maps as models. In: Chorley R J, Haggett P (eds.) *Models in Geography.* Methuen, London, pp. 671–725

Boehm B W (1981) *Software Engineering Economics.* Prentice-Hall, Englewood Cliffs New Jersey

Boehm B W (1987) Improving software productivity. *Computer (IEEE)* **20** (9): 43–57

Bolland J D (1986) Digital mapping and facilities management in a UK Water Authority. In: Blakemore M J (ed.) *Proceedings of AUTOCARTO London*, Volume 2. Royal Institution of Chartered Surveyors, London, pp. 162–70

Bonczek R H, Holsapple C W, Whinston A B (1981) *Foundations of Decision Support Systems.* Academic Press, New York

Bonczek R H, Holsapple C W, Whinston A B (1984) *MicroDatabase Management: practical techniques for application development.* Academic Press, New York

Bonham-Carter G F (1991) Integration of geoscientific data using GIS. In: Maguire D J, Goodchild M F, Rhind D W (eds.) *Geographical Information Systems: principles and applications.* Longman, London, pp. 171–84, Vol 2

Bonham-Carter G F, Agterberg F P (1990) Application of a micro-computer based geographic information system to mineral potential mapping. In: Hanley T, Merriam D F (eds.) *Microcomputers in Geology*, Volume 2. Pergamon Press, Oxford, pp. 49–74

Bonham-Carter G F, Agterberg F P, Wright D F (1988) Integration of geological data sets for gold exploration in Nova Scotia. *Photogrammetric Engineering and Remote Sensing* **54** (11): 1585–92

Bonham-Carter G F, Agterberg F P, Wright D F (1990) Weights of evidence modelling: a new approach to mapping mineral potential. *Geological Survey of Canada Paper* **89–9**, pp. 171–83

Bonham-Carter G F, Rogers P J, Ellwood D J (1987) Catchment basin analysis applied to surficial geochemical data, Cobequid Highlands, Nova Scotia. *Journal of Geochemical Exploration* **29**: 259–78

Bonoma T V (1985) *The Marketing Edge.* Free Press, New York

Boots B, Getis A (1988) Point pattern analysis. *Sage Scientific Geography Series, Number 8.* Sage Publications, London

Bouma J (1989) Land qualities in space and time. In: Bouma J, Bregt A K (eds.) *Land Qualities in Space and Time. Proceedings of a Symposium organised by the International Society of Soil Science (ISSS), Wageningen, The Netherlands, 22–26 August 1988.* PUDOC, Wageningen, pp. 3–14

Bouma J (1989) Using soil survey data for quantitative land evaluation. *Advances in Soil Science*. Volume 9. Springer-Verlag, New York, pp. 177–213

Bouma J, Bregt A K (eds.) (1989) *Land Qualities in Space and Time. Proceedings of a Symposium organised by the International Society of Soil Science (ISSS), Wageningen, The Netherlands, 22–26 August 1988.* PUDOC, Wageningen, 356 pp.

Bouma J, Laat P J M de, Awater R H C M, Heesen H C van, Holst A F van, Nes Th. J van de (1980) Use of soil survey data in a model for simulating regional soil moisture regimes. *Soil Science Society of America Journal* **44**: 808–14

Bouma J, Lanen H A J van (1987) Transfer functions and threshold values: from soil characteristics to land qualities. In: Beek K J, Burrough P A, McCormack D E (eds.) *Quantified Land Evaluation Procedures.* ITC Publication No 6, Enschede, pp. 106–10

Bouma J, Lanen H A J van, Breeuwsma A, Wösten H J M, Kooistra M J (1986) Soil survey data needs when studying modern land use problems. *Soil Use and Management* **2**: 125–29

Bourne L E, Dominowski R L, Loftus E F (1979) *Cognitive Processes.* Prentice-Hall, Englewood Cliffs New Jersey

Box E O, Holben B N, Kalb V (1989) Accuracy of the AVHRR Vegetation Index as a predictor of biomass, primary productivity and net CO_2 flux. *Vegetatio* **80**: 71–89

Bracken I, Higgs G, Martin D, Webster C (1989) A classification of geographical information systems literature and applications. *Concepts and Techniques in Modern Geography* **52**: Environmental Publications, Norwich

Bracken I, Higgs G (1990) The role of GIS in data integration for rural environments. *Mapping Awareness* **4** (8): 51–6

Bracken I, Webster C (1989) Towards a typology of geographical information systems. *International Journal of Geographical Information Systems* **3** (2): 137–52

Bracken I, Webster C (1990) *Information Technology in Geography and Planning: including principles of GIS.* Routledge, London

Brand M J D (1986) The foundation of a geographical information system for Northern Ireland. In: Blakemore M J (ed.) *Proceedings of AUTOCARTO London.* Royal Institution of Chartered Surveyors, London, pp. 4–9

Brand M J D, Gray S (1989) From concept to reality. *Proceedings of AGI '89* 5.2.1–5.2.7

Brandenberger A J, Ghosh S K (1985) The world's topographic and cadastral mapping operation. *Photogrammetric Engineering and Remote Sensing* **51** (4): 437–44

Brassel K E (1974) A model for automatic hill-shading. *The American Cartographer* **1** (1): 15–27

Brassel K E, Utano J J (1979) Design strategies for continuous tone area mapping. *The American Cartographer* **6** (1): 39–50

Brassel K E, Weibel R (1988) A review and conceptual framework of automated map generalization. *International Journal of Geographical Information Systems* **2** (3): 229–44

Brauer A (1985) Introduction to the Australian Standard Geographical Classification. *URPIS – Proceedings of the Urban and Regional Planning Information Systems Annual Conferences*, Volume 13. Australasian Urban and Regional Information Systems Association Inc., Sydney, pp. 365–97

Breeusma A, Reijerink J G A, Schoumans O F, Brus D J H van het Loo (1989) *Fosfaatbelasting van bodem, grond- en oppervlaktewater in het stroomgebied van de Schuitenbeek. Rapport 10.* Instituut voor Onderzoek van het Landelijk Gebied, Wageningen, The Netherlands, 95 pp.

Bregt A K (1989) Quality of representative profile descriptions for predicting the land quality moisture deficit at different scales. In: Bouma J, Bregt A K (eds.) *Land Qualities in Space and Time. Proceedings of a Symposium organised by the International Society of Soil Science (ISSS), Wageningen, The Netherlands, 22–26 August 1988.* PUDOC, Wageningen, pp. 169–72

Bregt A K, Beemster J G R (1989) Accuracy in predicting moisture deficits and changes in yield from soil maps. *Geoderma* **43**: 301–10

Brewer C A (1989) The development of process-printed Munsell charts for selecting map colors. *The American Cartographer* **16** (4): 269–78

Bridge J S, Leeder M R (1979) A simulation model of alluvial stratigraphy. *Sedimentology* **26**: 617–44

Briggs D, Mounsey H M (1989) Integrating land resource data into a European geographical information system: practicalities and problems. *Applied Geography* **9** (1): 5–20

Brodie M L, Bobrow D, Lesser V, Madnick S, Tsichritzis D, Hewitt C (1988) Future artificial intelligence requirements for intelligent database systems. In: Kerschberg L (ed.) *Proceedings from the Second International Conference on Expert Database Systems, Tysons Corner, Virginia, 25–27 April 1988.* The Benjamin/Cummings Publishing Company, pp. 45–62

Brodie M L, Mylopoulos J (1986) Knowledge bases versus databases. In: Brodie M L, Mylopoulos J (eds.) *On Knowledge Base Management Systems: integrating artificial intelligence and database technologies.* Springer-Verlag, New York, pp. 83–6

Bromley R D F, Coulson M G (1989) *Geographical Information Systems and the work of a local authority: a case study of Swansea City Council.* Department of Geography, University College Swansea, Swansea

Bromley R D F, Coulson M G (1989) The value of corporate GIS to local authorities. *Mapping Awareness* **3** (5): 32–5

Brooks F P (1987) Grasping reality through illusion: interactive graphics serving science. CHI '90. *SIGCHI Bulletin* (special issue): 1–11

Brooks F P (1987) No silver bullet – essence and accidents of software engineering. *Computer (IEEE)* **20** (4): 10–19

Brooks R A (1983) Model-based three-dimensional interpretations of two-dimensional images. *IEEE Transactions on Pattern Analysis and Machine Intelligence* **PAMI-5**: 140–50

Broome F R (1986) Mapping from a topologically encoded database: the US Bureau of the Census example. In: Blakemore M J (ed.) *Proceedings of AUTOCARTO London.* Royal Institution of Chartered Surveyors, London, pp. 402–11

Broome F R, Godwin L (1990) The Census Bureau's publication map system. *Cartography and Geographic Information Systems* **17** (1): 79–88

Broome F R, Meixler D B (1990) The TIGER database structure. *Cartography and Geographic Information Systems* **17** (1): 39–47

Brotchie J F, Dickey J W, Sharpe R (1980) *TOPAZ – General Planning Model and its Applications at the Urban and Facility Planning Levels.* Springer-Verlag, Heidelburg

Brown C W, Landgraf H F, Uzes F D (1969) *Boundary Control and Legal Principles*, 2nd edn. Wiley, London

Brown G, Atkins M (1988) *Effective Teaching in Higher Education.* Methuen, London

Brown M J, Norris D A (1988) Early applications of geographical information systems at the Institute of Terrestrial Ecology. *International Journal of Geographical Information Systems* **2** (2): 153–60

Bruegger B P, Frank A U (1989) Hierarchies over topological data structures. *Proceedings of the American Congress on Surveying and Mapping Annual Convention, Baltimore*, Vol. 4. ACSM, Falls Church Virginia, pp. 137–45

Bryant J (1990) AMOEBA clustering revisited. *Photogrammetric Engineering and Remote Sensing* **56**: 41–7

Bryden R (1989) GIS: an industry perspective. *Workshop on Strategic Directions for Canada's Surveying, Mapping, Remote Sensing and GIS Activities*. November 1989. Ottawa

Buchmann A, Günther O, Smith T R, Wang Y-F (1989) *Design and Implementation of Large Spatial Databases. Lecture Notes in Computer Science 409.* Springer-Verlag, New York

Bull G A (1960) Comparison of rain-gauges. *Nature* **185**: 437–38

Bunce R G H, Barr C J, Whittaker H A (1982) A stratification system for ecological sampling. In: Fuller R M (ed.) *Ecological Mapping from, Ground, Air and Space*. Institute of Terrestrial Ecology Symposium No. 10. Monk's Wood, Cambridgeshire, pp. 39–46

Bundock M (1987) An integrated DBMS approach for geographic information systems. *Proceedings of AUTOCARTO 8*. ASRPS, Falls Church Virginia, pp. 292–301

Bunge W (1966) *Theoretical Geography*. Gleerup, Lund Sweden

Bureau of the Budget (1947) *National Map Accuracy Standards*. US Government Printing Office, Washington DC

Bureau of the Census (1982) *Guide to the 1980 Census of Population and Housing*. US Department of Commerce, Washington DC

Bureau of the Census (1984) *Guide to the 1982 Economic Census and Related Statistics*. US Department of Commerce, Washington DC

Bureau of the Census (1984) *Guide to the 1982 Census of Agriculture and Related Statistics*. US Department of Commerce, Washington DC

Burgess T M, Webster R, McBratney A B (1981) Optimal interpolation and isarithmic mapping of soil properties: 4. Sampling strategy. *Journal of Soil Science* **32**: 643–59

Burgess T M, Webster R (1980) Optimal interpolation and isarithmic mapping of soil properties: 1. The semi-variogram and punctual kriging. *Journal of Soil Science* **31**: 315–31

Burgess T M, Webster R (1980) Optimal interpolation and isarithmic mapping of soil properties: 2. Block kriging. *Journal of Soil Science* **31**: 333–41

Burke K C, Dixon T M (eds.) (1988) *Topographic Science Working Group, Final Report*. National Aeronautics and Space Administration, Washington DC

Burns K L (1988) Lithologic topology and structural vector fields applied to subsurface prediction in geology. *Proceedings of GIS/LIS '88*. ACSM/ASPRS, Falls Church Virginia, pp. 26–34

Burns K L (1990) Three dimensional modelling and geothermal process simulation. *Proceedings of Symposium on Three Dimensional Computer Graphics in Modelling Geologic Structures and Simulating Processes*. Freiburger Geowissenschafliche Beitrage **2**: 10–12

Burrough P A (1980) The development of a landscape information system in the Netherlands, based on a turn-key graphics system. *GeoProcessing* **1** (3): 257–74

Burrough P A (1982) Computer assistance for soil survey and land evaluation. *Soil Survey and Land Evaluation* **2**: 25–36

Burrough P A (1983) Multi-scale sources of spatial variation in soil. I. The application of Fractal concepts to nested levels of soil variation. *Journal of Soil Science* **34**: 577–97

Burrough P A (1983) Multi-scale sources of spatial variation in soil II. A non-Brownian Fractal model and its application to soil survey. *Journal of Soil Science* **34**: 599–620

Burrough P A (1986) *Principles of Geographical Information Systems for Land Resources Assessment*. Clarendon Press, Oxford, 194 pp.

Burrough P A (1986) Five reasons why geographical information systems are not being used efficiently for land resources assessment. In: Blakemore M J (ed.) *Proceedings of AUTOCARTO London*, Vol. 2. Royal Institution of Chartered Surveyors, London, pp. 139–48

Burrough P A (1987) Natural resources databases: conceptual units, data structures and natural variation. In Beek K J, Burrough P A, McCormack D (eds.) *Quantified Land Evaluation. Proceedings of a Joint Meeting of ISSS Working Groups on Land Evaluation and Soil Information Systems, Washington 25 April–2 May 1986*. ITC, Enschede, pp. 60–5

Burrough P A (1989) Fuzzy mathematical methods for soil survey and land evaluation. *Journal of Soil Science* **40**: 477–92

Burrough P A (1989) Matching spatial databases and quantitative models in land resource assessment. *Soil Use and Management* **5**: 3–8

Burrough P A (1989) Fractals and geochemistry. In: Avnir D (ed.) *The Fractal Approach to Heterogeneous Chemistry*. Wiley, Chichester, pp. 383–406

Burrough P A (1990) Sampling designs for quantifying map unit composition. In: Mausbach M J, Wilding L (eds.) *Spatial Variability and Map Units for Soil Surveys*. International Soil Science Society Working Group of Soil and Moisture Variability in Time and Space/ American Society of Agronomy, the Crop Science Society of America and the Soil Science Society of America (in press)

Burrough P A (1991) Soil information systems. In: Maguire D J, Goodchild M F, Rhind D W (eds.)

Geographical Information Systems: principles and applications. Longman, London, pp. 153–69, Vol 2

Burrough P A, Beckett P H T (1971) The relations between cost and utility in soil survey. I. The design of the experiment. *Journal of Soil Science* **22**: 359–68

Burrough P A, Beckett P H T (1971) The relations between cost and utility in soil survey. III. The costs of soil survey. *Journal of Soil Science* **22**: 382–94

Burrough P A, Beckett P H T, Jarvis M (1971) The relations between cost and utility in soil survey. II. Conventional or free survey. *Journal of Soil Science* **22**: 369–81

Burrough P A, Bie S W (eds.) (1984) *Soil Information Systems Technology*. PUDOC, Wageningen, 178 pp.

Burrough P A, Veer A A de (1980) Cartographic processes. In: Machover C, Blauth R E (ed.) *The CAD/CAM Handbook*. Computervision Corporation, Massachusetts, pp. 97–120

Burrough P A, Veer A A de (1984) Automated production of landscape maps for physical planning in the Netherlands. *Landscape Planning* **11**: 205–26

Burton I (1963) The quantitative revolution and theoretical geography. *Canadian Geographer* **7**: 151–62

Burton W (1979) Logical and physical data types in geographic information systems. *Geo-Processing* **1** (4): 167–81

Bush V (1945) As we may think. *Atlantic Monthly* **176**: 101–8

Busoni E, Sanesi G, Torri D (1986) Soil moisture regimes and erodibility in the assessment of soil suitability for crops in Tuscany. *Soil Use and Management* **2**: 130–3

Buttenfield B P (1986) Digital definitions of scale-dependent line structure. In: Blakemore M J (ed.) *Proceedings of AUTOCARTO London*. Royal Institute of Chartered Surveyors, London, pp. 497–506

Buttenfield B P (1987) Automating the identification of cartographic lines. *The American Cartographer* **14** (1): 7–20

Buttenfield B P (1989) Scale-dependence and self-similarity in cartographic lines. *Cartographica* **26**: 79–100

Buttenfield B P, Mackaness W A (1991) Visualization. In: Maguire D J, Goodchild M F, Rhind D W (eds.) *Geographical Information Systems: principles and applications*. Longman, London, pp. 427–43, Vol 1

Buxton R (1989) Integrated spatial information systems in local government – is there a financial justification? *Mapping Awareness* **2** (6) 14–16

Buzzell R D (1985) *Marketing in an Electronic Age*. Harvard Business School Press, Boston

Buzzell R D, Gale B T (1987) *The PIMS Principles: linking strategy to performance*. Free Press, New York

CACI (1983) *1981 ACORN Classification*. CACI Market Analysis, 59/62 High Holborn, London.

CADalyst (1989) When reality is not enough. *CADalyst* December: 40–53

Calkins H W (1979) The planning monitor: an accountability theory of plan evaluation. *Environment and Planning A* **11**: 745–58

Calkins H W (1983) A pragmatic approach to geographic information system design. In: Peuquet D, O'Callaghan J (eds.) *Design and Implementation of Computer-based Geographic Information Systems*. International Geographical Union, New York, pp.92–101

Calkins H W (1991) GIS and public policy. In: Maguire D J, Goodchild M F, Rhind D W (eds.) *Geographical Information Systems: principles and applications*. Longman, London, pp. 233–45, Vol 2

Calkins H W, Marble D F (1987) The transition to automated production cartography: design of the master cartographic database. *The American Cartographer* **14**: 105–21

Callahan M, Broome F R (1984) The joint development of a national 1 : 100 000 scale digital cartographic database. *Proceedings of the Annual Conference of the American Congress on Surveying and Mapping*, Washington DC, pp. 246–53

Campbell J B (1981) Spatial correlation effects upon accuracy of supervised classification of land cover. *Photogrammetric Engineering and Remote Sensing* **47**: 355–63

Campbell J B (1987) *Introduction to Remote Sensing*. Guildford Press, New York

Campbell W G, Church M R, Bishop G D, Mortenson D C, Pierson S M (1989) The role for a geographical information system in a large environmental project. *International Journal of Geographical Information Systems* **3** (4): 349–62

Canada Department of Forestry and Rural Development (1965) *The Canada Land Inventory: objectives, scope and organisation*. Report No. 1. Ottawa, Canada Land Inventory

Card D H (1982) Using known map category marginal frequencies to improve estimates of thematic map accuracy. *Photogrammetric Engineering and Remote Sensing* **48**: 431–9

Carlbom I (1987) An algorithm for geometric set operations using cellular subdivision techniques. *IEEE Computer Graphics and Applications*. May: 45–55

Carlson E D (1983) An approach for designing decision support systems. In: House W C (ed.) *Decision Support Systems*. Petrocelli, New York, pp. 127–56

Carlson E D (1987) Three dimensional conceptual modelling of subsurface structures. *Proceedings of AUTOCARTO 8*. ACSM/ASPRS, Falls Church Virginia, pp. 336–45

Carlson E D, Bennett J L, Giddings G M, Mantey P·E (1974) The design and evaluation of an interactive geo-data analysis and display system. In: Rosenfeld J L (ed.) *Information Processing 74, The Proceedings of the IFIP Congress*. North-Holland, New York

Carruthers A, Waugh T C (1988) *GIMMS User Manual*. GIMMS Ltd, Edinburgh

Carter J R (1985) Curricula standards, certification, and other possibilities in cartographic education. *Technical*

Papers of the 45th Annual Meeting of the American Congress on Surveying and Mapping. ACSM, Falls Church, pp. 2–7

Carter J R (1987) Defining cartography as a profession. *ACSM Bulletin* August, 23–6

Carter J R (1989) On defining the geographic information system. In: Ripple W J (ed.) *Fundamentals of Geographic Information Systems: a compendium.* ASPRS/ACSM, Falls Church Virginia, pp. 3–7

Casley D J, Lury D A (1981) *Data Collection in Developing Countries.* Clarendon Press, Oxford

Cass R (1989) Digital databases for vehicle navigation: review of the state of the art. *Proceedings of the 20th International Symposium on Automotive Technology and Automation, Florence,* IEEE, Toronto, pp. 1241–54

Castner H W, Eastman J R (1985) Eye movement parameters and perceived map complexity. *The American Cartographer* **12** (1): 29–40

Catling I, Belcher P (1989) Autoguide – Route Guidance in the United Kingdom. In: Reekie D H M, Case E R, Tsai J (eds.) *Vehicle Navigation & Information Systems Conference, Toronto,* pp. 1127–44

Caulfield I (1989) The role of GISG and LAMSAC in local government. *Proceedings of the National Mapping Awareness Conference.* Miles Arnold, London

Cavill M V, Greener S (1988) Introducing Geographic Information Systems Technology: concepts, approval and implementation. *URPIS – Proceedings of the Urban and Regional Planning Information Systems Annual Conferences,* Volume 16. Australasian Urban and Regional Information Systems Association Inc., Sydney, pp. 323–30

CCITT, The International Telegraph and Telephone Consultative Committee of the International Telecommunications Union (1985) *CCITT-3 and CCITT-4 – Terminal Equipment and Protocols for Telematic Services. Series T Recommendations Geneva.* CCITT Volume VII, Fascicle VII.3

CEC (1990) CORINE: *Examples of the Use of the Results of the Programme 1985–90.* Directorate General of the Environment, Nuclear Safety and Civil Protection, Commission of the European Communities, Brussels

Cederholm T (ed.) (1989) *Utvecklingsradet for Landskapsinformation Geografiska Informationssystem.* Landmateriverket, Gävle Sweden

Central Office of Information (1988) *Britain 1988.* HMSO, London

Centre National d'Études Spatiales (1989) *SPOT Users Handbook,* Volume 2. Centre Spatial de Toulouse, Toulouse, France

Chadha S M (1989) Presidential Address. *IX INCA International Seminar on Digital Cartography and Potential Users.* Pre-Session Proceedings. Survey of India, Dehra Dun, p. 7

Chakravarthy U S (1985) *Semantic Query Optimization in Deductive Databases.* Unpublished PhD thesis, University of Maryland

Chamberlin D D, Astrahan M M, Eswaran K P, Lorie R A, Mehl J W, Reisner P, Wade B W (1976) SEQUEL 2: a unified approach to data definition, manipulation, and control. *IBM Journal of Research and Development* **20**: 560–75

Chamberlin D D, Boyce R F (1974) Sequel: a structured English query language. In: Rustin R (ed.) *Workshop on Data Description, Access and Control.* ACM SIGMOD, Ann Arbor, Michigan, 249–64

Chambers J M, Cleveland S, Kleiner B, Tukey P A (1983) *Graphical Methods for Data Analysis.* Duxbury, Boston

Chan K (1988) *Evaluating Descriptive Models for Prescriptive Inference.* Unpublished PhD thesis, Harvard University

Chandra N, Goran W (1986) Steps toward a knowledge-based geographical data analysis system. In: Optiz B (ed.) *Geographic Information Systems in Government.* A Deepak Publishing, Hampton

Chappuis A, Golbéry L (1984) Un atlas regional, outil d'aide a la décision en Inde. *Paper read to the 12th International Cartographic Conference, Perth, Australia*

Charlwood G, Moon G, Tulip J (1987) Developing a DBMS for geographic information: a review. *Proceedings of AUTOCARTO 8.* ASPRS, Falls Church Virginia, pp. 302–15

Chavez P S (1984) *US Geological Survey Mini Image Processing System.* USGS Open File Report 84–880

Chazelle B, Edelsbrunner H (1988) An optimal algorithm for intersecting line segments in the plane. *Proceedings, 29th Annual Symposium on Foundations of Computer Science, White Plains*

Chelst K, Schultz J, Sanfhvi N (1988) Issues and decision aids for designing branch networks. *Journal of Retail Banking* **10**: 5–17

Chen P P (1976) The Entity–Relationship Model – towards a unified view of data. *Association for Computing Machinery Transactions on Database Systems* **1** (1): 9–36

Chen P P (1983) English sentence structure and entity–relationship diagrams. *Information Sciences* **29**: 127–49

Chen S (1987) Geographical data handling and GIS in China. *International Journal of Geographical Information Systems* **1** (3): 219–28

Chen Z-T (1987) *Quadtree and Quadtree Spatial Spectra in Large Geographic Information Systems: the hierarchical handling of spatial data.* Unpublished PhD dissertation, University of California, Santa Barbara California

Chen Z-T, Guevara J A (1987) Systematic selection of very important points (VIP) from digital terrain models for constructing triangular irregular networks. *Proceedings of AUTOCARTO 8.* ASPRS, Falls Church Virginia, pp. 50–6

Chinese Academy of Sciences, Institute of Geography (1987) *Population Atlas of China.* Oxford University Press, Oxford

Chorley R (1988) Some reflections on the handling of geographic information. *International Journal of Geographical Information Systems* **2** (1): 3–9

Chorley R, Buxton R (1991) The government setting of GIS in the United Kingdom. In: Maguire D J, Goodchild

M F, Rhind D W (eds.) *Geographical Information Systems: principles and applications*. Longman, London, pp. 67–79, Vol 1

Chrisman N R (1982) A theory of cartographic error and its measurement in digital databases. *Proceedings of AUTOCARTO 5*. ASPRS, Falls Church, pp. 159–68

Chrisman N R (1982) Beyond accuracy assessment: correction of misclassification. *Proceedings International Society of Photogrammetry and Remote Sensing Commission IV*, 24-IV, pp. 123–32

Chrisman N R (1983) The role of quality information in the long-term functioning of a GIS. *Proceedings of AUTOCARTO 6*, Vol. 2. ASPRS, Falls Church, pp. 303–21

Chrisman N R (1984) The role of quality information in the long-term functioning of a geographical information system. *Cartographica* **21**: 79–87

Chrisman N R (1986) Quality report for Dane County soil survey digital files. In: Moellering H (ed.) *Report 7, National Committee for Digital Cartographic Data Standards*, pp. 78–88

Chrisman N R (1987) Design of geographic information systems based on social and cultural goals. *Photogrammetric Engineering and Remote Sensing* **53** (10): 1367–70

Chrisman N R (1987) Efficient digitizing through the combination of appropriate hardware and software for error detection and editing. *International Journal of Geographical Information Systems* **1** (3): 265–77

Chrisman N R (1988) The risks of software innovation: a case study of the Harvard Lab. *The American Cartographer* **15** (3): 291–300

Chrisman N R (1989) Modeling error in overlaid categorical maps. In: Goodchild M F, Gopal S (eds.) *Accuracy of Spatial Databases*. Taylor & Francis, London, pp. 21–34

Chrisman N R (1991) The error component in spatial data. In: Maguire D J, Goodchild M F, Rhind D W (eds.) *Geographical Information Systems: principles and applications*. Longman, London, pp. 165–74, Vol 1

Chrisman N R, Yandell B (1988) Effects of point error on area calculations. *Surveying and Mapping* **48**: 241–6

Christensen A H J (1987) Fitting a triangulation to contour lines. *Proceedings of AUTOCARTO 8*. ASPRS, Falls Church Virginia, pp. 57–67

Christiansen H N, Sederberg T W (1978) Conversion of complex contour line definitions into polygonal element mosaics. *ACM Computer Graphics* **12** (3): 187–92

Christianson C J (1986) Geoprocessing activities in the Fish and Wildlife Survey. *Proceedings of a Geographical Information Systems Workshop*, American Society of Photogrammetry and Remote Sensing, Falls Church Virginia, pp. 43–6

Churchman C W (1968) *The Systems Approach*. Dell Publishing Co. Inc., New York

Cibula W G, Nyquist M O (1987) Use of topographic and climatological models in a geographic database to improve Landsat MSS classification for Olympic National Park. *Photogrammetric Engineering and Remote Sensing* **53**: 67–75

Civco D (1989) Knowledge-based land use and land cover mapping. *Proceedings ASPRS/ACSM Annual Convention*, Vol. 3. ASPRS/ACSM, Falls Church Virginia, pp. 276–91

Claire R W (1982) Algorithm development for spatial operators. *Proceedings of PECORA9*, pp. 213–21

Clark D M, Hastings D A, Kineman J J (1991) Global databases and their implications for GIS. In: Maguire D J, Goodchild M F, Rhind D W (eds.) *Geographical Information Systems: principles and applications*. Longman, London, pp. 217–31, Vol 2

Clark D M, Kineman J J (1988) Global databases: a NOAA experience. In: Mounsey H M, Tomlinson R F (eds.) *Building Databases for Global Science*. Taylor & Francis, London, pp. 216–33

Clark I, Houlding S, Stoakes M (1990) Direct geostatistical estimation of irregular 3-D volumes. *Proceedings of Symposium on Three Dimensional Computer Graphics in Modelling Geologic Structures and Simulating Processes*. Freiburger Geowissenschafliche Beitrage **2**: 13–15

Clark J W (1977) Time–distance transformations of transportation networks. *Geographical Analysis* **9**: 195–205

Clark W F (1990) *North Carolina's Estuaries: a pilot study for managing multiple use in the State's public trust waters*. Albemarle-Pamlico Study Report 90-10. Albemarle-Pamlico Study Program, Raleigh North Carolina

Clarke A L (1988) Upgrading a digital mapping system. *Proceedings of the Seventh Australian Cartographic Conference*. Australian Institute of Cartographers, Sydney, pp. 238–47

Clarke A L (1991) GIS specification, evaluation and implementation. In: Maguire D J, Goodchild M F, Rhind D W (eds.) *Geographical Information Systems: principles and applications*. Longman, London, pp. 477–88, Vol 1

Clarke A L, Grün A, Loon J C (1982) The application of contour data for generating high fidelity grid digital elevation models. *Proceedings of AUTOCARTO 5*. ASPRS, Falls Church Virginia, pp. 213–22

Clarke K C (1986) Recent trends in geographic information systems. *Geo-Processing* **3**: 1–15

Clarke K C (1986) Advances in Geographic Information Systems. *Computers, Environment and Urban Systems* **10**: 175–84

Clarke K C (1988) Scale-based simulation of topographic relief. *The American Cartographer* **15** (2): 171–81

Clarke K C (1990) *Analytical and Computer Cartography*. Prentice-Hall, Englewood Cliffs New Jersey

Clarke M (1989) Geographical information systems and model based analysis: towards effective decision support systems. *Proceedings of the GIS Summer Institute* Kluwer, Amsterdam

Claussen H, Lichtner W, Siebold J, Heres L, Lahaije P (1989) GDF, a proposed standard for digital road maps to be used in car navigation system. In: Reekie D H M, Case E R, Tsai J (eds.) *Vehicle Navigation & Information Systems Conference, Toronto*, pp. 324–30

Clayton C, Estes J E (1980) Image analysis as a check on census enumeration accuracy. *Photogrammetric Engineering and Remote Sensing* **46**: 757–64

Clayton D, Kaldor J (1987) Empirical Bayes estimates of age-standardised relative risks for use in disease mapping. *Biometrics* **43**: 671–81

Cleveland W S (1985) *The Elements of Graphing Data*. Wadsworth, Monterey California

Cleveland W S, McGill R (1984) Graphical perception: theory, experimentation and application to the development of graphical methods. *Journal of the American Statistical Association* **79**: 531–54

Cliff A D, Ord J K (1981) *Spatial Processes: models and applications*. Pion, London

Cobb M C (1970) Changing map scales by automation. *Geographical Magazine* **4** (3): 786–8

Cocks K D, Walker P A, Parvey C A (1988) Evolution of a continental-scale geographical information system. *International Journal of Geographical Information Systems* **2** (3): 263–80

Cocks K D, Walker P A (1987) Edging towards a nation-wide resources information system for Australia. *Proceedings of the 21st Conference of the Institute of Australian Geographers, Perth*, pp. 319–25

Codd E F (1970) A relational model of data for large shared data banks. *Communications of the ACM* **13** (6): 377–87

Codd E F (1979) Extending the database relational model to capture more meaning. *Association for Computing Machinery Transactions on Database Systems* **4** (4): 397–434

Codd E F (1982) Relational database: a practical foundation for productivity. *Communications of the ACM* **25** (2): 109–17

Cohen J (1988) A view of the origins and development of Prolog. *Communications ACM* **31** (1): 26–36

Cohen P R (1985) *Heuristic Reasoning About Uncertainty: an artificial intelligence approach*. Pitman, London

Cohon J L (1978) *Multiobjective Programming and Planning*. Academic Press, New York

Cole G, Voller J (1988) Introduction of FM into British Telecom. *Proceedings of AM/FM Today. Nottingham Conference*. AM/FM European Division, PO Box 6, CH4005, Basel, Switzerland

Collins J (1982) *Review of Competitive Database Software*. Savant, Carnforth

Collins W G, El-Beik A H A (1971) Population census with the aid of aerial photographs: an experiment in the city of Leeds. *Photogrammetric Record* **7**: 16–26

Colwell R N (1983) *Manual of Remote Sensing*. American Society of Photogrammetry, Falls Church Virginia

Commager H S (1973) Quoted by Justice W O Douglas in EPA *v*. Mink. 410 US 73: 106

Commission on Geographical Data Sensing and Processing (1976) *Second interim report on digital spatial data handling in the US Geological Survey*. International Geographical Union, Ottawa

Committee on Earth Sciences (1989) *Our Changing planet: the FY90 research plan – the US global change research program*. Office of Science and Technology Policy, Washington DC

Committee on Global Change (1988) *Toward an Understanding of Global Change: Initial priorities for US contributions to the International Geosphere-Biosphere Program*. National Academy Press, Washington DC

Computer Graphics World (1989) Daratech survey. *Computer Graphics World* November, p. 22

Congalton R G (1986) Geographic information systems specialists. *Proceedings of Geographic Information Systems Workshop*. ASPRS, Falls Church, pp. 37–42

Congalton R G (1988) A comparison of sampling schemes used in generating error matrices for assessing the accuracy of maps generated from remotely sensed data. *Photogrammetric Engineering and Remote Sensing* **54**: 593–600

Congalton R G (1988) Using spatial autocorrelation analysis to explore the errors in maps generated from remotely sensed data. *Photogrammetric Engineering and Remote Sensing* **54**: 587–92

Congalton R G, Odervwald R, Mead R (1983) Assessing Landsat classification accuracy using discrete multivariate analysis statistical techniques. *Photogrammetric Engineering and Remote Sensing* **6**: 169–73

Conklin J (1987) Hypertext: an introduction and survey. *IEEE Computer* **20**: 17–41

Cook R N (1966) The CULDATA system. In: Cook R N, Kennedy J L (eds.) *Proceedings of a Tri-State Conference on a Comprehensive Unified Land Data System (CULDATA)*. College of Law, University of Cincinnati, pp. 53–7

Cook R N, Kennedy J L (1966) (eds.) *Proceedings of a Tri-State Conference on a Comprehensive Unified Land Data System (CULDATA)*. College of Law, University of Cincinatti

Cooke D F (1980) A review of geoprocessing systems and a look at their future. In: Krammer K, King J (eds.) *Computers in Local Government Urban and Regional Planning*. Auerbach Publishers Inc., Pennsauken, pp. (2.4.1) 1–16

Cooper M A R (1974) *Fundamentals of Survey Measurement and Analysis*. Crosby Lockwood Staples, London

Coote A M (1988) Current developments in field-based digital mapping systems at Ordnance Survey. *Proceedings of Mapping Awareness Conference*. Miles Arnold, Oxford

Copeland B J (1989) *Albemarle-Pamlico Esturine System: Preliminary Technical Analysis of Status and Trends*. Albemarle-Pamlico Study Report 89–13A. Albemarle-Pamlico Study Program, Raleigh North Carolina

Coppock J T (1988) The analogue to digital revolution: a view from an unreconstructed geographer. *The American Cartographer* **15** (3): 263–75

Coppock J T, Barritt M (1978) *Application of digital techniques to information systems for planning*. Consultants' report to the Scottish Development Department, Edinburgh

Coppock J T, Rhind D W (1991) The history of GIS. In: Maguire D J, Goodchild M F, Rhind D W (eds.) *Geographical Information Systems: principles and applications*. Longman, London, pp. 21–43, Vol 1

Corbett J P (1975) Topological principles in cartography. *Proceedings, International Symposium on Computer-Assisted Cartography, AUTOCARTO 2*. Reston, Virginia, US Department of Commerce, pp. 22–33

Corbett J P (1979) Topological principles in cartography. *Technical Paper* 48, US Bureau of the Census, Suitland (also published in *Proceedings of AUTOCARTO 4* 1975, pp. 22–33. American Congress on Survey and Mapping/ American Society for Photogrammetry, Washington DC)

Costanza R, Sklar F H, White M L (1990) Modeling coastal landscape dynamics. *Bioscience* **40**: 91–107

Couclelis H (1989) Geographically informed planning: requirements for a planning-relevant GIS. Presented to the North American meeting of the Regional Science Association, Santa Barbara, November

Coulson M R, Waters N (1990) Teaching the NCGIA curriculum in practice. In: Unwin D J (ed.) *GIS Education and Training, Collected Papers of a Conference, University of Leicester 20–21 March 1990*. Midlands Regional Research Laboratory, Leicester

Cowen D J (1983) Rethinking DIDS: the next generation of interactive colour mapping systems *Cartographica* **21**: 89–92

Cowen D J (1986) PC-CAD manages geographical data. *Computer Graphics World* **9** (7): 38–41

Cowen D J (1988) GIS versus CAD versus DBMS: what are the differences? *Photogrammetric Engineering and Remote Sensing* **54**: 1551–4

Cowen D J, Hodgson M, Santure L, White T (1986) Adding topological structure to PC-based CAD databases. *Proceedings of the 2nd International Symposium on Spatial Data Handling*. International Geographical Union, Columbus Ohio, pp. 132–41

Cowen D J, Mitchell L, Meyer W (1990) Industrial modeling using a Geographic Information System: the first step in developing an expert system for industrial site selection. *Proceedings of GIS/LIS '90*, Volume 1. ASPRS/ACSM/AAG/URISA/AM-FM, Bethesda Maryland, pp. 1–10

Cowen D J, Shinar W (1989) A GIS-based support system for economic development. *URISA Proceedings* **2**: 138–48

Cowen D J, Shirley W L (1991) Integrated planning information systems. In: Maguire D J, Goodchild M F, Rhind D W (eds.) *Geographical Information Systems: principles and applications*. Longman, London, pp. 297–310, Vol 2

Cowen D J, White T (1989) A versatile mapping system for the USGS 1:100 000 DLGs. *Proceedings of AUTOCARTO 9*. ACSM/ASPRS, Falls Church Virginia, pp. 705–14

Cox B J (1986) *Object-Oriented Programming: An evolutionary approach*. Addison-Wesley, Reading. Massachusetts. 274pp.

Cox C W (1976) Anchor effects and the estimation of graduated circles and squares. *The American Cartographer* **3**: 65–74

Cox N J, Aldred B K, Rhind D W (1980) A relational database system and a proposal for a geographical data type. *Geo-Processing* **1**: 217–29

Craig W J (1989) URISA's research agenda and the NCGIA. *Journal of the Urban and Regional Information Systems Association* **1** (1): 7–16

Crain I K (1990) Extremely large spatial information systems: a quantitative perspective. *Proceedings of the 4th International Symposium on Spatial Data Handling*, Volume 2. International Geographical Union, Columbus Ohio, pp. 632–41

Crain I K, MacDonald C L (1984) From land inventory to land management. *Cartographica* **21**: 40–6

Crapper P F (1980) Errors incurred in estimating an area of uniform land cover using Landsat. *Photogrammetric Engineering and Remote Sensing* **10**: 1295–301

Crapper P F, Walker P A, Nanninga P M (1986) Theoretical prediction of the effect of aggregation on grid cell data sets. *Geo-processing* **3**: 155–66

Crawley K J, Nitze R T (1989) One Hundred Million Connections. GIS/LIS for Public Utilities. *Proceedings of Surveying and Mapping '89*, Royal Institution of Chartered Surveyors, London, Paper F3

Cromley R G (1985) An LP relaxation procedure for annotating point features using interactive graphics. *Proceedings of AUTOCARTO 7*. ASPRS, Falls Church Virginia, pp. 127–32

Cromley R G (1986) A spatial allocation analysis of the point annotation problem. *Proceedings of the 2nd International Symposium on Spatial Data Handling*. International Geographical Union, Ohio, pp. 38–49

Croom F (1989) *Principles of Topology*. Saunders College Publishing, Philadelphia

Crossilla F (1986) Improving the outlier separability in geodetic networks according to the generalized orthomax criterion. *Manuscripta Geodaetica* **11**: 38–47

Croswell P L, Clark S R (1988) Trends in automated mapping and geographic information systems. *Photogrammetric Engineering and Remote Sensing* **54**: 1571–6

Cuddy S M, Laut P, Davis J R, Whigham P A, Goodspeed J, Duell T (1989) Modelling the environmental effects of training on a major Australian army base. *Proceedings SSA IMACS Biennial Conference on Modelling and Simulation, Canberra*

Curran P J, Hay A M (1986) The importance of measurement error for certain procedures in remote sensing at optical wavelengths. *Photogrammetric Engineering and Remote Sensing* **52**: 229–41

Curran P J, Williamson H D (1986) Sample size for ground and remotely sensed data. *Remote Sensing of Environment* **20**: 31–41

Cutter S L (1985) Rating places: a geographer's view on quality of life. *Resource Publications in Geography*. Association of American Geographers, Washington DC

Cuzick J, Edwards R (1990) Tests for spatial clustering of events for inhomogeneous populations *Journal of the Royal Statistical Society Series B* **52**: 73–104

Dacey M F (1970) Linguistic aspects of maps and geographic information. *Ontario Geography* **5**: 71–80
Dale M B, McBratney A B, Russell J S (1989) On the role of expert systems and numerical taxonomy in soil classification. *Journal of Soil Science* **40**: 223–34
Dale P F (1976) *Cadastral Surveys within the Commonwealth*. Her Majesty's Stationery Office, London
Dale P F (1988) Economic considerations in the development of land information systems. *Proceedings from the FIG Land Information Systems Workshop, Bali, Indonesia*, pp. 75–83
Dale P F (1990) All the world's a stage – but where are all the players? *Proceedings of National Mapping Awareness Conference*. Miles Arnold, Oxford, pp. 12.1–12.3
Dale P F (1990) Education in land information management. In: Unwin D J (ed.) *GIS Education and Training, Collected Papers of a Conference, University of Leicester 20–21 March 1990*. Midlands Regional Research Laboratory, Leicester, 6 pp.
Dale P F (1991) Land information systems. In: Maguire D J, Goodchild M F, Rhind D W (eds.) *Geographical Information Systems: principles and applications*. Longman, London, pp. 85–99, Vol 2
Dale P F, McLaughlin J D (1988) *Land Information Management – an introduction with special reference to cadastral problems in Third World countries*. Oxford University Press, Oxford
Dangermond J (1983) A classification of software components commonly used in geographic information systems. In: Peuquet D J, O'Callaghan J (eds.) *Design and Implementation of Computer Based Geographic Information Systems*. IGU Commission on Geographical Data Sensing and Data Processing, Amherst New York
Dangermond J (1986) The software toolbox approach to meeting the user's needs for GIS analysis. *Proceedings of the GIS Workshop, Atlanta, Georgia, 1–4 April 1986*, pp. 66–75
Dangermond J (1987) The maturing of GIS and a new age for geographic information modeling (GIMS). In: Aangeenbrug R T, Schiffman Y M (eds.) *International Geographic Information Systems (IGIS) Symposium, Arlington, Virginia*, Volume 2. ASPRS, Falls Church, pp. 55–67
Dangermond J (1988) A review of digital data commonly available and some of the practical problems of entering them into a GIS. *Proceedings of ACSM–ASPRS St Louis*. ACSM/ASPRS, Falls Church Virginia
Dangermond J (1988) A technical architecture for GIS. *Proceedings of GIS/LIS '88*. ACSM/ASPRS, Falls Church, pp. 561–70
Dangermond J (1989) The organizational impact of GIS technology. *ARC News* Summer: 25–6
Dangermond J (1991) The commercial setting of GIS. In: Maguire D J, Goodchild M F, Rhind D W (eds.) *Geographical Information Systems: principles and applications*. Longman, London, pp. 55–65, Vol 1
Dangermond J, Freedman C (1986) Findings regarding a conceptual model of a municipal database and implications for software design. *Geo-Processing* **3**: 31–49
Dangermond J, Freedman C, Chambers D (1986) Tongass National Forest natural resource management information study – a description of project methodology and recent findings. *Geo-Processing* **3**: 51–75
Dangermond J, Harnden E (1990) *Map Data Standardization*. Environmental Systems Research Institute, Redlands California
Dangermond J, Morehouse S (1987) Trends in computer hardware for geographic information systems. *Proceedings of AUTOCARTO 8*. ASPRS/ACSM, Falls Church: pp. 380–5
Dangermond J, Smith K L (1988) Geographic Information Systems and the revolution in cartography: the nature of the role played by a commercial organization. *The American Cartographer* **15** (3): 301–10
Danziger J N, Dulton W H, Kraemer K L (1982) *Computers and Politics: high technology in American local government*. Columbia University Press, New York
Dartington Institute (1986) *The Potential for Forestry on the Culm Measures Farms of south west England*. Dartington Institute, Dartington Devon
Date C J (1986) *An Introduction to Database Systems*. 2nd edn. Addison-Wesley, Reading Massachusetts
Davenport T H, Hammer M (1989) How executives can shape their company's information systems. *Harvard Business Review* **67** (2): 130–4
Davis D L, Elnicki R A (1984) User cognitive types for decision support systems. *Omega* **12**: 601–14
Davis F W, Dozier J (1990) Information analysis of a spatial database for ecological land classification. *Photogrammetric Engineering and Remote Sensing* **56** (5): 605–13
Davis F W, Dubayah R, Dozier J (1989) Covariance of greenness and terrain variables over the Konza Prairie. *Proceedings of IGARRS 89*, pp. 1322–5
Davis F W, Michaelsen J, Dubayah R, Dozier J (1990). Optimal terrain stratification for integrating ground data from FIFE. *Proceedings of the AMS Symposium on the First ISLSCP Field Experiment (FIFE)*. American Meteorological Society, Boston Massachusetts, pp. 11–15
Davis F W, Simonett D S (1991) GIS and remote sensing. In: Maguire D J, Goodchild M F, Rhind D W (eds.) *Geographical Information Systems: principles and applications*. Longman, London, pp. 191–213, Vol 1
Davis J C (1986) *Statistics and Data Analysis in Geology*, 2nd edn. Wiley, New York
Davis J R (1986) Giving directions: a voice interface to a direction giving program. *Proceedings, 1986 Conference, American Voice I/O Society*. September, pp. 77–84
Davis J R, Clark J L (1989) A selective bibliography of expert systems in natural resource management. *AI Applications in Natural Resource Management*. Moscow, Idaho

Davis J R, Grant I W (1987) ADAPT: a knowledge-based decision support system for producing zoning schemes. *Environment and Planning B* **14**: 53–66

Davis J R, Laut P (1989) An expert system to estimate trafficability in a remote region of Australia. *AI Applications in Natural Resource Management* **3** (1): 17–26

Davis J R, Nanninga P M, Clark R D S (1989) A decision support system for evaluating catchment policies. *Proceedings of the Conference on Computing in the Water Industry*, Melbourne, pp. 205–9

Davis J R, Schmandt C M (1989) The back seat driver: real time spoken driving directions. *Proceedings, First Vehicle Navigation & Information Systems Conference (VNIS '89)*. IEEE, New York, pp. 146–50

Davis J R, Whigham P A, Grant I W (1988) Representing and applying knowledge about spatial processes in environmental management. *AI Applications in Natural Resource Management* **2** (4): 17–25

Davis J S, Deter R S (1990) Hypermedia application: Whole Earth Decision Support System. *Information and Software Technology* **32** (7): 491–6

Dawson M (1989) Developing a sedimentological database on an Apple Macintosh II. *BP International Information Systems Services paper*

Day T, Muller J-P (1988) Quality assessment of digital elevation models produced by automatic stereo matchers from SPOT image pairs. *International Archives of Photogrammetry and Remote Sensing* **27** (B3): 148–59

DCDSTF (Digital Cartographic Data Standards Task Force) (1988) The proposed standard for digital cartographic data. *The American Cartographer* **15** (1): 9–140

De Floriani L, Falcidieno B, Pienovi C, Allen D, Nagy G (1986) A visibility-based model for terrain features. *Proceedings of the 2nd International Symposium on Spatial Data Handling*. International Geographical Union, Columbus Ohio, pp. 600–10

de Man E (1988) Establishing a geographical information system in relation to its use: a process of strategic choice. *International Journal of Geographical Information Systems* **2**: 245–61

Dear M (1978) Planning for mental health care: a reconsideration of public facility location theory. *International Regional Science Review* **3**: 93–111

Deering D (1989) Field measurements of bidirectional reflectance. In: Asrar G (ed.) *Theory and Applications of Optical Remote Sensing*. Wiley, New York, pp. 14–65

Demko G J, Hezlep W (1989) USSR: mapping the blank spots. *Focus* **39** (1): 20–1

Denham C, Rhind D W (1983) The 1981 Census and its results. In: Rhind D W (ed.) *A Census User's Handbook*. Methuen, London, pp. 17–88

Densham P J (1991) Spatial decision support systems. In: Maguire D J, Goodchild M F, Rhind D W (eds.) *Geographical Information Systems: principles and applications*. Longman, London, pp. 403–12, Vol 1

Densham P J, Armstrong M P (1987) A spatial decision support system for locational planning: design, implementation and operation. *Proceedings of AUTOCARTO 8*. ACSM/ASPRS, Bethesda Maryland, pp. 112–21

Densham P J, Goodchild M F (1989) Spatial decision support systems: a research agenda. *Proceedings of GIS/LIS '89*, Vol. 2. ACSM/ASPRS, Falls Church Virginia, pp. 707–16

Densham P J, Rushton G (1988) Decision support systems for locational planning. In: Golledge R, Timmermans H (eds.) *Behavioural Modelling in Geography and Planning*. Croom-Helm, London, pp. 56–90

Dent B D (1990) *Principles of Thematic Map Design*. Addison-Wesley, Reading Massachusetts

Denver L E, Phillips D C (1990) Stratigraphic geocellular modelling. *Geobyte* February: 45–7

Department of Health and Social Security (1989) *Working for Patients*. HMSO, London

Department of the Environment (DoE) (1971) Inter-departmental Committee, chaired by J. D. W. Janes. *Report of the Committee on the Ordnance Survey 1970–71*. Unpublished

Department of the Environment (DoE) (1972) *General Information Systems for Planning*, Department of the Environment, London

Department of the Environment (DoE) (1987) *Handling Geographic Information*. Report of the Committee of Enquiry chaired by Lord Chorley. HMSO, London

Department of the Environment (DoE) (1988) *Handling Geographic Information. The Government's response to the report of the Committee of Enquiry*. HMSO, London

Department of Trade and Industry (1990) *Profiting from Electronic Trading: the case study package*. HMSO, London

Devereux B J (1986) The integration of cartographic data stored in raster and vector formats. In: Blakemore M J (ed.) *Proceedings of AUTOCARTO London 1*. Royal Institution of Chartered Surveyors, London pp. 257–66

Devine H A, Field R C (1986) The gist of GIS. *Journal of Forestry* August, 17–22

Dewdney J C (1983) Censuses past and present. In: Rhind D W (Ed.) *A Census User's Handbook*. Methuen, London, pp. 1–15

Dewdney J C, Rhind D W (1986) The British and United States Censuses of Population. In: Pacione M (ed.) *Population Geography: progress and prospects*. Croom Helm, London, pp. 35–57

Dias H D (1987) Varying information needs for local and regional planning and their implications for planning. *Regional Development Dialogue* **8** (1): 24–8

Dias H D (1989) Initiatives in GIS applications at the Asian Institute of Technology. *Paper given to the International Conference on Geographical Information Systems: approaches for urban and regional planning*. Ciloto, Puncak, Indonesia

Diaz B M, Bell S B M (eds.) (1986) *Spatial Data Processing using Tesseral Methods (collected papers from Tesseral Workshops 1 and 2)*. NERC Unit for Thematic

Information Systems, Natural Environment Research Council, Swindon

Dickinson H J (1989) Techniques for establishing the value of geographic information and geographic information systems. *Proceedings of GIS/LIS '89.* ACSM/ASPRS, Falls Church, pp. 412–20

Dickinson H J, Calkins H W (1988) The economic evaluation of implementing a GIS. *International Journal of Geographical Information Systems* **2** (4): 307–27

Didier M (1990) *Utilité et valeur de l'Information Géographique.* CNIG Economica, Paris

Diello J, Kirk K, Callander J (1969) The development of an automated cartographic system. *Cartographic Journal* **6**: 9–17

Diepen C van, Wolf J, Keulen H van, Rappolt C (1989) WOFOST: a simulation model of crop production. *Soil Use and Management* **5**: 16–24

Diggle P J (1983) *Statistical Analysis of Spatial Point Patterns.* Academic Press, London

Dikau R (1989) The application of a digital relief model to landform analysis in geomorphology. In: Raper J F (ed.) *Three Dimensional Applications in Geographical Information Systems.* Taylor & Francis, London, pp. 51–77

Dimmick S (1985) *Pro-Fortran User Guide.* Oracle Corporation, Menlo Park California

Dixon J F, Openshaw S, Wymer C (1987) A proposal and specification for a geographical analysis sub-routine library. *Research Report 3 Northern Regional Research Laboratory.* NRRL, Department of Geography University of Newcastle, Newcastle-upon-Tyne

Dobkin D, Silver D (1988) Recipes for geometry and numerical analysis, part 1: an empirical study. *Proceedings of Fourth ACM Symposium on Computer Geometry*, pp. 93–105

Dobson M W (1986) Spatial decision support systems for early warning of disaster driven social emergencies. *Proceedings of the 2nd International Symposium on Spatial Data Handling* International Geographical Union, Williamsville New York, pp. 332–48

Dobson M W (1988) Digital cartography in the world of commercial publishing. *Proceedings of the 3rd International Symposium on Spatial Data Handling.* International Geographical Union, Columbus, Ohio, pp. 1–8

Doerschler J S (1985) Map data production for an expert name placement system. *Technical Report IPL-TR-073.* Image Processing Laboratory Rensselaer Polytechnic Institute, Troy

Doerschler J S (1985) Data structures required for overlap detection in an expert map name placement system. *Technical Report IPL-TR-077.* Image Processing Laboratory Rensselaer Polytechnic Institute, Troy

Doerschler J S (1987) A rule-based system for dense-map name placement. *Technical Report SR-005.* CAIP Centre, Rutgers University 08855–1390

Doerschler J S, Freeman H (1989) An expert system for dense-map name placement. *Proceedings of AUTOCARTO 9.* ACSM/ASPRS, Falls Church Virginia, pp. 215–24

DOI (1989) *Managing Our Land Information Resources.* Bureau of Land Management, US Department of the Interior, Washington DC

Dolk D R (1986) Data as models: an approach to implementing model management. *Decision Support Systems* **2**: 73–80

Dondis D A (1984) *A Primer of Visual Literacy.* MIT Press, Cambridge Massachusetts

Dougenik J A, Chrisman N R, Niemeyer D R (1985) An algorithm to construct continuous area cartograms. *Professional Geographer* **37**: 75–81

Douglas D H (1986) Experiments to locate ridges and channels to create a new type of digital elevation model. *Cartographica* **23** (4): 29–61

Douglas D H, Peucker T K (1973) Algorithms for the reduction of the number of points required to represent a digitized line or its caricature. *The Canadian Cartographer* **10**: 112–22

Dowers S, Gittings B M, Sloan T M, Waugh T C, Healey R G (1990) Analysis of GIS performance on parallel architectures and workstation-server systems. *Proceedings of GIS/LIS '90.* ASPRS/ACSM/AAG/URISA/AM-FM, Bethesda, pp. 555–61

Dowman I, Muller J P (1986) Real-time photogrammetric input versus digitized maps: accuracy, timeliness and cost. In: Blakemore M J (ed.) *Proceedings of AUTOCARTO LONDON*, Vol. 1. Royal Institution of Chartered Surveyors, London, pp. 538–43

Downs A (1967) A realistic look at the final payoffs from urban data systems. *Public Administrations Review* **27** (3): 204–10

Dowson E, Sheppard V L O (1952) *Land Registration.* Her Majesty's Stationery Office, London

Doytsher Y, Shmutter B (1981) Transformation of conformal projections for graphical purposes. *Canadian Surveyor* **35**: 395–404

Dozier J (1989) Spectral signature of alpine snow cover from the Landsat Thematic Mapper. *Remote Sensing of Environment* **28**: 9–22

Dozier J, Strahler A H (1983) Ground investigations in support of remote sensing. In: Colwell R N (ed.) *Manual of Remote Sensing.* American Society of Photogrammetry, Falls Church Virginia, pp. 959–86

Driessen P M (1989) Quantified land evaluation: consistency in time and space. In: Bouma J, Bregt A K (eds.) *Land Qualities in Space and Time. Proceedings of a Symposium organised by the International Society of Soil Science (ISSS), Wageningen, The Netherlands, 22–26 August 1988.* PUDOC, Wageningen, pp. 3–14

Drummond J, Bosma M (1989) A review of low-cost scanners. *International Journal of Geographical Information Systems* **3** (1): 83–95

Drysdale R L (1979) *Generalized Voronoi Diagrams and Geometric Searching.* Unpublished PhD dissertation, Department of Computer Science, Stanford University

Dubayah R, Dozier J, Davis F W (1990) Topographic

distribution of clear-sky radiation over the Konza Prairie, Kansas. *Water Resources Research* **26** (4): 679–90

Dueker K J (1974) Urban geocoding. *Annals of the Association of American Geographers* **64**: 318–25

Dueker K J (1979) Land resource information systems: a review of fifteen years experience. *Geo-Processing* **1**: 105–28

Dueker K J (1979) Land resource information systems: spatial and attribute resolution issues. *Proceedings of AUTOCARTO 4* Vol. 2. ASPRS, Falls Church, pp. 328–36

Dueker K J (1980) An approach to integrated information systems for planning. In: Krammer K, King J (eds.) *Computers in Local Government Urban and Regional Planning*. Auerbach Publishers Inc., Pennsauken, pp.(2.1.2) 1–12

Dueker K J (1985) Geographic information systems: towards a georelational structure. *Proceedings of AUTOCARTO 7*. ASPRS/ACSM, Falls Church, Virginia, 172–75

Dueker K J (1988) Urban applications of geographical information systems: a grouping into three levels of resolution. *URISA Proceedings*, Volume 2, pp. 104–9

Duffield B S, Coppock J T (1975) The delineation of recreational landscapes: the role of computer-based information systems. *Transactions of the Institute of British Geographers* **66**: 141–8

Duggin M J (1985) Factors limiting the discrimination and quantification of terrestrial features using remotely sensed radiance. *International Journal of Remote Sensing* **6**: 3–27

Duke J (1983) Interactive video: implications for education and training. *CET Working Paper 22*. Council for Educational Technology, London

Dumanski J B, Kloosterman B, Brandon S E (1975) Concepts, objectives and structure of the Canadian Soil Information System. *Canadian Journal of Soil Science* **55**: 181–7

Dumanski J B, Onofrei C (1989) Crop yield models for agricultural land evaluation. *Soil Use and Management* **5**: 9–15

Dunn C, Newton D (1989) Notes on shortest path algorithms for GIS. *North West Regional Research Laboratory Research Report 3*. North West Regional Research Laboratory, Lancaster

Dutton G (ed.) (1979) *First International Study Symposium on Topological Data Structures for Geographic Information Systems*. Addison-Wesley, Reading, Massachusetts

Dutton G (1989) The fallacy of coordinates. *Multiple Representations. NCGIA Technical Paper* **89–3** National Center for Geographical Information Analysis, Santa Barbara California, pp. 44–8

Earth System Sciences Committee (1988) *Earth System Science, a closer view*. NASA, Washington DC

Eastman J R (1988) *IDRISI: a grid-based geographic analysis system*. Graduate School of Geography Clark University, Massachusetts

Eather P T (1986) The HUB – the Queensland approach to land information system development. *URPIS – Proceedings of the Urban and Regional Planning Information Systems Annual Conferences*, Volume 16. Australasian Urban and Regional Information Systems Association Inc., Sydney, pp. 198–208

Ebdon D (1985) *Statistics in Geography: a practical approach*, 2nd edn. Basil Blackwell, Oxford

Ebinger L R, Goulette A M (1989) Automated names placement in a non-interactive environment. *Proceedings of AUTOCARTO 9*. ACSM/ASPRS, Falls Church Virginia, 205–14

Ebinger L R, Goulette A M (1990) Noninteractive automated names placement for the 1990 decennial census. *Cartography and Geographic Information Systems* **17** (1): 69–78

Ebner H, Reinhardt W, Hössler R (1988) Generation, management and utilization of high fidelity digital terrain models. *International Archives of Photogrammetry and Remote Sensing* **27** (B11): III556–65

Edelsbrunner H (1987) *Algorithms for Computational Geometry*. Springer-Verlag, Heidelberg

Edney P, Cavill M (1989) The Melbourne Knowledge Precinct GIS pilot project. *URPIS – Proceedings of the Urban and Regional Planning Information Systems Annual Conferences*. Volume 17. Australasian Urban and Regional Information Systems Association Inc., Sydney, pp. 325–31

Edralin J (1990) Conference Report. *International Conference on Geographical Information Systems: Application for Urban Regional Planning*. Nagoya, UNCRD

Egenhofer M J (1984) Implementation of MAPQUERY, a query language for land information systems (in German). *Report 79*. Institute for Geodesy and Photogrammetry, Swiss Federal Institute of Technology (ETH), Zurich

Egenhofer M J (1989) A formal definition of binary topological relationships. In: Litwin W, Schek H-J (eds.) *Third International Conference on Foundations of Data Organization and Algorithms (FODO), Paris* (Lecture Notes in Computer Science, Volume 367). Springer-Verlag, New York, pp. 457–72

Egenhofer M J (1989) *Spatial query languages*. Unpublished PhD Thesis, University of Maine, Orono

Egenhofer M J (1989) Spatial SQL: a spatial query language. *Report 103*. Department of Surveying Engineering, Orono Maine

Egenhofer M J, Frank A U (1987) Object oriented databases: database requirements for GIS. In: Aangeenbrug R T, Schiffman Y M (eds.) *International Geographic Information Systems (IGIS) Symposium, Arlington, Virginia II*. ASPRS, Falls Church Virginia, pp. 189–211

Egenhofer M J, Frank A U (1988) Designing object-oriented query languages for GIS: human interface aspects. *Proceedings of the 3rd International Symposium on Spatial Data Handling*. International Geographical Union, Columbus Ohio, pp. 79–96

Egenhofer M J, Frank A U (1988) Towards a spatial query language: user interface considerations. *Proceedings, 14th International Conference on Very Large Data Bases, Los Angeles.* Morgan Kaufmann, Los Altos, California, pp. 124–33

Egenhofer M J, Frank A U (1990) Lobster: combining AI and database techniques for GIS. *Photogrammetric Engineering and Remote Sensing* 56 (6): 919–26

Egenhofer M J, Frank A U, Jackson J (1989) A topological data model for spatial databases. In: Buchmann A, Gunther O, Smith T, Wang Y (eds.) *Symposium on the Design and Implementation of Large Spatial Databases* (Lecture Notes in Computer Science, Volume 409). Springer-Verlag, New York, pp. 271–86

Egenhofer M J, Herring J R (1991) High-level spatial data structures for GIS. In: Maguire D J, Goodchild M F, Rhind D W (eds.) *Geographical Information Systems: principles and applications.* Longman, London, pp. 227–37, Vol 1

Egger G (1990) Cost-effective automated data conversion using SysScan's (A)DC and GEOREC. *Proceedings of FIG 90*

Ehlers M (1989) Remote sensing and geographic information systems: towards integrated spatial information processing. *Proceedings of IGARRS 89*, pp. 63–6

Ehlers M, Edwards G, Bedard Y (1989) Integration of remote sensing with geographic information systems: a necessary evolution. *Photogrammetric Engineering and Remote Sensing* 55 (11): 1619–27

Eichhorn G (1981) Das FIG-Symposium in Darmstadt – Eine Zusammenfassung. *Proceedings of FIG XVI Congress, Montreux*, pp. 304.1/1–9

Elachi C (1987) *Introduction to the Physics and Techniques of Remote Sensing.* Wiley, New York

Ellis H (1985) Twenty years of data analysis. In: Holloway S (ed.) *Data Analysis in Practice.* Database Specialist Group, The British Computer Society, London, pp. 99–120

Ellis M Y (1978) *Coastal Mapping Handbook.* United States Government Printing Office, Washington DC

Enderle G, Grave M, Lillehagen F (1986) *Advances in Computer Graphics*, Vol. 1. Springer-Verlag, New York

Englund E, Sparks A (1988) *GEO-EAS User's Guide.* Environmental Monitoring Systems Laboratory, Office of Research and Development, Environmental Protection Agency, Las Vegas, Nevada

Eos Science Steering Committee (1987) *Earth Observing System Volume II. From pattern to process: the strategy of the Earth Observing System.* National Aeronautics and Space Administration, Washington DC

EPA (1987) *Sharing Data for Environmental Results.* State/EPA Data Management Program Project Report 1987. United States Environmental Protection Agency, Washington

Epstein E F (1987) Litigation over information: the use and misuse of maps. In: Aangeenbrug R T, Schiffman Y M (eds.) *International Geographic Information Systems (IGIS) Symposium, Arlington, Virginia*, Vol. I. NASA, Washington DC, pp. 177–84

Epstein E F (1988) Legal and institutional aspects of global databases. In: Mounsey H M, Tomlinson R F (eds.) *Building Databases for Global Science.* Taylor & Francis, London, pp. 10–30

Epstein E F (1991) Legal aspects of GIS. In: Maguire D J, Goodchild M F, Rhind D W (eds.) *Geographical Information Systems: principles and applications.* Longman, London, pp. 489–502, Vol 1

Epstein E F, Duchesneau T D (1984) *Use and Value of a Geodetic Reference System.* Federal Geodetic Control Committee National Oceanic and Atmospheric Administration, Rockville Maryland

Epstein E F, Roitman H (1987) Liability for information. *Proceedings of the Urban and Regional Information Systems Association*, Vol 4. URISA, Washington DC, pp. 115–25

ESRI (1989) *ARC/INFO V5.0 Users Guide*, Volumes I and II. ESRI Inc., Redlands California

ESRI (1989) Integration of geographic information technologies. *ARC News* Winter: 24–5

ESRI (1989) *Network Users Guide.* Environmental Systems Research Institute, Redlands California

ESRI (1990) *ARC News* Spring. ESRI, Redlands California

ESRI (1990) *Understanding GIS – the ARC/INFO Method.* Environmental Systems Research Institute, Redlands California

ESRI (1990) ESRI, IBM, and HTE develop interactive link between ARC/INFO and IBM AS/400 Parcel Management System. *ARC News* Winter: 30

ESSC (1988) *Earth System Science : a program for global change.* Report prepared by the Earth System Sciences Committee for the National Aeronautics and Space Administration, Washington DC.

Estes J E, Bredekamp J H (1988) Activities associated with global databases in the National Aeronautics and Space Administration. In: Mounsey H M (ed.) *Building Databases for Global Science.* Taylor & Francis, London, pp. 251–69

Estes J E, Hajic E J, Tinney L R (1983) Manual and digital analysis in the visible and infrared regions. In: Simonett D S, Ulaby F T (eds.) *Manual of Remote Sensing*, 2nd edn. Vol. 1. American Society of Photogrammetry, Falls Church Virginia, 987–1123

Estes J E, McGwire K E, Fletcher G E, Foresman T W (1987) Coordinating hazardous waste management activities using GIS *International Journal of Geographical Information Systems* 1: 359–77

Estes J E, Sailer C, Tinney L R (1986) Applications of artificial intelligence techniques to remote sensing. *Professional Geographer* 38: 133–41

ETAK (1988) *ETAK MapEngine, Programmers Guide.* ETAK, Menlo Park California

Evans I S (1972) General geomorphometry, derivatives of altitude, and descriptive statistics. In: Chorley R J (ed.)

Spatial Analysis in Geomorphology. Methuen, London, pp. 17–90

Evans I S (1979) *An integrated system of terrain analysis and slope mapping. Final report on DA-ERO-591-73-G0040: Statistical characterisation of altitude matrices by computer*. Department of Geography, University of Durham

Evans I S (1980) An integrated system of terrain analysis and slope mapping. *Zeitschrift fur Geomorphologie (supplements)* **36**: 274–95

Everett J, Simonett D S (1976) Principles, concepts and philosophical problems. In: Lintz J L, Simonett D S (eds.) *Remote Sensing of Environment*. Addison-Wesley, Reading Massachusetts, pp. 85–127

Experimental Cartography Unit (1971) *Automatic Cartography and Planning*. Architectural Press, London

Eyre L A (1989) JAMGIS, the first Jamaican Government comprehensive multi-data geographical information system: achievements and problems. *International Journal of Geographical Information Systems* 3 (4): 363–71

Eyton J R (1984) Raster contouring. *Geo-Processing* **2**: 221–42

Fagin R (1979) Normal forms and relational database operations. *Proceedings of the ACM SIG-MOD International Conference on Management of Data*, pp. 153–60

Fandrei G (1989) *Descriptive Characteristics of the Seven Eco-regions in Minnesota*. Minnesota Pollution Control Agency. Draft Report, State of Minnesota, St Paul

Fanon F (1963) *The Wretched of the Earth*. New York, Grove Press

Fanshawe J (1985) *Global Resource Information Database*. UNEP Global Environment Monitoring System, Nairobi

FAO (1976) *A Framework for Land Evaluation*. FAO Soils Bulletin 32, Rome

Federal Interagency Coordinating Committee on Digital Cartography (1989) *Co-ordination of Digital Cartographic Activities in the Federal Government*. FICCDC

Fedra K, Reitsma R (1989) Decision support and geographical information systems. *Proceedings of the GIS Summer Institute*. Kluwer, Amsterdam

Feuchtwanger M (1989) Geographic logical database model requirements. *Proceedings of AUTOCARTO 9*. ACSM/ASPRS, Falls Church Virginia, pp. 599–609.

Finch S, Rhind D W (1986) Cartographic and remote sensing digital databases in the UK. *British Library Information Guide 6*. British Library, London

Finch S (1987) *Towards a national digital topographic data base*. Unpublished PhD thesis, University of London.

Fisher P F (1987) The nature of soil data in GIS: error or uncertainty. In: Aangeenbrug R T, Schiffman Y M (eds.) *Proceedings of International Geographic Information Systems (IGIS) Symposium: the research agenda*, Vol. 3. NASA, Washington DC, pp. 307–18.

Fisher P F (1989) Geographical information system software for university education and research. *Journal of Geography in Higher Education* **13**: 69–78

Fisher P F (1989) Knowledge-based approaches to determining and correcting areas of unreliability in geographic databases. In: Goodchild M F, Gopal S (eds.) *Accuracy of Spatial Databases*. Taylor & Francis, London, pp. 45–54

Fisher P F (1991) Spatial data sources and data problems. In: Maguire D J, Goodchild M F, Rhind D W (eds.) *Geographical Information Systems: principles and applications*. Longman, London, pp. 175–89, Vol 1

Fisher P F, Pathirana S (1989) Evaluation of fuzzy membership of land cover classes in suburban areas of north-east Ohio. *ASPRS Technical Papers, 1989 ASPRS/ACSM Fall Convention*. ASPRS, Falls Church VA, pp. 125–32

Fisher P F, Pearson M P, Clarke S R, Ragg J M (1987) Computer program to assist the automation of soil description. *Soil Use and Management* **3**: 26–31

Fisher T, Wales R Q (1991) 3-D solid modelling of geo-objects using non-uniform rational B-splines (NURBS). In: Turner A K (ed.) *Three Dimensional Modelling with Geoscientific Information Systems*. Kluwer, Dordrecht

Fitzpatrick-Lins K (1978) Accuracy and consistency comparisons of land use and land cover maps from high-altitude photographs and Landsat multispectral imagery. *Journal of Research, US Geological Survey* **6** (1): 23–40

Fitzpatrick-Lins K (1981) Comparison of sampling procedures and data analysis for a land use and land cover map. *Photogrammetric Engineering and Remote Sensing* **47**: 343–51

Flew A G (1989) *An Introduction to Western Philosophy: ideas and argument from Plato to Popper*. Thames and Hudson, New York

Flowerdew R (1991) Spatial data integration In: Maguire D J, Goodchild M F, Rhind D W (eds.) *Geographical Information Systems: principles and applications*. Longman, London, pp. 375–87, Vol 1

Flowerdew R, Banting D (1989) Evaluating the potential role of GIS for a market analysis company. *North West Regional Research Laboratory, Research Report 2*. NWRRL, Lancaster

Flowerdew R, Green M (1989) Statistical methods for inference between incompatible zonal systems. In: Goodchild M F, Gopal S (eds.) *Accuracy of Spatial Databases*. Taylor & Francis, London, pp. 239–47

Flowerdew R, Openshaw S (1987) A review of the problems of transferring data from one set of areal units to another incompatible set. *Northern Regional Research Laboratory, Research Report 4*. NRRL, Lancaster and Newcastle-upon-Tyne

Flynn J J (1990) 3-D computing geosciences update. *Geobyte* February: 33–5

Foley J D (1987) Interfaces for advanced computing. *Scientific American* **257** (4): 83–90

Foley J D, van Dam A, Feiner S K, Hughes J F (1990) *Computer Graphics: Principles and Practice*, 2nd edn. Addison-Wesley, Reading Massachusetts

Foley M E (1988) Beyond the bits, bytes and black boxes – institutional issues in successful LIS/GIS management.

Proceedings of GIS/LIS '88. ACSM/ASPRS, Falls Church, pp. 608–17

Forshaw M R B, Haskell A, Miller P F, Stanley D J, Townshend J R G (1983) Spatial resolution of remotely sensed imagery: a review paper. *International Journal of Remote Sensing* **4**: 497–520

Foster M J, Shand P J (eds.) (1990) *The Association for Geographic Information Yearbook 1990*. Taylor & Francis and Miles Arnold, London

Fournier A, Fussel D, Carpenter L (1982) Computer rendering of stochastic models. *Communications of the ACM* **25** (6): 371–84

Frank A U (1981) Applications of DBMS to land information systems. In: Zaniolo C, Delobel C (eds.) *Proceedings of Seventh International Conference on Very Large Data Bases, Cannes, France*. Morgan Kaufmann Publishers, Los Altos, pp. 448–53

Frank A U (1982) MAPQUERY – database query language for retrieval of geometric data and its graphical representation. *ACM SIGGRAPH* **16** (3): 199–207

Frank A U (1984) Computer assisted cartography – graphics or geometry. *Journal of Surveying Engineering* **110** (2): 159–68

Frank A U (1984) Extending a network database with PROLOG. *Proceedings of the First International Workshop on Expert Database Systems, Kiawah Island, SC, October*, pp. 665–74

Frank A U (1984) Requirements for database systems suitable to manage large spatial databases. *Proceedings of the 1st International Symposium on Spatial Data Handling*, Volume 1. International Geographical Union, Zurich Irchel, pp. 38–60

Frank A U (1986) Integrating mechanisms for storage and retrieval of land data. *Surveying and Mapping* **46**: 107–21

Frank A U (1988) Requirements for a database management system for a GIS. *Photogrammetric Engineering and Remote Sensing* **54** (11): 1557–64

Frank A U, Barrera R (1990) The fieldtree: a data structure for geographic information systems. In: Buchmann A, Gunther O, Smith T R, Wang Y-F (eds.) *Design and Implementation of Large Spatial Databases*. Springer-Verlag, New York, pp. 29–44

Frank A U, Buyong T B (1991) Geometry for 3D GIS in geoscientific applications. In: Turner A K (ed.) *Three Dimensional Modelling with Geoscientific Information Systems*. Kluwer, Dordrecht

Frank A U, Kuhn W (1986) Cell graph: a provable correct method for the storage of geometry. *Proceedings of the 2nd International Symposium on Spatial Data Handling, Seattle*. International Geographical Union, Williamsville New York, pp. 411–36

Frank A U, Mark D M (1991) Language issues for GIS. In: Maguire D J, Goodchild M F, Rhind D W (eds.) *Geographical Information Systems: principles and applications*. Longman, London, pp. 147–63, Vol 1

Frank A U, Palmer B, Robinson V (1986) Formal methods for the accurate definition of some fundamental terms in physical geography. In: Marble D (ed.) *Proceedings of Second International Symposium on Spatial Data Handling, Seattle*. International Geographical Union, Ohio, pp. 583–99

Franklin J, Logan T L, Woodcock C E, Strahler A H (1986) Coniferous forest classification and inventory using Landsat and digital terrain data. *IEEE Transactions on Geoscience and Remote Sensing* **GE-24**: 139–46

Franklin S E, Peddle D R, Moulton J R (1989) Spectral/geomorphometric discrimination and mapping of terrain: a study in Gros Morne National Park. *Canadian Journal of Remote Sensing* **15**: 28–42

Franklin W R (1984) Cartographic errors symptomatic of underlying algebra problems. In: *Proceedings of the first International Symposium on Spatial Data Handling, Zurich*. International Geographical Union, Zurich Irchel, pp. 190–208

Franklin W R (1990) Calculating map overlay polygon areas without explicitly calculating the polygons – implementation. *Proceedings of the 4th International Symposium on Spatial Data Handling*. Zurich International Geographical Union, Columbus Ohio, pp. 151–60

Franklin Wm R (1991) Computer systems and low-level data structures for GIS. In: Maguire D J, Goodchild M F, Rhind D W (eds.) *Geographical Information Systems: principles and applications*. Longman, London, pp. 215–25, Vol 1

Franklin W R, Chandrasekhar N, Kankanhalli M, Akman V, Wu P Y F (1990) Efficient geometric operations for CAD. In Wozny M J, Turner J U, Preiss K (eds.) *Geometric Modeling for Product Engineering*. Elsevier, Amsterdam, pp. 485–98

Franklin W R, Chandrasekhar N, Kankanhalli M, Seshan M, Akman V (1988) Efficiency of uniform grids for intersection detection on serial and parallel machines. In: Magnenat-Thalmann N, Thalmann D (eds.) *New Trends in Computer Graphics (Proceedings, Computer Graphics International '88)*. Springer-Verlag, New York

Franklin W R, Chandrasekhar N, Kankanhalli M, Sun D, Zhou M-C, Wu P Y F (1989) Uniform grids: a technique for intersection detection on serial and parallel machines. *Proceedings of AUTOCARTO 9*. ASPRS/ACSM, Bethesda Maryland, pp. 100–9

Franklin W R, Wu P Y F, Samaddar S, Nichols M (1986) Geometry in prolog. In: Kunii T (ed.) *Advanced Computer Graphics, Proceedings of Computer Graphics Tokyo '86*, pp. 71–8

Franklin W R, Wu P Y F (1987) A polygon overlay system in PROLOG. *Proceedings of AUTOCARTO 8*. ASPRS/ACSM, Falls Church Virginia, pp. 97–106

Fraser-Robinson J (1989) *The Secrets of Effective Direct Mail*. McGraw-Hill, New York

Freedom of Information Act (1966) As amended. *5 USCA §552(a)(3)*

Freedom of Information Act (1966) As amended. *5 USCA §552(b)(1–9)*

Freeman H (1991) Computer name placement. In: Maguire D J, Goodchild M F, Rhind D W (eds.)

Geographical Information Systems: principles and applications. Longman, London, pp. 445–56, Vol 1
Freeman H, Ahn J (1984) AUTONAP – an expert system for automatic name placement. *Proceedings of the 1st International Symposium on Spatial Data Handling.* Universitat Zurich-Irchel, Zurich, pp. 544–69
Freeman H, Ahn J (1987) On the problem of placing names in a geographic map. *International Journal of Pattern Recognition and Artificial Intelligence* **1** (1): 121–40
Freeman J (1975) The modelling of spatial relations. *Computer Graphics and Image Processing* **4**: 156–71
French J R (1989) Hydrodynamics and sedimentation in a macrotidal salt marsh, north Norfolk, England. Unpublished PhD Thesis, University of Cambridge, England
French R (1986) Automobile navigation: where is it going? *IEEE Position Location and Navigation Symposium, Las Vegas*
Friedman L M (1984) *American Law.* Norton, New York
Fritsch D (1990) Towards three dimensional data structures in geographic information systems. *Proceedings of the EGIS '90,* pp. 335–45
Frost & Sullivan, Inc. (1989) *The U.S. Non-Entertainment Automotive Electronics Market.* Frost & Sullivan, New York
Fulton P N, Ingold J H (1989) Highlights of geographic coverage and content for the 1990 census data products program. In: Frazier J W, Epstein B J, Schoolmaster F A (eds.) *Papers and Proceedings of Applied Geography Conferences,* Vol. 12. pp. 215–17

Gaal G (1988) Exploration target selection by integration of geodata using statistical and image processing techniques: an example from Central Finland. *Geological Survey of Finland, Report of Investigation* **80**: 156 pp.
Gahegan M N, Hogg J (1986) A pilot geographical information system based on linear quadtrees and a relational database for regional analysis. In: Diaz B M, Bell S B M (eds.) *Spatial Data Processing Using Tesseral Methods.* Natural Environment Research Council, Swindon, p. 213–32
Gahegan M N, Roberts S A (1988) An intelligent, object-oriented geographical information system. *International Journal of Geographical Information Systems* **2**: 101–10
Gaits G M (1969) Thematic mapping by computer. *Cartographic Journal* **6**: 50–68
Gallaire H, Minker J, Nicolas J (1984) Logic and databases: a deductive approach. *ACM Computing Surveys* **16**: 153–85
Gamezo M U, Rubakhin V F (1964) The role of spatial concepts in map reading and the interpretation of aerial photographs. In: Ananyev B G, Lomov B F (eds.) *Problems of Spatial Perception and Spatial Concepts.* (Technical Translation F-164). NASA, Washington, DC
Gardiner V (1982) Stream networks and digital cartography. *Cartographica* **19** (2): 38–44
Gardiner-Hill R C (1971) Automated cartography in the Ordnance Survey. *Proceedings of the Conference of Commonwealth Survey Officers.* Cambridge, August 1971. Foreign and Commonwealth Office. Paper E3, pp. 235–41
Gardiner-Hill R C (1972) *Professional Paper New Series No. 23.* Ordnance Survey, Southampton
Gardiner-Hill R C (1974) The cosmetics of computer cartography. *Proceedings of the 7th International Conference on Cartography.* International Cartographic Association, Madrid
Garey M R, Johnson D S (1979) *Computers and Intractibility: a guide to the theory of incompleteness.* Freeman, San Francisco
Gargantini I (1982) An effective way to represent quadtrees. *Communications of the ACM* **25** (12): 905–10
Gargantini I (1991) Modelling natural objects via octrees. In: Turner A K (ed.) *Three Dimensional Modelling with Geoscientific Information Systems.* Kluwer, Dortrecht
Garner B J (1986) Geographical information systems technology at the University of New South Wales. *AURISA News* March/June: 3–5
Garnsworthy J (1990) The Tradeable Information Initiative. In: Foster M J, Shand P J (eds.) *The Association for Geographic Information Yearbook 1990.* Taylor & Francis, London, pp. 106–8
Gateaud J (1988) The use of cartography databases in multi-purpose utility applications – an experience report. *Proceedings of AM/FM International – European Division Conference Montreux.* AM/FM European Division, PO Box 6, CH4005, Basel, Switzerland, pp. 15–18
Gatrell A C (1983) *Distance and Space: a geographical perspective.* Oxford University Press, Oxford
Gatrell A C (1991) Concepts of space and geographical data. In: Maguire D J, Goodchild M F, Rhind D W (eds.) *Geographical Information Systems: principles and applications.* Longman, London, pp. 119–34, Vol 1
Gatrell A C, Vincent P (1990) Managing natural and technological hazards: the role of GIS. *Regional Research Laboratory Initiative Discussion Paper 7.* RRL Initiative, Sheffield University
Gault I, Peutherer D (1990) Developing geographical information systems in local government in the UK: case studies from Birmingham City Council and Strathclyde Regional Council. In: Worrell L (ed.) *Geographic Information Systems: developments and applications.* Belhaven, London, pp. 109–32
Gaydos L, Newland W L (1978) Inventory of land use and land cover of the Puget Sound region using Landsat digital data. *US Geological Survey Journal of Research* **6**: 807–14
Geoffrion A M (1983) Can OR/MS evolve fast enough? *Interfaces* **13**: 10–25
Geographical Survey Institute (ed.) (1989) *Digital Mapping.* Kashima Shuppankai, Tokyo
Getis A, Boots B (1978) *Models of Spatial Processes.* University Press, Cambridge
Giblin P (1977) *Graphs, Surfaces and Homology.* Chapman and Hall, London
Gibson R J (1974) The production of 1:10,000 scale mapping from large scale database. In: Wilford-Brickwood, Bertrand and van Zuylen (eds.) *Working*

Group Oceanic Cartography Commission III. International Cartographic Association, Enschede, pp. 121-32

Gibson W (1984) *Neuromancer* Ace Science Fiction.

Giles R H (1987) The creation, uses and demise of a Virginia USA Geographical Information System. *Proceedings of the International Geographical Union GIS Workshop Beijing, China*. IGU, pp. 507-24

Gill A (1976) *Applied Algebra for the Computer Sciences*. Prentice-Hall, Englewood Cliffs New Jersey

Gilmartin P P (1981) The interface of cognitive and psychological research in cartography. *Cartographica* **18** (3): 9-20

Gilmartin P P (1981) Influence of map context on circle perception. *Annals of the Association of American Geographers* **71**: 253-8

Giltrap D J (1984) MIDGE – a microcomputer soil information system. In: Burrough P A, Bie S W (eds.) *Soil Information Systems Technology*. PUDOC, Wageningen, pp. 112-19

Ginzberg M J, Stohr E A (1981) Decision support systems: issues and perspectives. In: Ginzberg M J, Reitman W, Stohr E A (eds.) *Decision Support Systems*. North-Holland, New York

Girard M-C (ed.) (1981) *Proceedings of the International Society of Soil Science Working Group on Soil Information Systems Colloquium, 14-17 Sept. 1981, Paris*. Institut National Agronomique, Paris, Grignon (3 volumes). Departement des Sols Nos 4, 5, 6

GISWorld (1990) *GIS Software Survey 1990*. GISWorld Inc., Fort Collins Colorado

GISWorld (1990) *GIS Technology '90: results of the 1990 GISWorld geographic information systems survey*. GISWorld, Fort Collins Colorado, 16 pp.

Gittings B (1989) Education and training – the missing link. In: Shand P, Moore R (eds.) *The Association for Geographic Information Yearbook*. Taylor & Francis and Miles Arnold, London, pp. 323-4

Gittings B, Mounsey H M (1989) GIS and LIS training in Britain: the present situation. *Proceedings of the First National Conference of the Association for Geographic Information, 'GIS as a Corporate Resource'*. AGI, Birmingham England, pp. 4.4.1-4.4.4

Goddard Space Flight Center (1984) Earth Observing System: Science and Mission Requirements, Working Group Report, Volume H 1. *NASA Goddard Space Flight Center Technical Memorandum 86129*. National Aeronautics and Space Administration, Greenbelt Maryland

Goel N S (1989) Inversion of canopy reflectance models for estimation of biophysical parameters from reflectance data. In: Asrar G (ed.) *Theory and Applications of Optical Remote Sensing*. Wiley, New York, pp. 205-51

Goetz A F H (1989) Spectral remote sensing in geology. In: Asrar G (ed.) *Theory and Applications of Optical Remote Sensing*. Wiley, New York, pp. 491-526

Gold C, Cormack S (1987) Spatially ordered networks and topographic reconstructions. *International Journal of Geographical Information Systems* **1** (2): 137-48

Goldberg A (1984) *Smalltalk-80: the interactive programming environment*. Addison-Wesley, Reading Massachusetts

Goldberg M, Alvo M, Karam G (1984) The analysis of LANDSAT imagery using an expert system: forestry applications. *Proceedings of AUTOCARTO 6*. ACSM/ASPRS, Falls Church Virginia, pp. 493-503

Goldstein H, Wertz J, Sweet D (1969) *Computer Mapping: a tool for urban planners*. Battelle Memorial Institute, Cleveland

Golledge R G (1982) Fundamental conflicts and the search for geographical knowledge. In: Gould P R, Olssen G (ed.) *A Search for Common Ground*. Pios, London: 11-21

Golledge R G et al. (1982) Commentary on 'The highest form of the geographer's art'. *Annals of the Association of American Geographers* **72**: 557-8

Gonzalez R C, Wintz P A (1987) *Digital Image Processing* 2nd edn. Addison-Wesley, Reading Massachusetts

Goodchild M F (1978) Statistical aspects of the polygon overlay problem. In: Dutton G (ed.) *Harvard Papers on Geographic Information Systems*, Vol 6. Addison-Wesley, Reading Massachusetts, pp. 1-22

Goodchild M F (1980) The effects of generalization in geographical data encoding. In: Freeman H, Pieroni G (eds.) *Map Data Processing*. Academic Press, New York, pp. 191-205

Goodchild M F (1985) Geographical information systems in undergraduate geography: a contemporary dilemma. *The Operational Geographer* **8**: 34-8

Goodchild M F (1986) Spatial autocorrelation. *CATMOG* 47 GeoAbstracts, Norwich

Goodchild M F (1987) A spatial analytical perspective on geographical information systems. *International Journal of Geographical Information Systems* **1** (4): 327-34

Goodchild M F (1987) Application of a GIS benchmarking and workload estimation model. *Papers and Proceedings of Applied Geography Conferences* **10**: 1-6

Goodchild M F (1988) A spatial analytical perspective on GIS. *International Journal of Geographical Information Systems* **1**: 327-34

Goodchild M F (1988) *Spatial Autocorrelation*. CATMOG (Concepts and Techniques in Modern Geography), Vol. 47. GeoBooks, Norwich

Goodchild M F (1988) Stepping over the line: technological constraints and the new cartography. *The American Cartographer* **15** (3): 311-19

Goodchild M F (1988) Towards an enumeration and classification of GIS functions. In: Aangeenbrug R T, Schiffman Y M (eds.) *International Geographic Information Systems (IGIS) Symposium: The research agenda*, Vol II. AAG, Falls Church Virginia: pp. 67-77

Goodchild M F (1989) Geographic information systems and market research. *Papers and Proceedings of Applied Geography Conferences*, Volume 12. 1-8

Goodchild M F (1990) Keynote address: spatial information science. *Proceedings of the 4th International*

Symposium on Spatial Data Handling, Vol 1. International Geographical Union, Columbus Ohio, pp. 3–14

Goodchild M F (1990) Spatial information science. *Proceedings of 4th International Symposium on Spatial Data Handling*, Vol. 1. International Geographical Union, Columbus Ohio, pp. 3–12

Goodchild M F (1991) Geographical data modelling. *Computers and Geosciences* **17**

Goodchild M F (1991) The technological setting of GIS. In: Maguire D J, Goodchild M F, Rhind D W (eds.) *Geographical Information Systems: principles and applications*. Longman, London, pp. 45–54, Vol 1

Goodchild M F, Anselin L, Deichmann U (1989) A general framework for the spatial interpolation of socio-economic data. Paper presented at the Regional Science Association meeting, Santa Barbara California

Goodchild M F, Dubuc O (1987) A model of error for choropleth maps with applications to geographic information systems. *Proceedings of AUTOCARTO 8*. ASPRS/ACSM, Falls Church, pp. 165–74

Goodchild M F, Gopal S (eds.) (1989) *Accuracy of Spatial Databases*. Taylor & Francis, London

Goodchild M F, Grandfield A W (1983) Optimizing raster storage: an evaluation of four alternatives. In: *Proceedings of AUTOCARTO 6 (2)*. ASPRS, Falls Church, pp. 400–7

Goodchild M F, Kemp K K (eds.) (1990) *Core Curriculum in GIS*. National Center for Geographic Information and Analysis, Santa Barbara

Goodchild M F, Kemp K K (1990) Developing a curriculum in GIS: the NCGIA Core Curriculum Project. In: Unwin D J (ed.) *GIS Education and Training, Collected Papers of a Conference, University of Leicester 20–21 March 1990*. Midlands Regional Research Laboratory, Leicester

Goodchild M F, Lam N S-N (1980) Areal interpolation: a variant of the traditional spatial problem. *Geo-Processing* **1**: 297–312

Goodchild M F, Mark D M (1987) The fractal nature of geographic phenomena. *Annals of the Association of American Geographers* **77**: 265–78

Goodchild M F, Rhind D W (1990) The US National Center for Geographic Information and Analysis: some comparisons with the Regional Research Laboratories. In: Foster M J, Shand P J (eds.) *The Association for Geographic Information Yearbook 1990* Taylor & Francis, London, pp. 226–32

Goodchild M F, Rizzo B R (1987) Performance evaluation and work-load estimation for geographic information systems. *International Journal of Geographical Information Systems* **1** (1): 67–76

Goodchild M F, Wang, Min-Hua (1988) Modeling error in raster based spatial data. *Proceedings of the 3rd International Symposium on Spatial Data Handling*. International Geographical Union, Columbus, Ohio, pp. 97–106

Goodenough D G (1988) The integration of remote sensing and geographic information systems. In: Damen M C J, Smit, G S, Verstappen (eds.) *Symposium on Remote Sensing for Resource Development and Environmental Management*, Balkema, Rotterdam, pp. 1015–28

Goodenough D G (1988) Thematic Mapper and SPOT integration with a geographic information system. *Photogrammetric Engineering and Remote Sensing* **54**: 167–76

Goodenough D G, Goldberg M, Plunkett G, Zelek J (1987) An expert system for remote sensing. *IEEE Transactions on Geoscience and Remote Sensing* **GE-25**: 349–59

Gorry G A, Morton M S (1971) A framework for management information systems. *Sloan Management Review* **13**: 56–70

Gorry G A, Morton M S (1989) A framework for management information systems. *Sloan Management Review* **30** (3): 49–61

Gorte B, Liem R, Wind J (1988) The ILWIS software kernel. *ITC Journal* **19**: 15–22

Gottschalk H-J (1972) Die Generalisierung von Isolinien als Ergebnis der Generalisierung von Flèchen. *Zeitschrift für Vermessungswesen* **97** (11): 489–94

Gould M D (1989) The value of spatial decision support systems for oil and chemical spill response. *Proceedings of the 12th Applied Geography Conference* Binghampton, pp. 75–83

Goward S N, Markham B, Dye D G, Dulaney W, Yang J (1991) Normalized difference vegetation index measurements from the Advanced Very High Resolution Radiometer. *Remote Sensing of Environment* **35**: 257–78

Grace B F (1975) A case study of man/computer problem solving. *IBM Research Report RJ1483*. International Business Machines, San Jose

Grant N G (ed.) (1989) *Proceedings of National Conference Challenge for the 1990s GIS*. Canadian Institute of Surveying and Mapping, Ottawa

Gray P, King W R, McLean E R, Watson E J (eds.) (1989) *Management of Information Systems*. Dryden Press, Chicago

Greasley I (1988) Data structures to organize spatial subdivisions. *Proceedings of ACSM-ASPRS Annual Convention, St. Louis*, pp. 139–48

Green D, McEwen L J (1989) GIS as a component of information technology courses in higher education. Meeting the requirements of employers. In: *Proceedings of the First National Conference of the Association for Geographic Information, 'GIS as a Corporate Resource'*. AGI, Birmingham England, pp. c1.1–c1.6

Green N P A (1987) Teach yourself geographical information systems: the design, creation and use of demonstrators and tutors. *International Journal of Geographical Information Systems* **1** (3): 279–90

Green N P A (1990) Towards truly distributed GIS. *Proceedings of the GIS Design Models and Functionality Conference*. Midlands Regional Research Laboratory, University of Leicester, 8pp.

Griffin J M, Hickman D L (1988) *Cost and Benefit Analysis of Geographic Information System Implementation. Final Report to the Bureau of Indian Affairs*. Battelle, Lakewood Colorado

Griffin M W (1987) A rapid method for simulating three dimensional fluvial terrain. *Earth Surface Processes and Landforms* **12**: 31–8

Griffith D A (1987) Spatial autocorrelation: a primer. *Association of American Geographers, Resource Publications in Geography.* Association of American Geographers, Washington

Grimshaw D J (1988) Land and property information systems. *International Journal of Geographical Information Systems* **2** (1): 67–79

Groop R E, Smith R (1982) A dot matrix method of portraying continuous statistical surfaces. *The American Cartographer* **9** (2): 123–30

Gruijter J J de (1977) *Numerical Classification of Soils and its Application in Survey.* PUDOC, Wageningen, 117 pp.

Grunreich D (1985) Computer-assisted generalization. *Papers CERCO-Cartography Course.* Frankfurt a.M

Guevera J A (1989) Latin America: geo-information for development. *ARC News* **11** (3): 16

Guibas L, Stolfi J (1985) Primitives for the manipulation of general subdivisions and the computation of Voronoi diagrams. *ACM Transactions on Graphics* **4** (2): 74–123

Guinn R (1990) The NJUG Perspective. In: Foster M J, Shand P J (eds.) *The Association for Geographic Information Yearbook 1990.* Taylor & Francis, London

Gulati A K (1989) Digital cartography or GIS for resource management and mapping. IX *INCA International Seminar on Digital Cartography and Potential Users.* Pre-Session Proceedings. Survey of India, Dehra Dun, pp. 128–37

Gunther O, Bilmes J (1989) The implementation of the cell tree: design alternatives and performance evaluation. *Proceedings BTW '89 – Database Systems for Office Automation, Engineering, and Scientific Applications.* Springer-Verlag, pp. 72–92

Guptill S C (ed.) (1988) A process for evaluating geographic information systems. *Federal Interagency Coordinating Committee on Digital Cartography, Technology Exchange Working Group, Technical Report 1.* US Geological Survey, Reston Virginia

Guptill S C (ed.) (1990) An enhanced digital line graph design. *US Geological Survey Circular 1048.* USGS, Reston Virginia

Guptill S C (1986) A new design for the US Geological Survey's National Digital Cartographic Database. In: Blakemore M J (ed.) *Proceedings of AUTOCARTO LONDON,* Volume 2. Royal Institution of Chartered Surveyors, London, pp. 10–18

Guptill S C (1987) Desirable characteristics of a spatial database management system. *Proceedings of AUTOCARTO 8.* ASPRS, Falls Church Virginia, pp. 278–281

Guptill S C (1988) A process for evaluating geographic information systems. Technology Exchange Working Group – Technical Report 1. Federal Interagency Coordinating Committee on Digital Cartography. *US Geological Survey Open-File Report 88–105.* USGS, Reston

Guptill S C (1989) Evaluating geographic information systems technology. *Photogrammetric Engineering and Remote Sensing* **55** (11): 1583–7

Guptill S C (1989) Speculations on seamless, scaleless cartographic databases. *Proceedings of AUTOCARTO 9.* ASPRS, Falls Church, pp. 436–43

Guptill S C (1991) Spatial data exchange and standardization. In: Maguire D J, Goodchild M F, Rhind D W (eds.) *Geographical Information Systems: principles and applications.* Longman, London, pp. 515–30, Vol 1

Guptill S C, Boyko K J, Domaratz M A, Fegeas R G, Rossmeissl H J, Usery E L (1990) *An enhanced Digital Line Graph Design.* US Geological Survey Professional Paper 1048, Washington DC

Gurd F B (1990) Requirements of Geographic Information Systems used for supply/demand analysis of real estate markets. *Proceedings of GIS/LIS '90* **1**: ASPRS/ACSM/AAG/URISA/AM-FM, Bethesda Maryland, pp. 21–5

Guttag J, Horowitz E, Musser D (1978) Abstract data types and software validation. *Communications of the ACM* **21** (12): 1048–64

Guttman A (1984) R-trees: a dynamic index structure for spatial searching. *Proceedings of the Annual Meeting ACM SIGMOD, Boston,* pp. 47–57

Haber R N, Wilkinson L (1982) Perceptual components of computer displays. *IEEE Transactions on Computer Graphics and Applications* **2** (3): 23–35

Hägerstrand T (1955) *Statistiska primäruppgifter, flygkartering och 'dataprocessing'-maskiner. Ett kombineringsprojekt. Svensk Geografisk Årsbok 1955.* Lund, Sweden

Hägerstrand T (1967) The computer and the geographer. *Transactions of the Institute of British Geographers* **42**: 1–20

Hägerstrand T (1973) The domain of human geography. In: Chorley R J (ed.) *Directions in Geography.* Methuen, London, pp. 67–87

Haggett P (1965) *Lotational Analysis in Human Geology.* Edward Arnold, London

Hake G (1975) Zum Begriffsystem der Generalisierung. *Nachrichten aus dem Karten- und Vermessungswesen.* Sonderheft zum 65 Geburtstag von Prof Knorr: 53–62

Hall F G, Badhwar G D (1987) Signature-extendable technology: global space-based crop recognition. *IEEE Transactions on Geoscience and Remote Sensing* **GE-25**: 93–103

Hall F G, Strebel D E, Sellers P J (1988) Linking knowledge among spatial and temporal scales: vegetation, atmosphere, climate and remote sensing. *Landscape Ecology* **2**: 3–22

Hall P A V, Papadopoulos S (1990) Hypertext systems and applications. *Information and Software Technology* **32** (7): 477–90

Hamilton A C, Williamson I P (1984) A critique of the FIG definition of a Land Information System. In: *The Decision Maker and Land Information Systems. Papers and*

Proceedings from the FIG International Symposium, Edmonton, Alberta, pp. 28–34

Hamilton W L (1989) Concurrent development of academic geo- computing facilities and curricula for undergraduate education: a case study. *Proceedings of GIS/LIS '89.* ASPRS/ACSM, Bethesda Maryland, pp. 495–505

Hammer M, Zdonik S B (1980) Knowledge-based query processing. *Journal of the IEEE* **6**: 137–46

Hammond N (1989) Hypermedia and learning: who guides whom? In: Maurer H (ed.) *Computer Assisted Learning.* Springer-Verlag, Berlin

Hammond N, Allinson L (1987) The travel metaphor as design principle and training aid for navigating around complex systems. In: Diaper D, Winder R (eds.) *People and Computers III.* Cambridge University Press, Cambridge, pp. 75–90

Hammond N, Allinson L (1989) Extending hypertext for learning: an investigation of access and guidance tools. In: Sutcliffe A, Macaulay L (eds.) *People and Computers V.* Cambridge University Press, Cambridge, pp. 293–304

Han K H (1985) *Estimation of Major City Population in Korea Using Landsat Imagery.* Unpublished PhD thesis, University of Utah

Hannah M J (1981) Error detection and correction in digital terrain models. *Photogrammetric Engineering and Remote Sensing* **47** (1): 63–9

Haralick R M (1980) Edge and region analysis for digital image data. *Computer Graphics and Image Processing* **12**: 60–73

Haralick R M, Fu K (1983) Pattern recognition and classification. In: Colwell R N (ed.) *Manual of Remote Sensing*, 2nd edn. American Society of Photogrammetry, Falls Church Virginia, pp. 793–805

Haralick R M, Shanmugam K, Dinstein I (1973) Textural features for image classification. *IEEE Transactions on Systems, Man, and Cybernetics* **SMC-3** (6): 610–21

Harding A E, Forrest M D (1989) Analysis of multiple geological data sets from the English Lake District. *IEEE Transactions on Geoscience and Remote Sensing* **27**: 732–9

Harig J (1990) Visualisation of 3-D finite element solutions of Navier–Stokes equations. *Proceedings of Symposium on Three Dimensional Computer Graphics in Modelling Geologic Structures and Simulating Processes.* Freiburger Geowissenschafliche Beitrage **2**: 36–8

Harper E A, Manheim M L (1989) Geographic information systems in transportation planning. *Paper given to the International Conference on Geographical Information Systems: approaches for urban and regional planning.* Ciloto, Puncak, Indonesia

Harris B (1965) New tools for planning. *Journal of the American Institute of Planners* **31** (2): 90–5

Harris D P (1984) *Mineral Resource Appraisal.* Clarendon Press, Oxford

Harris N (1989) Aid and urbanization – an overview. *Cities* **6** (3): 174–85

Hart A (1988) The New South Wales Land Information System in action. *URPIS – Proceedings of the Urban and Regional Planning Information Systems Annual Conferences*, Volume 16. Australasian Urban and Regional Information Systems Association Inc., Sydney, pp. 25–39

Hart J F (1982) The highest form of the geographer's art. *Annals of the Association of American Geographers* **72**: 1–29

Hart J F (1983) More gnashing of false teeth. *Annals of the Association of American Geographers* **73**: 441–3

Hart J F (1988) Keynote Address. *Proceedings of The International Symposium on the Challenge of Rural Poverty: How to Meet It.* Feldafing, FRG, FAO and DSE, pp. 21–4

Harvey D R (1986) *Countryside Implications for England and Wales of Possible Changes in the Common Agricultural Policy.* Centre for Agricultural Strategy, University of Reading UK

Hastings D A (1986) *Stereo-pair World Map.* NOAA National Geophysical Data Center, Boulder Colorado

Hastings D A (1986) *Global MAGSAT Scalar Anomaly Maps.* NOAA National Geophysical Data Center, Boulder Colorado

Hastings D A (1987) AVHRR Stereography. *Proceedings of the North American NOAA Polar Orbiter Users Group First Meeting.* NOAA National Geophysical Data Center, Boulder Colorado (USA), pp. 121–4. Reprinted in *Photogrammetric Engineering and Remote Sensing* **54**: cover and p. 105

Hastings D A, Moll S H (1986) Using Geographic Information Systems as an initial approach to Artificial Intelligence in the geological sciences. *Proceedings of the 1st Annual Rocky Mountain Conference on Artificial Intelligence.* BREIT International Inc, Boulder, pp. 191–200

Haugen E (1957) The semantics of Icelandic orientation. *Word* **13**: 447–60

Hawkins J M (1983) *Oxford Paperback Dictionary.* Oxford University Press, Oxford

Hayes G E, Romig H G (1977) *Modern Quality Control.* Bruce, Encino California

Haywood P E (ed.) (1986) *Final Draft Papers of the Working Party to Produce National Standards for the Transfer of Digital Map Data.* Ordnance Survey, Southampton

Haywood P E (1986) National transfer standards for Great Britain. *Land and Minerals Surveying* **4** (11): 569–78

Haywood P E (1987) The OS Topographic Database Study – the first stage report. In: Haywood P E (ed.) *Proceedings of Spatially-Oriented Referencing Systems Association (SORSA) Symposium, Durham.* Ordnance Survey

Haywood P E (1988) Structured digital data at OS. *Land and Minerals Surveying* **6** (3): 151–6

Haywood P E (1989) Structured topographic data – the key to GIS. *Proceedings of Association for Geographic Information Conference*, Birmingham, October 1989. AGI, London, pp. B1.1–1.4

Hazelton N W J, Leahy F J, Williamson I P (1990) On the design of a temporally-referenced, 3-D Geographical

Information System: development of a four dimensional GIS. *Proceedings of GIS/LIS '90*. AAG/ACSM/AMFM/ASPRS/URISA, Bethesda Maryland, pp. 357–372

Head C G (1984) A map as a natural language – new insight into cartographic communication. *Cartographica* **21** (31): 1–32

Healey R G (1983) Regional geography in the computer age: a further commentary on 'The highest form of the geographer's art'. *Annals of the Association of American Geographers* **73**: 439–41

Healey R G (1991) Database management systems. In: Maguire D J, Goodchild M F, Rhind D W (eds.) *Geographical Information Systems: principles and applications*. Longman, London, pp. 251–67, Vol 1

Hearnshaw H M, Maguire D J, Worboys M F (1989) An introduction to area-based spatial units: a case study of Leicestershire. *Midlands Regional Research Laboratory Research Report 1*. MRRL, Leicester

Helldén U (1987) An assessment of woody biomass, community forests, land use and soil erosion in Ethiopia. *Lund Studies in Geography, Ser C General, Mathematical and Regional Geography No. 14*. Lund University Press, Lund, 75 pp.

Heller M (1986) Triangulation and interpolation of surfaces. In: Sieber R, Brassel K E (eds.) *A Selected Bibliography on Spatial Data Handling: data structures, generalization and three-dimensional mapping. Geoprocessing Series 6*. Department of Geography, University of Zurich, Zurich, pp. 36–45

Heller M (1990) Triangulation algorithms for adaptive terrain modeling. *Proceedings of the 4th International Symposium on Spatial Data Handling*. International Geographical Union, Columbus Ohio, pp. 163–74

Hendrix G, Sacerdoti E, Sagalowicz D, Slocum J (1978) Developing a natural language interface to complex data. *ACM Transactions on Database Systems* **3** (2)

Her Majesty's Land Registry (1990) *Report on the work of HM Land Registry 1989–90*. Her Majesty's Stationery Office, London

Herndon L, Schertz D L (1989) The Water Erosion Prediction Project (WEPP) – SCS Implementation. *Poster Paper in 1989 ASA-CSSA-SSSA Annual Meetings, Las Vegas, Nevada, 16 October 1989*

Herring J R (1987) TIGRIS: topologically integrated geographic information system. *Proceedings of AUTOCARTO 8*. ASPRS/ACSM, Falls Church Virginia, pp. 282–91

Herring J R (1989) The category model of spatial paradigms. In: Mark D M, Frank A U, Egenhofer M J, Freundschuh S, McGranaghan M, White R M (eds.) *Languages of Spatial Relations: Report on the Specialist Meeting for NCGIA Research Initiative 2*. National Center for Geographic Information and Analysis, Santa Barbara, pp. 47–51

Herring J R (1989) A fully integrated geographic information system. *Proceedings of AUTOCARTO9*. ASPRS, Falls Church, pp. 828–37

Herring J R, Egenhofer M J, Frank A U (1990) Using category theory to model GIS applications. *Proceedings of the 4th International Symposium on Spatial Data Handling, Zurich*. International Geographical Union, Columbus Ohio, pp. 820–9

Herring J R, Larsen R C, Shivakumar J (1988) Extensions to the SQL query language to support spatial analysis in a topological database. *Proceedings of GIS/LIS '88*, Volume 2, ASPRS/ACSM, Falls Church Virginia, pp. 741–50

Herskovits A (1985) Semantics and pragmatics of locative expressions. *Cognitive Science* **9**: 341–78

Herskovits A (1986) *Language and Spatial Cognition: an interdisciplinary study of the prepositions in English*. Cambridge University Press, Cambridge

Herskovits A (1987) *Spatial Prepositions in English*. Cambridge University Press, Cambridge Massachusetts

Herzog A (1989) Modeling reliability on statistical surfaces by polygon filtering. In: Goodchild M F, Gopal S (eds.) *Accuracy of Spatial Databases*. Taylor & Francis, London, 209–18

Herzog A, L'Eplattenier R, Weibel R, Brassel K (1987) Experimental spatial data displays. *Proceedings of the 13th Conference of the International Cartographic Association*, Volume IV. ICA, Morelia, pp. 375–89

Heuvelink G B M, Burrough P A, Stein A (1989) Propagation of error in spatial modelling with GIS. *International Journal of Geographical Information Systems* **3** (4): 303–22

Heyn B N (1984) *An Evaluation of Map Color Schemes for Use on CRTs*. Unpublished MS thesis, Department of Geography, University of South Carolina

Heywood D I, Petch J R (1990) GIS education: a business perspective. In: Unwin D J (ed.) *GIS Education and Training, Collected Papers of a Conference, University of Leicester 20–21 March 1990*. Midlands Regional Research Laboratory, Leicester, 11 pp.

Hibbard W, Santek D (1989) Visualizing large data sets in the earth sciences. *IEEE Computer* **22** (8): 53–7

Hill G J E, Kelly G D (1987) A comparison of existing map products and Landsat for land cover mapping. *Cartography* **16**: 51–7

Hirsch S A (1980) *Algorithms for Automatic Name Placement of Point Data*. Unpublished MSc thesis, Department of Geography, State University of New York, Buffalo

Hittelman A M, Metzger D R (1983) Marine geophysics: database management and supportive graphics. *Computers and Geosciences* **9** (1): 27–33

HMSO (Her Majesty's Stationery Office) (1979) *Report of the Ordnance Survey Review Committee*. Chaired by Sir David Serpell. HMSO, London

HMSO (Her Majesty's Stationery Office) (1983) *Report of the Select Committee on Science and Technology – Remote Sensing and Digital Mapping*. Chaired by Lord Shackleton. HMSO, London

HMSO (1980) *People in Britain – a census atlas*. HMSO, London

Hoare C A R (1987) An overview of some formal methods for program design. *Computer (IEEE)* **20** (9): 85–91

Hodgson J M (1978) *Soil Sampling and Description*. Oxford University Press, Oxford

Hoff W A, Michalski R S, Stepp R E (1983) INDUCE 3: a program for learning structural descriptions from examples. *Final Draft Report*. Chicago, Department of Computer Science, Artificial Intelligence Lab, University of Illinois

Hoffer R M (1978) Biological and physical considerations in applying computer-aided analysis techniques to remote-sensor data. In: Swain P H, Davis S M (eds.) *Remote Sensing: the quantitative approach*. McGraw-Hill, New York, pp. 227–87

Hoffer R M (1989) President's Inaugural Address. *Photogrammetric Engineering and Remote Sensing* **55** (7): 1031–2

Hoffer R M, Fleming M D, Bartolucci L A, Davis S M, Nelson R F (1979) Digital processing of Landsat MSS and topographic data to improve capabilities for computerized mapping of forest cover types. *LARS Technical Report 011579*, p. 159

Hoffmann C (1989) The problems of accuracy and robustness in geometric computation. *IEEE Computer* **22** (3): 31–42

Hoffmeister E D (1978) Programmgesteurte Gebandegeneralisierung fur die Topographische Karte 1/25000. *Nachrichten aus dem Karten- und Vermessungswesen* 1 **75**: 51–62

Holben B N, Fraser R S (1984) Red and near-infrared sensor response to off-nadir viewing. *International Journal of Remote Sensing* **5**: 145–60

Holloway C A, Mantey P E (1976) Implementation of an interactive graphics model for design of school boundaries. *Research Paper 299*. Graduate School of Business, Stanford University

Holstein L (1988) LIS problems and issues in urban areas. *Proceedings from the FIG Land Information Systems Workshop, Bali, Indonesia*, pp. 53–9

Honey S, Milnes K, Zavoli W (1988) *Apparatus for generating a heading signal for a land vehicle*. US Patent 4,734,863.

Honey S, White M (1986) Cartographic databases. In: Lambert S S, Ropiequet S (ed.) *CD/ROM The New Papyrus*. Microsoft Press, Redmond WA, pp. 563–72

Honey S, Zavoli W, Milnes K, Phillips A, White M, Loughmiller G (1989) *Vehicle navigational system and method*. US Patent 4,796,191.

Hopgood F R A, Hubbold R J (eds.) (1986) *Advances in Computer Graphics II*. Springer-Verlag, New York

Hopkins L (1984) Evaluation of methods for exploring ill-defined problems. *Environment and Planning B* **11**: 339–48

Hopmans J W, Stricker J N M (1989) Applications of scaling techniques at a watershed scale. In: Bouma J, Bregt A K (eds.) *Land Qualities in Space and Time. Proceedings of a Symposium organised by the International Society of Soil Science (ISSS), Wageningen, The Netherlands, 22–26 August 1988*. PUDOC, Wageningen, pp. 181–4

Horn B K P (1986) *Robot Vision*. MIT Press, Cambridge Massachusetts

Horn D et al. (1989) Spatial access paths and physical clustering in a low level geo-database system. *Geologisches Janrbuch* **A 104** (Construction and display of geoscientific maps derived from databases)

Horn M, O'Callaghan J F, Garner B J (1988) Design of integrated systems for spatial planning tasks. *Proceedings of the 3rd International Symposium on Spatial Data Handling*. International Geographical Union, Columbus, Ohio, pp. 107–16

Horwood E M (1980) Planning information systems: functional approaches, evolution and pitfalls. In: Krammer K, King J (eds.) *Computers in Local Government Urban and Regional Planning*. Auerbach Publishers Inc., Pennsauken, pp. (2.1.1) 1–12

House of Lords (1984) *Remote sensing and digital mapping*. Report 98 of the House of Lords Select Committee on Science and Technology, Her Majesty's Stationery Office, London

House W C (ed.) (1983) *Decision Support Systems*. Petrocelli, New York, pp. 167–88

Howe D R (1985) *Data Analysis for Data Base Design*. Edward Arnold, London

Hsu S Y (1971) Population estimation. *Photogrammetric Engineering* **37**: 449–54

Hubert L, Golledge R G, Costanzo C M (1981) Generalized procedures for evaluating spatial autocorrelation. *Geographical Analysis* **13**: 224–33

Hudson J C (1979) (ed.) Seventy-five years of American geography. *Annals of the Association of American Geographers* **69** (1): 185pp.

Hummel J, Reck R (1979) A global surface albedo model. *Journal of Applied Meteorology* **18**: 239–53

Hurion R D (1986) Visual interactive modelling. *European Journal of Operational Research* **23**: 281–7

Hurle G (1989) The status of development of facility management systems within the Australian electricity supply industry. *URPIS – Proceedings of the Urban and Regional Planning Information Systems Annual Conferences*, Volume 17. Australasian Urban and Regional Information Systems Association Inc., Sydney, pp. 350–8

Hutchinson C F (1982) Techniques for combining Landsat and ancillary data for digital classification improvement. *Photogrammetric Engineering and Remote Sensing* **48**: 123–30

Hutchinson M F (1988) Calculation of hydrologically sound digital elevation models. *Proceedings of the 3rd International Symposium on Spatial Data Handling*. International Geographical Union, Columbus Ohio, pp. 117–33

Hutchinson M F (1989) A new procedure for gridding elevation and stream line data with automatic removal of spurious pits. *Journal of Hydrology* **106** (1/2): 211–32

ICA (International Cartographic Association) (1973)

Multilingual Dictionary of Technical Terms in Cartography. ICA, Wiesbaden

ICSU (International Council for Scientific Unions) (1989) *Guide to the World Data Center System: part I(a) Updates, Corrections and Additions to Part 1*. ICSU, Boulder Colorado

ICSU Panel on World Data Centers (1987) *Guide to the World Data Center System*. International Council of Scientific Unions, Boulder Colorado

IGBP Special Committee (1988) *The International Geosphere–Biosphere Programme: a study of global change – a plan for action*. Report No. 4. IGBP Secretariat, Stockholm

IGBP Special Committee (1989) *Pilot Studies for Remote Sensing and Data Management*. Report No. 8. IGBP Secretariat, Stockholm

Imhof E (1937) Das Siedlungsbild in der Karte. *Mitteilungen der Geographisch-Ethnographischen Gesellschaft*. Zurich, Band **37**: 17–85

Imhof E (1962) Die Anordnung der Namen in der Karte. *Annuaire International de Cartographie II*. Orell Fuessli Verlag, Zurich, pp. 93–129

Imhoff E (1982) *Cartographic Relief Presentation*. de Gruyter, Berlin

Inaba K, Aumann G, Ebner H (1988) DTM generation from digital contour data using aspect information. *International Archives of Photogrammetry and Remote Sensing* **27** (B8): III101–10

Indian Towing Co. v. United States [1955] 350 US 61, 76 S. Ct. 122, 100 L. Ed. 48

Ingram I K, Phillips W (1987) Geographic information processing using a SQL-based query language. *Proceedings of AUTOCARTO 8*. ASPRS/ACSM, Falls Church Virginia, pp. 326–35

Intergovernmental Oceanographic Commission (1987) GF3, A general formatting system for geo-referenced data, vol 2, Technical description of the GF3 Format and code tables. *Intergovernmental Oceanographic Commission, Manuals and Guides* **17**: UNESCO, Paris

Intergraph Corporation (1989) *Tigris Imager Reference Manual*. Intergraph Corporation, Huntsville

Intergraph Corporation (1989) *Microstation Analyst (MGA) Reference Manual*. Intergraph Corporation, Huntsville Alabama

Intergraph Corporation (1989) *Relational Interface (RIS) User Reference Manual*. Intergraph Corporation, Huntsville Alabama

International Cartographic Association (1973) *Multilingual Dictionary of Technical Terms in Cartography*. Franz Steiner Verlag GMBH

International Council of Scientific Unions (1989) *Yearbook 1989* ICSU Press, Paris

IOS (International Organisation for Standardisation) (1986) *Office Document Architecture (ODA)*. ISO 8613. ISO, Geneva

Iri M, Okabe A, Koshizuka T, Yomono H (1986) *Computer Geometry and Geoprocessing*, Special publication of *BIT* magazine. Kyoritu Shuppan, Tokyo

Irons J R, Weismuller R A, Petersen G W (1989) Soil reflectance. In: Asrar G (ed.) *Theory and Applications of Optical Remote Sensing*. Wiley, New York, pp. 66–106

ISO DP 10303 (1988) *Product Data Exchange Specification (PDES), STEP Version 1.0; also PDES Working Draft Version 1.0; also NTIS PB 89–144–794*. ISO

ISO 2nd DP 9636 (1988) *Computer Graphics Interfacing Techniques for Dialogues with Graphical Devices (CGI)*; also dpANSI X3.161. ISO

ISO 7942 (1985) *Graphical Kernel System (GKS)*; also ANSI X3.124–1985; also FIPS 120. ISO

ISO 8211 (1986) *Specification for a Data Descriptive File for Information Interchange*; also FIPS 123. ISO

ISO 8632 (1987) *Computer Graphics Metafile for the Storage and Transfer of Picture Description Information (CGM)* Parts 1–4; also ANSI X3.122–1986; also FIPS 128. ISO

ISO 8805 (1988) *Graphical Kernel System for Three Dimensions (GKS-3D)*. ISO

ISO 9582 (1989) *Programmer's Hierarchical Interactive Graphics System (PHIGS)*; also ANSI X3.144–1989. ISO

Ives M J, Lovett R (1986) Exchange of digital records between public utility digital mapping systems. In: Blakemore M J (ed.) *Proceedings of AUTOCARTO London*, Volume 2. Royal Institution of Chartered Surveyors, London, pp. 181–9

Jackson J E (1980) *Sphere, Spheroid and Projections*. Granada, London

Jackson J (1990) Developing an effective human interface for geographical information systems using metaphors. *ACSM/ASPRS Annual Convention* **3** (1): 117–25

Jackson M J (1987) Digital cartography, image analysis, and remote sensing: towards an integrated approach. *Interdisciplinary Science Reviews* **12**: 33–44

Jackson M J, Mason D C (1986) The development of integrated geo-information systems. *International Journal of Remote Sensing* **7**: 723–40

Jackson M J, Woodsford P A (1991) GIS data capture hardware and software. In: Maguire D J, Goodchild M F, Rhind D W (eds.) *Geographical Information Systems: principles and applications*. Longman, London, pp. 239–49, Vol 1

Jager E (1987) Computer-assisted symbolization by raster data processing. *Nachrichten aus dem Karten und Vermessungswesen* 1 **46**: 61–70

James P E, Martin G J (1978) *The Association of American Geographers: the first seventy-five years 1904–1979*. Association of American Geographers, Washington DC

Jankowski P (1989) *Knowledge-based Structured Modelling: an application to stream water quality management*. Unpublished PhD dissertation, Department of Geography, University of Washington

Jankowski P, Nyerges T (1989) Design considerations for MaPKBS-map projection knowledge-based system. *The American Cartographer* **16**: 85–95

Jarke M (1984) Semantic query optimization in expert

systems and database systems. *Proceedings of First International Conference on Expert Database Systems*, pp. 467–82

Jarvis R S (1984) Topology of tree-like networks. In: Gaile G L, Willmott C J (eds.) *Spatial Statistics and Models*. D. Reidel, Dordrecht, pp. 271–91

Jasinski M F, Eagleson P S (1989) The structure of red-infrared scattergrams of semivegetated landscapes. *IEEE Transactions on Geoscience and Remote Sensing* **27**: 441–51

Jenkins G M, Watts D G (1968) *Spectral Analysis and Its Applications*. Holden-Day, Oakland California

Jenks G F (1963) Generalization in statistical maps. *Annals of the Association of American Geographers* **53**: 15–26

Jenks G F (1967) The data model concept in statistical mapping. *International Yearbook of Cartography* **7**: 186–8

Jenks G F (1975) The evaluation and prediction of visual clustering in maps symbolized with proportional circles. In: Davis J C, McCullagh M J (eds.) *Display and Analysis of Spatial Data*. Wiley, London, pp. 311–27

Jenks G F (1981) Lines, computers and human frailties. *Annals of the Association of American Geographers* **71**: 1–10

Jensen J R (1986) *Introductory Digital Image Processing*. Prentice-Hall, Englewood Cliffs New Jersey

Jerie H C, Kure J, Larsen H K (1980) A system approach to Geo-Information Systems. *ITC Journal* 4, International Institute for Aerospace Survey and Earth Science, Enschedé

Jeworrek J (1988) *Untersuchungen zur automatischen generalisierung von flachen im Rasterdaten format*. Unpublished Master's Thesis, University of Hannover

Joffe B A and Wright W (1989) SimCity : Thematic mapping + City management Simulation = an entertaining, interactive gaming tool. *Proceedings of GIS/LIS '89*. ACSM\ASPRS\AAG\URISA\AM/FM, Bethesda Maryland, pp. 591–600

Johnson B D, Mott J J, Robey T (1989) Providing effective access to resources information – progress towards a national directory of Australian resources data. *URPIS – Proceedings of the Urban and Regional Planning Information Systems Annual Conferences*, Volume 17. Australasian Urban and Regional Information Systems Association Inc., Sydney, pp. 260–5

Johnson C G (1975) The role of automated cartography in soil survey. In: Bie S W (Ed.) *Soil Information Systems. Proceedings of the meeting of the ISSS Working Group on Soil Information Systems, Wageningen, The Netherlands, 1–4 Sept 1975*. PUDOC, Wageningen, pp. 48–51

Johnson M (1987) *The Body in the Mind: the bodily basis of meaning, imagination and reason*. University of Chicago Press, Chicago

Johnston R J, Gregory D, Smith D M (eds.) (1986) *The Dictionary of Human Geography*, 2nd edn. Blackwell, Oxford

Jones A R, Settle J J, Wyatt B K (1988) Use of digital terrain data in interpretation of SPOT HRV-1 multispectral imagery. *International Journal of Remote Sensing* **9**: 669–76

Jones C B (1989) Data structures for 3-D spatial information systems. *International Journal of Geographical Information Systems* **3**: 15–32

Jones C B, Abraham I M (1986) Design considerations for a scale-independent cartographic database. *Proceedings 2nd International Symposium on Spatial Data Handling, Seattle*. IGU, Columbus, pp. 384–98

Jones T A (1988) Modeling geology in 3 dimensions. *Geobyte* February: 14–20

Jordan T G, Rowntree L (1982) *The Human Mosaic: a thematic introduction to cultural geography*, 3rd edn. Harper and Row, New York

Journel A G, Huijbregts C J (1978) *Mining Geostatistics*. Academic Press, London

Jupp D L B, Strahler A H, Woodcock C E (1989) Autocorrelation and regularization in digital images: II. Simple image models. *IEEE Transactions on Geoscience and Remote Sensing* **27**: 247–56

Jupp D L B, Walker J, Penridge L K (1986) Interpretation of vegetation structure in Landsat MSS imagery: a case study in disturbed semi-arid Eucalypt woodlands. Part 2. Model-based analysis. *Journal of Environmental Management* **23**: 35–57

Justice C O, Townshend J R G, Holben B N, Tucker C J (1986) Analysis of the phenology of global vegetation using meteorological satellite data. *International Journal of Remote Sensing* **6**: 1271–318

Kainz W (1989) Order, topology, and metric in GIS. *Proceedings of ASPRS-ACSM Annual Convention, Baltimore*. ASPRS/ACSM, Falls Church, pp. 154–60

Kamata et al. (1989) *Introduction to Cartographic Analysis*. Nikkan Kogyo Shinbun, Tokyo

Kamijo S, Okumura K, Kitamura A (1989) Digital road map data base for vehicle navigation and road information systems. In: Reekie D H M, Case E R, Tsai J (ed.) *Vehicle Navigation & Information Systems Conference, Toronto*, pp. 319–23

Kaneda K, Kato F, Nakamae E, Nishita T (1989) Three dimensional terrain modeling and display for environmental assessment. *Computer Graphics (SIGGRAPH '89 Proceedings)* **23** (3): 207–14

Kanemasu E T, Asrar G, Fuchs M (1985) Application of remotely sensed data in wheat growth modeling. In: Day D W, Atkin R K (eds.) *Wheat Growth and Modelling*. Plenum, New York, pp. 407–25

Karjala D S (1987) Copyright, computer software, and the new protectionism. *Jurimetrics Journal* **33**: 51–4

Kates R W (1987) The human environment: the road not taken, the road beckoning. *Annals of the Association of American Geographers* **77** (4): 525–34

Katz S (1988) Emulating the Prospector Expert System with a raster GIS. In: Thomas H F (ed.) *GIS: Integrating Technology and Geoscience Applications*. National Resource Center, Connecticut, pp. 27–8

Kauth R J, Thomas G S (1976) The tasselled cap: a graphic description of the spectral-temporal development of crops as seen by Landsat. *Proceedings of the 3rd Symposium on Machine Processing of Remotely Sensed Data*, Vol. 4B. Purdue University, West Lafayette Indiana, pp. 41–51

Kavouras M, Masry S (1987) An information system for geosciences: design considerations. *Proceedings of AUTOCARTO 8.* ACSM/ASPRS, Falls Church Virginia, pp. 336–45

Kawauchi (ed.) (1988) Recent computer mapping systems. *PIXEL*, Gazou Joho Shori Centre, Tokyo

Keates J S (1982) *Understanding Maps*. Longman, London

Keates J S (1989) *Cartographic Design and Production*, 2nd edn. Longman, London

Keefer B J, Smith J L, Gregoire T G (1988) Simulating manual digitizing error with statistical models. *Proceedings of GIS/LIS '88*. ACSM, Falls Church, pp. 475–83

Keen P G W (1980) Adaptive design for decision support systems. *Data Base* **12**: 15–25

Keen P G W (1983) Interactive computer systems for managers: a modest proposal. In: House W C (ed.) *Decision Support Systems*. Petrocelli, New York, pp. 167–88

Keen P G W, Morton M S (1978) *Decision Support Systems: an organizational perspective*. Addison-Wesley, New York

Kehris E (1989) Interfacing ARC/INFO with GLIM: a progress report. *North West Regional Research Laboratory Research Report 5*. North West Regional Research Laboratory, Lancaster

Kelk B (1991) 3-D GIS for the geosciences. *Computers and Geosciences* **17**

Kelk B, Challen K (1989) Experiments with a CAD package for spatial modelling of geoscientific data. *International Colloquium on 'Digital maps in the Geosciences', Würzburg Germany*

Kelley A D, Malin M C, Nielson G M (1988) Terrain simulation using a model of stream erosion. *Computer Graphics (SIGGRAPH '88 Proceedings)* **22** (4): 263–8

Kelly P (1980) *Automated Positioning of Feature Names on Maps*. Unpublished MSc thesis, Department of Geography, State University of New York, Buffalo

Kemp Z (1990) An object-oriented data model for spatial data. *Proceedings of the 4th International Symposium on Spatial Data Handling*, Volume 2. International Geographical Union, Columbus Ohio, pp. 659–68

Kennedy S (1988) A geographical regression model for medical statistics. *Social Science and Medicine* **26**: 119–29

Kennedy S (1989) The small number problem and the accuracy of spatial databases. In: Goodchild M F, Gopal S (eds.) *Accuracy of Spatial Databases*. Taylor & Francis, London, pp. 187–96

Kent W (1983) A simple guide to five normal forms in relational database theory. *Communications of the Association for Computing Machinery* **26** (2): 120–25

Kidwell J (1990) Impact of copyright law. *Workshop on Managing the Risks and Recovering the Costs of Geographic and Facilities Management Systems*. University of Wisconsin-Madison, Madison, Wisconsin

Kijima Y (1983) *Urban Image*. Seichosha, Kumamoto

Kimball R C, Gregor W T (1989) Emerging distribution strategies in US retail banking. *Journal of Retail Banking* **11**: 4–16

Kimerling A J (1985) The comparison of equal value gray scales. *The American Cartographer* **12** (2): 119–27

Kimes D S (1981) Remote sensing of temperature profiles in vegetation canopies using multiple view angles and inversion techniques. *IEEE Transactions on Geoscience and Remote Sensing* **GE-19**: 85–90

Kindleberger C (1988) Planning support systems for the 1990s: local government information processing challenges and opportunities. *URISA Proceedings* **3**: 1–21

Kineman J J (1989) *Monthly composites of the NOAA Vegetation Index from April 1985 through December 1988 on a 10' grid*. National Geophysical Data Center, Boulder, Colorado

Kineman J J, Clark D M (1988) Connecting global science through spatial data and information technology. In: Aangeenbrug R T, Schiffman Y E (eds.) *Proceedings of the International GIS Symposium: the research agenda*, Volume 1. American Association of Geographers, Falls Church, pp. 209–27

Kineman J J, Clark D M, Croze H (1990) Data integration and modelling for global change: an international experiment. *Proceedings of the International Conference and Workshop on Global Natural Resource Monitoring and Assessments: preparing for the 21st Century*. Volume 2 American Society of Photogrammetry and Remote Sensing, Falls Church, pp. 660–9

Kineman J J, Hastings D A, Colby J D (1986) Developments in global databases for the environmental sciences: discussion and review. *Proceedings of the 12th International Symposium on Remote Sensing of the Environment*. Volume 2. Environmental Research Institute of Michigan, Ann Arbor, pp. 471–82

King C W B (1988) Computational formulae for the Lambert conformal projection. *Survey Review* **29**: 229, 230, 323–37, 387–93

King D, Daroussin J, Bonneton P, Nicoullaud J (1986) An improved method for combining map data. *Soil Use and Management* **2**: 140–5

King R (1989) Introduction to the special issue on non-English interfaces to databases. *IEEE Transactions on Database Engineering* **12** (4): 1–7

Knuth D E (1973) *The Art of Computer Programming*. Addison-Wesley, Reading Massachusetts

Konecny G (1988) Keynote address: current status of geographic and land information systems. *Proceedings of AM/FM European Conference IV, Montreux*

Konecny G, Lohmann P, Engel H, Kruck E (1987) Evaluation of SPOT imagery on analytical photogrammetric instruments. *Photogrammetric Engineering and Remote Sensing* **53** (9): 1223–30

Konecny G, Pape D (1981) Correlation techniques and devices. *Photogrammetric Engineering and Remote Sensing* **47** (3): 323–33

Konsynski B, Sprague R H (1986) Future research

directions in model management. *Decision Support Systems* 2: 103–9

Korth H F, Silberschatz A (1986) *Database System Concepts.* McGraw-Hill, New York

Korzybski A (1948) *Science and Sanity: an introduction to non-Aristotelean systems and general semantics*, 3rd edn. The International Non-Aristotelean Library Publishing Co., Lakeville CT

Koshkariov A V, Tikunov V S, Trofimov A M (1989) The current state and the main trends in the development of geographical information systems in the USSR. *International Journal of Geographical Information Systems* 3 (3): 257–72

Kosslyn S M (1988) *Image and Mind.* Harvard University Press, Cambridge Massachusetts

Köstli A, Sigle M (1986) The random access data structure of the DTM program SCOP. *International Archives of Photogrammetry and Remote Sensing* 26 (B4): 128–37

Kotler P (1988) *Marketing Management: analysis, planning implementation and control.* Prentice-Hall, Englewood Cliffs

Kowalski R (1974) Predicate logic as a programming language. *Proceedings of IFIP-74*, pp. 569–574

Kowalski R (1987) Algorithm = logic + control. *Communications of the ACM* 22: 424–36

Kraak M J (1988) *Computer Assisted Cartographical Three Dimensional Imaging Techniques.* Delft University Press, Delft

Kriegel H-P, Schiwietz M, Schneider R, Seeger B (1989) Performance comparison of point and spatial access methods. In: Buchmann A, Gunther O, Smith T, Wang Y (eds.) *Symposium on the Design and Implementation of Large Spatial Databases* (Lecture Notes in Computer Science, Volume 409). Springer-Verlag, New York, pp. 89–114

Krishnayya J G (1986) *C MAPS (Core System) Specifications.* Research and Systems Institute, Pune, India

Kubik K, Frederiksen P (1983) Automatic generalization of contour lines. *Paper presented at Eurocarto II, Bolkejo, Norway* 9pp.

Kubik K, Lyons K, Merchant D (1988) Photogrammetric work without blunders. *Photogrammetric Engineering and Remote Sensing* 54: 51–4

Kubo S (ed.) (1987–89) *Proceedings AUTOCARTO JAPAN 3–5.* Autocarto Japan Organizing Committee, Tokyo

Kubo S (1980) Recent trends in geographic data processing. *Jinbun Chiri* 32 (1): 40–62

Kubo S (1987) The development of geographical information systems in Japan. *International Journal of Geographical Information Systems* 1 (3): 243–52

Kubo S (1990) *GIS and the Population Census.* Bureau of Census, Tokyo

Kubo S (1991) The development of GIS in Japan. In: Maguire D J, Goodchild M F, Rhind D W (eds.) *Geographical Information Systems: principles and applications.* Longman, London, pp. 47–56, Vol 2

Kuennucke B H (1988) Experiments with teaching a GIS course within an undergraduate geography curriculum. *Proceedings of GIS/LIS '88.* ASPRS, Falls Church, pp. 302–07

Kuhn W (1991) Are displays maps or views? *Proceedings of AUTOCARTO 10.* ACSM/ASPRS, Bethesda Maryland

Kuilenburg J van, Bunschoten B, Burrough P A, Schelling J (1981) The digital soil map, scale 1 : 50 000 of The Netherlands. *Proceedings of the International Society of Soil Science Working Group on Soil Information Systems Colloquium, 14–17 Sept 1981, Paris.* Institut National Agronomique, Paris, Grignon Departement des Sols No. 4 pp. 73–86

Kuilenburg J van, Gruijter J J de, Marsman B A, Bouma J (1982) Accuracy of spatial interpolation between point data on soil moisture capacity, compared with estimates from mapping units. *Geoderma* 27: 311–25

Kuipers B (1978) Modelling spatial knowledge. *Cognitive Science* 2: 129–53

Kumar R S (1989) A case for Survey-Net. *IX INCA International Seminar on Digital Cartography and Potential Users.* Pre-Session Proceedings. Survey of India, Dehra Dun, pp. 182

Lacroix V (1984) An improved area-feature name placement. *Technical Report IPL-TR-064.* Image Processing Laboratory, Rensselaer Polytechnic Institute, Troy

Lai P C (1988) Resource use in manual digitization. A case study of the Patuxent Basin geographical information system database. *International Journal of Geographical Information Systems* 2 (4): 329–45

Laing A W, Puniard D J (1989) The Australian Defence Force requirements for land-related information. In: Ball D, Babbage R (eds.) *Geographical Information Systems: defence applications.* Pergamon Press, Sydney, pp. 61–79

Lakoff G (1987) *Women, Fire, and Dangerous Things: what categories reveal about the mind.* University of Chicago Press, Chicago

Lakoff G, Johnson M (1980) *Metaphors We Live By.* University of Chicago Press, Chicago

Lam S-N (1983) Spatial interpolation methods: a review. *The American Cartographer* 10 (2): 129–49

Lamp J (1983) Habilitation thesis. Christian-Albrecht University of Kiel, West Germany

LAMSAC (1989) *An Approach to Evaluating GIS for Local Authorities (Requirements Study).* LAMSAC, London

Land Agency (ed.) (1986) *Geographic Information System.* The Printing Bureau, The Ministry of Finance, Tokyo

Lanen H A J van, Bregt A K, Bulens J D, van Diepen C A, Hendriks C M A, de Koning G H J, Reinds G J (1989) *Crop Production potential of Rural Areas Within the European Community.* Dutch Scientific Council for Government Policy, The Hague

Langel R A, Phillips J D, Horner R G (1982) Initial scalar anomaly map from MAGSAT. *Geophysical Research Letters* 9: 269–72

Langford M, Maguire D J, Unwin D J (1989) Modelling population distribution using remote sensing and GIS. *Research Report 3 Midlands Regional Research Laboratory*. MRRL, Leicester UK

Langford M, Maguire D J, Unwin D J (1991) The area transform problem: estimating population using satellite imagery in a GIS framework. In: Masser I, Blakemore M J (eds.) *Geographic Information Management: methodology and applications*. Longman, London

Langran G, Chrisman N R (1988) A framework for temporal geographic information. *Cartographica* **25** (1): 1–14

Langran G (1988) Temporal GIS design tradeoffs. *Proceedings of GIS/LIS '88*, Volume 2. ASPRS/ACSM, Falls Church Virginia, pp. 890–99

Langran G (1989) A review of temporal database research and its use in GIS applications. *International Journal of Geographical Information Systems* **3**: 215–32

Langran G (1989) Accessing spatio-temporal data in a temporal GIS. *Proceedings of AUTOCARTO 9*. ACSM/ASPRS, Falls Church Virginia, pp. 191–98

Langran G (1989) *Representing Temporality as a Third GIS Dimension*. Unpublished PhD thesis, Department of Geography, University of Washington

Lasseter T (1990) An interactive 3-D modelling system for integrated interpretation in hydrocarbon reservoir exploration and production. *Proceedings of Symposium on Three Dimensional Computer Graphics in Modelling Geologic Structures and Simulating Processes*. Freiburger Geowissenschafliche Beitrage **2**: 45–6

Lauer D (1990) *An Evaluation of National Policies Governing the United States Civilian Satellite Land Remote Sensing Program*. Unpublished PhD dissertation, Department of Geography, University of California, Santa Barbara California

Laurillard D (ed.) (1989) *Interactive Media: working methods and practical applications*. Ellis Horwood, Chichester England

Laurini R, Milleret-Raffort F (1989) Principles of geomatic hypermaps *Ekistics* **56** (338–39): 312–17

Lavin S J, Archer J C (1984) Computer-produced unclassed bivariate choropleth maps. *The American Cartographer* **11** (1):49–57

Lavin S J (1979) *Region Perception Variability on Choropleth Maps: pattern complexity effects*. Unpublished PhD dissertation, University of Kansas

Lavin S J (1986) Mapping continuous distributions using dot density shading. *The American Cartographer* **13** (2): 140–50

Lay H G, Weber W (1983) Waldgeneralisierung durch digitale Rasterdaten verarbeitung. *Nachrichten aus dem Karten und Vermessungswesen* **1** (92): 61–71

Lay J C (1975) Mapping services in Fairfax County, Va. *Proceedings of AUTOCARTO 4*. American Congress on Survey and Mapping/American Society for Photogrammetry, Washington DC, pp. 143–7

Lee T S, Russell J S (1990) Potential applications of Geographic Information Systems to the construction industry. *Proceedings of GIS/LIS '90*, Volume 1. ASPRS/ACSM/AAG/URISA/AM-FM, Bethesda Maryland, pp. 11–20

Leenaers H, Burrough P A, Okx J P (1989) Efficient mapping of heavy metal pollution on floodplains by co-kriging from elevation data. In: Raper J F (ed.) *Three Dimensional Applications in Geographical Information Systems*. Taylor & Francis, London, pp. 37–50

Leenaers H, Okx J P, Burrough P A (1989) Co-kriging: an accurate and inexpensive means of mapping floodplain soil pollution by using elevation data. In: Armstrong M (ed.) *Geostatistics. Proceedings of the third Geostatistics Congress, Avignon, October 1988*. Kluwer, pp. 371–82

Lefschetz S (1975) *Applications of Algebraic Topology*. Springer-Verlag, New York

Leick A (ed.) (1982) Land information at the local level. *Proceedings of the International Symposium, Orono, Maine*

Leick A (1987) GIS point referencing by satellite and gravity. In: Aangeenbrug R T, Schiffman Y M (eds.) *Proceedings of International Geographic Information Systems (IGIS) Symposium: the research agenda*, Vol. 2. NASA, Washington DC, pp. 305–17

Lelewer D A, Hirschberg D S (1987) Data compression. *ACM Computing Surveys* **19** (3): 261–96

Lemmens M J P M (1988) A survey on stereo matching techniques. *International Archives of Photogrammetry and Remote Sensing* **27** (B8): V11–V23

Leonard J J, Buttenfield B P (1989) An equal value gray scale for laser printer mapping. *The American Cartographer* **16** (2): 97–107

L'Eplattenier R (1987) An interactive system for display and analysis of block diagrams. Unpublished MSc Thesis (in German). Department of Geography, University of Zurich, Zurich

Lesslie R G, Mackey B G, Preece K M (1988) A computer-based method of wilderness evaluation. *Environmental Conservation* **15** (3): 225–32

Lewis P (1987) Spatial data handling using relational databases. Unpublished MSc thesis, Department of Geography, University of Edinburgh, Scotland.

Li X, Strahler A H (1985) Geometric-optical modeling of a conifer forest canopy. *IEEE Transactions on Geoscience and Remote Sensing* **GE-23**: 705–21

Li X Z, Sun Y (1986) The research of agricultural information systems at a county level. *Resource and Environment System No 1*. LREIS, Beijing

Li Z N (1988) An algorithm for compressing digital contour data. *The Cartographic Journal* **25**: 143–6

Li Z N, Uhr L (1987) Pyramid vision using key features to integrate image-driven bottom-up and model-driven top-down processes. *IEEE Transactions on Systems, Man and Cybernetics*, SMC-17

Lichtner W (1979) Computer-assisted processes of cartographic generalization in topographic maps *Geo-Processing* **1** 183–99

Lieth H (1975) Primary production of the major vegetation units of the world. In: Lieth H, Whittaker R H (eds.)

Primary productivity of the Biosphere (Ecological Studies 14). Springer-Verlag, New York, pp. 203–15

Liley R (1985) Integration – the big pay-off for geobased municipal systems. *Papers of the Urban and Regional Information Systems Association – URISA '85*. URISA, Ottawa, Canada **2**: 11–27

Lillesand T M, Kiefer R W (1987) *Remote Sensing and Image Interpretation*, 2nd edn. Wiley, New York

Lloyd J W (1987) *Foundations of Logic Programming*. Springer-Verlag, New York

Lo C P, Welch R (1977) Chinese urban population estimates. *Annals of the Association of American Geographers* **67**: 246–53

Lobeck A K (1924) *Block Diagrams*. Wiley, New York

Lodwick W A, Monson W, Svoboda L (1990) Attribute error and sensitivity analysis of map operations in geographical information systems suitability analysis. *International Journal of Geographical Information Systems* **4** (4): 413–28

Lodwick W A (1989) Developing confidence limits on errors of suitability analyses in geographical information systems. In: Goodchild M F, Gopal S (eds.) *Accuracy of Spatial Databases*. Taylor & Francis, London, pp. 69–78

Logan T L, Bryant N A (1988) Spatial data software integration: merging CAD/CAM mapping with GIS and image processing. *Photogrammetric Engineering and Remote Sensing* **53** (10): 1391–5

Loomis R G (1965) Boundary networks. *Communications, Association for Computing Machinery* **8**: 44–8

Lorie R A, Meier A (1984) Using a relational DBMS for geographical databases. *Geo-Processing* **2**: 243

Lovejoy S, Schertzer D (1985) Generalised scale invariance in the atmosphere and fractal models of rain. *Water Resources Research* **21**: 1233–50

Loveland T R, Ramey B (1986) Applications of US Geological Survey Digital Cartographic Products, 1979–1983. *US Geological Survey Bulletin 1583*, United States Government Printing Office, Washington

LREIS (1987) *Proceedings of International Workshop on Geographic Information System, Beijing '87*. Laboratory of Resource and Environmental Information Systems, Academica Sinica, Beijing

Luger G L, Stubblefield W A (1989) *Artificial Intelligence and the Design of Expert Systems*. The Benjamin/Cummings Publishing Company Inc, New York

Lupian A E, Moreland W H, Dangermond J (1987) Network analysis in geographic information systems. *Photogrammetric Engineering and Remote Sensing* **53** (10): 1417–21

Lyall G A (1980) Planning and land assessment in Scotland – the role of the Rural Land Use Information Systems Working Party. In: Thomas M F, Coppock J T (eds.) *Land Assessment in Scotland*. Aberdeen University Press, Aberdeen, pp. 107–17

Lyons H G (1931) Land surveying in early times. *Proceedings of Conference of Empire Survey Officers* pp. 175–180

Lyytinen K, Hirschheim R (1987) Information systems failures – a survey and classification of the empirical literature. *Oxford Surveys in Information Technology* **4**: 257–309

Ma P (1987) An algorithm to generate verbal instructions for vehicle navigation using a geographic database. *East Lakes Geographer* **22**: 44–60

MacEachren A E (1982) Map complexity: comparison and measurement. *The American Cartographer* **9** (1): 31–46

MacEachren A E with **Buttenfield B P, Campbell J C, Monmonier M S** (1992) Visualization. In: Abler R F, Olson J M, Marcus N G (eds.) *Geography's Inner World*. Rutgers University Press, New Jersey

Mackaay E (1982) *Economics of Information and Law*. Kluwer Nijhoff, Boston

Mackaness W A, Fisher P F (1987) Automatic recognition and resolution of spatial conflicts in cartographic symbolization. *Proceedings of AUTOCARTO 8*. ASPRS, Falls Church, pp. 709–18

Mackaness W A, Scott D J (1988) The problems of operationally defining the map design process for cartographic expert systems *Proceedings of Austra Carto III, 22–26 Aug, 7th Australian Cartographic Conference, Sydney*. ACA, Sydney, pp. 715–23

Mackenzie H G, Smith J L (1977) Data storage and retrieval. In: Moore A W and Bie S W (eds.) *Uses of Soil Information Systems. Proceedings of the Australian Meeting of the ISSS Working Group on Soil Information Systems, Canberra, Australia, 2–4 March 1976*. PUDOC, Wageningen, pp. 19–36

Mackinlay J (1986) Automating the design of graphical presentations of relational information. *ACM Transactions on Graphics* **5** (2): 110–41

Maeder S R, Tessar P A (1988) *The Use of Geographic Information Systems for Lake Management in Minnesota*. Minnesota State Planning Agency, Minneapolis

Maes J, Vereecken H, Darius P (1987) Knowledge processing in Land Evaluation. In: Beek K-J, Burrough P A, McCormack D E (eds.) *Quantified Land Evaluation Procedures. Proceedings of the Joint Meeting of the ISSS Working Groups on Land Evaluation and Soil Information Systems, Washington 25 April–2 May 1986; ITC Publication No. 6*. ITC, Enschede, pp. 66–73

Maffini G (1987) Raster versus vector encoding and handling: a commentary. *Photogrammetric Engineering and Remote Sensing* **53**: 1397–8

Maffini G, Arno M, Bitterlich W (1989) Observations and comments on the generation and treatment of error in digital GIS data. In: Goodchild M F, Gopal S (eds.) *Accuracy of Spatial Databases*. Taylor & Francis, London, pp. 55–67

Maffini G, Saxton W (1987) Deriving value from the modelling and analysis of spatial data. In: Aangeenbrug R T, Schiffman Y M (eds.) *International Geographic Information Systems (IGIS) Symposium, Arlington, Virginia* Vol 3. NASA, Washington DC, pp. 271–90

Magnenat-Thalman N, Thalman D (1987) An indexed

bibliography on image synthesis. *IEEE Computer Graphics and Applications* **7** (8): 27–37

Maguire D J (1989) *Computers in Geography*. Longman, London

Maguire D J (1989) The Domesday interactive videodisc system in geography teaching. *Journal of Geography in Higher Education* **13** (1): 55–68

Maguire D J (1989) DEMOGIS Mark 1: an ERDAS based GIS tutor. *Proceedings of AUTOCARTO 9*. ASPRS/ACSM, Falls Church Virginia, pp. 620–30

Maguire D J (1990) A research plan for GIS in the 1990s. In: Foster M J, Shand P J (eds.) *The Association for Geographic Information Yearbook 1990*. Taylor & Francis and Miles Arnold, London, pp. 267–77

Maguire D J (1990) Computer cartography. In: Perkins C R, Parry R B (eds.) *Information Sources in Cartography*. Bowker-Saur, London, pp. 201–13

Maguire D J (1991) An overview and definition of GIS. In: Maguire D J, Goodchild M F, Rhind D W (eds.) *Geographical Information Systems: principles and applications*. Longman, London, pp. 9–20, Vol 1

Maguire D J, Dangermond J (1991) The functionality of GIS. In: Maguire D J, Goodchild M F, Rhind D W (eds.) *Geographical Information Systems: principles and applications*. Longman, London, pp. 319–35, Vol 1

Maguire D J, Goodchild M F, Rhind D W (1991) Section I. Introduction. In: Maguire D J, Goodchild M F, Rhind D W (eds.) *Geographical Information Systems: principles and applications*. Longman, London, pp. 3–7, Vol 1

Maguire D J, Hickin B W, Longley I, Mesev T (1991) Waste disposal site selection using raster and vector GIS. *Mapping Awareness* **5** (1): 24–7

Maguire D J, Raper J F (1990) Design models and functionality in GIS. *Proceedings of the GIS Design Models and Functionality Conference*. Midlands Regional Research Laboratory, Leicester, 10 pp.

Maguire D J, Worboys M F, Hearnshaw H M (1990) An introduction to object-oriented Geographical Information Systems. *Mapping Awareness* **4** (2): 36–9

Maher R V, Wightman J F (1985) A design for geographic information systems training. *The Operational Geographer* **8**: 43–6

Mahoney R P (1985) Digital mapping in SEGAS. *Proceedings of AM/FM International – European Division Conference. Montreux*. AM/FM European Division, PO Box 6, CH4005, Basel, Switzerland, pp. 112–22

Mahoney R P (1986) Digital mapping – an information centre. In: Blakemore M (ed.) *Proceedings of AUTOCARTO London*, Volume 2. Royal Institution of Chartered Surveyors, pp. 190–9

Mahoney R P (1991) GIS and utilities. In: Maguire D J, Goodchild M F, Rhind D W (eds.) *Geographical Information Systems: principles and applications*. Longman, London, pp. 101–14, Vol 2

Makarovic B (1973) Progressive sampling for digital terrain models. *ITC Journal* **1973** (3): 397–416

Makarovic B (1977) Composite sampling for digital terrain models. *ITC Journal* **1977** (3): 406–33

Makarovic B (1979) From progressive to composite sampling for digital terrain models. *Geo-Processing* **1**: 145–66

Makarovic B (1984) Structures for geo-information and their application in selective sampling for digital terrain models. *ITC Journal* **1984** (4): 285–95

Malin M C, Sheridan M F (1982) Computer-assisted mapping of pyroclastic surges. *Science* **217**: 637

Maling D H (1968) The terminology of map projections. *International Yearbook of Cartography* **8**: 11–65

Maling D H (1973) *Coordinate Systems and Map Projections*. George Philip, London

Maling D H (1989) *Measurements from Maps: principles and methods of cartometry*. Pergamon, Oxford

Maling D H (1991) Coordinate systems and map projections for GIS. In: Maguire D J, Goodchild M F, Rhind D W (eds.) *Geographical Information Systems: principles and applications*. Longman, London, pp. 135–46, Vol 1

Mallet J-L (1991) GOCAD: a computer-aided design program for geological applications. In: Turner A K (ed.) *Three Dimensional Modelling with Geoscientific Information*. Kluwer, Dortrecht

Malone T W, Yates J, Benjamin R I (1989) The logic of electronic markets. *Harvard Business Review* **67** (3): 166–72

Mandelbrot B B (1967) How long is the coast of Britain? Statistical self-similarity and fractional dimension. *Science* **156**: 636–8

Mandelbrot B B (1982) *The Fractal Geometry of Nature*. W H Freeman and Co, San Francisco

Mandelbrot B B (1986) Self-affine fractal sets; parts I, II, and III. In: Pietronero L, Tosati E (eds.) *Fractals in Physics*. Elsevier North-Holland, Amsterdam, pp. 3–28

Mann J F (1987) *Computer Technology and the Law*. Carswell, Toronto

Mapping Science Committee, National Academy of Science (1990) *Spatial Data Needs: the future of the National Mapping Program*. National Academy Press, Washington DC

Marble D F (1979) Integrating Cartographic and Geographic Information Systems education. *Technical Papers of the 39th Annual Meeting of the American Congress on Surveying and Mapping*. ACSM, Falls Church, pp. 493–9

Marble D F (1980) (ed.) *Computer Software for Spatial Data Handling*, 3 volumes. Commission on Geographical Data Sensing and Processing/International Geographical Union, Ottawa Canada

Marble D F (ed.) (1980) *Computer Software for Spatial Data Handling* 3 volumes. IGU Commission on Geographical Data Sensing and Processing for the US Department of the Interior Geological Survey, Ottawa

Marble D F (1989) Letter to PERS. *Photogrammetric Engineering and Remote Sensing* **55** (4): 434–5

Marble D F, Calkins H W, Dueker K, Gilliland J, Salmona J (1972) Introduction to the economics of geographical information systems, and geographical information system design: concepts and methods. In: Tomlinson R F (ed.) *Geographical Data Handling. UNESCO/IGU Second Symposium on Geographical Information Systems.* International Geographical Union, Ottawa

Marble D F, Lauzon J P, McGranaghan M (1984) Development of a conceptual model of the manual digitizing process. *Proceedings of the 1st International Symposium on Spatial Data Handling.* University of Zurich-Irchel, Zurich, pp. 146–71

Marble D F, Peuquet D J (1983) Geographic information systems. In: Colwell R N (ed.) *Manual of Remote Sensing,* 2nd edn. American Society of Photogrammetry, Falls Church, pp. 923–58

Marble D F, Peuquet D J, Boyle A R, Bryant N, Calkins H W, Johnson T (1983) Geographic information systems and remote sensing. In: Colwell R N (ed.) *Manual of Remote Sensing.* American Society of Photogrammetry, Falls Church Virginia, pp. 923–57

Marble D F, Sen L (1986) The development of standardised benchmarks for spatial database systems. *Proceedings of the 2nd International Symposium on Spatial Data Handling.* IGU, Columbus Ohio, pp. 488–96

Marchionini G, Schneiderman B (1988) Finding facts versus browsing knowledge in hypertext systems. *Computer* 3 (1): 70–80

Mark D M (1975) Geomorphometric parameters: a review and evaluation. *Geografiska Annaler* 57A (3–4): 165–77

Mark D M (1979) Phenomenon-based data structuring and digital terrain modeling. *Geo-Processing* 1: 27–36

Mark D M (1984) Automated detection of drainage networks from digital elevation models. *Cartographica* 21: 168–78

Mark D M (1985) Finding simple routes: 'ease of description' as an objective function in automated route selection. *Proceedings, Second Symposium on Artificial Intelligence Applications, Miami Beach*

Mark D M (1987) On giving and receiving directions: cartographic and cognitive issues. *Proceedings of AUTOCARTO 8.* ACSM/ASPRS, Falls Church Virginia, pp. 562–71

Mark D M (1987) Recursive algorithms for the analysis and display of digital elevation data. *Proceedings First Latin American Conference on Computers in Cartography, San José, Costa Rica,* pp. 375–97

Mark D M (1989) Cognitive image-schemata for geographic information: relations to user views and GIS interfaces. *Proceedings of GIS/LIS '89,* Vol. 2. ASPRS/ACSM, Falls Church, pp. 551–60

Mark D M (1989) Multiple views of multiple representations. *Multiple Representations. NCGIA Technical Paper* **89–3** National Centre for Geographic Information and Analysis, Santa Barbara California, pp. 68–71

Mark D M, Aronson P B (1984) Scale-dependent fractal dimensions of topographic surfaces: an empirical investigation, with applications in geomorphology and computer mapping. *Mathematical Geology* 16: 671–83

Mark D M, Cebrian J A (1986) Octrees: a useful method for the processing of topographic and subsurface data. *Proceedings of ACSM–ASPRS Annual Convention,* Volume 1. ACSM/ASPRS, Falls Church Virginia, pp. 104–113

Mark D M, Csillag F (1989) The nature of boundaries in 'area-class maps'. *Cartographica* 26 (1): 65–78

Mark D M, Frank A U, Egenhofer M J, Freundschuh S, McGranaghan M, White R M (1989) Languages of spatial relations: report on the specialist meeting for NCGIA Research Initiative 2. *Technical Report 89–2,* National Center for Geographic Information and Analysis, Santa Barbara

Mark D M, Gould M D, Nunes J (1989) Spatial language and geographic information systems: cross-linguistic issues. *Proceedings, II Conferencia Latinoamericana sobre el (Technologia de los Sistemas de Informacion Geograficos (SIG).* Universidad de Los Andes, Merida, Venezuela, pp. 105–30

Mark D M, Svorou S, Zubin D (1988) Spatial terms and spatial concepts: geographic, cognitive, and linguistic perspectives. In: Aangeenbrug R T, Schiffman Y M (eds.) *International Geographic Information Systems (IGIS) Symposium, Arlington, Virginia.* NASA, Washington DC, pp. 101–12

Marks D, Dozier J, Frew J (1984) Automated basin delineation from digital elevation data. *Geo-Processing* 2: 299–311

Marr D (1982) *Vision.* Freeman, San Francisco

Marsman B, Gruijter J J de (1984) Dutch soil survey goes into quality control. In: Burrough P A, Bie S W (eds.) *Soil Information Systems Technology.* PUDOC, Wageningen, pp. 127–34

Marsman B, Gruijter J J de (1986) Quality of soil maps. A comparison of survey methods in a sandy area. *Soil Survey Papers No. 15.* Netherlands Soil Survey Institute, Wageningen, 103 pp

Martin D (1989) Mapping population data from zone centroid locations. *Transactions of the Institute of British Geographers.* NS 14 (1): 90–7

Martin J (1976) *Principles of Database Management.* Prentice-Hall, Englewood Cliffs New Jersey

Martin J (1983) *4th Generation Languages,* Volume 1. Savant, Carnforth Lancashire

Martin P H (1983) Disclosure and use of proprietary data: task force report 15. *Natural Resources Lawyer 799.* American Bar Association, Chicago, pp. 802–3

Marx R W (1986) The TIGER system: automating the geographic structure of the United States census. *Government Publications Review* 13: 181–201

Marx R W (1990) The TIGER system: yesterday, today and tomorrow. *Cartography and Geographic Information Systems* 17 (1): 89–97

Mason D C, Corr D G, Cross A, Hoggs D C, Lawrence D H, Petrou M, Tailor A M (1988) The use of digital map data in the segmentation and classification of remotely-sensed images. *International Journal of Geographical Information Systems* 2 (3): 195–215

Mason D C, Townshend J R G (1988) Research related to

geographical information systems at the Natural Environment Research Council's Unit for Thematic Information System. *International Journal of Geographical Information Systems* **2**: 121–41

Mason K (1990) Cartographic applications of satellite remote sensing. In: Perkins C R, Parry R B (eds.) *Information Sources in Cartography*. Bowker-Saur, London, pp. 142–67

Masser I (1988) The Regional Research Laboratory Initiative: a progress report. *International Journal of Geographical Information Systems* **2**: 11–22

Masser I (1990) The Regional Research Laboratory initiative: an update. In: Foster M J, Shand P J (eds.) *The Association for Geographic Information Yearbook 1990*. Taylor & Francis and Miles Arnold, London, pp. 259–63

Mateo A, Burrough P A, Comerma J (1987) Analysis espacial de propiedadas de suelo para estudios de modelacion de cultivos en Venezuela. *Proceedings First Latin American GIS Conference, Costa Rica*. Ed. Lyen M, October 1987, Universidad Estatal a Distancia, San José, Costa Rica. pp. 164–78

Mather P M (1987) *Computer Processing of Remotely-sensed Images: an introduction*. Wiley, Chichester

Matheron G (1971) *The Theory of Regionalised Variables and its Applications*. Les Cahiers du Centre de Morphologie Mathématique de Fontainebleau. Ecole Nationale Superieure des Mines de Paris

Matheson G (1986) The implementation of a facilities information system with a major utility organisation. *URPIS – Proceedings of the Urban and Regional Planning Information Systems Annual Conferences*, Volume 14. Australasian Urban and Regional Information Systems Association Inc., Sydney, pp. 203–25

Matsui I (1930) Relations between grade and cultural landscape around Kamimizo. *Geographical Review of Japan* **6**: 1599–627

Matsui I (1931) Statistical observation of scattered village in Tonami Plain. *Geographical Review of Japan* **7**: 459–75

Matsui I (1933) Some problems in spatial distribution, especially in Tama Hill. *Geographical Review of Japan* **8**: 359–1627

Matthews E (1983) Global vegetation and land use: new high resolution databases for climate studies. *Journal of Climatology and Applied Meteorology* **22**: 474–87

Mausbach M J, Reybold W U (1987) In support of GIS in the SCS: SIS. In: Beek K-J, Burrough P A, McCormack D E (eds.) *Quantified Land Evaluation Procedures. Proceeedings of the Joint Meeting of the ISSS Working Groups on Land Evaluation and Soil Information Systems, Washington 25 April–2 May 1986. ITC Publication No. 6.* ITC, Enschede, pp. 77–80

Mausbach M J, Wilding L (eds.) (1990) *Spatial Variability and Map Units for Soil Surveys*. International Soil Science Society Working Group of Soil and Moisture Variability in Time and Space/American Society of Agronomy, the Crop Science Society of America and the Soil Science Society of America

McAleese R (ed.) (1989) *Hypertext: theory into practice*. Intellect Books, Oxford

McBratney A B, Webster R, Burgess T M (1981) The design of optimal sampling schemes for local estimation and mapping of regionalised variables. 1. Theory and method. *Computers & Geosciences* **7**: 331–4

McBratney A B, Webster R (1981) The design of optimal sampling schemes for local estimation and mapping of regionalized variables: 2 Program and examples. *Computers & Geosciences* **7**: 335–65

McBratney A B, Webster R (1983) How many observations are needed for regional estimation of soil properties? *Soil Science* **135**: 177–83

McBratney A B, Webster R (1983) Optimal interpolation and isarithmic mapping of soil properties. V. Co-regionalisation and multiple sampling strategy. *Journal of Soil Science* **34**: 137–62

McConalogue D J (1970) A quasi-intrinsic scheme for passing a smooth curve through a discrete set of points. *Computer Journal* **13** (4): 392–96

McCormick B H, Defanti T A, Brown M D (1987) Visualization in scientific computing. *SIGGRAPH Computer Graphics Newsletter* **21** (6)

McCormick S, Bratt P (1988) Some issues relating to the design and development of an interactive video disc. *Computers in Education* **12** (1): 257–60

McCullagh M J (1981) Creation of smooth contours over irregularly distributed data using local surface patches. *Geographical Analysis* **13** (1): 52–63

McCullagh M J (1982) Mini/micro display of surface mapping and analysis techniques. *Cartographica* **19** (2): 136–44

McCullagh M J (1988) Terrain and surface modelling systems: theory and practice. *Photogrammetric Record* **12** (72): 747–79

McEwen R B (1979) US Geological Survey digital cartographic data aquisition. In: *Mapping Software and Cartographic Data Bases*. Havard Library of Computer Graphics, pp. 136–42

McEwen R B (1980) USGS Digital Cartographic Applications Program. *Journal of Surveying and Mapping Division*. ASCE, **106** (1): 13–22

McEwen R B (1981) *A National Digital Cartographic Data Base*. Computer Graphics in Transportation. The Princeton University Conference

McEwen R B (1982) Observations and Trends in Digital Cartography. *Proceedings ISPRS Commission IV Symposium*. ASP, Falls Church Virginia, pp. 419–31

McEwen R B, Calkins H W (1982) Digital Cartography in the USGS National Mapping Division: a comparison of current and future mapping processes. *Cartographica* **19**: 11–26

McEwen R B, Jacknow H R (1980) USGS Digital Cartographic Data Base. *Proceedings of AUTOCARTO4*. SPRS, Falls Church Virginia, pp. 225–35

McGranaghan M (1989) Context-free recursive-descent parsing of location-description text. *Proceedings, Ninth*

International Symposium on Computer-Assisted Cartography. ACSM/ASPRS, Falls Church, pp. 580–7

McGranaghan M, Mark D M, Gould M D (1987) Automated provision of navigation assistance to drivers. *The American Cartographer* **14**: 121–38

McGranaghan M, Wester L (1988) Prototyping an herbarium collection mapping system. *Proceedings 1988 ACSM-ASPRS Annual Convention.* ACSM/ASPRS, Falls Church, pp. 232–8

McGuigan F J (1957) An investigation of several methods of teaching contour interpretation. *Journal of Applied Psychology* **41**: 53–7

McHarg I L (1969) *Design with Nature.* Doubleday, New York

McHarg I (1987) Keynote speech. *Proceedings of GIS '87.* ACSM/ASPRS, Falls Church Virginia

McKenna R (1988) Marketing in an age of diversity. *Harvard Business Review* **88** (5): 88–95

McKeown D M (1986) The role of artificial intelligence in the integration of remotely sensed data with Geographic Information Systems. *Report CMU-CS-86–174.* Department of Computer Science, Carnegie-Mellon University, Pittsburgh Pennsylvania

McKeown D M, Lai R C T (1987) Integrating multiple data representations for spatial databases. *Proceedings of AUTOCARTO 8.* ACSM/ASPRS, Falls Church Virginia, pp. 754–63

McLaren R A (1989) Choosing GIS/LIS. *FIG Newsletter No.3; Commission 3 Working Group on Land Information Systems in Developing Countries*

McLaren R A (1990) Establishing a corporate GIS from component data sets – the database issues. *Mapping Awareness* **4** (2): 52–8

McLaren R A, Kennie T J M (1989) Visualisation of digital terrain models: techniques and applications. In: Raper J F (ed.) *Three Dimensional Applications in Geographical Information Systems.* Taylor & Francis, London, pp. 79–98

McMaster R B (1987) Automated line generalization. *Cartographica* **24**: 74–111

McMaster R B, Monmonier M (1989) A conceptual framework for quantitative and qualitative raster-mode generalization. *Proceedings of GIS/LIS '89.* ACSM ASPRS, Falls Church Virginia, pp. 390–403

McMaster R B, Thrower N J (1987) University cartographic education in the United States: tracing the routes. *Proceedings International Cartographic Association Conference, Morelia* **2**: 343–59

McNamara T P, Ratcliff R, McKoon G (1984) The mental representation of knowledge acquired from maps. *Journal of Experimental Psychology, Learning, Memory and Cognition* **10** (4): 723–32

McRae S, Cleaves D (1986) Incorporating strategic data-planning and decision analysis techniques in geographic information system design. *Proceedings of Geographic Information Systems Workshop.* ASPRS, Atlanta, pp. 76–86

Meier A (1986) Applying relational database techniques to solid modelling. *Computer Aided Design* **18**: 319–26

Meijerink A M J, Valenzuela C R, Stewart A (1988) ILWIS: the Integrated Land and Watershed Management Information System. *ITC Publication No. 7.* International Institute for Aerospace Survey and Earth Sciences (ITC), Enschede, The Netherlands, 115 pp

Mel B W, Omohundro S M, Robinson A D, Skiena S S, Thearling K H, Young L T, Wolfram S (1988) Tablet: personal computer in the year 2000. *Communications ACM* **31** (6): 639–46

Menon S (1989) *Spatial Search for Multi-component Objects in a Geographic Information System Using Symbolic Models and Hierarchical Data Structures.* Unpublished PhD dissertation, University of California, Santa Barbara California

Merchant D C (1987) Spatial accuracy specification for large scale topographic maps. *Photogrammetric Engineering and Remote Sensing* **53** (7): 958–61

Methley B D F (1986) *Computational Models in Surveying and Photogrammetry.* Blackie, Glasgow

Meyer U (1987) Computer-assisted generalization of buildings for digital landscape models by classification methods. *Nachrichten aus dem Karten- und Vermessungswesen* 2 **46**: 193–200

Meyerson M (1956) Building the middle-range bridge for comprehensive planning. *Journal of the American Institute of Planners* **22** (2): 58–64

Mikhail E M (1976) *Observations and Least Squares.* IEP-Dun-Donnelly Harper & Row, New York

Miller A I (1984) *Imagery in Scientific Thought: creating 20th century physics.* Birkhauser, Boston

Miller C L, Laflamme R A (1958) The digital terrain model – theory and application. *Photogrammetric Engineering* **24** (3): 433–42

Miller E E (1980) Similitude and scaling of soil-water phenomena. In: Hillel D (ed.) *Applications of Soil Physics.* Academic Press, New York

Miller G A (1956) The magical number seven, plus or minus two: some limits on our capacity for processing information. *Psychological Review* **63**: 81–97

Millington A C, Townshend J R G, Kennedy P, Saull R, Prince S, Madams R (1989) *Biomass Assessment in the SADCC Region.* Earthscan Publications, London

Ministry of Construction (1987) *The Urban Information Database.* Keibun Shuppan, Tokyo

Minker J (1988) *Foundations of Deductive Databases and Logic Programming.* Morgan Kaufmann, Los Altos

Minker J (1988) Perspectives in deductive databases. *Journal of Logic Programming* **5** (1): 33–60

Minnesota Department of Natural Resources, Division of Forestry and Office of Planning (1984) *Modelling Direct Economic Returns to Timber Management as a Component of a Comprehensive, Multiple-Use Forest Management Model.* State of Minnesota, St Paul

Minnesota Department of Natural Resources, Division of Minerals (1989) *Glacial Drift Geochemistry for Strategic*

Minerals; Duluth Complex, Lake County, Minnesota. Report 262. State of Minnesota, St Paul

Minnesota Department of Natural Resources, Office of Planning (1986) *DNR-Administered Public Lands: their suitability to meet natural resource management objectives*. State of Minnesota, St Paul

Misra P (1989) Survey of India identification of user needs. *IX INCA International Seminar on Digital Cartography and Potential Users*. Pre-session Proceedings. Survey of India, Dehra Dun, pp. 223–35

Mitchell C P, Brandon O H, Bunce R G H, Barr C J, Tranter R B, Downing P, Pearce M L, Whittaker H A (1983) Land availability for production of wood energy in Great Britain. In: Strub A, Cartier P, Scleser G (eds.) *Energy from Biomass. Proceedings 2nd European Community Conference, Berlin*. Applied Science, London, pp. 159–63

Mitchell C W (1973) *Terrain Evaluation*. Longman, London

Mitchell T M, Keller R M, Kedar-Cabelli S T (1986) Explanation-based generalization: a unifying view. *Machine Learning* 1: 47–80

Mitchell W B, Guptill S C, Anderson E A, Fegeas R G, Hallam C A (1977) GIRAS – a Geographic Information Retrieval and Analysis System for handling land use and land cover data. *Professional Paper 1059*, USGS Reston Virginia

Moellering H (1973) The automatic mapping of traffic crashes. *Surveying and Mapping* 23: 467–77

Moellering H (1980) Strategies of real time cartography. *The American Cartographer* 7 (1): 67–75

Moik J G (1980) Digital processing of remotely sensed images. *NASA SP-431*. Scientific and Technical Information Branch National Aeronautics and Space Administration, Washington DC

Molenaar M (1990) A formal data structure for three dimensional vector maps. *Proceedings of EGIS '90*, pp. 770–81

Monkhouse F J, Wilkinson H R (1971) *Maps and Diagrams: their compilation and construction*. 3rd edn. Methuen, London

Monmonier M S (1974) Measures of pattern complexity for choropleth maps. *The American Cartographer* 1 (2): 159–69

Monmonier M S (1977) Maps, distortion and meaning. *Association of American Geographers Resource Paper in Geography*, **75–4**. Association of American Geographers, Washington

Monmonier M S (1982) *Computer-Assisted Cartography: principles and prospects*. Prentice-Hall, Englewood Cliffs New Jersey

Monmonier M S (1985) *Technological Transitions in Cartography*. The University of Wisconsin Press, Madison

Monmonier M S (1988) Geographical representation in statistical graphics: a conceptual framework. *Proceedings of the American Statistical Association Conference Section on Statistical Graphics*, pp. 1–10

Monmonier M S (1990) Geographic Information Systems. In: Perkins C R, Parry R B (eds.) *Information Sources in Cartography*. Bowker-Saur, London, pp. 214–31

Montgomery D, Urban G (1969) *Management Science in Marketing*. Prentice-Hall, Englewood Cliffs

Moon W M (1989) Application of evidential belief theory in geological, geophysical and remote sensing data integration. *Proceedings of IGARRS '89*, pp. 838–41

Mooneyhan D W (1988) Applications of Geographic Information Systems within the United Nations Environmental Programme. In: Mounsey H M, Tomlinson R F (eds.) *Building Databases for Global Science*. Taylor & Francis, London, pp. 315–29

Moore A W, Bie S W (1977) Uses of soil information systems. *Proceedings of the Australian Meeting of the ISSS Working Group on Soil Information Systems, Canberra, Australia, 2–4 March 1976*. PUDOC, Wageningen, 103 pp

Moore A W, Cook B G, Lynch L G (1981) Information systems for soil and related data. *Proceedings of the Second Australian Meeting of the ISSS Working Group on Soil Information Systems, Canberra, Australia, 19–21 February 1980*. PUDOC, Wageningen, 1–10

Morehouse S (1985) ARC/INFO: a geo-relational model for spatial information. *Proceedings of AUTOCARTO 8*. ASPRS, Falls Church Virginia, pp. 388–97

Morehouse S (1989) The architecture of ARC/INFO. *Proceedings of AUTOCARTO 9*. ASPRS/ACSM, Falls Church, pp. 266–77

Morgan J M (1987) Academic geographic information systems education: a commentary. *Photogrammetric Engineering and Remote Sensing* 53: 1443–5

Morgenstern M, Borgida A, Lassez C, Maier D, Wiederhold G (1988) Constraint-based systems: knowledge about data. In: Kerschberg L (ed.) *Proceedings of the Second International Conference on Expert Database Systems, Tysons Corner, Virginia 25–27 April 1988*. Benjamin/Cummings Publishing Company, pp. 23–44

Morrill R L (1987) A theoretical imperative. *Annals of the Association of American Geographers* 77 (4): 535–41

Morrison J L (1974) A theoretical framework for cartographic generalization with emphasis on the process of symbolization. *International Yearbook of Cartography* 14: 115–27

Morrison J L (1991) The organizational home for GIS in the scientific professional community. In: Maguire D J, Goodchild M F, Rhind D W (eds.) *Geographical Information Systems: principles and applications*. Longman, London, pp. 91–100, Vol 1

Morse B W (1987) Expert interface to a geographic information system. *Proceedings of AUTOCARTO 8*. ACSM/ASPRS, Falls Church Virginia, pp. 535–41

Morton G M (1966) *A Computer Oriented Geodetic Data Base and New Technique in File Sequencing*. IBN Ltd, Ottawa Canada

Morton Index (1966) In: Tomlinson R F (1972) (ed.) *Geographic Data Handling*. Commission on Geographical Data Sensing and Processing. International Geographical Union, Ottawa Canada

Mosteller F, Tukey J W (1977) *Data Analysis and Regression*. Addison-Wesley, Reading Massachusetts

Mott J (1990) The National Resource Information Centre – data directory, data broker. In: Parvey C, Grainger K (eds.) *A national Geographic Information System – an achievable objective?* AURISA Monograph 4. AURISA, Eastwood New South Wales, pp. 57–60

Mounsey H M (1991) Multisource multinational environmental GIS: lessons learnt from CORINE. In: Maguire D J, Goodchild M F, Rhind D W (eds.) *Geographical Information Systems: principles and applications*. Longman, London, pp. 185–200, Vol 2

Mounsey H M, Tomlinson R F (eds.) (1988) *Building Databases for Global Science*. Taylor & Francis, London

Muehrcke P C (1969) *Visual pattern analysis: A look at maps*. Unpublished Doctoral Thesis, University of Michigan

Muehrcke P C (1978) *Map Use: reading, analysis and interpretation*. J P Publications, Madison Wisconsin

Muehrcke P C (1986) *Map Use*, 2nd edn. JP Publications, Madison Wisconsin

Muehrcke P C (1990) Cartography and geographic information systems. *Cartography and Geographic Information Systems* **17** (1): 7–17

Muessig L F, Robinette A, Rowekamp T (1983) *Application of the USLE to define critical erosion and sedimentation in Minnesota*. Paper given at 38th Annual Meeting of the Soil Conservation Society of America, 31 July–3 August. Hartford, Conneticut.

Mulla D M (1988) Using geostatistics and spectral analysis to study spatial patterns in the topography of southeastern Washington State, USA. *Earth Surface Processes and Landforms* **13**: 389–405

Muller J-C (1977) Map griding and cartographic errors: a recurrent argument. *The Canadian Cartographer* **14**: 152–67

Muller J-C (1978) The mapping of travel time in Edmonton, Alberta. *Canadian Geographer* **22**: 195–210

Muller J-C (1982) Non-Euclidean geographical spaces: mapping functional distances. *Geographical Analysis* **14**: 189–203

Muller J-C (1983) Ignorance graphique ou cartographie de l'ignorance. *Cartographica* **20**: 17–30

Muller J-C (1984) Canada's elastic space: a portrayal of route and cost distances. *Canadian Geographer* **28**: 46–62

Muller J-C (1985) Geographic information systems: a unifying force for geography. *The Operational Geographer* **8**: 41–3

Muller J-C (1987) Fractal and automated line generalization. *The Cartographic Journal* **24**: 27–34

Muller J-C (1991) Generalization of spatial databases. In: Maguire D J, Goodchild M F, Rhind D W (eds.) *Geographical Information Systems: principles and applications*. Longman, London, pp. 457–75, Vol 1

Muller J-C, Honsaker J L (1983) Visual versus computerized seriation: the implications for automated map generalization. *Proceedings of AUTOCARTO 6*. ASPRS, Falls Church, pp. 277–88

Muller J-C, Johnson R D, Vanzella L R (1986) A knowledge based approach for developing cartographic expertise. *Proceedings of the 2nd International Symposium on Spatial Data Handling, Seattle*. International Geographical Union, Ohio, pp. 557–71

Muller J-P (1989) Real-time stereo matching and its role in future mapping systems. *Proceedings of Surveying and Mapping 89*. Royal Institution of Chartered Surveyors, London, Paper C5, 15 pp

Muller J-P, Anthony A, Brown A T, Deacon A T, Kennedy S A, Montgomery P M, Robertson G W, Watson D M (1988) Real-time stereo matching using transputer arrays for close-range applications. *Proceedings of the Joint IAPR Workshop on 'Computer vision – Special Hardware and Industrial Applications'*. Tokyo, Japan. 12–14 October 1988, pp. 45–9

Muller J-P, Day T, Kolbusz J, Dalton M, Richards S, Pearson J C (1988) Visualization of topographic data using video animation. *International Archives of Photogrammetry and Remote Sensing* **27** (B4): 602–14

Muller J-P, Day T, Kolbusz J, Dalton M, Richards S, Pearson J (1988) Visualisation of topographic data using video animation. In: Muller, J-P (ed.) *Digital Image Processing in Remote Sensing*. Taylor & Francis, London, pp. 21–38

Munkres J (1966) *Elementary Differential Topology*. Princeton University Press, Princeton,

Murai S (ed.) (1986) *Proceedings of AUTOCARTO JAPAN 2*. Autocarto Japan Organizing Committee, Tokyo

Murata T (1930) A method for analysing distribution of scattered village. *Geographical Review of Japan* **6**: 1744–53

Murayama Y (1990) *Regional Analysis*. Kokon Shoin, Tokyo

Murphy P A, Zehner R B, Robertson P A, Hirst R (1988) *Computer Use by Local Government Planners: an Australian perspective*. School of Town Planning University of New South Wales, Sydney

Musgrave F K, Kolb C E, Mace R S (1989) The synthesis and rendering of eroded fractal terrains. *Computer Graphics (SIGGRAPH '89 Proceedings)* **23** (3): 41–50

Mylopoulos J (1986) On knowledge base management systems. In: Brodie M L, Mylopoulos J (eds.) *On Knowledge Base Management Systems: integrating artificial intelligence and database technologies*. Springer-Verlag, New York, pp. 3–8

Nag P (1984) *Census Mapping Survey*. International Geographical Union Commission on Population Geography/Concept Publishing Company, New Delhi

Nag P (1987) A proposed base for a Geographical Information System for India. *International Journal of Geographical Information Systems* **1** (2): 181–7

Nagao M, Mukai Y, Sugimura T, Ayabe K, Arai K, Nakazawa T (1988) A study of reducing abnormal elevations in automatic computation of elevations from satellite data. *International Archives of Photogrammetry and Remote Sensing* **27** (B4): 280–8

Nagy G, Wagle S (1979) Geographic data processing. *ACM Computing Surveys* **11** (2)

Nagy Z, Siderelis K C (1990) A GIS model for local water use planning and zoning. *Proceedings of the Tenth Annual ESRI User Conference, Volume 2.* Environmental Systems Research Institute, Redlands California

Naithani K K (1989) The SOI PC/AUTOCAD Photogrammetric Monoplotter System: a tool for rural-urban mapping. *IX INCA International Seminar on Digital Cartography and Potential Users.* Pre-session Proceedings. Survey of India, Dehra Dun, pp. 239–46

Naqvi S (1986) Discussion. In: Brodie M L, Mylopoulos J (eds.) *On Knowledge Base Management Systems: integrating artificial intelligence and database technologies.* Springer-Verlag, New York, p. 93

Naqvi S, Tsur S (1989) *A Logical Language for Data and Knowledge Bases.* Computer Science Press, New York

Nash K (1986) The application of computers to planning tasks in the city of Sydney. *Australian Planner* **24**: 19–23

Nash K (1988) The Sydney City Council Land Information System – a decade on, the dream and the reality. *URPIS – Proceedings of the Urban and Regional Planning Information Systems Annual Conferences*, Volume 16. Australasian Urban and Regional Information Systems Association Inc., Sydney, pp. 1–13

Nastelin J (1985) Optimization of baseline determination for area map annotation. *Technical Report IPL-078.* Image Processing Laboratory, Rensselaer Polytechnic Institute, Troy

Natal/KwaZulu Association for Geographic Information Systems (1989) *NAGIS NEWS* June. Institute of Natural Resources, Pietermaritzburg 3200 Natal South Africa

National Academy of Sciences (1983) *Procedures and Standards for a Multipurpose Cadastre.* National Academy Press, Washington DC

National Computer Graphics Association (1989) *Standards in the Computer Graphics Industry.* NCGA, Fairfax Virginia

National Geophysical Data Center (1985) *Relief of the Surface of the Earth (maps, scale approximately 1 : 39 000 000).* Report MGG-2. National Geophysical Data Center, Boulder Colorado

National Joint Utilities Group (1986) *NJUG Specification for the Digitisation of Large Scale OS Maps. No. 12.* NJUG, London

National Joint Utilities Group (1988) *The quality control procedure for large scale Ordnance Survey maps digitized to OS 1988. Publication Number 13* NJUG, London

National Research Council (1989) *Numerical Data Advisory Board Annual Report 1988–1989.* National Academy Press, Washington DC

Navon D (1977) Forest before trees: the precedence of global features in visual perception. *Cognitive Psychology* **9**: 353–83

NCGIA (1989) Multiple representations. *NCGIA Technical Paper 89–3*

NCGIA (1989) The research plan of the National Center for Geographic Information and Analysis. *International Journal of Geographical Information Systems* **3** (2): 117–36

Neal J G, Shapiro S C (1990) Intelligent multi-media interface technology. In: Sullivan J W, Tyler S W (eds.) *Architectures for Intelligent Interfaces: elements and prototypes.* Addison-Wesley, Reading Massachusetts

Neal J G, Thielman C Y, Dobes Z, Haller S M, Shapiro S C (1989) Natural language with integrated deictic and graphic gestures. *Proceedings, DARPA Speech and Natural Language Workshop.* Morgan Kaufmann, Los Altos CA

Needham J (1959) *Science and Civilization in China*, Volume 3. Cambridge University Press, Cambridge

Needham J (1981) *The Shorter Science and Civilization in China* (Abridged C A Ronan), Volume 2. Cambridge University Press, Cambridge

Neiser U (1976) *Cognition and Reality: principles and implications of cognitive psychology.* Freeman, San Francisco

Nelson T (1981) *Literary Machines.* (2nd edn) Theodore Holm Nelson, Swarthmore

Nelson T (1987) *Computer Lib.* Microsoft Press, Redmond, WA

NERC (1988) *Geographical Information in the Environmental Sciences.* (Report of the Working Group on Geographic Information), Natural Environment Research Council, Swindon

Newell R G, Theriault D G (1990) Is GIS just a combination of CAD and DBMS? *Mapping Awareness* **4** (3): 42–45

Newell R G, Theriault D G, Easterfield M (1990) Temporal GIS – modelling the evolution of spatial data in time. *Proceedings of GIS Design Models Conference.* Midlands Regional Research Laboratory, Leicester

Newkirk P (1987) Municipal information systems: challenges and opportunities. *Plan Canada* **27**: 94–100

Newman W M, Sproull R F (1979) *Principles of Interactive Computer Graphics*, 2nd edn. McGraw-Hill, New York

Newton P W, Crawford J R (1988) Microcomputer-based geographic information and mapping systems. In: Newton P.W, Taylor M A P, Sharpe R (eds.) *Desktop Planning: microcomputer applications for infrastructure and services planning and management.* Hargreen, Melbourne, pp. 31–43

Newton P W, Taylor M A P, Sharpe R (eds.) (1988) *Desktop Planning: microcomputer applications for infrastructure and services planning and management.* Hargreen, Melbourne

NEXPRI (1989) *Geographical Information Systems for Landscape Analysis Research Programme.* NEXPRI, University of Utrecht

Nichol D G, Fiebig M J, Whatmough R J, Whitbread P J (1987) Some image processing aspects of a military geographic information system. *Australian Computer Journal* **19** (3): 154–60

Nicholson R (1990) Public access to spatial information:

the use of value added networks in the UK. *Proceedings of EGIS '90*, Volume 2. EGIS Foundation, Utrecht, pp. 782–8

Nickerson B G, Freeman H R (1986) Development of a rule-based system for automatic map generalization. *Proceedings of the 2nd International Symposium on Spatial Data Handling, Seattle*. International Geographical Union, Ohio, pp. 537–56

NICOGRAPH (ed.) (1988) *Computer Mapping*. Nihon Keizai Shinbunsha, Tokyo

Nielsen D R, Bouma J (1985) *Spatial Analysis of Soil Data*. PUDOC, Wageningen

Nielsen J (1990) The art of navigating through hypertext. *Communications of the Association of Computing Machinery* **33** (3): 296–310

Nielsen J (1990) *Hypertext and Hypermedia*. Academic Press, San Diego California

Nievergelt J, Hinterberger H, Sevcik K (1984) The grid file: an adaptable, symmetric multi-key file structure. *ACM Transactions on Database Systems* **9** (1): 38–71

Nievergelt J, Schorn P (1988) Line problems with supra-linear growth (in German). *Informatik Spektrum* **11** (4)

Nijkamp P (1979) *Multidimensional Spatial Data and Decision Analysis*. Wiley, New York

Nijkamp P, De Jong W (1987) Training needs in information systems for local and regional development and planning. *Regional Development Dialogue* **8** (1): 72–119

Nilsson N J (1971) *Problem Solving Methods in Artificial Intelligence*. McGraw-Hill, New York

Nilsson N J (1980) *Principles of Artificial Intelligence*. Tioga Publishing Co., Palo Alto

Nishikawa O, Kubo S (1986) Intensive Utilisation of Geographic Information, In: Hirayama H (ed.) *Perspectives and Tasks Towards an Information Society*. The Science Council of Japan, Tokyo, pp. 131–40

NJUG (1986) *Proposed Data Exchange Format for Utility Map Data*. NJUG 11. National Joint Utilities Group, 30 Millbank, London, SW1P 4RD

NJUG (1986) *NJUG Specification for the Digitisation of Large Scale OS Maps*. NJUG 12. National Joint Utilities Group, 30 Millbank, London, SW1P 4RD

NJUG (1988) *Quality Control Procedures for Large Scale OS Maps Digitised to OS 1988*. NJUG 13. National Joint Utilities Group, 30 Millbank, London, SW1P 4RD

NOAA (1987) *Climate and Global Change: An integrated NOAA program in Earth System Science*. NOAA, Washington DC

Nordbeck S (1962) Location of areal data for computer processing. *Lund Studies in Geography, Series C, General, Mathematical and Regional Geography No. 2*, Lund University Sweden

Norman J (1979) Modeling of complete crop canopy. In: Barfield B G, Gerber J F (eds) *Modification of the Aerial Environment of Plants*. American Society of Agricultural Engineers, St Joseph Mississippi, pp. 249–77

Norris P (1983) Microdata from the British census. In: Rhind D W (ed.) *A Census User's Handbook*. Methuen, London, pp. 301–19

NRC (1980) *Need for a Multipurpose Cadastre*. National Research Council, Washington DC

NRC (1983) *Procedures and Standards for a Multipurpose Cadastre*. National Research Council, Washington DC

NSSDC (National Space Science Data Center) (1989) *Directory Interchange Format Manual, Version 1.0*. NASA Goddard Space Flight Center, Greenbelt Maryland

Nyerges T L (1980) *Modelling the Structure of Cartographic Information for Query Processing*. Unpublished PhD thesis, Ohio State University

Nyerges T L (1989) Components of model curricula development for GIS in university education. *Proceedings of AUTOCARTO 9*. ASPRS/ACSM, Bethesda Maryland, pp. 199–204

Nyerges T L (1989) Information integration for multipurpose land information systems. *URISA Journal* **1** (1): 27–38

Nyerges T L (1989) Schema integration analysis for the development of GIS databases. *International Journal of Geographical Information Systems* **3** (2): 153–83

Nyerges T L, Chrisman N R (1989) A framework for model curricula development in cartography and geographic information systems. *Professional Geographer* **41** (3): 283–93

Obermeyer N J (1989) A systematic approach to the taxonomy of geographic information use. *Proceedings GIS/LIS '89*, Volume 2. ASPRS/ACSM/AAG/URISA/AM-FM, Bethesda, pp. 421–9

O'Callaghan J F, Garner B J (1991) Land and Geographical Information Systems in Australia. In: Maguire D J, Goodchild M F, Rhind D W (eds.) *Geographical Information Systems: principles and applications*. Longman. London, pp. 57–70, Vol 2

O'Callaghan J F, Mark D M (1984) The extraction of drainage networks from digital elevation data. *Computer Vision, Graphics, and Image Processing* **28**: 323–44

Odland J (1988) Spatial autocorrelation. *Sage Scientific Geography Series Number 9*. Sage Publications, London

OECD (1988) *Activities of the OECD, Report of the Secretary General*. OECD Publications, Paris

Office of Technology Assessment (1981) *Computer-Based National Information Systems*. Congress of the United States, Washington DC, pp. 58–9

Official Journal of the European Community (1985) Council Decision on 27 June 1985 on the adoption of the Commission work programme concerning an experimental project for gathering, coordinating and ensuring the consistency of information on the state of the environment and natural resources in the Community. OJ L 176, 6 July 1985

Ogrosky C E (1975) Population estimates from satellite imagery. *Photogrammetric Engineering and Remote Sensing* **41**: 707–12

Oliver M A, Webster R (1986) Combining nested and linear sampling for determining the scale and form of spatial variation of regionalised variables. *Geographical Analysis* **18**: 227–42

Oliver M A, Webster R (1986) Semi-variograms for modelling the spatial pattern of landform and soil properties. *Earth Surface Processes and Landforms* **11**: 491–504

Oliver M A, Webster R, Gerrard J (1989) Geostatistics in physical geography. Part 1. *Transactions of the Institute of British Geographers* NS **14**: 259–69

Oliver M A, Webster R, Gerrard J (1989) Geostatistics in physical geography. Part 2. *Transactions of the Institute of British Geographers* NS **14**: 270–86

Olle T W (1978) *The Codasyl Approach to Database Management*. Wiley, Chichester. 287pp.

Olson J M (1972) Autocorrelation as a measure of complexity. *Proceedings American Congress on Surveying and Mapping*. ACSM, Falls Church Virginia, pp. 111–19

Olson J M (1979) Cognitive cartographic experimentation. *The Canadian Cartographer* **16** (1): 34–44

Olson J M (1986) Color and the computer in cartography. In: Durrett H J (ed.) *Color and the Computer*. Academic Press, Boston, pp. 205–21

Olson J S (1989) *World Ecosystems* (WE2.0) NOAA/National Geophysical Data Center, Boulder, Colorado

Olson J S, Watts J, Allison L (1983) *Carbon in Live Vegetation of Major World Ecosystems*. US Department of Energy contract No. W-7405–ENG-26. Oak Ridge Laboratory, Oak Ridge Tennessee

Olsson L (1988) Automation of the pipeline register in the City of Stockholm. *Proceedings of AM/FM International – European Division Conference, Montreux*. AM/FM European Division, PO Box 6, CH4005, Basel, Switzerland, pp. 173–7

Olsson L (1989) Integrated resource monitoring by means of remote sensing, GIS and spatial modelling in arid environments. *Soil Use and Management* **5**: 30–7

O'Neill M O, Mark D M (1987) The Psi–s Plot: a useful representation for digital cartographic lines. *Proceedings of AUTOCARTO 8*. ASPRS, Falls Church, pp. 231–40

Openshaw S (1983) Multivariate analysis of census data: the classification of areas. In: Rhind D W (ed.) *A Census User's Handbook*. Methuen, London, pp. 243–64

Openshaw S (1984) The modifiable areal unit problem. *Concepts and Techniques in Modern Geography*. Vol. 38. Geo Abstracts, Norwich

Openshaw S (1988) Building an automated modelling system to explore a universe of spatial interaction models. *Geographical Analysis* **20**: 31–46

Openshaw S (1989) Learning to live with errors in spatial databases. In: Goodchild M F, Gopal S (eds.) *The Accuracy of Spatial Databases*. Taylor & Francis, London, pp. 263–76

Openshaw S (1989) Computer modelling in human geography. In: Macmillan W (ed.) *Remodelling Geography*. Blackwell, Oxford, pp. 70–88

Openshaw S (1989) Making geodemographics more sophisticated. *Journal of the Market Research Society* **31**: 111–31

Openshaw S (1989) Automating the search for cancer clusters. *The Professional Statistician* **8** (9): 7–8

Openshaw S (1990) Spatial referencing for the user in the 1990s *Mapping Awareness* **4** (2): 24–9

Openshaw S (1990) Towards a spatial analysis research strategy for the Regional Research Laboratory initiative. In: Masser J, Blakemore M J (eds.) *Geographical Information Management: methodology and applications*. Longman, London

Openshaw S (1990) Spatial analysis and GIS: a review of progress and possibilities. In: Scholten H J, Stillwell J C H (eds.) *Geographic Information Systems for urban and regional planning*. Kluwer, Dordrecht, 156–63

Openshaw S (1990) Automating the search for cancer clusters: a review of problems, progress, and opportunities. In Thomas R W (ed.) *Spatial Epidemiology. London Papers in Regional Science 21*. Pion, London, pp. 48–78

Openshaw S (1991) Developing appropriate spatial analysis methods for GIS. In: Maguire D J, Goodchild M F, Rhind D W (eds.) *Geographical Information Systems: principles and applications*. Longman, London, pp. 389–402, Vol 1

Openshaw S, Charlton M, Craft A W, Birch J M (1988) An investigation of leukaemia clusters by use of a geographical analysis machine. *The Lancet* **1**: 272–73

Openshaw S, Charlton M, Wymer C (1987) A Mark 1 Geographical Analysis Machine for the automated analysis of point data. *International Journal of Geographical Information Systems* **1**: 335–43

Openshaw S, Cross A E, Charlton M E (1990) Building a prototype Geographical Correlates Exploration Machine. *International Journal of Geographical Information Systems* **3**: 297–312

Openshaw S, Cross A E, Charlton M, Brunsdon C, Lillie J (1990) Lessons learnt from a post-mortem of a failed GIS. *Proceedings of AGI '90*, AGI, London, pp. 2.3.1–2.3.5

Openshaw S, Cullingford D, Gillard A A (1980) A critique of the national census classifications of OPCS and PRAG. *Town Planning Review* **51**: 421–39

Openshaw S, Goddard J (1987) Some implications of the commodification of information and the emerging information economy for applied geographical analysis in the United Kingdom. *Environment and Planning A* **19**: 1423–39

Openshaw S, Mounsey H M (1987) Geographic information systems and the BBC's Domesday interactive videodisk. *International Journal of Geographical Information Systems* **1** (2): 173–9

Openshaw S, Wilkie D, Binks K, Wakeford R, Gerrard M H, Croasdale M R (1989) A method for detecting spatial clustering of disease. In: Crosbie W A, Gittus J H (eds.) *Medical Responses to the Effects of Ionising Radiation*. Elsevier Applied Science, London, pp. 295–308

Openshaw S, Wymer C, Charlton M (1986) A geographical information and mapping system for the

BBC Domesday optical disks. *Transactions of the Institute of British Geographers* NS **11**: 296–304
Ordnance Survey Review Committee (1979) *Report of the Ordnance Survey Review Committee*. HMSO, London
Ordnance Survey (1984) *Report of the Small Scales Digital Map User Needs Study*. OS, Southampton
Ordnance Survey (1985) *Report of the Investigation into Demand for Digital Data from 1:50 000 Mapping*. OS, Southampton
Ordnance Survey (1987) *National Transfer Format, Release 1.0*. OS, Southampton UK
Ordnance Survey (1988) *Annual Report 1987/88*. OS, Southampton
Ordnance Survey (1988) *Ordnance Survey's Contractors' Specification for Digital Mapping*. OS, Southampton
Ordnance Survey (1989) *Annual Report 1988/89*. OS, Southampton
Ordnance Survey (1989) *National Transfer Format, Release 1.1*. OS, Southampton UK
Ordnance Survey (1990) *Annual Report*, HMSO, London
Orenstein J A (1990) An object-oriented approach to spatial data processing. *Proceedings of the 4th International Symposium on Spatial Data Handling*, Volume 2. International Geographical Union, Columbus Ohio, pp. 669–78
Orman L (1986) Flexible management of computational models. *Decision Support Systems* **2**: 225–34
Oswald H, Raetzsch H (1984) A system for generation and display of digital elevation models. *Geo-Processing* **2**: 197–218
Ottoson L (1977) Information systems at the National Land Survey of Sweden. *Cartographica Monograph* 20: 104–14
Ottoson L (1987) *A programme for National Geographic Data Bases in Sweden*. LMV-rapport 1987:8, ISSN 0280-5731. Gävle, Sweden
Ottoson L, Rystedt B (1991) National GIS programmes in Sweden. In: Maguire D J, Goodchild M F, Rhind D W (eds.) *Geographical Information Systems: principles and applications*. Longman, London, pp. 39–46, Vol 2
Ozemoy V M, Smith D R, Sicherman A (1981) Evaluating computerized geographic information systems using decision analysis. *Interfaces* **11**: 92–8

Pandey M K, Dave V S, Kumar S (1989) Relevance of application of digital cartography for development planning process in India. *IX INCA International Seminar on Digital Cartography and Potential Users*. Pre-session Proceedings. Survey of India, Dehra Dun, pp. 304–19
Parent P (1988) Universities and Geographical Information Systems: background, constraints and prospects. *Proceedings of Mapping the Future*. URISA, Washington, pp. 1–12
Parent P, Church R (1987) Evolution of geographic information systems as decision making tools. *Proceedings of GIS '87*. ASPRS/ACSM, Falls Church VA, pp. 63–71
Park S E, Miller K W (1988) Random number generators: good ones are hard to find. *Communications ACM* **31** (10): 1192–201
Parker H D (1988) The unique qualities of a geographic information system: a commentary. *Photogrammetric Engineering and Remote Sensing* **54** (11): 1547–49
Parker H D (1989) GIS software 1989: a survey and commentary. *Photogrammetric Engineering and Remote Sensing* **55**: 1589–91
Parker H D (1989) *The GIS Sourcebook*. GIS World Inc., Fort Collins Colorado
Parrott R, Stutz F P (1991) Urban GIS applications. In: Maguire D J, Goodchild M F, Rhind D W (eds.) *Geographical Information Systems: principles and applications*. Longman, London, pp. 247–60, Vol 2
Parry R B, Perkins C R (1987) *World Mapping Today*. Butterworths, London
Parsloe E (ed.) (1983) *Interactive Video*. John Wiley, Chichester England
Parthasaradhi, E U R, Krishnanunni K (1989) Specifications of a digital topographic base for GIS applications: some experiences from project Vasundharsa. *IX INCA International Seminar on Digital Cartography and Potential Users*. Pre-session Proceedings. Survey of India, Dehra Dun, pp. 320–8
Pascoe R T, Penny J P (1990) Construction of interfaces for the exchange of geographic data. *International Journal of Geographical Information Systems* **4** (2): 147–56
Pavlidis T (1982) *Algorithms for Graphics and Image Processing*. Computer Science Press, Rockville Maryland
Pazner M, Kirby K C, Thies N (1989) *MAP II Map Processor*. Wiley, New York
Peacock D, Rutherford I (1989) Concepts into reality – an account of a GIS implementation in SWEB. *Proceedings of AGI 89 Conference, Birmingham*. AGI, 12 Great George Street, London, SW1P 3AD, pp. 2.3.1–2.3.6
Peano G (1890) Sur une courbe qui remplit toute une aire plane. *Mathematische Annalen* **36** A:157–60
Pearce D, Markandya A, Barbier E B (1989) *Blueprint for a Green Economy*. Earthscan Publications, London
Pech R P, Graetz R D, Davis A W (1986) Reflectance modelling and the derivation of vegetation indices for an Australian semi-arid shrubland. *International Journal of Remote Sensing* **7**: 389–403
Pellew R A, Harrison J D (1988) A global database on the status of biological diversity: the IUCN perspective. In: Mounsey H M, Tomlinson R F (eds.) *Building Databases for Global Science*. Taylor & Francis, London, pp. 330–9
Peplies R W, Keuper H F (1975) Regional analysis. In: Reeves R G, Anson A, Landen D (eds.) *Manual of Remote Sensing*, Vol. 2. American Society of Photogrammetry, Falls Church Virginia, pp. 1947–98
Perkal J (1965) Translated by Jackowski W. An attempt at objective generalization. *Michigan Inter-University Community of Mathematical Geographers. Discussion Paper* **9**
Perkins C R, Parry R B (eds.) (1990) *Information Sources in Cartography*. Bowker-Saur, London

Perl Y, Itai A, Avni H (1978) Interpolation search – a log log n search. *Communications ACM* **21** (7): 550–3

Perrett P, Lyons K J, Moss O F (1989) Overview of GIS activities in Queensland. In: Ball D, Babbage R (eds.) *Geographical Information Systems: defence applications.* Pergamon Press, Sydney, pp. 152–79

Perring F H (1964) Contribution to Session 6, The mapping of vegetation flora and fauna. In: Bickmore D P (ed.) *Experimental Cartography – Report of the Oxford Symposium.* Oxford University Press, Oxford

Perring F H, Walters S M (1962) *Atlas of the British Flora.* Nelson, London

Petach M, Wagenet R J (1989) Integrating and analyzing spatially variable soil properties for land evaluation. In: Bouma J, Bregt A K (eds.) *Land Qualities in Space and Time. Proceedings of a Symposium organised by the International Society of Soil Science (ISSS), Wageningen, The Netherlands, 22–26 August 1988.* PUDOC, Wageningen, pp. 145–54

Petchenik B (1989) The road not taken. *The American Cartographer* **16** (1): 47–50

Peters T (1987) *Thriving on Chaos.* Macmillan, London

Peterson D L, Running S W (1989) Applications in forest science and management. In: Asrar G (ed.) *Theory and Applications of Optical Remote Sensing.* Wiley, New York, pp. 429–73

Peterson M (1979) An evaluation of unclassed cross-line choropleth mapping. *The American Cartographer* **6** (1): 21–37

Petrie G, Kennie T (eds.) (1990) *Terrain Modelling in Surveying and Civil Engineering.* Whittles, Latheronwheel

Peucker T K (1972) Computer cartography. *Commission on College Geography, Resource Paper No.17.* Association of American Geographers, Washington DC

Peucker T K (1975) A theory of the cartographic line. *Proceedings of AUTOCARTO 2.* ASPRS, Falls Church, pp. 508–18

Peucker T K (1978) Data structures for digital terrain models: discussion and comparison. *Harvard Papers on Geographic Information Systems 5 (Proceedings First International Advanced Study Symposium on Topological Data Structures for Geographic Information Systems, held in 1977).* 1–15

Peucker T K, Chrisman N R (1975) Cartographic data structures. *The American Cartographer* **2** (2): 55–69

Peucker T K, Cochrane D (1974) Die Automation der Reliefdarstellung – Theorie und Praxis. *International Yearbook of Cartography* **XIV**: 128–39

Peucker T K, Douglas D H (1975) Detection of surface specific points by local parallel processing of discrete terrain elevation data. *Computer Graphics and Image Processing* **4**: 375–387

Peucker T K, Fowler R J, Little J J, Mark D M (1978) The triangulated irregular network. *Proceedings of the ASP Digital Terrain Models (DTM) Symposium.* American Society of Photogrammetry, Falls Church Virginia, pp. 516–40

Peuquet D J (1981) An examination of the techniques for reformatting digital cartographic data Part 1: the raster-to-vector process. *Cartographica* **18** (1): 34–48

Peuquet D J (1981) An examination of the techniques for reformatting digital cartographic data Part 2: the vector-to-raster process. *Cartographica* **18** (3): 21–33

Peuquet D J (1984) A conceptual framework and comparison of spatial data models. *Cartographica* **21** (4): 66–113

Peuquet D J (1988) Issues involved in selecting appropriate data models for global databases. In: Mounsey H M, Tomlinson R F (eds.) *Building Databases for Global Science.* Taylor & Francis, London, pp. 66–78

Peuquet D J (1988) Representations of geographic space: toward a conceptual synthesis. *Annals of the Association of American Geographers* **78**: 375–94

Peuquet D J, Zhan C-X (1987) An algorithm to determine the directional relationship between arbitrarily-shaped polygons in a plane. *Pattern Recognition* **20**: 65–74

Pevsner S (1989) Image processing in a GIS environment. In: Barrett E C, Brown K A (eds.) *Remote Sensing for Operational Applications.* The Remote Sensing Society, Nottingham England, pp. 323–30

Pfefferkorn C, Burr D, Harrison D, Heckman B, Oresky C, Rothermel J (1985) ACES: a cartographic expert system. *Proceedings of AUTOCARTO 7.* ASPRS, Falls Church Virginia, pp. 399–407 and *Cartographic Journal* **15** (2): 72–7

Phillips A (1987) *Flux gate sensor with improved sense winding gating.* US Patent 4,646,015.

Phillips M, Blackburn J (1989) The Chrysalis Project: a regional GIS over Jervis Bay. In: Ball D, Babbage R (eds.) *Geographical Information Systems: defence applications.* Pergamon Press, Sydney, pp. 204–31

Phillips R J, DeLucia A, Skelton N (1975) Some objective tests of the eligibility of relief maps. *Cartographic Journal* **12** (10): 39–46

Piercy N, Evans M (1983) *Managing Marketing Information.* Croom Helm, London

Pike R J (1988) The geometric signature: quantifying landslide terrain types from digital elevation models. *Mathematical Geology* **20** (5): 491–510

Pike R J, Rozema W J (1975) Spectral analysis of landforms. *Annals of the Association of American Geographers* **65** (4): 499–516

Pinker S (1985) Visual cognition: an introduction. In: Pinker S (ed.) *Visual Cognition.* MIT Press, Cambridge Massachusetts: pp. 1–96

Piscator I (1987) The Swedish Land Data Bank and its use by local authorities. *Proceedings of Land Use Information in Sweden.* Swedish Council for Building Research, Stockholm Sweden. ISBN 91-540-4665-3, pp. 56–68

Piwowar J M, Le Drew E F, Dudycha D J (1990) Integration of spatial data in vector and raster formats in a geographic information system. *International Journal of Geographical Information Systems* **4** (4): 429–44

Pixar Inc. (1988) *Renderman Interface.* Pixar, San Rafael California

Pleijsier L K (1986) The laboratory methods and data

exchange programme. *Interim Report on the Exchange Round 85–2*. International Soil Reference and Information Centre, Wageningen

Pleijsier L K (1989) Variability in soil data. In: Bouma J, Bregt A K (eds.) *Land Qualities in Space and Time. Proceedings of a Symposium organised by the International Society of Soil Science (ISSS), Wageningen, The Netherlands, 22–26 August 1988*. PUDOC, Wageningen, pp. 3–14

Poiker T K (1985) Geographic information systems in the geographic curriculum. *The Operational Geographer* **8**: 38–41

Porcher E (1989) *Ground Water Contamination Susceptibility in Minnesota*. Minnesota Pollution Control Agency, St Paul

Powitz B M, Meyer U (1989) Generalization of settlements by pattern recognition methods. *Paper presented at the ICA Conference, Budapest* 7pp

Preparata F P, Shamos M I (1985) *Computational Geometry: an introduction*. Springer-Verlag, New York

Press L (1990) Compuvision or teleputer? *Communications of the Association for Computing Machinery* **33** (9): 29–36

Preusser A (1984) Computing contours by successive solution of quintic polynomial equations. *ACM Transactions on Mathematical Software* **10** (4): 463–72

Price S (1989) Modelling the temporal element in land information systems. *International Journal of Geographical Information Systems* **3**: 233–44

Price Waterhouse (1991) Price performance trends. *Computer Weekly* 17 January: 1

Prisley S P, Gregoire T G, Smith J L (1989) The mean and variance of area estimates computed in an arc-node geographic information system. *Photogrammetric Engineering and Remote Sensing* **55** (11): 1601–12

Prisley S P, Mead R A (1987) Cost-benefit analysis for geographic information systems. *Proceedings of GIS '87*. ASPRS, San Francisco, pp. 29–37

Przymusinski T C (1989) On the declarative and procedural semantics of logic programs. *Journal of Automated Reasoning* **5**: 167–205

Puissegur A (1988) Does charging eradicate the defense of sovereign immunity? *Proceedings of the Urban and Regional Information Systems Association*, Vol. 4. URISA, Washington DC, pp. 358–70

Puissegur A (1989) An overview of state open records laws. *Workshop on Managing the Risks and Recovering the Costs of Geographic and Facilities Management Systems*. Department of Engineering Professional Development, University of Wisconsin-Madison, Madison, Wisconsin

Pullar D, Egenhofer M J (1988) Towards formal definitions of topological relations among spatial objects. *Proceedings of the 3rd International Symposium on Spatial Data Handling*. International Geographical Union, Columbus Ohio, pp. 225–42

Pullar D, Egenhofer M J (1988) Towards formal definitions of topological relations amongst spatial objects. *Proceedings of the 3rd International Symposium on Spatial Data Handling*. International Geographical Union, Columbus Ohio, pp. 225–42

Pyle I C (1985) *The Ada Programming Language: a guide for programmers*. Prentice-Hall, Englewood Cliffs New Jersey

Quade E S (1982) *Analysis of Public Decisions*, 2nd edn. North-Holland, New York

Quarmby N A, Saull R J (1990) The use of perspective views in local planning. *International Journal of Remote Sensing* **11**: 1329–30

Quarterman J S, Silberschatz A, Peterson J L (1985) 4.2bsd and 4.3bsd as examples of the Unix system. *ACM Computing Surveys* **17** (4): 379–418

Rada J (1982) The microelectronics revolution: implications for the Third World. *Development Dialogue* **2**: 41–67

Raisz E J (1931) The physiographic method of representing scenery on maps. *Geographical Review* **21**

Raisz E J (1948) *General Cartography*. McGraw Hill, New York

Ramachandran A (1990) The global strategy for shelter: a new challenge for surveys. *Keynote address to the XIX Congress of the International Federation of Surveyors*, Helsinki

Ramer U (1971) An iterative procedure for the polygonal approximation of plane curves. *Computer Graphics and Image Processing* **1** (3): 244–56

Rao M K, Pathan S K, Matieda I Cm, Majumder K L, Yogarajan N, Padmavathy A S (1989) Development of a Geographic Information System around ISROVISION. *IX INCA International Seminar on Digital Cartography and Potential Users*. Pre-session Proceedings. Survey of India, Dehra Dun, pp. 502–3

Raper J F (1988) A methodology for the investigation of landform-sediment relationships in British glaciated valleys. Unpublished PhD Thesis Queen Mary College, University of London

Raper J F (1989) *Three Dimensional Applications in GIS*. Taylor & Francis, London

Raper J F (1989) The geoscientific mapping and modelling system: a conceptual design. In: Raper J F (ed.) *Three Dimensional Applications in Geographical Information Systems*. Taylor & Francis, London, pp. 11–20

Raper J F (1990) An atlas of 3-D functions. *Proceedings of Symposium on Three Dimensional Computer Graphics in Modelling Geologic Structures and Simulating Processes*. Freiburger Geowissenschafliche Beitrage **2**: 74–5

Raper J F (ed.) (1989) *Three Dimensional Applications in Geographical Information Systems*. Taylor & Francis, London

Raper J F, Green N P A (1989) Development of a hypertext based tutor for geographical information systems. *British Journal of Educational Technology* **9**: 3–23

Raper J F, Green N P A (1989) GIST: an object-oriented

approach to a GIS tutor. *Proceedings of AUTOCARTO 9.* ACSM/ASPRS, Falls Church Virginia, pp. 610–19

Raper J F, Kelk B (1991) Three-dimensional GIS. In: Maguire D J, Goodchild M F, Rhind D W (eds.) *Geographical Information Systems: principles and applications.* Longman, London, pp. 299–317, Vol 1

Raper J F, Rhind D W (1990) UGIX (A): the design of a spatial language interface to a topological vector GIS. *Proceedings of the 4th International Conference on Spatial Data Handling.* International Geographical Union, Columbus Ohio, pp. 405–12

Rapp S, Collins T (1987) *Maxi Marketing.* McGraw-Hill, New York

Rasmussen J (1986) *Information Processing and Human Machine Interaction: an approach to cognitive engineering.* North Holland, New York

Rasool S I, Ojima D S (1989) Pilot studies for remote sensing and data management. *International Geosphere Biosphere Program, Global Change Report No. 8.*

Redfern P (1987) *A Study on the Future of the Census of Population: alternative approaches.* EUROSTAT Report 3C, Luxembourg

Redfern P (1989) Population registers: some administrative and statistical pros and cons. *Journal of the Royal Statistical Society A* **152** (1): 1–41

Reed C N (1986) DELTAMAP just another new GIS? *Proceedings of the 3rd International Symposium on Spatial Data Handling.* IGU Commission on Geographical Data Sensing and Processing, Williamsville NY, pp. 375–83

Reed C N (1988) A minimum set of criteria for selecting a turn-key geographic information system: an update. *Proceedings of GIS/LIS '88.* ACSM ASPRS AAG URISA, Falls Church, pp. 867–73

Reeuwijk L P van (1982) *Laboratory methods and data quality. Program for soil characterisation: a report on the pilot round. Part I. CEC and texture. Proceedings of the 5th International Classification Workshop.* Khartoum, Sudan, 58 pp

Reeuwijk L P van (1984) *Laboratory methods and data quality. Program for soil characterisation: a report on the pilot round. Part II. Exchangeable bases, base saturation and pH.* International Soil Reference and Information Centre, Wageningen, 28 pp.

Reeves R, Anding D, Mertz F (1987) First principles deterministic simulation of IR and visible imagery. *Photon Research Associates Report R-024–88.* PRA Inc., La Jolla California

Reisner P, Boyce R F, Chamberlin D D (1975) Human factors evaluation of two database query languages – Square and Sequel. *Proceedings, National Computer Conference (AFIPS)*, pp. 447–52

Reminga v. United States [1978] 448 F. Supp. 45 (W. D. Mich.)

Requicha A A G (1980) Representations for rigid solids: theory, methods, and systems. *ACM Computing Surveys* **12** (4): 437–64

Reybold W, TeSelle G W (1989) Soil geographic databases. *Journal of Soil and Water Conservation* **44** (1): 28–9

Rhind D W (1971) The production of a multi-colour geological map by automated means. *Nachr. aus den Karten und Vermessungswesen* Heft Nr. **52**: 47–51

Rhind D W (1974) An introduction to the digitising and editing of mapped data. In: Dale P F (ed.) *Automation and Cartography.* British Cartographic Society Special Publication, Volume 1, pp. 50–68

Rhind D W (1976) Geographical Information Systems. *Area* **8** (1): 46

Rhind D W (1981) Geographical Information Systems in Britain. In: Bennett R J, Wrigley N (eds.) *Quantitative Geography: retrospect and prospect.* Routledge and Kegan Paul, London, pp. 17–35

Rhind D W (1984) The SASPAC story. *BURISA 60*: 8–10

Rhind D W (1985) Successors to the Census of Population. *Journal of Economic and Social Measurement* **13** (1): 29–38

Rhind D W (1986) Remote sensing, digital mapping and Geographical Information Systems: the creation of government policy in the UK. *Environment and Planning C: Government and Policy* **4**: 91–102

Rhind D W (1987) Recent developments in geographic information systems in the UK. *International Journal of Geographical Information Systems* **1** (3): 229–41

Rhind D W (1988) A GIS research agenda. *International Journal of Geographical Information Systems* **2**: 23–8

Rhind D W (1988) Geografische Informatiesystemen en Kartografie. *Kartografisch Tijdschrift* **14**: 25–7

Rhind D W (1988) Personality as a factor in the development of a new discipline: the case of computer-assisted cartography. *The American Cartographer* **15** (3): 277–89

Rhind D W (1990) Global databases and GIS. In: Foster M J, Shand P J (eds.) *The Association for Geographic Information Yearbook 1990.* Taylor & Francis and Miles Arnold, London, pp. 218–23

Rhind D W (1990) Topographic databases derived from small scale maps and the future of Ordnance Survey. In: Foster M J, Shand P J (eds.) *The Association for Geographic Information Yearbook 1990.* Taylor & Francis, London, pp. 87–96

Rhind D W (1991) Counting the people: the role of GIS. In: Maguire D J, Goodchild M F, Rhind D W (eds.) *Geographical Information Systems: principles and applications.* Longman, London, pp. 127–37, Vol 2

Rhind D W (ed.) (1983) *A Census Users Handbook.* Methuen, London

Rhind D W, Clark P (1988) Cartographic data inputs to global databases. In: Mounsey H M, Tomlinson R F (eds.) *Building Databases for Global Science.* Taylor & Francis, London, pp. 79–104

Rhind D W, Cole K, Armstrong M, Chow L, Openshaw S (1990) An on-line, secure and infinitely flexible database system for the national population census. *Working Report 14 South East Regional Research Laboratory.* SERRL, Birkbeck College, London

Rhind D W, Green N P A (1988) Design of a geographical information system for a heterogeneous scientific community. *International Journal of Geographical Information Systems* **2**: 171–89

Rhind D W, Green N P A, Mounsey H M, Wiggins J C (1984) The integration of geographical data. *Proceedings of Austra Carto Perth*. Australian Cartographic Association, Perth, pp. 273–93

Rhind D W, Green N P A, Mounsey H M, Wiggins J C (1984) The integration of geographical data. *Proceedings of Austra Carto Perth*, Volume 1. Australian Institute of Cartographers, Perth, pp. 237–53

Rhind D W, Hudson R (1980) *Land Use*. Methuen, London

Rhind D W, Mounsey H M (1989) The Chorley Committee and 'Handling Geographic Information'. *Environment and Planning A* **21**: 571–85

Rhind D W, Mounsey H M (1989) GIS/LIS in Britain in 1988. In: Shand P J, Moore R V (eds.) *The Association for Geographic Information Yearbook 1989*. Taylor & Francis, London, pp. 267–71

Rhind D W, Openshaw S (1987) The BBC Domesday system: a nation-wide GIS for $4448. *Proceedings of AUTOCARTO 8*. ACSM/ASPRS, Falls Church Virginia, pp. 595–603

Rhind D W, Tannenbaum E (1983) Linking census and other data. In: Rhind D W (ed.) *A Census User's Handbook*. Methuen, London, pp. 287–300

Rhind D W, Visvalingham M, Evans I S (1980) Making a national atlas of population by computer. *Cartographic Journal* **17** (1) 3–11

Rhind D W, Whitfield R A S (1983) *A Review of the OS Proposals for Digitising the Large Scale Maps of Great Britain*. Consultancy report – unpublished.

Rhind D W, Wyatt B K, Briggs D J, Wiggins J C (1986) The creation of an environmental information system for the European Community. *Nachrichten aus dem Karten und Vermessungswesen Series 2*, **44**: 147–57

Rich C, Waters R C (1988) The programmer's apprentice: a research overview. *Computer (IEEE)* **21** (11): 10–25

Richards J A (1986) *Remote Sensing Digital Image Analysis: an introduction*. Springer-Verlag, New York

Richards J A, Sun G Q, Simonett D S (1987) L-band radar backscatter modeling of forest stands. *IEEE Transactions on Geoscience and Remote Sensing* **GE-25**: 487–98

Richardson D E (1988) *Rule based generalization for base map production*. Unpublished Master's Thesis, ITC Enschede

Richardson L F (1961) The problem of contiguity: an appendix to the statistics of deadly quarrels. *General Systems Yearbook* **6**: 139–87

Richardus P, Adler R K (1972) *Map Projections for Geodesists, Cartographers and Geographers*. North-Holland, Amsterdam

Riezebos H Th. (1989) Application of nested analysis of variance in mapping procedures for land evaluation. *Soil Use and Management* **5**: 25–9

RIN (1990) NAV 90. Land Navigation and Information Systems. *Proceedings of the 1990 Conference of the Royal Institute of Navigation*. Royal Institute of Navigation, London

Ripley B D (1981) *Spatial Statistics*. Wiley, New York

Ripley B D (1984) Present position and potential developments: some personal views. *Journal of the Royal Statistical Society* A **147**: 340–48

Robert P (1989) Land evaluation at farm level using soil survey information systems. In: Bouma J, Bregt A K (eds.) *Land Qualities in Space and Time. Proceedings of a Symposium organised by the International Society of Soil Science (ISSS), Wageningen, The Netherlands, 22–26 August 1988*. PUDOC, Wageningen, pp. 289–98

Robert P, Anderson J (1987) Use of computerised soil survey reports in county extension offices. In: Beek K-J, Burrough P A, McCormack D E (eds.) *Quantified Land Evaluation Procedures. Proceedings of the Joint Meeting ISSS Working Groups on Land Evaluation and Soil Information Systems, Washington 25 April–2 May 1986*. ITC Publication No. 6. ITC, Enschede, 165 pp.

Robertson P K (1988) Choosing data representations for the effective visualization of spatial data. *Proceedings of the 3rd International Symposium on Spatial Data Handling, Sydney*. International Geographical Union, Ohio, pp. 243–52

Robinette A (1991) Land management applications of GIS in the state of Minnesota. In: Maguire D J, Goodchild M F, Rhind D W (eds.) *Geographical Information Systems: principles and applications*. Longman, London, pp. 275–83, Vol 2

Robinove C J (1981) The logic of multispectral classification and mapping of land. *Remote Sensing of Environment* **11**: 231–44

Robinove C J (1986) Principles of logic and the use of digital geographic information systems. *US Geological Survey Circular 977*. USGS, Reston Virginia

Robinson A H (1953) *Elements of Cartography*. Wiley, New York

Robinson A H (1960) *Elements of Cartography*, 2nd edn. Wiley, New York

Robinson A H (1961) The cartographic representation of the statistical surface. *International Yearbook of Cartography* **1**: 53–184

Robinson A H (1962) Mapping the correspondence of isarithmic maps. *Annals of the Association of American Geographers* **52**: 414–25

Robinson A H (1975) Map design. *Proceedings of AUTOCARTO 2*. ASPRS, Falls Church Virginia, pp. 9–14

Robinson A H (1976) Revolutions in cartography. *Proceedings of the American Congress on Surveying and Mapping*. ACSM, Falls Church, pp. 403–08

Robinson A H, Bryson R A (1957) A method for describing quantitatively the correspondence of geographical distributions. *Annals of the Association of American Geographers* **47**: 379–91

Robinson A H, Petchenik B B (1976) *The Nature of Maps: essays toward understanding maps and mapping*. University of Chicago Press, Chicago

Robinson A H, Sale R D, Morrison J L, Muehrcke P C (1984) *Elements of Cartography*, 5th edn. Wiley, New York

Robinson G K (1950) Ecological correlation and the behaviour of individuals. *American Sociological Review* **15**: 351–7

Robinson G M, Gray D A, Healey R G, Furley P A (1989) Developing a geographical information system (GIS) for agricultural development in Belize, Central America. *Applied Geography* **9**: 81–94

Robinson G R (1991) The UK digital Marine Atlas Project: an evolutionary approach towards a Marine Information System. *International Hydrographic Review*, Monaco. **68**: 39–51

Robinson J (1987) The role of fire on earth: a review of the state of knowledge and a systems framework for satellite and ground based observations. *NCAR Cooperative Thesis 112*. National Center for Atmospheric Research, Boulder Colorado

Robinson V B, Frank A U, Karimi H A (1987) Expert systems for geographic information systems in resource management. *AI Applications in Natural Resource Management* **1** (1): 47–57

Robinson V B, Miller R, Klesh L (1988) Issues in the use of expert systems to manage uncertainty in geographic information systems. In: Aangeenbrug R T, Schiffman Y M (eds.) *International Geographic Information Systems (IGIS) Symposium, Arlington, Virginia*, Vol 2. NASA, Washington DC, pp. 89–100

Rodney W (1974) *How Europe Underdeveloped Africa*. Howard University Press, Washington

Roe K (1989) Information overload. *Science* **356** (11): 563

Rogers D F (1985) *Procedural Elements for Computer Graphics*. McGraw-Hill, New York

Roo A de, Hazelhoff L, Burrough P A (1989) Soil erosion modelling using ANSWERS and Geographical Information Systems. *Earth Surface Processes and Landforms* **14**: 517–32

Roo A P J de, Hazelhoff L (1988) Assessing surface runoff and soil erosion in watersheds using GIS technology. *Proceedings EUROCARTO 7, ITC Publication 8*. ITC, Enschede, pp. 172–83

Rosch E (1973) On the internal structure of perceptual and semantic categories. In: Moore T E (ed.) *Cognitive Development and the Acquisition of Language*. Academic Press, New York, pp. 111–44

Rosch E (1978) Principles of categorization. In: Rosch E, Lloyd B B (eds.) *Cognition and Categorization*. Erlbaum, Hillsdale New Jersey, 27–48

Rosenfield G, Melley M (1980) Applications of statistics to thematic mapping. *Photogrammetric Engineering and Remote Sensing* **46**: 1287–94

Rosinski R R (1977) *The Development of Visual Perception*. Goodyear Publishing, Santa Monica California

Rossiter D (1989) ALES: a microcomputer program to assist in land evaluation. In: Bouma J, Bregt A K (eds.) *Land Qualities in Space and Time. Proceedings of a Symposium organised by the International Society of Soil Science (ISSS), Wageningen, The Netherlands, 22–26 August 1988*. PUDOC, Wageningen, pp. 113–16

Rothman J (ed.) (1989) Geodemographics. *Journal of the Market Research Society* (Special Edition) **31** (1): 1–131

Rowe L A (1986) A shared object hierarchy. In: Stonebraker M R, Rowe L A (eds.) *The POSTGRES Papers. Memorandum No. UCB/ERL M86/85*. College of Engineering, University of California, Berkeley

Rowe L A, Stonebraker M R (1987) The progres data model. *Proceedings of the 13th Conference on very large databases*, Brighton, England, pp. 83–96

Rowley J (1990) Land Information Systems. In: Foster M J, Shand P J (eds.) *The Association for Geographic Information Yearbook 1990*. Taylor & Francis, London, pp. 278–84

Rowley J, Gilbert P (1989) The market for land information services, systems and support. In: Shand P J, Moore R V (eds.) *The Association for Geographic Information Yearbook 1989*. Taylor & Francis and Miles Arnold, London, pp. 85–91

Roy A G, Gravel G, Gauthier C (1987) Measuring the dimension of surfaces: a review and appraisal of different methods. *Proceedings of AUTOCARTO 8*. ASPRS, Falls Church Virginia, pp. 68–77

Roy J R, Anderson M (1988) Assessing impacts of retail development and redevelopment. In: Newton P W, Taylor M A P, Sharpe R (eds.) *Desktop Planning: microcomputer applications for infrastructure and services planning and management*. Hargreen, Melbourne, pp. 172–9

Royal Society (1966) *Glossary of Technical Terms in Cartography*. Royal Society, London

RRDN (1986) *Rural Regional Development Newsletter*. AIT, Bangkok

Rüber O (1989) Interactive design of faulted geological surfaces. *Geologisches Jahrbuch* **A 104** (Construction and display of geoscientific maps derived from databases)

Ruggles C L N (1990) An abstract model for the structuring of a spatially indexed set of images. *Proceedings of EGIS '90*, Volume 2. EGIS Foundation, Utrecht, pp. 948–57

Running S W, Nemani R R, Peterson D L, Band L E, Potts D F, Pierce L L, Spanner M A (1989) Mapping regional forest evapotranspiration and photosynthesis by coupling satellite data with ecosystem simulation. *Ecology* **70**: 1090–101

Rushton G (1969) A comprehensive model for the study of agricultural land use patterns. *Computer Assisted Instruction in Geography. Commission on College Geography, Technical Paper No. 2*. Association of American Geographers, Washington DC, pp. 141–50

Rystedt B (1987) *The New National Atlas of Sweden*. LMV-rapport 1987:17, ISSN 0280–5731. Gävle, Sweden

Saalfeld A (1985) Lattice structure in geography. *Proceedings of AUTOCARTO 7*. ASPRS, Falls Church, pp. 482–97

Saalfeld A (1988) Conflation: automated map compilation. *International Journal of Geographical Information Systems* **2** (3): 217–28

Sadovski A, Bie S W (1978) Developments in soil information systems. *Proceedings of the Second Meeting of the ISSS Working Group on Soil Information Systems, Varna/Sofia, Bulgaria, 30 May–June 1977*. PUDOC, Wageningen, 113 pp

Sakashita S, Tanaka Y (1989) Computer-aided drawing conversion (an interactive approach to digitize maps). *Proceedings of GIS/LIS '89, Orlando*. Vol. 2. ASPRS/ACSM, Bethesda Maryland, pp. 578–90

Salgé F, Piquet-Pellorce D (1986) The IGN small scale geographical database (1 : 100 000 to 1 : 500 000). In: Blakemore M J (ed.) *Proceedings of AUTOCARTO London*, Vol. 1. Royal Institution of Chartered Surveyors, London, pp. 433–46

Salgé F, Sclafer M N (1989) A geographic data model based on HBDS concepts: the IGN cartographic database model. *Proceedings of AUTOCARTO 9*. ACSM/ASPRS, Falls Church, pp. 110–17

Salmon R, Slater M (1987) *Computer Graphics*. Addison-Wesley, Reading Massachusetts

Samet H (1984) The quadtree and related hierarchical data structures. *ACM Computing Surveys* **16** (2): 187–260

Samet H (1988) Recent developments in the use of hierarchical data structures for image databases. *Proceedings Ausgraph 88, Melbourne*, pp. 207–19

Samet H (1990) *The Design and Analysis of Spatial Data Structures*. Addison-Wesley, Reading Massachusetts

Satterwhite M, Rice W, Shipman J (1984) Using landform and vegetation factors to improve the interpretation of LANDSAT imagery. *Photogrammetric Engineering and Remote Sensing* **50**: 83–91

Saxena M (1989) Satellite remote sensing for thematic maps. *IX INCA International Seminar on Digital Cartography and Potential Users*. Pre-session Proceedings. Survey of India, Dehra Dun, pp. 400–5

Schacter B J (1983) (ed.) *Computer Image Generation*. John Wiley, New York

Schaeben H (1989) Improving the geological significance of computed surfaces by CADG methods, *Geologisches Jahrbuch* **A 104** (Construction and display of geoscientific maps derived from databases)

Schek H-J, Waterfeld W (1986) A database kernel system for geoscientific applications. *Proceedings of the 2nd International Symposium on Spatial Data Handling*. International Geographical Union, Columbus Ohio, pp. 273–88

Schmidt A H, Zafft W A (1975) Progress of the Harvard University Laboratory for Computer Graphics and Spatial Analysis. In: Davis J C, McCullagh M J (eds.) *Display and analysis of spatial data*. Wiley, London, pp. 231–43

Schönhage S, Strassen V (1971) Schnelle multiplikation grosser zahlen. *Computing* **7**: 281–92

Schott J R, Salvaggio C, Volchok W J (1988) Radiometric scene normalization using pseudoinvariant features. *Remote Sensing of Environment* **26**: 1–16

Schultze C L (1970) Director, Bureau of the Budget, Statement in *Planning, Programming, Budgeting*, 91st Congress, 2nd Session, Subcommittee on National Security and International Operations. US Government Publications Office, Washington DC. pp. 172–3

Schumaker L L (1976) Fitting surfaces to scattered data. In: Lorentz G G et al. (eds.) *Approximation Theory II*. Academic Press, New York, pp. 203–68

Schut G H (1976) Review of interpolation methods for digital terrain models. *The Canadian Surveyor* **30** (5): 389–412

Schweitzer R H (1973) *Mapping Urban America with Automated Cartography*. Bureau of the Census US Department of Commerce, Suitland Maryland

Scott D J (1987) *Mental Imagery and Visualization: their role in map use*. Unpublished PhD thesis, Department of Geography, London School of Economics

SCS (1984) *Soil Survey Manual*. Government Printing Office, Washington DC

SCS (1984) *Technical Specifications for Line Segment Digitizing of Detailed Soil Survey Maps*. Government Printing Office, Washington DC

Seaborn D W (1988) Distributed processing and distributed databases in GIS – separating hype from reality. *Proceedings of GIS/LIS '88*, Volume 1. ASPRS/ACSM, Falls Church Virginia, pp. 141–4

Sedgewick R (1983) *Algorithms*. Addison-Wesley, Reading Massachusetts

Sedunary M E (1988) Land Information Systems – their reasons and rewards. *Proceedings from the FIG Land Information Systems Workshop, Bali, Indonesia*, pp. 66–74

Seldon D D (1987) Success criteria for GIS. In: Aangeenbrug R T and Schiffman Y M (Eds.) *International Geographic Information Systems (IGIS) Symposium, Arlington, Virginia*. Vol 3. NASA, Washington DC, pp. 239–43

Sellers P J (1985) Canopy reflectance, photosynthesis, and transpiration. *International Journal of Remote Sensing* **6**: 1335–72

Sellers P J, Hall F G, Asrar G, Strebel D E, Murphy R E (1988) The first ISLSCP field experiment (FIFE). *Bulletin of the American Meteorological Society* **69**: 22–7

Selvin S, Merrill D W, Sacks S (1988) Transformations of maps to investigate clusters of disease. *Social Science and Medicine* **26**: 215–21

Senior M L (1979) From gravity modelling to entropy maximizing: a pedagogic guide. *Progress in Human Geography* **3**: 179–210

Seymour W A (ed.) (1980) *A History of the Ordnance Survey*. Dawson, Folkestone

Shand P J, Moore R V (eds.) (1989) *The Association for Geographic Information Yearbook 1989*. Taylor & Francis and Miles Arnold, London, pp. 85–91

Shapiro L G, Haralick R M (1980) A spatial data structure. *Geo-Processing* **1**: 313–37

Shepherd I D H (1985) Teaching geography with the

computer: possibilities and problems. *Journal of Geography in Higher Education* **9**: 3–23

Shepherd I D H (1990) Mapping with desktop CAD: a critical review. *Computer Aided Design* **22** (3): 136–50

Shepherd I D H (1990) Computer mapping: 21 roles for AutoCAD. *Bulletin of the Society of University Cartographers* **23** (2): 1–15

Shepherd I D H (1990) Build your own desktop GIS? *Land and Minerals Surveying* **8** (4): 176–83

Shepherd I D H (1991) Information integration and GIS. In: Maguire D J, Goodchild M F, Rhind D W (eds.) *Geographical Information Systems: principles and applications*. Longman, London, pp. 337–60, Vol 1

Shetler T (1990) Birth of the BLOB. *BYTE* **15** (2): 221–6

Shiryaev E E (1987) *Computers and the Representation of Geographical Data*. Wiley, New York

Shmutter B (1981) Transforming conic conformal to TM coordinates. *Survey Review* **26**: 130–6, 201

Shneiderman B (1981) A note on human factors issues of natural language interaction with database systems. *Information Systems* **6** (2): 125–9

Shneiderman B (1983) Direct manipulation: a step beyond programming languages. *Computer* **16**: 57–69

Shneiderman B (1987) *Designing the User Interface: strategies for effective human-computer interaction*. Addison Wesley, Reading Massachusetts

Shortridge B G, Welch R B (1980) Are we asking the right questions? *The American Cartographer* **7** (1): 19–24

Shortridge B G, Welch R B (1982) The effect of stimulus redundancy on the discrimination of town size on maps. *The American Cartographer* **9** (1): 69–80

Shumway C (1986) Summary of the US Forest Service Geographical Information Systems activities. *Proceedings of Geographical Information Systems Workshop*. American Society for Photogrammetry and Remote Sensing, Falls Church, pp. 49–52

Shyue S W (1989) *High Breakdown Point Robust Estimation for Outlier Detection in Photogrammetry*. Unpublished PhD dissertation, University of Washington

Siderelis K C (1991) Land resource information systems. In: Maguire D J, Goodchild M F, Rhind D W (eds.) *Geographical Information Systems: principles and applications*. Longman, London, pp. 261–73, Vol 2

Siderelis K C, Tribble T N (1988) Using a Geographic Information System to prepare a site proposal for the Superconducting Super Collider. *Proceedings of GIS/LIS '88 Volume 1*. ACSM/ASPRS/AAG/URISA, Falls Church Virginia, pp. 459–68

Siegel M D (1989) Automatic rule derivation for semantic query optimization. In: Kerschberg L (ed.) *Proceedings of Second International Conference on Expert Database Systems, Tysons Corner, 25–27 April 1988*. Benjamin/Cummings Publishing Company, pp. 69–98

Sievers J, Bennat H (1989) Reference systems for maps and digital information systems of Antarctica. *Antarctic Science* **1**: 351–62

Silverman B G (ed.) (1987) *Expert Systems for Business*. Addison-Wesley, Reading Massachusetts

Simonett D S (1988) Considerations on integrating remote sensing and Geographic Information Systems. In: Mounsey H, Tomlinson R F (eds.) *Building Databases for Global Science*. Taylor & Francis, London, pp. 105–28

Simonett D S, Reeves R G, Estes J E, Bertke S E, Sailer C T (1983) The development and principles of remote sensing. In: Colwell R N (ed.) *Manual of Remote Sensing*. American Society of Photogrammetry, Falls Church Virginia, pp. 1–32

Simpson S R (1976) *Land Law and Registration*. Cambridge University Press, Cambridge

Singh C B (1989) Indian perspective for automatic cartography – a poser. *IX INCA International Seminar on Digital Cartography and Potential Users*. Pre-session Proceedings. Survey of India, Dehra Dun, pp. 424–6

Singh G (1989) Grid referenced data as a decision support system. *Proceedings of the 2nd National Mapping Awareness Conference*. Miles Arnold, Oxford, pp. 22.1–22.3

Singh S M, Saull R J (1988) The effect of atmospheric correction on the interpretation of multitemporal AVHRR-derived vegetation index dynamics. *International Journal of Remote Sensing* **25**: 37–51

Sinha A K, Waugh T C (1988) Aspects of the implementation of the GEOVIEW design. *International Journal of Geographical Information Systems* **2**: 91–100

Sinton D (1978) The inherent structure of information as a constraint to analysis: mapped thematic data as a case study. In: Dutton G (ed.) *Harvard Papers on Geographic Information Systems*, Volume 6. Addison-Wesley, Reading Massachusetts

SIS (1986) *pMAP User's Guide and Technical Reference, Professional Map Analysis Package (pMAP)*. Spatial Information Systems, Springfield Virginia

Slama C C, Theurer C, Henriksen S W (1980) (eds.) *Manual of Photogrammetry*, 4th edn. American Society of Photogrammetry, Falls Church Virginia

Slingerland R, Keen T R (1990) A numerical study of storm driven circulation and 'event bed' genesis. *Proceedings of Symposium on Three Dimensional Computer Graphics in Modelling Geologic Structures and Simulating Processes*. Freiburger Geowissenschafliche Beitrage **2**: 97–9

Slocum T A (1983) Predicting visual clusters on graduated circle maps. *The American Cartographer* **10** (1): 59–72

Smallworld Systems (1990) GIS in Europe – summary report. *Geodetical Info Magazine* **4** (4): 28–9

Smith A B (1986) Developments in inertial navigation. *The Journal of Navigation* **39** (3): 401–15

Smith A B (1989) Geographical Information for European Vehicle Navigation Systems. In: Perry (ed.) *Proceedings of Government Computing 1989 (GC 89)*. HMSO, London. pp. 15–17.

Smith A B (1989) Prototyping a navigation database of road network attributes (PANDORA), In: Reekie D H M, Case E R, Tsai J (ed.) *Vehicle Navigation & Information Systems Conference, Toronto*, pp. 331–6

Smith D C, Harslem E, Irby C, Kimball R, Verplank W

(1983) Designing the Star user interface. *Proceedings, European Conference on Integrated Interactive Computing Systems: Stresa, Italy*. North-Holland, Amsterdam

Smith D R, Paradis A R (1989) Three-dimensional GIS for the earth sciences. In: Raper J F (ed.) *Three Dimensional Applications in Geographical Information Systems*. Taylor & Francis, London, pp. 149–54

Smith D R, Paradis A R (1989) Three-dimensional GIS for the Earth Sciences. *Proceedings of AUTOCARTO 9*. ACSM/ASPRS, Falls Church Virginia, pp. 324–35

Smith E A, Crosson W L, Cooper H J, Weng H (1990) Heat and moisture flux modeling of the FIFE grassland canopy aided by satellite derived canopy variables. *Proceedings of the Symposium on FIFE*. American Meteorological Society, Boston Massachusettes, pp. 154–62

Smith E E, Medin D L (1981) *Categories and Concepts*. Harvard University Press, Cambridge Massachusetts

Smith G H (1935) The relative relief of Ohio. *Geographical Review* **25**: 272–84

Smith J L, Mackenzie H G, Stanton R B (1988) A knowledge-based decision support for environmental planning. *Proceedings of the 3rd International Symposium on Spatial Data Handling*. International Geographical Union, Columbus Ohio, pp. 307–20

Smith J M, Smith D C P (1977) Database abstractions: aggregation and generalization. *Association for Computing Machinery Transactions on Database Systems* **2** (2): 105–33

Smith L, Eden R (1989) GIS and natural resource management: the Murray–Darling Basin *URPIS – Proceedings of the Urban and Regional Planning Information Systems Annual Conferences*, Volume 17. Australasian Urban and Regional Information Systems Association Inc., Sydney, pp. 452–60

Smith N S (1987) Data models and data structures for Ordnance Survey. *Proceedings of the Ordnance Survey/SORSA Symposium, Durham, May 1987*.

Smith P (1989) Tomorrow's open land registry and the dawn of a national information system. *Proceedings of National Mapping Awareness Conference*. Miles Arnold, Oxford

Smith T R, Ye Jiang (1991) Knowledge-based approaches in GIS. In: Maguire D J, Goodchild M F, Rhind D W (eds.) *Geographical Information Systems: principles and applications*. Longman, London, pp. 413–25, Vol 1

Smith T R, Menon S, Star J L, Estes J E (1987) Requirements and principles for the implementation and construction of large-scale geographic information systems. *International Journal of Geographical Information Systems* **1** (1): 13–31

Smith T R, Peuquet D J, Menon S, Agarwal P (1987) KBGIS-II: a knowledge-based geographical information system. *International Journal of Geographical Information Systems* **1** (2): 149–72

Snodgrass R (1987) The temporal query language TQUEL. *Association for Computing Machinery Transactions on Database Systems* **12**: 247

Snyder J P (1985) Computer-assisted map projection research. *US Geological Survey Bulletin* **1629**. US Government Printing Office, Washington

Snyder J P (1987) Map projections – a working manual. *US Geological Survey Professional Paper 1395*. Government Printing Office, Washington

Snyder J P (1987) Differences due to projection for the same USGS quadrangle. *Surveying and Mapping* **47**: 199–206

Snyder J P (1987) Labeling projections on published maps. *The American Cartographer* **14**: 21–7

Soil Survey Staff (1976) *Soil Taxonomy*. US Government Printing Office, Washington DC

Somerville I (1989) *Software Engineering*, 3rd edn. Addison-Wesley, Reading Massachusetts, 653pp.

Sommers R (1987) Geographic information systems in local government: a commentary. *Photogrammetric Engineering and Remote Sensing* **53**: 1379–82

South African Society for Photogrammetry, Remote Sensing and Cartography (1987) *Proceedings of Earth Data Information Systems, EDIS 87*. South African Society for Photogrammetry, Remote Sensing and Cartography, Pretoria

Southard R B, Anderson K E (1983) A National Program for Digital Cartography. *AUTOCARTO 5 Proceedings*. ACSM, Falls Church Virginia, pp. 41–9

Sowa J F (1984) *Conceptual Structures*. Addison-Wesley, Reading Massachusetts

Sowton M (1971) Automation in cartography at the Ordnance Survey using digital output from a plotting machine. *Bildmessung und Luftbildwesen* **39** (1): 41–4

Sowton M (1991) Development of GIS-related activities at the Ordnance Survey. In: Maguire D J, Goodchild M F, Rhind D W (eds.) *Geographical Information Systems: principles and applications*. Longman, London pp. 23–38, Vol 2

Sowton M, Green P (1984) Digital map data for computerised land and utility information systems. *Proceedings 10th European Symposium for Urban Data Information Systems – Urban Data Management and the End Users*. Padua, pp. 34–49

Sowton M, Haywood P E (1986) National Standards for the Transfer of Digital Map Data. In: Blakemore M J (ed.) *Proceedings of AUTOCARTO London*, Vol. 1. Royal Institution of Chartered Surveyors, London, pp. 298–311

Spanier E (1966) *Algebraic Topology*. McGraw-Hill, New York

Spiegelhalter D J, Knill-Jones R P (1984) Statistical and knowledge-based approaches to clinical decision-support systems, with an application to gastro-enterology. *Journal of the Royal Statistical Society* **A 147** (1): 35–77

Sprague R H, Carlson E D (1982) *Building Effective Decision Support Systems*. Prentice-Hall, Englewood Cliffs New Jersey

Sprague R H (1980) A framework for the development of decision support systems. *Management Information Sciences Quarterly* **4**: 1–26

Sprinsky W H (1987) Transformation of positional

geographic data from paper-based map products. *The American Cartographer* **14**: 359–66

SSC Central Design Group (1986) *SSC Conceptual Design of the Superconducting Super Collider*. Universities Research Association, SSC-SR-2020C, Washington DC

Star J, Estes J E (1990) *Geographic Information Systems: an introduction*. Prentice Hall, Englewood Cliffs New Jersey

Starr L E (1990) USGS National Mapping Division: preparing for the Twenty-First Century. *Proceedings of GIS/LIS '90*. AAG/ACSM/AM/FM/ASPRS/URISA, Bethesda Maryland, pp. 872–81

Starr L E, Anderson K E (1982) Some Thoughts on Cartographic and Geographic Information Systems for the 1980s. *Pecara VII Symposium Proceedings*. ASP, Falls Church Virginia, pp. 41–55

Starr L E, Anderson K E (1991) A USGS perspective on GIS. In: Maguire D J, Goodchild M F, Rhind D W (eds.) *Geographical Information Systems: principles and applications*. Longman, London, pp. 11–22, Vol 2

Starr L E, Guptill S C (1984) The US Geological Survey and the National Digital Cartographic Data Base. *Proceedings from the FIG International Symposium*. Edmonton Alberta, pp. 166–75

Starr M K, Zeleny M (1977) *Multiple Criteria Decision Making*. North-Holland, Amsterdam

State of North Carolina (1987) *North Carolina Site Proposal for the Superconducting Super Collider (SSC)*, Volumes 1–8. State of North Carolina, Raleigh NC

Staufenbiel W (1973) *Zur automation der generalisierung topographischer karten mit besonderer berucksichtigung Grobmabstabiger Gebaudedarstellungen*. Unpublished Doctoral Thesis, University of Hannover

Stefanovic P, Drummond J, Muller J-C (1989) ITC's response to the need for training in CAC and GIS. *IX INCA International Seminar on Digital Cartography and Potential Users*. Pre-session Proceedings. Survey of India, Dehra Dun, pp. 450–60

Stein A, Hoogerwerf M, Bouma J (1988) Use of soil map delineations to improve (co)kriging of point data on moisture deficits. *Geoderma* **43**: 163–77

Steinitz C F, Parker P, Jordan L (1976) Hand-drawn overlays: their history and prospective uses. *Landscape Architecture* **66** (8): 444–55

Steinke T R (1987) Eye movement studies in cartography and related fields. *Cartographica* **24** (2): 40–73

Steneker M, Bonham-Carter G F (1988) *Computer Program for Converting Arc-Node Vector Data to Raster Format*. Geological Survey of Canada, K1Z 8R7, 300pp.

Stevens S S (1946) On the theory of scales of measurement. *Science* **103**: 677–80

Stewart J C (1987) Geographic criteria for the siting of low level waste disposal sites. *Proceedings of the International Geographic Information Systems (IGIS) Symposium: the research agenda*, Volume 3. AAG, Washington, pp. 87–101

Steyaert L T (1989) Investigating the use of geographic information systems technology in the computer workstation environment for global change research. *Proceedings of the ASPRS/ACSM 1989 annual meeting*, April 1989, Volume 4. American Society of Photogrammetry and Remote Sensing, Falls Church, pp. 46–53

Stiefel M (1987) Mapping out the differences among geographic information systems *The S. Klein Computer Graphics Review*, Fall: 73–87

Stone R A (1988) Investigations of excess environmental risks around putative sources: statistical problems and a proposed test. *Statistics in Medicine* **7**: 649–60

Stonebraker M, Hanson E N (1988) The POSTGRES rule manager. *IEEE Transactions on Software Engineering* **14** (7): 897–907

Stonebraker M, Hearst M (1989) Future trends in expert database systems. In: Kerschberg L (ed.) *Expert Database Systems*. The Benjamin/Cummings Publishing Company, Redwood City, pp. 3–20

Strahler A H (1981) Stratification of natural vegetation for forest and rangeland inventory using Landsat digital imagery and collateral data. *International Journal of Remote Sensing* **2**: 15–41

Strahler A H, Woodcock C E, Smith J A (1986) On the nature of models in remote sensing. *Remote Sensing of Environment* **20**: 121–39

Stroustrup B (1987) *The C++ Programming Language*. Addison-Wesley, Reading Massachusetts

Stroutstrop B (1988) What is object-oriented programming. *IEEE Software* **5** (3): 10–20

Su S (1988) *Database Computers: principles, architectures and techniques*. McGraw-Hill, New York, 497pp.

Suh S, Kim M P, Kim T J (1988) ESMAN: an expert system for manufacturing selection. *Computers, Environment and Urban Systems* **12**: 239–52

Suits G, Malila W, Weller T (1988) Procedures for using signals from one sensor as substitutes for signals of another. *Remote Sensing of Environment* **25**: 395–408

Sullivan J G, Chow A L K (1990) The Wisconsin legislative redistricting project: design interface, training, and policy issues. *Proceedings of GIS/LIS '90*, Volume 1. ASPRS/ACSM/AAG/URISA/AM-FM, Bethesda Maryland, pp. 26–41

Sun Microsystems (1985) *Programming Utilities for the Sun Workstation*. Sun Microsystems

Sun Y, Wang R, Tang Q (1987) Automated cartographic system for population maps. *Proceedings of International Workshop on Geographic Information System, Beijing '87*. LREIS, Beijing, pp. 402–13

Sundaram K V (1987) Integrated approach to training for the establishment and use of information systems for subnational development planning. *Regional Development Dialogue* **8** (1): 54–70

Svorou S (1988) *The Experiential Basis of the Grammar of Space: evidence from the languages of the world*. Unpublished PhD dissertation, Department of Linguistics, State University of New York at Buffalo

Sweet D C (1970) An industrial development screening matrix. *The Professional Geographer* **22**: 124–7

Swiss Society of Cartography (1987) *Cartographic Generalization*, 2nd edn. SGK-Publikationen, Zurich

Switzer P (1975) Estimation of the accuracy of qualitative maps. In: Davis J C, McCullagh M J (eds.) *Display and Analysis of Spatial Data*. Wiley, New York, pp. 1–13

Switzer R (1975) *Algebraic Topology-Homotopy and Homology*. Springer-Verlag, New York

Szegö J (1987) Geocoded real property data in urban and regional planning. *Proceedings of Land Use Information in Sweden*. Swedish Council for Building Research, Stockholm Sweden. ISBN 91–540–4665–3, pp. 87–94.

Szelinski R, Terzopoulos D (1989) From splines to fractals. *Computer Graphics (SIGGRAPH '89 Proceedings)* **23** (3): 51–60

Talmy L (1983) How language structures space. In: Pick H, Acredolo L (eds.) *Spatial Orientation: theory, research, and application*. Plenum, New York, pp. 225–82

Talmy L (1988) How language structures space. In: Mark D M (ed.) *Cognitive and linguistic aspects of geographical space*. National Center for Geographic Information and Analysis Publication. NCGIA, Santa Barbara California

Tanic E (1986) Urban planning and artificial intelligence: the URBYS system. *Computers, Environment, and Urban Systems* **10** (3–4): 135–46

Tarjan R E (1987) Algorithm design. *Communications ACM* **30** (3): 205–12

Tarpley J D (1979) Estimating incident solar radiation at the earth's surface from geostationary satellite data. *Journal of Applied Meteorology* **18**: 1172–81

Tavernier R (1985) *Soil Map of the European Communities. 1 : 1 000 000*. Office for Official Publications of the European Communities, Luxembourg

Taylor D R F (1991) GIS and developing nations. In: Maguire D J, Goodchild M F, Rhind D W (eds.) *Geographical Information Systems: principles and applications*. Longman, London, pp. 71–84, Vol 2

Taylor M A P (1988) Computer models for traffic systems applications. In: Newton P W, Taylor M A P, Sharpe R (eds.) *Desktop Planning: microcomputer applications for infrastructure and services planning and management*. Hargreen, Melbourne, pp. 264–98

Taylor P J (1976) An interpretation of the quantification debate in British geography. *Transactions of the Institute of British Geographers* New Series **1**: 129–42

Taylor P J (1977) *Quantitative Methods in Geography*. Houghton Mifflin, Boston

Taylor P J (1990) Editorial comment: GKS. *Political Geography Quarterly* **9** (3): 211–12

Taylor R M, Hopkin V D (1975) Ergonomic principles and map design. *Applied Ergonomics* **6** (4): 196–204

Teorey T J, Fry J P (1982) *Design of Database Structures*. Prentice Hall, Englewood Cliffs New Jersey

Terada T (1930) Statistical methods on distribution of slopes using maps. *Geographical Review of Japan* **6**: 653–61

Tetzloff D M, Harbaugh J W (1989) *Simulating Plastic Sedimentation*. Van Nostrand Reinhold, New York

Thapa K (1988) Automatic line generalization using zero-crossings. *Photogrammetric Engineering and Remote Sensing* **54**: 511–17

Thatte S (1988) Report on the object-oriented database workshop: implementation aspects. In: Power L, Weiss Z (eds.) *OOPSLA '87 Addendum to the Proceedings. Special Issue of SIGPLAN Notices* **23** (5): 87

Thom R (1973) La theorie des catastrophes: etat present et perspectives. *Manifold* **14**: 16–23

Thomas E N (1960) Maps of residuals from regression: their characteristics and use in geographical research. *Geographical Publication No 2*. University of Iowa

Thomas P J, Baker J C, Simpson T W (1989) Variability of the Cecil map unit in Appomattox County, Virginia. *Soil Science Society of America, Journal* **53** (5): 1470–4

Thompson C N (1978) Digital mapping in the Ordnance Survey 1968–1978. In: Allam (ed.) *Proceedings of the International Society for Photogrammetry Commission IV International Symposium – New Technology for Mapping*. Ottawa, pp. 195–219

Thompson C N (1979) The need for a large scale topographic database. *Proceedings of the Conference of Commonwealth Survey Officers, July 1979*, Foreign and Commonwealth Office. Paper F4

Thompson D (1990) GIS – a view from the other (dark?) side: the perspective of an instructor of introductory geography courses at University level. In: Unwin D J (ed.) *GIS Education and Training, Collected Papers of a Conference, University of Leicester 20–21 March 1990*. Midlands Regional Research Laboratory, Leicester, 16 pp.

Thompson M M (1988) *Maps for America*, 3rd edn. US Government Printing Office, Washington DC

Thoone M (1987) CARIN, a car information and navigation system, *Philips Technical Review* **43** (11/12): 317–29

Tobler W R (1959) Automation and cartography. *Geographical Review* **49**: 526–34

Tobler W R (1961) *Map Transformations of Geographical Space*. Unpublished PhD dissertation, Department of Geography, University of Washington

Tobler W R (1966) Numerical map generalization. *Michigan Inter-University Community of Mathematical Geographers Discussion Paper* **8**

Tobler W R (1969) Satellite confirmation of settlement size coefficients. *Area* **3**: 30–3

Tobler W R (1970) A computer movie simulating urban growth in the Detroit Region. *Economic Geography* **46**: 234–40

Tobler W R (1973) Choropleth maps without class intervals? *Geographical Analysis* **3**: 262–65

Tobler W R (1973) A continuous transformation useful for redistricting. *Annals, New York Academy of Sciences* **219**: 215–20

Tobler W R (1977) *Bidimensional Regression*. Department of Geography, University of California, Santa Barbara

Tobler W R (1979) Cellular geography. In: Gale S, Olsson

G (eds.) *Philosophy in Geography*. D. Reidel Publishing Company, Dordrecht Holland, pp. 379–86

Tobler W R (1979) Smooth pycnophylactic interpolation for geographical regions. *Journal of the American Statistical Association* **74**: 519–30

Tobler W R (1982) Surveying multidimensional measurement. In: Golledge R G, Rayner J N (eds.) *Proximity and Preference: problems in the multidimensional analysis of large data sets*. University of Minnesota Press, Minneapolis, pp. 3–4

Tobler W R (1984) Application of image processing techniques to map processing. *Proceedings of the 1st International Symposium on Spatial Data Handling, Zurich*. Universitat Zurich-Irchel, Zurich (1): 140–44.

Tobler W R (1988) Geographic information systems research agenda: the scientific community perspective. In: Aangeenbrug R T, Schiffman Y M (eds.) *International Geographic Information Systems (IGIS) Symposium, Arlington, Virginia*, Vol 1. NASA, Washington DC, pp. 49–52

Tobler W R (1988) Resolution, resampling and all that. In: Mounsey H M, Tomlinson R F (eds.) *Building Databases for Global Science*. Taylor & Francis, London, pp. 129–37

Tobler W R, Kennedy S (1985) Smooth multidimensional interpolation. *Geographical Analysis* **17** (3): 251–7

Tobler W R, Moellering H (1972) The analysis of scale-variance. *Geographical Analysis* **4**: 34–50

Tomasi S G (1990) Why the nation needs a TIGER system. *Cartography and Geographic Information Systems* **17** (1): 21–6

Tomatsuri Y (1985) Geographic research and data base. *Jinbun Chiri* **37** (3): 270–86

Tomlin C D (1975) *The Tomlin Subsystem of IMGRID*. Unpublished Master's thesis, Harvard University

Tomlin C D (1983) A map algebra. *Harvard Computer Graphics Conference 1983*. Harvard University Graduate School of Design Laboratory for Computer Graphics and Spatial Analysis, Cambridge Massachusetts

Tomlin C D (1983) *Digital Cartographic Modeling Techniques in Environmental Planning*. Unpublished PhD dissertation, Yale University

Tomlin C D (1983) A map algebra. *Proceedings, Harvard Computer Graphics Conference*. Cambridge, Massachusetts

Tomlin C D (1985) The IBM Personal Computer Version of the Map Analysis Package. Laboratory for Computer Graphics and Spatial Analysis, Graduate School of Design, Harvard University

Tomlin C D (1990) *Geographic Information Systems and Cartographic Modelling*. Prentice-Hall, Englewood Cliffs New Jersey

Tomlin C D (1991) Cartographic modelling. In: Maguire D J, Goodchild M F, Rhind D W (eds.) *Geographical Information Systems: principles and applications*. Longman, London, pp. 361–74, Vol 1

Tomlin C D, Berry J K (1979) A mathematical structure for cartographic modelling in environmental analysis.

Proceedings of the 39th Symposium of the American Conference on Surveying and Mapping, pp. 269–83

Tomlin C D, Tomlin S M (1981) An overlay mapping language. *Regional Landscape Planning: Proceedings of Three Educational Systems*. American Society of Landscape Architects: 155–64

Tomlinson R F (1967) *An Introduction to the Geographic Information System of the Canada Land Inventory*. Department of Forestry and Rural Development, Ottawa Canada

Tomlinson R F (1970) (ed.) *Environment Information Systems*. Commission on Geographical Data Sensing and Processing. International Geographical Union, Ottawa Canada

Tomlinson R F (1972) (ed.) *Geographic Data Handling*. Commission on Geographical Data Sensing and Processing. International Geographical Union, Ottawa Canada

Tomlinson R F (ed.) (1972) *Geographical Data Handling* 2 volumes. IGU Commission on Geographical Data Sensing and Processing for UNESCO/IGU Second Symposium on Geographical Information Systems, Ottawa

Tomlinson R F (1974) *The application of electronic computing methods to the storage, compilation and assessment of mapped data*. Unpublished PhD thesis, University of London

Tomlinson R F (1985) Geographic Information Systems – the new frontier. *The Operational Geographer* **5**: 31–6

Tomlinson R F (1987) Current and potential uses of geographical information systems – the North American experience. *International Journal of Geographical Information Systems* **1** (3): 203–8

Tomlinson R F (1988) The impact of the transition from analogue to digital cartographic representation. *The American Cartographer* **15** (3): 249–62

Tomlinson R F (1989) Letter to PERS. *Photogrammetric Engineering and Remote Sensing* **55** (4): 434–5

Tomlinson R F (1989) Recent trends in GIS technology. *Workshop on Strategic Directions for Canada's Surveying, Mapping, Remote Sensing and GIS Activities*, November 1989, Ottawa

Tomlinson R F (1989) Canadian GIS experience. *CISM Journal* **43** (3): 227–32

Tomlinson R F, Calkins H W, Marble D F (1976) *Computer Handling of Geographical Data*. Natural Resources Research Series XIII, UNESCO Press, Paris

Tomlinson R F, Petchenik B B (1988) (eds.) Reflections on the revolution: the transition from analogue to digital representations of space, 1958–1988. *The American Cartographer* **15** (3): 243–334

Tong L, Richards J A, Swain P H (1987) Probabilistic and evidential approaches for multisource data analysis. *IEEE Transactions on Geoscience and Remote Sensing* **GE-25**: 283–93

Topographic Science Working Group (1988) *Topographic Science Working Group Report to the Land Processes Branch, Earth Science and Applications Division*. NASA Headquarters Lunar and Planetary Institute, Houston

Toppen F (1990) GIS education in the Netherlands: a bit of everything and everything about a bit? In: Unwin D J (ed.) *GIS Education and Training, Collected Papers of a Conference, University of Leicester 20–21 March 1990.* Midlands Regional Research Laboratory, Leicester, 10 pp.

Townshend J R G (1991) Environmental databases and GIS. In: Maguire D J, Goodchild M F, Rhind D W (eds.) *Geographical Information Systems: principles and applications.* Longman, London, pp. 201–16, Vol 2

Townshend J R G, Justice C O (1988) Selecting the spatial resolution of satellite sensors required for global monitoring of land transformations. *International Journal of Remote Sensing* **9**: 187–236

Townshend J R G, Justice C O (1990) The spatial variation of vegetation at very coarse scales. *International Journal of Remote Sensing* **11**: 149–57

Trollegaard S (1985) *Land Information Systems in Denmark.* Ministry of Housing, Copenhagen

Tsichritzis D C, Klug A (eds.) (1975) *The ANSI/X3/SPARC DBMS Framework Report of the Study Group on Database Management Systems.* AFIPS Press, Montvale, New Jersey

Tsichritzis D C, Lochovsky F H (1977) *Data Base Management Systems.* Academic Press, New York

Tsichritzis D C, Lochovsky F H (1982) *Data Models.* Prentice-Hall, New York

Tsichritzis D C, Nierstrasz O M (1988) Fitting round objects into square databases. In: Gjessing S, Nygaard K (eds.) *Proceedings of ECOOP '88, the European Conference on Object-Oriented Programming.* Springer-Verlag, Berlin, pp. 283–99

Tsuzawa M, Okamoto H (1989) Advanced mobile traffic information and communication system (AMTICS). In: *Proceedings of the 20th International Symposium on Automotive Technology and Automation, Florence,* pp. 1145–60

Tucker C J, Townshend J R G, Goff T E (1985) African land-cover classification using satellite data. *Science* **227**: 369–75

Tucker D F, Devine H A (1988) GIS education – eclectic, integrated and evolving *Proceedings GIS/LIS '88.* ASPRS, Falls Church, pp. 528–40

Tufte E R (1983) *The Visual Display of Quantitative Information.* Graphic Press, Cheshire Connecticut

Tukey J W (1977) *Exploratory Data Analysis.* Addison-Wesley, Reading Massachusetts

Tuori M, Moon G C (1984) A topographic map conceptual data model. *Proceedings of the 1st International Symposium on Spatial Data Handling,* Volume 1, International Geographical Union, Columbus Ohio, pp. 28–37

Turnbull M, McAulay I, McLaren R A (1990) The role of terrain modelling in computer aided landscape design. In: Petrie G, Kennie T (eds.) *Terrain Modelling in Surveying and Civil Engineering.* Whittles, Latheronwheel, pp. 262–75

Turner A K (1989) The role of 3-D GIS in subsurface characterisation for hydrogeological applications. In: Raper J F (ed.) *Three Dimensional Applications in Geographical Information Systems.* Taylor & Francis, London, pp. 115–28

Turner A K (1990) *Three-Dimensional Modeling with Geoscientific Information Systems.* NATO Advanced Research Workshop

Turner A K, Kolm K, Downey J (1990) Potential applications of geoscientific information systems (GSIS) for regional ground water flow systems. *Proceedings of Symposium on Three Dimensional Computer Graphics in Modelling Geologic Structures and Simulating Processes.* Freiburger Geowissenschafliche Beitrage **2**: 108–10

Turner M G, Costanza R, Sklar F H (1989) Methods to evaluate the performance of spatial simulation models. *Ecological Modelling* **48**: 1–18

TYDAC (1989) *SPANS User Guide, Version 4.3.* Tydac Technologies Inc., 1600 Carling Ave., Ottawa, Ontario, Canada

Tyrie A (1986) LIS education versus training: a surveying perspective. In: Blakemore M J (ed.) *Proceedings of AUTOCARTO London,* Vol. 2. London, Royal Institution of Chartered Surveyors: 340–50

Ullman J D (1982) *Principles of Database Systems.* Computer Science Press, Rockville Maryland

Ullman J D (1986) Logic and database systems. In: Brodie M L, Mylopoulos J (eds.) *On Knowledge Base Management Systems: integrating artificial intelligence and database technologies.* Springer-Verlag, New York, pp. 121–24

Ullman J D (1986) An approach to processing queries in a logic-based query language. In: Brodie M L, Mylopoulos J (eds.) *On Knowledge Base Management Systems: integrating artificial intelligence and database technologies.* Springer-Verlag, New York, pp. 147–64

UN (1989) *United Nations 1987 Demographic Yearbook.* UN, New York

UNEP Global Resource Information Database (1988) *Report on the meeting of the GRID Scientific and Technical Management Advisory Committee, Jan. 1988.* Report No. 15. UNEP/GEMS/GRID, Nairobi

UNICEF (1988) *The State of the World's Children.* UNICEF Publications, New York

United Nations (1989) Modern mapping techniques. *United Nations Inter-Regional Seminar, Honefoss, Norway.*

United States Congress, Office of Technology Assessment (1990) *Helping America Compete: the role of federal scientific and technical information.* US Government Printing Office, Washington DC

United States Department of Energy, Office of Energy Research, Superconducting Super Collider Site Task Force (1987) *Invitation for Site Proposals for the Superconducting Super Collider (SSC).* DOE/ER-0315 US Department of Energy, Washington DC

Universities Research Association (1987) *To The Heart of*

Matter – The Superconducting Super Collider. Universities Research Association, Washington DC

Unninayar S (1988) The global system: observing and monitoring change, data problems, data management and databases. In: Mounsey H M, Tomlinson R F (eds.) *Building Databases for Global Science*. Taylor & Francis, London, pp. 357–77

Unwin D J (1980) Make your practicals open-ended. *Journal of Geography in Higher Education* **4**: 37–42

Unwin D J (1981) *Introductory Spatial Analysis*. Methuen, London

Unwin D J (1991) The academic setting of GIS. In: Maguire D J, Goodchild M F, Rhind D W (eds.) *Geographical Information Systems: principles and applications*. Longman, London, pp. 81–90, Vol 1

Unwin D J, Dale P (1990) An educationalist's view of GIS. In: Foster M J, Shand P J (eds.) *The Association for Geographic Information Yearbook*. Taylor & Francis, London, pp. 304–12

Unwin D J et al. (1990) A syllabus for teaching geographical information systems. *International Journal of Geographical Information Systems* **4** (4): 457–65

Upstill S (1990) *The RenderMan Companion: a programmer's guide to realistic computer graphics*. Addison-Wesley, Reading Massachusetts

Upton G, Fingleton B (1985) *Spatial Data Analysis by Example. Volume 1. Point Pattern and Quantitative Data*. Wiley, New York

USBC (1969–73) *Census Use Study Reports 1 to 12*. US Bureau of Census, Washington DC

USGS (1984) *Landsat 4 Data Users Handbook*. Government Printing Office, Reston Virginia

USGS (1986) *Goals of the US Geological Survey*. US Geological Survey Circular 1010

USGS (1986) Digital line graphs from 1:24 000–scale maps. *Data User's Guide*, Vol. 1. US Department of the Interior, Reston

USGS (1986) Land use and land cover digital data from 1:250 000- and 1:100 000-scale maps. *Data User's Guide*, Vol. 4. US Department of the Interior, Reston

USGS (1987) *Digital Elevation Models, US Geological Survey Data Users Guide 5*. USGS, Reston Virginia

USGS (1989) *Digital Line Graphs from 1:100 000-Scale Maps*. US Geological Survey Data Users Guide 2. USGS, Reston Virginia

USGS (1990) *Digital Line Graphs from 1:24 000-Scale Maps. US Geological Survey Data Users Guide 1*. USGS, Reston Virginia

USGS (1991) *The Spatial Data Transfer Format*. US Geological Survey National Mapping Division, Washington DC

Ustin S L, Adams J B, Elvidge C D, Rejmanek M, Rock B N, Smith M O, Thomas R W, Woodward R A (1986) Thematic Mapper studies of semiarid shrub communities. *Bioscience* **36**: 446–52

van der Vlugt M (1989) The use of a GIS based decision support system in physical planning. *Proceedings of GIS/LIS '89*. ASPRS, Bethesda Maryland, pp. 459–67

van Roessel J W (1987) Design of a spatial data structure using the relational normal form. *International Journal of Geographical Information Systems* **1** (1): 33–50

van Roessel J W, Fosnight E A (1984) A relational approach to vector data structure conversion. *Proceedings of the 1st International Symposium on Spatial Data Handling*, Volume 1. International Geographical Union, Columbus Ohio, pp. 78–95

Varvel D A, Shapiro L (1989) The computational completeness of extended database query languages. *Journal of the IEEE* **15** (5): 632–8

Vazsonyi A (1978) Decision support systems: the new technology of decision making? *Interfaces* **9**: 74–8

Vazsonyi A (1982) Decision support systems, computer literacy, and electronic models. *Interfaces* **12**: 74–8

Ventura S, Sullivan J G, Chrisman N R (1986) Vectorization of Landsat TM land cover classification data. *Proceedings URISA* **1**: 129–40

Veregin H (1989) A taxonomy of error in spatial databases. *Technical Paper 89–12*. National Center for Geographic Information and Analysis University of California, Santa Barbara California

Veregin H (1989) Error modeling for the map overlay operation. In: Goodchild M F, Gopal S (eds.) *Accuracy of Spatial Databases*. Taylor & Francis, London, pp. 3–18

Verhey W H (1986) Principles of land appraisal and land use planning within the European Community. *Soil Use and Management* **2**: 120–4

Verhoef W (1984) Light scattering by leaf layers with application to canopy reflectance modeling: the Sail model. *Remote Sensing of Environment* **16**: 125–41

Verplank W L (1988) Graphic challenges in designing object orientated user interfaces. In: Helender M (ed.) *Handbook of Human Computer Interfaces*. Elsevier, North Holland

Vevany M J (1987) A critical evaluation of the proliferation of automated mapping systems in local governments. In: Aangeenbrug R T, Schiffman Y M (eds.) *International Geographic Information Symposiums: The Research Agenda*, Vol 3. Association of American Geographers, Washington, pp. 165–77

Vincenty T (1971) The meridional distance problem for desk computers. *Survey Review* **21**: 136–40, 161

Vincenty T (1989) The flat earth concept in local surveys. *Surveying and Mapping* **49**: 101–2

von Hohenbalken B and West D S (1984) Manhattan versus Euclid: market areas computed and compared. *Regional Science and Urban Economics* **14**: 19–35

Vonderohe A P, Chrisman N R (1985) Tests to establish the quality of digital cartographic data: some examples from the Dane County Land Records Project. *Proceedings of AUTOCARTO 7*. ASPRS/ACSM, Falls Church, pp. 552–9

Vose M (1990) Hot links to go. *BYTE* **15** (12): 373–7

Wadge G (1988) The potential of GIS modelling of gravity flows and slope instabilities. *International Journal of Geographic Information Systems* 2: 143–52

Wadge G, Isaacs M C (1988) Mapping the volcanic hazards from Soufriere Hills Volcano, Montserrat, West Indies using an image processor. *Journal of the Geological Society* 145: 541–52

Wagner G (1990) SICAD: profile of a raster indexed topological vector GIS. *Proceedings of the Conference on GIS Models and Functionality*. Midlands Regional Research Laboratory, University of Leicester

Wainer H, Thissen D (1981) Graphical data analysis. *Annual Review of Psychology* 32: 191–241

Waldrop M M (1990) Learning to drink from a fire hose. *Science* 248 (11): 674–5

Walker P A, Cocks K D (1984) Computerised choropleth mapping of Australian resources data. *Cartography* 13 (4): 243–52

Walker P A, Hutton P G (1986) Grid cell representation of soil maps: an Australian example. *Australian Geographical Studies* 24 (2): 210–21

Walker P A, Moore D M (1988) SIMPLE – an inductive modelling and mapping tool for spatially-oriented data. *International Journal of Geographical Information Systems* 2 (4): 347–63

Walker T C, Miller R K (1990) *Geographic Information Systems – an assessment of technology, applications, and products*. SEAI Technical Publications, Madison Georgia USA

Wallin E (1990) The map as hypertext: on knowledge support systems for the territorial concern. *Proceedings of EGIS '90*, Volume 2. EGIS Foundation, Utrecht, pp. 1125–34

Walsh S J (1985) Geographic information systems for natural resource management. *Journal of Soil and Water Conservation* 40: 202–5

Walsh S J, Lightfoot D R, Butler D R (1987) Recognition and assessment of error in geographic information systems. *Photogrammetric Engineering and Remote Sensing* 53: 1423–30

Walters D K (1987) Selection of image primitives for general-purpose visual processing. *Computer Vision, Graphics and Image Processing* 37: 261–98

Walters D K (1990) Computer vision. In: Ralston A, Reilly E (eds.) *Encyclopedia of Computer Science and Engineering*. Van Nostrand Reinhold, New York

Wang F, Hall G B, Subaryono (1990) Fuzzy information representation and processing in conventional GIS software: database design and application. *International Journal of Geographical Information Systems* 4 (3): 261–83

Wang S, Elliott D B, Campbell J B, Erich R W, Haralick R M (1983) Spatial reasoning in remotely sensed data. *IEEE Transactions on Geoscience and Remote Sensing* GE-21: 94–101

Ware C (1990) Using hand position for virtual object placement. *The Visual Computer* 6 (5): 245–53

Ware C, Osborne S (1990) Exploration and virtual camera control in virtual three dimensional environments. *1990 Symposium on Interactive 3D Graphics: Computer Control* (special issue)

Warntz W (1964) A new map of the surface of population potentials for the United States, 1960. *Geographical Review* 54: 170–84

Warthen B (1988) Move over IGES: Here comes PDES/STEP. *Computer Graphics Review* Nov-Dec, 34–40

Wasielewski P (1988) Overview of PATHFINDER. *Proceedings of Research and Development Conference, California Department of Transportation, Sacramento*, September 263–4

Waters N M (1989) Expert systems within a GIS: knowledge aquisition for spatial decision support systems. *Proceedings of Challenge for the 1990s* Ottawa, pp. 740–59

Waters R S (1989) Data capture for the Nineties: VTRAK. *Proceedings of AUTOCARTO 9*. ACSM/ASPRS, Bethesda, Maryland, pp. 377–83

Watson G P, Rencz A N, Bonham-Carter G F (1989) Computers assist prospecting. *GEOS* 18 (1): 8–15

Waugh T C (1980) The development of the GIMMS computer mapping system. In: Taylor D R F (ed.) *The Computer in Contemporary Cartography*. Wiley, London, pp. 219–34

Waugh T C, Healey R G (1986) The GEOLINK system, interfacing large systems. In: Blakemore M J (ed.) *Proceedings of AUTOCARTO London*, Volume 1. Royal Institution of Chartered Surveyors, London, 76–85

Waugh T C, Healey R G (1987) The GEOVIEW design. A relational database approach to geographical data handling. *International Journal of Geographical Information Systems* 1: 101–18

WCED (1987) *Our Common Future*. World Commission on Environment and Development. Oxford University Press, Oxford

Webster C J (1988) Disaggregated GIS architecture: lessons from recent developments in multi-site database management systems. *International Journal of Geographical Information Systems* 2 (1): 67–79

Webster C J (1989) Point-in-polygon processing in PROLOG. *Technical Reports in Geo-Information Systems* 17. Wales and the South West RRL, University of Wales College of Cardiff

Webster R (1968) Fundamental objections to the 7th Approximation. *Journal of Soil Science* 19: 354–66

Webster R (1977) *Quantitative and Numerical Methods in Soil Classification and Survey*. Oxford University Press, Oxford

Webster R (1978) Mathematical treatment of soil information. *Proceedings of the 11th International Congress of Soil Science, Edmonton, Canada*, Volume 3. pp. 161–90

Webster R (1985) Quantitative spatial analysis of soil in the field. *Advances in Soil Science* 3: 2–70

Webster R, Burgess T M (1984) Sampling and bulking strategies for estimating soil properties in small regions. Journal of Soil Science 5: 127–40

Webster R, Burrough P A (1972) Computer-based soil mapping of small areas from sample data: I. Multivariate classification and ordination. *Journal of Soil Science* **23**: 210–21

Webster R, Burrough P A (1972) Computer-based soil mapping of small areas from sample data: II Classification smoothing. *Journal of Soil Science* **23**: 222–34

Webster R, Burrough P A (1974) Multiple discriminant analysis in soil survey. *Journal of Soil Science* **25**: 120–34

Webster R, Butler B E (1976) Soil classification and survey studies at Ginninderra. *Australian Journal of Soil Science* **14**: 1–24

Webster R, Oliver M (1989) Optimal interpolation and isarithmic mapping of soil properties: VI. Disjunctive Kriging and mapping the conditional probability. *Journal of Soil Science* **40**: 497–512

Webster R, Oliver M (1990) *Statistical Methods in Soil and Land Resource Survey. Spatial Information Series.* Oxford University Press, Oxford

Weibel R (1989) Concepts and experiments for the automation of relief generalisation. Unpublished PhD dissertation (in German). *Geoprocessing Series 15*, Zurich, Department of Geography, University of Zurich.

Weibel R, Buttenfield B P (1988) Map design for geographic information systems. *Proceedings GIS/LIS '88*, Vol. 1. ASPRS/ACSM, Falls Church Virginia pp. 350–9

Weibel R, DeLotto J L (1988) Automated terrain classification for GIS modeling. *Proceedings of GIS/LIS '88*, Volume 2: ASPRS/ACSM, Falls Church Virginia, pp. 618–27

Weibel R, Heller M (1990) A framework for digital terrain modelling. *Proceedings of the 4th International Symposium on Spatial Data Handling.* International Geographical Union, Columbus Ohio, pp. 219–29

Weibel R, Heller M (1991) Digital terrain modelling. In: Maguire D J, Goodchild M F, Rhind D W (eds.) *Geographical Information Systems: principles and applications.* Longman, London, pp. 269–97, Vol 1

Weibel R, Heller M, Herzog A, Brassel K (1987) Approaches to digital surface modeling. *Proceedings First Latin American Conference on Computers in Cartography, San José, Costa Rica*, pp. 143–63

Weibel R, Herzog A (1988) Automatische Konstruktion panoramischer Ansichten aus digitalen Geländemodellen. *Nachrichten aus dem Karten- und Vermessungswesen Series I/100*: 49–84

Weir S (1975) *Getting around town: modifications in a local travel time space caused by expressway construction.* Unpublished MSc thesis. Department of Geography, Pennsylvania State University

Weiser R L, Asrar G, Miller G P, Kanemasu E T (1986) Assessing grassland biophysical characteristics from spectral measurements. *Remote Sensing of Environment* **20**: 141–52

Weizenbaum J (1976) *Computer Power and Human Reason.* Freeman, San Francisco

Welch R A (1990) 3-D terrain modelling for GIS applications. *GIS World*, October/November: 26–30

Welch R A, Usery E L (1984) Cartographic accuracy of Landsat-4 MSS and TM image data. *IEEE Transactions on Geoscience and Remote Sensing* **GE-22**: 281–8

Welch T A (1984) A technique for high performance data compression. *IEEE Computer* **17** (6)

Wellings C (1989) A review of the Association for Geographic Information Yearbook 1989. *Mapping Awareness* **3** (4): 51

Wells D (1988) How object-oriented databases are different from relational databases. In: Power L, Weiss Z (eds.) *OOPSLA '87 Addendum to the Proceedings. Special Issue of SIGPLAN Notices* **23** (5): 81

Werner C (1988) Formal analysis of ridge and channel patterns in maturely eroded terrain. *Annals of the Association of American Geographers* **78** (2): 253–70

Westcott T, Reiman R (1987) Siting the Superconducting Super Collider: a case study of the role of Geographic Information Systems in macro site analysis. *Paper presented at the 42nd Annual Meeting of the Southeast Division of the Association of American Geographers, Charlotte, NC*

Weyer S A, Borning A H (1985) A prototype electronic encyclopedia. *ACM Transactions on Office Information Systems* **31** (1): 63–88

Wharton S W (1989) Knowledge-based spectral classification of remotely sensed image data. In: Asrar G (ed.) *Theory and Applications of Optical Remote Sensing.* Wiley, New York, pp. 548–77

Wheeler P H (1988) *Olmsted County's Farmland Soil Loss Controls.* Rochester–Olmsted Consolidated Planning Department.

Whelan S D (1983) The MIDAS project: considerations for success. *Proceedings of AM/FM International, Keystone, USA.* AM/FM International, 8775 E. Orchard Rd, Suite 820, Englewood, CO80111

Whimbrel Consultants Ltd (1989) *CORINE Database Manual, Version 2.1.* Brussels

White B (1973) Supreme Court opinion in EPA *v.* Mink. 410 US 73

White B (1985) Modelling forest pest impacts – aided by a geographic information system in a decision support system framework. *Proceedings of Geographic Information Systems Workshop.* ASPRS, Falls Church Virginia, pp. 238–248

White D (1985) A taxonomy of space–time relations. *Proceedings of the Princeton Conference on Computer Graphics and Transportation Planning.* American Society of Landscape Architects

White D (1985) Relief modulated thematic mapping by computer. *The American Cartographer* **12** (1): 62–7

White M S (1984) Technical requirements and standards for a multi-purpose geographic data system. The *American Cartographer* **11**: 15–26

White M (1978) A geometric model for error detection and correction. *Proceedings of AUTOCARTO 3.* ASPRS, Falls Church, pp. 439–56

White M (1991) Car navigation systems. In: Maguire D J, Goodchild M F, Rhind D W (eds.) *Geographical*

Information Systems: principles and applications. Longman, London, pp. 115–25, Vol 2

Whittaker E, Robinson G (1944) *The Calculus of Observations*, 4th edn. Blackie and Son, London

Wiederhold G (1983) *Database Design*. 2nd edn. McGraw-Hill, London, 751pp.

Wiederhold G (1986) Knowledge versus data. In: Brodie M L, Mylopoulos J (eds.) *On Knowledge Base Management Systems: integrating artificial intelligence and database technologies*. Springer-Verlag, New York, pp. 77–82

Wiggins J C (1986) Performance considerations in the design of a map library: a user perspective. *Proceedings of the ARC/INFO Users' Conference*. ESRI, Redlands California

Wiggins J C, Hartley R P, Higgins M J, Whittaker R J (1987) Computing aspects of a large geographic information system for the European Community. *International Journal of Geographical Information Systems* **1** (1): 77–87

Wilding L P, Jones R B, Schafer G M (1965) Variation of soil morphological properties within Miami, Celina and Crosby mapping units in West-Central Ohio. *Proceedings of the Soil Science Society of America* **29**: 711–17

Williams E P J (1971) Digitisation of Large Scale Maps. *Proceedings of ICA Commission III meeting, Paris*. ICA, Paris, Paper II/a

Williams R B G (1984) *Introduction to Statistics for Geographers and Earth Scientists*. Macmillan, London

Williams R B G (1986) *Intermediate Statistics for Geographers and Earth Scientists*. Macmillan, London

Williams R L (1960) Map symbols: the curve of the gray spectrum – an answer. *Annals of the Association of American Geographers* **50**: 487–91

Williams W B P (1982) The Transverse Mercator Projection – simple but accurate formulae for small computers. *Survey Review* **26**: 205, 307–20

Williamson I P (1986) Trends in land information system administration in Australia. In: Blakemore M J (ed.) *Proceedings of AUTOCARTO London 1*. Royal Institution of Chartered Surveyors, London, pp. 71–82

Williamson I P, Blackburn J W (1987) Current developments in Land Information Systems in Australia. *Proceedings of the 21st Conference of the Institute of Australian Geographers, Perth*, pp. 289–97

Willmott C J (1984) On the evaluation of model performance in physical geography. In: Gaile G L, Willmott C J (eds.) *Spatial Statistics and Models*. D. Reidel, Dordrecht, pp. 443–60

Wilson A G (1974) *Urban and Regional Models in Geography and Planning*. Wiley, London

Wilson A G, Bennett R J (1985) *Mathematical Methods in Human Geography and Planning*. Wiley, London

Winograd T, Flores F (1986) *Understanding Computers and Cognition: a new foundation for design*. Addison-Wesley, Reading Massachusetts

Winston P H (1984) *Artificial Intelligence*, 2nd edn. Addison-Wesley, Reading Massachusetts

Wischmeier W H, Smith D D (1978) *Predicting Rainfall Erosion Losses. Agricultural Handbook 537*. USDA, Washington DC

Wise S, Burnhill P (1990) GIS: models of use and implications for service delivery on higher education computing campuses. In: Unwin D J (ed.) *GIS Education and Training, Collected Papers of a Conference, University of Leicester 20–21 March 1990*. Midlands Regional Research Laboratory, Leicester

Witkin A P (1986) Scale-space filtering. In: Pentland A P (ed.) *From Pixels to Predicates*. Ablex Publishing, Norwood New Jersey, pp. 5–19

Woelk D, Kim W (1987) Multimedia information management in an object oriented database system. In: Stocker P M, Kent W (eds.) *Proceedings of the 13th Very Large Databases Conference, Brighton*, pp. 319–29

Woodcock C E, Strahler A H (1987) The factor of scale in remote sensing. *Remote Sensing of Environment* **21**: 311–32

Woodcock C E, Strahler A H, Jupp D L B (1988) The use of variograms in remote sensing: I. Scene models and simulated images. *Remote Sensing of Environment* **25**: 323–48

Woodcock C E, Strahler A H, Jupp D L B (1989) Autocorrelation and regularization in digital images: II. Simple image models. *IEEE Transactions on Geoscience and Remote Sensing* **27**: 247–56

Woodcock J, Loomes M (1989) *Software Engineering Mathematics*. Addison-Wesley, Reading Massachusetts

Worboys M F, Hearnshaw, H M, Maguire D J (1990) Object-oriented data modelling for spatial databases. *International Journal of Geographical Information Systems* **4**: 369–83

Worboys M F, Hearnshaw H, Maguire D J (1990) Object-oriented data and query modelling for geographical information systems. *Proceedings of the 4th International Symposium on Spatial Data Handling*. International Geographical Union, Columbus Ohio, pp. 679–88

World Commission on Environment and Development (1987) *Our Common Future*. Oxford University Press, Oxford

Wösten J H M, Bannink M H, Bouma J (1989) Relation between the questions being asked and the sales and costs at which land evaluation is performed. In: Bouma J, Bregt A K (eds.) *Land Qualities in Space and Time. Proceedings of a Symposium organised by the International Society of Soil Science (ISSS), Wageningen, The Netherlands, 22–26 August 1988*. PUDOC, Wageningen, pp. 213–5

Wray T (1974) The seven aspects of a general map projection. *Cartographica Monograph* **11**, 72 pp.

Wright D F, Bonham-Carter G F, Rogers P J (1988) Spatial data integration of lake-sediment geochemistry, geology and gold occurrences, Meguma Terrane, Nova Scotia. In: MacDonald D R, Mills K A (eds.) *Prospecting in Areas of Glaciated Terrain – 1988*. Canadian Institute of Mining and Metallurgy, pp. 501–15

Wrigley N (ed.) (1988) *Store Choice, Store Location and Market Analysis*. Routledge and Kegan Paul, London

Wrigley N (1985) *Categorical Data Analysis for Geographers and Environmental Scientists*. Longman, London

Wu, Zhong-xing, Yang, Qi-he (1981) A research on the transformation of map projections in computer-aided cartography, *Paper presented at the 10th International Cartographic Conference Tokyo*, 22 pp.

Wyatt B K, Briggs D J, Mounsey H M (1988) CORINE: An information system on the state of the environment in the European Community. In: Mounsey H M, Tomlinson R F (eds.) *Building Databases for Global Science*. Taylor & Francis, London, pp. 378–96

Yan S Y (1988) *A Logic Foundation for Expert Geographic Database Systems*. Melbourne, Australia, Department of Computer Science, University of Melbourne.

Yan S, Zhou M, Shi Z (1987) Chinese Tourism Resource Information System. *Proceedings of International Workshop on Geographic Information System Beijing '87*. LREIS, Beijing, pp. 377–83

Yapa L S (1988) Computer-aided regional planning: a study in rural Sri Lanka. *Environment and Planning B* **15**: 285–304

Yapa L S (1989) Peasants, planners and microcomputers in the Third World. *Earth and Mineral Sciences* **58** (2): 31–3

Yarbus A L (1967) *Eye Movement and Vision*. (Tr. Haig B). Plenum, New York

Yarrow G J (1987) Joint utility mapping. *Proceedings of NJUG 87 First National Conference, Birmingham*. National Joint Utilities Group, 30 Millbank, London, SW1P 4RD

Yarrow G J (1989) Dudley – the lessons. *Proceedings of the National Joint Utilities' Conference*

Yates S R, Yates M V (1988) Disjunctive kriging as an approach to management decision making. *Soil Science Society of America Journal* **62**: 1554–58

Yeh A G (1990) A land information system for the monitoring of land supply in the urban development of Hong Kong. In: Worrell L (ed.) *Geographic information systems: developments and applications*. Belhaven, London, pp. 163–87

Yeorgaroudakis Y (1990) The GIS of the future. *Proceedings of EGIS '90*, Volume 2. EGIS Foundation, Utrecht, pp. 1188–99

Yeung A K W, Lo C P (1985) Cartographic digitizing for geographical application: some hardware and software considerations. *Asian Geographer* **4**: 9–22

Yoeli P (1965) Analytical hill shading. *Surveying and Mapping* **25**: 573–9

Yoeli P (1967) Mechanisation in analytical hill-shading. *Cartographic Journal* **4**: 82–8

Yoeli P (1972) The logic of automated map lettering. *Cartographic Journal* **9** (2): 99–108

Yoeli P (1982) Cartographic drawing with computers. *Computer Applications* **8**

Yoeli P (1983) Shadowed contours with computer and plotter. *The American Cartographer* **10** (2): 101–10

Yoeli P (1985) The making of intervisibility maps with computer and plotter. *Cartographica* **22** (3): 88–103

Yoeli P (1985) Topographic relief depiction by hachures with computer and plotter. *Cartographic Journal* **22** (2): 111–24

Yoshimura S (1930) A method for area measurement and its example. *Geographical Review of Japan* **6**: 1569–84; and 1708–43

Youngman C (1978) A linguistic approach to map description. In Dutton G (ed.) *Spatial Semantics: understanding and interacting with map data*. Laboratory for Computer Graphics and Spatial Analysis, Graduate School of Design, Harvard University

Youngmann C (1989) Spatial data structures for modelling subsurface features. In: Raper J F (ed.) *Three Dimensional Applications in Geographical Information Systems*. Taylor & Francis, London, pp. 129–36

Zadeh L A (1974) *Fuzzy Logic and its Application to Approximate Reasoning, Information Processing*. North-Holland, Amsterdam

Zarzycki J M, Jiwani Z (1986) Canadian standards for exchange of digital topographic data. *Proceedings of the XVIII FIG Congress, Commission V*: 171–181

Zavoli W B (1989) Navigation and digital maps interface for fleet management and driver information systems. *Proceedings, First Vehicle Navigation & Information Systems Conference (VNIS '89)*. IEEE, New York, pp. A9–A14

Zhang Q, Kou Y (1987) A study on the information system for agricultural resources and economy. *Proceedings of International Workshop on Geographic Information System Beijing '87*. LREIS, Beijing, pp. 90–4

Zheng W, Ren F, Cheng Ji-Cheng (1989) Building of micro-GIS tool and its application. *Proceedings of International Conference in Urban Planning and Urban Management*. University of Hong Kong, Hong Kong, pp. 299–314

Zhong S, Zhong E (1987) A preliminary research on Land Resources Information System (LRIS) at Fushui County. *Proceedings of International Workshop on Geographic Information System Beijing '87*. LREIS, Beijing, 433–7

Zhou Q (1989) A method for integrating remote sensing and geographic information systems. *Photogrammetric Engineering and Remote Sensing* **55**: 591–6

Zilles S (1984) Types, algebras, and modelling. In: Brodie M, Mylopoulos J, Schmidt J (eds.) *On Conceptual Modelling*. Springer-Verlag, New York, pp. 441–50

Zinn v. State [1983] 112 Wis. 2nd 417, 334 N.W. 2nd 67

Zobrist A L (1983) Integration of Landsat image data with geographic databases. In: Peuquet D J, O'Callaghan J (eds.) *Proceedings of the United States/Australia Workshop on Design and Implementation of Computer-based Geographic Information Systems*. IGU Commission on Geographical Data Sensing and Processing, Amherst New York, pp. 51–63

Zoraster S (1986) Integer programming applied to the map label placement problem. *Cartographica* **23** (3): 16–27

Zoraster S, Davis D, Hugus M (1984) *Manual and*

Automated Line Generalization and Feature Displacement, ETL-Report ETL-0359 (plus ETL-0359–1). US Army Engineer Topographic Laboratories, Fort Belvoir Virginia
Zuboff S (1988) *In the Age of the Smart Machine*. Heinemann, London
Zusne L (1970) *Visual Perception of Form*. Academic Press, New York

Zycor N C (1984) Manual and automated line generalization and feature displacement. *Report for the US Army Engineer Topographic Laboratories Fort Belvoir, Virginia 22060 USA, unclassified material*, 2 vols, 204pp.
Zyda M J (1988) A decomposable algorithm for contour surface display generation. *ACM Transactions on Graphics* **7** (2): 129–48

LIST OF ACRONYMS

A-P	Albemarle-Pamlico	AURISA	Australasian Urban and Regional Planning Information Systems Association
AAG	Association of American Geographers		
ABS	Australian Bureau of Statistics		
ACORN	A Classification of Residential Neighbourhoods	AUSLIG	Australian Surveying and Land Information Group
ACSM	American Congress on Surveying and Mapping	AVHRR	Advanced Very High Resolution Radiometer
ADMATCH	Address Matching Software		
ADT	Abstract Data Type		
AGI	Association for Geographic Information	BBC	British Broadcasting Corporation
AGNPS	Agricultural Nonpoint Source Pollution Model	BEM	Basic Employment Allocation Model
		BIOS	Basic Input Output System
		BLOB	Binary Large Object
AID	Automated Interaction Detector	BP	British Petroleum
AIS	Address Information System	BR	Boundary Representation
AIS	Australia Information System	BURISA	British Urban and Regional Information Systems Association
AIT	Asian Institute of Technology		
ALIC	Australian Land Information Council		
AM/FM	Automated Mapping/Facilities Management	CAD	Computer-Aided Design
AMEDAS	Automated Meteorological Data Acquisition System	CAD	Computer-Aided Drafting
		CADD	Computer-Aided Design and Drafting
		CAL	Computer-Assisted Learning
AML	ARC Macro Language	CAM	Computer-Aided Mapping
AMTICS	Advanced Mobile Traffic Information and Communication System	CAMA	Coastal Area Management Act
		CARD	Cartographic Representation of Data
ANSI	American National Standards Institute	CARP	Computer-Assisted Regional Planning
ARDA	Canadian Agricultural Rehabilitation and Development Association	CASS	Crime Analysis Statistical System
		CBRED	Central Bureau for Real Estate Data
ARIS	Australia Resources Information System	CCD	Charge-Coupled Device
		CD-ROM	Compact Disk Read Only Memory
ARJIS	Automated Regional Justice Information System	CFD	Central Board of Real Estate Data
		CGIA	Center for Geographical Information and Analysis
ASCII	American Standard Code for Information Interchange		
ASPRS	American Society for Photogrammetry and Remote Sensing	CGIS	Canada Geographic Information System
		CHEST	Combined Higher Education Software Team
ATM	Adaptive Triangular Mesh		
ATM	Automated Teller Machine	CIA	Central Intelligence Agency

List of acronyms

CISM	Canadian Institute of Surveying and Mapping	DR	Dead Reckoning
CLDS	Canada Land Data System	DRIVE	Dedicated Road Infrastructure for Vehicle Safety
CLI	Canada Land Inventory	DSS	Decision Support System
CLISG	Commonwealth Land Information Support Group	DTED	Digital Terrain Elevation Data
CNES	Centre National d'Etudes Spatiales	DTI	Department of Trade and Industry
CODASYL	Conference on Data Systems Languages	DTM	Digital Terrain Model
CODATA	Committee on Data for Science and Technology	EC	European Commission
CORINE	Coordinated Information on the European Environment	ECU	Experimental Cartography Unit
		ED	Enumeration District
		ED Group	Department of Employment Group
CRIES	Comprehensive Resource Inventory and Evaluation System	EDA	Exploratory Data Analysis
		EDI	Electronic Data Interchange
CRISP	Computerized Rural Information Systems Project	EDP	Electronic Data Processing
		EFTPoS	Electronic Funds Transfer at Point of Sales
CRT	Cathode Ray Tube		
CSG	Constructive Solid Geometry	EGA	Extended Graphics Array
CSIRO	Commonwealth Scientific and Industrial Research Organisation	EGIS	European Geographical Information Systems Symposia
CZCS	Coastal Zone Color Scanning	EMR	Department of Energy, Mines and Resources Canada
DBMS	Database Management System	EMS	Emergency Management System
DBS	Database System	EMS	Engineering Modelling Software
DCDSTF	Digital Cartographic Data Standards Task Force	EOS	Earth Observation Satellite
		EPA	Environmental Protection Agency
DCM	Digital Cartographic Model	EPoS	Electronic Point of Sales
DDE	Dynamic Data Exchange	ERDAS	Earth Resources Data Analysis System
DEFM	Demographic and Economic Forecasting Model	ERE	Effective Resolution Element
		ERIN	Environmental Resources Information Network
DEM	Digital Elevation Model		
DFUS	Digital Field Update System	ES	Expert System
DG XI	Directorate General of the Environment	ESA	European Space Agency
		ESRC	Economic and Social Research Council
DGIWG	Digital Geographic Information Working Group	ESRI	Environmental Systems Research Institute
DHA	District Health Authority	ESSC	Earth Systems Science Committee
DID	Digital Image Document		
DIDS	Decision Information Display System	FAA	Federal Aviation Administration
DIDS	Desktop Information and Display System	FGDC	Federal Geographic Data Committee
		FICCDC	Federal Interagency Coordinating Committee on Digital Cartography
DIDS	Domestic Information Display System	FIG	Fédération International de Géomètres
DIME	Dual Independent Map Encoding		
DIP	Document Image Processing	FIPS	Federal Information Processing Standard
DLG	Digital Line Graph		
DLG-E	Digital Line Graph – Enhanced	FOIA	Freedom of Information Act
DLM	Digital Landscape Model	FPC	Family Practitioner Committee
DMA	Defense Mapping Agency		
DMSP	Defense Meteorological Satellite Program	GAM	Geographical Analysis Machine
		Gb	Gigabyte
DOE	Department of Energy	GCDP	Global Change Database Project
DoE	Department of the Environment	GCEM	Geographical Correlates Exploration Machine
DOI	Department of the Interior		
DP	Data Processing		

List of acronyms

GCM	Global Climate Model	ICSU	International Council of Scientific Unions
GD	Geologic Division		
GDF	Geographic Data File	IfAG	Institut fur Angewandte Geodasie
GEBCO	General Bathymetric Chart of the Oceans	IFOV	Instantaneous Field of View
		IGBP	International Geosphere-Biosphere Programme
GEMS	Global Environmental Monitoring System		
		IGES	Initial Graphics Exchange Specification
GENESSIS	Generic Scene Simulation Software	IGIS	Integrated Geographical Information System
GEODAS	Geophysical Data System		
GF3	General Formatting System for Geo-Referenced Data 3	IGU	International Geographic Union
		IJGIS	International Journal of Geographical Information Systems
GIA	Geographical Information Analysis		
GIMMS	Geographic Information Mapping and Management System	ILI	Institute for Land Information
		ILWIS	Integrated Land and Watershed Management Information System
GIPS	Geographical Information Processing System		
		IMM	Interactive Multimedia
GIRAS	Geographical Information Retrieval and Analysis System	IMS	Information Management System
		IOC	International Oceanographic Commission
GIS	Geographical Information System		
GISG	Geographic Information Steering Group	IODE	International Oceanographic Data and Information Exchange
GISP	General Information System for Planning		
		IS	Information System
GIST!	Geographical Information Systems Tutor	ISD	Information Systems Division
		ISDN	Integrated Services Digital Network
GKS	Graphical Kernel System	ISIF	Intermediate Standard Transfer Format
GPS	Global Positioning Satellite	ISM	Interactive Surface Modelling
GPS	Global Positioning System	ISO	International Standards Organisation
GPV	General Parametric Videoshow	ISPRS	International Society of Photogrammetry and Remote Sensing
GRASS	Geographical Resources Analysis Support System		
		ISSS	International Soil Science Society
GRID	Global Resource Information Database	IT	Information Technology
GSD	Geographical Data of Sweden	ITC	International Institute for Aerospace Survey and Earth Science
GSI	Geographical Survey Institute		
GSM	General Systems Model	ITE	Institute of Terrestrial Ecology
GSS	Government Statistical Service	ITT	Invitation to Tender
GTS	Global Telecommunications System	ITU	Integrated Terrain Unit
GUI	Graphical User Interface	ITU	International Telecommunications Union
		IU	Intelligence Unit
HCI	Human-Computer Interaction	IV	Interactive Video
HCI	Human-Computer Interface	IVM	Interactive Volume Modelling
HDGCP	Human Dimensions of Global Change Program		
HMLR	Her Majesty's Land Registry	JAMGIS	Jamaica GIS
HMSO	Her Majesty's Stationery Office	JANET	Joint Academic Network
HPGL	Hewlett Packard Graphics Language	JDRMA	Japan Digital Road Map Association
		JIS	Japan Industrial Standard
IAC	Inter-Application Communications		
IBG	Institute of British Geographers	Kb	Kilobyte
IBM	International Business Machines	KB	Knowledge Base
ICA	International Cartographic Association	KBGIS	Knowledge Based Geographical Information System
ICES	International Council for the Exploration of the Sea		
		KBT	Knowledge Based Technique
ICL	International Computers Limited	KUB	Knoxville Utilities Board

List of acronyms

LAI	Leaf Area Index	NAGIS	Natal/KwaZulu Association for Geographic Information Systems
LAMIS	Local Authority Management Information System	NASA	National Aeronautics and Space Administration
LAMSAC	Local Authorities Management Services and Computer Committee	NATO	North Atlantic Treaty Organization
LAN	Local Area Network	NCDC	National Climate Data Center
LAS	Land Analysis System	NCGA	National Computer Graphics Association
LCG	Harvard Laboratory for Computer Graphics	NCGIA	National Center for Geographic Information and Analysis
LDBS	Land Data Bank System	NCHS	National Center for Health Statistics
LDC	Less Developed Countries	NCIC	National Cartographic Information Center
LIS	Land Information System		
LMI	Labour Market Information	NDCDB	National Digital Cartographic Data Base
LOTS	Land Ownership and Tenure System		
LR	Land Register	NEC	Nippon Electric Corporation
LREIS	Laboratory for Resource and Environmental Information Systems	NERC	Natural Environmental Research Council
LRIS	Land Resources Information System	NEXPRI	Nederlands Expertise Centruum voor Ruimtelijke Informatiererwerkig
LRU	Least Recently Used		
LTER	Long Term Ecological Research	NGDC	National Geophysical Data Center
LUDA	USGS Land Use Data Analysis	NHS	National Health Service
LZW	Lempel-Zif and Welch	NIC	Newly Industrialized Countries
		NIMBY	Not In My Back Yard
MAFF	Ministry of Agriculture, Forestry and Fishery	NJUG	National Joint Utilities Group
		NL	Natural Language
MAGI	Maryland Automatic Geographic Information	NLA	National Land Agency
		NLS	National Land Survey
MAI	Mean Annual Increment	NMD	National Mapping Division
MAP	Map Analysis Package	NMP	National Mapping Program
MAUP	Modifiable Areal Unit Problem	NNRIS	National Natural Resources Information System
Mb	Megabyte		
MDS	Multi-Dimensional Scaling	NOAA	National Oceanographic and Atmospheric Administration
MFlops	Millions of Floating Point Operations per Second		
		NODC	National Oceanographic Data Centres
MGRA	Master Geographical Reference Area	NOMIS	National On-Line Manpower Information System
MIAS	Marine Information Advisory Service		
MIMD	Multiple Instruction Multiple Data	NP	Non-Deterministic Polynomial Time
MIPS	Million Instructions Per Second	NRC	National Research Council
MIS	Management Information System	NRIC	National Resources Information Centre
MITI	Ministry of International Trade and Industry	NSF	National Science Foundation
MLMIS	Minnesota Land Management Information System	NSSDC	National Space Science Data Center
		NSW	New South Wales
MMS	Materials Management Service	NTF	National Transfer Format
MOSS	Map Overlay and Statistics System	NTT	Nippon Telephone and Telegram
MS	Metropolitan Map Series	NURBS	Non-Uniform Rational B-Splines
MS-DOS	MicroSoft Disk Operating System		
MSA	Major Statistical Areas	OCR	Optical Character Reader
MSD	Master Survey Drawing	ODA	Office Document Architecture
MSS	Multi-Spectral Scanner	ODA	Official Development Assistance
MTS	Michigan Terminal System	OECD	Organization for Economic Cooperation and Development
NA	Network Analysis	OHWM	Ordinary High Water Mark
NAG	Numerical Algorithm Group	OLWM	Ordinary Low Water Mark

List of acronyms

OMB	Office of Management and Budget	RGB	Red, Green and Blue
ONC	Operational Navigation Charts	RGF	Regional Growth Forecast
OODB	Object-Orientated Database	RGS	Royal Geographical Society
OODBMS	Object-Oriented Database Management System	RHA	Regional Health Authority
		RIN	Royal Institute of Navigation
OPCS	Office of Population Census and Surveys	RISC	Reduced Instruction Set Chip
		RLE	Run Length Encoding
OPIS	Oakland Planning Information System	RLUIS	Rural Land Use Information System
OS	Ordnance Survey	RMS	Root Mean Square
OS/2	Operating System/2	RMSE	Root Mean Square Error
OSAC	Oxford System of Automated Cartography	RNODC	Responsible National Oceanographic Data Centres
OSNI	Ordnance Survey of Northern Ireland	ROADIC	Road Administration Information Centre
OSTF	Ordnance Survey Transfer Format		
OSTF+	Ordnance Survey Transfer Format Plus	RPR	Real Property Register
		RRDN	Rural Regional Development Newsletter
PANDORA	Prototyping a Navigation Database of Road Network Attributes	RRL	Regional Research Laboratory
PANIC	Potential And Needs, Investments and Capabilities	RSA	Republic of South Africa
		RTPI	Royal Town Planning Institute
PC	Personal Computer	SA	South Australia
PCA	Parliamentary Constituency	SACS	Small Area Census Studies
PCB	Polychlorinated Biphenyl	SAE	Society of Automotive Engineers
PDES	Product Data Exchange Specification	SAHSU	Small Area Health Statistics Unit
PDF	Probability Density Function	SANDAG	San Diego Association of Governments
PEX	PHIGS-Extended-to-X	SASPRSC	South African Society for Photogrammetry, Remote Sensing and Cartography
PHIGS	Programmers Hierarchical Integrated Graphics System		
PI	Primitive Instancing	SAV	Submerged Aquatic Vegetation
PIES	Portable Interactive Editing System	SCS	Soil Conservation Service
PIMS	Profit Impact of Market Strategy	SDSS	Spatial Decision Support System
PIOS	Planning Information Overlay System	SDTS	Spatial Data Transfer Standard
PIOS	Polygon Intersection and Overlay System	SET	Système d'Exchange et de Transfer
		SIC	Standard Industrial Classification
PLUM	Projective Land Use Model	SIF	Standard Interchange Format
pMAP	Professional Map Analysis Package	SIM	Survey Information on Microfilm
PR	Peano Relation	SIMD	Simple Instruction Multiple Data
PS	Production System	SIMPLE	Spatial and Inductive Modelling Package for Land Evaluation
PSF	Point Spread Function		
PSS	Packet Switching Stream	SIS	Spatial Information System
PUSWA	Public Utilities Street Works Act	SLDS	Swedish Land Databank System
QA	Quality Assurance	SMHI	Swedish Meteorological and Hydrological Institute
QC	Quality Control		
QLD	Queensland	SOAP	Sophisticated Allocation Process
QMSG	Quantitative Methods Study Group	SOE	Spatial Occupancy Enumeration
QTM	Quaternary Triangulation Mesh	SOI	Survey of India
		SORSA	Spatially Orientated Referencing Systems Association
RAM	Random Access Memory		
RAWP	Resource Allocation Working Party	SOTER	Soil and Terrain Database
RB	Rule Base	SQL	Structured Query Language
REGIS	Regional Geographical Information Systems Project	SR	Sweep Representation
		SRA	Sub-Regional Areas
RFP	Request for Proposal	SSC	Superconducting Super Collider

List of acronyms

STEP	Standard for the Exchange of Product Data	URA	User Requirement Analysis
STI	Scientific and Technical Information	URISA	American Urban and Regional Information Systems Association
SUSI	Sale of Unpublished Survey Information	URPIS	Urban and Regional Planning Information Systems
SWEB	South-Western Electricity Board	USBC	United States Bureau of the Census
TA	Training Agency	USDA	United States Department of Agriculture
TAS	Tasmania		
TAZ	Traffic Analysis Zones	USGS	United States Geological Survey
Tb	Terabyte	USLE	Universal Soil Loss Equation
TC	Training Commission	UTM	Universal Transverse Mercator
TEED	Training Education and Enterprise Division	VADS	Value Added and Data Services
TIFF	Tag Image File Format	VIC	Victoria
TIGER	Topologically Integrated Geographic Encoding Referencing	ViSC	Visualization in Scientific Computing
		VNIS	Vehicle Navigation and Information Systems Conference
TIIWG	Inter-Departmental Working Group on the Tradeable Information Initiative		
TIN	Triangulated Irregular Network	WA	Western Australia
TJUG	Taunton Joint Utilities Group	WAN	Wide Area Network
TM	Thematic Mapper	WCED	World Commission on Environment and Development
TRIP	Tourism and Recreation Information Package		
		WDDES	World Digital Data for the Environmental Sciences
UIS	Urban Information System	WEDSS	Whole Earth Decision Support System
ULI	Council for Research and Development in Land Information Technology	WEE	Wind Erosion Equation
		WEGS	Western European Geological Surveys
ULI	Utvecklingsradet for Landskapsinformation	WMO	World Meteorological Organization
		WOCE	World Ocean Climate Experiment
UN/ECLAC	United Nations Economic Commission for Latin America and the Caribbean	WORM	Write Once Read Many
		WRD	Water Resources Division
UNEP	United Nations Environmental Programme	WYSIWYG	What You See Is What You Get
UNITAR	United Nations Institute for Training and Research	ZUM	Zones for Urban Modelling

AUTHOR INDEX

Numbers in roman refer to volume 1, numbers in italic refer to volume 2.

Aangeenbrug R T 4, 104, *314*
Aanstoos R 377
Abel D J 262, *67*, *214*
Abler R F 33, 84, 101, 122, 154, 348
Abraham I M 472
Acquista C 207
Adams J B 122, 203
Adedeji A *71*, *72*
Adlam K H *214*
Adler R K 135, 137, 143
Aerospatiale Direction Technique 528
Aetna Casualty & Security Co. v. Jeppeson & Co. 500
Agarwai P 199, 420, 421, 422
AGI News 96
Aglinfou *43*
Agterberg F P *172*, *173*, *174*, *177*, *178*, *183*, *184*
Ahn J 423, 436, 446, 451, 452
Aho A V 217, 220
Akima H 277
Akman V 219
Aldersey-Williams H 315
Aldred B K 151, 372
Aldus Corporation 245
Alegiani J B *124*
Alemi M H *163*
Alexander F E 392
Alexandroff P 150, 231, 233, 235
ALIC 58, *61*
Allen D 286
Allen J H *204*
Allinson L 355, *208*
Alter S L 403, 406, 410

Alvo M 422
Ambron S 352
American Bar Association 494
American Cartographer, The 181, 186
American National Standards Institute 156, 228, 528
Amin S *73*
Amos L L *17*
Amrhein C 185
Anderson D E 30
Anderson D R 277
Anderson E A 31, 262, *13*, *131*, *133*
Anderson J *165*
Anderson J E 202
Anderson J J 181
Anderson J R 179, 180, 186, *264*, *276*
Anderson K E 31, *3*, *12*, *13*, *16*, *23*, *304*, *305*
Anderson M 66
Andersson S 38, *92*, *93*
Anding D 207
Andresson S 186
Angel J C 30
Angus Leppan P 39, *92*, *94*
Annand K P *109*
Annoni A 344, 345
Anselin L 13, 102, 203, 205, 385, 391
Anthony A *223*
Anuta P E 193
Apple Computer Incorporated 278, 431
Applegate L M 409
Arai K 285
Arbia G 170

Archer H *298*
Archer J C 430
Archibald P D 198, 201
Ardrey R *88*
Armstrong M P 122, 257, 407, 410, 411, *133*
Arnheim R 428, 437
Arno M 185, 381, 384
Aronoff S 5, 10, 15, 83, 87, 301, 320, 325, *317*
Aronson P B 193, 260, 263, 339
Arthur D W G 140
Artin E 233
Arur M G *78*
Asano Y *47*
ASPRS 169
Asrar G 192, 205, 206
Astrahan M M 156
AT&T Bell Laboratories 215
Atkey R G *26*
Atkins M 86
Auerbach S 305
Aumann G 278
AURISA 58, *62*, *65*, *67*
AUSLIG *60*
Avni H 222
Awater R H C M *155*
Ayabe K 285
Aybet J 338, 345

Babbage R *64*
Bachi R 429, 430
Badhwar G D 195, 202
Baerwald T J 95
Bak P 299, 308, 310

397

Author index

Baker A M 171
Baker H H 351
Baker J C 180
Baker K *144*
Ballard D H 434
Balodis M 446
Band L E 206, 283, 284, 285
Bannink M H *156*
Banting D 84, 383
Barbier E B *10*
Barker G R 198
Barnard S T 272
Barr A 414, *229*
Barr C J *213*
Barrera R 197, 199
Barritt M 36
Bartolucci L A 191, 203
Barton B A 140
Barwinski K 517
Basoglu U 446
Bates M 422
Batjes N H *165*
Batten L G 299
Batty M 435
Baumgardner M F *155, 156, 224*
Bayard-White C 352
Beard C *134*
Beard M K 171, 182, 344, 435, *302*
Beaumont J R 33, 37, *4, 6, 109, 128, 140, 144*
Beckett P H T *154*
Bedard Y 47, 191, 192, 198, 200, 201, 206, 498, *304*
Bedell R 344
Beek K-J *155*
Beemster J G R *155, 156*
Belcher P *117, 120*
Bell S B M 149, 199, 232
Benjamin R I *148*
Bennett J L 406, 411
Bennett R J 389, *140*
Bentley J L 219
Bentley T J 82
Benyon D 10, *186*
Berry B J L 171, 389
Berry J K 13, 124, 130, 323, 329, 339, 361, 372, *9, 247, 286, 287, 298*
Berry J L 27
Bertin J 155, 430, 431, 437, 458
Bertke S E 193
Besag J E 392, 398, 399
Best R G *164*
van Beurden S A H A *164*
Bhatnagar S C 411

Bickmore D P 23, 34, *25, 223*
Bie S W *153, 154*
Billingsley F C 193, *227*
Bilmes J 435
Binks K 399
Birch J M 399
Bird D *148*
Birkoff G 277
Birugawa S *47*
Bishop M M *184*
Bishton A *134*
Bitterlich W 185, 381, 384
Bittlestone R *149*
Black J 59
Blackburn J W *58, 59, 60*
Blais J A R 271
Blakemore M J 116, 185, 245, 382, *8, 244*
Blalock H M 434
Blanning R W 409
Blatchford R P *192*
Blum H 449
Bobrow D 418
Boehm B W 217, 483, 484
Bolland J D *111*
Bonczek R H 406, 407
Bonham-Carter G F 344, 390, *7, 173, 174, 176, 177, 178, 179, 183, 184*
Bonneton P *155*
Bonoma T V *140*
Boots B 126, 193
Borgida A 418
Borning A H 355
Bosma M 244
Bouma J 390, *154, 155, 156, 160, 163, 164*
Bourne L E 433
Bouwman A F *165*
Box E O 205
Boyce R F 156
Boyko K J *15, 16*
Boyle A R 191
Bracken I 5, 15, 260, 338, 339, 347, 378, 385
Brand M J D 35, 73
Brandenberger A J 179
Brandon O H *213*
Brandon S E *154*
Brassel K E 274, 288, 290, 292, 430, 464
Bratt P 353
Bredekamp J H 201
Breeuwsma A *155, 164*

Bregt A K *155, 156, 164*
Brewer C A 430
Bridge J S 313
Briggs D J 137, 342, 343, 344, 385, *187, 193, 198, 199*
Brodie M 415
Brodie M J 515
Brodie M L 418
Bromley R D F 478, *89, 297*
Brooks F P 217, 354
Broome F R 30, 122, *134*
Brotchie J F *66*
Brown A T *223*
Brown C M 434
Brown G 86
Brown H 233
Brown M D 428, 432, 439
Brown M J 36
Bruegger B P 435
Brüggermann H 517
Brunsdon C *9*
van het Loo Brus D J H *164*
Bryant J 202
Bryant N A 191, 192, 198, 200, 344
Bryden R *74*
Bryson R A 429
Buchanan A 49
Bulens J D *164*
Bull G A *208*
Bunce R G H *213*
Bundock M 261, 262
Bunge W 168
Bunschoten B *154, 160*
Burgess T M 170, *155, 159, 160*
Burke K C *223*
Burnhill P 86
Burns K L 308
Burr D 446
Burrough P A 5, 11, 83, 122, 168, 170, 185, 193, 198, 199, 200, 206, 227, 230, 269, 301, 305, 320, 330, 339, 341, 381, 390, *7, 153, 154, 155, 156, 158, 159, 160, 163, 164, 165, 177, 194, 195, 209, 224, 261, 317*
Burton I 88
Burton W 151
Bush V 352
Busoni E *155*
Butler B E *209*
Butler D R 203, 204
Buttenfield B P 102, 115, 287, 398, 429, 430, 432, 434, 436, 458, 460, 465
Buxton J *124*

Author index

Buxton R 4, 36, 37, 96, *28, 29, 30, 89, 94, 132*
Buzzell R D *143*

CACI *144*
CADalyst 354
Calkins H W 6, 10, 11, 17, 30, 45, 46, 106, 191, 407, 478, 481, 508, *8, 13, 139, 185, 192, 237, 239, 242, 244, 276, 297, 298, 301, 314*
Callaghan M 30
Callahan G M *13, 16*
Callander J 23, 27
Campbell J B 183, 185, 186, 202
Campbell J C 429, 432
Campbell J R 203
Canada Department of Forestry and Rural Development *185*
Card D H 203
Carlbom I 308
Carlson E D 309, 406, 407, 411
Carpenter L 271
Carr J L 193
Carruthers A 512
Carter J R 10, 11, 102, 104
Casley D J 342
Cass R *121*
Castner H W 438, 439
Catling I *117, 120*
Caulfield I 76
Cavill M V 67
CCITT 245
Cebrian J A 308
Cederholm T 98
Centre National d'Etudes Spatiales 523
Chadha S M 76
Chakravarthy U S 421
Challen K 300, 305
Chamberlin D D 156
Chambers D 478
Chambers R J M 431
Chan K 373
Chandra N 422
Chandrasekhar N 219
Chapman M A 271
Chappuis A 77
Charlton M E 385, 397, 399, *9*
Charlwood G 261, 263
Chavez P S *13*
Chazelle B 219
Chelst K 404
Chen P P 253, 407
Chen S 79, *80*

Chen Z 199
Chen Z-T 280
Chen Shupeng 39, *5*
Cheng Ji-Cheng 80
Chinese Academy of Sciences 79
Chorley R 4, 36, 37, 96, 481, *28, 29, 30, 94, 132*
Chow A L K 247
Chow L *133*
Chrisman N R 22, 28, 30, 33, 84, 112, 122, 132, 165, 168, 169, 171, 172, 178, 180, 182, 185, 200, 204, 227, 235, 285, 323, 324, 341, 344, 381, 383, 384, *89, 194, 196, 298, 318, 319*
Christensen A H J 277, 278
Christiansen H N 304
Christianson C J 30
Church R 11
Churchman C W *235*
Cibula W G 203
Civco D 436
Claire R W 373
Clark D M 16, 39, 64, 178, 325, *3, 7, 8, 12, 63, 185, 186, 196, 201, 203, 220, 223, 227, 228*
Clark I 309
Clark J L 422
Clark J W 129
Clark P 175, 178, 182, 204, *223*
Clark P K *188, 194*
Clark R D S 67
Clark S R 15, *300*
Clark W F *263*
Clarke A L 61, 116, 278, 478, 508, *94, 191, 192*
Clarke D M *9, 74*
Clarke K C 10, 12, 103, 271, 435
Clarke M 411
Claussem H *124*
Clayton A R *214*
Clayton C *128*
Clayton D 392
Cleaves D 479
Cleveland W S 428, 431, 438
Cliff A D 170, 193, 391
Clifford P 392
Cobb M C *32*
Cochrane D 288
Cocks K D 38, 135, 136, 139, *63, 66, 225*
Codd E F 149, 228, 229, 257, 258, 416
Cohen J 217

Cohen P R *183*
Cohon J L 403
Colby J D *218, 223*
Cole G *111*
Cole K *133*
Collins J 252
Collins T *143*
Collins W G *128*
Colwell R N 192
Comerma J *160*
Commanger H S 494
Commission of the European Communities *186, 188, 193*
Committee on Earth Sciences *220*
Committee on Global Change *220*
Congalton R G 101, 203
Conklin J 352
Cook B G *153*
Cook R N 23, 26
Cooke D F *297*
Cooper H J 206
Cooper M A R *144*
Coote A M *32*
Copeland B J *263*
Coppock J T 3, 4, 9, 34, 35, 36, 45, 111, *73, 87, 305, 313, 321*
Corbett J P 31, 151, 327, *134*
Cormack S 288
Corr D G 185, 186, 191, 203, *210*
Costanza R 206, 207, 208
Costanzo C M *128*
Couclelis H 112, *316*
Coulson M G 478, *89, 297*
Coulson M R 84, 86
Cowen D J 11, 12, 13, 261, 338, 341, *3, 9, 247, 250, 302, 303, 305, 307*
Cox B J 264
Cox C W 430
Cox N J 151, 372
Craft A W 399
Craig W J *301, 315*
Crain I K 16, 17, 48
Crapper P F 199
Crawford J R 66
Crawley K J *88*
Croasdale M R 399
Cromley R G 446
Croom F 231
Cross A E 185, 186, 191, 203, 397, *9, 210*
Crossilla F 171
Crosson W L 206
Croswell P L 15, *298, 300*
Croze H *220, 223*

Csillag F 168
Csillag M 468, 469
Cuddy S M 67
Cullingford D *144*
Cunningham C G 181
Curran P J 204, 205
Cutter S L 376
Cuzick J 399

Dacey M F 372
Dale P F 6, 38, 82, 87, 88, 138, 181, 331, *4*, *6*, *58*, *86*, *91*, *92*, *93*, *94*, *97*, *156*, *304*, *319*
Dalton M 292, 354
Dangermond J 3, 10, 13, 15, 23, 32, 51, 59, 114, 124, 319, 323, 330, 338, 344, 348, 478, 479, 480, 515, *9*, *80*, *94*, *191*, *297*, *300*, *303*, *304*, *322*
Danziger J N 105
Darius P *156*
Daroussin J *155*
Dartington Institute *214*
Date C J 254, 255, 256, 258, 261
Dave V S *78*
Davenport T H *149*
David S M 191
Davis A W 207
Davis D L 278, 405
Davis F W 13, 47, 112, 186, 193, 199, 205, 206, 240, 325, 339, 385, *171*, *207*
Davis J C 390
Davis J R 159, 411, 422, *66*, *67*
Davis J S 353
Davis S M 203
Dawson M 315
Day T 272, 285, 292, 354
De S 410
De Floriani L 286
De Jong W *75*
de Man E 10
Deacon A T *223*
Dear M 403
Deering D 195, 204, 205
Defanti T A 428, 432, 439
Deichmann U 385
DeLotto J L 283
DeLucia A 432
Demko G J 384
Denham C 183
Densham P J 11, 115, 257, 392, 403, 407, 410, 411, *9*, *77*, *139*, *142*, *149*, *244*, *276*, *299*, *301*
Dent B D 430, 437

Department of Health and Social Security 75
Department of the Environment 37, 69, 71, 73, 74, 76, 96, 186, 485, *25*, *29*, *30*, *66*, *88*, *101*, *193*, *297*
Department of the Interior *88*
Department of Trade and Industry *141*
Deter R S 353
Devereux B J 385
Devine H A 11, 82, 84
Dewdney J C 30, 184, *128*
Dias H D *74*
Diaz B M 149, 199, 232
Dickey J W *66*
Dickinson H J 10, 11, 17, 46, 481, 508, *244*
Didier M *10*, *192*
Diello J 23, 27
van Diepen C A *155*, *164*
Diggle P 128, 390, 396
Digital Cartographic Data Standards Task Force 125, 165, 166, 169, 180, 322, 346, 523, 524, *318*
Dikau R 283
Dimmick S 262
Dinstein I 283
Dixon J F 409, *142*
Dixon T M *223*
Dobes Z 155, 160
Dobkin D 228
Dobson M W 411, *77*
Doerschler J S 446, 449, 452, 454, 455
Dolk D R 409
Domaratz M A *15*, *16*
Dondis D A 437
Donimowski R L 433
Dougenik J A 132
Douglas D H 185, 247, 283, 284
Dowers S *321*
Dowman I 185
Downey J 314
Downing P *213*
Downs A 105, 106
Dowson E 85
Doytsher Y 138
Dozier J 193, 199, 203, 204, 205, 206, 284, 285
Driessen P M *155*
Drown C W 181
Drummond J 244, *75*, *81*
Drysdale R L 220
Dubayah R 193, 199, 205

Duboc O 166
Duchesneau T D 498
Dudycha D J 343
Dueker K J 11, 26, 166, 341, 478, *247*, *299*, *300*, *304*, *305*
Duell T 67
Duffield B S 35
Duggin M J 193, 195
Duke J 352
Dulaney W *209*
Dulton W H 105
Dumanski J B *154*, *155*, *164*
Dunn C 122
Dutton G 160, 463
Dye D G *209*

Eagleson P S 207
Earth System Sciences Committee 7, *207*, *217*, *220*
Easterfield M 314, 344
Eastman J R 15, 124, 439
Eather P T *59*
Ebdon D 127
Ebinger L R 446, *134*
Ebner H 273, 278
Edelsbrunner H 219, 227, 275
Eden R *64*
Edney P 67
Edralin J *74*, *75*, *78*
Edwards G 47, 191, 192, 198, 200, 201, 206, *304*
Edwards R 399
Egenhofer M J 92, 103, 113, 124, 154, 155, 156, 157, 160, 198, 227, 229, 230, 231, 233, 235, 236, 245, 264, 310, 320, 323, 325, 330, 339, 461, 515, 517, *122*, *134*, *172*, *174*, *314*
Ehlers M 47, 191, 192, 198, 200, 201, 206, 207, *304*
Eichhorn G *87*
El-Beik A H A *128*
Elachi C 192, 195
Elliot D B 202
Ellis H 253
Ellis M Y *202*
Ellwood D J *176*
Elnicki R A 405
Elvidge C D 203
Emerson R W 438
Enderle G 528
Engel H 185
Englund E *155*
Environmental Protection Agency *185*

Environmental Systems Research
    Institute 86, 97, 159, 261, 338, 339,
    340, 349
Eos Science Steering Committee 196
Epstein E F 4, 116, 186, 496, 498,
    499, *54, 94, 194*
Erich R W 202
Estes J E 5, 6, 10, 11, 83, 103, 120,
    191, 193, 194, 198, 199, 201, 202,
    203, 320, *128, 218, 227, 250, 317*
Eswaran K P 156
Etak 159
Evans I S 282, *132*
Evans M *143*
Everett J 192, 208
Eyre L A 38, 186
Eyton J R 288

Fagin R 259
Falcidieno B 286
Fandrei G *278*
Fanon F *73*
Fanshawe J *224*
FAO *155*
Fedra K 411
Fegeas R G 31, *13, 15, 16*
Feigenbaum E A 414, *229*
Feuchtwanger M 330
FICCDC *18*
Fiebig M J 67
Field R C 11
Fienberg S E *184*
Finch S 21, 35, 186
Fingleton B 390, 396
Fischler M A 272
Fisher P F 46, 87, 112, 137, 166, 176,
    180, 186, 240, 241, 248, 376, 427,
    460, 473, *104, 194*
Fisher T 305, 309
Fitzpatrick-Lins K 171, 180, 186
Flemming M D 191, 203
Fletcher G E *250*
Flew A G 429
Flores F 161
Flowerdew R 114, 124, 184, 323, 328,
    340, 342, 343, 383, 384, 385, 506,
    189, 262
Flynn J J 300, 302
Foley J D 288, 290, 354
Foley M E 481
Foresman T W *250*
Forrest M D 203
Forshaw M R B 193
Fosnight E A 254

Foster M J 56
Fotheringham A S 435
Fournier A 271
Fowler R J 273
Frank A U 13, 50, 103, 112, 122, 150,
    155, 156, 160, 197, 199, 227, 229,
    232, 233, 235, 236, 260, 264, 323,
    330, 342, 422, 435, 438, *318*
Franklin S E 203
Franklin W M R 3, 15, 113, 217, 219,
    220, 228, 230, 299, 422, *134, 321*
Fraser R S 195
Fraser-Robinson J *148*
Frederiksen P 465
Freedman C 478, *297, 300, 303, 304*
Freedom of Information Act 494, 495
Freeman H R 115, 330, 423, 436, 446,
    449, 451, 452
Freeman J 153, 230, 310
French J R 308
French R *118*
Freundschuh S M 160, 229
Frew J 284, 285
Friedman L M 491
Fritsch D 309, 314
Frost and Sullivan Incorporated *115*
Fry J P 515
Fu K 201, 202
Fuchs M 206
Fulton P N 183
Furley P A 342, 385
Fussel D 271

Gaal G *172*
Gahegan M N 261
Gaits G M 35
Gale B T *143*
Gallaire H 417
Gamezo M U 432
Gardiner V 176
Gardiner-Hill R C *26, 31*
Garey M R 222
Gargantini I 230
Garner B J 38, 67, 136, *4, 5, 67, 92, 93*
Garnsworthy J 74
Gateaud J *104*
Gatrell A C 112, 120, 121, 129, 130,
    149, 228, 231, 234, 322, 376, 390,
    460, 461, *255*
Gault I *260*
Gauthier C 283
Gaydos L 203
Geoffrion A M 406

Gerrard J 390
Gerrard M H 399
Getis A 126, 193
Ghosh S K 179
Giblin P 150
Gibson R J *26, 32*
Gibson W 354
Giddings G M 411
Gilbert P 15
Giles R H 23, *9*
Gill A 230
Gillard A A *144*
Gilliand J 478
Gilmartin P P 430, 437
Giltrap D J *155*
Ginzberg M J 406
Girard M-C *153, 154*
GIS World 299, 319, 324, 477
Gittings B M 82, 84, *321*
Goddard J 10
Goddard Space Flight Center 196,
    197, 198
Godwin L *134*
Goel N S 207
Goetz A F H 204
Goff T E *210*
Golbéry L *77*
Gold C 288
Goldberg A 217
Goldberg M 202, 203, 422
Golledge R G 83, 102, 128
Golstein H 30
Gonzalez R C 278
Goodchild M F 3, 6, 11, 13, 14, 37,
    46, 57, 82, 84, 85, 96, 101, 102, 103,
    119, 124, 126, 128, 149, 166, 170,
    194, 199, 240, 241, 299, 301, 310,
    320, 323, 341, 381, 384, 385, 389,
    411, 479, 484, 485, *8, 74, 78, 105,
    142, 299, 300, 301, 314, 315, 318,
    319, 321*
Goodenough D G 200, 201, 202, 203,
    344
Goodspeed J 67
Gopal S 6, 103, 166, 381, 384, *318*
Gopalan N *78*
Goran W 422
Gorry G A 403, 406, *141*
Gorte B 345
Gottschalk H-J 279
Gould M D 159, 160, 411
Gould P R 122
Goulette A M 446, *134*
Goward S N *209*

Author index

Grace B F 411
Graetz R D 207
Grandfield A W 124
Grant I W 411, 66, 67
Grant N G 97
Grave M 528
Gravel G 283
Gray D A 342, 385
Gray P *142*
Gray S 73
Greasley I 230
Green D 84
Green M 184, 323, 385
Green N P A 37, 87, 200, 338, 341, 347, 353, 375
Green P *28*
Greener S 67
Gregoire T G 185, 200
Gregor W C 404
Gregory D 389
Griffin J M 481
Griffin M W 271
Griffith D A 128, 185, 391
Grimshaw D J 35
Groop R E 430
de Gruijter J J *154*, *155*, *156*
Grun A 278
Grunreich D 458, 469
Guevara J A 280, *81*
Guibas L 275, 280
Guinn R 69
Gulati A K *78*
Günther O 49, 435
Guptill S C 31, 51, 116, 261, 262, 263, 319, 320, 324, 325, 330, 345, 462, 473, 478, 479, 480, 484, 517, *12*, *13*, *15*, *16*, *17*, *30*, *61*, *108*, *193*, *214*, *318*
Gurd F B *247*
Gurney A J 30
Guttag J 232
Guttman A 233

Haber R N 431
Hägerstrand T 23, 389, *4*, *39*, *40*
Haggett P 124
Hajic E J 202
Hake G 457
Hall F G 195, 202, 204, 205
Hall G B 341
Hall P A V 352
Hallam C A 31, *13*
Haller M 277
Haller S M 155, 160

Hamilton A C *87*
Hamilton W L 84
Hammer M 421, *149*
Hammond N 355
Han K H *128*
Hannah M J 285
Hanson E N 417, 421
Haralick R M 200, 201, 202, 283, 372
Harbaugh J W 315
Harding A E 203
Hardy E E 179, 180, 186, 202, *264*, *276*
Harig J 301
Harnden E 59
Harper E A 78
Harris B *237*
Harris D P *172*
Harris N *92*
Harrison D 446
Harrison J D *205*
Harslem E 156
Hart A *59*
Hart J F 83, *73*
Hartley R P 39, *188*
Harvey D R *213*
Haskell A 193
Hastings D A 16, 39, 64, 178, 325, *3*, *7*, *8*, *12*, *63*, *74*, *185*, *186*, *196*, *201*, *203*, *218*, *223*, *229*
Haugen E 154
Hawkins J M 457
Hay A M 204, 205
Hayes G E 165
Haywood P E 165, 346, 526, 527, 529, *30*, *33*, *34*, *36*
Hazelhoff L 282, *155*
Hazelton N W J 301, 314
Head C G 437
Healey R G 12, 83, 113, 127, 262, 328, 342, 345, 385, *321*
Healey R J 339
Hearnshaw H M 103, 120, 253, 254, 263, 264, 323, 379
Hearst M 414, 418, 419
Heckman B 446
van Heesen H C *155*
Helldén U *155*, *165*
Heller M 50, 113, 127, 199, 204, 235, 270, 274, 275, 278, 280, 301, 304, 325, 376, 380, 460, 469, *12*, *15*, *314*
Hendriks C M A *164*
Hendrix G 422
Henriksen S W 290
Her Majesty's Land Registry *88*

Her Majesty's Stationery Office *28*, *132*
Heres L *124*
Herndon L *155*
Herring J R 15, 92, 113, 124, 156, 157, 198, 231, 236, 245, 263, 264, 320, 325, 339, 461, 515, 517, *122*, *134*, *172*, *174*, *314*
Herskovits A 154, 229
Herzog A 274, 290, 464
Heuvelink G B M 206, 339, 341, *164*
Hewitt C 418
Heyn B N 430
Heywood D I 82, 83
Hezlep W 384
Hibbard W 290
Hickin B W *250*
Hickman D L 481
Higgins M J 39, *188*
Higgs G 5, 338, 347, 385
Hill G J E 191
Hinterberger H 233
Hirsch S A 446
Hirschberg D S 223
Hirschheim R 485
Hirst R 67
Hittelman A M *225*
Hoare C A R 217
Hodgson J M *157*
Hodgson M 261
Hoff W A 420
Hoffer R M 94, 191, 202, 203
Hoffmann C 228
Hoffmeister E D 469
von Hohenbalken B 121
Hogg D C 185, 186, *210*
Hogg J 261
Hoggs D C 191, 203
Holben B N 195, 205, *209*, *210*
Holland P W *184*
Holloway C A 411
Holroyd F 199
Holsapple C W 406, 407
van Holst A F *155*
Holstein L 89
Honey S *119*, *121*, *124*
Honsaker J L 464
Hoogerwerf M *156*, *160*, *163*
Hooper C 352
Hopcroft J E 217, 218, 220
Hopgood F R A 528
Hopkin V D 438
Hopkins L 403
Hopmans J W *156*

402

Horn B K P 435
Horn D 314
Horn M 67
Horowitz E 233
Horwood E M *297, 299, 302*
Hössler R 273
Houlding S 309
House W C 406
House of Lords 36, 68, 526
Howe D R 253
Hsu S Y *128*
Hubbold R J 528
Hubert L 128
Hudson J C 27
Hudson R 36
Hugus M 278
Huijbregts C J *159, 160*
Hummel J *208*
Hurion R D 410
Hurle G *64*
Hutchinson C F 203
Hutchinson M F 48, 278, 283
Hutton P G 341

ICSU Panel on World Data Centres *224*
IGBP Special Committee *217, 218, 219*
Imhoff E 47, 429, 447, 448, 467
Inaba K 278
Indian Towing Co v. United States 500
Ingold J H 183
Ingram I K 15
Ingram K J 156, 263
Intergovernmental Oceanographic Commission *208*
Intergraph Corporation 156, 261
International Cartographic Association 135, 457
International Council of Scientific Unions 93, *204*
International Organisation for Standardisation 355
International Standards Organization 525, 528
Irby C 156
Iri M *52*
Irons J R 204
Isaacs M C *212*
Itai A 222
Ives M J *111*

Jacknow H R *13*
Jackson J E 137, 235

Jackson M J 46, 47, 48, 63, 113, 185, 191, 199, 324, 338, 344, 345, *90, 96, 104, 276*
Jager E 465
Jajoo B H 411
James P 27
Jankowski P 145, 146, 411, 465
Janks G F 429
Jarke M 421
Jarvis M *154*
Jarvis R S *285*
Jasinski M F 207
Jenkins G M 195
Jenks G F 430
Jensen J R 470
Jerie H C 75
Jeworrek J 471, 472
Jiwani Z 346
Joffe B A 82, *8*
Johnson B D *63*
Johnson C G *154*
Johnson C R 308
Johnson D S 222
Johnson M 152, 153, 154, 229, 310
Johnson R D 436
Johnson T 191
Johnston R J 389
Jones A R 203
Jones C B 308, 472
Jones R B *154*
Jones T A 308
Jordan L 339, 372
Jordan T G 103
Journel A G *159, 160*
Jupp D L B 194, 207
Justice C O 193, 195, 196, *209, 210*

Kainz W 230
Kalb V 205
Kaldor J 392
Kamijo S *124*
Kaneda K 292
Kanemasu E T 205, 206
Kankanhalli M 219
Karam G 422
Karimi H A 422
Karjala D S 495
Kata F 292
Kates R W 102
Kauth R J 202
Kavouras M 308
Kawauchi *53*

Keates J S 176, 177, 178, 181, 436, 438
Kedar-Cabelli S T 420
Keefer B J 185
Keen P G W 406, 407, 410
Keen T R 299
Kehris E 127, 385
Kelk B 50, 114, 149, 269, 300, 305, 313, *201, 207, 214*
Keller R M 420
Kelley A D 271
Kelly G D 191
Kelly P 446
Kemp K K 84, *319*
Kemp Z 264
Kennedy J L 26
Kennedy P *210, 211*
Kennedy S A 184, 380, 391, *223*
Kennie T J M 271, 299, 300
Kent W 259
van Keulen H *155, 164*
Keuper H F 191
Kidwell J 495
Kiefer R W 185
Kijima Y *49*
Kim M P *302*
Kim T J *302*
Kim W 350, 355, 418
Kimball R C 156, 404
Kimerling A J 430
Kimes D S 207
Kindleberger C *298, 299, 302, 303*
Kineman J J 16, 64, 178, 325, *3, 7, 8, 12, 63, 74, 185, 186, 196, 201, 203, 218, 220, 223, 227, 228*
King C W B 138
King D *155*
King R 160
King W R *142*
Kinneman D 39
Kinto Y *47*
Kirby K C 156
Kirk K 23, 27
Kitamura A *124*
Kleiner B 431
Klesh L 122, 324
Kloosterman B *154*
Klug A 148
Knill-Jones R P *183*
Knuth D E 218, 220, 229
Kolb C E 271, 292
Kolbusz J 292, 354
Kolm K 314
Konecny G 185, 239, 272

Author index

de Koning G H J *164*
Konsynski B R 409
Kooistra M J *155*
Korth H F 417
Korzybski A 167
Koshizuka T *52*
Kosskariov A V 11, 38
Kosslyn S M 428
Kostli A 273
Kotler P *140*
Kou Y *79, 81*
Kowalski R 417
Kraak M J 431
Kraemer K L 105
Kriegel H-P 233
Krishnanunni K *77*
Krishnayya J G *77*
Kruck E 185
Krum G L 308
Kubik K 171, 465
Kubo S 38, 67, 97, *5, 6, 14, 49, 81*
Kuennucke B H 84
Kuhn W 150, 235
van Kuilenburg J *154, 160*
Kuipers B 438
Kumar R S *77*
Kumar S *78*
Kure J *75*

L'Eplattenier R 290
de Laat P J M *155*
Lacroix V 449
Laflamme R A 269
Lahaije P *124*
Lai P C 480
Lai R C T 356
Laing A W *64*
Lakoff G 152, 153, 229, 435
Lam W K 271
Lam N S-N 274, 275, 380, 385
Lamp J *154*
LAMSAC *89, 90*
Landgraf H F 181
van Lanen H A J *155, 163, 164*
Langford M 385, *128*
Langran G 168, 178, 264, 436, 207, 323
Lanigan J C 181
Larsen H K *75*
Larsen R C 156, 263
Lasseter T 309
Lassez C 418
Lauer D 196
Laurillard D 352

Laut P 67
Lauzon J P 245, 324
Lavin S J 430
Lawrence D H 185, 186, 191, 203, *210*
Lay H G 470
Lay J C 30
Le Drew E F 343
Leahy F J 301, 314
Leanoard J J 430
Lee T S *247*
Leeder M R 313
Leenaers H 305, *163, 164, 165*
Lefschetz S 233
Leick A 186, 87
Lelewer D A 223
Lemmens M J P M 272
Lesser V 418
Lesslie R G *63*
Lewis P 262
Li X Z 207, *79*
Li Z N 434, 464
Lichtner W *124*
Liem R 345
Lieth H *208*
Lightfoot D R 203, 204
Liley R 347
Lille J *9*
Lillehagen F 528
Lillesand T M 185
Little J J 273
Lloyd J W 414, 416, 417
Lo C P 245, *128*
Lobeck A K 429
Lochovsky F H 46, 51, *186*
Lochovsky L C 253
Lodwick W A 341, 384
Loftus E F 433
Logan T L 192, 198, 200, 344
Lohmann P 185
Lolonis P 410
Longley I *250*
Longley P 435
Loomes M 148
Loon J C 278
Lorie R A 156, 261
Loughmiller G *119*
Lovejoy S 195
Loveland T R *154*
Lovett R *111*
LREIS *79*
Luger G L 463
Lupian A E *300*
Lury D A 342
Lyall G A 35

Lynch L G *153*
Lyons H G 85
Lyons K J 171, *65*
Lyytinen K 485

MacDonald C L 16, 17
Mace R S 271, 292
MacEachren A E 429, 430, 432
Mackaay E 491
Mackaness W A 102, 115, 287, 398, 437, 473
Mackenzie H G *154, 198*
Mackey B G *63*
Mackinlay J 429, 436, 437, 440
Madams R *210, 211*
Madnick S 418
Maeder S R *278*
Maes J *156*
Maffini G 185, 200, 381, 384, 480
Magnenat-Thalman N 354
Maguire D J 3, 5, 6, 10, 13, 16, 21, 22, 45, 49, 51, 56, 82, 87, 101, 103, 104, 111, 114, 120, 124, 227, 253, 254, 263, 264, 319, 322, 323, 324, 325, 328, 329, 333, 337, 351, 379, 385, 405, 479, 490, 506, 515, *5, 8, 88, 128, 191, 226, 250, 302, 314, 315, 316, 317, 322*
Maher R V 84
Mahoney H M *304*
Mahoney R P 33, 121, *6, 28, 29, 88, 92, 104, 113, 247*
Maier D 418
Majumder K L *77*
Makarovic B 271, 272
Malila W 195
Malin M C 271, *212*
Maling D H 50, 68, 112, 120, 124, 135, 137, 138, 140, 144, 145, 183, 248, 329, 376, 378
Malone T W *148*
Mandelbrot B B 125, 283, 465, *156*
Manheim M L *78*
Mann J F 495
Mansfield L 277
Mantey P E 411
Mapping Awareness 477
Mapping Science Committee, National Academy of Sciences *19*
Marble D F 5, 6, 13, 22, 27, 30, 45, 93, 102, 111, 191, 245, 324, 389, 407, 478, 480, 484, *185, 314*
Marchionini G 353
Mark D M 50, 112, 122, 124, 126,

152, 153, 154, 159, 160, 168, 193,
229, 272, 273, 274, 282, 284, 286,
308, 310, 355, 438, 458, 463, 465,
468, 469, 473, *318*
Markandya A *10*
Markham B *209*
Marks D 284, 285
Marr D 431, 433
Marsman B *155, 156*
Martin D 5, 385
Martin G J 27
Martin J 251, 252, 253, 257
Martin P H 495
Marx R W 338, *134, 135, 305*
Mason D C 185, 186, 191, 199, 203, 338, 345, *210, 214*
Mason K 5
Masry S 308
Masser I 77, 84, 96, *315*
Mateo A *160*
Mather P M 12, 139, *173*
Matheron G *159*, 59
Matieda I Cm 77
Matsui I *47*
Matthews E *208*
Mausbach M J *154, 155, 165*
Mauzon J P 480
McAleese R 352
McAulay I 301
McBratney A B *154, 155, 156, 160, 163*
McConalogue D J 29
McCormack D E *155*
McCormick B H 428, 432, 430
McCormick S 353
McCullagh M J 269, 274, 277, 288
McEwen L J 84
McEwen R B *12, 13*
McGill R 428, 438
McGillem C D 193
McGranaghan M 158, 159, 160, 229, 245, 324, 480
McGuigan F J 432
McGwire K E *250*
McHarg I L 13, 102, 330, 372, *300*
McKenna R *143*
McKeown D M 203, 356
McKoon G 438
McLaren R A 261, 271, 300, 301, 347, 94
McLaughlin J D 6, 181, *4, 86, 92, 97*
McLean E R *142*
McMaster R B 429, 468, 469, 470
McNamara T P 438

McRae S 479
Mead R A 203, 480
Medin D L 152
Mehl J W 156
Meier A 261, 307
Meijerink A M J *165*
Meixler D B *134*
Mel B W 216
Melley M 171
Menon S 11, 120, 198, 199, 201, 420, 421, 422, *218, 227*
Merchant D C 171, 179
Merrill D W 132
Mertz F 207
Mesev T *250*
Methley B D F 144
Metzger D R *225*
Meyer U 465, 469
Meyer W *247, 302, 305, 307*
Meyerson M *234, 298*
Michaelsen J 205
Michalski R S 420
Mikhail E H 172
Mikhail E M 142, 144
Mill A 299, 308, 310
Miller A I 432
Miller C L 269
Miller E E *156*
Miller G A 433
Miller G P 205
Miller K W 222
Miller P F 193
Miller R K 56, 122, 324
Millington A C *210, 211*
Milnes K *119*
Minker J 417, 418
Minnesota Dept of Natural Resources, Division of Forestry 280
Minnesota Dept of Natural Resources, Division of Minerals 281
Minnesota Dept of Natural Resources, Office of Planning 280
Misra P 77, 78
Mitchell C P *209, 213*
Mitchell L *247, 302, 305, 307*
Mitchell T M 420
Mitchell W B 31, *13*
Moellering H 398, 430, 461, 524
Moik J G 194, 201
Molenaar M 309, 314
Moll S H *229*
Monkhouse F J 429

Monmonier M S 5, 103, 126, 132, 393, 429, 430, 432, 469, 470
Monson W 341
Montgomery D *142*
Montgomery P M *223*
Moon G C 254, 261, 263
Moon W M *183*
Mooneyhan D W *205*
Moore A W *153*
Moore D M 66, *180*
Moore R 56, 96
Moran L 161
Morehouse S 15, 260, 261, 341
Moreland W H *300*
Morgan J M 83
Morgenstern M 418
Morrill R L 102
Morrison J L 4, 33, 67, 82, 111, 124, 165, 175, 176, 323, 467, *30, 317*
Morse B W 422
Morton G M 463
Morton M S 403, 406
Moser M G 422
Moss O F 65
Mosteller F 431
Mott J J 63, *185, 193*
Moulton J R 203
Mounsey H M 6, 16, 22, 37, 39, 70, 84, 137, 177, 338, 341, 342, 343, 344, 348, 351, 375, 385, *3, 7, 29, 193, 198, 199, 201, 208, 225, 302, 305*
Mozzi E 344, 345
Muehrcke P 124, 129, 132, 165, 168, 175, 176, 323, 428, 436, 439, 466
Muessig L F 277
Mukai Y 285
Mulla D M 193
Muller J-C 116, 126, 129, 130, 176, 199, 278, 292, 329, 423, 436, 460, 464, 465, 469, *33, 75, 81, 105, 189, 300*
Muller J-P 185, 272, 285, 292, 354, *223*
Munkres J 233
Murphy P A 67
Murphy R E 205
Musgrave F K 271, 292
Musser D 233
Mylopoulos J 414, 415, 515

Nag P 77, *129*
Nagao M 285
NAGIS 98

Author index

Nagy G 227, 286
Nagy Z *264*
Naithani K K 77
Nakamae E 292
Nakazawa T 285
Nanninga P M 199, *67*
Naqvi S 415, 419, 420
Narayan L R A *78*
Nash K *66*
Nastelin J 449
National Academy of Sciences 499
National Center for Geographic Information and Analysis 95, 396, 460, *315*
National Computer Graphics Association 528
National Geophysical Data Center 227
National Joint Utilities Group 37, 70, 248, *29, 30, 31, 111*
National Oceanographic and Atmospheric Administration *222*
National Research Council 93
National Space Science Data Center *214*
Natural Environmental Research Council *202, 203, 206, 209*
Navon D 428
NCDCDS 227
Neal J G 155, 158, 160
Needham J *76*
Neiser N 152
Nelson R F 191, 203
Nelson T 352
Nemani R R 206
van de Nes Th. J *155*
Newell J 399
Newell R G 12, 314, 344
Newkirk P *247*
Newland W L 203
Newman W M 290
Newton D 122
Newton P W *66*
NEXPRI 97
Nichol D G *67*
Nichols M 217
Nicholson R 347
Nickerson B G 436
Nicolas J 417
Nicoullaud J *155*
Nielsen D R 390, *154, 155, 163*
Nielsen J 352, 355
Nielson G M 271
Niemeyer D R 132

Nierstrasz O M 264
Nievergelt J 228, 233
Nijkamp P 403, *75*
Nilsson N J 414, 418, 451
Nishita T 292
Nitze R T *88*
Nordbeck S 23, 27, *39*
Norman J 207
Norris D A 36
Norris P 184
NRC *87*
Nunamaker J F 409
Nunes J 160
Nyerges T L 84, 145, 146, 342, 343, 347, 372, 465, *319*
Nyquist M O 203

O'Callaghan J F 38, 67, 136, 284, *4, 5, 67, 92, 93*
O'Neill M O 465
Obermeyer N J *302*
Odervwald R 203
Odland J *128*
OECD *73*
Office of Technology Assessment 496
Official Journal of the European Community *187*
Ogrosky C E *128*
Ojima D S *205*
Okabe A *52*
Okamoto H *120*
Okumura K *124*
Okuno T *47*
Okx J P 305, *163, 164, 165*
Oldeman L R *155, 156*
Oliver M A 193, 390, *159, 163, 164*
Olle T W 256
Olson J M 430, 439
Olson J S *208*
Olsson L *101, 155, 165*
Omohundro S M 216
Onofrei C *155, 164*
Openshaw S 10, 14, 17, 72, 73, 115, 119, 127, 184, 323, 333, 351, 384, 385, 391, 393, 396, 397, 398, 399, 405, 409, 439, *9, 130, 132, 133, 140, 142, 144, 145, 299, 314, 325*
Ord J K 170, 193, 391
Ordnance Survey 241, 526, *25, 27, 30, 36*
Ordnance Survey Review Committee 68
Orenstein J A 264
Oresky C 446

Orman L 409
Osborne S 354
Oswald H 278
Ottmann T A 219
Ottoson L 38, 67, 98, *4, 5, 40, 41, 92, 93, 128, 133*
Ozemoy V M 11

Padmavathy A S 77
Palmer B 235
Pandey M K *78*
Papadopoulos S 352
Pape D 272
Paradis A R 299, 309, *201*
Parent P 11, 101
Park S E 222
Parker H D 11, 94, 191, 200
Parker P 339, 372
Parrott R 8, *297, 303, 314*
Parry R B 5, 179, 325
Parsloe E 352
Parthasaradhi E U R 77
Parvey C A 38, 135, 136, 139, *66, 225*
Pascoe R T 345, 515
Paterson D L 202
Pathan S K 77
Pathirana S 186
Pavlidis T 436
Pazner M 156
Peacock D *111*
Peano G 463
Pearce D *10*
Pearce M L *213*
Pearson J C 292
Pech R P 207
Peddle D R 203
Pellew R A *205*
Penny J P 345, 515
Penridge L K 194, 207
Peplies R W 191
Perkal J 464, 471
Perkins C R 5, 179, 325
Perl Y 222
Perrett P *65*
Perring F H 23
Petach M *164*
Petch J R 82, 83
Petchenik B B 23, 92, *116*
Peters T *140*
Petersen G W 204
Peterson D L 206
Peterson J L 215
Peterson M 430
Petrie G 299

Author index

Petrou M 185, 186, 191, 203, *210*
Peucker T K 33, 166, 185, 200, 227, 235, 247, 272, 273, 274, 284, 288, 464
Peuquet D J 5, 6, 13, 51, 120, 154, 191, 198, 199, 200, 227, 320, 321, 325, 328, 329, 330, 339, 343, 420, 421, 422, 435, 515, 517
Peuther D *260*
Pevsner S 345
Pfefferkorn C 446
Philips W 263
Phillips A *118, 119*
Phillips M *60*
Phillips R J 432
Phillips W W 15, 156
Pienovi C 286
Piercy N *143*
Pierece L L 206
Pike R J 282, 283
Pinker S 433, 434
Piquet-Pellorce D 517
Piscator I *43*
Piwowar J M 343
Pixar Incorporated 299, 300
Pleijsier L K *155*
Plunkett G 202, 203
Poiker T K 84
Porcher E *280*
Potts D F 206
Powitz B M 469
Preece K M *63*
Preparata F P 220, 227, 275, 278, 280
Press L 349
Preusser A 288
Price S 264
Price Waterhouse *321*
Prince S *210, 211*
Prisley S P 185, 200, 480
Przymusinski T C 414, 417
Puissegur A 494, 498
Pullar D 156, 230, 231, 310
Puniard D J *64*
Pyle I C 217

Quade E S *233, 238*
Quarmby N A *212*
Quarterman J S 215

Rada J 76
Raetzsch H 278
Raisz E J 429
Ramachandran A 78

Ramer U 449
Ramey B *154*
Rao M K 77
Raper J F 10, 37, 50, 82, 87, 104, 114, 149, 269, 301, 310, 312, 314, 319, 324, 325, 353, *201, 207, 323*
Raper K B *88*
Rapp S *143*
Rappolt C *155, 164*
Rasmussen J 437
Rasool S I *205*
Ratcliff R 438
Reck R *208*
Redfern P *128, 129, 130, 136*
Reed C N 15, 484
van Reeuwijk L P *155*
Reeves R G 193, 207
Reijerlink J G A *164*
Reiman R *270*
Reinds G J *164*
Reinhardt W 273
Reisner P 156
Reitsma R 411
Rejmanek M 203
Reminga v. United States 500
Ren F *80*
Rencz A N *178, 179*
Requicha A A G 299, 307
Reybold W U 177, *154, 165*
Rhind D W 3, 4, 9, 11, 13, 16, 22, 23, 29, 30, 31, 34, 35, 36, 37, 45, 70, 72, 81, 82, 96, 104, 111, 116, 151, 175, 178, 182, 183, 186, 200, 204, 245, 324, 332, 338, 341, 343, 351, 372, 375, 439, 462, *6, 8, 16, 23, 28, 29, 39, 73, 87, 123, 128, 129, 132, 133, 136, 139, 187, 188, 192, 194, 223, 255, 256, 304, 305, 313, 315, 321, 323*
Rice W 203
Rich C 217
Richards J A 192, 201, 202, 203, 207
Richards S 292, 354
Richardson D E 465, 466
Richardson L F 125, 428
Richardus P 135, 137, 143
Ricketts T J 392
Riezebos H Th. *164*
Ripley B D 390, 396
Rizzo B R 46, 479, 484
Roach J T 179, 180, 186, 202, 264, 276
Robbins A M *134*
Robert P *165*

Roberts S A 261
Robertson A H 431
Robertson G W *223*
Robertson P A 67
Robey T *63*
Robinette A *3, 8, 261, 262, 272, 277, 297, 303, 314*
Robinove C J 202, 330
Robinson A 175, 176
Robinson A D 216
Robinson A H 47, 92, 124, 165, 167, 323, 429, 439, 457
Robinson G 458
Robinson G K 184
Robinson G M 342, 385
Robinson G R *214*
Robinson J 196
Robinson V 235
Robinson V B 122, 324, 422
Rock B N 203
Rodney W *73*
Roe K 103
van Roessel J W 254, 261, 372
Rogers D F 286, 288, 290
Rogers P J *176, 177*
Roitman H 496
Romig H G 165
de Roo A P J 282, *155*
Rosch E 152
Rosenfield G 171
Rosinski R R 433
Rossiter D *156*
Rossmeissl H J *15, 16*
Rothermel J 446
Rothman J *140*
Rowe L A 263, 264
Rowekamp T 277
Rowley J 15, 78
Rowley P D 181
Rowntree L 103
Roy A G 283
Roy J R 66
Royal Institute of Navigation *124*
Royal Society 135
Rozema W J 282
Rubakhin V F 432
Rüber O 306
Ruggles C L N 351
Running S W 202, 206
Rural Regional Development Newsletter 75
Rushton G 27, 257, 403, 407, 410, *299*
Russell J S *156, 247*
Rutherford I *111*

407

Author index

Rystedt B 38, 67, 98, *4*, *5*, *43*, *92*, *93*, *128*, *133*

Saalfeld A 230, 343, 344
Sacerdoti E 422
Sacks S 132
Sadovski A *153*
Sagalowicz D 422
Sailer C T 193, 203
Sakashita S 246
Sale R D 124, 165, 175, 176, 323
Salgé F 165, 517
Salijevic R *59*
Salmon R 299, 300
Salmona J 478
Salvaggio C 195
Samaddar S 217
Sambura A *59*
Samet H 5, 6, 49, 124, 149, 199, 227, 230, 233, 234, 325, 434, 463, *174*
Sanesi G *155*
Sanfhvi N 404
Santek D 290
Santure L 261
SASPRSC 98
Satterwhite M 203
Saull R J 195, *210*, *211*, *212*
Saxena M 77
Saxton W 480
Schacter B J 354
Schaeben H 305
Schafer G M *154*
Schek H-J 314
Schelling J *154*, *160*
Schertz D L *155*
Schertzer D 195
Schettini R 344, 345
Schiwietz M 233
Schmandt C M 159
Schmidt A H 287
Schneider R 233
Schneiderman B 160, 353, 354
Schönhage S 221
Schorn P 228
Schott J R 195
Schoumans O F *164*
Schultz J 404
Schultze C L *238*
Schumaker L L 274, 275
Schut G H 274, 380
Schweitzer R H 30
Sclafer M N 165
Scott D J 432, 436, 437
Scott Morton M S *141*

Seaborn D W 261
Sederberg T W 304
Sedgewick R 220, 436
Sedunary M E *89*, *93*
Seeger B 233
Seldon D D 481
Sellers P J 204, 205
Selvin S 132
Sen L 484
Senior M L 130
Seshan M 219
Settle J J 203
Sevcik K 233
Seymour W A *23*
Shamos M I 220, 227, 275, 278, 280
Shand P J 56, 96
Shanmugam K 283
Shapiro L G 372, 417
Shapiro S C 155, 158, 160
Shariari M R *163*
Sharpe R 66
Shaw M A 23, 34
Shepherd I D H 49, 87, 114, 323, 341, *74*
Sheppard V L O *85*
Sheridan M F *212*
Shetler T 349
Shi Z *79*
Shinar W *305*
Shipman J 203
Shirley W L *3*, *9*, *247*, *250*
Shiryaev E E 47, 242
Shivakumar J 156, 263
Shmutter B 137, 138
Shneiderman B 156
Shortridge B G 430, 437
Shumway C 30
Shyue S W 171
Sicherman A 11
Siderelis K C *3*, *8*, *247*, *250*, *264*, *270*, *275*, *297*, *303*
Siebold J *124*
Siegel M D 421
Sigle M 273
Sigmund J M 181
Silberschatz A 215, 417
Silver D 228
Silverman B G *143*
Simonett D S 13, 23, 47, 112, 186, 192, 193, 200, 206, 207, 208, 240, 325, 339, 385, *171*, *207*
Simpson S R *85*
Simpson T W 180
Singh C B *79*

Singh G *93*
Singh S M 195
Sinha A K 262
Sinton D 167, 168, 169, 171, 323
Skelton N 432
Skiena S S 216
Sklar F H 206, 207, 208
Slama C C 290
Slater M 299, 300
Slingerland R 299
Sloan T M *321*
Slocum J 422
Slocum T A 430
Smith A B *35*, *118*, *124*
Smith D C P 156, 415
Smith D D *164*
Smith D M 193, 389
Smith D R 11, 299, 309, *201*
Smith E A 206
Smith E E 152
Smith G H 429
Smith J A 193, 194, 201
Smith J L 185, 200, 262, *154*, *198*
Smith J M 415
Smith K L 23, 32
Smith L *64*
Smith M O 203
Smith N S 262
Smith P 73
Smith R 430
Smith T R 11, 49, 64, 115, 120, 198, 199, 201, 264, 420, 421, 422, *143*, *198*, *218*, *227*, *229*
Snodgrass R 264
Snyder J P 137, 138, 139, 141, 143, 144, 248
Soaw J F 462
Soil Conservation Service 177, 180, 186
Soil Survey Staff *153*, *157*
Somerville I 263
Sommers R *247*, *307*
Southard R B *12*
Sowton M 4, 35, 68, 70, 127, 178, 241, 262, 526, 527, 529, *3*, *13*, *14*, *25*, *28*, *30*, *108*, *111*, *123*, *131*, *132*, *133*, *304*
Spanier E 150, 233
Spanner M A 206
Sparks A *155*
Spatial Information Systems *287*
Spiegelhalter D J *183*
Sprague R H 406, 407, 409
Sprinsky W H 142

Sproull R F 290
SSC Central Design Group 270
Stallard D 422
Stanley D J 193
Stanton R B *198*
Star J L 5, 6, 10, 11, 83, 103, 120, 191, 193, 198, 199, 201, 320, *218, 227, 317*
Starr L E 31, 67, 127, 262, *3, 12, 13, 20, 23, 131, 133, 304, 305*
Starr M K 403
State of North Carolina *270*
Staufenbiel W 469
Stefanovic P 75, *81*
Stein A 339, 341, *156, 160, 163, 164*
Steinitz C F 339, 372
Steinke T R 438
Steneker M 344
Stepp R E 420
Steven T A 181
Stevens S S 322
Stewart A *165*
Stewart J C *250*
Steyaert L T *227*
Stiefel M *297*
Stoakes M 309
Stohr E A 406
Stolfi J 275, 280
Stone R A 400
Stonebraker M R 263, 414, 417, 418, 419, 421
Strahler A H 191, 193, 194, 201, 203, 207
Strand T C 193
Strassen V 221
Strebel D E 204, 205
Stricker J N M *156*
Stroustrup B 217, 264
Stubblefield W A 463
Stutz F P *8, 297, 303, 314*
Su S 262
Subaryono 341
Sugimura T 285
Suh S *302*
Suits G 195
Sukaviriya P 161
Sullivan J G 171, *247*
Sun D 219
Sun G Q 207
Sun Y 79
Sun Microsystems 224
Sundaram K V 76, *77*
Svoboda L 341
Svorou S 122, 154

Swain P H 203
Sweet D C 30, *299*
Swiss Society of Cartography 458
Switzer P 199
Switzer R 233
Szegö J *45*
Szelinski R 271

Tailor A M 185, 186, 191, 203, *210*
Talmy L 153, 229
Tanaka Y 246
Tang Q *79*
Tanic E 422
Tannenbaum E 343
Tarjan R E 220
Tarpley J D 204
Tavernier R *194*
Taylor D R F 26, 38, 63, 67, *5, 92, 314*
Taylor M A P 66
Taylor P J 88, 389, 390, *319, 323*
Taylor R M 438
Teorey T J 515
Terada T *47*
Terzopoulos D 271
TeSelle G W 177
Tessar P A *278*
Tetzloff D M 315
Tewari V K 410
Thalman D 354
Thapa K 464
Thatte S 264
Thearling K H 216
Theriault D G 12, 314, 344
Theurer C 290
Thielman C Y 155, 160
Thies N 156
Thissen D 429
Thom R 466
Thomas E N 429
Thomas G S 202
Thomas P J 180
Thomas R W 203
Thompson C N 28, *33*
Thompson D 82
Thompson M M 179, 186, *12*
Thoone M *117*
Thornton J D *277*
Thrower N J 429
Tikunov V S 11, 38
Tinney L R 202, 203
Tobler W R 23, 27, 124, 129, 132, 166, 176, 183, 373, 380, 385, 398, 428, 430, 457, 461, 469, *128, 321*

Tomasi S G *133, 305*
Tomatsuri Y *50*
Tomlin C D 5, 6, 13, 15, 51, 102, 114, 149, 232, 233, 329, 330, 339, 341, 361, 372, *285*
Tomlin S M 372
Tomlinson R F 5, 22, 23, 26, 27, 28, 30, 33, 39, 45, 93, 111, 485, *73, 185, 314*
Tong L 203
Topographic Science Working Group *209*
Toppen F 82, 84
Torri D *155*
Townshend J R G 39, 193, 195, 196, *3, 7, 12, 171, 185, 186, 196, 209, 210, 211, 214, 218, 224*
Tranter R B *213*
Tribble T N 270
Trofimov A M 11, 38
Trollegaard S *85*
Tsichritzis D C 46, 51, 148, 253, 264, 418, *186*
Tsur S 419, 420
Tsuzawa M *120*
Tucker C J *209, 210*
Tucker D F 82, 84
Tufte E R 429, 439
Tukey J W 431, 438
Tukey P A 431
Tulip J 261, 263
Tuori M 254
Turnbull M 301
Turner A K 149, 299, 308, 313, 314
Turner M G 208
TYDAC *172*
Tyrie A 82, 84

Uhr L 434
Ullman J D 217, 218, 220, 257, 415, 417
UNEP Global Resources Information Database *224*
UNICEF 72, *73*
United Nations 468, *127*
United States Bureau of the Budget 169
United States Bureau of the Census 183
United States Geological Survey 177, 186, 523, *11, 12, 13, 16, 17*
Universities Research Association *270*
Unninayar S *218, 221*

409

Author index

Unwin D J 4, 16, 62, 77, 82, 84, 85, 86, 88, 111, 124, 125, 128, 322, 323, 376, 385, 389, 390, *128*, *319*
Upstill S 292
Upton G 390, 396
Urban G *142*
Urena J L *227*
URISA *315*
US Congress, Office of Technology Assessment *19*
US Department of Energy, Office of Energy Research *270*
Usery E L 204, *15*, *16*
Ustin S L 203
Utano J J 430
Uzes F D 181

Valenzuela C R *165*
Van Dam A 288, 290
Varvel D A 417
Vazsonyi A 410
Ventura A D 344, 345
Ventura S 171
Vereecken H *156*
Veregin H 168, 200, 203, 381, 384
Verhey W H *164*
Verhoef W 207
Verplank W L 156, 439
de Verr A A *154*
Vevany M J 105
Vincent P *255*
Vincenty T 138
Visvalingham M *132*
van der Vlugt M 411
Volchok W J 195
Voller J *111*
Vonderohe A P 169, 180
Vose M 346

Wade B W 156
Wadge G *212*, *213*
Wagenet R J *164*
Wagle S 227
Wagner G 341
Wainer H 429
Wakeford R 399
Waldrop M M 103
Wales R Q 305, 309
Walker J 194, 207
Walker P A 38, 135, 136, 139, 199, 341, *63*, *66*, *180*, *225*
Walker T C 56
Wallin E 353
Walsh S J 203, 204, *164*

Walters D K 433, 434, 435
Walters S M 23
Wang F 341
Wang Min-Hua *78*
Wang R *79*
Wang S 202
Wang Y-F 49
Wanzell L R 436
Ware C 354
Warntz W 429
Warthen B 528, 529
Wasielewski P *120*
Wastman J R 438
Waterfeld W 314
Waters N M 84, 86, 410, 411
Waters R C 217
Waters R S 246
Watson D M *223*
Watson E J *142*
Watson G P *178*, *179*
Watts D G 195
Watts J *208*
Waugh T C 36, 262, 345, 512, *321*
Weber W 470
Webster C 5, 15, 260, 261, 339, 347, 378, 385, 422
Webster R 170, 193, 390, *154*, *155*, *156*, *159*, *160*, *163*, *164*, *209*
Van der Weg R F *155*, *156*, *164*
Weibel R 50, 113, 127, 199, 204, 235, 270, 274, 278, 279, 283, 290, 292, 301, 304, 325, 376, 380, 430, 460, 464, 469, *12*, *15*, *314*
Weir S 130
Weiser R L 205
Weismuller R A 204
Weitzel L 377
Weizenbaum J 434
Welch R 204, *128*
Welch R A 302
Welch R B 430, 437
Welch T A 245
Weller T 195
Wellings C 96
Wells D 264
Weng H 206
Werner C 285
Wertz J 30
West D S 121
Westcott T *270*
Wester L 158
Westin F C *164*
Weyer S 355
Wharton S W 194, 202

Whatmough R J 67
Wheeler P H 277
Whelan S D *112*
Whigham P A 67
Whimbrel Consultants Limited *188*
Whinston A B 406, 407
Whitbread P J 67
White B 411, 493
White D 290, 373
White M 122, 166, *6*, *14*, *54*, *314*, *321*
White M L 206, 207
White M S *119*, *121*, *300*
White R M 160, 229
White T 261, *305*
Whitfield R A S *28*, *29*
Whittaker E 458
Whittaker H A *213*
Whittaker R J 39, *188*
Wiederhold G 255, 415, 418
Wiggins J C 39, 375, *187*, *188*, *196*
Wiggins J S 338, 341
Wilding J P *154*
Wilding L *155*
Wilkie D 399
Wilkinson H R 429
Wilkinson L 431
Williams E P J 27
Williams J 392
Williams R B G 380
Williams R L 430
Williams W B P 138
Williamson H D 205
Williamson I P 301, 314, *58*, *59*, *87*
Willmott C J 285
Wilson A G 389, 390
Wind J 345
Winograd T 161
Winston P H 515
Wintz P A 278
Wischmeier W H *164*
Wise S M 86
Witkin A P 434
Witmer R E 179, 180, 186, *264*, *276*
Woelk D 350, 355
Wolf J *155*, *164*
Wolfram S 216
Wood E F 206, 283
Woodcock C E 193, 194, 201, 207
Woodcock J 148
Woodsford P A 46, 47, 48, 63, 113, 185, 324, *90*, *96*, *104*, *276*
Woodward R A 203
Worboys M F 103, 120, 253, 254, 263, 264, 323, 379

World Commission on Environment and Development 7, 72
Wösten H J M 155, 156
Wray T 140
Wright D F 173, 174, 176, 177, 178, 183, 184
Wright W 82, 8
Wrightman J F 84
Wrigley N 380, 434, 140, 145
Wu P Y F 217, 219, 422
Wu Zhong-xing 144
Wyatt B K 203, 187, 198, 199
Wymer C 385, 399, 409, 142

Yamamoto S 47
Yan S Y 422, 79
Yandell B S 169, 185
Yang J 209
Yang Qi-he 144
Yapa L S 74
Yarbus A L 438

Yarrow G J 92, 111
Yates J 148
Yates M V 163
Yates S R 163
Ye Jiang 64, 264, 413, 143, 198, 229
Yeh A G 260
Yeorgaroudakis Y 355
Yeung A K W 245
Yoeli P 286, 288, 430, 445, 446
Yogarajan N 77
Yomono H 52
Yoshimura S 47
Young L T 216
Youngman C 372
Youngmann C 299

Zadeh L A 148, 152
Zafft W A 28
Zarzycki J M 346
Zavoli W B 159, 119
Zdonik S B 421

Zehner R B 67
Zelek J 202, 203
Zeleny M 403
Zhan C-X 154
Zhang Q 79, 81
Zheng W 80
Zhong E 79
Zhong S 79
Zhou M 79
Zhou Q 192, 198, 200, 201
Zhou M-C 219
Zilles S 233
Zinn v. State 500
Zobrist A L 344
Zoraster S 278, 446
Zubin D 122, 154
Zuboff S 149
Zusne L 428
Zycor N C 464
Zyda M J 288

SUBJECT INDEX

Numbers in roman refer to volume 1, numbers in italic refer to volume 2, numbers in bold refer to main entry.

0–Cell *134*
1-Cell *134*
2-Cell *134*
2.5D 269, *272*
    Visualization 302, 304
2D 24, 50, 124, 135, 153, 280, 290, 292, 293, 299, 302, 325, *203*, *206*, *272*, *319*
    Cartographic Form 369
    Coordinate Information 262
    Isoline Map 305
    Matrices 234
    Projections 225
    Spatial Data *201*
    Visualization 302
3D 50, 53, 114, 124, 135, 149, 153, 167, 170, 269, 290, 302, 325, 516, 527, *201*, *202*, *203*, *206*, *209*, *319*, *320*
    Applications *317*
    Cartographic Form 369
    Clipping 290
    Coordinates 141
    Data 7, *88*
        Display 280
        Structures 439
    Digital Terrain Model *113*
    GIS **299–317**
    Imaging 431
    Modelling 373, *15*
        Systems 299
    Representation Techniques 307
    Run Encoding 308
    Spatial Data Structuring 299
    Surface *289*

Technology *319*
Topography *104*
Transformation 290
Triangulated Irregular Network 309
Vectors Per Second *319*
Visualization 302–4, *320*
4D 7, *201*, *202*, *207*

A Classification of Residential Neighbourhoods *144*
A/E/C Systems 93
Abstract Data
    Structure 215
    Types 417, 418
Abstraction 242
Access to Data and Information 492
Accuracy 242, *315*
    of Plant Recording *106*
    of Spatial Databases 95
Ada 217, 252
ADABAS 255
ADAMS *49*
ADAPT 66
Adaptive
    Filtering 464
    Modification 407
    Triangular Mesh Filtering 279, 280
Address
    Coding Guide 25
    Geocoding *300*
    Information System 24
    Matching 343, *304*
        Software 27

Admatch 25
Administrative
    Boundaries 71, 322
    District *131*
    Management Agency 48
ADR 255
Advanced
    Mobile Traffic Information and Communication System *120*
    Visualization Techniques 290–2
Aerial
    Photograph 29, 271, *55*, *288*, *298*, *304*
    Photography 141, 192, 239, *92*, *123*, *128*
    Photointerpretation 192
Aeronautical
    Charting and Information Center, St. Louis 27
    Information Services and Central Photographic Establishment *64*
Affine Transformation 141, **142–3**, 329
AFI3G 98
Agency for International Development 38
Aggregation 103, 343, 390
AGI
    NEWS 96
    Yearbook 51, 56
Agricultural
    Nonpoint Source Pollution Model *278*, *279*
    Research Service *278*
Agriculture 59, 197, 293, 422

Subject index

Air Photography 49, 201, 202
Aircraft Simulator 75
Airfield Design 293
Airport Noise Zones 105
Albemarle-Pamlico *8*
    Estuarine Study *262*, **263-7**
Alberta LRIS 260
ALES *156*
Algebraic Topology 150, 231
Algorithm Analysis 215
Algorithmic
    Probability 396
    Solution Methods 409
Algorithms 84, **220-3**
ALI/SCOUT *120*
ALIS *49, 50*
Allocation Model *239*
ALSCAL 130
Alternative Reality 354
Ambient Light Transparency 288
Amdahl 503, 509, *133*
American
    Association for Geodetic Surveying 94
    Cartographer, The 23, 94, 524
    Cartographic Association 94
    Congress on Surveying and Mapping 7, 93, 94, 524
    National Standards Institute 252, 525, 527
    Society for Photogrammetry and Remote Sensing 7, 93, 94, 169, 170, 179
    Urban and Regional Information Systems Association 6
AMTECS *54*
Analogue 47
    Attribute Data 175
    Data 175, 272
        Sources **175-83**
    Scanning 244
    Spatial Data 175
Analytical
    Computation 428
    Geometry 228
    Model *281*
    Modelling 405, 408
        Techniques 371
    Photogrammetry 458, *42*
    Stereoplotter 271
    Transformation **139-41**
Angular Field of View 192
Animated Graphics 53
Animation 87, 115

Antarctica 137
Anthropology 152
Anti-Aliasing 290, 300
AOS/VS 58
Apple
    Computer Incorporated 50
    Macintosh 49, 156, 352
Application
    Logic 418
    -Independent Benchmark 484
Applications of GIS *3*, **5-10**
    in the Environmental Sciences *210-14*
    in the Utilities *106*
Appropriate
    Spatial Analysis for GIS **395-6**
    Technology *81*
Arc 47
ARC 341
    Macro Language 341, *257*
ARC/INFO 15, 24, 32, 51, 52, 96, 113, 159, 168, 235, 241, 261, 325, 328, 341, 345, 512, *14, 15, 52, 53, 55, 67, 74, 75, 77, 189, 196, 250, 257, 258, 262, 316, 319, 321*
    Allocate *256, 257*
Arc/Node *153, 157*
    Spatial Data Model 341
    Topological Model 339
ARCDEMO 87
Archaeological Site Recording and Monitoring *90*
Architectural
    CAD Diagram 427
    Planning 301
Architecture 59
    of Very Large GIS Databases 95
Archival Data *201*
Archives 48
ARCNEWS 32, *75*
Arctic *225*
ARCView *324*
Area 85, 102
    Attribute 383
    Cartogram 132
    Class Map 168
    Measurement 114
    Quadtree *172*
Areal
    Interpolation 385
    Weighting 385
Argentina *123, 227*
ARISTOWN *51*

ARITHMICON 24, 31
Array 149, 218, 320
    Fetch 262
Artifacting 208
Artificial
    Intelligence 64, 95, 185, 417, 515, *143, 228, 229, 293, 301, 325*
    Neural Nets 396
ARX *67*
ASCII 224, 325, 346, *174, 176, 180, 228*
Asian Institute of Technology *74*
Aspatial 12, 27
    Object 301
Aspect Vector 278
ASPENEX 422
Assessment of Risk *192*
Association 103
    for Geographic Information 4, 7, 37, 51, 71, **77-8**, 96, 99, *9, 30, 317*
    of American Geographers 7, 33, 93, 94, 97
    of Computer Machinery 33
    of Local Authorities *42*
Asymptotic Assumptions 392
Atlantic Institute 96
Atlas
    of Great Britain and Northern Ireland 23
    of the British Flora 23
ATLAS*GIS 53, *317, 320, 322*
Atlases 92
Atmospheric
    Attenuation 204
    Correction 203
    Model 207
    Path Radiance 204
    Science 114
    Sciences Data *205-6*
Atomic Fragment *135*
Attribute 12, 46, 114, 120, 127, 166
    Accuracy **170-1**, 181, 459
        Test 172
    Association 349
    Attachment *33*
    Change 470
    Conceptual Error 383
    Consistency Checking 344
    Data **183-5**, 324, 338, 339, 340, 341, 343, 347, 479, 525, *205*
        Resolution 342
        Table 350
    Definition 170

Subject index

Error 440
Information 340, 341
Similarity 128
Audio Tape 349
AUSNOMA *60*
AUSSAT 66
Australia 38, 67, 93, *4, 5, 92, 93, 94, 95, 225*
    Information System 135
    Resources Information System 38
Australian
    Bureau of Statistics 65
    Centre for Remote Sensing *60*
    Defence Force *61*
    Federal Resources Database *185*
    Heritage Commission *63*
    International Development Assistance Bureau 39
    Key Centre in Land Information Studies *67*
    Land Information Council *58, 60, 61, 62, 67*
    National
        Parks and Wildlife Service *63*
        University *67*
    Natural Resources Information Centre *193*
    Resources
        Data Bank *66*
        Information System *66*
    Standard Geographical Classification *65*
    Survey
        and Land Information Group *5, 60*
        Office and Division of National Mapping *60*
Authoritative Map 165
AUTOCAD 261, 325, 523, *74*
AUTOCARTO 5, 6, 22, 33, 84, 85, 86
Autocorrelation *195*
    and Regularization in Satellite Imagery **193–5**
Autocovariance 194
Autofact 93
Autoguide *117, 120, 121, 123*
Automap II 24
Automated 23
    Address Matching 26–7
    Cartographic
        Production 52
        Systems *11*
    Cartography 27, 30, *144, 262, 321*
    Classification *210*
    Digital Terrain Model Extraction 285
    Generalization 463, *26*
    Geographical Databases 56
    Graphic Indexing *214*
    Intelligence 115
    Interaction Detector 398
    Interpretation of Aerial Photography 422
    Land Titles System *60*
    Map
        Making 499
        Production *33*
    Mapping/Facilities Management 97, 104, 292, *5, 6, 49, 51, 92*
        International 94, 95
        TODAY Conference 77
    Meteorological Data Acquisition System 52
    Regional Justice Information System 257
    Spatial Analysis 394
    Teller Machine *145, 150*
    Terrain
        Feature Extraction 422
        Analysis 280
    Thematic Mapping *155*
    Zone Design 397
Automatic
    Digitizing 435, 436
    Image Enhancement *31*
    Line Following *31*
    Name Placement 454, 455
        System 445
    One-pass Generalization 329
    Snapping 344
    Spatial Response Modeller 397
    Text Annotation 344
    Zoning 398
Automobile Association 512
AUTONAP 423, 452
Autoregressive Model 185
Autoroute *35*
Availability of Digital Data *206–7*
Average Variogram *162*
AVHRR 193, 195, 196, *202, 209, 222, 223, 228*
AVL Tree 220
Awareness of GIS *3*
Azimuthal Equal-Area Projection 145

B-reps 309
Backface Elimination 290
Backward Chaining 419
Baghdad *260*
Band Location 195
Bandwidth Encoding 464
Bangladesh *127*
Bartholomews *6*
Baseline Determination Algorithm 449
BASIC 74
Basic
    Employment Allocation Model *248, 249*
    Guidelines for SSSpatial Analysis in GIS 396
    Input Output System *124*
    Terms of Error **166**
Basin Area 285
Batch 45
    Processing 480, *13*
Bathometric Charts *64*
Baud 504
Bayes Rule *171*
Bayesian
    Estimator 202
    Mapping 390
    Methods 392, 396, *172*
    Principles *173*
BBC 83
Beijing Astronomical Observatory *204*
Benchmark 116, 484–5, *96, 189, 322*
Benefits
    of a Land Registration Scheme *92*
    of GIS **14–15**
    of Information Integration 337–8
Benetton Company *143*
Bessell Function *159, 160*
Bias 166, 169, 203, 204
Bideford Experiment *25, 26, 32*
Bijective 231
    Transformation 467
BILDED 306
Binary
    Conversion *176*
    Large Object 349
    Representation 29
    Segmentation 398
    Signature Map *174*
    Tree 219, 220, 463
Bioclimatology 197

Subject index

Biological Conservation 32
Biophysical Resources 57
Birkbeck College, University of London 86, 87, *188*, *189*
Birmingham *28*
Bitmap 325
Bivariate
    Interpolation 430
    Quadratic Simplicial B-Spline 306
Black
    Inquiry 74
    Report (1984) 74
Blind Digitizing *26*
Block
    Encoding 199
    Kriging *164*
Boehm's Figure of Merit 483
Bonne Projection 145
Boolean Operation 308, 321, 330
Borehole 308
    Log *203*
    Records 270
Bosch *115*
    Travelpilot *115*, *116*, *117*, *119*, *120*, *121*
Botswana *211*
Boundary
    Representation 307
    Approximation Algorithm 449
Bounding Nodes 227
Boyce-Codd 259
BP 315
Branch Location Analysis *139*, *140*, *143*, **145–8**
British
    Cartographic Society 96
    Census 380, *131–3*
    Gas *111*
    Geological Survey 186, *203*, *204*
    Library 186
    Military Board of Ordnance *23*
    Oxygen Company *26*
    Telecom 504, 513, *111*
Britton Lee *33*
    IDM Database Computer 262
Brundtland Report 7, *72*
Buffer Zone *191*, *307*
Buffering 322, 329, 389
Building
    Asset Management *90*
    Permit Control *90*
    Walk-Through 354
Bulgaria *153*

Bureau
    of Mineral Resources *63*
    of Rural Resources *63*
Business (Development) Planning *140*, *141*
Byte-Oriented Run-Length Encoding 245

C 215, 219, 224, 252
C++ 216
Cable
    Television *51*
    Utilities *102–3*
CAD-Based Systems 261
CAD/CAM 32
Cadastral 38, 138
    Data *261*
    Information 466
        System 12, 332, *58*
    Mapping 137, 292, *76*
    Plan *91*
    Records 97
    Station *106*
    Survey *86*
    Surveying 85
    System *4*
Cadastre 12, 181, *58*, *85*
Calcomp 31, *26*
CALFORM 24, 28
Calibration 191
    Models **204–6**
Calliper 53
Canada
    Geographic Information System 17, 22, 23, **28–9**, 45, *314*
    Land
        Data System 17
        Inventory 23, 29, 111, *185*
    Agricultural Rehabilitation and Development Administration 29
    Hydrographic Survey 27
    Institute of Surveying and Mapping 97
Cancer Screening *130*
Capability Model *300*
Car
    Guidance System *6*
    Navigation *34*, *318*, *321*
    Systems *54*, **115–24**
CARIN *121*
Cartesian
    Axes 143
    Coordinates 124, 135, 136, 139, 140, 141, 299, 364, *271*

Cartogram 119, **132**, 430
Cartographic
    Acceptability of Data 242
    and Spatial Analytical Concepts of GIS 85
    Comparison 385
    Conceptual Error 383
    Data 221, 344, *224*
        Exchange Standard 227
        Interpretation 367
        Sources 272
    Database 385
    Design 427
        Rules 438
    Display 405, 408
    Error 206, 381
    Form 371, 391
    Generalization 247, 292, 457, 460, 462, 464, *17*
        of Digital Terrain Models 278, 279, 283
    Image 361
    Information 191, 200
    Measurement Error 381
    Modelling 102, 103, **361–73**, *291*
        Capabilities **367–71**
        Conventions **364–7**
        System 340
        Techniques **371–2**
    Projection 365, *218*, *228*
    Rectification 191
    Representation 125, 471
        of Data 77
    Reprojection 365
    Symbolization *17*
    Symbols 50
Cartography 22, 55, 57, 59, 88, 91, 92, 101, 115, 139, 141, 167, 168, 169, 172, 221, 430, 435, 436, 437, 439, *15*, *102*, *116*, *317*
    and Geographic Information Systems 6, 94, **102–3**, *134*
Cartometry 345
Catastrophe Theory 466, 474
Catastrophic Approach to Cartographic Generalization 466–8
Categorical
    Attribute 383
    Coverage 168, 383
    Data 376
    Analysis 380
Cathode Ray Tube 302, 438
CD-ROM 5, 48, 55, 183, 215, 343,

Subject index

349, 352, 513, *15*, *53*, *54*, *65*, *74*, *121*, *122*, *149*, *197*, *220*, *324*
CDA 346
CDATA-86 65
CDF 346
Cell 150, 233
Cellular
    Automata 398
    Decomposition 235
    Topology 235
Census 6, *128*, *263*, *298*, *303*, *304*, *324*
    Data 183, *261*
    District 253
    Map Production 331, 332
    of Population 71, 504, 513
        and Housing *307*
    Statistics *128*
    Tract *239*, *240*, *249*, *250*, *256*, *257*, *305*
        Descriptor 516
Center for Urban and Regional Analysis 31
Central
    Board of Real Estate Data 38, *43*
    Government 67
        Reporting 90
    Intelligence Agency 27, 30
    Office of Information 67
    Population Register *129*
Centralized GIS 480
Centre
    for Recent Crustal Movements *203*
    for Renewable Resources and Environment *205*
    for Resource and Environmental Studies 67
    for Soil Geography and Classification *205*
    for Spatial Information Systems 67
Centroid 126, 150
CGIS-CLI 260
CGM 346
Chain Code *314*
Change-Detection in LANDSAT Images 422
Channel Pixel 284
Chaotic Model 435
Character Representation *29*
Characteristics
    of an Education System 84
    of Environmental Data Sets ***202–7***
    of Environmental Databases *206–7*
    of Geographical Data 103
    of Geoprocessing Systems **405–7**
Characterization 312
Characterizing Neighbourhoods *213*
Charge-Coupled Device 243
Chemistry 92, 93
Chernobyl *186*, *193*
China 39, 98, *5*, *9*, *75*, *224*, *324*
    Tourism Resource Information System *79*
Chinese Academy
    of Geological Sciences *204*
    of Sciences *205*
Chorley
    Committee 68, 69, 96, 487, *29*, *30*, *35*
    Report 22, *88*, *94*, *132*
Chorochromatic Map *156*
    Model *158*
Choropleth 28
    Map 168, 438, *120*, *156*, *158*, *257*
Cinematic Animation 300
City
    Block Distance 231
    Growth *78*
    of Knoxville *112*
    Planning *54*
Civil
    Engineering 59, 286, 287, 293, 299
    Service 72, 507, 508, 509, 510
Clarion NAVI *117*
Classification 168, **201–4**, 383
    Accuracy 204
    Bias 203
    Errors 202–3, 285
    of Landslide Hazards 283
    of Systems **215–17**
    of Water Tracts 265–7
Classifying Geographical Data 323
Climatology 92, 197, 293, *205*
Cluster Analysis 201, 391
Clustering 434
Co-Kriging 305, *153*, *163*, *164*
Co-Regionalized Variable 305
Co-Registered Data Sets *208–9*
Co-Registration 343
Co-Variogram *163*
Coarsening
    of a Digital Terrain Model 280
    of Rectangular Grids 274
Coastal
    Area Management Act *264*, *265*
    Planning 59
    Zone Color Scanning System *202*
COBOL 256
CODATA Task Group 93
Codd Normal Forms 261
Code
    Management 217
    of Federal Regulations *267*
Cognitive Science **151–4**, 439
COGO 345
Collection of Spatial Information 429
Colliding Record 218
Colombia *75*
Colour 434
Combined Higher Education Software Team 96
Combining Data Sets 280
Commercial
    GIS **56–60**
    Values 494
Commission for Integrated Survey of Natural Resources *205*
Committee
    of Enquiry into the Handling of Geographic Information 67, 68, **69–78**, *29*, *66*
    of Geographical Names in Australia *60*
    on Data for Science and Technology 93
Commodity Market 492
Common Agricultural Policy *213*
Commonwealth
    Land Information Support Group *60*
    Scientific and Industrial Research Organization 38, *66*
    Surveyor General *61*
Communications 59
    Planning 75
    Map 458
Community Charge 76
Comparative
    Analysis *262*
    Study 392
Compass *119*
Competitive Tendering *90*
Completeness 242
Composite
    Map Model 339–40, 356
    Sampling 271, 272

Subject index

Comprehensive Resource Inventory and Evaluation System 38, 75
Compulsory Purchase Order 90
Computational
 Geometry 227, 275
 Vision 435
Computer
 -Aided
  Design 12, 101, 299, 326, 329, 341, 439, 527
   and Drafting 64
  Drafting 56, 24
  Mapping 24
  Analysis of Spatial Data 48
 -Assisted
  Cartography 84, 45, 75, 80
  Generalization 458, 473
  Learning 87
  Map Analysis 287, 294
  Regional Planning 74
 Cartography 12, 83, 86, 329, 330, 436
 Display of Spatial Data 48
 Error 497
 Graphics 290, 463
  Interface 527
  Metafile 527
  Standards 527–9
 Mapping 385, 512
 Matching 253
 Name Placement **445–55**
 Photomontage 354
 Science 22, 57, 113, 149, 152, 215, 15, 102, 156, 314
Computerized
 Data Analysis 218
 Rural Information Systems Project 77
Conceptual
 Data Model 515, 516
 Error 381
 Fuzziness 384
 Generalization 466, 467
 Model 112–13, 113, 320
 Modelling 515
Conceptualization of Reality 51
Concurrency Control 418
Concurrent Processors 15
Conditional
 Execution 366
 Independence 171, 174, 183, 184
  Assumption 174, 180
Conflict Resolution Model **292–3**
Confusion Matrix 203

Connectivity 330, 213
Conquest 25
Conservation
 Model 290
 Monitoring Centre 205
Constraint
 Introduction 421
 Removal 421
 Replacement 421
Constructive Solid Geometry 307
Consulting 60
Containment 330
 Relationship 421
Contiguity 440
 Constraint 391
Continental Environmental Database 186
Contingency Table 203
Continuous 231
 Coordinate Space 200
 Data 376
  Collection 207
 Feed Scanner 243, 244
 Spectral Change 195
 Tone Isoplethic Map 430
Contour 287
 Data Model 113
 Digitizing 13
 Interpolation 288
 Polygon 278
 -to-Grid
  Conversion 280
  Interpolation 278
 -to-TIN Conversion 280
Contouring 287
Conversion Algorithm 378
Convex Hull 275
Convolution 470
Coordinate
 Conversion 13
 Density Equalization 343
 Geometry 322
 Registration 343
 System 85, 112, 135
 Transformation 85, 248
Coordinating Committee on Locational References 69
Copyright 72, 99
 Law 495
 Design and Patents Act 94
Core GIS Theory 319
CORINE 137, 260, 342, 344, 385, 7, 164, **185–99**, 225, 305
Cost of Data Collection 77

Cost-Effectiveness
 Analysis 477
 Estimate 244
 Evaluation 485
Cost/Benefit 85, 95, 192
 Analysis 61, 85, 477, 478, 479, 480–1, 9, 43, 150, 244
 of GIS 315
 of Land Information Systems **88–9**
 Ratio 244, 314
Costs of GIS 46, 3
Council
 for Research and Development in Land Information Technology 43
 of Europe Convention 495
Count Data 376
Countryside Commission for Scotland 35
County 131
 Administration Board 43
 Council 76
Course Development Project 84
Covariance Matrix 202
Coverage 48, 52, 168
 Database 168
CPU 219, 252, 257, 484, 485, 49, 123, 133
Creation of a Spatial Decision Support System 301–2
Credit
 Referencing Agency 143
 Scoring 140, 143, 149
Crime
 Analysis
  Mapping System 257
  Statistical System 257
 Control 8, 247, 250
 Pattern Analysis 90
 Prevention Planning 257
 Reporting 257
  and Interactive Mapping Environment 257, 258
Critical Erosion Targeting 277–8
Crop
 Disease 433
 Modelling 157, 164
 Suitability Study 293
 -Specific Phenology 202
Cross
 Area Estimation 396
 Linguistic Transfer 160
 -Hairs 243

418

Subject index

-Indexing 351
-Selling *144*
Crown Copyright 512
CRT *54*
Cubic Interpolation 278
CUBRICON 155
Cultural Landscape *47*
Curriculum
    Content 87
    Requirements *319*
Curvilinear Transformation 329
Customer
    Billing *90*
    Database *149*
    Origin Survey *145*
Customized Zone Design 397
Cut-and-Fill 287
Cybernetics 439
Cyberspace 354

Dangling Chain 382
Danish Meteorological Institute *204*
Daratech Incorporated 14, 56
Data
    Absorption 347
    Access 93, 418, *193*
    Accuracy 112, 395, *17*, *194*
    Acquisition 85, 338, 498, *87*
    Analysis 253–4, 324, 419, 498, *127*, *189–91*, *315*
    and Knowledge **415–16**
    Availability *193*
    Capture 60, 239, 319, 324, 480, *201*, *206*, *207*, *208*, *210*, *315*
        and Processing Algorithms 247–8
        for Digital Terrain Models 270
        Technology 276
    Cataloguing *207*
    Classification 78
    Collection 239, 432, 481, *4*, *6*, *12*, *195*, *318*
        Technology 191
    Combination 498
    Communications *43*
    Compaction 458, 509
    Compilation *127*
    Compression 458, *174*
    Confidentiality *325*
    Conversion 349, *96*
    Definition *197*
    Descriptive File for Information Interchange 78
    Differences 380
    Directory Project *219*

Display 111, *127*
Dissemination *127*
Dredging 420, 421
Editing 319, 324
Entry 113, *276*
Environment 529
Error 398, 496
Exchange 515, 518
    Standards *111*
Exploration 115
Export 515
Format 112, *209*, *319*
Gathering Agencies 116
General *263*
Generalization 324
Glove 315, 354, 439
Import 515
Inconsistency 342
Indexing 29, *207*
Input 252, *189*
Integration 112, 324, 328, 340, 384, 385, *7*, *96*, *189*, *262*
    Modelling ***172–4***, 180
    Tools *300*
Integrity 262, *61*
Interpolation 114, 428, 438
Key 348
Layer Intersection 263
Logger 325, 349
Management 93, *5*, *20*, *222*, *242*, *300*
    Support *263*
Manipulation 260, 389, 499
Measurement Scale 375
Media 342
Model **51**, 85, 228, 254, 269, 320, 342, 347, *96*, *318*
Modelling 113, 251, 253, 428, *315*, *318*
    Techniques 251
Models for Soil Survey *156*
Normalization *79*
Observation 375
Oriented Raster Structure 200
Output *191–2*
Presentation 324, 366
Privacy Legislation *149*
Processing 55, 93, 113, 154, 361, 481, *87*, *194*
    System *142*
Quality 78, 93, 395, 459, 523, 525, 526, 529, ***89–91***, *155*, *193–6*, *197*, *220*, *319*
    Assessment 293

Query 324
Redundancy 256, 258, 279
Reliability 93
Restructuring 324
Retrieval 113
Robustness 457
Sales *4*
Security 262, *106*
Segregation 232
Sharing *59*
Signposting *193*
Simplifier 397
Sources *318*
    for Digital Terrain Models 270
Standards 116–17, *79*
Storage 85, 113, 252, 324
Structure 85, 112, 113, 114, 228, 324, 342, 434
    Conversion 192, 280
    for Digital Terrain Models 272
    Examples of **218–20**
Switchyard 518, 522, 523
Transfer 112, 319, 324, 515
Transformation 324, 365, 367
Type *209*
Uncertainty 85
Unit 379
Validation 324, *12*
Verification 497
Visualization 115, 354
Volume *315*
    of Digital Terrain Models 279
Database 22, 57, 59, 85, 111, 187, 218, 223, 227, 251, 405, 415, 492, 495, *32*, *55*, *77*, *262*
    Analysis 111
    Computer 262
    Construction *43*
    Creation 479
    Design 111, 251, **252–4**, *17*
    Development *287*
    Generalization 464
    Interfaces **154–6**
    Linkages 232
    Locks 419
    Management 12, 83, 84, 329, 435, 439, 479, 515, *33*, *144*, *291*
        System 12, 13, 46, 56, 57, 172, 228, 251, 325, 330, 349, 385, 408, 419, *33*, *142*, *228*, *229*
        Interfacing 347, 349
        Software Components 252
    Manager 217
    Modelling 398

Subject index

Database – *cont.*
    Models 463
    Representation *107*
    Structures 95
    Systems 413
    Tables 257
    Task Group of the Conference on Data Systems Language 256
    Theory 416
    Tools 216, 251
    Update *196*
    View of GIS 13–14
    Volume *196*
DATACOM/DB 255
Dataquest Incorporated 56
DB2 259
DBASE 346, *74*, *322*
DBF 346
Dbmap 25
DCA 346
DDBMS 347
DDIF 346
Dead Reckoning *116*, *117*
Debugging 223
Decision
    Analysis 479
    Declaration on Transborder Data Flows 495
    Declarative Query Language 421, 422
    Dedicated Road Infrastructure for Vehicle Safety *124*
    Deductive Database 414, 416, 417
    Estimation 181
    Information Display System *300*, *302*
    Making *60*, *61*, *74*, *301*, *302*
        in a GIS Context 85
        Model *286*
        Tools *300*
    Model *142*
    Modelling 479
    Research 403
    Resources 24
    Space *236*, *237*
    Support 391
        System 10, 11, 17, 404, *67*, *77*, *142*, *145*, *149*, *276*, *299*, *300*, *301*
            Generator 407
    Tree Analysis *180*
Defence 59, 67, 71
    GIS **75–6**
    Scientific and Technology Organization 67
Defence
    Mapping Agency 48, 518
    Meteorological Satellite Program 202
Defining
    Areas for Development 289–92
    Conservation Areas 288
    Ecological Research Areas 288–9
Definition
    Limited 313
    of GIS **10–12**
    of a Land Information System 87
Definitions of Visualization 432
Delaunay Triangulation 220, 275, 276, 278, 305
Delivery Scheduling *35*
Deltamap/Genamap 15
DEMOGIS 87
Demographic
    Analysis *90*
    and Economic Forecasting Model *248*
    Data *261*
    Profile *250*
Demography 197, 503
Dempster-Scafer Theory *183*
Denmark *129*
Densification
    of a Digital Terrain Model 280
    of Gridded Digital Terrain Models 280
    of Rectangular Grids 274
Department
    of Administrative Services *60*
    of Agriculture 177, 179, 180, 182, *75*, *154*, *163*, *278*
    of Commerce 495
    of Economic Development 507
    of Employment 503
        Group 507, 508
    of Energy *17*, *213*, *270*, *271*
        Mines and Resources Canada 97
    of Environment, Health and Natural Resources *262*
    of Health 279
    of Housing and Urban Development 30
    of Natural Resources, Division of Forestry *280*
    of Primary Industries and Energy *63*
    of Roads *53*
    of Science Programming and Earthquake Monitoring *205*
    of the Environment 35, 69, 72, 74, 508, *23*, *27*, *132*, *209*
    of the Interior 495, 524, *12*, *13*, *15*, *19*
    of Trade and Industry 74, 508, 510
    of Transport 72, 508
    of Treasury 495
Depth Cuing 300
Derived
    Map *26*, *27*, *289*, *290*
Descriptive
    Cartographic Model 371
        Modelling Techniques 371
    Mapping *285*
Desktop
    Information Display System 24
    Publishing 348, *314*
Destination
    Finding *115*, *121*, *124*
Determination of Name Baseline 449
Deterministic
    Model **206–7**
    Solution *292*
Developing Countries 67
Development 59
    Areas Model *289*, *291*
    Control 76, 90
    Planning *298*
Device Control 366
DFAULT 306
DG XI *189*
Diagnostic Signature *171*
Dialogue Understanding 158
Dichotomous Data 376
DIF 346
Differential Rectification 290
DIGEST 346, *318*
Digital
    Array 427
    Atlas *304*
    Camera 243
    Cartographic
        Data 251, 254, 260, 516, *11*, *12*, *13*
        Base *76*, *77*
        Standard *17*

Standards Task Force 165, 523
Feature Representation 523
Model 459
Cartography *11*, *12*, *78*, *154*
Data 175, *298*
  Donor Programme *20*
  Sources **185–6**
Database 324, *317*
Elevation
  Data 203, 527
  Matrices 168
  Model 37, 177, 269, 279, 345, 523, *12*, *18*, *36*, *212*, *213*, *223*, *315*, *319*
Equipment Company 52, *33*, *321*, *324*
Field Update System *31*, *32*
Flow Line *28*
Geographic Information Working Group 75
Image Document 343
Landscape Model 458, 459, 460, 465, 471
Line Graph 177, 219, 221, 235, 325, 345, 346, 435, 523, *9*, *13*, *16*, *17*, *228*, *305*, *306*
  -Enhanced 517, 519, 522, 529, *17*
Mapping 73, 127, 299, *28*
Orthophotograph 192, *14*
Photogrammetry 26
Processing 361
Representation 85, **112–14**
  of Information 113
Road Map Association *54*
Simulation 271
Soil Information *155*
Sound Sampler 349
Spatial Data 427, 515, *19*
  Quality *20*
Stereo
  Correlation 271, 272
Street Network *123*
Technology 111
Terrain
  Elevation Data 75, *17*, *228*
  Model 126, 170, 345, 349, 464, *47*
    Application 270, 292–3
    Editing 278
    Filtering 278
    Generation **270–8**
    Interpolation from
      Topographic Samples 274
      Interpretation 270, **280–7**
      Joining 280
      Manipulation 270, **278–80**
      Merging 280
      Quality Control 285
      Visualization 270, **287–92**
    Modelling **269–97**
    Thematic Global Database *219*
    Topographic Mapping 69
      in Australia *64*
Digitizer 15, 57, 242, 243, *80*, *250*, *287*
Digitizing 46, 49, 59, 70, 113, 124, 137, 175, 185, 272, 328, 379, *43*, *90*, *110*, *188*, *203*, *207*, *222*, *250*, *324*
  Error 200, 381
  Model 185
  Spatial Data 232
  Station *317*
  Table 377, *30*
  Tablet 56, *74*
DIME 25, 27, **30**, 327, 345, *65*, *256*, *257*, *305*
Dimensionality of Spatial Data **301–4**
Dip Angle *118*
Direct
  Data
    Conversion 515
    Retranslation 518
    Translation 518
  Mail *139*, *140*, *143*, **148–9**
  Manipulation Interface 354
  Marketing *148*
  Surveying 240
  Transformation 139, **141–3**
Director General of the Military Survey 75
Directorate General of the Environment *187*
Dirichlet
  Polygon *132*
  Tessellation 28, 275, 276
Disaster Management *316*
Disclosure of Information 494
Discrete
  Feature 168
  Sampling 458
  Speech 158
Discretization 312
Disease Database 393
Disjunctive Kriging *153*, *163*
Disk
  Drive 253
  Storage 485
Disparate
  Geographical Data 192
  Information 68
Dispersion 365
Display 85
  Issues **115–16**
  of Spatial Information 429
Dispute Settlement 491
Distance
  Learning 87
  Queue 280
Distortion
  Isogram 145
  Pattern 144
Distributed
  Database 45
  GIS 480
  Spatial Database *67*
District
  Council 76
  Health Authority 68, 74
  of Columbia 26
Division of Advanced Scientific Computing 432
DMV *30*
Document
  Digitizing 325
  Image Processing 343
  Scanning 325
Domain
  Consistency Rules *210*
  Modelling 420
  Partition 313
  -Dependent Knowledge 421
  -Independent Knowledge 421
Domains of Visualization Research 432
Domesday
  Community Disk 351
  System 83, 353
  Videodisc 385
Domestic Information Display System 24
Donnelley Marketing Information Service 25
Dot
  Map *45*
  Matrix Printer *287*
  Per Inch 244
Douglas-Peucker Algorithm 246, 247
DPMAP 25
Draft Proposed Standard for Digital Cartographic Data 524

Subject index

Drainage
    Area Transform 284
    Basin Monitoring 293
    Density 283
    Enforcement Algorithm 278
DRASTIC *279, 280*
Drum Scanner 29, 244
Dual Data Storage 340
Dudley Project 27–8, 34, 111
Dutch
    National Science Foundation 97
    Soil Survey *154, 164*
        Institute 163
DXF 325, 345, 346, 523
Dynamatch 25
Dynamic
    Data 419
        Exchange 346
    Graphics *263*
        Incorporated 309
    Optimization 421
    Simulation *291*
    Stormwater Simulation Program 278
    Thresholding 244
    Vehicle Routing *247*
    Visualization 440

Earth
    Data Information Systems Conference 98
    Observation
        Satellite 47, 53, 198, 216
        System 196, *229*
    Science 293, *217*
        Data *202–3*
            Directory *15*
            Information Network *15*
    Surface Process 191
Earthwork Calculation in Site Planning 293
Easements *109*
East Africa 23, 29
Eastern Europe 98
Ecodisk 353
Ecological
    Characterization *213*
    Fallacy 184
    Interference Error 391
Ecology 59, 197
Economic
    and Social Research Council 37, 77, 81, 84, 96, 396, *66*
        Data Archive 513

Atlas of China 79
Development *57*
Geography 275
Implications of GIS in Australia **64–6**
Map Series *41, 42*
Edge
    Based Database 218
    Detection 390, 398
    Detector 397
    Matching 248, 343, 378, *194, 305*
Edifact 346
EDIS87 98
Education 45, 60, 62, 71, 76, 81, 85, 86, 87, 88, 319, 318
    and Training *325*
Effective Resolution
    Element 193
    of Sensors 193
Egypt 85
Einstein 222
ELAS *13*
Elastic Scaling 460
Electoral Ward *131*
Electricity 69
Electromagnetic
    Flux *6*
    Properties 1193
    Response *176*
    Signal 202
Electronic
    Data
        Interchange *141, 143*
        Processing *142*
    Drafting *300*
    Funds Transfer at the Point of Sales *145*
    Mail 5, *317*
    Market *148*
    Messaging 355
    Point of Sales *144, 150*
Electrostatic Plotter 50, 56, *305*
Elements of a GIS **15–16**
Elevation 168
    Database 48
    Matrix 273
    Zonation 203
EM Algorithm 385
Emergency
    Management 49, *53*
        System *53*
    Planning *8, 90, 110, 247, 250, 255*

Response 47, 104
Services *113*
    Management *90*
Employment Service 513
EMPRESS DBMS 15
Enclosure 373
End-to-End Systems Study on Surface Temperature Data *219*
Energy Assessment 75
Engineering *102, 317*
    CAD Diagram 427
    Modelling Software 305
Enhancement
    of Digital Terrain Models 278
    of the National Digital Cartographic Database *20*
Entity
    -Categorical-Relationship 408
    Construction 313
    Relationship 255
        Model 253
        Modelling 257
    Sets 253
Enumeration District 126, 385, 504, *131, 132, 133*
Environmental
    Applications of GIS *3, 201*
    Change 105, *209*
    Classification System 202
    Constraints *289*
        to Development *291*
    Control and Enforcement *90*
    Crisis 55
    Data 191, *192, 201, 202*
        Holdings *202*
    Database *3, 7, 59, 185, 186, 187, 188, 189, 192, 193, 196,* 197, 198
        and GIS **201–15**
    Dimension of GIS *6–8*
    Fly-Over 354
    Geochemistry *208*
    Impact
        Analysis 350
        Assessment *90*
        Study 282, 293
    Knowledge 410
    Law 422
    Management 356, *9, 185, 261*
    Modelling 191, 299, 356, *188, 229–30*
    Monitoring *81, 222*
    Observation 222
    Overlay *303*
    Planning 59, 293, 422, *53, 185*

Protection 22, *53*
   Agency 186, *185, 263, 278, 279, 280*
   Department *52*
   Regulation 59
   Resources Information Network *63*
   Science 84
   Survey 192
   Systems Research Institute 3, 21, 23, 24, **31–3**, 51, 52, 96, 113, 168, 328, 349, 512, *74, 75, 250, 257, 262, 314, 316, 319, 322*
Epidemiology 132
EPPL7 53
EPS 346
Epsilon
   Band 471
   Distance 382
   Filtering 464
Equal-Area Projection 377
Equivalence Relations 421
Equivalent Dimensionality 440
ERDAS 241, 344, 345, 372, *15, 263*
Erode Smoothing 470
Eroding 470
   Blanket 471, 472
   Technique 470
Erosion 197
Error 85, 165, 217, 242, 396
   and Accuracy **381–4**
   Correcting Modem 511
   Correction 278, 285
   Detection 285
   Handling 366
   Location 376
   Measurement 376
   Modelling 85, 112
   Propagation 435, *164, 229*
   Tracking 373
Errors 114
   in Representing Location 499
   in Spatial Databases 166, 167, 458
ERS-1 198
ESMAN *302*
Estimate of Population 504
Estimated Point Density Map *173*
Etak 24, 6, *115, 122, 124*
   Map Engine 24
   Navigator *116, 117, 119, 120, 121*
Euclidean 121, 301
   Dimensionality 322
   Distance 119, 120, 129, 130, 132, 438

Geometry 149, 228, 229, 232
   Representation 122
   Space 126, 231
EUROCARTO 6
European
   Commission 39, *7, 185, 187*
   Community 137, 342, 494, 513, *7, 186, 187, 188, 196, 199, 213, 225, 323, 324*
   Division of AM/FM 77
   Environment Agency *185*
   Space Agency *7*
EVA *121*
Evaluating GIS Functions 114
Evaluation of Alternative Fire Station Locations *257*
Evolution **23–6**
Exact Matching 340
Examples
   of Low-Level Spatial Data Structures **233–5**
   of Spatial Data Models **232–3**
Exchange
   Format *205*
   of Data 69
Executive
   Agency 71, 72, 513
   Information System *149*
   Office of the President *303*
Experimental
   Cartography Unit 3, 21, 23, **34–5**, 37, *24, 25*
   Variogram *160*
   Realism 152
Expert System 64, 95, 202, 419, 420, 422, 423, 446, 469, *33, 142, 143, 155, 156, 198, 228, 229, 302, 307, 318*
   Shell 418
Explanation-Based Learning 420
Exploratory
   Data Analysis 431, *228, 229, 299*
   Geographical Analysis 397
   Spatial Analysis 399
Extendible Array 215, 219
External Attribute Database 232
Exxon 308
Eye Fixation Pattern 438

Facility
   Management *298, 304, 316*
   Mapping Systems *317*
   Siting *298*
Factor Loading Plot 434

Factoring 434
Failed GIS *9*
False 3D Image *281*
Family Practitioner
   Committee 74
   Area 506
Far Eastern Research Centre 38
Fault Location *109*
FAX 346, *317*
Feasibility Analysis 61
Feature
   Association 349
   Code *29*
      Specification *29*
   Coded Vector Data *30, 35*
   Database 168
   Density 447
   Extraction 373, 435, *15*
   Generalization 343
   Overlay *15*
   Programming 373
   Recognition *324*
Features of the Variogram *159*
Federal
   Aviation Administration 500
   Geographic
      Data Committee *19*
      Exchange Format 524
   Geographical Data Committee 20
   Information Processing Standard 524, 525
   Interagency
      Committee on Digital Cartography *19*
      Coordinating Committee on Digital Cartography 524, *18*
   Republic of Germany *4*
Fédération Internationale de Géomètres 93, *87*
   Symposium on Land Information Systems 87
Ferranti *26*
FES 422
Field
   Survey 324, 338
   Tree 199
FIFE 205
Figure-Ground Relation 430
File
   Management *33*
   Reformatting 365
   Structure 518
   Transfer Protocol 510

Filter Mapping 339
Financial
    Analysis *139*, *149*
    Control *90*
    Information System *57*
Finite Computer 228, 229
Finland *129*
Fire
    Service 76
    Services Management *90*
First Order Logic 414, 416
Fish and Wildlife
    Management *261*
    Service 30
Fisheries 197
Flatbed Scanner 244
FLINT 306
Floating
    Horizon Algorithm 290
    Point Performance 215
Flood Control 59, *109*
Floodplain Management 32
Floppy Disk 5, *220*
Flow Simulation 373
Flowline 239
FMS/AC *317*
Focal
    Bearing 370
    Combination 370
    Data Transformation 370–1
    Gravitation 370
    Insularity 370
    Majority 370
    Maximum 370
    Mean 370
    Minimum 370
    Minority 370
    Neighbour 370
    Percentage 370
    Percentile 370
    Product 370
    Proximity 370
    Ranking 370
    Rating 370
    Sum 370
    Variety 370
Footpath Maintenance *90*
Footprint 168
Ford Foundation 28
Forest
    Canopy Damage 105
    Management *53*, *62*
    Resource Management 331, 332, *280–1*, *316*

Forestry 56, 59, 197, 293, 422, *261*
    Commission 35
    Management System 52
Formal Logic 413
Formalization 229
    of Spatial Concepts 230
Formatting System for Geo-referenced Data *206*
Fortran 217, 252, *29*, *271*
Fortran77 215, 452, 509
Forward
    Chaining 419
    Solution 139
Fourier Transform 278
Fourth Generation Language 216, 217, 252
Fractal **125–6**, *156*
    Behaviour 194
    Dimension 125, 283, 390, 465, 469
    Geometry 465
    Model 435
France 98, *123*, *154*, *324*
Free Duct Analysis *109*
Freedom of Information Act 494, *94*
Freight Transport Cost 321
Fujitsu *50*, *51*, *52*, *53*
Functional
    Capabilities of GIS 114
    Classification of GIS 319
    Dependency 421
    Issues **114–15**
Functionality of GIS 324–31
Fuzzy
    Analysis 398
    Classification 170
    Data Attribute 341
    Features *194*
    Geodemographic Targeting System 398
    Logic 324
    Matching 340
    Pattern Analysis 397
    Reasoning 148
    Set 122, 170
        Theory 152, *156*
    Space 122

Gamma Radioactivity *176*
Ganesa Group International 24
Gas 69
Gaussian
    Error 171

Function *159*
    Model *160*
Gazetteer 512, *60*, *107*
GCEM 400
GDS/AMS 341
GEDDEX 422
GEM 346
Genasys 52
General
    Bathymetric Chart of the Oceans *206*
    Format-3 *207*, *208*
    Geomorphometry 282
    Information Systems for Planning 34, 69
    Reference Map of Australia *60*
    Register Office 507
    Systems Model *235*
Generalization 111, 115, 292, 329, 390, 437, 457, *33*, *189*, *194*, *209*
    and Accuracy 460
    and Resolution 460–1
    and Scale 459–60
    Decision Rules 472
    in Data Quality **459–61**
    of Spatial Databases **457–74**
    of Volumetric Objects 471
    Operators 472
    Definition of **115–16**
Generalized Mapping System *305*
Generating Binary Predictor Maps *174–6*
Generic
    Scene Simulation Software *207*
    Spatial Analysis Functions **396–8**
Geo-Object 308, 309
Geo-Relational Model 339, 340–1, 356
Geo/SQL 53
GEOBASE 512
Geochemical Anomaly *171*
Geochemistry 197
Geocoding 85, 384, *49*, *121*, *135*, *304*, *305*
GEODAS *49*, *50*, *226*
Geodemographic Discriminator *144*, *149*
Geodemographics *139*
Geodesic Hierarchy 463
Geodesist 92
Geodesy 137, 138, 169, 171, 172, *60*
Geodetic Control *3*
    Coordinates 227
    Data *11*

Subject index

Position 365
Reference 169, 499
Survey 433
Geographic
  Data
    Technology Incorporated 25
  Information 167
    Steering Group 72, 76
    Systems Speciality Group 94
Geographical 12
  Analysis 103, 191, 395, 406, *144*
    Machine 399
  Concepts 152
  Correlates Exploration Machine 397
  Data 15–16, 45, 81, 196, *124*
    Handling 422, *318*
    Matrix 323
    Models **320–2**
    of Sweden *40, 41–2*
    Structures **320–2**
  Database 175, 324, 328, 342, 394, 397, 446
    Design 319, 320
  Information 68, 69, 70, 71, 73, 77, 78, 96, 167, 191, 489, 490, 529
    Analysis 405
    for Vehicle Navigation *35*
    Institution 489
    Management System Committee *303*
    Processing 269, *13*
    Retrieval and Analysis System 31, *13*
    Science *313*
    Systems in Australia **57–68**
  Intelligence 9
  Names Information *11*
  Partitions 48
  Reality 113
  Reference 14
    System 12, *249, 314*
  Relationships 113
  Sensitivity Analysis 341
  Space 113, 153, 157
  Survey Institute 38, *14, 48, 55*
Geography 22, 57, 92, 439
Geoid 137
Geoidal Reference *203*
Geoinformation *81*
Geokernal 314
Geologic Division *15*
Geological
  Interpretation 293

Map *272*
Mapping 293
  Survey of Canada *172*
Geology 50, 92, 114, 126, 139, 168, 178, 197, 293, *15*
Geomatic Hypermap 353
Geometric
  Classes 229
  Concepts 233
  Data Model 157, 230
  Error 285
  Model 207
  Object 230
  Phenomena 102
  Registration 195
  Resolution 195
  Transformation 135, 467
Geometrical
  Encoding *122*
  Generalization 466, 467, 468
  Knowledge 464
  Search 421
Geometry 84, 157
Geomorphological
  Classification 293
  Modelling 283
  Simulation 293
Geomorphology 84, 293
Geomorphometric
  Analysis 282, 286
  Mapping 203
GEONET *15*
Geophysical Data System 225
Geophysics *15*
Geoprocessing 6, 22, 292
Georeferencing 85
Geoscience 93
  Database 314
Geosciences Data Index *214*
Geoscientific
  Analysis 301
  Spatial Data 301
GEOSET 308
Geosight 24
Geostatistics 170, *154, 164*
GeoVision 52, 261, 328, *316*
Gerber 29
  Plotter 27
Germany *124, 127, 324*
Gestalt
  Approach 103
  Perceptual Task 430
  PhotoMapper *13*
GFIS 52, *314, 316, 319*

GIF 346
Gigabyte 215, 241, 509
GIMMS 36, 510, 512
GIRAS 31, 345
GIS 111, 112, 119, 121, 126, 127, 130, 139, 167, 172, 191, 217, 227, 230, 240, 248, 251, 269
  2000 *320–2*
  Acquisition 116, 477
  and Developing Nations **71–82**
  and Infrastructure **5–6**
  and Knowledge Based Techniques **420–3**
  and Land **5–6**
  and Management 85
  and Market Analysis **139–50**
  and Organizations 105–6
  and People **5–6**
  and Public Policy **233–44**
  and Utilities **101–13**
  Applications for Urban and Regional Planning Conference 75
  as a Discipline *316–17*
  Database 239, 241, 247
  Design *244*
  Education *319*
  Evaluation **477–87**
  for Policy Analysis and Monitoring **239–41**
  for Public Policy Analysis **237–8**
  Framework **137–9**
  Functionality 85, 114
  Implementation **477–87**
  in China **76–80**
  in India **76–80**
  in Island Resource Planning **285–94**
  in Japan **47–55**
  in the Utilities in the United States *112*
  in Urban Planning in San Diego County **250–9**
  in Utilities in the United Kingdom *110–12*
  Modelling 280, *294*
  News 94
  Plus 53
  Primitives 114
  Programmes in Sweden **39–46**
  Query Language 158
  Research and Education **76–7**
  Society *313*
  Sourcebook 51
  Specification **477–87**

Subject index

GIS – *cont.*
   Support for Public Policy
    Analysis *241–3*
   Terminology 86
GIS/LIS 7, 93, 94, *317*, *320*
GIST! 353
GISTutor 87
GISWorld 6, 15, 51, 56, *316*
Glasgow *260*
GLIM 127, 329, 385, 396
Global
   Analysis 428
   Area Coverage *228*
   Atmospheric Research
    Programme *219*
   Change 92, 93, *217*, *219*
    Database Project *219*
    Diskette Project *219*
    Studies *220*
   Climate Model *208*
   Databases 177, *205*, **217–30**
    in GIS *225–8*
    Systems *225–8*
   Environmental
    Change Project *5*, *47*
    Database *186*
    Monitoring System *74*, *205*, *224*
   Forcing Functions *219*
   Information System for Land
    Cover *205*
   Interdisciplinary Studies *227*
   Interpolation 279
   Modelling *223*
   Monitoring *8*
    Data Sets *218*
   Optimization 419
   Positioning
    Satellite *54*, *105*, *124*, *324*
    System 47, 169, 186, 240, 318, 324, *6*, *118*, *123*, *317*, *319*, *320*, *321*
   Programmes **218–24**
   Reference Data Sets *218*
   Resource Information Database *74*, *205*, *224*, *225*
   Scale Use 85
   Science 112
   Systems 104
   Telecommunications System *206*
   Thematic Data *217*
   Topological Database *223–4*
   Vegetation Index *209*
   Warming *127*
Goal Planning *292*

GOCAD 306
GOES 198
Goodness-of-Fit *174*, *184*
Gouraud Shading 288
Government Statistical Service 511
GPL 247
GPS World 47
GPV 346
Grained Analysis 428
Graph
   Theory 390, 421
   Theoretic Mapping 462
   Theoretic Representation 462
Graphic 46
   Communication 432
   Fudging 344
   Overlay *300*
   Survey *102*
Graphical
   Encoding of Information 431
   Interfaces 437–9
   Kernel System 300, 527
   Presentation 438
   Report Generator 409–10
Graphics
   Accelerator Chip 300
   Package 46
   Processor 300
GRASS 53, 345, 372, *15*, *314*
Graticule 136, 139
Great
   Barrier Reef Marine Park
    Authority *63*
   Lakes *278*
Greece *188*, *193*
Greenhouse Effect *186*
Greyscale
   Normalization 343
   Thinning 285
GRID 28, 32, 345, 372
   Analysis 49
   Cell *153*
   Cell Database 168
   Cell GIS 341
   Cell Tessellation 339
   Data 525
    Model 113
   Map *45*
   -on-Grid Transformation 139, **141–3**
   -to-Contour Conversion 280
   Resolution 280
   Smoothing 329
   TOPO 32

Gridded
   Database 5
   Digital Terrain Model 278, 280
Grids 25
Ground
   Landscape Photography *55*
   Survey 270, 271, 458
Groundwater Modelling *15*
Group Decision Support System *150*
Growth Rates by Sector 56
GUI 50, 52
Gyro *115*
Gyroscope *118*

H-Resolution Model 194
Halobias 470
Hard Disk 48, *50*
Hardware 85, **243–5**
   Environment for GIS 113
Harvard
   Computer Graphics Weeks 28, 33
   Laboratory for Computer Graphics 21, 23, 25, **27–8**, 31, 34
    and Spatial Analysis 3, 328
   Mapping Collection 7
   University 160, *48*
Hash Table 215, 218, 219, 224
Hashing 218, 222
Hazardous
   Vehicle Routing 331
   Waste Management *261*, **267–70**
Health and Safety
   at Work Act *111*
   Control 90
   Board 74
Heathrow Airport *123*
Helmert Transformation **141–2**
Her Majesty's
   Land Registry 67, 68, 71, **73–4**, 78, 181, *93*
   Treasury 508, *25*, *28*
Heuristic Search Procedure 201
Hextree 199
Hidden
   Element Removal 290
   Surface Removal 300
Hierarchical
   Classification 462
   Data Structure 199, 200
   Database
    Models 113
   Structure 251
   System 254, **255–6**

Dominance *292*
Land Classification 206
Matching 340
Model Structure 255
Raster Data Structures **199–200**
Sampling Pattern 272
Tessellation 463
Hierarchically Structured Database 472
High-Level
    Programming Languages 234
    Spatial Data Structure 228
Higher
    Education 86, 87
    Level Image Description 434
Highpass Filter 278
Highway
    Maintenance *90*
    Network 72
Hillshading 288
History of Visualization in GIS **428–31**
Hitachi *49, 50, 53*
    CAD-Core Tracer 246
Hitosubashi University *47*
Hokkaido Gas *51*
Holistic Approach to GIS 324
Home Office 508
Honda *14*
    Gyrocator *116*
Hong Kong 75, *76, 123*
Horn Clause Rule 416
House of
    Commons 503
    Lords Select Committee on Science and Technology 67, 68, 526, *29*
HPGL 49, 345, 346
Huffman Run-Length Encoding 245
Human
    Computer
        Interaction 115, 437, 439
        Interface 431
    Dimensions
        of Global Change Programme 55
        of Global Environmental Change Programme *63*
    Error 382
    Information Processing System 428
    Settlements Development Group *74*
    System 112
    Visual Processing 428
    System 429
Hybrid
    Data
        Model **260–1**, 341
        Storage 340
    Model 207
Hydrogeological Runoff Modelling 293
Hydrogeology 299
Hydrographer of the Navy 75
Hydrographic
    Charts *64*
    Department of the Admiralty *93*
Hydrologic Phenomena 105
Hydrological Runoff Simulation 282, 283
Hydrology 48, 50, 197, 204, 293, *15*
HyperCard 87, 352
    Tutorial 512
Hypercube 216, 219
Hyperdocument 353
Hypermapping 439
Hypermedia 355
    GIS 356
Hypertext 352, 355, 439
    Tutorial 512
Hypothesis Testing 389
Hypsometric
    Intergral 282
    Tint Display 288

I/O 215, 222
Iberian Peninsula 378
IBM 26, 29, 52, 55, 300, 328, 411, *50, 51, 53, 74, 224, 314, 316, 319, 322, 324*
    PC 223, *9, 287, 291*
    PS/2 223
    RS/6000 *319*
    -PC-MAP 372
Iceland 154
ICL 36, *28, 30*
Identification Error 171
IDMS 256
IDRISI 15, 52, 53, 124, 372, *314*
IGES 345, 346
IGU 33
IIS-MAP *54*
Illumination
    Geometry 195
    Model 288
    Vector 288
ILWIS 341
Image
    Abstraction 434
    Analysis 433, 439
    Based Information System 12
    Brightness 194
    Classification 191, 192, 470
    Correlation 435
    Description 435
    Enhancement 193
    Generation 433
    Local Variance 194
    Overlay 349
    Processing 47, 56, 59, 60, 64, 86, 240, 278, 283, 339, 340, 344, 390, 398, 435, 469, *67, 171, 172, 229, 262*
    Pyramid 194, 199
    Rectification 193
    Resolution 194
    Schema Model of Cognition 152
    Schemata 153, 310
    Segmentation 202, 204
    Sharpening 470
    Smoothing 470
    Space Algorithm 290
    Synthesis 434, 435
    Texture 194
    -to-Image Registration 343
    Understanding 435
Imaging Frequency 195
IMG 346
IMGRID 372
Implementation
    of Irregular Tessellation **234–5**
    of Regular Tessellation 233
IMSL 409
Inclined Contour 288
Inclinometer *118*
Incompatible Areal Units **384–5**
Incremental
    Data Transformation 369
    Triangulation 280
IncrementalArea 369
IncrementalAspect 369
IncrementalDrainage 369
IncrementalFrontage 369
IncrementalLength 369
IncrementalLinkage 369
IncrementalPartition 369
IncrementalVolume 369
Indeterminacy 208
Indexes 49
Indexing 87
India 74, 75, *92, 127*

Indian Ocean *64*
Indicators of Accuracy 112
Indonesia *75, 92*
Inductive Learning 420
Industrial
    Location Modelling *247*
    Screening Matrices *299*
    Site Location 293
Inertial
    Device *115*
    Navigation Sensor *118*
Inference Net *180*
INFO 260, 341
INFO-MAP 24
Information 10
    Acquisition 491
    Based Planning Strategy *247*
    Consistency 338
    Exchange *28, 230*
    Handling *41, 207*
    Infrastructure *299*
    Integration **337–56**
    Interchange 338
    Linkage 338
    Management 255, 314
    Overload 103–4
    Processing 431
    System 148, 191
        Failure 487
        Division *15*
    Technology 70, *96, 142, 150, 186, 189, 192, 324*
Informix 260, 349
    On-Line 349
Infrared 427
INGRES 259, 260, 263
INGRES(QUEL) 417
Inheritance Tree 463
Initial Graphics Exchange Specification 527
INS SPACER *54*
INSECT 307
Installation 57
Instance
    Method 263
    Variable 263
Instantaneous Field of View 192
Institut fur Angewandte Geodasie *4, 188, 195*
Institut Géographique National 517
Institute
    for Geophysics *204*
    for Land Information 95, 96
    of British Geographers 81, 96
    of Geography of the Chinese Academy of Sciences *79*
    of Physical and Chemical Research *204*
    of Space and Aeronautical Research *204*
    of Terrestrial Ecology 36, 186, *213*
Institutional
    Change *267*
    Issues 85
Instrumental Survey *32*
Intangible Benefits *244*
Integrated
    Data Model **261–2**
    Database Management System 406
    Geographical
        Analysis 192, 197
        Information System 191, 200
    Geometry 150
    Land and Watershed Management Information System *75*
    Planning Information Systems **297–308**
    Rural Development *74*
    Services Digital Network 216
    Software 81
    Spatial Database *11*
    Terrain Unit 344
    Topology 52
    Use of Data Sets *212*
Integrating
    Data *201*
    Remote Sensing and GIS **196–201**
Integration
    Model 348
    of Disparate Data Structures 200
    of Geoscientific Data ***171–81***
    of Remote Sensing and GIS 191
Integrity of Data Sets *209*
Intel 223
    /386 *74*
    /8088 *123*
Intelligence Unit 508
Intelligent
    Filtering 47
    Raster *37*
Intensity Edge 434
Inter-
    Application Communications 346
    Departmental Working Group on the Tradeable Information Initiative 74
Interactive 45
    Automatic Systems 246–7
    Computer Graphics 73
    Editing *32*
    Generalization *36*
    Hypermedia Systems **352–3**
    Processing 480
    Spatial Display 105
    Surface Modelling *263*
    Transformation 300
    Visualization 287
    Volume Modelling 309, 313
Intercellular Relationship 233
Interface Translation 160
Interfaces to GIS 104
Intergraph 24, 32, 52, 300, 305, 325
    IGDS/DMRS 261
    Microstation GIS 261
    Microstation-32 261
    TIGRIS 264
Intermediate Standard Transfer Format *108*
Internal Revenue Service 495
International
    Cartographic Association 39, 93, 523
    Centre for Recent Crustal Movements *204*
    Council
        for the Exploration of the Sea *206, 208*
        of Scientific Unions 92, *55, 219*
    Data Handling Symposia 7
    Date Line *226*
    Developments in GIS *3*
    Geographical
        Union 93, *223*
            Commission 84
            on Geographical Data Sensing and Processing 29–30
    Geophysical Year *219, 224*
    Geosphere-Biosphere Programme 92, *55, 63, 205,* **219–20**
    Gravity Bureau *206*
    Institute for Aerospace Survey and Earth Science 97
    Journal
        of Geographical Information Systems 6, *33, 58*
        of Imaging 6

Subject index

Oceanographic
   Commission *206, 206, 208*
   Data and Information
     Exchange *206*
   Organisations **92–3**
   Policy 104
   Society
     of Photogrammetry and
       Remote Sensing 93
     of Soil Science *153*
   Soil
     Reference and Information
       Center *204*
     Science Society *155*
   Standards Organisation 525,
     527
   Symposium on Computer-
     Assisted Cartography 33
   Telecommunications Union 245
   Union for Conservation of
     Nature and Natural Resources
     205
Interpolation 195, 373, 376, *4, 158,*
   175, 176, 177
   Algorithm 275
   from Contour Data 277–8
   Methods 380
   of Digital Terrain Models 274–5
Interpretation 115
   of Digital Terrain Model Quality
     Assessment 285
   of Digital Terrain Models 269
     for Engineering 286
     for Planning 286
Interpreted Map *289, 290*
Intersection 16
   Frequencies 391
Interspersion 373
Interval Data 322, 437, 439
Intervisibility 114
   Problem 286
Inverse Solution 139
Inverted List Database
   Structure 251
   System **254–5**
Invertible Model 201
Investment Appraisal 406, *9, 139,*
   149, 192
Invitation to Tender *96*
Iran *127*
Iraq *323*
Ireland 377
Irish Grid 70
IREX 309, 312

Irregular Tessellation 151, 198, 227,
   233
   Models **150–1**
Irrigation
   Studies *154*
   Water Rights *15*
IRS IA 77
Isarithm 287
Isarithmic Map 45
ISLAND *50, 51*
ISM 345
ISO-8211 78
Iso-Surface 309
Isochrone Map 129
Isogram 145
Isoline 28, 302, 304
Isomorphic Mapping 467
Isotrophic Variogram 194
Israel *128*
ISROVISION 77
ISSCO 32
ITA 67
Italy *130, 324*

Jamaica 186
   GIS 38
Janes Committee 25
Japan 67, *5, 14, 123, 124, 224, 324*
   Digital Road Map Association
     14, 123
   Industrial Standard *48*
   Meteorological Agency *204*
   Standard Grid System *48*
   Surveyors Association 97
Job Centre 504, 506
Joint Academic Network 87, 504, 510
Journal of the Urban and Regional
   Information Systems Association 6
Juridical Cadastre 85

Kantian Viewpoint 148
Kauth-Thomas Tassled Cap
   Transformation 202
Kawasaki *51*
KBGIS-II 420, 421, 422
KDB-Tree 325
Keiyo Gas *51*
Kenya 75, *224*
Key to Bucket Transformation 222
Kingston Polytechnic 77, *317*
Knowledge
   Acquisition 418
   Base 413, 415

Based
   Approach *210*
   Geographical Information
     System 201
   Management Systems 414
   Search 473
   System 264, 527, *318*
   Techniques **413–23**
     in Non-Spatial Databases
       416–18
   Organization 435
   Representation 414, 515
Knox County *112*
Knoxville Utilities Board *112, 113*
Kokusai *52*
Kriging 170, 206, *159, 164, 177*
KUMAP 49
Kuwait *323*
Kyoto University *204*

L-Resolution Model 194
Label 115
Labor Market Information 513
Laboratory
   of Resource and Environment
     Information Systems *5, 79*
Lagrange Multiplier *161*
LAIRD 66
Lambert Conformal Conical
   Projection 137, 139, 377
Lambertian Shading 288
LAMIS 28
LAMM 66
Land
   Administration System 58
   Analysis System *14*
   Characterization *213*
   Classes 111
   Classification Scheme *213*
   Cover
     Change Pilot Project *219*
     Classification *212*
     Data Set 177
     Map 180, 186
   Data System 12
   Development 365
   Evaluation *164*
     in Developed Countries *165*
     Model *164*
   Gazetteer 27
   Information 489, 490
     Management 57
     Products and Services 97

429

Subject index

Land – *cont.*
    Steering Advisory Committee 58
    System 12, 73, 94, 191, 192, 201, 239, 347, 490, *4*, *5*, *11*, *43*, *86*
        Hub *59*
        Systems 94, 95, *85–97*
        in Australia *57–68*
    Management 22, 59, 121, 205, 490, 498, *3*, *11*, *262*, *278*
        Applications of GIS *275–83*
        Information Center *277*, *280*, *281*
    Market Monitoring *90*
    Ownership 71, *6*
        Information System 332
        Modelling 331
        Records *86*, *90*
    Parcel *91*
        -Based Systems *85*, **91–3**
        Referencing *93*
    Policy Formulation 490
    Reclamation 32
    Register *45*
    Registration *4*, *85*
        Act (1988) 73, 74
        Systems 94
    Registry Records *93*
    Resource
        Information System *8*, ***261–72***
        Management *272*
    Resources Information Service *262*
    Surface
        Analysis 191
        Classification 192, 204
    Survey 83, 88
    System Mapping *209*
    Taxation *45*, *59*, *92*
    Titles Office *59*
    Titling 38, *92*
    Use 105, 126, 168, *9*
        Analysis *47*
        Code *253*
        Conflict *198*
        Data Set 177
        Decision Making *293*
        Management *90*
        Map 178, 180, 186
        Planning *298*
        Regulation 497
        Valuation *58*

Landesvermessungamt Nordrhein-Westfalen 517
Landform Analysis 283
Landmateriet *4*
Landsat 31, 47, 48, 185, 193, 195, 196, 198, 240, 523, *9*, *77*, *228*
    Multi-Spectral Scanner 135, 141, 185, *195*
    Thematic Mapper 141, 185, 194, *178*, *202*, *228*, *264*
Landscape
    Architecture 59, 299
    Depiction 429
    Design 301
    Ecological Planning 75
    Planning 102, 339
LANDSEARCH *60*
Landtrac 24
Language 147
    Primitives 153
    Representation 423
    Universals 153
Languages of Spatial Relations 95
Lanzhou Institute for Glaciology and Geocryology *204*
Laplacian Filter 470
Large-Scale Databases *33*
Laser
    Altimetry 270, *223*
    Disk 215
    Printer 511
Laser-Scan 345
    VTRAK 246
Latin American Demographic Centre 75
Latitude 377, *202*, *203*, *225*, *228*
Lattice 320, 345
Laura Ashley *144*, *147*
Layer 48, *104*
    Concept 150
    Orientation 364
    Resolution 364
Leaf Area Index 204
Leakage Survey *109*
Least-Squares
    Estimation 172
    Fitting 248
Lecture Course 87
Legal
    Aspects of GIS **489–501**
    Cadastre *85*
    Implications *85*
    Liability *106*

Lempel-Zif and Welch Compression 245
Less Developed Countries *89*, *92*
Li-Strahler Geometric-Optical Canopy Model 207
Liability
    for Data and Information 496
    for Misuse of Information 498
Licensed Cadastral Surveyor *93*
Light List 500
Limitations of Spatial Analysis 394–5
Line 85, 102, 328
    Attribute 383
    Continuity 436
    Digitizing 365
    Enhancement 126
    Following 272, *31*
        Algorithms 436
    Generalization 126, 200, 272, 468
    Intersection 436
    -of-Sight 75, 365
    Printer 23, 50, 511
    Segment 125
    Smoothing 329
    Snapping 344
    Symbolization 290
Lineament Interpretation *179*
Linear
    Cartogram 129
    Conformal Transformation 141
    Feature Name Placement 448
    Generalization *195*
    Interpolation 271, 277, 278
        within Triangles 275
    Planning 292
    Programming 446
    Quadtree 230, 233, *172*
Linguistics 152
Link
    Length 285
    Magnitude 285
Link/Node 29
Linkages 113
Linking
    Environmental Data Sets *207–9*
    of Data 69, 70
Literature 5
Live-Link 241
Liveware 15
LOBSTER 422
Local
    Authorities Management Services and Computer Committee 89

Subject index

Authority 72, 73
    Management Information System 36
    Data Transformation 367–8
    Government 67, 71, **76**, 104, 116, 8
LocalArcCosine 367
LocalArcSine 367
LocalArcTangent 367
LocalCombination 367
LocalCosine 368
LocalDifference 368
LocalMajority 368
LocalMaximum 368
LocalMean 368
LocalMinimum 368
LocalMinority 368
LocalProduct 368
LocalRating 368
LocalRatio 368
LocalRoot 368
LocalSine 368
LocalSum 368
LocalTangent 368
LocalVariety 368
Local Area
    Coverage *228*
    Network 216, 244, *228*
Locating Waste Disposal Sites *250*
Location 92
    Allocation Modelling 329, 390
    Code 348
Locational
    Accuracy 459
    Analytic Work 389
    Attribute *286*
    Coordinates 125
    Data 183, 341, 408
    Information 119
    Reference 348
    Referencing 71, 122, *206*
    System 70, *203*
    Specificity *286*
Log Odd *173*
Logic
    Based
        Database 421
        System 418
    Program 418
    Programming 217, 416, 418, 422
Logical
    Consistency **171–2**
    Data Model 516
    Database Design 252–3, 254

Intersection 419
    Programming 417
Logit *173*
London Underground 438
Long Term Ecological Research 205
Longevity of Databases *206*
Longitude *377, 202, 203, 225, 228*
Lookup Table 341, *173*
Loose Coupling 418, 419
LORAN-C *118, 124*
Loss of Information 113
Lotus 1–2–3 *322*
Lotus PIC 346
Low-Level
    Data Structure 215, **217–20**
    Spatial Data Structure 228, 229–30, 233
Lowland Flooding 102
Lowpass Filter 278
Lynx Incorporated 309

MacArthur Foundation *294*
MacGIS 372
Machine Vision 435–6, *229*
Macintosh 52, 53, 87, 431, *317*
Macro 59
Magnetic
    Resonance Scanning Imagery 427
    Susceptibility *176*
    Tape 46, 48, 216, 527, *13, 25, 29, 30, 54, 226*
    Drive *228*
MAGSAT *222*
    Anomaly Map *222*
Mailing Target Group *149*
Mainframe 49, 50, 52, 57, 58, 63, 215, 216, 328, 503, *9, 49, 50, 51, 81, 107, 113, 314, 317*
Major Statistical Area *249, 253*
MAL *49*
Malaysia 75
Management
    Applications of GIS *3*
    Information *101*
        System 11, 36, 406, *142, 324, 325*
    of Environmental Data *201*
    of GIS Acquisition **486–7**
    of Information *192*
    of Large-scale Databases 96
    Problems 116
    using GIS *8*

Managing Land Information Systems **94–7**
Manchester *34*
Manhattan
    Distance 121, 122, 129, 231
    Metric 121
    Space 126
Manifold 233
Manipulation of Digital Terrain Models 269
Manpower Services Commission 508
Manual
    Data Capture 245
    Digitizing 480
    Map Analysis *294*
    Stereoplotter 271
Many-to-Many
    Mapping 253
    Relationship 256, 257
MAP 51, 53, 168, 372
Map
    Accuracy **179–80**
    Assessment 203
    Algebra 149, 330, 361, 365
    Analysis *286,* **287–92**, *293*
        Package 75
    Animation 430
    Attribute Data 251
    Audience 177
    Conflation 343, 344
    Coverage **178–9**
    Data 527
    Design 427, 437, 439
    Display *115*
    Distortion 144
    Drawing 366
    Function 467
    Generalization 423
    Integration *172*
    Interpretation 432
    Layer Zones 367
    Layers 364
    Matching 116, *119–20, 122*
        Algorithm *119, 122, 123*
    Overlay 111, 217
    and Statistical System *13, 226*
    Processing 13, 330, *285*
        Model *325*
    Projection 85, 88, 112, 135, 137, 138, 344, 452
        Knowledge-Based System 145
        Standardization 343
    Reproduction 102
    Retrieval *122–3*

Map – *cont.*
   Revision Cycle *12*
   Structure *285*
   Theme 467
   Transformation 119
   Update 191
   View of GIS 13
Map-ematics *286*, *293*
Map-Oriented Vector Structure 200
MAP/INFO 24, 53, *319*
MAP2 372
MapBox 373
MAPEX 423
MAPICS 512
MAPII 372
MAPMASTER 24
MAPOI 25
Mapping
   Awareness 6, *316*
   Science *12*
      Committee of the National Academy of Science *19*
   Soil Properties *7*
   Tools *6*
MAPS 114, 372, 422
   as Data **285–6**
Marine
   Atlas Project *214*
   Data *203*
   Information
      Advisory Centre *208*
      Service *206*
      System *214*
   Navigation *6*, *116*
MARK II *16*, *17*, *18*, *20*
Market
   Analysis **140–2**, *143*, *145*
      Information System 12
   Research 53, 59, *316*
   Survey *144*
   Share 56, *145*
Marketing Information System *139*, *140*, **143–5**
Markov Techniques 313
Markovian Model
   of Cycling 313
   of Succession 313
Mars *223*
Marsden Square *203*
Maryland 30
   Automatic Geographic Information 32

Master
   Geographical Referencing Area *249*, *250*, *256*, *257*
   Survey Drawing *31*, *32*, *37*
Masters Plotter *26*
Matchmaker 25
Mathematical
   Analysis 390
   Primitive 307
   Spline *29*
Mathematics 22
Matrix 75, 320
Max Metric 231
Maxi Marketing *143*, *144*
Maximum Likelihood 202, 470
Maxwell Communications Group 513
Mazda *123*
MDBS Associates 408
MDBS III 256, 408
Mean Slope 285
Measurement
   Error 381
   Topology 323
Measures of Spatial Proximity **130–2**
Medicine 92
Megabyte *319*
Megapel 49
Memory 57
   Caching 262
Mensuration 76
Mental
   Map 438
   Model 437
Menu Handler 252
Mercator 140
Merchants Association *287*
Merge Rules *210*
Meta-Information *214*
Metadata 420, 421, *226*
Meteorological
   Agency *52*
   Data 105
   Space-Time Data 290
Meteorology 92, 275, 293, 299, *202*
Method
   of Agreement 420
   of Concomitant Variation 420
   of Difference 420
   of Residues 420
Methods for Counting People **128–9**
Metric
   Representation 459
   Space **120–2**, 231
Metropolitan Map Series *133*, *134*

Mexico *224*
   City *260*
MIADS 345
Micad 93
Michigan
   State University 75
   Terminal System 509, 510
Micro-Analytical Technology 398
Microcomputer 399, *15*, *49*, *74*, *75*, *149*
Migration 504, 516
Military
   Application of Digital Terrain Models 293
   Intelligence 22
   Tactics 22
Mineral Exploration *281*
Minerals 59
   Management 495, *90*
Minicomputer 52, 57, 58, 63, 69, 215, 216, *15*, *66*, *321*
Minimal Tension Interpolation 309
Minimum
   Change in Angularity 460
   Distance to Means 470
   Interpolation Error *161*
   Variance *161*
   Vector Displacement 460
Mining 59, 87, 299
Ministry
   of Agriculture 67
      Forestry and Fishery *48*, *52*
   of Construction *49*, *51*, *53*, *54*
   of Defence 67, 74, *36*, *78*, *195*
   of Education *49*, *52*, *55*, *204*
   of Home Affairs *53*
   of International Trade and Industry *48*, *51*
   of Posts and Telecommunications *204*
   of the Environment 67
   of the Treasury *48*
   of Transport 67
   of Transportation *52*
MINITAB 13, 127, 128, 329
Minnesota 30, *8*, *9*
   Department of Natural Resources *282*
   Forest Inventory *281*
   Geological Survey *281*
   GIS 275
   Land Management Information System 31
   Pollution Control Agency 277, *280*

Subject index

MIPS 49, 57, 215
Misclassification Matrices 181
Misregistration 203
Missing Data Problem 380
Mississippi River *278*
Misuse of Data and Information 501
Model
    204 Database *133*
    Articulation 253
    Base Management System 408–9
    Construction 272
    Curricula 81
    Development in 3D **310–15**
    for GIS Acquisition **477–86**
    Generalization 458
    of Urban Structure 435
Modelling 27, 55, 312, *7*
Models 103
    of Data Interrelationship 253
    of Spatio-Temporal Domains 413
Modifiable Areal Unit Problem 170, 184, 391, *130*
Modified Mercalli Intensity Scale *268*
Modula 215
Modular Course 87
MONARCH 308
Monitoring Energy Use *90*
Monotonic Curvature 448
Monte Carlo
    Method 400, 401
    Significance Test 392, 399
    Simulation 384
Morphism 157
Morton
    Order 308, *314*, *325*
MOS/LOS 198
Mosaic Surface 168
MOSS 345, 372, 422
Motion 434
Motivations for Generalization **458–9**
Mount St Helens 105
MS-DOS 49, 52, 53, *314*
MULATM *66*
Multi
    -Image Mosaic 343
    -Resolution Imagery 194
    -Scale Database 398
    -Sensor Imagery 240
    -State
        Categorical Map *175*
        Distance Map *175*
        Ordinal-scale Map *176*
    -Surface Modelling *271*

    -Temporal
        Analysis 195
        Imagery 196, 240
    -Thematic Environmental Data 225
    -User Data Access 262
Multidimensional 46
    Data 129, 429, 440
Multidisciplinary Database *217*
Multimedia 47, 55, 115, *320*
    Databases **348–52**
    GIS 323, 351, 356, *52*, *317*
Multinational
    Database *196*
    GIS Collaboration *3*
Multiple
    Instruction Multiple Data 216
    Representations 95
    Testing 399
    Valued Attribute 522, 523
Multipurpose
    Cadastre 86, *304*
    Geographical Database *303*
Multiscale Line Tree 472
Multisensory
    Feedback 354
    GIS 356
    Simulation 354
Multispectral Scanner 193, *80*, *202*
Multiuser 45
Multivariable Signature *172*
Multivariate 102
    Analysis 391
    Classification of Landforms 283
    Spatial Database 222
    Statistical Analysis *172*, *180*
Munsell *157*
Murray-Darling Basin Commission *63*
MVS 58

Nadir 193
NAG 409
NAGIS News 98
Nagoya *48*
    University *204*
Name Placement 423
    Freedom 447
NAPLPS 346
Narrowness 373
NASA 186, *7*, *204*, *223*, *229*, *303*
    Earth System Science Programme *220*
Natal/KwaZulu Association for Geographic Information Systems 98

National
    Academy of Sciences *204*, *220*
    Agricultural Information System *79*, *81*
    Atlas of Sweden *39*, *41*, *42–3*
    Bureau of Surveying and Mapping, Beijing 98
    Cartographic Information Center 186
    Center
        for Geographic Information and Analysis 4, 7, 33, 55, 81, 84, 95, 96, 99, 111, 381, 396, *66*, *302*, *315*, *319*
            Core Curriculum 84, 86, 111
        for Health Statistics *16*
    Climate Data Center *206*
    Committee on Digital Cartographic Data Standards 94
    Computer Graphics Association 93
    Council of Science and Technology 55
    Court Administration *43*
    Decision Systems 24
    Developments
        in GIS *3*
        in Official Mapping and GIS *3–5*
    Digital Cartographic Database *11*, *12*, *13*, *14*, *16*, *18*, *20*, *21*
    Estuary Program *263*
    Forest Inventory *63*
    Gazetteer Pilot Study 35
    GEO-DATA System *20*
    Geodetic Vertical Datum of the United States *202*
    Geophysical Data Center *204*, *222*, *225*
    Grid 37, 68, 69, 70, *29*, *36*, *104*, *131*, *132*, *213*
        Data *48*
    Health
        Service 67, **74–5**, 513
            Family Practitioners Areas 504
        Statistics Database *16*
        Survey 71
    Informatics Centre 77
    Institute for Polar Research *204*
    Joint Utilities Group 69, 70, 248, *28*, *30*, *31*, *105*, *111*

Subject index

National – cont.
  Land
    Agency 48, 50
    Survey 4, 39, 40, 41, 42, 43, 46
  Mapping 59
    Agencies 3
    Division 524, 12, 15, 16, 18, 20
    Program 11, 12, 16, 17, 18, 21
  Meteorological Center 205
  Museum of Cartography 5, 47, 55
  Oceanographic
    and Information Centre 205
    Data Centres 206
  On-Line Manpower Information System 116, **503–13**
  Organizations **93–8**
  Park Management 62
  Parks 38
  Partition File 135
  Police Agency 52, 54
  Property Line Base 42
  Resources Information 63
  Rivers Authority 111
  Science Foundation 84, 95, 96, 111, 432, 66
  Society for Professional Surveyors 94
  Strategy for Land Information Management 61, 62
  Surveys Coordinating Committee 78
  Tax Board 45
  Topographic Database 23, 29
  Transfer
    Format 77, 78, 325, 346, 526, 527, 30, 108, 318
    Standards 77
  Water
    Summary 15
    Well Association 279
  Well Record Collection 209
  Wetland Inventory 186
  Wilderness Inventory 63
  Workshop on Natural Resources Data Management 62
NATMAP 5
NATO 376, 196
Natural
  Environment Research Council 34, 37, 77, 206, 214
    Unit for Thematic Information Systems 34
  Language 112, 264, 420, 422, 229

Resource
  Data 185
  Management 163
    Information System 12
Resources
  Advisory Committee 34
  Data Management System 77
  Information System 77
  Management 63, 64
Nature
  Conservation 62, 198
  of GIS 3
  of Planning **297–9**
  of Space 112
  of Spatial Data 85, **112**, 167
Nautical Chart 168
Navigation 75, 112, 6, 117
Navigator 115
Navy Hydrographic Service 64
NCMM 198
Nearest Neighbour 231, 330, 390
NEC 50
Nederlands Expertise Centruum voor Ruimtelijke Informatiererwerkig 7, 97
Negligence 497–8
Neighbourhood 232
  Query 227
  Weighted Kernel 470
Netherlands, The 123, 153, 154, 164
Network 58, 322
  Analysis 329, 390, 108, 304
  Communication 320
  Configuration 371
  Data 391, 261
  Database 113, 251, 254, **256–7**
  Routing 329, 250
  Topology 285
Neutral Exchange
  File Structure 518
  Structure 516
New
  Brunswick 178
  Directions in GIS 85
  Haven Census Use Study 25, 27, 30
  York 30
NICNET 77
NIMBUS-7 198
Nippon Telephone and Telegram 51, 52, 53, 54
Nissan 14, 115
  Cedric 115, 116, 117, 119, 120
Nitrate Leaching 155

NOAA 186, 193, 196, 198, 7, 202, 204, 206, 209, 220, 222, 223, 225, 226, 227, 287
Node 257, 306, 27
Nominal
  Data 322, 437, 439
  Record Linkage 343
Non
  -Deterministic Polynomial Time 222
  -Geometric Classes 229
  -Linear Bidimensional Regression 430
  -Metric Spaces **122–4**
  -Satellite Remote Sensing 192
  -Spatial
    Analytical Model 409
    Database Application 419
  -Statistical Interpolation 164
  -Transitional Variogram 159
    Model 160
  -Uniform Rational B-Spline 305, 309
  -Weighted Kernel 470
Normal Forms in a Database 258
North
  Carolina 8
    Administrative Code 267
    Center for Geographic Information and Analysis 8, 261, 262, 267, 269, 272
    General Statutes 267
    Hazardous Waste Management Commission 267, 269
    Sea Grant College Program 264
  Central Soil Conservation Research Laboratory 279
  East London Polytechnic 317
  WesternTechnical Institute 28
    University 28
Northern Ireland Land Registry 73
Norway 129, 153, 224
Nottingham 145, 148
Nuggett Variance 160
Numerical
  Algorithm Group 216
  Categorization 470
  Raster Generalization 470
  Transformation **143–4**
Nyquist
  Frequency 195
  Limit 193

Subject index

Oakland Planning Information
   System 30
Object
   Concept 150
   Generalization 458
   Geometry 193
   Localization 434
   Orientation 120, 324, 417
   Recognition 434
   Rendering 290
Object-Oriented 85, 323, 418, 462, 472
   Database 113, 127, 418, 462, *110*
      Design 328
      Management System **263–4**, 355
   Programming 373, 398, 462, 463
   System **103**, 463
Objective Knowledge 371
Observatoire de Paris *204*
Ocean Surface Monitoring 196
Oceanography 50, 114, 197
Octree 124, 308, 310, 325
ODA 346, *73*
ODYSSEY 24, 28, 32, 328
OECD 495, *73*
Office
   Document Architecture 355
   of Management and Budget 524, *17*, *18*, *19*
   of Population Censuses and Surveys 67–8, 507, 508
Official Development Assistance *72*
Ohio State University 524
Oil Exploration 299
Oman *76*
OMB/Whitehouse 24
On-Line
   Grid Control *109*
   Transformation 344
One-to-Many
   Mapping 253
   Relationship 256, 257
ONKA 66
Open
   -Cast Mining 271, 293
   Data Format *108*
   System 57
Operating
   System 216, *318*
   Considerations 85
Operational
   Data *276*
   Geographer, The 84
   Issues **116–17**

Navigation Chart *188*, *223*
   Planning *276*
Optical
   Character Reader 325
   Disk 106, 215, 352, *15*
   Line Following 244
   Speed Sensor *118*
   Storage 245
Optimal
   Interpolation *158–63*
   Location 121
   Spatial Interpolation *7*
Optimization Model *292*
Optimizing Sampling Networks *154*
ORACLE 216, 259, 260
Orbital
   Inclination 195
   Orientation 195
Order 230
   Relation 230
   Data 376
Ordinal Data 322, 437, 439
Ordnance Survey 27, **34–5**, 67, 68, 69, 70, **72–3**, 77, 78, 124, 127, 138, 186, 241, 248, 262, 512, 513, 526, *3*, *4*, *13*, *23*, *93*, *105*, *111*, *123*, *131*, *132*
   Data *29–30*, *31*
   Database Project *33–4*
   Digital Map Stock 70
   Digitizing Methods *31*
   Feature Coding *30*
   Map Revision *31–2*
   National Grid 377
   of Northern Ireland **73**, *23*
      Topographic Database 73
   of the Republic of Ireland *23*
   Review 36, 67, 68, *28*
   Topographic Database 36
   Transfer Format *29*, *30*
Oregon 30
Origins of Land Information Systems *85–7*
Orthogonal Coordinate Axes 377
Orthographic Display Techniques 287
Orthophoto 182, 183, 288, 290, *12*
   Mapping *41*
   Production 293
Orthophotoquad *18*
OS (1988) 70
OS/2 49, 52
Osaka *48*
   Gas *51*
   Metropolitan University *49*
OSBASE *35*

OSCAR 35, *123*
OSLAND *35*
OSU-MAP 372
Overground Networks *103*
Overlap 330
Overlay 57, 114, 324, 341, 389, *213*, *265*
   Digitizing 245–6
   Mapping 102
Oversampling of Contours 272
Ownership and Tenure System *89*
Oxford System of Automated Cartography 23, 34
Ozone Hole *186*

Pacific Ocean *64*
PackBits 245
Packet Switching Stream 504
Painter's Algorithm 290
Pair-wise Test *174*
PAMAP *316*
PANACEA 372
PANDA 422
Paper Maps *4*
Papua New Guinea *64*
Paradigm 47
Parallel
   Processing 207, 216, 240, *321*
   Programming 410
   Recognition 473
Parameterization 91, 92, 314
Parcel-Based Land Information Systems *62*
Parent-Child Linkage 256
Parliamentary Constituency 506
Parochialism 65
ParrallelPiping 470
Partial 230
   Order 230
Pascal 252
PASCO *52*
Passkey 510
PATHFINDER *120*
Pathfinding *115*, *122*
   Algorithm *121*
Pattern
   Detection 399
   Generation 459
   Recognition 45, 435, 439, 469
   Spotter 397
   Tester 397
PC 52, 57, 58, 63, 215, 216, 244, *15*, *35*, *52*, *53*, *74*, *77*, *156*, *172*, *177*, *180*, *220*, *293*, *314*, *317*, *322*

Subject index

PC – cont.
    ARC/INFO 24
    GIS 53
PC-Atlas 43
PC-Based GIS *132*
PC-DBMS 261
PC-MAP 24
PCMAPICS 512
PCX 346
PDES 346
Peano
    Curve 463
    Relation 463
    Tuple Algebra 463
Peanokey 463
Pedology 197
Pen Plotter 439
Pennsylvania State University *74*
Perceived Spatial Variation 195
Perception 428
Performance
    Evaluation *141*
    Monitoring 218
Periodicals 6
Perspective 300
    Block Diagram 290
    Display Techniques 290
    Transformation 290
Pesticide Distribution *155*
Phantom Line 235
Phenomenon Fluctuation 381
Phenomenal Generalization 473, 474
Phillips CARIN *117*
Philosophy 152
Phong Shading 288
Photo-Essays 106
Photo-Journalism 106
Photogrammetric
    Data 275, 278
        Capture 270, 271, 293
    Digitizing *26*
    Engineering and Remote Sensing 6, 22, 94
    Sampling Techniques 271
    Survey 308, 312
Photogrammetry 47, 56, 59, 60, 138, 142, 168, 169, 171, 172, 338, 345, *12, 31, 32, 41, 317*
Photographic
    Archiving 429
    Imagery 378
    Reduction *32*
Photography 433
Photoimage Map *11*

Photointerpretation 56, 59
Photomultiplyer Tube 244
Photorealistic Scene Rendering 292
Physical
    Data Model 516
    Database Design 252–3
    Model 206
    Modelling 191, 192
    Realization 217
    System 112
Physics 93, 275
Picture Cells 232
Pilot
    Application 64
    Studies 62, *96*
Pinpoint Analysis Limited 37, 124
PIOS 345
Pipe Utilities *102*
Pivot Number 221
Pixel 49, 51, 124, 135, 193, 194, 197, 199, 201, 202, 203, 204, 207, 234, 320, 434
    Magazine *53*
    Radiance Value 203
    Re-classification *213*
Placement 449
    of Line-Feature Names **451–2**
    of Point-Feature Names **450–1**
Plan
    d'Occupation du Sol *297*
    Development *234*
Planar
    Enforcement 52, 324
    Graph 217
PLANES 28
PLANET *51*, *52*
Planimetric
    Data 269
    Footprint 362
    Information *41*
    Map *113*
Planimetrically Rectified Locational Data 185
Planimetry *113*
Planner 92, 104
Planning 84, 119, 197, 286, 293, *8, 57*
    Commission of the Government of India 77
    Control 76
    Database *303*
    Information
        Overlay System 32
        System 12, ***299–302***

    Models 294
    Tools 391
Planogram *145*
Plotter 15, 56, 511, *80, 110, 250*
pMAP 124, 130, 372, *287, 291*
Point 85, 102, 328
    Pollution 104
    Referencing of Areal Data *39*
    Spread Function 192
    Variogram 194
Point-Feature Placement Triangle 450
Point-in-Polygon 128, 172, 422, *158*
Point-Mode Digitizing 435
Poisson 397, 399, 400, 401
Polar Coordinates 135, 136
Polarization 194
Polarizing Filter 50
Police Management *90*
Policy
    Analysis *8, 238*
    Evaluation *242*
    Formulation *262*
Political
    Districting *298*
    Geography 84
    Geography Quarterly *314*
Politicians 105
Poll Tax 76
Pollution 97, 197, *9, 109*
    Control 76, *90*
    Dispersion Model 293
Polychlorinated Biphenyl *268*
Polygon 111, 115, 124, 125, 138, 169, 172, 199, 200, 217, 218, 219, 233, 247, 263, 269, 308, 328, 377, 382, 383, 468, *7, 30, 32, 34, 35, 36, 48, 153, 157, 158, 172, 202, 209, 210, 222, 250*
    Attribute *34*
    Based Database 218
    Closure 436
    Creation 378
    Data Layer *269*
    Filtering 469
    Intersection and Overlay System 24
    Lumped Average *164*
    Merging 464
    Network *164*
    Object 264, *34*
    Overlay 126, 128, 149, 169, 170, 172, 181, 231, 322, 339, 422, *13, 209, 261, 262*
Polygonization 300

Polyhedral Rendering *319*
Polyline 305
Polynomial
    Transformation 139
    Trend *159*
        Surface 391
Polytree 308
POLYVRT 327
Population
    Atlas of China *79*
    Cartogram 132
    Characteristics 322
    Density 168
    Forecasting *90*
    Register *128*, *129–31*, *135*
    Shift 255
Portable
    Field Computer *154*
    Interactive Editing System *32*
Position Determination **117–21**
Positional
    Accuracy **169–70**
    Completeness *195*
    Data 135
    Error 440
Post
    Census Data Processing 133
    Code 69, 70, 506, *132*, *133*
    Office 71
Posterior
    Logit *173*
    Probability *173*, *174*, *181*
POSTGRES 263, 417, 419, 421
Postscript 346
Potential and Needs, Investments and Capabilities Audit *140*
Practical Class 87
Pre-Census
    Data Processing *133*
    Planning *129*
Pre-Journey Route Planning *35*
Predicate Calculus 417, 422
Prediction 119
Preference Weighting Sub-Model *291*
Prescriptive
    Cartographic Modelling Techniques 371–2
    Map *290*
    Mapping *285*
Presentation Graphics *324*
Price Waterhouse *321*
Primary
    Data Capture **240–1**

Map *289*, *290*
Mapping Economic Analysis Study *18*
Prime 52
    SYSTEM/9 262
Prime/Wild 320
Primitive
    Entities 373
    Instancing 307, 326
Primitives 12
Primos 52
Principles
    of Graphic Design 432
    of Map Design 115
Prior Probability *174*
Private Values 493
Probability
    Density Function 202, *174*
    Map *174*
Problem
    Clarification *234*
    Sensing *234*
    Translation 231
Procedural
    Data Types 417
    Knowledge 464
    Tools for Generalization of Spatial Databases **464–8**
Procedures for Detecting Patterns and Relationships **399–400**
Proceedings of the International Spatial Data Handling Symposia 58
    Workshop on Geographical Information Systems *79*
Process Knowledge 393
Processor 85
Product Data Exchange Specification 527, 529
Production
    GIS 86
    System Language 418
    Systems 86
Profit Impact or Market Strategy *143*
Programmers Hierarchical Integrated Graphics System 300, 527
Programming Language Interface 252
Progressive Sampling 271, 272
Project
    Data 276
    Management 85, 87
    Planning *276*
    Vasundharsa 77

Projection
    Conversion *189*
    Error 220
Projective Land Use Model *248*, *249*
PROLOG 418, 422
Properties 103
    of a Polygon 217
Property
    Database 350
    Development 76
    Gazetteer *27*
    Information System 12
    Investment 76
    Management *54*
    Ownership 22
    Rights 492
    Tax Database *50*
    Taxation 53
PROSPECTOR 422
Protectionism 65
Prototyping 152, *185*, *189*
Proximal 28
    Polygon *132*
Proximity 330, 440
    Analysis 329
    Beacon Detection *117*
Proxy Data 395
Psi-s Plot 465
Psychologist 104
Psychology 152
Public
    Decision Making *243*
    Facilities
        Model 256
        Modelling 256–7
        Planning 248
    Health 76
    Policy
        Analysis *233*, *234*, *235*, *242*
            Paradigm *234–5*
        Decision Making *233*
        Support System *238*
    Protection 76
    Utilities Street Works Act *88*, *111*
    Values 493
Publishing 60
Punch Card 23
PURSIS *80*
Pycnophylactic Interpolation 385
Pyroclastic Surge *212*
Pythagoras 120
Pythagorean Distance 130, 231

Subject index

Q-Net 65
Quadrangle 136
Quadrat Analysis 390
Quadtree 124, 149, 199, 200, 201, 230, 233, 234, 261, 308, 325, 328, 463, *174, 175, 314*
    Map *176, 177*
Qualitative
    Benchmark 484
    Uncertainty 181
Quality
    Assurance 85, *320*
    Control 116, *223, 225, 320*
        Procedure *29*
    of Generalization 468
Quantification
    in Human Geography *47*
    of Attributes *238*
    of Goals *238*
    of Objectives *238*
    of Specific Targets *238*
Quantitative
    Analysis 88, 287, 390, *223*
        of Digital Terrain Data 282
    Benchmark 484, 485
    Geography 81, 88, 173, 389, 390, 393
    Land Evaluation 97
    Methods 88, 173, *319*
        Study Group 81
    Model *212*
    Revolution 87, 88, 91, 429, 439
    Visualization 287
Quantization 192
Quaternary Triangulation Mesh 463
Quebec *179*
Queensland
    Centre for Surveying and Mapping Studies 67
    Department of Geographic Information 67
    University 67
QUEL* 417
Query 147, 389
    Function 405
    Language 228, 252, 417, *96*
    Optimization 420, 421
Querying Geographical Variation 112

R-Tree 199, 233
Radar 324
    Altimetry 270
    Interferometry *223*
RADARSAT 198
Radial Distance *250*
Radiance 191
Radiation 193, 197
Radio Location *115, 117*
    Signal *119*
Radiometer 204
Radiometric
    Calibration 195
    Precision 199
    Rectification 202
    Resolution 192
RAM 49, *117, 122, 319*
Rand McNally 24
Rand-Map 24
Random Error 166
Randomization 221
Randomized Algorithm 215, 221
Rangeland Management *164*
Ranked Data 376
RAPID *59*
Rapid Prototyping 215, 223–4
Raster 13, 21, 50, 51, 52, 53, 56, 75, 85, 92, 111, 114, 124, 130, 135, 136, 149, 155, 196, 198, 199, 200, 201, 230, 233, 239, 240, 244, 245, 246, 247, 248, 269, 290, 293, 299, 302, 304, 308, 309, 310, 312, 321, 325, 328, 329, 338, 348, 364, 385, 413, 422, 452, 457, 479, *15, 30, 37, 42, 77, 81, 157, 161, 172, 192, 206, 207, 212, 213, 218, 222, 262, 278, 306, 314, 315, 318*
    -based GIS 85
    Contouring 288
    Data 525, 527
    Model 343
    Storage 85
    Structures 200
    Database 330
    Generalization 470
    Handling 345
    Model 320, 516
    Overlay *164*
    Remote Sensing System 191, 324
    Scanning 272, 325, *16, 52, 203*
    Space 461
    Spatial Structuring 310
    -to-Vector Conversion 246, 247, *228, 314*
    -Vector
        Contrasts 85
        Dichotomy 325
        Restructuring 329

Rasters 232, 234
Rating Matrix 465
Ratio Data 322
Rational Planning Model *237–8*
Ray Tracing 288, 292
Rayner Review 511
Re-Triangulation 280
Real
    Estate 59
    Property Register *45*
Reality 433
Realization in a Computing Environment 85
Rebotics 439
Recent Ordnance Survey Developments **33–6**
Reclassification 343
Recording Utility Plant *105–6*
Recreation 59
Recreational Planning 32
Rectangular Grid 273
Rectification 343
Recursive Query 416
REDATAM 75
Reduced Instruction Chip Set 299
Redundancy *172*
    in Data 253
Reference Systems **376–8**
Referential Integrity Constraints 419
Reflectance 168
Reflected Radiance of a Surface 194
Refuse Collection 76
Region *131*
    Growing 185
    Re-classification *213*
Regional
    Analysis 192
    Board of Forestry *43*
    Database Systems *225*
    Geographical Information Systems Project 65
    Growth Forecasting *248, 253*
    Health Authority 68, 74, 75
    Information System *259*
    Land Survey *43*
    Planning 22, 59
    Research Laboratory 7, 77, 81, 84, 96, 396, *66, 315*
    Urban Information System *257*
Regionalization 314, 390
Regionalized
    Variable Theory *159–63*
    Variables *159*

Subject index

Register
   of Population 39
   of Property 39
Registered Overlay System 499
Registers of Scotland 93
Registration Error *220*
Registry of Deeds 159
Regression 380, 434, *177*
   Analysis 205, *278*
   Score Map *177*
   Tree Analysis 205
Regular
   Sampling 271
   Tessellation **149–50**, 198, 227, 232–3
Regularization 193, 194
Regulation of Behaviour 491
Relational
   Algebra 257
   Base 419
   Based System 418
   Calculus 416
   Data
      Management Techniques 373
      Model 229
   Database 251, 416, *33*, *158*
      Management System 201, *314*
      System 254, **257–9**
   Geographical Information System 200
   Joins in a Database 258
   Matching *300*
Relationship
   Prover 397
   Seeker 397
Relative
   Accuracy 166
   Nonpoint Source Pollution Potential Study *278*
   Sensor *119*
Relief
   Contour 288
   Shading 371
   Shadow Analysis 286
Remote
   Scanning System 191
   Sensing 6, 12, 22, 47, 53, 56, 83, 84, 92, 101, 112, 124, 168, 170, 185, **191–208**, 192, 239, 240, 271, 290, 293, 329, 338, 353, 432, 434, 436, 439, 470, *28*, *43*, *57*, *60*, *63*, *74*, *77*, *78*, *155*, *157*, *171*, *172*, *186*, *196*, *198*, *207*, *218*, *227*, *281*, *306*, *317*

   as a Resource of Geographical Data **192–6**
   Data 344
   Database 385
   Models 201, 204
   Principles 192
   Systems 192
Remotely Sensed Imagery 516
RenderMan 292, 300
Reorientation of a Digital Terrain Model 280
Report
   Generation 366
   of the House of Lords Select Committee on Science and Technology **36**
   Writer 252
Representation 242
Representative Polygon *176*
Request for Proposals 482, 483, 484
Resel 469
Reservoir Design 287
Residual
   Error 341
   From Regression 429
Resolution
   of Scanners 244
   Theorem Proving 422
Resource
   Allocation Working Party 75
   Analysis 197, 201, *21*
   Assessment *280*
   Based Course 87
   Management 22, 47, 53, 76, 119, 293, 339, *3*, *8*, *11*, *21*, *314*, *316*, *317*
   Optimization *90*
   Planning *250*, *285*
   Provision 83
   Shortage 55
Response Modelling 396
Responsibility for Education in GIS 84
Responsible
   Marine Information Advisory Centre *208*
   National Oceanographic Data Centres *206*
Restricted Zone Design 397
Restrictive Covenant 73
RFT 346
RGB 245
Ridge Line 278
River Rhine *193*

Road
   Administration Information Centre 53
   Design 287, 293
   Network 59
Roads 271
   Service 73
Robotics 435
Rome Air Development Center 27
Root Mean Square 243, 285
Rosch-Lakoff-Johnson Model of Cognitive Categories 152
Rotation 231
Route
   Finding *314*
   Planning *26*, *90*
Routeplanner Map Series 36
Royal
   Australian Army Survey Corps 64
   College of Art *24*, *25*
   Geographical Society 96
   Observatory of Belgium *204*
   Town Planning Institute 36
RTSI 24
Rubber Sheeting 344, 499, *189*, *194*, *324*
Rule
   Base 414
   Set *267*, *268*, *269*
Rule-Based
   Applications 420
   Expert System 420
   System 419, *37*
Run-Length Encoding 124, 199, 230, 233, 234, 245, 325
Runoff 114
Rural Land Use Information System 35

SAC 372
SACS 24
Sage 25
SAGIS 372
SAGIS89 98
SALADIN 75
Sales
   by Sector 56
   Force Automation *141*
   Forecasting *141*
Sammamish Data Systems 24
Sampling 307–8
   Bias *171*
   Limitation 312

Subject index

Sampling – *cont.*
   Resolution 460
   Strategy 428
   Techniques 270
San Diego
   Association of Governments 8, *247, 248, 249, 250, 256, 257, 259*
   Council of Governments 24
Sanitary Engineering 59
Sapir-Wharf Hypothesis 153
SAS 13
SASPAC 513, *132*
Satellite 191, 223, 427, *80*
   Data 191, *210*
   Image 349, *55*
   Imagery 271, 458, *14, 128, 135, 178, 195*
   Photography 378
   Radiances 195, 204
   Reflectance Measurement 203
Satimage *43*
Saudi Arabia 76, *123*
Scale
   Conversion 343
   Dependency 193, 323
      in Vegetation Patterns 193
   -Dependent Database **471–3**, 472
   -Free 37
   Data 25
   Database *33, 35, 189, 192*
   -Independent Database 472, 473
   of Measurement 193
Scaleless Database **471–3**
Scaling 231
Scanner 15, 57, 241, 243–4, 245, 324, 328, 345, 349, *314*
Scanning 46–7, 59, 64, 113, 185, 433, 436, *12, 15, 31, 37, 194, 324*
Scatter Diagram 434
Scene Analysis 434
Schema 152
   Integration Analysis 343, 344
School
   Districting *298*
   Resource Planning *90*
Schönhage-Strassen 221
Science
   and Engineering Research Laboratory *204*
   Council of Japan 55
Scientific Analysis 191
SCMAP 372
Scope and Domain of Visualization **431–9**

Scott Polar Research Institute *204*
Scottish
   Development
      Agency 508
      Department 35, 36
   Tourist Board 35
Screen Forms Management System 252
Screening 105
   Matrix 299
SCRIS 25
SCS 345
SDF 346
Seamless Database 182, *116*
Secondary Data Capture **241–3**
Secretary of State for the Environment 69
Security 76, 418, *61, 96, 325*
SEDMAC 315
SEDSIM 315
Segment 27
Seibu Gas *51*
SEISCO 306
Seismic 270, 308, 516, *171*
Selective Sampling 271, 272
Self-Similarity 435, 460, 465
Semantic
   Data Modelling 103, 515
   Equivalence 421
   Frame 417
   Integrity Constraints 419
   Knowledge 421
   Network 414, 417, 421, 515
Semi
   -Automatic Digitization 435
   -Structured Spatial Problems 403
   -Variogram 194
   -variance *159*
Sensitivity Analysis 439
Sensor
   Calibration 191, 192, 204
   Model 207
   Resolution 194, 204
Sensory Bandwidth 354
Sequent 216, 219
Series Mapping *80*
Serpell Committee *28*
Server 58
Service Planning 76
Set 346
Sewage Disposal *109*
SGML 346
Shackelton Committee 68, *28*

Shaded Contour 288
Shaft Encoder 25
Shape Analysis 434
Sharebase *33*
Shell 308
Shibata Gas *51*
Shortest Path Algorithm 122
Shuttle 198
SICAD 341
SICAD-HYGRIS 345
Sieve Mapping 339
SIF 345, 346
Silicon Graphics 300, *319*
SimCity *8*
Similarity Transformation 141
Simplex 235
Simplicial
   Decomposition 235
   Topology 235
Simulation 75
Single Instruction Multiple Data 216
SIRO-DBMS 67
Site
   Finding *90*
   Planning 297
Siting a Superconducting Super Collider **270–2**
SLF 345
Sliver Polygon 341, 382, 383, *195*
Slope Analysis 282
Small Area
   Census Studies 25
   Health Statistics Unit 74
Smalltalk 217
Smallworld Systems 14, 15, *320*
Smoothing
   of Digital Terrain Models 278
   Operations 458
Social
   Control 491
   Engineering 491
   Implications of GIS in Australia **64–6**
   Scientists 92
   Services 76, *57*
      Optimization and Management *90*
      Committee on Vehicle Navigation *124*
Socio-Economic
   Applications of GIS *3*
   Attributes **183–4**
   Data *6*
   Databases *219*

Subject index

Software 81, **85–6**, 104, **245–8**
   Development Strategy **223–4**
   Engineering 215, 217
   Exploitation 111
   Integration *320*
Soil 168, *7*
   and Terrain Database Project *224*
   and Water Conservation Board *277*
   Classification *156*
   Conservation 177, 179, 180, 182, 186, *62, 163*
   Data Model *156*
   Database 177, *164*
   Erosion 282, 293, 365
   Information
     Base *155*
     System 12, **153–65**
   Map
     Database *155*
     Quality *156*
   Mapping *154*
     Unit *157*
   Maps 103
   Moisture Regime *155*
   Pollution Studies *164, 165*
   Polygon *155, 156, 158, 162, 163, 164*
   Profile *154, 155, 157*
   Science 293
   Survey 179, 186, *153*
Solid
   Modelling 307
   State Compass *115, 118*
   Voxel 309
Sonar 270
Sophisticated Allocation Process 248, 249, 250, 253
Sorting Order 421
SOTER 260, *164*
Source
   Document Distortion 248
   Zone 385
South
   African Society for Photogrammetry, Remote Sensing and Cartography 98
   Australia 89
   Carolina 9
     Infrastructure and Economic Development Project *308*
     Infrastructure and Economic Planning Project *302, 305*

Wales 305
Western Electricity Board *104*
Soviet
   Geophysical Committee of the Academy of Sciences of the USSR *204*
   Union 38, 98, *224*
Space 119
   Images 112
     -Bounding 309
     -Filling 309
   -Time
     Interaction in Remote Sensing 196
     Model 323
     Relationships *141*
Spaghetti
   Data Structure 232
   Tessellation 227
Spain 130
SPANS 51, 53, 124, 261, 344, *15, 172, 174, 175, 177, 178, 316, 317*
Spatial 12, 45, 49, 55, 56, 59, 69, 71, 74, 76, 91, 102
   Analysis 13, 27, 55, 83, 84, 95, 97, 101, 103, 104, 111, 114, 115, 119, 124, 128, 185, 200, 231, 260, 329, 345, 391, 392, 406, 439, 464, *36, 47, 55, 145, 262, 316, 317, 318*
     Methods for GIS **389–401**
   System *316*
   Tools 389, *139, 300*
   View of GIS 14
   and Inductive Modelling Package for Land Evaluation 66
   Association *171, 173, 175, 176, 179, 180*
   Autocorrelation 102, 128, 170, 194, 390, 464
   Autocovariance *164*
   Base *189*
   Characteristics of Remotely Sensed Data **192–3**
   Clustering 314
   Cognition 112, 440
   Complexity *293*
     of a Landscape *286*
   Comprehensive Database *208*
   Concepts 85, 122, 227, **228–9**, 232
   Configuration 304
     Engineering 396
   Conflict 473

Consistency 506, *188*
Constraint Propagation 421
Content *109*
Context 197
Control 168, 170
Covariance *159*
Coverage 375, *193*
Data 83, 85, 96, 98, 119, 128, 165, 166, 170, 207, 228, 233, 261, 338, 339, 341, 343, 347, 385, 391, 417, 421, 437, 439, 458, 461, 479, 516, *5, 76, 94, 143, 158, 175, 228, 298, 302, 314*
   Aggregation 397
   Analysis *37, 180*
   Display 95
   Exchange **515–30**
     Standard 524
   Exploratory Techniques 389
   Handling 81, 93, 292, 394, 420, *9, 66, 77, 78, 241*
   Integration **375–85**
   Model 227, 229, 233, 352, 479, 516, 517
   Query 285
   Representation 302
   Resolution 342
   Retrieval *214*
   Set 222
   Source *186*
   Standard *11*
   Structure **197–200**, 227, 228, 229, *7, 172*
   Technology *19*
   Transfer 94, 523, 525, *17*
Database 98, 114, 167, 251, 299, 420, 439, 457, 460, 462, 473, 484, *171, 172, 174,* **302–4**
   Application 419
   Design *11, 15*
   Management 285
   Models 113
   System *134*
   Toolkit 67
Decision 115
   Making 114, 116, 438, 440, *308*
   Support
     System 12, 115, **403–11**, *9, 139, 308, 314, 318*
        Architecture **408–10**
        Toolbox 407
     in Planning *301*
   Techniques 392
Deduction 122

441

Spatial – *cont.*
    Dependency 391
    Detail *220*, *304*
    Disaggregation 203
    Distribution 168, 429
        of Error 203
    Domain 105, 301, *162*
    Engineering 397
    Entity 340, 373, 375, 462
    Environmental Variation 195
    Error Budget 208
    Evidence 166
    Feature 183, 340
    Filtering 470
    Form 299
    Frame 304
    Framework *3*
    Function 310
    Heterogeneity 206
    Impact *293*
    Incompatibility 344
    Index Structure 233
    Indexing 113, 301, 308
    Information 111, 113, 166, 338, 428, 429, 432, 433, 434, 437, 458, 477, *104*, *261*, *285*, *293*, *294*, *298*, *299*, *300*, *302*, *307*, *323*
        Handling *214*
        Management *94*
        Paradigm *316*
        Processing 166, *285*
        Science 14
        Systems 12, *287*
        Technology 64, *57*
    Integration 207
    Interaction 130, 206, 390, *145*
    Interpolation 380, *157*
    Key 340, 348, *262*
    Knowledge 175, 438, 440, 437
    Language 440
    Location 120, 227, 356, *297*
    Measurements 168
    Model 104, 341, 409, 517, *262*
    Modelling 203, 392, 460, 464, *222*, **286–9**
    Nonsense 428
    Object 85, 113, 119, 120, 124, 125, 126, 127, 128, 227, 228, 229, 230, 232, 304, 421, 460, 525
    Occupancy Enumeration 307
    Optimization 67
    Overlay 338, 339
    Paradigm 236
    Partitioning *196*
    Pattern 301, 391, 429, 438, *210*, *291*
        Description 391
        Detection 396
        Relationships 391–3
    Planning 391, *75*
    Position 194
    Primitive 408
    Problem 403, 405, 406
    Process 193, 299, 305, 457, 468
    Properties 229
    Proximity 119, 121, 462
    Query 122, 197, 227, 314, 329, 408, 463, 463
        Languages **154–6**, **262–3**
    Reference *36*, *59*
    Referenced Data 299
    Referencing 72, 74, 350, 352, 499, *39*, *202*, *208*
    Regression 390, 391
    Relation 373, 406
    Relationship 92, 95, 132, 200, 373, 445, 461, 473, *195*, *286*, *291*, *293*
    Representation 165, 310
    Resolution 192, 193, 196, 199, 428, 460, 463, *49*, *164*, *172*, *196*, *238*
    Response Modelling 398
    Sampling 171
    Search 329, 338, 339, *154*
    Separation 122, 129
    Similarity 128
    Simulation Modelling 206
    Situations 158
    Specificity *287*
    Statistics 95, 200, 373, 393, 394
    Structure 406
    Template *188*, *189*, *194*
    Theory 301, *302*
    Thesaurus *49*
    Trend 438
    Unit 341, *85*, *241*, *249*
    Variation 170, 192, 193, 380, *156*
        in a Satellite Image 193
        of Soil Properties *154*
    Video Analysis 397
Spatially
    Autocorrelated Data 392
    Orientated Referencing Systems
    Association 27
    Referenced Data 191, *202*
    Registered Information *303*
    Related Data 68

Spatio-Temporal Statistical Analysis 206
Special
    Purpose GIS 5
    Transformation 421
Specific Geomorphometry 283–5
Specification Error 205
Spectral
    Analysis 271
    Band Width 192
    Contrast 193
    Coverage Spectral Band
    Location 192
    Dimensionality 192
    Mapping 203
    Resolution 192, 428
    Response Properties 195
    Separation 203
Specular Reflection 288
Speed of Processing 46
Spherical Variogram *161*
Spheroid 137
Spit Tape 25
Splay Tree 220
Spline
    Curve 233
    Generation Software *29*
Split
    Rules *210*
    System *209*
SPOT 141, 185, 194, 198, 271, 523, *9*, *77*, *202*, *223*, *228*, *306*
Spottiness 373
Spreadsheet *142*, *291*
SPSS 127, 130, 329
Spurious Precision 382
SQL 114, 349, 422
Square
    Lattice 460
    Misclassification Index 171
    Tessellation 199
Sri Lanka *74*, *75*
St Lucia *93*
Standard
    for Digital Cartographic Data Quality 165
    for Exchange of Spatial Data 165
    for the Exchange of Product Data 527, 529
    Industrial Classification *251*
    Interchange Format 325
    Meridian 377
    Query Language 155

Standards
  Australia *61*
  Manual 78
Standing Committee on Rural Land Use 35
Staring Institute for Integrated Land, Water and Rural Survey *163*
State
  Database *272*
  Land Information Council 59, *94*
  Plane System 377
  Planning Commission 79
Static
  Query Optimization 421
  Visualization 287
Statistical 22
  Analysis 88, 390, *191*, *300*, *304*
  Correlation *277*
  Data 417
  Description 428
  Generalization 460, 464, 468
  Geography 389, 390
  Graphics 409
  Mapping 429
  Methods 88
  Modelling 435, *7*
  Pattern Recognition 203
  Self Similarity 460, 465
  Survey 433
Statistics 439
  Bureau 52
  Graphics System *228*
  Sweden *45*
Statmap 24
Status of Biological Diversity *205*
Step 346
Stereo
  Aerial Photograph *157*
  Depth 434
  Digitizing *113*
  Visualization System 302
Stereoplotter 325, *13*
STIBOKA *154*
Stochastic
  Analysis in Human Geography *47*
  Uncertainty 206
Stockholm *260*
Storage **48–9**, 409
Storm Surge 102
Straight-Line Graticule 377
Strain Ellipsoid 409
Stratamodel 309

Strategic
  Data *276*
  Planning 479
  Information System 53
  Mapping 53, *317*, *320*
  Planning 406, *276*
Stream
  Line 278
  -Mode Digitizing 435
Street
  Address Matching System 25
  Cleaning 76
  Gazetteer 72
  Light Maintenance *90*
  Map 377
  Network
    Database *318*
    Topology *121*, *124*
Striation 373
Strict-Order Relations 230
Strings 341
Strip Tree 463
Structural
  Generalization 469
  Knowledge 464
Structural-Conceptual Generalization 469
Structure 92
  Preserving Transformation 468
  Signature 460, 465
Structured
  Data 242, *32*
  Query Language **156**, 252, 263, *156*
  Topographic Data *34*
  Vector Data *32*
Student Learning 81
Sub-Regional
  Area *249*
  Forecast *249*, *250*
Sub-Surface Hydrology 114
Subdivision 330
Subjective Judgement 371
Submerged Aquatic Vegetation *265*, *266*
Subregion 330
Subsetting Mechanism 253
Suitability
  Model *300*
  Ranking *291*
Sumitomo Forestry *52*
Sun
  Microsystems 219, 220, *263*
  -Earth-Satellite Geometry 193

Super
  cluster 399
  computer 215, 394, 399, 427, 439, *15*, *218*, *219*
  computing 432
  conducting Super Collider *8*, *9*, *261*, *262*, *271*
  fund *280*
  plan 35
  position 330
Supervised Classification 202, 203
Supply and Demand Forecasting *247*
Surface 85
  Classification 191
  Flow Modelling 329
  Inflection 371
  Modelling in 3D **304–7**
  Variation 194, 283
Surface-Sensor Geometry 193
Surrogate
  Data 395
  Walk 354
Survey
  Data Capture 293
  Information on Microfilm *34*
  of India 76, *78*
Surveying 22, 59, 121, 137, 169, 172, *12*, *102*, *317*
  and Mapping 94
  and Photogrammetry 292–3
Surveyor 92
Swansea 145
Sweden 38, 67, 98, 186, *4*, *93*, *129*
Swedish
  Central Board for Real Estate 92
  Land Data Bank 38, *39*, *40*, *41*, *42*, **43–6**
  Meteorological and Hydrological Institute *42*
  National Road Administration *42*
  Water Archive *42*
Sweep Representation 307
Switzerland *224*
SYLK 346
SYMAP 24, 28, 33, 34, 36, 372, *48*
Symbolic
  Logic 330
  Manipulation 231
Symbolization 437, 464, *26*
Symbology 232, 440, *17*
Symmetry 430
Symposia 6, 60
Synercom 24, 32

443

Subject index

Syntactic Pattern Recognition 202
Synthesising Cartographic Data 371
Synthetic
    Aperture Side-Scan Radar *80*
    Imagery 435
    Modelling Techniques 371
SysScan GEOREC 247
System
    Cycle Support **60–1**
    Evaluation 483–5
    Implementation 85
    Planning 85
    Security 509
    Software 85
System/9 15, 52, *320*
Systematic
    Error 166
    Survey 308
Système d'Exchange et de Transfer 527
Systems Analysis 101, *234*, *235*

Tables 113
Tabular Report Generator 409–10
Tachymetry 345
Tactical
    Data *276*
    Planning *276*
Tag Image File Format 245, 345
Tagging *16*
Tangible Benefits *244*
Tape 183
    Drive 15
    Triangulation *102*
Target
    Group Index *144*, *147*
    Zone 385
Taunton Joint Utilities Group 69, *111*
Taxation 22, *91*
Taxicab
    Distance 121
    Metric 231
Taxonomy of Error in GIS Data **168–72**
Teaching 33, 81, 85
Technical Institute of Darmstadt *87*
Technological Imperialism *5*
Tektronix 50, 87
    4010 49
TeleAtlas *123*
Telecom *67*
Telecommunications 69
Telescoping *276*
Teleshopping *148*

Television 222, 349
Template Matching 465
Templating 344
Temporal
    Attributes in Spatial Databases 264
    Characteristics of Remotely Sensed Data **195–6**
    Data 101, 251, 342, 431, 439
    Dynamics 373
    Resolution 192
    Variation 195
Terminal 49
    Emulator 512
Terrain
    Analysis 75, 469, 67
    Data Editing 293
    Intervisibility Calculation 329
    Modelling 113, 114, 235
    Related Information 75
    Representation 114
TerraSoft 341
Terrestrial
    Ecological Data *203–5*
    System 136
Tessellation 329, 440, *225*
    Model 320, 321, 322, 324, 516
Terabyte 216, 229
Text
    Placement 437
    Processor 217
Textbooks **5–6**
Textual Database 341
Textural Analysis 283
Texture 434
TGA 346
Thailand 38, *75*, *76*, *92*, *224*
    Land Titling Project *94*
The Times *127*
Thematic
    Attribute 168, *286*
    Cartography 166, 167
    Data 341, 408, *189*, *224*
    Error 381, 383, 384
    Map 92, 176, 429
        Accuracy 203
    Mapper 135, 205, 207, *209*
    Specificity *286*, *287*
Themes 48
Theorem Proving 421
Theoretical
    Analysis **220–1**
    Modelling Systems *218*
Theories on Liability 496–8

Theory
    of Error 168
    of Normal Forms 258
Thickening 470
    Blanket 471, 472
Thiessen Polygon 28, 121, 126, 275, 276, *132*, *176*
Thinking Machine Corporation 216
Third Generation Language 252
Thresholding 285
TIGER 24, 29, 31, 33, 122, 186, 325, 345, *6*, *9*, *16*, *65*, *123*, *133*, *136*, *256*, *305*, *306*, *307*
    Database 48
    Line Files 24
    Spatial Data Structure *135*
    Spatial Database *134*
    System *134–5*
TIGER/Line *134*, *135*
Tight Coupling 419
TIGRIS 15, 52, 235
Tile 48, 277, *196*
Time
    Distance 119
    in GIS 323
    Projections 105
    Series Analysis 170, 464
Time-Dynamic Spatial Information 393
TIN-to-Contour Conversion 280
Title Registration 58
Tokyo *48*, *49*
    Astronomical Laboratory *204*
    Gas *6*, *49*, *51*, *54*
    Metropolitan Government *48*
Tolerance 383
TOPAZ *66*
Topographic
    Archive 72
    Base Map *103–5*
    Data *4*
    Database 59, *188*
    Elevation 113
    Features 71
    Incline 363
    Information *25*
    Map 92, 168, 169, 176, 182, *41*, *42*
    Mapping 139, 287, 293, *3*, *4*, *23*
    Slope 363
    Surface 269
Topographical Mapping 138, *6*
Topography 113, 193, *113*
Topological
    Attribute 285

Data 408
 Structure 231, *11, 27, 30, 32, 33, 36*
 Dimension 125
 Encoding *115, 116*
 Genus 371
 Invariant 231
 Linking 200
 Order 285
 Overlay *300*
 Relation 151, 312
 Relationship 382, *34*
 Space 122
 Spatial Data Model 341
 Transformation 231
 Validation *13, 16*
Topology 31, 58, 122, **124–5, 128–32**, 230–1, *32*
Torrens Systems of Land Registration 58
Toshiba *53*
Total Transfer Package 529
Tourism and Recreation 35
Town and Country Planning Act 69, *297*
Toyota *14, 54, 116*
Tracking Vehicle 47
Tradeable Information Initiative 70, 71, **74**, 78, 510, *94*
Traffic 105, *35, 90*
 Accident Analysis *90*
 Analysis 115, 276, *249, 250, 255, 256, 298*
Trafficability Analysis 283
Training 57, 59, 60, 83, 85, 319, 506, 508, *319*
Transaction
 Loggers 14
 Processing System 10, 17
Transfer
 Function *163*
 Model *163*
Transformation 52, 112, 138, **139–44**, 231, 312
Transforming Objects **126–7**
Transitional Variogram *159, 160*
Translation 231
Transnational Information Access 493
Transport
 Planning *90, 110*
 Survey Coding Guide 25
Transportability 69
Transportation 26, 59, 76, 472, *248*

Transverse Mercator 138
 Graticule 377
 Projection 68, 139, 141
 Travel *145, 148, 265*
 Trend
  Analysis *264*
  Surface *159*
Tri-state Transport 25
Triangle
 Data Model 113
 Inequality 121
 Nodes 277
Triangulated Irregular Network 125, 126, 235, 273, 274, 306, 325, 376, 460, *314*
 Based Interpolation 275
Triangulation 275
 Based Interpolation 278
Tribal Designated Statistical Area *133*
Trigonometrical Survey 68
Trilateration 129
TRINITY *52*
Tropical Resources Institute *294*
TRW Incorporated *143*
TUMSY *54*
Tuple 113, 257, 463
Turbid Medium Model 207
Turing
 Test 157
 -Computable 414, 415
Turnaround Test 410
TYDAC 51, 52, 53, *316*
Types of Database Management Systems Structure **254–63**

UMTA 24
Uncertainty *175, 184*
Unclassed Choropleth Map 430
Underground Networks *103*
Undersampling of Contours 272
UNESCO Natural Resources Research Series 30
UNICEF *72, 73*
Uniform Grid 215, **219–20**, 460
Unimatch 25
Unintended Use of Maps 500
Uniqueness Property 258
United
 Nations
  Centre for Regional Development *75*
  Economic Commission for Latin America and the Caribbean *75*
  Environmental Programme *74, 187, 205*
  Food and Agriculture Organization *187*
  Institute for Training and Research *224*
 States 67
  Bureau
   of the Budget 26, 179
   of the Census 3, 21, 25, 26, 30, 33–34, 48, 122, 183, 186, 325, 327, 495, 507, 529, *6, 9, 16, 65, 129, 131, 134, 135, 136, 256, 303, 304, 305, 318*
  Census *6, 133*
  Defense Mapping Agency 182, *17, 223*
  Fish and Wildlife Service 186
  Forest Survey 30
  Forestry Service *281*
  Geological Survey 3, 21, 25, 27, 30, 33, 48, 127, 136, 177, 179, 180, 186, 219, 221, 223, 262, 325, 377, 434, 500, 501, 517, 523, 524, 529, *3, 4, 9, 11, 12–13, 21, 133, 134, 136, 154, 203, 204, 209, 263, 276, 287, 304, 305, 306, 318*
  Global Change Research Programme *220*
  National
   Bureau of Standards 524
   Committee for Digital Cartographic Data Standards 166
   Institute of Standards and Technology 524
   Map Accuracy Standard 169, 172, 179, 180
   Ocean Survey 27
  Naval Observatory *204*
  Postal Service 24, *131*
  Soil Conservation Service 434
  Standard for Digital Cartographic Data 180
  Standards for Map Accuracy *194*
Univariate Analysis 391
Universal
 Soil Loss Equation *164, 277*
 Transverse Mercator 137, 377, *202, 203*

Subject index

University
  College London 512
  of Amsterdam 97
  of California 32, 33, 95, 223
  of Chicago 28
  of Cincinnati 26
  of Delft 97
  of Durham 36, 81, 503, 507, 508, 509
  of Edinburgh 36, 77
  of Essex 513
  of Leicester 77, 84
  of London 36, 88, *188*, *189*
  of Lund *39*
  of Maine 33, 95, 96
  of Melbourne 67
  of Michigan 38
  of Minnesota 31
  of Nanjing 98
  of New South Wales 67
  of New York at Buffalo 33, 95
  of Newcastle 508, 509
  of Ohio State 84
  of Oregon 24
  of Reading 34
  of Saskatchewan 33
  of Tokyo *47*, *49*, *52*
  of Utrecht 97
  of Wageningen 97
  of Washington 24, 26
Unix 15, 49, 50, 52, 58, 215, 217, 224, 300, 509, 510, *263*, *323*
Unlinking Data Sets 209
Unstructured Tessellation Model 321
Unsupervised Classification 201, 202, 203
Urban 104
  and Regional
    Information Systems
      Association 7, 26, 33, 36, 93, 94, 97, *65*, *301*, *315*
    Planning *58*, *68*
  Atlas 24, 30–1
  Data 25, 105
  GIS Applications **247–60**
  Growth Management **236–7**, *238*, *239*
  Information System 12, *49*, *248*
  Infrastructure 92, *314*
  Management 89, *243*
  Planning 22, 59, 104, 293, *218*
  Transportation Studies 111
URBYS 422
USAID *75*

Use and Value of Geographic Information 95
USEMAP *75*
User
  Interface 483, *315*
  Requirement Analysis 95, *96*
Uses of Information 490
USI II *51*
USSR
  Academy of Sciences 38
  State Committee for Hydrometeorology and Control of the Environment *204*, *206*
Utilities Mapping 292
Utility
  Management 22
  Network *59*
Utvecklingsradet for Landskapsinformation 98

Validation 99, 399
Valuation and Property Assessment *90*
Value
  Added Services *142*, *143*, *325*
  of GIS 106, 116
Valuer General's Department *58*
Variable
  Resolution Display *280*
  Scaling 460
Variogram 194, 271, *159*
Vaster 328
VAX *33*, *51*, *321*
Vector 28, 32, 50, 51, 52, 53, 56, 75, 85, 111, 124, 130, 135, 149, 197, 198, 199, 201, 202, 233, 235, 239, 245, 246, 247, 248, 299, 304, 306, 308, 309, 310, 312, 314, 324, 325, 328, 329, 330, 338, 342, 345, 348, 364, 378, 381, 385, 452, 457, 479, *13*, *15*, *37*, *75*, *104*, *157*, *192*, *206*, *207*, *218*, *223*, *306*, *315*, *318*
  Algorithms 85
  Boundary *175*
  Data 200, 242, 343, 525, 527, *49*
  GIS 191, 340, *172*, *222*, *226*, *262*
  Interchange Format *175*
  Model 320, 322, 324, 517
  Overlay 341
  Polygon *175*, *224*
  Representation System 376
  Space 461
  Spatial Structuring 310
Vector-Mode Generalization **468–9**

Vector-Raster 85, 329, 344, *228*
Vector-Topological System 261
Vectorization 247, 272, *324*
Vegetation 103, 168, 176, 178, 422
Vehicle
  Location Tracking 240
  Navigation 59, 159, *124*
  Routing *298*
Venezuela *161*
Vertex Extraction Algorithm 247
Vibrating Rod Sensor *118*
Video 5, 47, 55, 115, 349, 365, 512
Videodisc 349
Videotape 59
Virgin Islands 9, *287*, *294*
Virtual
  Memory 46, 216, 314
  Reality 315, **353–5**
Visibility Analysis 286
Vision/Pattern Recognition 432
Visual
  Balance 430
  Feedback 278
  Interactive Modelling 410
  Interpretation 287
  Perception 47, 428, 430
  Realism 429
  Simulation 366
  Variable 430
Visualization 75, 85, 91, 92, 102, 115, 132, 240, 280, 299, 312, 315, **427–40**, *67*, *202*
  Enhancer 397, 398
  in Scientific Computing 432
  of Digital Terrain Models 269
  of Geoscientific Data 290
  of Spatial Information 439
  of Terrain *212*
VM/CMS 52, 58, *314*
VMS 52, 58, 87
Voice Recognition 325, 439
Volume of Data 46
Volumetric
  Computation *13*
  Spatial Function 299
Volygon 308
Voronoi
  Diagram 215, 220, 275, 276
  Polygon 126, *175*
Voxel 308, 309, 439
VPT 346

Walking Generalization Algorithm 469

446

Waseda University *49*
Wastewater Management 32
Water 69
    Area Use Classification System *264*, *266*
    Quality *109*, *278*
    Resources 59, 422, *15*, *109*, *209*, *278–280*
    Service 73
Waterfall Model 215, 223
Wayleaves *109*
WDDES 260
Weapons Sighting 75
Weather Balloon 308
Weights of Evidence *180*
    Modelling *172*, *173–4*, *183–4*
Welsh Office 507, 508
West
    Germany *123*
    Indies *212*
Western European Geological Survey *203*
WGS84 Ellipsoid *123*
What You See Is What You Get 217
Wheel Rotation Sensors *115*
Whole Earth Decision Support System 353
Wide Area Network 216
Wild A8 Autograph *25*
Wildlife Modelling 422
Wind 293, *277*
Window Retrieval *122*
Windows Metafile 346
WING *50*

Wisdom 490
WK1 346
WKS 346
Word 346, *322*
    Processing *314*
    Processor *291*
WordPerfect 346, *322*
Wordstar 346
Working
    Committee on International Oceanographic Data Exchange *206*
    Group
        on Data and Information Systems *219*
        on Quantitative Land Evaluation *156*
        on Soil Information Systems *153*, *155*
Workstation 46, 49, 50, 52, 53, 57, 58, 215, 216, 241, 244, 260, 262, 290, 300, 485, *9*, *15*, *31*, *32*, *34*, *52*, *53*, *110*, *305*, *306*, *307*, *313*, *317*, *319*, *321*
    and Data Compaction 244–5
World
    Data Center System *203*, **204–5**, *224*
    Database II 39
    Digital Database for Environmental Science 39, *223*
    Meteorological Organization *206*, *208*
    Ocean Climate Experiment *206*

WORM 48, 343, 352, *74*
Wuhan Technical University 98

X-OS 58
X-Windows 217, 300, *323*
Xerox 50

Yale University *294*

Z-Buffer Algorithm 290
Z-MAP *53*
Zenrin *123*
Zero Dimension 137
Zipping 280, 344
Zonal
    Data Transformation 368–9
    System Overlap 385
ZonalCombination 368
ZonalMajority 369
ZonalMaximum 369
ZonalMean 369
ZonalMinimum 369
ZonalMinority 369
ZonalPercentage 369
ZonalPercentile 369
ZonalProduct 369
ZonalRanking 369
ZonalSum 369
ZonalVariety 369
Zone Design 396
Zone Reclassification 365
Zones for Urban Modelling *248*, *249*
Zoning Maps *298*
Zoology 92